SCHOLARSHIP AND CONTROVERSY

Also available from Bloomsbury

GREEK HOMOSEXUALITY
by K. J. Dover

MARGINAL COMMENT: A MEMOIR REVISITED,
by K. J. Dover
(edited by Stephen Halliwell and Christopher Stray)

WHAT IS A JEWISH CLASSICIST?
by Simon Goldhill

SCHOLARSHIP AND CONTROVERSY

CENTENARY ESSAYS ON THE LIFE AND WORK OF SIR KENNETH DOVER

Edited by Stephen Halliwell and Christopher Stray

BLOOMSBURY ACADEMIC
LONDON • NEW YORK • OXFORD • NEW DELHI • SYDNEY

BLOOMSBURY ACADEMIC
Bloomsbury Publishing Plc
50 Bedford Square, London, WC1B 3DP, UK
1385 Broadway, New York, NY 10018, USA
29 Earlsfort Terrace, Dublin 2, Ireland

BLOOMSBURY, BLOOMSBURY ACADEMIC and the Diana logo are
trademarks of Bloomsbury Publishing Plc

First published in Great Britain 2023
Paperback edition published 2025

Copyright © Stephen Halliwell, Christopher Stray & Contributors, 2023

Stephen Halliwell and Christopher Stray have asserted their right under the Copyright,
Designs and Patents Act, 1988, to be identified as Editors of this work.

Cover image: Sir Kenneth Dover, 2001 © Robin Gillanders

All rights reserved. No part of this publication may be reproduced or transmitted
in any form or by any means, electronic or mechanical, including photocopying,
recording, or any information storage or retrieval system, without prior
permission in writing from the publishers.

Bloomsbury Publishing Plc does not have any control over, or responsibility for,
any third-party websites referred to or in this book. All internet addresses given
in this book were correct at the time of going to press. The author and publisher
regret any inconvenience caused if addresses have changed or sites have
ceased to exist, but can accept no responsibility for any such changes.

A catalogue record for this book is available from the British Library.

Library of Congress Cataloging-in-Publication Data
Names: Dover, K. J. (Kenneth James), 1920–2010, honouree. | Halliwell, Stephen, editor. |
Stray, Christopher, editor.
Title: Scholarship and controversy : centenary essays on the life and work of Sir Kenneth Dover /
edited by Stephen Halliwell and Christopher Stray.
Other titles: Centenary essays on the life and work of Sir Kenneth Dover
Description: London : Bloomsbury Academic, 2023. | Includes bibliographical references and index.
Identifiers: LCCN 2022046402 | ISBN 9781350333451 (hardback) |
ISBN 9781350333499 (paperback) | ISBN 9781350333468 (ebook) | ISBN 9781350333475 (epub)
Subjects: LCSH: Dover, K. J. (Kenneth James), 1920-2010. | Dover, K. J. (Kenneth James),
1920-2010–Influence. | Classicists–Great Britain–Biography. | Scholars–Great Britain–Biography. |
Greek philology–Study and teaching–Great Britain–History–20th century. | Civilization, Classical–
Study and teaching–Great Britain–History–20th century. | LCGFT: Festschriften.
Classification: LCC PA85.D725 S35 2023 | DDC 813/.6—dc23
LC record available at https://lccn.loc.gov/2022046402

ISBN:	HB:	978-1-3503-3345-1
	PB:	978-1-3503-3349-9
	ePDF:	978-1-3503-3346-8
	eBook:	978-1-3503-3347-5

Typeset by RefineCatch Limited, Bungay, Suffolk

To find out more about our authors and books visit www.bloomsbury.com
and sign up for our newsletters.

CONTENTS

List of Images   vii
Notes on Contributors   viii
Preface   xii
List of Abbreviations   xiv

Introduction *Christopher Stray*   1

Part I The Life

1. **Dover at School and University** (with an Appendix: Two poems by Kenneth Dover) *Christopher Stray*   13
2. **Dover, Oxford and the Study of Classical Literature: The Making of a Professional Scholar** *Tim Rood*   31
3. **Dover and St Andrews** *Elizabeth Craik*   51
4. **Dover and Corpus** (with two Appendices) *Ewen Bowie*   61
5. **Dover, Blunt and the British Academy** *Robin Osborne*   81
6. *Marginal Comment*: **Composition, Publication and Reception** *Christopher Stray*   99

Part II The Work

7. **Dover on Thucydides** *Christopher Pelling*   113
8. **Dover and Plato's *Symposium*: Attraction, Aversion and Intemperance** *Frisbee C.C. Sheffield*   131
9. **Dover and Greek Popular Morality** *Christopher Carey*   149
10. **Dover and Greek Drama** *Constanze Güthenke*   167
11. **After *Greek Homosexuality*** *Carol Atack*   181
12. **Dover's 'Inch': Reflections on the Art-Historical Method in *Greek Homosexuality*** (with an Appendix: Dover's list of vases collated against Beazley's corpora by provenance) *Jaś Elsner*   203
13. **Dover and Theocritus** *Richard Hunter*   237
14. **No Stone Unturned: Dover as Historian of Greek Language between Epigraphy and Literature** *Lucia Prauscello*   251

15 **Dover on Style** *Ben Cartlidge* 271

Epilogue

16 **Dover and the Public Face of Classics** (with an Appendix: Kenneth Dover, 'The value of Classics', an article translated from the Italian original) *Stephen Halliwell* 291

17 **Memories of Kenneth Dover** *Rebecca Dover, Sir Brian Harrison, Jay Parini, David Stuttard* 315

Bibliography 333
Index 355

IMAGES

0.1	The Dover family: a characterological analysis, May 1940	3
7.1	Commentary on Thucydides 6.18.3–7 from Dover 1965a, 31	123
12.1	Dover's B65. Lydos Painter, black-figure belly amphora, *c.* 540 BC, found in Tamassos, Cyprus. Cyprus Museum, Nicosia C440. Side A. Photograph: By permission of the Department of Antiquities, Cyprus.	206
12.2	Dover's B65. Side B. Photograph: By permission of the Department of Antiquities, Cyprus	207
12.3	Dover's B64. Lydos Painter, black-figure belly amphora, *c.* 540 BC, found in Vulci, Etruria. Cabinet des médailles Paris, no. 206. Side A. Photograph: Bibliothèque nationale de France	209
12.4	Dover's B64. Side B. Photograph: Bibliothèque nationale de France	210
12.5	Dover's B76. Painter from Beazley's 'Group E', black-figure belly amphora, *c.* 550 BC, found in Vulci, Etruria. Vatican, Museo Gregoriano Etrusco 352, renumbered as 17829. Photograph: Copyright of the Governorate of the Vatican City-State Directorate of the Vatican Museums	211
12.6	Dover's B114. Taleides Painter, black-figure Lekythos, *c.* 530 BC, provenance unknown. Princeton University Art Museum 86.53. Photograph: Princeton University Art Museum/ Art Resource NY	213
12.7	Dover's B342. Fragment from an incense burner by a 'Painter akin to that of the Nicosia Olpe', *c.* 530 BC, provenance unknown. Boston Museum of Fine Arts 08.31i. Photograph: Boston Museum of Fine Arts	214
12.8	Dover's B250. The Painter of Berlin 1686, black-figure amphora, *c.* 540 BC, from Vulci, Etruria. British Museum 1865,1118.39. Photograph: British Museum	215
12.9	Dover's B250. The side Dover neither cites nor illustrates. Photograph: British Museum	216
12.10	Dover's R196. Red-figure cup signed by 'Peithinos' as painter, *c.* 500 BC, from Vulci, Etruria. Berlin Antikensammlung, no. F2272. Side A. Photograph: Antikensammlung/Johannes Laurentius/Art Resource NY	221
12.11	Dover's R196. Side B. Photograph: Antikensammlung/Johannes Laurentius/Art Resource NY	221
12.12	Dover's R196. Interior with Peleus and Thetis. Photograph: Antikensammlung/Johannes Laurentius/Art Resource NY	223

CONTRIBUTORS

Carol Atack is Director of Studies in Classics and Fellow of Newnham College, University of Cambridge. Her research interests centre on ancient Greek political thought and its contemporary reception. She has published articles and chapters on Aristotle's account of kingship, conjectural history in Plato's *Laws*, the pseudo-Platonic Eighth Letter, Foucault's interpretation of Platonic parrhesia, and the political thought of Plato, Xenophon and Isocrates. Her books include *The Discourse of Kingship in Classical Greece* (2019) and *Anachronism and Antiquity* (2020, with Tim Rood and Tom Phillips).

Ewen Bowie, Emeritus Fellow of Corpus Christi College, Oxford, was its Praelector in Classics 1965–2007, and successively University Lecturer, Reader, and Professor of Classical Languages and Literature at the University of Oxford. He writes on early Greek elegiac, iambic and melic poetry; Aristophanes; Herodotus; Hellenistic poetry; and Greek literature and culture under the Roman Empire. He has published a commentary on Longus, *Daphnis and Chloe* (2019), edited a collection, *Herodotus: Narrator, Scientist, Historian* (2018), and co-edited *Archaic and Classical Choral Song* (2011) and *Philostratus* (2009). Cambridge University Press is publishing his collected papers (3 volumes: volume 1, 2021).

Christopher Carey is Emeritus Professor of Greek at University College London. He was educated at Jesus College, Cambridge, and has taught at Cambridge, St Andrews, University of Minnesota, Carleton College, Royal Holloway, and UCL. He has published on Greek lyric, epic, drama, history, historiography, Hellenistic poetry, oratory and law.

Ben Cartlidge is Lecturer in Greek Culture and Classical Receptions at the University of Liverpool. Previously he was a Leverhulme Early Career Research Fellow at Liverpool and held teaching posts at St John's College, Worcester College and Christ Church, Oxford. His teaching covers both Greek and Latin literature, and his research focuses on Greek comedy (particularly Menander), Greek Imperial literature (particularly Athenaeus), literary texts on papyrus, and linguistics. He has also published on the history of scholarship, editing a fragmentary lecture and correspondence by E. R. Dodds.

Elizabeth Craik is an honorary professor in the School of Classics at the University of St Andrews; she previously taught at St Andrews and Kyoto University, Japan. She has published widely on tragedy, social history and the history of medicine in ancient Greece. Publications include critical editions and translations of several Hippocratic works and a significant monograph, *The 'Hippocratic' Corpus: Content and Context* (2015).

Rebecca Dover is Kenneth Dover's granddaughter. Educated at Duncan of Jordanstone College of Art and Design and Edinburgh Telford College, she has worked as an artist, specializing in paintings of Scottish landscapes, for the past twenty years: see http://www.rebeccadover.com/about

Jaś Elsner is Humfry Payne Senior Research Fellow in Classical Art and Archaeology at Corpus Christi College, Oxford. His interests include the history and historiography of Greek and Roman art and issues in the reception of art more broadly, including viewing, pilgrimage and ekphrasis. His most recent book is *Eurocentric and Beyond: Art History, the Global Turn and the Possibilities of Comparison* (2022).

Constanze Güthenke is Professor of Greek Literature at the University of Oxford and E.P. Warren Praelector at Corpus Christi College, Oxford. She works on Greek literature and its reception and on disciplinary histories; she is, most recently, the author of *Feeling and Classical Philology: Knowing Antiquity in German Scholarship, 1770–1920* (2020) and a co-author of The Postclassicisms Collective's *Postclassicisms* (2020).

Stephen Halliwell is Wardlaw Professor Emeritus of Greek at the University of St Andrews and a Fellow of both the British Academy and the Royal Society of Edinburgh. His books include *The Aesthetics of Mimesis: Ancient Texts and Modern Problems* (2002, winner of the Premio Europeo d'Estetica 2008), *Greek Laughter: A Study of Cultural Psychology from Homer to Early Christianity* (2008, winner of the Criticos Prize 2008), *Between Ecstasy and Truth: Interpretations of Greek Poetics from Homer to Longinus* (2011), verse translations of Aristophanes for the Oxford World's Classics Series (1997–2022), and a commentary on pseudo-Longinus, *On the Sublime* (2022).

Sir Brian Harrison FBA is Emeritus Professor of Modern History, University of Oxford, and Emeritus Fellow of Corpus Christi College, Oxford, where he was Tutorial Fellow in history and modern politics 1967–2004 and Senior Tutor 1984–6 and 1988–90. His books include two volumes in the New Oxford History of England series, *Seeking a Role: The United Kingdom 1951–1970* (2009) and *Finding a Role? The United Kingdom 1970–1990* (2010). He was editor of *The History of the University of Oxford, Volume VIII: The Twentieth Century* (1994).

Richard Hunter is Regius Professor of Greek Emeritus at the University of Cambridge and a Fellow of Trinity College, Cambridge. His most recent books are *The Measure of Homer* (2018), *Euripides, Cyclops* (with Rebecca Laemmle, 2020), *The Layers of the Text: Collected Papers on Classical Literature 2008–2021* (2021) and *Greek Epitaphic Poetry: A Selection* (2022).

Robin Osborne has been Professor of Ancient History at the University of Cambridge since 2001. His work ranges across Greek History and Classical Archaeology. His most recent books are *The Transformation of Athens: Painted Pottery and the Creation of Classical Greece* (2018) and (with P. J. Rhodes) *Greek Historical Inscriptions 478–404* (2017). He has been President of the Society for the Promotion of Hellenic Studies, Chair of the Council of University Classical Departments, and Chair of the Classics Sub-Panel for the Research Excellence Framework 2014. He has been a Fellow of the British Academy since 2006.

Contributors

Jay Parini is D.E. Axinn Professor of English and Creative Writing at Middlebury College, Vermont, and the author of numerous works of poetry, fiction and criticism, including biographies of John Steinbeck, Robert Frost, William Faulkner and Gore Vidal, and the memoir *Borges and Me* (2020). His *The Last Station: A Novel of Tolstoy's Last Year* (1990) was made into an Academy Award-nominated film starring Helen Mirren and Christopher Plummer in 2009. He received a PhD in English Literature from the University of St Andrews in 1975. His personal website is http://jayparini.com/

Christopher Pelling is Emeritus Regius Professor of Greek at the University of Oxford. His books include *Literary Texts and the Greek Historian* (2000), *Plutarch and History* (2002), *Herodotus and the Question Why* (2019), *Twelve Voices from Ancient Greece and Rome* (with Maria Wyke, 2014) and commentaries on Plutarch, *Antony* (1988) and *Caesar* (2011), Herodotus 6 (with Simon Hornblower, 2017), and Thucydides 6 and 7 (2022). His chapter in this volume is a companion piece to a similar essay on A.W. Gomme in the volume he co-edited with Stephen Harrison, *Classical Scholarship and Its History: Essays in Honour of Christopher Stray* (2021).

Lucia Prauscello is a Senior Research Fellow of All Souls College, Oxford. She is the author of *Singing Alexandria: Music between Practice and Textual Transmission* (2006) and *Performing Citizenship in Plato's Laws* (2014), and co-editor of *Greek Comedy and the Discourse of Genres* (2013) and *Simonides Lyricus* (2020). She has published critical and papyrological articles on authors including Sappho and Callimachus, as well as on various aspects of ancient Greek literature and culture. She is currently working with Giovan Battista D'Alessio on an edition of Corinna and with Peter Parsons on the new OCT of Menander.

Tim Rood is Professor of Greek Literature and Dorothea Gray Fellow and Tutor in Classics at St Hugh's College, Oxford. His main research interests are Greek historiography and its reception. He is the author of *Thucydides: Narrative and Explanation* (1998), *The Sea! The Sea! The Shout of the Ten Thousand in the Modern Imagination* (2004), *American Anabasis: Xenophon and the Idea of America from the Mexican War to Iraq* (2010) and *Anachronism and Antiquity* (with Carol Atack and Tom Phillips, 2020). With Luuk Huitink he has edited *Xenophon: Anabasis Book III* for the Cambridge Greek and Latin Classics series (2019).

Frisbee Sheffield is Associate Professor of Classics at the University of Cambridge and a Fellow of Downing College. Areas of expertise are ancient Greek philosophy, particularly ethics, moral psychology, aesthetics and politics. She has also published on Hannah Arendt and the reception of Greek philosophy. She is the author of *Plato's Symposium: The Ethics of Desire* (2006) and co-editor of *Plato's Symposium: Issues in Interpretation and Reception* (2006), an annotated translation of Plato's *Symposium* (2008) and *The Routledge Companion to Ancient Philosophy* (2013). She has written numerous articles on Plato and is currently writing a book on Plato's *Phaedrus*.

Christopher Stray is Honorary Research Fellow in the Department of History, Heritage and Classics, Swansea University. His books include *Classics Transformed: Schools,*

Universities, and Society 1830–1960 (1998, Runciman Prize 1999), *An American in Victorian Cambridge: Charles Bristed's* Five Years in an English University (2008), and *Student Life in Nineteenth-Century Cambridge* (2022), a new edition of J.M.F. Wright's 1827 memoir, *Alma Mater: or, Seven Years at the University of Cambridge* (2023). His Festschrift, *Classical Scholarship and Its History Since the Renaissance*, edited by Stephen Harrison and Christopher Pelling, was published in 2018.

David Stuttard is an historian, translator and lecturer. Founder of the classical theatre company Actors of Dionysus, he edits Bloomsbury's *Looking at...* series on Greek drama. His own books include *Power Games: Ritual and Rivalry at the Ancient Greek Olympics* (2012), *A History of Ancient Greece in Fifty Lives* (2014), *Greek Mythology: A Traveller's Guide from Mount Olympus to Troy* (2016), *Nemesis: Alcibiades and the Fall of Athens* (2018) and *Phoenix: A Father, A Son, and the Rise of Athens* (2021). He is currently writing *Hubris: Pericles' Parthenon Project and the Invention of Athens*. His personal website is http://www.davidstuttard.com/

PREFACE

Kenneth Dover's scholarly career almost exactly filled the second half of the twentieth century: he was appointed to his first academic position, a fellowship of Balliol College, Oxford, in 1948, and he published his last book, *The Evolution of Greek Prose Style*, in 1997. Over the five decades between those dates, he rapidly acquired and long sustained the status of one of the world's leading authorities on ancient Greek literature and culture, fashioning himself as a figure who combined daunting philological prowess (including expertise in stylistics, textual criticism and metrics) with a distinctive conception of historical interpretation as the master-art not just of Classics but of the humanities in general. It is in keeping with the importance which Dover attached to history, in the widest sense, that his own career, together with the development of Classics as a discipline during that same period, should now be a fitting subject in its own right for historical scrutiny and investigation. Between them, the essays collected here aim to shed light both on Dover as an individual scholar and on the web of academic and intellectual relationships in which he stood to the changing structures of his discipline. They also inevitably (and rightly) represent a variety of perspectives and judgements, especially where controversial aspects of Dover's career are concerned. The editors have tried to encourage strong independent thinking (something that Dover himself valued highly); needless to say, they should not be taken to agree with all the views advanced by contributors. It is certainly testimony to the remarkable range and character of Dover's work that it can be profitably approached from so many angles.

The present volume was originally planned to mark the centenary of Dover's birth in 2020, as was the conference at Corpus Christi College, Oxford, on which it is based and which took place belatedly in September 2021. Given the disruptions caused by the coronavirus pandemic, it is with a feeling of considerable relief (as well as gratitude to all contributors, including the writers of 'memories', for their cooperation and efficiency) that the editors are now able to bring the volume to publication with the centenary at least in recent memory. The book makes a special point of encompassing discussion of the 'life' alongside the 'work'; when Dover published his memoir, *Marginal Comment*, in 1994, he himself was preoccupied with the interaction between the personal and the professional in the shaping of his career. It is worth adding in this connection that the present volume is appearing in conjunction with a reissue of *Marginal Comment*, now furnished with annotations (by the same editors) which provide historical information and guidance for those who wish to engage closely with Dover's own account of his life.

The editors would like to record their warm thanks to Helen Moore (President), Constanze Güthenke and Henner Petin for enabling the 2021 conference to take place so productively and enjoyably at Corpus Christi College; to the Corpus archivist, Julian

Reid, and the Oxford University Press archivist, Martin Maw, for arranging access to papers in the College's and the Press's archives; to Sir Brian Harrison and Sir Keith Thomas for sharing materials relating to Dover and his career; to Catherine Brown, Kenneth Dover's daughter, for the invaluable loan of, and permission to quote from, Dover's letters to his parents; and, finally, to Alice Wright and Lily Mac Mahon at Bloomsbury for their constructive help and advice throughout the preparation of the book.

SH and CS

August 2022

ABBREVIATIONS

(= indicates entries in the Bibliography, where further details can be found)

EGPS	Dover, *The Evolution of Greek Prose Style* (= Dover 1997a)
G&G	Dover, *Greek and the Greeks* (= Dover 1987)
G&L	Dover, *The Greeks and their Legacy* (= Dover 1988a)
GH	Dover, *Greek Homosexuality* (= Dover 1978, 1989, 2016)
GPM	Dover, *Greek Popular Morality* (= Dover 1974)
HCT	*A Historical Commentary on Thucydides* (= Gomme, Andrewes, Dover 1945–81)
LSJ	H.G. Liddell and R. Scott, eds, *A Greek-English Lexicon*, 9th edn (Oxford, 1940), with a revised supplement, ed. P.G.W. Glare (Oxford, 1996)
MC	Dover, *Marginal Comment: A Memoir* (= Dover 1994 and 2023)
ODNB	*Oxford Dictionary of National Biography* (https://www.oxforddnb.com/)
Retribution	D. Cannadine, ed., *A Question of Retribution?* (= Cannadine, ed., 2020)

INTRODUCTION
Christopher Stray

This book derives from a conference originally planned to celebrate the centenary of Kenneth Dover's birth in 1920. Centenaries are curious things. It is common for birthdays celebrating ages ending in a zero to be seen as special, and so the double-zero of 100 has an even greater conventional claim to our attention. As the Oxford ancient historian Oswyn Murray remarked in 2008, reviewing a book about his teacher Arnaldo Momigliano (1908–87):

> A centenary is a difficult age. You will have been dead some twenty years; those who celebrate you fall into three groups: ageing disciples who knew you (and perhaps revere you too much; your enemies will hopefully keep silent); those who have become famous since your death, who are as concerned for their own reputations as for yours; and young Turks out to kill or at least appropriate their predecessor.[1]

Murray went on to say:

> The younger generation see Momigliano as a predecessor rather than a model – the worst fate of being a centenarian, not forgotten but reinterpreted simply as a stage in the inexorable progress of a discipline.

In his introduction to the book Murray was reviewing, its editor wrote that Momigliano had not yet made the transition 'from a remembered figure to a fully historical one ... Our volume ... is an attempt to move him in that direction'.[2] The aim of the present volume can be summarized more simply: to explore and appraise the achievements of an outstanding scholar for whom life and work were intimately connected, and whose publications included an autobiography. Similarly, its contributors do not belong to the groups cynically identified by Murray: their project is historical, not political – a project of recovery.[3]

Kenneth Dover remembered Momigliano himself as an exemplary figure: 'For learning, accuracy of recall, speed of absorption and breadth of historical interests he was a man whose like I have not known' (*MC* 64). Something similar might, mutatis mutandis, be said of Dover himself. He was remarkable for pursuing advanced scholarship in both language and history. His first and last books (Dover 1960, 1997a) were significant contributions to the study of Greek language, but he also produced work on literature (Aristophanes, Plato, Thucydides) and social history (homosexuality, popular morality).

On top of this, he made a considerable reputation as an accomplished administrator, from his precocious appointment as senior tutor of Balliol aged thirty-one to the positions he later held as Dean of Arts and later Chancellor at St Andrews, President of Corpus Christi and later of the British Academy.[4]

Parents and son

One of Dover's final achievements was to compose a striking and controversial account of his own life, which necessarily mentioned his life as a scholar but which was, as he himself emphasized, the autobiography of a man who happened to be an academic, rather than an 'academic autobiography' as one of the Oxford University Press readers suggested.[5] Dover's *Marginal Comment* was noted (and in some ways notorious) for its revelations, especially about the sexual activity of both the author and others. This has perhaps taken attention away from the absence of other aspects of his life. In this respect it resembles Dodds' autobiography (Dodds 1977), whose very title hints at absences, a theme echoed in the book's epigraphs: 'The persons we have been are lost rather than fulfilled in what we become' (John Cowper Powys); 'Each half lives a hundred different lives' (Matthew Arnold).[6] Dover's typically forensic analysis of his and his parents' lives can be seen in the characterological analyses he produced in 1940, apparently at the suggestion of his then teacher Max Beck (see Figure 0.1).[7]

The analytical approach they represent might be linked with the stemmatic timeline of the development of his own interests (reproduced at the end of Halliwell 2011) that he produced for an autobiographical lecture in Rome in 1993, and perhaps also with his forensic deployment of statistics in response to criticism of *Marginal Comment*. The categories in question stem from a long tradition of such analyses, which began with the *Characters* of Theophrastus (c. 371–287 BC). The system used by Beck probably derived from the work of the Dutch philosopher Gerard Heymans (1857–1930), who recognized eight personality types. Four were emotional: nervous, choleric, sentimental, and passionate; four lacking in emotion: amorphous, sanguine, apathetic, and phlegmatic.[8] Percy Dover is identified as 'nervous and choleric'.

One of the absences in *Marginal Comment* has to do with the dialogues Dover conducted with his parents by letter when he was away from home.[9] These conversations, which can be seen in the surviving correspondence, throw light on an ongoing epistolary relationship that has been overshadowed by Dover's account of his father's moody and aggressive character.[10] It is worth remembering that the diagram above was shared with his parents, to be the subject of conversation rather than Dover's private introspection; but such conversations are not mentioned in *Marginal Comment*.

Some of Dover's scholarship was also controversial, though not to the same degree as *Marginal Comment*. According to his British Academy memoirists Donald Russell and Stephen Halliwell, *Greek Homosexuality* was 'the most widely known and controversial' achievement of his long and productive scholarly career.[11] Most of the controversy in which he was involved, however, sprang from events outside his life as a scholar: the

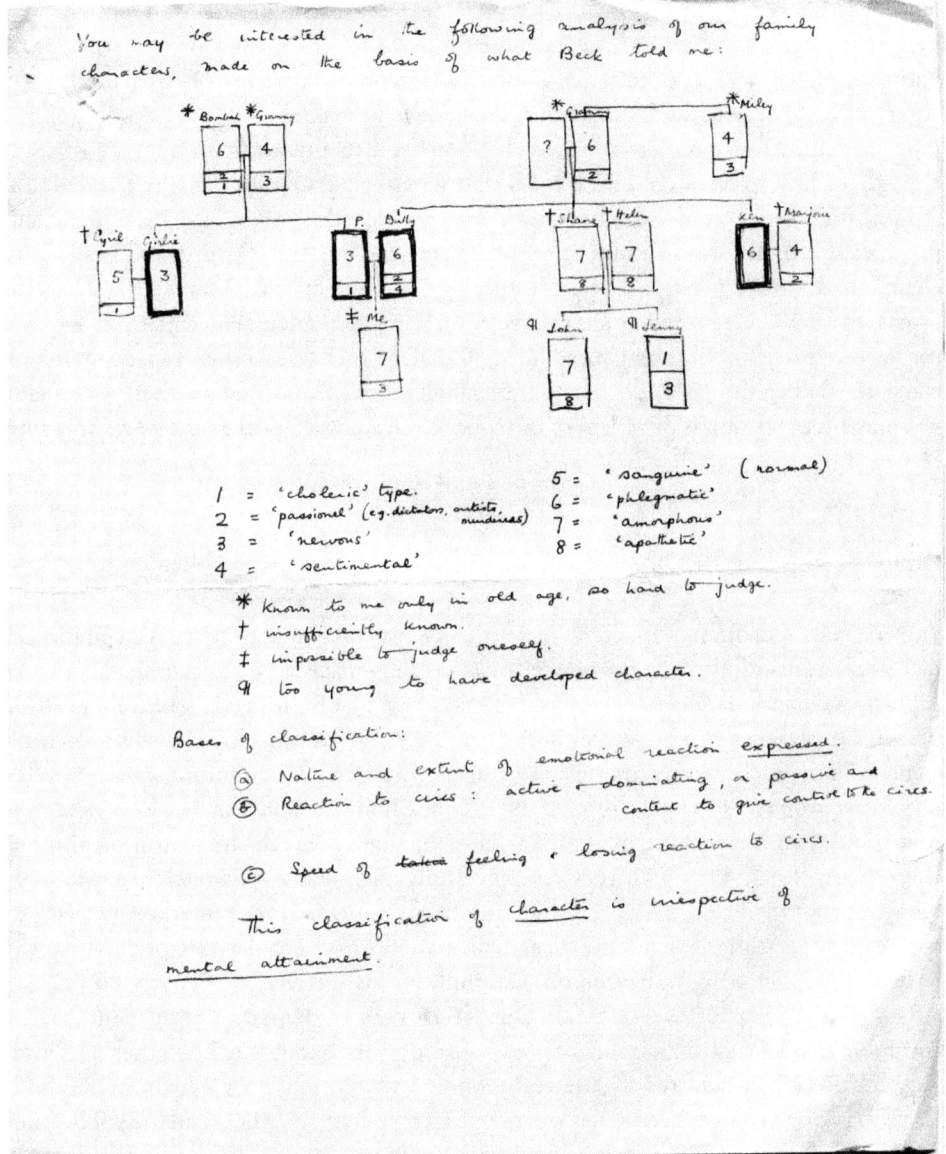

Figure 0.1 The Dover family: a characterological analysis, May 1940.

Aston affair (see Bowie's chapter), the Blunt affair (see Osborne's chapter), and the publication of his memoir *Marginal Comment* (see Stray's chapter on this, and Halliwell's introduction to the reissue of the memoir, in Dover 2023). Dover's undergraduate career at Oxford, on the other hand, was a model of conventional academic achievement, and his success in winning prizes brought him, as he himself noted, to the attention of the local dons. As he told his parents in June 1939, 'It looks as if my two fords (Gaisford and

Hertford) have put me on the ladder of fame'.[12] He consolidated his reputation by successful performances in seminars run by Eduard Fraenkel, the Corpus Professor of Latin, and later by Theodore Wade-Gery, the Wykeham Professor of Ancient History. After military service and graduation, he taught at Balliol and at St Andrews and published numerous books and articles: by 1960 his academic reputation was substantial enough for him to be offered the Regius chair of Greek at Oxford.[13] His refusal led to a striking divergence from the conventional success story that might have been predicted, in which all roads for an ambitious and talented scholar led to Oxford, and the Regius chair was the most prestigious position there. The character of Oxford as a collegiate university, however, provided alternative routes to academic achievement, in Dover's case as president of Corpus Christi, a small college that was known especially for its classical staffing. In 1988, during the Triennial classical meeting of that year, Keith Thomas, his successor as president of the college, referred to Dover as 'the world's leading Hellenist'.[14]

Dover as scholar and analyst

Dover's analytical orientation complicates a conventional distinction between empiricist fact-grubbing and theorizing; his self-declared empiricism was accompanied by a sophisticated and meticulous analysis. His insistence that he always began from his own personal experience can be seen as both energizing and limiting: his remarks on gender transposition in 'Eros and nomos' (1964a, 35) are curiously reminiscent of Jowett's notorious proposal to render references to Greek homosexuality in Plato's *Symposium* innocuous: 'had [Plato] lived in our times, he would have made the transposition himself' (see Turner 1981, 425).[15] Dover was powerfully inclined to self-reference and self-reflection, but he displayed, as Halliwell points out in his chapter, 'a marked aversion to sustained theorization of his practices or his values as a scholar'. This tendency was noticed, less flatteringly, by Simon Goldhill in his review of Dover's edition of Aristophanes' *Frogs* (Dover 1993a): 'One of Dover's trademarks is the bluff use of common sense laced with modern and often personal analogies.' Another reviewer, Kenneth Reckford, referred to 'the common and comic sense for which Sir Kenneth Dover has long been admired'.[16] It is worth noting that in the year between the publication of the edition and of these reviews, the appearance of *Marginal Comment* had thrown light on Dover's ways of thinking.[17]

Dover and others

One way to look at Kenneth Dover is to consider his relationship with others. His parents' difficult relationship posed problems for his own relationship with them, but he was able to manage this when he was away from home, in part by focusing on interests he shared with them. Among these were music and books, but also the life of Gangtown, the imaginary world he had created as a child and populated with simian figures based on the stuffed toys he had accumulated, especially the glamorous and ruthless Wimpee (*MC* 13, 17, 29). Such fantastic creations were not uncommon in children's lives, but it was much less common for their parents to be involved. It was perhaps the absence of siblings that encouraged the emergence of this shared inter-generational involvement.

Once at school, Dover found other adults to whom he could relate. At St Paul's, the most important were his classical teachers George Bean (Greek), Philip Whitting (Ancient History) and Robert James (Latin). Whitting, he thought 'the most memorable teacher I have ever known' (*MC* 36), but Bean's understanding of Greek was 'extraordinary', and he was 'subtle and imaginative' in composition (ibid.). Dover's relationship with Bean will also have been deepened by their going on a holiday to Greece together with another pupil in 1938 (*MC* 38). At Oxford he was impressed by the professors of Latin and Greek, Eduard Fraenkel and E.R. Dodds, but came into closer contact with his Balliol tutor Russell Meiggs; Meiggs and Fraenkel competed to recruit Dover to work on literature (Fraenkel) or history (Meiggs). His tutorials began a lifelong friendship with his tutorial partner Donald Russell, whose interests and skills complemented Dover's own: he was a talented literary critic but less good at ancient history and headed toward a career in Mods teaching while Dover aimed for Greats. Russell's generous and benign character contrasted with that of a slightly younger friend, Hugh Lloyd-Jones, who was given the Regius chair of Greek in 1960 after Dover refused it. Lloyd-Jones' Greek scholarship was on a par with Dover's own, but much more centred on literature, and he was a spiky and sometimes aggressive individual, competitive where Russell was cooperative. Unlike Dover, Lloyd-Jones also had a considerable interest in the history of scholarship (see e.g. Lloyd-Jones 1982). Dover's papers include several typically pugnacious letters from the Manchester Latinist Harry Jocelyn, a keen student of the history of scholarship, and it is unfortunate that there is no sign of any replies from Dover.[18] Looking further afield, we might compare Dover with the American scholar of ancient history Moses Finley (1913–86), who emigrated to Britain in 1954 after being sacked by Rutgers University for refusing to say whether he had belonged to the Communist Party. Finley was almost employed by Christ Church, but went instead to Jesus College, Cambridge. Dover admired Finley's ability to ask new questions about the ancient world; Finley however was critical of Dover's historical work (Finley 1973, 111 n. 25), and the two men seem never to have corresponded, though they might both be seen, in different ways, as outsiders.[19]

Oxford and elsewhere

One of the most striking aspects of Dover's career is the way he disturbed the conventional topography of Classics in Britain by moving to St Andrews in 1955 and then, five years later, rejecting the opportunity to return to Oxford. Since the mid-nineteenth century a number of new universities had been founded in Britain, most of which had Classics departments. In some cases, their strengths lay in science, and the inclusion of Classics was a concession to a notion of the university as an institution that necessarily had a humanities component. In this new, expanded world of higher education, Oxford and Cambridge retained their traditional prestige, if not supremacy: it became common for promising young academics to make their name in Oxbridge before moving to provincial departments, where they rose to chairs, and in some cases later returned to Oxford or Cambridge. This informal cursus honorum can be seen in the career of the Cambridge scholar Richard Jebb (1841–1905), who was elected to the Glasgow Greek chair in 1875 and returned to Cambridge when he became Regius Professor of Greek in 1889, and of Gilbert Murray (1866–1957), who succeeded Jebb at Glasgow and moved back to Oxford to the Regius chair of Greek in 1908. For an ambitious academic, a move to a provincial university involved a trade-off between power and prestige; the choice lay between being one of many fish in a large pond and being a big fish in small pond.[20] Here the career of E.R. Dodds represents a transitional phase in that history: having been helped by the support of his teacher Gilbert Murray to gain chairs at Reading and then at Birmingham, he returned to the Oxford Regius chair in 1936. In his case his provincial posts were more than simply way-stations on the way to Oxford. Already an outsider as an Irishman, a supporter of Sinn Fein and a student of postclassical thought (Neoplatonism), he encountered resentment and opposition on his arrival in Oxford.[21]

As Dover remarked in his letter of refusal in 1960, he thought it would be impossible to change the teaching of Classics in Oxford as Regius Professor, whereas in his position as a professor at St Andrews he could control or at least influence the curriculum and teaching. The Scottish universities were run differently from those in England, though St Andrews differed from the other major Scottish universities, Glasgow, Aberdeen and Edinburgh, in being rural and residential – the nearest Scottish equivalent to Oxbridge. Looking further back in Dover's career, when we consider the individual factors that led him to the decentring of his own alma mater, we cannot overestimate the role of his experience in military service. His years as a junior officer, interacting daily with the rank and file, had a lasting effect on him (cf. *MC* 52). This makes it all the more intriguing that he apparently used Aeneas' morale-boosting speech in the first book of Vergil's *Aeneid* to help quell an incipient mutiny among the troops (Dover 1988b, translated in this volume as an appendix to Halliwell's chapter). It is surely likely, however, that he quoted it in translation and did not identify the source.

Dover in the history of Classics

Where are we to locate Kenneth Dover as a scholar and as a public intellectual? He was certainly one of the leading classical scholars of his generation and stood out among his contemporaries both for the wide range of his work and for his methodological sophistication. This made him a significant figure in what might, in Oswyn Murray's terms, be called the 'progress of a discipline' (Murray 2008, quoted above), though we can hardly assume that this is 'inexorable', or indeed that it is, in any Whiggish sense of the word, 'progressive'.

The history of Classics in Britain since 1900 shows a steady marginalizing of the subject in the public sphere. I have mentioned the cases of Gilbert Murray and Richard Jebb, both with a high public profile, but we can also find cases of professionalism associated with lower profiles. An example is Murray's predecessor Ingram Bywater, Regius Professor of Greek in Oxford 1893–1908, who was content to pursue scholarship and bibliophily, in marked contrast both to Murray and to his own predecessor Benjamin Jowett, Regius Professor 1855–93 (Chapman 1922). In Cambridge, Jebb's successor Henry Jackson, Regius Professor 1906–21, was an important liberal reformer in the university, but lacked a national profile. His Trinity College colleague James Frazer acquired one, but only after finishing a large-scale commented translation of Pausanias' *Description of Greece* (Frazer 1898) and emigrating to the wider and more exotic world of the *Golden Bough* (Frazer 1890–1905). Another Trinity colleague, A.E. Housman (Professor of Latin 1911–36), encapsulated the split between professionalism and cultural production by being at once professor and poet (see, most recently, Vincent 2018). Dover's place in a later stage of this history was noted by Mary Beard in her review of his memoir (Beard 1995): '*Marginal Comment* may well come to be seen as the book that finally marked [the departure of Classics] from the centre of the cultural stage in this country . . . there is a wide change here; . . . the growing professionalisation of Classics has removed it decisively from its place in the wider, non-university, intellectual culture of Britain.'

Life and work together

How can Dover's life and his work be considered as a unity? A striking example relates to verbal and written style, both his own and that of the authors he studied. His publications included books on Greek word order and Greek prose style (Dover 1960, 1997: see Cartlidge's chapter), and he saw through the press a second edition of Denniston's 1934 classic *Greek Particles* (1954).[22] Behind this lay a long involvement in the study of other languages, especially those of Melanesia; it was only in the 1940s that Dover focused his attention entirely on Greek (and even after that, he occasionally returned to the subject, for example in his 1977 Bowra lecture on 'Song-language in primitive cultures' (Dover 1987, chapter 1). As Cartlidge remarks in his chapter: 'It is interesting that Dover's analysis of style begins with self-reflection: "I try to make every sentence not only clear and precise but also architecturally, phonologically and rhythmically attractive"' (see *MC* 201). This could mean taking five minutes over a sentence, just as he had spent six to twelve hours on a prose composition (*MC* 67). The importance of style in Dover's thinking is shown by the fact that the extract I have just quoted comes from a chapter in *Marginal Comment* entitled 'Style 1977–1994' (*MC* 199–204).[23] 'Phonologically attractive' reminds us of his remark in the preface to *Marginal Comment* that he rejected the alternative title 'Unfenced Roads' as being 'phonologically repellent' (*MC* [vii]). Cartlidge's point can be reinforced by David Stuttard's memories of Dover, which are included in this volume:

> During my undergraduate and postgraduate years Kenneth did, of course, return occasionally to St Andrews ... to give the occasional public lecture, and I experienced at first-hand what I had only heard about from others – the precise yet elegant style; the inimitably cultured smoker's voice; the delivery which, though always measured, was never dull. As I listened, I was struck by how he always spoke in perfectly formed sentences – no hesitations; no discourse markers; no filler words – sentences that were so well-honed and so entirely discrete that at the end of each you could almost hear the full-stop. It was something that I noticed in my later conversations with him, too: no matter how informal the setting, his sentence structure, his choice of vocabulary, his ability to express the most complex ideas with limpid clarity and razor-sharp precision suggested that, before he said a word, each utterance was fully weighed and each idea was fully shaped and formed, like an Athena emerging from the head of Zeus.

Stuttard's account of Doverian sentences chimes with Dover's own account of his writing: we might imagine titles like *The Evolution of ... Prose Style* and ... *Word Order* (Dover 1997a, 1960) in which 'Greek' was replaced by 'Doverian'.

This volume is one of a pair, co-edited with Stephen Halliwell, which link biography and autobiography: such linkage between the two genres is not common. Gilbert Murray's unfinished autobiography (Smith and Toynbee 1960) was accompanied by essays on him written by his friends, but that must have been motivated in part by a desire to make a commemorative volume after his death in 1957: his autobiographical fragment runs only to eighty pages, little more than a third of the book. In Dover's case his autobiography had been published sixteen years before his death, and the project of reissuing it alongside a centenary volume has made it possible to add new material to a book that both needed and deserved annotation.[24] The present volume is intended to complement the autobiography; we hope that together the chapters that follow will provide a rounded portrait of a remarkable scholar. Part I (Chapters 1–6) deals with Dover's life, Part II (Chapters 7–15) with his work. The volume ends with an epilogue by Stephen Halliwell, who has a good claim to know the man and his work better than anyone else.

Notes

1. Murray 2008, 414. In a later musing on this theme, Murray (who was born in 1937) remarked that: 'As imperceptibly one approaches ripe old age, time becomes an ever more problematic concept. One's relationship to events changes, for they lie in the past rather than the future: so time past overtakes time future, as one becomes truly an ancient historian' (Murray 2011, 301).
2. Miller 2007, 8.

3. The same can be said of two earlier celebrations, of Gilbert Murray (Stray, ed., 2007a) and of E.R. Dodds (Stray, Pelling and Harrison, eds, 2019).
4. See the chapters by Craik, Bowie and Osborne, as well as Sir Brian Harrison's 'Memory'.
5. In his response, Dover insisted that the book was 'an autobiography *simpliciter* ... academics are non-academic for much of their waking lives'. See Stray's chapter on *Marginal Comment*, pp. 99–103.
6. Arnold's dictum would be easier to understand if it read 'half-lives' (cf. Stray and Pelling 2019, 4).
7. The contemporary context of this kind of analysis is discussed by Wyatt and Teubner 1944.
8. Heymans' terminology constitutes a link between ancient schools of thought and modern experimental psychology (Crocq 2013). An earlier system of four temperaments had influence in a variety of genres: for example, Carl Nielsen's second symphony is entitled 'The Four Temperaments'.
9. These are discussed in Stray's chapter on Dover at school and university.
10. *MC* 7 and 10.
11. Russell and Halliwell 2012, 164.
12. Dover to his parents, 12 June 1939.
13. He also refused an offer of a tenured chair at Berkeley after his Sather lectures there in 1967 (*MC* 139). Refusals of the Oxford Greek chair have been rare, though one occurred in 2015, and as with Dover himself, from outside Oxford. Dover also rejected an offer from Pittsburgh in 1961 and the chair of Greek at University College London in 1966.
14. The remark came in an unpublished address on the history of Classics given during the Triennial meeting in Oxford. My thanks to Sir Keith Thomas for sending me a copy of his address, and for allowing me to quote from it.
15. Their motivations were of course very different; Dover was explicitly comparing homo- and hetero-, and in his article on expurgation (Dover 1980b) was himself scathing about the *evasive* use of gender transpositions.
16. Simon Goldhill, *Classical Philology* 90 (1995): 86–91, at 89; Kenneth Reckford, *American Journal of Philology* 116 (1995): 488–90, at 488.
17. In a recent volume, Simon Goldhill has stated that Dover mistook self-exposure for self-reflection (Goldhill 2022, 10); my own view is that it would be hard for an unprejudiced reader of *Marginal Comment* to come to this conclusion.
18. This would usually be signified by a tick in red ink, often with a comment, but they are absent from Jocelyn's letters.
19. Cf. Peter Garnsey's discussion of Finley's relationship with Arnaldo Momigliano, in Jew et al., eds, 2016, 193–209.
20. As this suggests, institutions play a large role in such histories; cf. the recent analysis in Tribe 2022.
21. For a discussion of what Dodds brought to Oxford from the provinces, see Stray 2019.
22. Dover insisted that his role in the revision of Denniston's book was 'editorial' (*MC* 72); the main text was in fact photographically reproduced from the first edition. A similar procedure had been followed with the 'Oxford red' editions of Euripides, using the plates of Gilbert Murray's OCT; this led to conflicts between the editors' readings and those of Murray's text (Henderson 2007).

23. The start date is the year in which Dover, having been elected President of Corpus Christi College, began giving lectures on the history of Greek prose style at the invitation of the Oxford Classics Faculty.
24. Needed, because, inter alia, some references in Dover's text would not be clear to twenty-first-century readers, and the index is inadequate. Deserved, because *Marginal Comment* is a remarkably frank account of the life of a remarkable man who was also a great scholar. The new edition, by the editors of the present volume (Dover 2023), will, it is hoped, remedy both defects.

PART I
THE LIFE

CHAPTER 1
DOVER AT SCHOOL AND UNIVERSITY
Christopher Stray

The young Kenneth Dover wrote frequently to his parents Percy and Dorothy Dover when he was away from home. As a teenager he addressed them as 'Darling Both'; as an undergraduate he wrote to 'Dear Dully and Pop'. As this suggests, he was closer to his warm and affectionate mother than to his father, a minor civil servant at the Ministry of Transport, who was often irascible and at times furious. The tension between affectionate closeness and defensive distance ran deep in Dover's upbringing.[1] Father and son did however find common ground in some areas. Percy Dover was a keen pianist, and father and son bonded over music; Dover's letters home are full of references to concerts, and he regularly enclosed programmes for local events when at Oxford. Some of his comments on music suggest a more than casual perception: for example, he declared that the opening bar of the last movement of Mozart's 'Jupiter' Symphony (for which he wrote out a musical example) could 'claim first place as the clearest expression in music of pure happiness, beating the last movement of the Franck violin sonata for this claim because of its greater element of a sort of pagan exultance'.[2] Dover and his father also discussed wants and acquisitions of second-hand books. In retirement in Algarkirk in Lincolnshire, Percy Dover devoted himself to research on the history of his local community, and his son tried, though in vain, to have his book on the subject published by Oxford University Press.

In the days when people wrote letters, they did so when they were at a distance from their family and friends. Kenneth Dover's first letters to his parents were written when he was 14, from a hospital where he was being treated for scarlet fever. He went to a day school so for the most part had no need to write to his parents but did so when he went on two holidays to Greece in 1937 and 1938. Later series of letters were prompted by his going up to Oxford in 1938, by his British and foreign postings during World War II, and then by his appointments in Oxford (1948) and St Andrews (1955). This material provides detailed and fascinating insights into Dover's work and character; it will be much harder for future historians of scholarship to track the lives and careers of our contemporaries, whose correspondence is largely electronic and evanescent.

Dover spent six weeks in hospital recovering from scarlet fever in the spring of 1934; he wrote home regularly and about two dozen letters survive. They report on the state of health, his co-patients, food and treatment, but also on his reading, and in particular on the state of the secondary literature on comparative philology and on Indo-European and Oceanic languages. (Bear in mind that at this point he was fourteen years old.) A running theme in his letters is the life of Gangtown, a place run by the despotic Wimpee. In his memoir *Marginal Comment*, Dover described Wimpee as 'female, resolute, charming and unscrupulous' (p. 13). The only known portrait, from one of Dover's letters, shows Wimpee made up for the Gangtown beauty contest. Wimpee was in fact a stuffed toy, and like all the inhabitants of Gangtown, a monkey. She was overthrown in 1933 in an internal coup, made a comeback in 1936, but after that faded from Dover's life, though she is referred to occasionally in later letters. In his first term at Oxford, Dover narrowly escaped embarrassment when he opened his notebook in a lecture, only to find that it contained a map of 'Wimpeeland' he had drawn.[3] While in hospital Dover sent his parents several games based on Gangtown which he asked them to type up. As Dover himself pointed out, children tended either to form real gangs, or to imagine them; he did the latter, perhaps because as an only child he lacked the company of siblings.[4] What is striking about Wimpee and the other inhabitants of Gangtown is that they were often discussed by both Dover and his parents. In one letter home from hospital, he reported that he had had a letter from Wimpee. He then told them about the strange creatures he found crawling on his pillow: BLWUP, OODZ, and GISWASHK, and the king of them all, a long creature with a long name: KCHOQTLOTLETPQOSKKCHEM. Dover reported finding hundreds of them all over the pillow at night. The centrality of Wimpee and her clan to Dover's life was surely reflected in his memory that he had fantasized about 'growing a prehensile tail covered with dense fur'.[5]

The family lived in Putney, in SW London, so that Dover was able to attend St Paul's School, where he was taught by some of the best classical teachers in the country. He later recalled that

> there was great pressure to follow (and excel in) an academic career of traditional type, and I was persuaded that for an ambitious boy with strong linguistic interests, there were only two options: Greek + Latin and French + German. I was not encouraged to respect the latter, and in any case it wouldn't have been Other enough for my taste. Within Classics, Greek was not only more Other than Latin, but also, to my mind, then as now, the vehicle of a more powerfully appealing literature.[6]

Dover got on especially well with George Bean and Philip Whitting. Bean taught Greek but also had an interest in archaeology; after the war, he helped to found the department of Classics at the University of Istanbul and taught there for more than 20 years.[7] Whitting, a numismatist of some distinction and a Byzantinist, taught Dover ancient history.

In 1937 Dover went on an organized holiday in Greece, travelling by steamer to Athens, Santorini, Crete and Ithaca. His letters home give a vivid picture of the country, its inhabitants, his fellow travellers and life on board ship. This was SS *Cairo City*, chartered by a London-based Greek firm run by the Livas family. Dover's opinion of Greeks was very much of its time: 'The crew are entirely Greek, and more dago than you would ever think dagoes could be.' The lecturing staff included John Myres, Stanley Casson and Andrew Burn, all of them approved by Dover. In one letter he gave thumbnail sketches of some of his fellow travellers. 'Mellhuish: a Tottenham schoolmaster, a funny little man whose humour and classical knowledge are both considerable.'[8] Dover's description of Naomi Mitchison was brutal: 'a horse thinly disguised as a pig. She has abominable artist's capes, and legs like oak trees.' A few days later Mitchison gave a lecture on Socrates which Dover called 'uncritical bosh'. Naomi Mitchison was the daughter of the physiologist J.S. Haldane and sister of the biologist J.B.S. Haldane, with whom she worked on genetics. She was the author of over ninety books, including *Memoirs of a Spacewoman* (1962). Her best-known book, *The Corn King and the Spring Queen* (1932), was a striking and wide-ranging historical novel. It was set in Sparta and Egypt and included frank discussions of rape and homosexuality. Mitchison herself was polyamorous and had taken advice on Greek historical contexts from Theodore Wade-Gery, who had been her lover until his marriage in 1928. We shall meet him later on, in his role as Wykeham Professor of Ancient History at Oxford from 1939.

In 1938 Dover went on another trip to Greece, this time with his Greek teacher George Bean and a fellow pupil. They spent six weeks travelling through mainland Greece by mule and car, roughing it in what Dover called 'the old Greece', a peasant society very different from the relative luxury of Athens. His letters paint an unvarnished picture of conversational expectoration and revolting toilet practices.[9]

Oxford

George Bean and his colleagues were a team well-equipped to stretch a very talented pupil, and so it was not surprising that Dover gained the top scholarship to Balliol. He went up to Oxford in October 1938. His Mods tutor was Cyril Bailey, one of the most popular classical dons in Oxford. Bailey was an important link between dons and undergraduates and was widely known by his first name.[10] Dover got on very well with Bailey, who liked Dover's Greek compositions, though he thought some were a little strange – had they been written by an ancient Greek, he said, they would need a lot of annotation if published in modern times. Dover came to recognize Bailey's signs of approval – first of all a chuckle, and then a slap on the thigh – Bailey's own thigh, that is. Of his lecturers, the most impressive was E.R. Dodds, whose first lecture on the *Oresteia* made a considerable impact on Dover. He told his parents that 'His first lecture interested me enormously because he made just the same points about Aeschylus as I have always made in my essays, quite out of my own head and without any corroboration (indeed, opposed to such authorities as I did read at the time)' (12 October 1938). Dover described Dodds as 'a quiet, middle-aged, simian man with penetrating eyes.'[11] 'Simian' is surprising, until we remember the inhabitants of Gangtown: Dover was very fond of monkeys, and for him 'simian' was a term of praise.

In his second term, Dover encountered Eduard Fraenkel for the first time: 'Fraenkel is the last survival of German-Jewish scholarship. His English is not perfect ... his Greek pronunciation is unintelligible and his right hand is only a tenth the size of the left, but he's very good. . . . very clear, slow emphatic English – his Latin diction is so emphatic that he nearly falls off the dais' (16 January 1939). Dover won the Gaisford (Greek composition) prize this year, a remarkable achievement for a freshman, and was runner-up for the Hertford; the following year he gained a first in Mods. He realized that the local dons noticed the prizes; Fraenkel congratulated him and asked him to attend his *Agamemnon* class. As Dover told his parents, 'The Agamemnon classes are attended by dons, and if you make a name there half the classical world of Oxford knows about it. It looks as if my two fords (Gaisford and Hertford) have put me on the ladder of fame' (12 June 1939).

Dover was keen to begin ancient history in Greats, and also helped to found an undergraduate classical archaeology society. He was in fact about to engage with the tensions between individual interests and career planning and with the unique topography of Oxford Classics, in which the linguistic and literary work in Mods in the first five terms was succeeded by a mixture, not found elsewhere in Britain, of history and philosophy (ancient and modern) in the seven terms of Greats. E.R. Dodds commented in his autobiography that by the 1950s Greats was 'on the way to becoming ... a bizarre combination of two wholly unrelated subjects, epigraphically based history and modern logic'.[12] Relations between the Mods subfaculty and those of history and philosophy were strained at times. In his first term Dover told his parents of

> a wrong reasoning on my part that because we take Mods two years before Greats a Mods tutor is ipso facto inferior in intellect and salary to a Greats tutor. That ... is quite wrong, because Mods and Greats involve different subjects. The importance and pay among the Fellows of a College is graded solely by the numbers of years of service as a Fellow.
>
> 10 October 1938

As Donald Russell later described the situation, 'There were still people around for whom the subspecies Mods don was an inferior breed, not up to handling the more mature minds and capable only of donnish games and a sort of sophisticated proof-reading. That was offensive, and bred much ill-will.'[13] In the Easter term of 1940, Dover began the Greats course and had his first encounter with philosophy. At this point he found it a great stimulus: 'I have really fallen in love with philosophy; after only two essays I find it has induced a staggering increase in clarity of thinking' (4 May 1940). The Balliol tutors being engaged in war work, Dover had been farmed out to a Czech refugee he referred to as 'Beck'.[14] After the war, Dover returned to philosophy in the Greats course, but his teachers were Oxford men with rather different ideas, and he disliked their 'bloodless abstractions'.[15] It is striking that his first exposure to philosophy was at the hands of a representative of such a different tradition. An intriguing chart of family intellectual characteristics drawn in May 1940, and mentioned in the Introduction (see Figure 0.1, p. 3), was apparently inspired by Beck's teaching. The only mention of this teaching in Dover's memoir was to the effect that his Greats tutors were not very exacting and that he had written two essays on Hegel (*MC* 41).

The letter Dover sent to his parents at this point illustrates the continuing communication between them that complicates the picture of love and hate that can be drawn from the narrative in *Marginal Comment*. At his parents' request, Dover destroyed their letters after reading them, but they kept his own letters, which remained in a cupboard in Percy Dover's home at his death in 1978 and were only identified for what they were in 1990 (*MC* 2).[16] Dover's only reference to them is his statement that they were 'mainly narrative (with a disagreeably argumentative strain in the earlier years' (ibid.). The narrative strain can be illustrated from Dover's account of his Mods examinations in March 1940:

> Latin special books this afternoon: quite the worst paper I've ever seen. The essay question on Catullus was extremely difficult ... the translation pieces and pieces for comment from Catullus were all out of the dullest and least typical part of his work; one of the comment pieces was out of a poem not included in the syllabus, another clearly expected you to remember parts of the poem not quoted in the question, which is unfair on principle; ... I am reminded of what Barrington-Ward said to us in his last lecture: 'Whatever sort of paper you get on Catullus, it won't be worse than last year's. I happen to know who set that paper, and I strongly doubt whether the person in question knew anything at all about it.'[17] Well, I think they've let the same person loose again, and I also think he or she is jest a plain bastard. The trouble arises, probably, from the nature of Catullus, who is an author not read by many people because of his difficulty, and needs some appreciation, which the Moderators, who are all five of them Graecists, apparently have not got.
>
> 2 March

Here Dover's parents were probably simply an audience, but at times they were clearly in dialogue with him. In May, at the beginning of his Greats course, they challenged him 'to trace a historical event to purely economic causes', as he put it in a letter of 7 June in which he responded to the challenge. 'I thereupon took an event absolutely at random; at a battle in the 3rd Cy BC between two of the "Successors" – kings of large kingdoms in the E. Mediterranean after the time of Alexander.... when one of them defeated the other, instead of massacring the defeated army, he took them prisoner and they afterwards fought for him.'[18] He then pursued both sides of the dialogue himself, providing a series of questions and answers, and arguing that polis-loyalty had crumbled in the new post-Alexander situation. He concluded that a crucial factor in these changes was the suitability of Macedon and Thessaly for breeding horses on their plains, adding that 'I genuinely took that example at random, and I'd no idea when I started typing the argument where it was going to lead'. Whatever we may think of the argument, this is an impressive example of improvised historical analysis by a twenty-year-old undergraduate.[19]

Dover's letters also reveal that he corresponded with his parents about music. They both played the piano, his father at a high level, and joined in duets, and Dover reported to them on concerts he had attended and compared notes with them on recently released records. An anonymous contributor to the Balliol College magazine *Floreat Domus* recalled a question put to him in interview as an intending Balliol student: 'If Virgil had written a symphony rather than an epic, what key-colour might he have used to express the spirit of the age?'[20] The question was ascribed to Jasper Griffin, but it has been authoritatively described, by his former colleague Richard Jenkyns, as very unlike him.[21] Such anecdotes have often gravitated from their original location to well-known figures: could Dover be the original source? In the Lent term of 1939, Dover had to read rapidly through the *Aeneid*. When he reached the end, he told his parents that 'I have come for the first time to like Vergil. That sounds funny from a classical scholar, doesn't it? . . . he was really a great tragic dramatist who was obliged by his times to write in the epic medium.'[22] The inter-generic reference suggests that the Balliol anecdote might originally have featured Dover rather than Griffin.

In July 1940 Dover was called up, and was in the army until the autumn of 1945, when he resumed his Greats course. In Michaelmas term 1939 he had been one of ninety students who sat a special cut-down Mods examination arranged as part of wartime planning; then in Hilary term 1940 he was one of twenty who sat the regular full-blown examination. This unusual history, which ended in his gaining a distinction, is not mentioned in *Marginal Comment*.[23]

I shall not discuss Dover's army service in any detail, but it is worth mentioning that it was his experience in giving instruction in gunnery that convinced him that he was a good teacher. His military service was spent in charge of anti-aircraft batteries, and we might wonder why he was allocated to such work, while other talented classicists, including Donald Russell and Hugh Lloyd-Jones, were set to codebreaking and related activities.[24] During his military service he travelled to Egypt, Libya and Italy, taking classical texts with him to read when he could. During the North African campaign in July 1942, he was forced to abandon the rucksack containing his books. To his parents he reported that 'Some German now has most of my books' (13 July 1942). But he was writing as well as reading – he sent his parents twenty-eight chapters in all of a novel entitled *Paul's Rock*, before eventually abandoning it. In November 1939 he told his parents that he had written about twenty poems in the last three years; two have survived in his papers and are printed as an appendix to the present chapter. He also continued to explore the comparison of languages, wrote an essay on spelling reform, and was very pleased to find that his batman spoke Esperanto. In North Italy in 1944, when he was in charge of a Bofors gun unit, he was made responsible for captured German soldiers, and noticed that some of them spoke rather strange German, while the local Italian dialect was 'rough and consonantal'. His linguistic interests were clearly still alive, and he meditated a project on reduplication in Australian languages. This was given up on methodological grounds, but in 1946 he won the British Academy's Cromer prize for an essay on the translation of Greek poetry. This might be seen as marking the point at which Dover abandoned his ambition of specializing in the comparative study of languages, especially those of Melanesia.[25] He was however able to draw on this expertise. For example, in November 1946, at a meeting of the Oxford University Classical Society, George Thomson, the Marxist Professor of Greek at Birmingham, read a paper on 'The Origins of Poetry'. As Dover commented, 'This was right up my street, and I floored him on chimp language, and also on a point about poetry in Dobu' (16 November 1946). Dobu, as every schoolgirl knows, is an island off the coast of Papua; Dover had presumably read the anthropologist Reo Fortune's classic 1932 study *The Sorcerers of Dobu*.[26]

Dover gained a first in Greats, but his history marks were better than those in philosophy, which he found less engaging; nor was he impressed by the lecturers and tutors: 'I heard no lectures which aroused my interest in the subject ... The kind of linguistic analysis associated with the name of Oxford was not much in evidence when I was an undergraduate, though its great days were not far off' (*MC* 60–1). Ironically, while Dover had been away on military service, a group of women philosophers in Oxford had been developing a very different style of philosophizing.[27] In November 1946, Dover had a long talk with Fraenkel, who urged him not to be drawn by history too far away from classical literature, and professed himself very worried by the state of classical learning in England, which he thought Dover could do a lot to remedy if he got a job as a Mods don. 'Until Germany revives, if ever', he told Dover, 'the survival of the Classics depends almost entirely on this country. France has not produced any first-rate work on the Classics since the 16th century. The Americans never will, altho' they try so hard. Here at Oxford you have the best ancient historians in the world. But pure Classics, no: there are very few really good people' (28 November 1946).

The contrast between the literary study of Mods and the history and philosophy of Greats came into play in the relationship between Dover and his friend, rival, colleague and contemporary Donald Russell, who was paired with him for Greats as a pupil of the Balliol ancient historian Russell Meiggs. Meiggs recognized that Dover and Russell were very different, and at one point told them he should not have paired them for tutorials. In Meiggs' opinion, Russell had a better all-round brain than Dover, but was not as good at ancient history. Dover thought that the whole nature of the study of ancient history had been transformed by the publication of the Athenian tribute lists, and commented that 'I'm quite sure, the real tragedy of 1939–1945 is the holding up of the publishing of Vols XI-onwards of the new Corpus of Inscriptions of the Berlin Academy' (14 December 1945). The tribute lists were familiar to him, as he went to lectures given by Wade-Gery and Benjamin Meritt, two of the three editors. In February 1946 he told his parents, 'Meritt ... gave me a squeeze ... at the last class. A squeeze is a papier maché impression of an inscription, so don't misunderstand. ... I'll bring the one I have home with me. It's only about 5ft x 2, so it could be hung over the mirror in the bathroom to be read while shaving' (19 February 1946). The contrast between Dover and Russell was highlighted by their attitude to the Athenian tribute lists, which Dover loved but Russell viewed with distaste.

Dover's next move in getting himself noticed was to attend a Hesiod class run by Wade-Gery. At first it looked as if the only other member would be Arnaldo Momigliano, but eventually a few others joined in. After one meeting Dover wrote that he had spoken about the lawsuit between Hesiod and his brother: 'I stuck to my guns during an hour and a half's sustained attack on it from Wade-Gery ... as an undergraduate effort against a Professor it wasn't bad' (23 October 1946). After the next meeting, Dover commented, 'I see my difference of opinion with Wade-Gery coming in about a fortnight's time, and I am already bringing up artillery under cover of darkness' (5 November 1946). The metaphor evidently derived from his wartime career as officer in charge of a light anti-aircraft battery.[28]

In 1947 Dover married Audrey Latimer, the sister of a schoolfriend. They had a long and happy marriage and had two children. Dover's fascination with language led to detailed accounts, in his letters to his parents, of his son's and daughter's linguistic inventions. In 1948 he was appointed to a fellowship at Balliol, to teach both Greek language and literature and Greek history – an interesting crack in the wall between Mods and Greats, and one due to the then master, A.D. Lindsay.[29] His teaching of Greek composition is remembered by the playwright and director Kenneth Cavander:

> You would bring your work to Dover and then, seated on his left, you would wait for his diagnosis. It would come in the form of suggestions, perhaps a slight change of order here ... could you think of a less prosaic word here? .... perhaps, if you changed this for this ... and under his direction your clumsy pastiche would start to look a little more like a specimen from a lost fragment of some minor Greek poet – and then he would deliver his verdict. Kenneth Dover's moustache hedged a cautious smile, his spectacles planted and never, so far as I saw, removed, his frame, athletic and tall, supported by long legs fit for tramping miles over rocks. But it was his voice I remember best, the syllables softly rounded, the precise tone of the public school man, delivered like a doctor reassuring a patient – a reassurance that yes, this was not bad, you are not ailing too much, and you will surely, with practice, become better. It was all done with the tact of a friend, talking to someone he wanted to retain among his circle of other friends, knowing that what he was about to say might not be good news, but at least it could be couched in such a way that you would gladly come back and visit him again next week.[30]

Earlier in 1948, Dover had begun work on a DPhil thesis on late fifth-century Athens, supervised by Momigliano, but now gave it up and concentrated on teaching and publishing. Hearing that OUP planned to expand the OCT series, he offered them a volume on Antiphon. In his view, the Press were capitalizing on what he called 'the extinction of Teubner', that is, the collapse of the German publisher during the war. His work on the OCT was made easier when John Denniston's widow gave him her husband's Greek typewriter, which he used the following year to prepare the text of Denniston's book on Greek particles for republication.

As a teaching fellow, Dover could take pride in the achievements of his pupils, but, characteristically, he compared their achievements with his own. When the Mods results for 1949 came out, he remarked that 'My best pupil, the Scotsman Nisbet, I regret to say got a much better first than I did! An astonishing array of alpha and alpha, unmarred by anything as vulgar as an alpha beta. I console myself by reflecting that Mods is not such a stiff exam as it was in my day' (27 April 1949). In 1963, as Professor of Greek at St Andrews, he was external examiner for Martin West's DPhil thesis, an edition of and commentary on Hesiod's *Theogony*, and commented that 'I've nearly finished reading it, and it is so good that it almost depresses me; I don't think I could have done anything so good in the time at his age. Still he did for some inexplicable reason manage only a Second in Greats, so he must have an Achilles heel.'[31] West was in fact only the latest in a long line of Oxford men whose interests lay in language and literature, and whose high achievements in Mods preceded lower scores, and in some cases failure, in Greats. Dover and Russell had shared Mods teaching at Wadham and planned a new system whose long-term object was to create a much greater interest in getting to grips with the real problems of ancient civilization than the current Mods syllabus and the current way of teaching it were likely to create.

In 1951, Dover was appointed senior tutor of Balliol. He was then only 31, and his promotion was a recognition of his power of work and administrative talents. He saw his main task as securing a good intake of average men: as he told his parents, 'the great problem will be to get good commoners – the people who do well at sport. Balliol has no problem getting brighter men' (25 April 1951). At this point he was beginning to travel to other universities to give papers. At the University of Exeter, he met W.F. Jackson Knight, whom he called 'their tame lunatic' (26 May 1951). Later in the year, in Cambridge, he claimed to have put people right on a number of issues, and 'silenced both professors'.[32] Dover's friend Hugh Lloyd-Jones, who was now teaching in Cambridge, described his performance as 'throwing professors right and left' (19 August 1951). By the beginning of 1952 his long-term plans were laid to produce three large-scale works: a new edition of Aristophanes, a book on the language of Attic inscriptions, and a volume on Lysias.

In 1953 Eduard Fraenkel, Corpus Professor of Latin, and Theodore Wade-Gery, Wykeham Professor of Ancient History, reached retirement age. Embarrassingly enough, some members of the Faculty of Literae Humaniores recommended prolonging Wade-Gery's tenure but not Fraenkel's.[33] In Dover's view this was partly because Maurice Bowra, who was very anti-Fraenkel, was currently vice-chancellor. His own ideal scenario was for Wade-Gery to retire and be succeeded by Russell Meiggs, thus allowing Dover himself to gain more control over Classics in Balliol. As this suggests, Dover was now into the full swing of Oxford academic politics, and rather enjoying its machinations. In the event Wade-Gery did retire and was succeeded by Tony Andrewes. Meiggs was encouraged to apply but did not; Dover thought this was because it was not financially worthwhile for him to uproot himself from his Balliol accommodation in Holywell Manor, as he would have to, and find himself a house at his own expense. Dover's comment was, 'It's awful, the extent to which one's acceptance or refusal of a professorial chair turns nowadays on the availability of houses' (30 May 1953). This problem recurred, and I will return to it later on.

In Balliol itself, a vacant tutorial fellowship attracted several good candidates. One of them was described by Fraenkel as 'A superb technician, with no heart! Don't have him as a tutor.'[34] Another was seen by Dover as 'brilliant, but intolerable as a person and with a voice like a foghorn'.[35] The candidate who was best qualified on paper was a member of the Communist Party, something which as he himself admitted probably doomed his application.[36] In the end, the job went to Dover's own favourite, Gordon Williams, later well known for his 1968 book on tradition and originality in Roman poetry.

Another highlight of 1953 was Dover's trip to London to see the coronation of Queen Elizabeth II. He went armed with a groundsheet, food, and glucose and Horlicks tablets, and spent the night on the pavement. As soon as ambulance men had put stretchers on the islands in the middle of The Mall, one of the soldiers lining the route fainted and was carried away; Dover suspected that had the stretchers not been there, he might not have thought of fainting.

I mentioned above that Dover had visited Cambridge, where his friend Hugh Lloyd-Jones was teaching. In November, Lloyd-Jones gave a paper in Oxford, staying with the Dovers. He brought with him his new bride; a few months earlier, Dover had reported their engagement, adding 'I hope his wife is tolerant – she'll need to be'. Now he commented that 'she seems to have him fairly well under control & fortunately lacks reverence for his eccentricities'. Lloyd-Jones' paper went very well, 'but his extremely forceful delivery made us feel rather battered by the end of it.'[37] The two men were firm friends, but Dover later declared that while Lloyd-Jones had always been nice to him, he always felt he needed to watch his back.[38] In February 1954, Dover found that Lloyd-Jones was thinking of applying to be the first holder of the Warren praelectorship at Corpus, Oxford, which then had very limited teaching responsibilities and a ban on lecturing to women. He commented:

> It would be a considerable financial sacrifice, but the lure of Oxford is likely to prove too strong for him, especially with such a good chance to get on with his own work. I must say, if he takes the job and sits in Oxford with nothing to do but research for the next seven years, I don't see what's to stop him becoming the next Regius Professor of Greek.
>
> 6 February 1954

These were prophetic words, though as we shall see, not in a straightforward way.

Among the peripheral tasks to which Dover had committed himself was examining at Winchester College. He was alarmed to find that he was required to set a paper on the Epistle to the Romans. Taking courage from the reflection that it was at any rate in Greek, he put in a couple of days' work with three modern commentaries and produced what he called 'a masterpiece of a paper. I could even do it myself, which is more than I could say for some papers I've set' (16 May 1954).

In the autumn of 1954, Dover told his parents that he had completed an index verborum of all Attic inscriptions down to 446:

> I can't believe that I've really done it, because the path of Classical Scholarship is strewn with unfinished indices. It meant transcribing thousands of words onto columns of paper, cutting up all the columns into word-slips, arranging all the slips in alphabetical order, and pasting them all onto fresh strips, so that one ends up with a few hundred sheets made up of a couple of dozen slips. This sounds more laborious than a card-index system, but a bit of time-and-motion done for the Latin Dictionary established that it's in fact twice as quick.[39] . . . my future book on the language of Attic Inscriptions can be said to have taken shape.
>
> 4–5 September 1954

This task had occupied much of his time for several years. In February 1950 he had told his parents that 'I think I must do something about joining either the Times lending library at Christmas, or Boots: I'm finding myself at a conversational disadvantage through reading Greek inscriptions after supper instead of novels' (14 February 1950).

On the career front, the most significant event was Dover's decision to apply for the Greek chair at St Andrews. The deciding factor was that Fraenkel and Meiggs thought it a good stepping-stone for the Oxford chair, from which Dodds would retire in 1960; but Dover was also impressed by the library: he told his parents that 'The library is astonishing ... fully up to Oxford standards, and all readily accessible' (4 October 1954). Dover had registered with the Bodleian Library as an undergraduate, but often complained at the time taken to deliver books; college libraries were quicker but smaller. The St Andrews library thus seemed to be the perfect solution, easy to use and with very good coverage – in December 1955 Dover took out a Dutch book on New Guinea languages. The library was also only three minutes' walk away – as he commented, better than waiting two hours for a book in Bodley. The professorial body at St Andrews Dover described before he moved there as 'mostly old Scots, in a fairly rapid process of dilution by young English' (29 January 1955). He found some very congenial colleagues, though also some who were obstructive or otherwise difficult. In 1960 he was made Dean of the Arts Faculty and enormously enjoyed the multifarious challenges of the job. He also oversaw a rise in the recruitment of students to Classics. Overall, he was happily embedded in St Andrews when in 1960 the retirement of E.R. Dodds from the Oxford Regius chair of Greek was announced.

The decision point came in March 1960, when Dover received a letter from the prime minister, Harold Macmillan, offering him the Greek chair.[40] He was presumably unaware that Macmillan's appointments secretary had asked Dodds for advice, just as in 1936 Gilbert Murray had been asked to advise on who should be invited to succeed him.[41] Dodds had mentioned Dover, Lloyd-Jones and Spencer Barrett. The appointments secretary, David Stephens, told Dodds that he found all three men had substantial books coming out, and had asked for comments on them from those who had seen them and were qualified to comment.[42] Stephens was a Christ Church man himself, and probably enquired there. Dodds' letter of advice has not survived, but Stephens' response made it clear that he had stressed the importance of qualities other than technical scholarship. In December 1959 Dover had told his parents, 'The betting on the whole seems to be on me, though the danger of Lloyd-Jones is taken very seriously; no-one thinks there's any real danger of Webster or, unfortunately, any real likelihood of Barrett.'[43] Dover had thought long and hard about the Oxford chair, and took the precaution of touring Oxford estate agents to see what houses were available, but found very few of the right size and price. It appears that Macmillan's appointments secretary David Stephens recognized the problem; the prime minister's formal letter offering him the chair had been followed up next day by a note from Stephens offering to help with 'practical problems' arising from Macmillan's offer, 'in relation to housing etc'.[44]

A few days after receiving Macmillan's letter, Dover replied with a refusal. His main points were:

1. I believe ... that the patent anxiety of many professors in a score of universities to return to Oxford or Cambridge at the earliest opportunity has had many bad effects on the educational system of the whole country.
2. Oxford is the only major university which makes no provision for Classics (as normally understood) as a Final Honours School. My experience of participation in attempts to remedy this situation during 1953–55 was not at all encouraging.
3. Whereas a professor at St Andrews has effective control over the prescription, teaching and examination of his subject from first to last, an Oxford professor has little or no control.

He added that he would be happy to see Spencer Barrett in the chair.

Evidently Dodds heard a rumour that Dover had refused the chair and wrote to him to express his disappointment. Something of what he wrote, in a letter which does not survive, can be guessed at from Dover's response, which does.[45] Dover admitted that for more than twenty years, the chair had been the summit of his ambition. But his experience of the Mods subfaculty had been that the continuing power of the collegiate system made it impossible for strong leadership to be exercised. The members of the subfaculty, he insisted, thought they wanted a leader, but they were deceiving themselves, and he could see this clearly from his position outside Oxford, while he was still able to make an effective comparison of the two places. Looking at the situation of Classics in the country as whole, he thought it was unhealthy to have provision concentrated so much in two places (i.e. Oxford and Cambridge). He went on, 'the remedy must be the actual refusal of people like me to do the expected thing'. He ended by telling Dodds that he had suggested to Macmillan that Barrett would make a good Regius Professor. He admitted that this had been impertinent, since he had not been asked for his opinion; and also treacherous, since Lloyd-Jones was a friend. But, he concluded, 'Barrett's complete integrity as a scholar would be better for Oxford than Lloyd-Jones's philotimia, and better than some of the elements in my own make-up'.

Conclusion

What was remarkable about Kenneth Dover was his combination of advanced skills in fields that were usually separate. He carried off the highest prizes in the traditional field of Greek composition. Perhaps the most remarkable example of his skill came much later, when in 1956 the St Andrews Student Classical Society planned to put on the *Bacchae* in Greek, but it was thought that 60 lines of the final scene were missing. Dover wrote 60 lines himself on the day after Boxing Day 1956, and told his parents, 'I think I've produced lines which don't compare too unfavourably with Euripides'.[46] He also made himself a master of the evidence for Greek history, including inscriptions and lawcourt speeches: Momigliano declared that Dover knew more than anybody else about fifth-century Athens; something reported dismissively by Dover, who nevertheless was clearly flattered by it.[47] The combination of these skills enabled him to produce pioneering work on Aristophanes, Thucydides and Greek homosexuality. Other scholars have done something similar when given a catalyst.[48] In Dover's case, however, the catalyst appears to have been internal, and Momigliano simply a facilitator, though we lack evidence of the discussions they had while Momigliano was Dover's supervisor.

Dover's relationships with other scholars varied, as one might expect: we could contrast his friendship and rivalry with Hugh Lloyd-Jones, and his friendship without rivalry with Donald Russell, with whom he taught at one point. Dover and Russell had complementary skills and mutual admiration, though Russell disapproved of Dover's memoir *Marginal Comment*, which he thought did not reflect the nature of the man he knew so well. With Lloyd-Jones too Dover shared mutual admiration, but in this case mixed with merited caution – it was Lloyd-Jones, as I have mentioned, who blocked Dover's application for the Cambridge Regius chair in 1974. On a larger canvas, the most striking phenomenon to point to is perhaps the decentring of Oxford, seen by most of his contemporaries as the pinnacle and centre of British Classics. A Cambridge equivalent was recorded from an earlier generation: in the radio talk he gave about his father in 1958, Raymond Postgate suggested that for John Percival Postgate, the civilized world was firmly centred on Cambridge; but it also encompassed Oxford, TCD, Harvard and Yale, and a few foreign universities: 'The recognition given to Rome, Athens and Madrid was almost wholly a matter of Christian charity. Outside this civilised world there existed, but were neither understood nor discussed, what were in effect the wild lands. Here people earned their living by working with their hands, trading, owning property or engaging in politics.'[49] Dover's move to St Andrews in 1955, seen by himself and others as a preparation for a triumphant return to Oxford in 1960, became instead the basis for a revaluation of the topography of Classics in this country. Dover's happy and productive time in Scotland led him to redefine St Andrews as different but not marginal, though he later tried to move to Cambridge to secure more postgraduate teaching, and finally came back to Oxford when he felt his teaching powers were failing.

Appendix:
Two Poems by Kenneth Dover

In a letter to his parents of 22 November 1939, Dover said that he had written about twenty complete poems over the previous three years, in a variety of metrical forms, and would not be averse to seeing them 'printed'. The two poems in this appendix survive with the letters home. The first is preserved in the collection before a letter of 4 April 1941; it may have been written in the early months of 1941, when Dover was undergoing training for military service, though an earlier date cannot be ruled out. The second appears with the letter for 28 April/4 May 1942, when Dover was stationed in Libya: it is set out like a tripartite piece of Greek choral lyric, with abbreviations for strophe, antistrophe, and epode (together with marginal line numbers). In the letter in question, he says the poem has 'got off my chest some phrases and ideas about the desert which have been beating around quite a bit inside'.

Christophor Stray

The Wicked Man

He honoured no man's right.
How could he, so different from us?
His threats he kept, his oaths he broke,
And how he stared! We listened untrusting
        When he spoke.

We stared him from our sight.
He shut his door and spun
His web round all he called his own.
We saw his shadow and heard him laugh
        Working alone.

He died on a windy night.
As his soul crept from his body,
And the bed was lightened where he lay,
A black bull came out of the sea
        And took him away.

An In Memoriam for a Man Killed in Libya

Str.   I was one of those who went
        to live and die in Africa.
And here, when all had passed, I stayed behind.

        Lest I grow cold,
        the fierce sun at midday   5
        the hot sand and forever
        the dust shall be my covering.
        Lest I be hot,
        the frozen lips of night
        shall breathe the bitter wind   10
        across my bones. The wind,
        the sun, no more.

Antistr.   And I would have it so; a life
        is not enough. Live twenty times
and outgrow language; even then, the desert ...   15

        The desert speaks
        in the beating of tent-flaps,
        a wild beat, pausing
        fitfully with the vague wind.

>   The desert writes   20
>   its history in tiny trails,
>   delicate marks in sand,
>   stories of dim lizards
>   and black scorpions.

Ep.   But when the deep wall of the sandstorm moves,   25
         whirled in brown darkness, I shall move, and know
         the distant secret dunes as I knew London.
         I shall see manless valleys; withered wells
         and barren hills shall teach me, as my friends,
         the lonely sturdy music of their names.   30

Notes

1. In the present account I draw on the Dover papers at Corpus Christi College, Oxford, where I must thank Sir Brian Harrison for arranging unrestricted access and the college archivist Julian Reid for helpful discussions, and also on family papers, including a series of Dover's letters to his parents from the 1930s to the 1960s, very kindly loaned to me by his daughter Catherine Brown.
2. Letter to parents, undated but late July 1941.
3. Letter to parents, 21 October 1938.
4. We could compare the realms of Angria and Gondal, invented by the four Brontë children.
5. MC 69. Old World monkeys do not have prehensile tails, and not all New World monkeys have them; but the distinction should not be insisted on in this context.
6. Dover to the author, 12 August 1995, in response to being sent a draft of a review of *Marginal Comment*.
7. George Bean (1903–77) published four guides to the archaeological sites of Turkey. The second edition of his *Turkey Beyond the Maeander* (1989) includes a memoir by J.M. Cook, who described him as 'enormous – broad in the shoulder and almost six feet six inches tall; and to that imposing exterior he added a perfect command of educated Turkish' (p. v). Bean's battered suitcase, containing over 3,000 photos of Turkey, was deposited in Cambridge in 1990, unearthed in 2014 and then catalogued: see https://www.classics.cam.ac.uk/museum/collections/collection-videos-1/the-bean-archive-1
8. T.W. (Tommy) Melluish in fact taught in Tooting, south London, where he was senior classical master at the Bec Grammar School. He became a mainstay of several British classical organizations in Britain, and a serious obstacle to change in the early 1960s, when the Joint Association of Classical Teachers was being founded by John Sharwood Smith and his allies. He was a skilled composer in Latin and Greek, and also a talented crossword setter; Colin Dexter gave his name to a character in one of his Morse books.
9. Twelve MS letters survive in the Dover family papers, running from 21 March to 21 April. Later in 1938, Dover typed these up with changes and deletions, and added typed versions of seven more covering the period 24–30 April. These were bound up into a booklet, presumably for circulation in Dover's family; the booklet was sold with the rest of his library

after his death; a copy is now in the possession of Dr Frederick Naerebout of Leiden University, who very kindly sent me copies of the additional letters.

10. For Bailey, see the entry in *ODNB* (J. Griffin). Bailey taught at Balliol from 1902 to 1939 and was Public Orator 1932–9. He was a Delegate of OUP 1920–46, and had, for example, taught all the editors of the Latin editions ('Oxford Reds') published by the Press: Henderson 2006, 61 n. 14.

11. See the 1945 photograph of Dodds reproduced in Stray, Pelling and Harrison, eds, 2019, 31.

12. Dodds 1977, 177. In 1856 the author of a student handbook had commented that 'the acquaintance required in [the] First Examination is almost entirely restricted to a knowledge of the languages in which they wrote and has little regard for the subject matter of their works': Farrar 1856, 9.

13. Russell 2007, 237.

14. Beck is not named in *Marginal Comment* (p. 41), but in his original typescript Dover had written, 'Beck was an interesting man who launched me on Hegel' (p. 78). Maximilian Beck (1887–1950) had been a follower of Alexander Pfaender in the Munich phenomenological circle and had rejected the transcendental turn in Husserl's philosophy. In 1928 he founded the journal *Philosophische Hefte*, which he edited until 1936, when the Nazi invasion of Czechoslovakia forced him to leave for Britain. He emigrated to the USA in 1941 and held a fellowship at Yale until 1944. His treatise *Psychologie: Wesen und Wirklichkeit der Seele* was published in 1938.

15. The phrase is Stephen Halliwell's, from his *ODNB* article on Dover; it well summarizes Dover's own attitude.

16. It may be that this discovery was what made Dover think of writing an autobiography.

17. John Barrington-Ward (Christ Church) was a member of the Composition Club, a small group of Oxford men who had met from 1923 to compare their Latin and Greek compositions. This activity led to the publication of *Some Oxford Compositions. Translations into Greek and Latin Prose and Verse* (Oxford, 1949), and later, after Barrington-Ward's death in 1946, to *More Oxford Compositions* (Oxford, 1964), perhaps the last collection of its kind, except for celebratory occasional volumes such as that published to mark the 80th birthday of Anthony Bowen, Orator of the University of Cambridge 1993–2007 (Tyrrall 2022).

18. Perhaps the battle of Koroupedion (281 BC), fought between Lysimachus and Seleucus I Nicator. Surviving accounts of the battle, however, do not mention mercenaries. Dover may have been thinking of the late fourth century, when the transfer of defeated troops to the victor was not uncommon. The Macedonians who fought for Neoptolemus went over to Eumenes of Cardia after a battle in 322/1 (Diodorus Siculus 18.29.4), and both mercenaries and Macedonians went over to Antigonus after Eumenes' first defeat (18.41.4). My thanks to Paul Cartledge for identifying Koroupedion, and to Robin Waterfield for comments on fourth- and third-century battles and the sources for identifying them.

19. The intellectual style is reminiscent of Max Weber's work on historical sociology in his *Wirtschaft und Gesellschaft* (Weber 1921). There is however no evidence that Dover knew this work, which was not translated into English for nearly fifty years.

20. *Floreat Domus*, May 2020, 5.

21. Personal communication with the author. But note a remark of Griffin's on the *Georgics* in his *Virgil* (Oxford, 1986), 50: 'a suggestive parallel to this alternation of moods would be the movements of a symphony or other extended piece of music' (brought to my attention by Stephen Halliwell).

22. Letter to parents, 5 February 1939. The transfer of anecdotes to well-known figures is exemplified in the case of Thomas Gaisford, Dean of Christ Church 1831–55: Stray 2018, 73–6. This particular story in fact sounds rather Doverian.
23. My thanks to Tim Rood for an account of this moment in Dover's undergraduate career.
24. His contemporary R.M. Hare, later White's Professor of Moral Philosophy, was also sent to a gunnery unit.
25. Cf. Dodds' moving away from Neoplatonism to mainstream Classics with his edition of Euripides' *Bacchae* (1944).
26. He was probably unaware that Fortune also published speculations on number theory, and that a particular class of prime numbers came to be named for him: Fortunate numbers.
27. See Lipscomb 2021. One of them recalled in 2013 that 'It was clear that we were all more interested in understanding this deeply puzzling world than in putting each other down. That was how Elizabeth Anscombe, Philippa Foot, Iris Murdoch, Mary Warnock and I, in our various ways, all came to think out alternatives to the brash, unreal style of philosophizing – based essentially on logical positivism – that was current at the time. And these were the ideas that we later expressed in our own writings.' Mary Midgley, letter, *The Guardian*, 8 November 2013. For Dover's relationship to philosophy, see Sheffield's chapter in this volume.
28. One might see this as a (very) distant echo of Gibbon's remark that his experience as a captain in the Hampshire militia was of use to him as a historian of the Roman empire.
29. In 1945 Lindsay was ennobled as Lord Lindsay of Birker, a title which according to Dover caused some amusement to old Egypt hands, who remembered that 'Birker' sounded just like the name given to the most unsavoury district of Cairo.
30. My thanks to Kenneth Cavander for supplying me with his memories of Dover's teaching. Another ex-pupil, Sir Geoffrey Owen, remembered Dover as 'a very kind and attentive tutor, gently correcting my mistakes and pointing me in the right direction without in any way parading his vastly superior knowledge. I don't recall him being hugely interested in his tutees as people like say Russell Meiggs (whom I got to know much better)'.
31. 17 October 1963. West's supervisor was Hugh Lloyd-Jones. His second in Greats is explained by his lack of aptitude for ancient history and his lack of interest in philosophy: see Lightfoot 2019.
32. 19 August 1951; the reference is presumably to Roger Mynors, Kennedy Professor of Latin 1944–53, and Denys Page, Regius Professor of Greek 1950–73.
33. In the event, the Faculty decided to prolong neither.
34. 7 February 1953: Robert Browning.
35. 25 January 1953: Brian Shefton, whose foghorn voice I heard in Tunisia in January 1971.
36. Robert Browning again.
37. This sounds a little like Fraenkel's dais-shaking style – perhaps it had been learned from him.
38. This was certainly advisable during the election to the Cambridge Regius chair of Greek in 1974, when Lloyd-Jones, as an external elector, made sure that Geoffrey Kirk was appointed rather than Dover.
39. The Latin dictionary was the *Oxford Latin Dictionary*, in preparation since 1933 but much affected by the mental breakdown of its editor James Wyllie, who was dismissed this same year. See Stray 2012, and cf. Gilliver 2016, 424–5.
40. Macmillan to Dover, 3 March 1960. Dover family papers.
41. Stray 2019, 20–2.

42. In a set of notes on *Marginal Comment,* Dover stated that when Maurice Bowra found that Barrett was being considered for the chair, he had 'worked on the secretary to rule him out' (Dover papers, Corpus Christi College archive). This suggests that Bowra was one of those consulted by Stephens.
43. 28 December 1959. T.B.L. Webster, Professor of Greek at University College London, was an influential teacher, but in Oxford his scholarship was not well regarded. Spencer Barrett of Keble College was at work on an edition of the *Hippolytus*, which after long delays appeared to acclaim in 1964; he also worked on Pindar. His interests were narrower than those of Dover or Lloyd-Jones.
44. Stephens to Dover, 4 March 1960. Dover family papers.
45. Dover to Dodds, 24 March 1960; Dodds papers, Bodleian Library, 22.71–2. Dover had written in a similar vein to his parents on 28 December 1959: see n. 43 above.
46. No trace has been found of the lines in question; but Dover habitually destroyed such material after the occasion of its use.
47. Momigliano's remark is referred to by Dover in a letter to his parents of 12 January 1950.
48. I think of Robert Kaster's work on Roman imperial grammarians, where the depth and sophistication of his previous philological grounding was combined with an imaginative historical analysis fostered by contact with Arnaldo Momigliano at the University of Chicago. See Kaster 1988. (Information from Bob Kaster.)
49. Postgate 1958.

CHAPTER 2
DOVER, OXFORD AND THE STUDY OF CLASSICAL LITERATURE: THE MAKING OF A PROFESSIONAL SCHOLAR
Tim Rood

'At the start of my own professional career as a classical scholar, vestiges of schism were still apparent. I find them very hard to discern nowadays.'[1] So Kenneth Dover reflected in 1992 in his introduction to the edited volume *Perceptions of the Ancient Greeks*. The schism he had in mind was the lingering tension between historicism and classicism which, according to Anthony Grafton's chapter in that volume, prevailed in nineteenth-century German scholarship: the historical attempt to recreate the world of the Greeks in all its breadth sat uneasily alongside the humane ideals which classical education was alleged to promote.[2] Dover tweaked Grafton by using a term with religious associations, 'schism', and by associating this fracturing with the 'unGreek' inheritance of eschatological disputes. While Dover's formulation hints at his characteristic hostility to dogmatic Christianity, he did not attribute the disappearance of scholarly schism to the waning of religious belief. Rather, what united classical scholars by the end of the twentieth century was a shared need to defend the discipline from attack while themselves attacking popular misunderstandings of ancient Greece.

In this chapter I will be looking back to the start of Dover's career and reading his approach to classical literature against his undergraduate studies at Oxford, where he took first Classical Moderations (Mods), the initial examination in language and literature, and then Literae Humaniores (Greats), the final examination in Ancient History and Philosophy. The first section will sketch the development of the Oxford course, especially its literary component. Following that, I will analyse with the help of his letters to his parents Dover's account of reading for Mods in *Marginal Comment*, and relate this Oxford background to his literary interests, including his self-positioning as a 'historian of literature' – a category that he allowed to stand in under-theorized opposition to 'literary critic'.[3] In the final section, I turn from the substance to the spirit of the Oxford course. Dover, as we shall see, measured German professional standards against most Mods dons' less strenuous approach to understanding the Greek past. But he saw strengths as well as weaknesses in some of their work. I will focus here on his response to the image of Hellenism fostered by Gilbert Murray, the Oxford scholar whom Dover acknowledged as the most influential British Hellenist of his time (even if he chose not to follow him in the Regius chair). Throughout, I will be concerned with fragmentation – between literature and history and between generalized and specialized approaches to the classical past – and with Dover's attempts to negotiate it.

Tim Rood

The changing faces of Mods and Greats

Literae Humaniores was one of two Honour Schools created at Oxford in reforms to the previously undifferentiated Bachelor of Arts course at the start of the nineteenth century.[4] For the remainder of the nineteenth century, it enjoyed the greatest prestige and drew the largest numbers of any course; it was often regarded as an ideal general education from which graduates could progress to more specialized academic study or else to a career in public service or the professions.[5] The rise of Modern History, and later of Politics, Philosophy, and Economics ('Modern Greats'), had dented the glory of Literae Humaniores slightly by the time Dover studied, and it was no longer as strongly promoted as the quintessential Oxford degree in the student handbook. Even so, Greats had still been read by a majority of the Fellows of Oxford colleges in the late 1930s,[6] and Classics Mods remained a prestigious route into other Final Honour Schools, some of which did not have a first examination of their own.[7]

To understand the role played by literature in the Classics course at Oxford, we need to consider the course's re-structuring in the middle of the nineteenth century. Prior to these reforms, candidates for Honours offered a variable number of 'books', i.e. texts prepared for examination; while there were conventions on which books should be offered, no generic distinctions were applied. The result of the reforms was that the course was split into an examination 'in literis Graecis et Latinis' ('in Greek and Latin letters/literature') after five terms (Mods) and a final examination after four years, Literae Humaniores proper. The statutes specified that particular attention was to be paid in Mods to poets and orators (Homer, Virgil, Demosthenes and Cicero), while the final examination was to cover a broader range of topics, including ancient history, philosophy, and rhetoric. In practice, the literary element in Mods was initially confined to a subordinate role in a largely philological Critical Paper. A further reform in 1872, however, stipulated for Mods that 'questions directly bearing upon the contents, style, and literary history of the Books offered, will be considered an essential part of the examination';[8] at the same time, Greats was restricted to historical and philosophical books.

The reforms of 1872 specified how literature was to be studied in Mods. While some books – including the compulsory epic writers and orators – were tested through translation alone, others were to be 'specially prepared'; for these, commentary questions were set with a focus on textual criticism as well as essays on literary and textual topics. In addition, there was a requirement to offer one Special Subject among a range of literary, archaeological and philosophical options, and the Critical Paper was re-named the General Paper and given stronger literary content. From 1886, moreover, it was allowed that questions would be set on 'literary criticism' in this paper; while that phrase was dropped from the Regulations in 1922, literary critical essays were still set.

The reforms in the second half of the nineteenth century seem to point to a dichotomy between a linguistic and literary Mods and a philosophical and historical Greats. This perception needs, however, to be complicated. It is not just that candidates could offer a paper on material culture or Logic in Mods. It was also that the Statutes specified 'the

Greek and Latin Languages' as one of the three parts of Greats, and the student handbook from the ninth edition (1888) onwards stated that 'This head includes Literature'[9] – presumably an acknowledgement that candidates could offer a literary topic as an optional Special Subject, even if the burdens of the compulsory syllabus meant that very few of them did so.

More importantly, Mods was typically seen not so much as an exercise in literary study as in 'scholarship', which was understood as embracing translation, composition and textual criticism. Thus when Mods was first being established, Benjamin Jowett argued that 'scholarship rather than history or science' should be required,[10] and later in the nineteenth century Thomas Case, President of Corpus, advocated a three-year Literae Humaniores with more 'scholarship' in the final exam and more subject-matter in the first.[11] When J.D. Denniston made a similar proposal in the aftermath of the First World War, moreover, a colleague took him to be increasing the weight attached to 'scholarship' in Greats – whereas Denniston was actually promoting the introduction of literary study in Greats (exactly anticipating reforms introduced half a century later).[12]

It was not that 'scholarship' in this narrow sense had no part in the second part of the course. The *Student Handbook* for many years defined Philosophy, History and Scholarship as the three departments of Greats, since, besides translation of prepared books, unseen translation into and from English formed part of the examination. This usage of 'scholarship' persisted in the *Handbook* when Dover was an undergraduate: mention of the translation papers leads to the conclusion that 'a good classical scholar ... starts with a great advantage in the examination', but owing to excellence in Philosophy and History, it is conceded, 'men have appeared from time to time in the first class who were not in the narrow sense of the word good scholars'.[13]

The formal requirements for Mods did not result in much serious attention being paid to the literary qualities of the books on which candidates were examined. Tutorials on prose composition and lectures on the intricacies of textual points had long been the staple teaching of the Mods don, and this pattern continued well into the twentieth century. Nor was the lack of tutorial teaching made up by a wide range of good available criticism.[14] It is no surprise, then, that the standard of essays in Mods was generally regarded as low, at least by those who campaigned for literature to be taken seriously: one such reformer, L.R. Farnell, Fellow (and later Rector) of Exeter College, complained in an 1898 pamphlet that examiners were indulgent towards 'puerilities' in essays if the answers on translation and textual criticism were good, and that it frequently occurred that 'a man gets first class marks in Homer, Vergil, Demosthenes and Cicero, and yet remains as ignorant as he was at school of the great questions of Literature and History that inevitably arise in the intelligent and mature study of these authors'.[15]

Dover himself took Mods at a time when a new reform had been implemented with the aim of improving the literary aspect of the course. The most notable shift was the dropping of compulsory translation from the full oratorical corpora of Cicero and Demosthenes (often regarded as the most tedious part of the course).[16] This shift was accompanied by a change in the way other books were examined. The purpose of the reforms was explained in the *Oxford Magazine* as 'enlarging the scope of the candidates' reading of the best classical authors' and 'reducing the amount of textual criticism (and the consequent necessity for memorizing a mass of detail) in the specially prepared books'. More texts than 'the Four Beasts' were now to be tested by translation alone, and 'their brute nature has been transformed into something more humane', with the expectation that 'candidates will find the examination both more interesting from the literary point of view', and (in the peculiar Oxford terminology of the day) 'it will not, in future, be so easy for a second-class man to get a First, or indeed for a first-class man to get a Second'.[17] As part of this reform, the single General Paper was replaced by two papers, partly to allow more questions on the literary texts.[18] The *Magazine*'s justification of the reform only underscores, however, the failure of earlier attempts to meet these goals: a generation earlier the University *Handbook* had similarly spoken of the 1886 reforms as designed 'to encourage rather wider reading and lay more stress on the literary side of the training'.[19]

Further scope for literary study was allowed by the Special Subjects. The paper that Dover took, 'Aristotle's *Poetics* and the History of Greek Drama', was introduced when Special Subjects were created in 1872 and lasted until the 1960s. In Dover's time, it was recommended in the *Student Handbook* for 'those who are interested in literary criticism',[20] even if the sort of criticism it permitted was circumscribed: it required candidates to translate two passages from the *Poetics* (of 12–14 lines); to translate and comment on three much shorter passages; to write an essay on Aristotle (with a choice of two); and to answer at least two further questions. While there were a small number of broader literary questions, those questions could be dauntingly technical: typically, candidates might be invited to explain a list of terms such as ὀκρίβας, προαγών, and διστεγία or to write notes on the titles of fragmentary plays (in Dover's year: Πυτίνη, οἱ Δῆμοι, Λόγος καὶ Λογίνα, Περικειρομένη) or on the names of playwrights (Sophron, Phrynichus, Agathon, Theodectes). The paper was not generally seen as an exercise in literary criticism: Hugh Lloyd-Jones complained in 1956 that it 'seems to encourage most of those who take it to spend more time on Aristotle and Pickard-Cambridge than on the surviving plays',[21] while John Gould (a Cambridge student of Lloyd-Jones whose election to a Christ Church fellowship was thought to reflect on the failings of Oxford's own products[22]) picked it out in 1959 as one of the Mods papers 'done with least intelligence and insight into the overall problems of interpretation'.[23]

The historical and technical approach taken in the Greek Drama paper was typical of the other Special Subjects at this time. There were two other 'literary' papers, 'The History of Roman Poetry to the End of the Augustan Age' and 'The History of Greek Lyric and Elegiac Poetry to the time of Aristotle inclusive'. The first of these was particularly close to the Greek drama paper in that it was rooted in ancient criticism and included works now lost: students were expected to study Horace, *Epistles* II and *Ars Poetica* 'with special reference to the literary criticism contained therein', and in addition 'to show such knowledge of the works of the earlier Roman Poets as may be obtained from Merry, *Selected Fragments of Roman Poetry*'.[24] This focus on reading ancient literature through the lens of ancient criticism was expressly articulated in the Statutes that came into force in 1872 and were still in place when Dover was an undergraduate, which defined one of the remits of Mods as being study of 'the History of Greek and Latin Literature or of some periods thereof, with such portions of ancient Writers on the Arts of Poetry and Style as shall be specified by the Board of the Faculty'.[25]

Some of the non-literary Special Subjects shared the historical approach and the focus on direct study of the relevant ancient evidence. 'The History of Greek Sculpture, 700–320 BC', for instance, was studied through Henry Stuart Jones' *Select Passages from Ancient Writers, Illustrative of the History of Greek Sculpture*; 'Homeric Archaeology' was tied to passages in the Homeric poems that illustrated the 'material civilization' described therein as well as to relevant objects in the Ashmolean Museum.[26] A similar ethos can be found in the special subjects which candidates were allowed to create themselves, subject to the permission of the Literae Humaniores Board. The papers set in the five years up to and including the year of Dover's Mods were as follows: 'Latin Palaeography' (1936, 1938, 1940), 'The History of Greek Vase Painting' (1936, 1940), 'Greek Music' (1937, 1939, 1940), 'The Acropolis of Athens and its Monuments' (1937, 1939), 'The Elements of Greek Epigraphy' (1939), 'The History of Greek Mathematics' (1939). These papers were variously marked by a technical, historical or textual focus: the 'Greek Music' papers included 'a special study of Aristoxenus, Book I, and Plutarch, *De Musica*', while gobbets from Pausanias were set for the Acropolis paper.[27] It was not the case, however, that the historical approach required for Mods necessarily dug very deep: one of Dover's Balliol contemporaries attributed achieving his highest mark on the classical art paper to his tutor's 'ingenious plan for circumventing the examiners', namely learning by heart 'a list (it wasn't long) of all the major artists and their surviving works, with a view to permuting them like home draws in the Pools' depending on the precise question asked.[28]

One further characteristic of Literae Humaniores deserves mention at this point. Since 1830 it had been specified in the Statutes that ancient books could be illustrated through modern ones. While this stipulation initially applied primarily to the study of philosophy, the study of history and literature too was informed by a dialogue between ancient and modern. Oscar Wilde, for instance, who took a First in Mods in 1876, wrote in his journal of talking at his viva of Shakespeare and Walt Whitman in relation to an essay in the Greek Drama paper.[29] This sort of cross-temporal perspective, aimed at 'relat[ing] historically earlier to historically later stages of thought',[30] continued to feature in Mods shortly before Dover's arrival in Oxford: candidates for the paper that Wilde took were asked in 1932, for instance, to 'criticize, from the point of view of Aristotle, any tragedy of Shakespeare, and estimate the validity of such criticism', and in 1935 they were invited to make an even broader transhistorical speculation ('What do you think would have been Aristotle's views on (a) Shakespeare's historical plays, (b) Wordsworth's theory of poetic diction?'). This readiness to presuppose knowledge of canonical works of English literature was related to the conception of Mods as a general course from which students might choose to proceed to courses other than Greats. In retrospect, however, we can see the 1930s as the swansong for this sort of transhistorical approach; it receded as other disciplines achieved greater autonomy and prestige and as the cohesion of Greats was undermined by developments in modern philosophy and the more specialized types of evidence now required for the study of ancient history.

This section has sketched the background against which Dover's reaction to the Oxford course may be understood. In the next section, we shall probe his experience of reading Mods, and point both to the suggestiveness of reading his later scholarly interests against this background and to the need to complicate any simple correlations.

Dover's Mods: *Marginal Comment* and beyond

Kenneth Dover offers in *Marginal Comment* (39–43) a five-page account of his undergraduate career reading the Classics degree at Oxford prior to his departure for military service. While the account offers some vivid detail on the texture of Oxford life as shaped by the imminence, then the reality, of war, it is with Dover's own academic studies that the account starts and ends. First comes a paragraph on routine college work:

> Work at Oxford was essentially similar to work at school. I was required to produce two compositions a week for my tutors and to attend a dozen lectures a week on prescribed texts and a Special Subject. I had already studied most of the texts at school, but now had to think about them harder and learn much more about textual criticism and the reconstruction of relationships between manuscripts. I found all this entirely congenial and sometimes exciting ... I was never required to write an essay on any Classical subject for my tutors, but in our first year we were all expected, in accordance with a long-standing Balliol custom, to read essays on general topics to the Master and miscellaneous tutors.
>
> *MC* 39

More details are given later, on Dover's performance in university examinations: early success in the Gaisford Verse university prize was followed by 'a good First in Mods' – even if he 'lapsed to an alpha–beta on one paper, where a startling memory-blank caused me to answer a question about Aristotle's definition of tragedy without ever mentioning pity and fear' (*MC* 41). Picking up the Oxford thread after the war, Dover offers some personal impressions of his tutors in Ancient History and Philosophy (the subjects studied in the second half of the course) before ending with the expected climax – a distinguished performance in his final examinations, even if here too a clean run of alphas was spoiled by one alpha–beta.[31]

In some ways Dover's account of his studies in the first part of the Classics course is quite conventional. The comparison with schoolwork was a trope in memoirs of nineteenth-century and early twentieth-century Oxford,[32] in pamphlets promoting syllabus reform,[33] and even in the student handbook, which suggested that 'the course for Classical Moderations is a continuation of school work but with more intensive study'.[34] Also typical is Dover's stress on the spirit of competition fostered at Oxford – a culture which he fully absorbed: his disappointment at his one lapse from alphas can be gauged from a letter to his parents in which he anticipated getting fourteen (i.e. a full range of) alphas ('I should say my mark for the whole exam was 85–88%').[35]

In some other respects the account Dover offers of reading for Mods is unusual. One of the academic tasks that he mentions – writing general essays for the Master – was, as he notes, a distinctive Balliol practice, but Dover is more reticent about what these sessions involved than some other Balliol memoirists: Denis Healey, who read Greats two years above Dover, recalled writing on T.S. Eliot,[36] while one of the other classicists in Dover's cohort, the composer Geoffrey Bush, noted that the topics ranged 'from the politics of Munich to the achievement of Thomas Hardy'.[37] How much such sessions advanced students' literary analysis is another matter: Healey had already been well drilled at school by a Leavisite, while Bush confesses to having constructed his essay on Hardy 'out of a publisher's blurb'. Another distinctive college practice omitted by Dover is the Balliol Players' annual production of an Aristophanes play – in 1939, *Birds* – performed in loose translations with modern references.[38] Nor is there any hint of the sort of college club lectures on Greek drama and society by the likes of Gilbert Murray and E.R. Dodds that Healey recalls.[39]

The class to which Dover devotes most attention was likewise not a standard part of student experience – Eduard Fraenkel's famous seminar on Aeschylus' *Agamemnon*.[40] Dover asserts that this seminar, 'attended by some dons and a select number of undergraduates recommended by their tutors', 'mattered most at Oxford'. But his explanation of why it mattered highlights local fissures. Fraenkel's ability to present the Greeks and Romans as 'real people' who can be understood with enough work led Dover to form the 'arrogant judgement' that 'the older generation of Oxford scholars, for the most part, had not worked at it hard enough, but thought of the Classical poets as interesting neighbours who called in at the vicarage for tea and entertained the company by quoting from their poems' (*MC* 39). The high standards Fraenkel expected from students, Dover concludes, were what started him on his professional career.[41]

Dover's account of Mods is unusual, too, in its positive attitude to this part of the course. While the Oxford examination system as a whole was deplored by many critics for placing rote learning ahead of originality and research and for pandering to a spirit of college patriotism, Mods came in for particularly intense criticism. Many students viewed it as a grim prelude to the intellectual allure of Greats,[42] and some were even deterred by the perceived similarity to schoolwork from sitting the examination at all.[43] Dover bucks the trend – even if his confession that the work was 'entirely congenial and sometimes exciting' nods to conventional depreciations and concedes that the pleasure was contingent on his own character.

The oddest feature of the account in *Marginal Comment* is that it omits altogether the fact that, owing to the outbreak of war, Dover sat a special shortened Mods in October 1939 as well as the regular examination the following term.[44] He thereby makes the first part of the course seem more academically conventional than was in fact the case.

Dover's account can be fleshed out with the help of his regular letters to his parents. In one of these, Dover mentions that when he sat the full Mods in 1940, the passage he attempted for Latin verse composition was the poem 'Report on Experience' by Edmund Blunden (an English Tutor at Merton). While he told his parents that he found the passage 'difficult ... but quite satisfactory', he offered no comment on what strikes the modern reader, the choice of a poem that evoked the First World War ('I have seen a green country, useful to the race, / Knocked silly with guns and mines, its villages vanished'). Nor did Dover comment on the still more conspicuous military resonance of the Latin Prose passage – a section of a parliamentary speech by William Pitt the Younger which concluded with the peroration that the war against Napoleon was a contest for 'our very name as Englishmen', 'for everything dear and valuable to man on this side of the grave'.[45] The examination paper carefully dated the speech to 1803, the height of British fears of a French invasion. That combination of topicality and historicization had been matched by Latin prose passages set during the First World War: in 1916 an appeal made by T.E. Page dated 19 October 1915 ('We need leadership, and leadership in great crises must be personal ...'), in 1917 an extract from an article ('Stern Rebuke to Pacifists') in the *Times* dated 20 September 1916 which quoted the French Prime Minister Aristide Briand ('Think of the effort of Great Britain ...').[46] Dover, however, was understandably more absorbed by the technical challenges of composition than by its ideological undercurrents. We may note, too, that Dover does not use the word 'scholarship' to refer to prose and verse composition. He was already adopting the viewpoint of a scholar of the Fraenkel sort.[47]

Dover's letters shed fascinating light on his development as a literary scholar. When he sat the special Mods in October 1939, one of the changes made was the merging of the two General Papers into one. This merging left candidates with a generous range of questions to answer. The questions Dover himself answered (as shown by a letter to his parents on 27 October) offer a hint of the level of discussion that was expected:

- '"The orations of Cicero are among the greatest works of fiction ever produced." Do the speeches you have read lend support to this statement?'
- '"Take from Virgil his metre and diction, and what do you leave him?" (S.T. Coleridge). How would you answer this?'
- 'Need we regret the loss of Roman Tragedy?'
- 'Examine the development of Greek ideas about an after-life down to the end of the fifth century BC.'
- 'Trace the development of the idea of the unity and brotherhood of mankind in the ancient world.'

With our knowledge of Dover's later scholarly interests we may be surprised by all those answers on Latin literature:[48] he let pass juicy questions on Aristophanes ('Has Aristophanes any claim to be taken seriously as a critic either of literature or of politics?') and on the freedom of the intellectual ('Is it true that the Greeks believed in the unrestricted right of the individual to think for himself?'). The one purely Greek question he chose was a historical one about the afterlife – a 'pet subject' which he had pursued in studying the *Oresteia*. Despite his Latin-focussed responses to this paper, Dover's immersion in the trilogy as an undergraduate goes some way towards explaining its prominence in his later writings on Greek tragedy.[49]

There is a stronger foreshadowing of Dover's later literary interests in his answers on specially prepared texts when he sat the full Mods in 1940. He found the Greek Special

Books paper 'first-rate'; 'over breakfast I read up the interrelation of the manuscripts of the Eumenides, and that was the essay question, so within an hour of mugging it up I was writing it out.'[50] Dover here ignores the existence of an alternative question on theatrical performance ('"The true drama of the *Eumenides* is revealed only by production." With this in view, how would you produce the *Eumenides*?') – an odd omission in view of his experience as a theatre critic and his later sensitivity to the importance of imagining the performance of Greek drama.[51] At any rate, the gleeful response to the question on manuscripts, far from being the mark of the 'intellectual window-dresser',[52] could be seen as anticipating the crisp logic of Dover's later technical scholarship, as seen in his editions or his articles on textual criticism or literary chronology.[53]

Another of the mature Dover's characteristic concerns, poetic voice and originality, can be detected in his remarks on the Latin Special Books paper. Dover found this 'quite the worst paper I've ever seen':

> The essay question on Catullus was extremely difficult and the alternative one on Propertius (which I did) so obscurely and ambiguously worded that I had to make my essay two-faced, to be taken either way; the translation pieces and pieces for comment from Catullus were all out of the dullest and least typical part of his work; one of the comment pieces was out of a poem not included in the syllabus, another clearly expected you to remember parts of the poem not quoted in the question, which is unfair on principle; and to crown it all, one of the Propertius pieces contained a misleading misprint, which cost me five minutes puzzling.[54]

He further commented on the difficulty of understanding Catullus: the poet required a degree of appreciation which 'the Moderators, who are all five of them Graecists, apparently have not got'. His conclusion about the paper's setter was that 'he or she is jest a plain bastard'.[55]

The implications of Dover's response will be clearer if we look at the paper itself. The Catullus question ('"The poetry of Catullus is the poetry of a coterie of aristocrats and intellectuals." Discuss the social and political background of Catullus's work') was of a type by no means unprecedented in Dover's time;[56] that he found it 'extremely difficult' may be explained by the lack of tutorial support for literary study.[57] As for the question that Dover actually answered ('How far was Propertius influenced by the Augustan principate and its literary ideals?'), that seems obscure only if it is presupposed that the phrasing of an essay should offer a clue to the examiners' own view. Most interesting for its insight into Dover's aesthetic sensitivities, however, is his comment that the Catullus passages were from 'the dullest and least typical part of his work'. The passages for translation were 64.100–15 and 66.47–64, while those for comment were 11.9–12, 62.59–60, 64.285–7 and (wrongly set) 67.9–12. Dover shows a preference for the shorter poems over the longer hexameter and elegiac poems – that is, for the poems that are generally thought to show a strong personal voice and vividly express strong emotions over the poems that are commonly seen as more self-conscious literary exercises.

One point to emerge from my sketch of the developing study of literature at Mods was that there was more concern for the history of literature, broadly conceived, than for literary criticism as twenty-first-century classicists conceive it. The language used at Mods might be thought to suggest a link with Dover's conception of himself as a historian of Greek literature; more specifically, the 'History of Greek Drama' paper's concern with the full range of evidence, and not just the extant plays, finds an echo in his scholarly study of lost plays such as the *Presbeis* and *Hellas* of Plato Comicus.[58] But neither in *Marginal Comment* nor in his letters does Dover directly make such a connection. Perhaps the general 'history of literature' approach, though it had notable German exponents,[59] was too far removed from the more rigorous analysis of specific literary forms undertaken by German scholars in the first half of the twentieth century and subsequently pursued by Dover himself.

Dover was nonetheless prepared to link his dual interest in literature and history with his training in Mods and Greats. In one essay he suggests that other scholars may have neglected a significant parallel in Thucydides for the tapestry scene in the *Agamemnon* (two texts well known to him from Oxford teaching) because 'Greek literature and Greek history are commonly studied in separate compartments', whereas 'a fortunate combination of circumstances' had enabled him 'to study and teach both at the same time'.[60] In view here is (besides the greater freedom allowed him at St Andrews) the position he held at Balliol from 1948 to 1955, which offered him, unusually, the chance to combine some ancient history teaching with the functions of a traditional Mods don;[61] earlier (as we learn from his letters but not from *Marginal Comment*) he had been torn between pursuing a professional career in ancient history (as his tutor at Balliol, Russell Meiggs, encouraged him) and in literature (the direction in which Fraenkel pushed him).[62]

Amidst the blend of self-revelation and occlusion that marks Dover's account of his undergraduate career in *Marginal Comment*, one comment stands out. He reports that after leaving Oxford for military service a term after Mods, he had doubts 'about the morality of continuing with Classics' and thought of switching to PPE (*MC* 58); he credits his decision not to change in part to the cautious words of the Master of Balliol, the philosopher A.D. Lindsay (himself a product of Greats). There was in itself nothing unusual about changing course after Mods;[63] earlier it had been common, too, for students to read for another Final Honours School in a single year after Greats.[64] What is striking is that abandoning Classics should have seemed a moral choice – a perception that seems to remove the course from the humanistic tradition from which it had sprung and from the integration with broader social and political issues that was its hallmark in its heyday. As it was, the aspiring professional won the day – and Balliol won more prizes.

The value of Hellenism: Dover and Murray

Dover's thoughts about the morality of studying Classics provide a helpful bridge from the content of the Oxford course to the spirit underlying it. The paradox of that comment emerges more strongly if it is read against the explanation he offers elsewhere in *Marginal Comment* for the 'strong tendency among classicists of my generation to go for Greek in preference to Latin': 'We were all the grandchildren of Gilbert Murray' (*MC* 37). That Dover highlights Murray's influence on the study of Greek is no surprise. Murray's stirring teaching is attested by older Oxford scholars such as his successor as Regius Professor, E.R. Dodds, and two of Dodds' rivals for that position, Maurice Bowra and J.D. Denniston;[65] and among those, like Dover, too young to have been taught by Murray, Hugh Lloyd-Jones (Dodds' successor as Regius Professor) recalled being inspired by his teenage reading of Murray's *Euripides and his Age*.[66] The power of Murray's Hellenism sprang, moreover, from its integration with a lifetime's devotion to public service. As we shall see, however, Dover's attitude to Murray was marked by reservations that point to a clash between an older, partly idealizing and a newer, more self-consciously professional approach to the study of classical Greece.

Murray had been appointed to the chair of Greek at Glasgow in 1889, only a year after the conclusion of a spectacular undergraduate career at Oxford. The national attention he attracted there through his 1897 *History of Ancient Greek Literature* boomed after his resignation from that position in 1898 owing to the publication and performance of his translations of Euripides.[67] His return to Oxford in 1905 carried hopes of a revival of literary study in Oxford,[68] and these hopes were soon realized by his monograph *The Rise of the Greek Epic*, which promoted Greek literature 'as an embodiment of the progressive spirit, an expression of the struggle of the human soul towards freedom and ennoblement'.[69] Murray's influence was soon detected in the writings of younger colleagues such as Richard Livingstone, a Mods don (and later President) at Corpus: a *Times Literary Supplement* review of Livingstone's *The Greek Genius and its Meaning to Us*, for instance, hailed Murray as the inspiration for a 'new Hellenism' based in Oxford which had 'struck out its fibres ... into the efforts towards self-realization and self-education of the organized democracy'.[70] The wider influence claimed for Murray here stemmed from his involvement in educational projects such as the series for which he wrote *Euripides and his Age*, the Home University Library, and in national causes; with the onset of the First World War, moreover, Murray became prominent in international politics, notably through his chairmanship of the League of Nations Union.

Despite hailing Murray as the spiritual grandfather of his generation of Hellenists, Dover did not present Murray in a uniformly positive light in *Marginal Comment*. Some reservations can be detected in his silences: he is noticeably less specific than Lloyd-Jones about his affiliation to Murray, and he does not mention some of the pedagogical innovations of Murray's which remained in force, such as the class in literary translation held by Dodds.[71] Dover's distance from Murray is most pronounced, however, when he discusses the 1980s debates on Western civilization that he experienced at Stanford. In this context he mentions a letter Murray wrote after hearing Arnold Toynbee (his former son-in-law) deliver the BBC Reith lectures in 1952:

Gilbert Murray's reaction to Arnold Toynbee's Reith Lectures was: 'He wilfully ignored the fact that our Western or Christian civilisation is *better* than that of Asia or Africa' (the inclusion of 'Christian' is strange, coming from a man who found Assisi 'mad'). Anyone who said that to a student audience nowadays would probably be vilified as a racist and pelted with dung.

Dover does go on to defend the right to offer adverse judgements on different cultures ('confusion of acquired culture with genetically determined race has been disastrous') and to exercise that right himself by expressing a preference for the statues of Olympia over those which he had seen in Mexico. But he acknowledges that in Murray's case it is clear from his correspondence that he 'did not shake free of belief in a correlation of skin, hair and face with intelligence and virtue'.[72]

Dover's ambivalence about Murray can be traced in his correspondence too. In his final term at Oxford before joining the army, he attended a Classical Association lecture by Murray on 'The Euripides Trilogy of 415 BC', and told his parents 'whether or not it was good stuff is hard to say, because Murray has a unique style which paralyses criticism'.[73] Worse, once established as a tutor at Balliol he described the *Oxford Book of Greek Verse* – for which Murray was among those responsible – as giving 'in many cases a bad text, wrong attributions, misleading titles, and absurd comment'.[74] If that remark reflects the amateurishness of some earlier Oxford scholarship,[75] a perception of generational difference is confirmed by a letter he wrote about a paper he gave in Oxford soon after his departure for St Andrews. The paper was attended by Murray, then aged ninety: 'he looks like a bit of parchment flapping in the breeze, and said his doctor had forbidden him to come out – and wrote me a nice note about it afterwards'. But that his argument 'won Fraenkel's approval' evidently pleased him more.[76]

Dover elsewhere showed reservations not just about Murray's professional standards but also about his vision of Hellenism. In a 1979 essay 'Expurgation of Greek literature', he offered thoughtful reflections on the tension we noted at the start of this chapter between an idealized image of Greece and the actual contents of Greek literature. Now back in Oxford as President of Corpus, he turned to a number of Oxford scholars whose writings instantiated this tension – among them Murray and Livingstone. Dover's criticism related to attitudes towards Greek sexuality: he noted in Murray 'a tendency to excuse the obscenity of comedy as a ritual ingredient' owing to the influence of late nineteenth-century anthropology, and added in a footnote a reminder that 'Murray became a professor of Greek as early as 1889' – the formula 'as early as' serving as a rhetorical means of distancing Murray in time.[77] Dover's thoughts may have turned to Murray through recollection of Murray's conception, vividly expressed in *The Rise of the Greek Epic*, that the Homeric poems were marked by an 'expurgation' of earlier, darker elements.[78]

Despite this distancing, there is good reason to trace Murray's influence on Dover's aesthetic appreciation of ancient Greece. This influence can be seen in the value given to originality as one of the most appealing elements of Greek literature and in the perception that this element waned in the fourth century BC (except in comedy), in part because a developing classicism laid too much stress on imitation.[79] Common to both scholars, too, is a concern for free-thinking (even if with Dover this concern emerges in the relish he takes in irreverence) combined with reservations about excessive competitiveness.[80] More striking still when read against Dover's literary interests is Murray's statement in his 1897 *History of Ancient Greek Literature* that 'at the present day' Aristophanes 'seems to share with Homer and Aeschylus and Theocritus the power of appealing directly to the interest and sympathy of almost every reader'.[81] Grouped together here are the four Greek poets to whom Dover paid most attention in his scholarly career.[82] The overlap of interests is the closer because Murray omits from his list the poet whose plays he did much to popularize over the coming decades, Euripides – an author to whom Dover paid scarcely any scholarly attention. Dover's literary tastes show a commitment to early stages of cultural development, a preference that revealingly underlies his judgements on sculpture too.[83]

With growing years Dover can be seen reflecting in different ways on his relationship with Murray. These reflections can be read into the sympathetic review he wrote for the *Times Literary Supplement* of Duncan Wilson's 1987 biography of Murray.[84] Though conscious that Murray's classical scholarship did not fulfil his promise, in part owing to a 'gravely limited...capacity for enjoying historical enquiry', there is due acknowledgement of Murray's capacity to inspire interest in Classics. But there are also signs of personal identification with Murray. Dover himself is surely in view in the statement that 'Greek captured (as it is apt to do) the interest and love of a boy in whom intellectual ability and the need for emotional attachment were both very strongly developed'. His account of Murray's decision to resign from Glasgow and subsequently return to Oxford can be read, moreover, against his own decision to leave Oxford for Scotland and then turn down what had once been one of his 'wilder ambitions', the Regius Professorship at Oxford (*MC* 69); Murray's perception that improvements in scholarship needed to start with Oxford contrasts with Dover's conviction that threats to classical education could be defused most successfully by raising the standard of classical education at universities across Britain, but both men were thinking of the bigger national picture. Besides this, there is clear *parti pris* in Dover's allusion to Murray's opposition to 'the sharp division between "Mods" work and "Greats" work' and to the subsequent reforms in which Dover himself was initially involved and the slowness of which played a part in his decision in 1960 to turn down the Oxford chair.[85]

That Dover was in some ways identifying with Murray is shown, too, by his stress on Murray's non-classical work. This focus is not in itself surprising given Murray's tireless work for causes such as the League of Nations Union. But rather than lamenting Murray's failure to live up to his promise as a classical scholar, Dover suggests that he 'redirected his energies to much more important ends'. The remote Murray known for his idealizing platitudes on fifth-century Athens is revealed instead as 'a painstaking and infinitely patient chairman of committees', a practical man who understood that some progress towards a goal is better than none and who could lower the temperature on contentious issues when necessary. Dover himself was writing this appreciation as a scholar with a strong sense of public service and an interest in administrative efficiency, who had been both President of the British Academy and head of an Oxford college.[86]

There is a continuity between this distinguished figure and the Dover who had had doubts 'about the morality of continuing with Classics' (*MC* 58). For all Dover's hesitation about some of what passed for classical education in Oxford, the priority he himself gave to the needs of the community over the individual can be assimilated to the tradition which saw Literae Humaniores at Oxford as an intellectually demanding and rounded preparation for national service – and which looked on Periclean Athens as a utopian space for the imagining of a sort of national cohesion and greatness that nonetheless gave scope for individual advancement. It is in this light that we can understand Dover's own commitment to the causes of education and Hellenism – including his decision not to return to Oxford, for the better interests not just of his family but also of the broader study of Classics in the nation at large. Perhaps at some level he asked himself the question with which he closed his review of Murray's biography: 'Did anyone do better?'

Conclusion

In an essay published in 1972, the literary critic Niall Rudd offered some reflections on the ways in which the distinctive shaping of the Oxford degree had affected attitudes to the study of classical literature:

> Some very able Oxford men have been known to say that the structure of Mods and Greats signified that literature (by which they mean classical philology) was useful mainly as a propaedeutic to the more serious disciplines of history and philosophy. An outsider is afraid to laugh at a remark like that. It is safer simply to ask whether literary criticism had much chance to develop in a system where philology itself had a subordinate role.[87]

Rudd was one of a number of prominent scholars in the post-Second World War years who were highly critical of the reluctance of classicists to adopt the sort of critical approaches that were now standard in the study of English literature – approaches the adoption of which did perhaps lead to the sort of schism among Classicists by the end of the century that Dover passed over in the autobiographical snippet from which this chapter began.[88] As it happens, Rudd was writing at the very time the traditional division between Mods and Greats had been permanently weakened by the introduction of Literature in Greats, albeit in a form which was not immediately (and is perhaps still not) amenable to new theoretical approaches. But that Rudd was right to highlight this curricular division is suggested by Dover's career as we have followed it in this chapter. It is not just that his attitude to the study of literature can profitably be read against the way in which ancient literature was studied at Oxford. It is also that Dover himself was a perceptive critic of the tradition in which he had himself been educated – even as his passionate assertion of the value of studying Greek offered a personal inflection of an Oxonian myth that grew less and less powerful over the course of his lifetime.

Notes

1. Dover 1992, xii. Thanks to Constanze Güthenke, Chris Pelling and the editors for comments, and to Chris Pelling for permission to quote from E.R. Dodds' unpublished lectures.
2. Grafton 1985.
3. See Pelling, this volume.
4. For the development of Greats, see Jenkyns 1997, 2000, Murray 1997, 2000, Walsh 2000, Stray 2007a, Ellis 2012.
5. See further Rood 2022.
6. For changes in the *Handbook*, see Currie 1994, 110–11, 115–16; for the figures for Fellows, Harris 1994, 232.
7. Thus the creation of a FHS in English Language and Literature was agreed in 1893, but English Mods were first set in 1949; even then there was a compulsory paper on classical literature in the original until 1969. J.R.R. Tolkien and George Dangerfield were among those to move from Classics Mods to English.
8. [University of Oxford] 1872, 15.
9. [University of Oxford] 1888, 154. Murray 1997, 237 (on the identical phrasing in the 1906 edition) wrongly says that 'literature' was one of the three headings.
10. Jowett 1848, 20.
11. Case 1891. For the usage, see e.g. Papillon 1880, 3.
12. Denniston 1919–20a, b, Owen 1919–20.
13. [University of Oxford] 1939, 144. For similar qualifications, cf. Joseph 1939, 4 ('pure scholarship'), Murray 1946, 227 ('scholarship in the linguistic and imaginative sense of the word').
14. Rudd 1972, vii–viii surveys the literary criticism available to a student in 1939.
15. Farnell 1898, 4–5. Cf. Lloyd-Jones 1982, 29 (from his 1961 inaugural).
16. e.g. Bodleian Library, MSS Zimmern 10.69 (J.M. Thompson on his 'pet aversions'), Lewis 1955, 137 ('the Two Great Bores'). Even Gilbert Murray could recall finding Demosthenes wearisome because the political issues were not explained (1946, 220).
17. *Oxford Magazine*, 22 November 1934, 173. For the terminology, cf. Dover on H.D.F. Kitto as 'not a first class man by a long way' (letter to parents, 1 December 1956, expressing admiration all the same for Kitto's popular book *The Greeks*) and *MC* 89 on how St Andrews knocked this classificatory habit out of him. Collini 1999, 201 discusses the same trope in Isaiah Berlin.
18. In practice, owing to the introduction of the emergency war regulations (see my text at p. 37), only one General Paper was set from the Trinity 1941 examination; the second paper was formally abolished with effect from 1948.
19. [University of Oxford] 1906, 135.
20. [University of Oxford] 1939, 138.
21. Lloyd-Jones 1956, 611.
22. As Dover noted in a letter to his parents (20 March 1953): 'of the last five Mods dons elected by Oxford Colleges not one is an Oxford man – which makes a wonderful argument for the committee that's trying to get the "Mods option" into Greats.'
23. Gould 1958–9, 384.

24. An earlier paper, 'The History of Attic Oratory', had been studied with sections first of Aristotle's *Rhetoric*, then of Dionysius of Halicarnassus. Bailey 1918–19, 99 proposed replacing them with Longinus and establishing an equivalent Latin paper using Cicero, *Orator*, and Tacitus, *Dialogus*.
25. [University of Oxford] 1872, 6 – an amendment (*Oxford University Gazette*, 20 May 1871, 178) by E.L. Hicks and D.B. Monro of a formulation ('Poetic and Rhetoric, as treated by ancient authors') evocative of eighteenth-century professors such as Hugh Blair.
26. The other standard options, 'Comparative Grammar of the Classical Languages' and 'Logic', were both technical.
27. This option followed in method what had previously been a regular Special Subject, 'The detailed study of a Greek or Roman site'; in the 1920s first Delphi, and then the Athenian acropolis, were prescribed, in both cases with the relevant portions of Pausanias.
28. Bush 1990, 121.
29. Ross 2013, 37. The essay question was: 'What account do you gather that Aristotle would have given of the nature and office of Poetry? Compare any later definitions of Poetry with that which in your opinion he would have drawn, and explain his point of view.'
30. Shuter 2003, 250.
31. *MC* 58–61, 63–4.
32. e.g. Oman 1941, 78, Marett 1941, 77; Ellis 2012 offers numerous instances. The trope is noted by Jenkyns 1997, 519 and Brockliss 2016, 420. E.R. Dodds tried in his 1937 introductory lecture to first-years to convince them of the difference ('The nature of university studies in the Classics', Bodleian Library, E.R. Dodds papers, Box 27/12).
33. Farnell 1898, 4, Denniston 1919–20a, 147. In 1910 the Board of Literae Humaniores consulted tutors on this issue; the survey produced an even split (Oxford University archives).
34. [University of Oxford] 1939, 138. Female students, by contrast, were aware that they typically arrived with a less rigorous training in the classical languages: revealing female perspectives on Oxford around Dover's time can be found in Warnock 2000 and Midgley 2005. Iris Murdoch took a second class in Mods the term Dover gained a first.
35. Letter dated 6 April 1940; the use of a numerical marking system is perhaps a carry-over from the language of school (cf. *MC* 36). For Dover's concern with the quality of his First, cf. a letter to his parents (dated 27 April 1949) on his first Balliol cohort to sit Mods: 'My best pupil, the Scotsman [R.G.M.] Nisbet [later Corpus Professor of Latin at Oxford], I regret to say got a much better first than I did! An astonishing array of a and a–, unmarred by anything as vulgar as an ab. I console myself by reflecting that Mods is not such a stiff exam as it was in my day.' Cf. Dover's astonishment at M.L. West's Second in Greats, though his doctoral thesis is 'so good that it almost depresses me; I don't think I could have done anything so good in the time at his age' (letter dated 17 October 1963).
36. Healey 1989, 29.
37. Bush 1990, 110.
38. Wrigley 2011, 165–70.
39. Healey 1989, 37.
40. The *Agamemnon* was available on the Greek authors translation paper, and could be combined with other tragedies (including *Choephoroe* and *Eumenides*) in the specially prepared books paper (an option Dover seized); for *Agamemnon* short passages were set for comment, but discussion of textual problems was not required.

41. *MC* 40. Cf. Dover 1993b, 365 for praise of Russell Meiggs' emphasis on seeing the Greeks as real people.
42. See e.g. Farnell 1898, 7 ('the sick man of the University'), Oman 1941, 79 ('nightmare'), Gordon 1945, 16–17 ('blasphemous rage'), Bowra 1966, 99, MacNeice 1965, 90, 102, 110, Mitchell 2009, 34–5.
43. Thus another 1930s matriculand, A.J. Ayer, chose after Eton to sit the less respectable alternative of Pass Mods in his second term, so as to start Greats work sooner (1977, 75).
44. See Stray, this volume, on Dover at school and university. The Special Mods is erased, too, in Dover's entry in the *Balliol College Register*.
45. The passage was printed in a selection of Pitt's War Speeches first published in 1915, a new edition of which appeared in 1940.
46. The *Times*, 19 October 1915, 9; 20 September 1916, 8.
47. Dodds in his introductory Mods lectures (n. 32) similarly insisted that '"a good composer" and "a good scholar" are not convertible terms'.
48. Though see Stray, this volume, on Dover at school and university, for his new-found liking for Virgil. Cf. Bowra's recollection of impressing Gilbert Murray at Mods through his paper on Roman poetry (1966, 126–7).
49. Dover 1987, Chs 15–17 (Agamemnon's dilemma, the red fabric, and the politics of *Eumenides*; orig. 1973, 1977, 1957); also the focus on the *Oresteia* in Dover 1982, Ch. 5. Cf. Güthenke, this volume.
50. 4 March 1940. The question was: 'Describe the manuscript evidence for the *Eumenides* and illustrate the value of the younger MSS. for constituting the text.'
51. Dover 1954, 125 claimed that envisaging comedy as performed is one of the advances made in recent scholarship on Greek comedy. Cf. Dover 1973, Ch. 2, 1987, Chs 26–7 (articles on the *skene* and portrait-masks in Aristophanes, orig. 1966, 1968); also 1997b, 54 (recommending people suspend judgement 'until they have read (or better, seen) a Greek tragedy and have reflected on it').
52. MacNeice 1965, 113 (describing his own Mods). For the trope, cf. Hirst 1947, 95.
53. Dover 1988a, Ch. 2 (Antiphon's speeches: orig. 1950), Ch. 10 (Plato's *Symposium*: orig. 1965).
54. 2 March 1940. The misprint was at Prop. 4.1.49 ('Avernales' for 'Avernalis').
55. The examiners were F.C. Geary (Corpus Christi), E.R. Dodds, Christina Keith (St Hilda's), who lectured on Sophocles, *Trachiniae*, and Euripides, *Orestes*, K.J. Maidment (Merton), later editor of the Loeb Antiphon, and Colin Hardie (Magdalen). Hardie is better known as a Latinist: he was Director of the British School at Rome, 1933–6, and later introduced a special subject on Virgil (Russell 2007, 231). Dover probably attended his lectures on Aristotle's *Poetics*.
56. Compare a question from the 1934 paper for the short-lived 'Alexandrian Poetry' Special Subject: 'Sketch the political and social background of Alexandrian Poetry, and indicate the chief centres of productivity.' Dodds' introductory Mods lecture (n. 32) promoted the General Papers as encouraging study of 'the social roots and the social reference of literature, its meaning as a product, and a criticism, of a particular age'.
57. See pp. 33–4.
58. Dover 1987, Ch. 23 (orig. 1950).
59. Cf. Dover's perception that Rose 1934 exemplified the derivative character of most British attempts at literary history (letter dated 12 January 1956).

60. Dover 1987, 157.
61. *MC* 66. Dover commented on the unusualness of the position in a letter to his parents (11 February 1948).
62. Letters to parents dated 14 September, 26 October, and 28 November 1946.
63. Among Dover's near-contemporaries in the *Oxford Dictionary of National Biography*, Baron Keith of Kinkel (a judge) and the civil servants Sir Wilfrid Bourne and Sir Leo Pliatzy all moved from Firsts in Classics Mods to Final Honours in Jurisprudence or PPE. Note too the trajectories of Alan Bullock and Hugh Trevor-Roper (both born 1914) from Classics Mods to Modern History finals.
64. As Isaiah Berlin did with PPE. Cf. the degrees taken by the philosopher Richard Wollheim, who overlapped with Dover at Balliol: first Modern History, then PPE.
65. See Dodds 1977, 28–9, Bowra 1966, 252 (the same point Dover makes on the preference for Greek), with 110 for Murray's teaching as his one source of inspiration in Mods, and Wilson 1987, 329 (on Denniston).
66. Lloyd-Jones 1982, 208.
67. On Murray see especially Wilson 1987 and Stray 2007b.
68. e.g. *Oxford Magazine*, 25 January 1905, 135, Bodleian Library, MSS Gilbert Murray 11.98–9 (R.W. Macan), 144–5 (H.E. Butler).
69. Murray 1907, 3.
70. [Mackail] 1912, 249. The author was a former Balliol Fellow who worked for the Board of Education and was Professor of Poetry at Oxford from 1906 to 1911.
71. Contrast Healey 1987, 29, who recalls a visit by MacNeice.
72. *MC* 249. The quotation was known to Dover from Wilson 1987, 392. The inclusion of 'Christian' presumably reflects Toynbee's schema of civilizations, to which Murray frequently adverts; cf. a 1956 contribution to the *Sunday Times* quoted by Ceadel 2007, 239.
73. Letter dated 16 May 1940. The lecture was published in Murray 1946, 127–48.
74. Letter dated 1 January 1954. He continued: 'One day I must pluck courage and ask the sub-faculty to prescribe some text other than the OBGV, but it isn't easy when the five people responsible for its production [i.e. Murray, Bailey, Barber, Higham, Bowra] are still alive and kicking'. For other denigrations of the book's use in Oxford, see Warnock 2000, 42 (citing Rudolf Pfeiffer, one of the émigré scholars who raised Oxford standards) and Russell 2007, 235.
75. For Murray as amateur, cf. Highet 1976, 163, West 1984, 224, Fowler 1991, 94, Griffith 2007, 56; also n. 77 below and Henderson 1960, 144 on how Murray (unlike Housman) 'defended the spirit of the amateur'.
76. Letter dated 9 November 1956.
77. Dover 1988a, 282. Murray 1908, 64 revealingly classed himself among 'amateur anthropologists'.
78. Murray 1907, 116–35 (with e.g. 116 on 'certain forms of sexual irregularity'). Cf. Turner 1981, 61–76 on 'evolutionary humanistic Hellenism'.
79. e.g. Murray 1897, 371, 377. Cf. Lloyd-Jones 1982, 210.
80. Cf. e.g. Murray 1946, 18–19 and Dover 1982, 146 (from a popular book in which he nonetheless could not resist 'Prizes for coming first' as the heading for a section on Greek exceptionality (8–15)).
81. Murray 1897, 293.

82. The preference for Theocritus over other Hellenistic poets was embodied in the Oxford curriculum: he was the only post-classical specially prepared author, while he and Apollonius Rhodius were included in the General Books. 'What claims has the poetry of Theocritus to originality?' was the question posed to Mods candidates in 1942. Cf. Hunter, this volume.

83. Cf. Dover 1982, 58, 66 on his preference for the 'starker and less sophisticated' Olympia statues and for the Siphnian frieze over the Elgin Marbles; he rebuts the 'charge of thoughtless primitivism' (66) by appealing to the excitement of imagining sculptors' experience as they attempted to solve technical problems – a formulation redolent of the Greats philosopher R.G. Collingwood, but with roots in Murray (e.g. 1909, 19 on understanding ancient works as requiring the effort 'to re-think the thoughts as if they were our own').

84. Dover 1988c, one of only three reviews that he wrote for that journal: a letter to his parents dated 19 October 1962 shows that he refused invitations to contribute while reviews were unsigned (an interesting spotlight on his concern for the personal voice).

85. Cf. Russell 2007, 236 on Dover's motivation. Dover's further comment that 'part of the reform [Murray] desired came thirty years later, and the rest after another thirty' alludes in its second part to the introduction of literature as an equal partner in Greats – though Murray himself seems only to have pushed for reformed teaching of Mods. The reforms of the 1930s (pp. 33–4), moreover, though highlighted by Dodds (nn. 32, 56) as lessening the Mods–Greats divide, were scarcely as significant, and Murray had attempted to bridge that divide from the outset of his professorship through the 'Seven against Greats' lecture series (promised in his inaugural lecture (1909, 7–8)).

86. Dover even indexed the term 'chairmanship' in *MC*, as Stephen Halliwell points out to me. Cf. Osborne, this volume.

87. Rudd 1972, 13.

88. Especially pertinent is the Cambridge-educated J.P. Sullivan, Junior Research Fellow at Queen's College in Dover's last year at Balliol, and then Tutorial Fellow at Lincoln College: following his emigration to the United States, where he co-founded the journal *Arion* with the goal of modernizing literary approaches to Greek and Roman texts, he frequently looked back with irony on the stultifying approach to literary study at Oxford (e.g. 1964, 175: 'Oxford must have become a more exciting place than it was when I was there!').

CHAPTER 3
DOVER AND ST ANDREWS
Elizabeth Craik

Kenneth James Dover began his academic career in 1948 with a fellowship at Balliol College, Oxford; after that he spent twenty-one years, 1955-76, as professor at the University of St Andrews, followed by ten years as president of Corpus Christi College, Oxford. He arrived at St Andrews aged thirty-five: that is, by conventional ancient reckoning, just approaching the time of his coming floruit.

I agreed to write this chapter because my close personal experience of the main events and people involved in Dover's life and work over the years at St Andrews is surely unique among those still living. A summary of the course of my own career will substantiate. From 1956 to 1960 I studied for an MA degree at St Andrews. After graduation with first class honours, I spent three years in Cambridge, and acquired an MLitt degree. I was research fellow in Greek at the University of Birmingham for one year (1963-4), then returned to St Andrews to a temporary post (1964-5) as assistant lecturer in the Department of Humanity (Latin), led at that time by Gordon Williams. In the course of that year, a vacancy arose for a 'permanent' post in the Department of Greek with Kenneth Dover. Having been appointed, I remained in the department for some thirty years, including time preceding and time following Dover's departure for Oxford in 1976, until the award of a Wellcome research leave fellowship, held in London, changed the direction of my research interests and the course of my life. I did not return to teach at St Andrews, as I was offered and accepted a post as Professor in Classics at Kyoto University, Japan, and stayed there for five years until retirement to Scotland in 2002. In 2000, I was awarded a DLitt degree at St Andrews and since retirement I have been honorary professor in the School of Classics there. The years spent 'full time' in St Andrews when Dover too was here in a different capacity were: 1956-60, 1964-76 and 2002-10. At other times of coming and going our paths crossed frequently, most notably just before 1990 when I was editing the Festschrift *Owls to Athens*.

The chapter, while focussed on Dover's career, will illustrate incidentally how tertiary education was structured, and how Classics was taught, at a particular time in Scotland. It is based primarily on my own recollections, supplemented by notes made for different purposes at different times, and by private correspondence. It is my intention ultimately to deposit these papers in the archives of St Andrews University Library. The existence of *Marginal Comment* has at times served as an *aide-mémoire* but has occasionally been a complication, where my own recollection or interpretation of past events differs somewhat; for this reason, I have minimized allusion to matters treated there.[1]

Kenneth Dover was about to commence his second year as professor at St Andrews when I matriculated as a very young undergraduate in October 1956, coming from an unacademic family and a local high school. Although I knew nothing of departmental structures or staffing in this – or any other – university, the discrepancy between the classical subjects was immediately evident: the Latin (Humanity) department was very large while the Greek department was relatively small. At that time, Latin was a compulsory subject for almost all students in the Faculty of Arts, avoidable only by the few who could and did opt for the alternative, mathematics. The then professor, T. Erskine Wright, was a somewhat remote figure, and many other teachers, notably Terence Mitford who lectured in staccato military mode on Tacitus, *Agricola*, and Nan Dunbar who bravely conducted mass tutorials, helped to instruct the 'general' class of hundreds. In 1956–7, Greek had a teaching staff of three: Douglas Young and Ian Kidd with Kenneth Dover. In the Arts Faculty there were three levels of instruction: 'general', 'special' and honours. All students chose three subjects in the first year (at 'general' level); in the second year, students aiming, as most did, at a four-year honours course continued with two of these subjects (at 'special' level) while adding one further subject (at 'general' level). The honours course, devoted to the two main subjects, occupied years three and four. In 1956–7 my subjects were Greek, Latin and Moral Philosophy. It was compulsory for all students in the Arts Faculty to study a philosophical subject: either Logic and Metaphysics or Moral Philosophy. Philosophy was taught and examined in parallel classes at St Andrews and at Dundee, but typically without cooperation even on the syllabus. I recall a warning, before the end-of-year degree exam, not to attempt questions on topics that we did not recognize, as these were set for the other constituency.

A brief sketch of the local situation, in personal and academic terms, at the time of Dover's appointment follows. The two institutions of higher education in St Andrews and Dundee had coexisted, with complex interconnections, for many decades. University College Dundee, as it was originally named, was founded in 1881 and began teaching in 1883. Affiliation with St Andrews, attempted in 1890, was partial and union unrealized. There followed a long period of uneasy coexistence between new Dundee and old St Andrews: in this, questions of specialization and duplication were evident but unresolved. Following a Royal Commission and the consequent Universities of Scotland Act, there was, in 1953, a serious attempt to reorganize the University of St Andrews and the (renamed) Queen's College Dundee into an integrated academic whole. However, the single structure imposed then was short lived and some ten years later – ironically, just as a long-projected road bridge over the river Tay was completed – the separate university of Dundee was fully and finally established by a decree of 1964, implemented in 1967. An early professorial recruit to Dundee, in 1884, was the young D'Arcy Wentworth Thompson, who was famously said to be equally proficient in Greek and natural history; subsequently, from 1917 until his death in 1948, he was Professor of Natural History in St Andrews. Decades later he was still remembered (notably for such idiosyncrasies as the pet parrot perched on his shoulder) by many in town and university, including many of my own acquaintance. When Dover arrived in 1955, there were two former professors of Greek still resident in St Andrews and both very visible in the library and elsewhere around the university: H.J. Rose (in post 1927–53) and his successor W.L. Lorimer (in post 1953–5). Postcards preserved in the university archives attest to a lively intellectual exchange between Rose and D'Arcy Thompson over many years.

The careers of Lorimer and Young are in certain respects parallel: both were Scots with an active interest in the language and literature of Scotland. Lorimer was closely involved in the Scottish National Dictionary project and in retirement translated the New Testament into Scots (a work posthumously completed and finally published by his son in 1983), while Young, a gifted poet writing primarily in the more artificial literary medium of Lallans, translated into Scots verse two plays of Aristophanes, *The Puddocks* (*Frogs*) and *The Burdies* (*Birds*). These were successfully staged at the Byre Theatre St Andrews and the Edinburgh Festival Fringe in 1958 and 1959. Furthermore, to a certain extent, the professional relationship of Rose and Lorimer prefigures that of Dover and Young. The local man Lorimer was already employed in the department of the previous professor John Burnet and seemed destined to succeed him. But his candidature was unsuccessful and Rose, a Canadian who was then Professor of Latin at Aberystwyth, was appointed. Young, not just a Scot but a Scottish nationalist, seemed likely to succeed Rose and many were surprised when the apparent outsider Dover was appointed. At that time, Dover had published very little, and few, in Scotland at least, could have foreseen his stellar career. Both Lorimer and Young were committed Hellenists, but Lorimer held a post teaching Latin in Dundee after failing to secure the chair; similarly, Young, who was recruited to join Dover at the start of his second term in Candlemas 1956, was previously in charge of Latin in Dundee. There was, however, a difference in their later careers: Lorimer became professor at St Andrews when Rose retired in 1953; Young left Scotland in 1968 for a post at McMaster University in Canada, and later moved to the University of North Carolina, where he died.

It must be remembered that, even in the fifties, St Andrews was a very small university in a very small town. In the session 1949–50, regarded as a peak year, there were only some 2200 students in Dundee and St Andrews combined: approximately 1300 in St Andrews and 900 in Dundee. Furthermore, St Andrews was dominated by a limited and close-knit coterie of men. Classics and related subjects were hugely influential. When the classical scholar and educationist James Donaldson was appointed principal in 1886, a post he held until his death in 1915, Lewis Campbell, who had been Professor of Greek since 1863, was also a candidate. When Dover was appointed in 1955, Malcolm Knox, principal since 1953, had previously been Professor of Moral Philosophy. Informal consultation and formal committees notwithstanding, by and large principals appointed professors and professors ruled in the organization of their departments. Historically, there had been a long hegemony and it did not quickly die. It may be supposed that the degree of professorial autonomy came as a welcome discovery to a new incumbent from beyond Scotland. Dover does reflect on his considerably greater freedom to impose his own ideas on the teaching of his subject, notably on shaping the syllabus, acknowledging that at Oxford there was no comparable opportunity (*MC* 82–3).

To me as a student, the first and most enduring impression of Kenneth Dover was of a commanding intellectual presence, dominating his department. At enrolment, the syllabus for the entire year was laid out in detail, with set books and bibliography prescribed (to be ordered from Tom Jessiman at Henderson's bookshop in Church Street) and arrangements made for weekly language work, alternately prose composition and unseen translation. Throughout the Martinmas term Dover himself taught the 'general' class daily, at 10 o'clock, in a small lecture room just off the main university quadrangle with its large 'Schools'. After the first session of language work, when prose compositions were returned, Dover remarkably showed that he knew all members of the class by name (quite formally, as Miss This or Mr That, and these titles were used also on notice boards where marks given were openly displayed). The lectures on Aristophanes' *Clouds* were a revelation to a group of innocents, who did not expect obscenity to feature so prominently (or perhaps at all). But before then, there were introductory lectures on a great range of topics, occupying the first month of instruction: language, dialect and accidence, word order and sentence structure (much on postpositives), style, metre, translation of texts, and the history, with dating, of literature. There followed a background lecture on Greek comedy (Dionysiac festivals, selection of plays) and a rather brief introduction to *Clouds* (textual tradition, Socratic theme, matters of staging). In the course of the ensuing term, the entire play was covered in some detail, averaging fifty to seventy lines per lecture. In the second term the set texts were Plato, *Laches* and *Ion*; in the third term Herodotus Book 1 was studied. In the second year of 'special' Greek for the session 1957–8 the set texts were works of Thucydides, Aeschylus and Homer. In the Martinmas term, Dover lectured on Thucydides Book 6, with Thucydides Book 7 prescribed as additional reading: he had lectured on the same books for Mods at Oxford (*MC* 71–2).[2]

It was characteristic of Dover that even his elementary teaching incorporated material from his current research. His early book with the title *Greek Word Order*, to appear in 1960, evinced the same deep concern with the rather esoteric feature termed 'postpositives' as had appeared in his first-year lectures (cf. *MC* 73–4). Dover was first and foremost a linguist. In all his publications, linguistic precision is prominent. The course on *Clouds* was a step towards his magisterial edition of the play, though this was not completed until much later. His lectures on Thucydides, delivered to the 'special' class in 1957–8, were challenging, again work in progress. One major change in the syllabus, made in his earliest years at St Andrews, was the introduction to the honours classes of a 'special subject' studied at the end of the third and beginning of the fourth year and examined in one of the five final Greek papers. (For joint honours in Greek and Latin there were eleven papers, each of three hours duration: five in Greek, five in Latin and an essay paper common to both.) Dover himself offered a special subject in Greek drama: three tragedies (the Electra plays of Aeschylus, Sophocles and Euripides), two comedies (Aristophanes' *Frogs* and Menander's *Dyskolos*) and Aristotle's *Poetics*. Individual private reading was prescribed and presupposed before teaching by discussion of essays in small group tutorials. Other special subjects were similarly demanding. One particular innovation was a subject allowing specialization in the history of the Greek language, starting with Linear B (the decipherment still being controversial and disputed both by Douglas Young and by Arthur Beattie, who was then Professor of Greek in Edinburgh) and continuing with focus on dialectal differences. The last course of lectures to finalists delivered by Dover in 1960 was on Pindar, perhaps because Pindar was viewed (wrongly, he argued) as peculiarly difficult.

Dover and St Andrews

In 1965, five years after graduation, I became the fifth teaching member of the augmented Greek department, joining Kenneth Dover, Douglas Young, Ian Kidd and the recently appointed Robert Reid. A few years later, when Douglas Young left, Malcolm Campbell was appointed in his place. There was a similar expansion under Gordon Williams in Humanity. (Robert Ogilvie was appointed to the chair in 1975, following Williams' departure for Yale.) It is remarkable that whereas in Greek all three new appointees were Scots and primarily Scottish-educated, in Latin all those appointed were English and exclusively English-educated: Christopher Carter, Peter George, Adrian Gratwick and Peter Woodward. Perhaps this was a coincidence. This may be the place to remark that I was the only one of his former undergraduate students to be appointed to a permanent post by Dover, though over the years several others did hold temporary positions in his department. Dover seemed to see me as forever young and forever junior. (The last time I visited him in Stratheden hospital, shortly before he died there, he did not recognize me but when prompted did remember me by my unmarried name, Farmer, as 'one of my very first students'.) It is perhaps the place to remark also that in Scotland of the sixties very few women were employed as university teachers, and certainly none as professors. Two women classicists preceded me: Nan Dunbar in Latin and Ursula Hall (née Ewins) in Ancient History, a separate one-person department which at that time was viewed as ancillary to Latin and Greek. Both were lost to Classics in St Andrews. Nan accepted a fellowship at Somerville College, Oxford. Ursula, who had married a colleague in moral philosophy, had children and resigned her post. (I fear that it was assumed by her senior colleagues that she would do so. There was, of course, no precedent and no provision for maternity leave.)

It was at once exhilarating and daunting to teach where I had recently been a student: exhilarating because from the first I had complete autonomy in deciding how to teach particular courses assigned to me; daunting because I knew the formidable standard set at the top of the department. My abiding memory of departmental meetings is of smoke-filled rooms, as my Hellenic colleagues, smokers one and all, chain-smoked throughout. By this time there were several graduate students, including Morrison Marshall (on postpositives) and Alan Henry (on epigraphy), almost all of whom had begun as undergraduates at St Andrews. But the supervision of graduate work was a relatively new activity and there were as yet no provisions for its management. Under the old regulations, long unrepealed, there was no set time limit for completion of advanced degrees. With a perfectionist supervisor like Dover, a PhD degree was liable to become the work not of three years but of three, or more, decades. I found there were already some changes apparent in the organization of the department's teaching, for example there was at all levels much more teaching in small tutorial groups. Also, some new topics had been introduced, for instance at second year level a course on Greek lyric metre. More far-reaching changes followed. A significant innovation – soon to be followed by Greek departments in other universities – was the introduction of a beginners' language course. Beginners, in Greek 'general B', were taught separately for the first two terms. Dover devised his own language course, and it was typically idiosyncratic and typically demanding, the sort of course he himself would have liked had he been an adult beginner.

Grammatical and syntactical rules were not stated and then illustrated in the conventional way; rather, examples were set out, from which the students had to deduce and then apply linguistic usage. In conjunction with this intensive language course, they were required to read, in an unadulterated text, several speeches of Lysias (including the accessible Lysias 1 and the much less accessible, both long and difficult, Lysias 2); in the third term they joined the regular class, Greek 'general A', and read a play of Euripides, which at that time was regularly taught by me. According to several of these wonderfully well-motivated students, their arrival at this rewarding destination made the long slog of language learning worthwhile.

Later, another far-sighted innovation was the introduction of a course in 'classical culture', primarily literature in translation but incorporating also some lectures on art and architecture. This immediately took off, with a very large enrolment. Dover was always emphatic that it ought to remain only a 'general' class, not to be extended to an honours subject. But there were new forces at work in St Andrews as elsewhere. An expansionist view of ancient history, taught without the languages, capitalized on the opportunity to expand: student choice played a part and the easier options were liable eventually to prevail. Another novelty instituted by Dover in the late sixties was a regular summer school attended by school teachers of Classics. On these occasions, he and most of his close colleagues, some participating more enthusiastically than others, gave advanced lectures on particular academic subjects, strictly eschewing matters of purely pedagogic interest. Today such extra-curricular activities have become routine: 'public engagement' or 'impact' is a desideratum and 'knowledge transfer' from university to community is mainstream; but in its day Dover's initiative was unusual and avant garde. At the time, student recruitment was the main aim. These summer schools doubtless enhanced the reputation of St Andrews among the teachers, some local but many from further afield, who were responsible for their pupils' choice of destinations; the experiment was repeated over the years and the activity was undoubtedly popular as well as successful. Dover was ahead of his time also in his concern with student welfare. He was quite excited by a move in 1975 to appoint a professional student counsellor and himself volunteered to participate in amateur counselling in lieu of an appointment being made (*MC* 154).

Dover never seemed to make allowance for inherent shortcomings or frailties in others, especially in those he taught. On one occasion, when a student had to retake a class, Dover felt it was necessary to change the texts set, so that the student would not be 'bored' by repetition, as of course he himself would have been. There were some unrealistic expectations in administrative matters too. When it was decreed that all departments must have a staff-student council, Dover enthusiastically embraced this democratic principle and devised a scheme whereby the council would, instead of having a regular president, be chaired by a changing *prytanis*, appointed by lot at the start of each meeting (so that all of us would experience and understand just how ordinary Athenians felt): this terrifying role always seemed to fall on the most nervous and timid first year student who happened to be a member of the council. Despite his formidable range and seemingly effortless clarity in exposition, Dover was not himself a natural popularizer. This was one reason for the disastrous failure of his series on The Greeks, televised in 1980 soon after he had left St Andrews for Oxford; though perhaps more important was a lack of rapport between him and a pushy producer who sought the limelight to the exclusion of Dover, even in exposition (cf. *MC* 131–4).³

In university administration Dover made substantial contributions, serving on two occasions as Dean of the Faculty of Arts (1960–3 and 1973–5). He was a cool and neutral chairman, unfailingly patient and polite.⁴ There was a natural affinity between Greek and other small language departments, of which there were several in the faculty, but he usually contrived scrupulously to avoid bias both at faculty and at smaller committees such as the annual meetings of boards of studies where matters including details of syllabus, proposed after departmental debate, were routinely rubber-stamped. When he became Chancellor of the university in 1981, there were still more committees to be chaired, including the General Council, comprising all alumni and all current staff members. Dover gives a rather revealing account of his own reactions at a General Council meeting in 1983, where members debated, with right to comment but no power to act, the recommendation of the University Grants Committee that several small departments should be axed: Archaeology, Linguistics, Music and Theoretical Physics (*MC* 173–4). Here Dover's own inclination to support Linguistics (which historically he had always favoured) emerges in a snide parenthesis, 'why not close the Faculty of Divinity instead?' There were certainly occasions where he incurred hostility, and he was capable of returning it implacably (*MC* 100–2). Doubtless such occasions are bound to occur in academic, as in other, communities; and it is unusual only that Dover reports them so freely. As he once said, frankly, to a colleague who confessed an antipathy to a certain student, 'One cannot help disliking the dislikeable'. At the same time, he was willing to stand up in support of any junior colleagues whom he believed to be unjustly treated (cf. *MC* 102; other instances are known to me).

On 3 April 1990, *'Owls to Athens': Essays on Classical Subjects for Sir Kenneth Dover* was presented at a reception in the Senate House, University of London. When I first suggested that a Festschrift for Dover would be a good idea and that his coming seventieth birthday would be a fitting occasion, there was immediate agreement among colleagues (though it was noticeably muted on the part of one senior colleague, who probably felt that any such initiative ought to have waited for him to think of it). Opinions were canvassed in Oxford and once again there was a unanimous expression of enthusiasm by associates. Although I was willing to edit, I did not expect to do so unaided and originally hoped to find a joint editor either in St Andrews or, preferably, in Oxford. However, although everyone wished to contribute to the volume, no one was willing to collaborate greatly, and especially not to co-edit. However, Stephen Halliwell, from his post in Birmingham, kindly offered to take over the organization of the fund set up in conjunction with the publication and to be responsible for the associated tabula gratulatoria.⁵ Later, the Jowett Copyright Trustees, through Jasper Griffin and under the aegis of Balliol College, offered a generous subvention towards editorial expenses. I had originally hoped to keep quiet about the plan; but colleagues argued, probably rightly, that secrecy and surprise would be impossible. Without my knowledge, some details were leaked to Hilary Feldman at OUP and then to Dover himself. Contributions were invited from pupils and close colleagues only and restricted to 5,000 words. The designation 'close colleagues' was open to debate and among letters from Dover are some very frank comments on and criticisms of contenders, sent at the planning stage of the Festschrift, in which he took a disconcertingly active interest: 'There are at least five people in the world of Classics who would be extremely unwilling to do anything which would give me pleasure or confer honour on me ...'

This active interest extended to the final presentation. It would have been easy to arrange an event in either St Andrews or Oxford, but Dover was emphatic in his preference for London as 'neutral ground'. And so it was managed there, with the help of John Barron and of Ana Healey (librarian at Gordon Square who happened to be a cousin of Dover).[6] The Festschrift was graced with a Prologos in Greek contributed by Donald Russell, and Dover himself provided a valuable list of all his publications (up to 1989) for the end of the volume (401–9). The title was an inspired suggestion made by Martin West. There are forty-two chapters in six sections (Drama; Other Poetry; History; Beliefs, Society and Art; Language, Metre and Rhythm; Texts and Scholars) reflecting the breadth of Dover's own contributions to scholarship. I believe it met with his approval. Dover's own copy in a special presentation binding was given to me after his death by Catherine Brown, his daughter, and it shows signs of having been read closely.

Dover's first abode in St Andrews was a large, terraced house, rented from the university, in Queens Gardens near the centre of town. Later, in 1966, he and Audrey moved to a house with a very large garden on the west side of town, in Hepburn Gardens. There, his main relaxation became 'horticultural engineering' and he tended his large plot with tremendous vigour. It was there that 'Pop' Dover came, in 1973, to live happily with his son, of whom he was inordinately proud, and his daughter-in-law. Pop made many friends and was terribly disappointed by the family move to Oxford. Both Kenneth and Audrey Dover valued the amenity of life in St Andrews and there was never any doubt that one day they would retire there. At the same time, they were great travellers. During his time at St Andrews there were two periods spent in the USA – as visiting lecturer at Harvard (1960–1) and as Sather Professor at the University of California at Berkeley (1967) – as well as a term of study leave spent at Lucca in Italy. And he made many academic visits to universities in Europe and beyond, lecturing with impressive and impartial linguistic fluency. In the early years after retiring, he was a regular annual visitor to Stanford.

To the end of his life, Dover used an ancient manual typewriter, for which ribbons could be procured only from one particular old-fashioned Edinburgh supplier, for his many publications. Greek was written in by hand. Attempts to interest him in word processors were doomed to failure (*MC* 121, 203). Without computer 'backups' for files, he relied on the hazardous old technology of carbon copies. In 1989, leaving on a short journey, he entrusted me with the second copy of his testimonia and app. crit. to the *Frogs*. 'So much work has gone into them that I couldn't bear the idea of their existing in only one copy, so the first copy is in my study and I'd be most grateful if you could look after the second until our return. That way, not much short of a nuclear bomb will set me back to square one.'

Dover's lifestyle was unassuming in youth and remained so in old age. From his cars (like the rugged Jowett Bradford much remarked by students in the early days) to his garb (sweaters with holes, a source of wonder to visiting academics in his later life) he was indifferent to any kind of luxury in his surroundings and possessions. He valued simple comfort and plain good food but little else. Even books were not collected but viewed rather in terms of their use. Much has been written, especially in the aftermath of the 'Aston Affair' (*MC* 222–31) about Dover's character, generally regarded as aloof, unemotional and obsessively rational. But, really, he was not uncaring and was even quite vulnerable, hurt and perplexed when he felt misunderstood. If he was uncompromising and occasionally naïve in his judgments (uncompromising in his relations with his father, naïvely trusting in his dealings with television producers), he was unrivalled in the searing honesty he applied to everyone and everything, but first and foremost to himself. Dover's contributions to academic life, and especially to the study of Greek Classics, in St Andrews are vast and evident. But it was a two-way process: St Andrews presented him with opportunities and challenges at significant points in his career. In sum, Scotland suited him and he suited Scotland.

Notes

1. Also relevant in various ways to points touched on in this chapter are Cant 1992, Donaldson 1911, Russell and Halliwell 2012, Young 1969, and the articles by myself in the *ODNB* on Lewis Campbell (1830–1908), Sir James Donaldson (1831–1915) and Herbert Jennings Rose (1883–1961).
2. On Dover and Thucydides, see Pelling's chapter in this volume.
3. On the reception of the TV series The Greeks, cf. Halliwell, this volume, p. 308 n. 4.
4. On Dover's principles of chairing committees, see Osborne in this volume.
5. The fund in question was used to create an endowment with the Society for the Promotion of Hellenic Studies, London, whose Dover Fund, in accordance with its honorand's own wishes, makes awards to postgraduates and young scholars in support of work related to the history of the Greek language 'from the Bronze Age to the 15th century AD'.
6. On Ana Healey, cf. Stray's chapter on *MC*, this volume, p. 106.

CHAPTER 4
DOVER AND CORPUS
Ewen Bowie

When Kenneth Dover was elected President of Corpus Christi College, Oxford, in the academic year 1975/6, I was in my eleventh year as E.P. Warren Praelector in Classics. The Governing Body was only slightly larger than when I had joined it in 1965 – some twenty-six rather than nineteen – but still the smallest (so we thought) among Oxford colleges. It had an unparalleled proportion of classical Fellows – four Tutorial Fellows, the Corpus Professor of Latin, and in most cases the White's Professor of Moral Philosophy (since until recently many eminent philosophers had read *Literae Humaniores* at Oxford as undergraduates).[1] In deciding to elect Dover as President, the Governing Body was following the proposal of one of his most distinguished Balliol pupils, Robin Nisbet, who had read Mods and Greats at Balliol (1947–51) as a Snell Exhibitioner from Glasgow and was chiefly responsible for building up undergraduate classics in Corpus as its Latin Tutorial Fellow (1952–70). Fortunately for the college, he remained a Fellow when he himself was elected to the Corpus chair of Latin (1970). By 1975, when Derek Hall's sad death in office precipitated a presidential election, he was among the most influential figures in the Governing Body. In suggesting that Corpus elect somebody recognized as a leading international Hellenist, Robin was confident (rightly) of my own support, and probably confident of the support of the Tutorial Fellows in philosophy, Jim Urmson and Christopher Taylor, the latter of whom had, like Nisbet, read for a second undergraduate degree at Balliol, though after Dover had left it for St Andrews. Choosing Dover was especially attractive because no other convincing external candidate had been fielded.

Persuasion of other senior Fellows may not have been so straightforward. Dick (Richard M.) Hare, the White's Professor of Moral Philosophy since 1966, could claim to know Dover better than Nisbet did. A year older than Dover, he had overlapped with him as an undergraduate at Balliol; like him, he had joined the Royal Artillery (but was unfortunately captured by the Japanese at Singapore and spent the rest of the war as their prisoner). He had been elected a Tutorial Fellow at Balliol in 1947, the year before Dover himself. Between 1948 and Dover's departure in 1955 he had spent seven years working with him as a close colleague. He voiced reservations about Dover's suitability for the presidency, but he never explained them.[2]

The ancient history Tutorial Fellow, Frank Lepper, must have been more of a challenge even to Nisbet's negotiating skills. Born in 1913, Lepper was now 62, and had been a Tutorial Fellow since 1939. He had held important college offices (Dean and Senior Tutor), written plays for performance by the college dramatic society, the 'Owlets', and possessed all the qualities of a 'good college man'. He was much loved by many colleagues, pupils, and alumni. Being elected President would have crowned a career of unstinting service to the college: his term would not have been long, but if the Statutes in 1975 did not already set a president's retiring age at 70, they could be altered in time for him to stay in office until 1983. Change, however, was in the air, the admission of women to read for graduate degrees had already been agreed (in December 1971), and there was pressure from younger Fellows and some junior members for Corpus to join other colleges which had decided to admit women as undergraduates. Nisbet, whether alone or after consulting Trevor Aston, must have decided that Lepper was not the right president for Corpus in 1976, and have persuaded him that he would not get sufficient backing. I recall no attempt by Lepper to canvass support. Nor, once Dover was in office, am I aware that he was anything other than a good colleague. The only betrayal of perhaps deep disappointment that I recall is how, the day after Dover's post-prandial talk to the Senior Common Room (1978) which shocked some Fellows by its detailed discussion and photographic illustrations of male homosexual acts depicted on Greek vases, Lepper asked me in the car park what I thought of the talk, limiting his own verdict to some eloquent facial expressions.

As for Trevor Aston, there were several reasons why he might have supported Nisbet's proposal. In earlier years he could have hoped to become president himself, but his hopes of election when Frank Hardie retired (1969) were dashed by the serious depression from which he suffered in the late 1960s, and he had two other important irons in the fire. Since 1960 he had been editor of *Past and Present*, already prestigious when a committee of distinguished historians appointed him, and enjoying even more success under his editorship, about which I never heard any complaints other than the bursar's irritation that so much of the college space allocated to Aston was occupied by his research assistants. At least one more research assistant arrived when Aston accepted the general editorship of the projected multi-volume *History of the University of Oxford* (1968). At this point he resigned his Tutorial Fellowship, in which he had proved himself to be a brilliant tutor, and was elected to a Senior Research Fellowship: he retained rooms in college, but his salary was thereafter paid entirely by the university, something which later had repercussions when he came into conflict with the bursars. In 1968/69, then, he was not seen by himself (so far as I know) or by others as a candidate for the presidency. Nor, I think, was he so seen in 1975, though by then treatment by May Davidson at the Warneford Hospital had helped him resume an apparently happier, and certainly academically active, life. But he had little reason to be a candidate in a potentially contested and bruising election, and may have been swayed by Nisbet's own decision (despite himself also being in many respects an excellent candidate) to give his time and talents to making his mark as Corpus Professor of Latin. Though these two senior Fellows were not as close to each other as they had been when together they sent a telegram to Eden in 1956 demanding that he abort the Suez campaign, I doubt that at this point there was any friction between them.

When the presidency was offered to Dover he did not take long to accept it. This may seem surprising, since in 1960, when offered the Regius Professorship of Greek at Oxford, a position for which the outgoing incumbent, Eric Dodds, had recommended him, and which had been his target over the previous decade, he had turned it down. The reasons he gave in his letter of refusal to the Prime Minister, Harold Macmillan, are discussed by

Christopher Stray in Chapter 1. Here I note his mentioning the general issue of the impact on classics in the UK ('I believe ... that the patent anxiety of many professors in a score of universities to return to Oxford or Cambridge at the earliest opportunity has had many bad effects on the educational system of the whole country') and two issues particular to Oxford: (a) 'Oxford is the only major university which makes no provision for Classics (as normally understood) as a Final Honours School. My experience of participation in attempts to remedy this situation during 1953–55 was not at all encouraging'; and (b) 'Whereas a professor at St Andrews has effective control over the prescription, teaching and examination of his subject from first to last, an Oxford professor has little or no control'. It is also clear from his correspondence that finding an appropriate house (something then offered to Tutorial Fellows by most colleges but not part of a professorial package from the university) was an issue.

The offer of the presidency in 1975 differed in important ways. Housing, in the President's Lodgings in the college, was guaranteed. Although Dover would be a member of the Faculty of *Literae Humaniores*, he would have no teaching obligations on which the syllabus might impinge; and anyway by 1975 Robin Nisbet, Donald Russell and Godfrey Bond had successfully pushed through the sub-faculties, the Faculty Board and the General Board a reform that introduced the study of Greek and Latin Literature into the Final Honour School of *Literae Humaniores* (first examined in 1972), a huge change. Moreover, as head of a college Dover would have control of a sort: not of the sort then enjoyed by a professor in a Scottish university, but a much greater opportunity to affect the direction taken by a college than an Oxford professor had to influence his university colleagues. That he thought carefully about the sort of leadership being head of a college involved emerges from something later written to Trevor Aston: 'leadership in an institution where ultimately everything is decided by a majority vote is totally different [sc. from that of an officer in a military context].[3] If you lose the respect of the people you command, the fact that you are invested with power can help you in many ways to regain respect. If you lose the respect of people over whom you have no power at all, it is a much harder and longer job to get it back'.[4]

It also seems from other things Dover wrote in 1975 that he felt that his teaching in St Andrews was becoming a little stale, and that he was making mistakes: for somebody for whom getting things absolutely right was important, this may have been a crucial factor. On the other hand, he may not have given enough thought, or enough weight, to the possible consequences for his wife Audrey, who was very happy in St Andrews (and in the event not very happy in Oxford).

On many counts Dover's presidency was a success. He was popular with junior members of the college, both graduate and undergraduate. When the Governing Body decided (1981) to move the main Senior Common Room from the dark-panelled, modestly-sized room at the east end of the cloisters, with two windows overlooking Merton Grove, and instead take over as its main sitting room what had hitherto been a shared set, with two bedrooms and a sitting room, on the first floor of the Gentleman Commoners' Building, and other rooms on the same floor as a new dining room, Dover supported giving the dark-panelled room to the Middle Common Room, an offer that was much appreciated. Its president somewhat earlier, Ford Weiskittel, also credits Dover with letting them have a fine watercolour of Egypt for their previous common room (in the Gentleman Commoners' Building, ground floor), and writes: 'Kenneth Dover was very easy to work with as President. He listened to whatever concerns I might have had on behalf of the MCR and acted accordingly ... he was very supportive of efforts to make the MCR a central point in the life of the college for graduates...'[5] Graduates may also have liked Dover for not putting pressure on them to complete their doctoral theses in good time, something for which many of them took against his successor, Keith Thomas, who instituted a system of regular meetings with each graduate (analogous to the system of end-of-term 'collections', long customary for undergraduates): the presence of the graduate's college advisor did not diminish the terror some felt during these brief encounters, and several left in tears.

So far as I can recall or discover Dover's presidency was popular with undergraduates too. As a historian of ancient democratic Athens, he gave considerable importance to communities' autonomy, and saw the Junior Common Room as a body which should be allowed to make its own decisions and whose voice should be heard in college meetings. Following the turbulent events – sit-ins and demonstrations – of 1968 and 1969, a university Commission of Enquiry recommended formal participation of junior members both on university committees and on college governing bodies and committees: when Dover arrived in Corpus, this had been partly implemented in some college and university bodies but had been resisted by the Corpus Governing Body. It took Dover some time to persuade the Governing Body to accept this change, initially involving representation on committees, but by 1983 at meetings of the Governing Body – in each case with some 'reserved' business, of which neither the agenda nor the minutes were made available to junior members; nor were they present for discussion of 'reserved' items.[6]

A related response to controversial issues was already evident at the first Governing Body Dover chaired (October 1976). The Junior Common Room had requested the installation of a condom dispenser in the beer cellar. The debate was long. Most Fellows who spoke addressed the morality of actions that might be seen as encouraging casual sex: Dover was chiefly concerned with the constitutional question of whether the Governing Body should instruct the junior members on such matters.[7] A further issue on which many junior members may have approved of Dover's stance was that of admitting women undergraduates. The question had been opened by a letter circulated by the Warden of New College as early as 1964, and in Michaelmas Term 1971 the Governing Body had voted by thirteen to twelve to change the statutes to allow the admission of women to read for undergraduate degrees. But changing the statutes required a two-thirds majority, and some Fellows opposed to 'co-residence' fielded a diversionary proposal for an alliance with Somerville, then an all-women college: this proposal was made in June 1971 and accepted in December 1971. On 6 December 1971 it was also agreed to change the statutes to allow the admission of women as Fellows and as graduates; on 12 February 1972 the Governing Body opened the presidency too to women. But on the admission of women undergraduates, Corpus remained among many colleges which hung back. Only in 1976 was a committee appointed to 'consider the long-term issues arising from the possibility of co-residence'. In February 1977, the report of this 'Working Party on Co-residence' was unanimously accepted, and at the college meeting of 14 March 1977 Statute 28 was amended so that: 'Both men and women shall be eligible for election or appointment as President, Fellow, Tutor, Officer, Chaplain or Lecturer of the College and for admission as members of the College to read for any degree, diploma or certificate of the University.'[8] Neither my memory nor the minutes reveal how important Dover's support for this change was, but support it he did. That the thinking of some undergraduates – still all male – was comparable is shown by a Junior Common Room meeting in February 1977, at which nineteen voted for the admission of women undergraduates and four against, while there were four abstentions.

If the attendance at that Junior Common Room meeting betrayed lukewarm interest (by then Junior Common Room membership exceeded 150), the arrival of the first twenty undergraduate women in Michaelmas 1979 was welcomed by junior and senior members alike, and their integration went relatively smoothly (excepting some issues relating to communal shower rooms and the like). Dover deserves credit for getting the decision taken in 1977 and for its successful implementation. He had already shown support for the graduate women who had been arriving in small numbers since 1974, not least in going down to the boathouse to cheer them on in their achieving five bumps in Eights in Trinity Term 1978 and thereby earning the commemorative feast called 'a bump supper'. At that dinner most were tolerant of what some saw as a *faux pas,* when (making a joke inconceivable now) Dover somehow worked into his congratulatory speech, noting how physiology had not held back the rowers, a quotation from Tennyson's *The Lady of Shalott*:

Out flew the web and floated wide—
the mirror crack'd from side to side;
'The curse is come upon me', cried
the Lady of Shalott.

This was the only hint junior members had of Dover's interest in human reproductive organs, a hint reinforced by the publication in that year of *Greek Homosexuality.*[9]

A thorough and balanced account of how Dover was seen by junior members would require much more oral historical research than I have been able to conduct. But correspondence with a small sample (unrepresentative, no doubt, since they are all classicists) suggests he was perceived as a good president. For some, that perception was first formed as he carried out the duties of Tutor for Admissions, an office that still went with the presidency, though the president no longer had any substantial role in choosing among applicants for undergraduate places, something now entirely in the hands of the Tutorial Fellows and lecturers who would teach them. The days were past when a president could, as Frank Hardie reputedly had, press the case for admitting good golfers. Perhaps if Dover had thought that an applicant's interview with him during the admissions process revealed that that person might be a danger to the college community, he would have tried to impede the offer of an award or a place, but so far as I know this never happened. I certainly recall no attempt to veto acceptance of somebody whom tutors agreed in December 1976 to be a borderline candidate to read for the relatively new version of Honour Moderations designed for people with 'A' levels in Latin but little or no Greek – they learned Greek on arrival, for the first two terms chiefly in university language classes, and for the remaining three *via* a mixture of university and college teaching. Concerned about this person's slow progress under these arrangements and recalling Dover had expressed an interest in doing some teaching and was a major contributor to the JACT *Reading Greek* volumes designed precisely for people learning Greek from scratch (another 1978 publication), in the pupil's third or fourth term I asked Dover if he might have time to give him some help. He agreed, but rapidly got back to me: 'To all intents and purposes this man knows no Greek.'[10]

Another sort of help I sought from Dover was in giving revision classes to finalists for the paper on Greek literature of the fifth century BC: this would require no preparation by him, and it would benefit pupils to hear a different voice from that of the tutor who had set and commented on their essay work. Different memories survive of these classes, given in the summer of 1977. One pupil recalls that his own inadequately formulated contributions were very patiently handled, but that Nick Denyer (the year's star, who has since had a distinguished career as an ancient philosopher) was treated very roughly, with Dover putting him down on several points (and also ignoring questions from one of the cohort's weaker members). Nick Denyer himself remembers things differently. He writes: 'Two of Dover's remarks in those classes stick in my mind. One was about the uppity women in *Lysistrata*: any uprising among the women was the same kind of absurd fantasy as the uprising of the Birds. Another was that questions of literary style arise only when there is the possibility of saying the same thing in different ways. I had been reading Quine on synonymy, and objected. Dover treated my objection with perhaps greater courtesy than it deserved.'[11]

Patience with lesser intellects, however, was something noticed by Ross Leckie. Ross became a friend of Dover's son Alan in the two years before coming up to Oxford (they were both in a travelling troupe of theatrical players which toured Fife in a caravan drawn by two mules), helped him and his wife Wendy in their restoration of an old mill in Glenfarg, and benefited from several Dover lifts from Oxford to his native east of Scotland, stopping for tea and Audrey's sandwiches off the northern M6. Ross was never taught by Dover but recalls once asking him something about the *Frogs*, with which he was struggling: Dover 'was kind enough to respond by giving me thirty minutes in his study. I remember vividly not the details but how very gently, if rightly, he made me feel rather stupid, *via* his *reductio ad absurdum* of my position/understanding. Such was his intellect that I think I would have been greatly daunted to be taught by him.' Ross also had some dealings with him when President of the Junior Common Room and writes: 'I found him exemplary: patient, considerate, open.'[12]

A similar sort of patience was observed by Judith Mossman (recently President of the Society for the Promotion of Hellenic Studies). I quote at length from her email since it touches on many issues that arise here or in other chapters:[13]

I remember very well when I first met KJD – he was at that time acting as admissions tutor as well as president and I wrote to him and asked to come and look round, as the prospectus encouraged one to do. My parents dropped me off and I enquired at the lodge, and after a short interval KJD appeared, in gardening attire, and kindly showed me around and answered with patience the questions which occurred to me to ask.

When I was subsequently interviewed, we ... were seen by him separately for a sort of general interview. I cannot honestly remember what he asked me – they were not Classics questions ... He was formidable but kindly.

I was a JCR officer for a while and sat on the Library Committee with him and with Aston.[14] I never remember him being anything other than courteous to Aston in public – as he was indeed to everyone, as I recall – though I don't think he appreciated the noise of dramatic productions in the college garden.

He and Lady Dover entertained all the freshers, and knew our names, too – they learned off the photographs, which greatly impressed me.

Generally I remember people liking KJD, and Lady Dover, too, though she was famous for talking about the price of carrots at parties. Odd, really, as we all ate in hall and had little occasion to buy carrots.

It very definitely made a difference to us that he was an eminent classicist. Not a few of us had encountered either his *Clouds* or his *Aristophanic Comedy* book, and soon became aware of his other achievements.... Overall we were very positive about him and we were sorry when he and Lady Dover left.

In retrospect the fact that the food became so much better under Keith Thomas, and also the fact that graduate students were told that theses were for finishing, not eternal contemplation, suggests to my now more experienced mind that KJD might have been a more active president. But he was very friendly and polite (he used to raise his hat to me, which I enjoyed very much). I do remember in one of his lectures (which had to start in one of the big exam schools, it was so full) thinking that portentously using English swearwords as examples was maybe a little childish. That was the only hint I ever picked up of what was later revealed in his autobiography, and, like Donald Russell, I rather wish it had remained hidden. At the time, one really had no idea.

Nothing I know counters the impression of these communications that Dover was widely liked and respected by junior members. No disrespect was conveyed by the nickname acquired after his 1978 publication of *Greek Homosexuality* – Ben. 'Why Ben?' an innocent would ask. 'Ben Dover' was the reply. I never discovered if this nickname became known to its bearer. But that some graduates might have benefited from firmer encouragement to finish their theses is borne out by the last witness I cite, David Moncur. David had studied classics under Dover at St Andrews – where he observed 'that he was extremely sociable and took pleasure in human company (although he did not "suffer fools gladly")' – and on Dover's advice chose Corpus when applying to do a DPhil in Oxford. Like Dover, he arrived in Michaelmas 1976. I was initially appointed his supervisor (David was thinking of working on Aristophanes, and I was then lecturing on *Wasps*), but with 'no idea of what aspect of his work I wanted to study'. We worked through various ideas, and I also suggested he consider less well-worked subjects (e.g. Lucian). Later that academic year I had leave and David was transferred to Dover's supervision: Dover 'asked if I wished to continue to pursue research into Aristophanes, and although I still had no idea of a suitable topic, but thinking this was a chance to work with one of the leading Aristophanic scholars of the day, I said yes. Eventually we decided on dramatic discontinuity, or rather he suggested it and I agreed.' What ensued again merits quotation *verbatim*:

> Working with KJD was a genuinely formative intellectual experience – not only in giving me a better understanding of Greek language and literature, but also in terms of teaching me how to analyse an issue, ask the right questions, subject received opinion to scrutiny, find or make unlikely connections, consider no detail to be insignificant and take nothing at face value simply because it appears to provide the obvious answer. It would be no exaggeration to say that KJD taught me how to think effectively, and I have benefited hugely from that in everything I have done since. What I do not have are the letters DPhil after my name. Responsibility for this must lie squarely with me: I valued the experience of regular exchange of ideas with one of the most acute minds of the day and allowed myself the luxury of exploring the vast set of possibilities opened up by every question we discussed. I did not however manage to focus this intellectual energy into producing written material that could be moulded into something which might eventually turn into an Oxford DPhil. This failure is wholly mine, and in retrospect I should have realised that my researches were not progressing towards their intended goal. I have no doubt that had I voiced this concern to KJD, he would, in his usual forthright way, have told me so and given help and advice on what to do about it. But I did not and, as far as I recall, I was never formally confronted with the consequences of this lack of focus, or encouraged or indeed required to sit down, get my thoughts in order and write a draft chapter or two. Possibly KJD did not feel it was his responsibility to 'lay down the law' in this respect, or believed that his role was to encourage but not prescribe.

There is some similarity between Dover's views on the communal decisions of the Junior Common Room and on the decisions of individual students. In each case they should be given the opportunity to decide for themselves.

I now return to Dover's relations with senior members of the college: again space compels me to be selective. One Fellow enthusiastic about Dover, right from his first interview by the electors, was Brian Harrison. His thoughtful and well-written assessment of Dover's presidency, with particular reference to the 'Aston affair', was published in *THES* in reply to a piece by Valentine Cunningham that was extremely critical of the revelations of *Marginal Comment*,[15] and no summary could do it justice. I pick out just one point: Brian's support for Dover at that interview was secured by Dover's response when asked if he thought the college should admit women – 'of course'.

I too was enthusiastic. I had already heard about Dover in the late 1950s, when, as an undergraduate at Pembroke College, Oxford, I had a friend (from the same Scottish burgh, Coupar Angus) who, after reading English at St Andrews, came to do a doctorate at Oxford. He had attended and admired some of Dover's lectures at St Andrews, and also recalled a remark of Dover that on completing his undergraduate career he had decided to read all Greek literature. I think I did not meet Dover until his Corpus interview in 1975, but I greatly admired his work, and devoured both his commentary on Aristophanes' *Clouds* (1968) and his monograph *Aristophanic Comedy* (1972) soon after publication. When I lectured for some years on Theocritus, I found his commentary (1971) less rewarding, though its analysis of what he presented (misleadingly, in my view) as *all* possible ways of understanding Lycidas in *Idyll* 7 pushed me to develop my own ideas.[16] I was also much impressed by *Greek Popular Morality* (1974). So when he became president of Corpus, I was in almost as much awe of him as those quoted above, and was chuffed when, some time after his arrival, he asked me to write the Hellenistic and imperial Greek section of a short book *Ancient Greek Literature* that OUP had invited him to write (it appeared in 1980). I happily took on imperial Greek literature, but doubted I was right for Hellenistic literature, so that was offered to Jasper Griffin: the first two chapters were written by Martin West, the following five by Dover himself. I never discovered, then or later, whether Dover's decision to read 'all Greek literature' had taken him beyond the death of Demosthenes. Nor did I discover if he really thought me the right choice for imperial Greek literature, or if he was simply being courteous to someone now a colleague.

Not unrelated is the fact that in Dover's ten years in Corpus we had few conversations about classical literature. That was surprising, in retrospect, and I may be as responsible as he (it takes two to tango); and having discovered from some non-classical conversations that he disliked being outdone in argument I may have hesitated to broach topics where I was sure his erudition and analytic ability exceeded mine. The two occasions I remember on which we had classical conversations are both revealing. After examining the doctoral thesis of one of his pupils I remarked at lunch that, while it was in almost all respects an excellent thesis, one of the readings defended in a passage of Aristophanes was unmetrical. Dover's eyebrows shot up, but without missing a beat he said 'He can't have shown me these pages'. To Dover it was either inconceivable or not to be admitted that he could have let defence of an unmetrical reading slip past. On the other hand, at another lunch – but this lunch was bibulous, since it was the lunch then held termly to conclude (or in some unfortunate cases to punctuate) a statutory Governing Body meeting – by chance I found myself next to Dover, and late in the meal became bold enough to make a suggestion about a passage in his *Clouds* commentary. When instructing Strepsiades on knowledge of metre and rhythms (ῥυθμοί, 638), Socrates explains how this will make him κομψὸν ἐν συνουσίαι (649), ἐπαΐονθ' ὁποῖός ἐστι τῶν ῥυθμῶν / κατ' ἐνόπλιον, χὠποῖος αὖ κατὰ δάκτυλον. 'Smart in *synousia* ... knowing what sort of rhythm goes with the *enoplion*, which rhythm with the dactyl.' Pages 180–1 of the commentary have a long and valuable note on ancient metrical terminology, but miss the possibility (or certainty?) that there is an obscene *double entendre*, initiated by the term συνουσία which Dover's note on 649 explains as 'party', while commenting that 'it can also refer to any other kind of meeting or association'. I pointed out that sexual intercourse is a well-established sense of συνουσία (LSJ *s.v.* I.4) and that this choice of word prepares the audience to understand κατ' ἐνόπλιον as 'using your weapon' and κατὰ δάκτυλον as 'using your finger', an understanding doubtless encouraged by obscene miming by the actor (cf. Dover on 652 and on οὑτοσί in 654). Dover accepted my suggestion at once, with great grace, remarking γηράσκω δ' αἰεὶ πολλὰ διδασκόμενος, 'I grow old always learning many things' (Solon fr. 18 West).

Finally, I recall his generous response when, as editor of *JHS*, I sent him some points concerning an article he had submitted (Dover 1983b): they were a collage of referees' observations and my own. He replied that he had never had so helpful and carefully formulated comments from an editor.

Overall, then, I was a fan. But there was an indefinable remoteness that I found hard to handle. Nor was I entirely surprised when, during my years as Senior Tutor (1981–4), he made no move before meetings to discuss important items on the Governing Body and Tutorial Committee agenda – presumably because he thought this might infringe these bodies' autonomy. We also had very different attitudes to the Mediterranean landscapes of the ancient Greek *diaspora* and to their modern Greek inhabitants. I perceived a good knowledge of landscapes and urban remains as essential to my attempts to understand the Greek world of the Roman Empire, and from my first visit to Greece as an undergraduate (Easter 1960) made repeated summer visits to Greece, several to Turkey, two to Syria and Lebanon, and one to Egypt. Dover seemed little interested in the natural environment or the impact on it of human habitation,[17] was apparently unresponsive to an enthusiastic account by James Howard-Johnston in the summer of 1975 (just before his assumption of the presidency) of Macedonia's 'rolling hills, fertile upland plains and deciduous forests stretching over ridge after ridge into the distance', and is reported by James (in the same context) as saying he twice 'had to' go to Greece.[18] Undoubtedly Dover would no longer have written, as he did on his first visit to Greece (on a cruise as a schoolboy at St Paul's), 'The crew are entirely Greek, and more dago than you would ever think dagoes could be';[19] and he was a stimulating and attentive supervisor to at least one Greek graduate pupil, John Petropoulos, studying 'Eroticism in ancient and medieval Greek poetry'. But so far as I know Dover never developed the good relations with Greek academia that has marked the careers of Pat Easterling and Chris Carey.

In these and other respects, Trevor Aston, to whom I now turn, was very different. In the eleven years between my arrival in Corpus and Dover's I had come to know Trevor well. Initially overawed by the forceful manner of the tall, lean figure who most often dressed in black, I was impressed by his apparently total commitment to the college and by the energy with which he built up the holdings of its library and expanded its physical space, an energy also directed to many aspects of the college's management of its then chiefly agricultural investments. He seemed equally at home discoursing eloquently in the Senior Common Room on diverse 'high culture' subjects and examining the roof-structure of the medieval mansion in Kent, Netherhale, from which the college's tenant wanted to move to a modern, purpose-built farmhouse. One evening we went together to a pub in Temple Guiting, a Cotswold village where Corpus was the principal landowner, hoping to assess local views of the possible impact of selling off several properties, as was proposed by the college's land agents.

Already in 1969, my first wife, Rosemary Fleck, and I had invited Trevor to join us on a visit to Istanbul and the Aegean coast of Turkey: he had had nothing resembling a holiday for years, he was throwing himself into organizing the *History* of the university of which he became General Editor in 1968, and he still devoted much time to *Past and Present* and to the library. We felt he desperately needed a change of scene, though we knew little of the breakdown that had hospitalized him for six months in 1959.

Trevor agreed. He would fly to join us in Istanbul; we drove *via* Hungary, Yugoslavia and Bulgaria. When we reached Istanbul, he was in hospital with a back problem, seemingly triggered by attempts to move the bed in the modest hotel in Sultan Ahmet where we had agreed to stay, so we saw little of Istanbul together. We were halfway through our planned tour of the great cities of the Aegean coast, and had just explored Ephesus, when over dinner I remarked that on my next Turkish trip I wanted to see the late Hellenistic sculptures on the summit of Nemrut Dağı, in what had once been the kingdom of Commagene. It was a mistake. Trevor's interest was at once aroused, and when told more about the cult of Antiochus and its context he insisted we change our plans and go to Nemrut. I pointed out that driving to the nearest village, Eski Kahta, would alone take three days, even stopping to see nothing *en route*; another day would be needed for the ascent from Eski Kahta (there was then no motor road, and we would have to use mules); then at least one more for return to the nearest airport, whence Trevor would need to fly immediately to Istanbul to connect with the flight he had already (apparently irrevocably) booked back to London. It was an irrational use of time hitherto earmarked for Lycia and Pamphylia. A few glasses of rakı and many persuasive Aston arguments later we resolved to leave Söke early the next morning. As I drove my ageing Ford Anglia across the Anatolian plateau, now conveying not just me, my wife, and Trevor, but also his teenage niece, who had joined us in Istanbul, and a large stringed instrument (a 'suz') she had acquired in Bursa, Trevor took picture after picture of agricultural implements, installations and practices, which related to what he knew in the medieval West. Somehow Kahta was reached, Nemrut ascended, and we even drove hours along a rock-littered track to see Lucian's city Samosata (already threatened by the planned Euphrates dam); Trevor and his niece got back to Adana in time.

I tell this much-pruned story because it shows Trevor at his best, happy and flamboyant in a context different from most in which other accounts set him. Alas, the break was not enough: in September 1969 he entered a deep depression and spent a year in a hospital in London.[20] By 1971, when James Howard-Johnston was elected university lecturer in Byzantine History and a Fellow by Special Election of Corpus, Trevor was much better, and was the most active Corpus member of the joint college/university committee for that election. On James' arrival, there were few other senior members living in college – sometimes a Junior Research Fellow, sometimes a lecturer – and James became Trevor's closest friend and chief support. Ruth Padel, then better known as a classicist than – as now – as a poet, was a lecturer who often dined, though she did not live in college. I too was quite often in dinner and stayed for post-prandial conversation, and I vividly recall an occasion in Common Room when Ruth and Trevor competed for the most plausible suggestion concerning the Archbishop of Canterbury's bedtime reading. I forget which proposed calling Lambeth Palace, but one of them made such a phone call, without establishing the answer. By the mid-1970s, with psychiatric help, Trevor seemed fully recovered and was a major and positive figure in college life.

When Dover arrived, no friction with Trevor was apparent. Dover made no attempt to obstruct the implementation of a decision, taken before his election,[21] to expand the west end of the library into the existing president's study and College Office, though it involved him moving the study to a small room on the ground floor in the south-west corner of the main quadrangle. This small room had no window overlooking the quadrangle, unlike that through which it was reached, and which now became the College Office, occupied by the person who was both college secretary and secretary to the president. This was quite unlike previous presidents' first-floor study, whose location in the quadrangle's south-west corner Frank Hardie judged ideal for discreet observation of college life, something he believed important to the president's role (and hence deplored the college's decision). Nor did Dover oppose another major scheme for library expansion, the conversion to library space of Lecture Room 3 (on the ground floor on the quadrangle's south side). Trevor presented plans for both, drawn up by the college architect Geoffrey Beard, to Governing Body on 14 February 1979: works were completed in 1980.

That relations between Dover and Trevor Aston were still good is also indicated by the fact that in 1979, seeing few suitable candidates for the position of Dean when Thomas Charles-Edwards left it as planned in 1980, Dover invited Trevor to take on this major college office. This Trevor would only consider if he were allowed simultaneously to continue as librarian, something Dover rightly would not allow. Dover probably made the suggestion that Trevor become Dean partly hoping it might dislodge him from a college office in which he was becoming increasingly autocratic and in which his insufficiently monitored expenditure was alarming the Library Committee and the bursars.

The library, however, was not the only part of the college where Trevor's input resulted in expenditure greater than planned. Frank Lepper's retirement made available the elegant seventeenth-century house he had occupied, 3 Merton Street. Trevor asked to be allowed to move from his large set in the Fellows' Building to 3 Merton Street, to be rented for occupation by himself and his second wife Judith (whom he had married in June 1975), with ample room for his research assistants. The expense of restoring it, over the long vacation of 1980, to how Trevor believed a seventeenth-century house should look, expense to which he somehow obtained the college's agreement, worsened his relations with the bursars, already bad because of library expenditure. Moreover, the

Senior Common Room's move to new premises, although initially opposed by Trevor, involved many decisions in which he played a great part over the autumn and winter of 1981/2, especially concerning furnishing, where his vigorous researches resulted in the purchase of the Bauhaus chairs and settees that still furnish the large and small Senior Common Rooms, and comparably expensive chairs in the dining room.

Relations between Trevor and his colleagues improved for a time, and Trevor may have been pleased that in Michaelmas Term 1981, Dover sounded out Fellows on the possibility of sacking the Domestic Bursar, Don Wild, while he was on leave: by then Trevor certainly saw Wild as an enemy. But earlier in 1981 he had complained to James Howard-Johnston about Dover's weakness as president – he felt he should have taken his side against the bursars – and several incidents in 1982 further damaged his relations with some colleagues.

First, Trevor was suspected, along with another Fellow, of having drunk (over two occasions) more than three bottles of Glenmorangie (the Senior Common Room's favoured malt) without signing for them as was required. At a common room meeting in spring 1982 its master, Thomas Charles-Edwards, Trevor's former pupil and his successor as Tutorial Fellow in medieval history, proposed a ban on spirits in the common room until the missing whisky was accounted for. Only Trevor voted against.

Second, an incident in June 1982 provoked a long letter from Dover to Trevor, dated 29 June, which in the event was not sent. It mentions threats of legal action by Trevor and an abusive letter he sent to the Domestic Bursar on 7 June, and shows Dover keen to reason with Trevor, even when his patience had worn very thin.[22]

Third, a Dover letter dated 2 November 1982 concerns a drunken outburst by Trevor in the lodgings.

Finally, at the end of 1982,[23] a college agent was sent to look over 3 Merton Street, to assess its rental for the next three-year period. Trevor, maintaining he had not been told this was the purpose of the visit, sent Dover an angry note resigning his Fellowship, an action he telephoned to reverse the next day.

By 1984, however, Trevor had decided to relinquish 3 Merton Street and to return to a large set in the Fellows' Building, having its spacious bathroom (which I remember from my occupation of that set in 1965–7) converted to create more space for research assistants: he and they would use the communal bathroom on the staircase. A suggestion by Thomas Charles-Edwards that even so the set could hardly accommodate Trevor and his assistants caused Trevor to leave the Governing Body meeting and write at length to Dover, accusing Thomas of envy and complaining of persecution by the Governing Body.[24]

It was also in 1984 that the bursars became increasingly concerned about Trevor's unpaid battels (totalling £1544 by 18 December). Meanwhile in 1982 the Library Committee, disturbed by growing library expenditure, sometimes on expensive art books unrelated to subjects in which the college admitted students, had begun asking for accessions lists, requests which were fobbed off. By Hilary Term 1985, it had adopted a scheme (with details devised by Robin Nisbet) that essentially shifted control of purchases from the librarian to the committee. It also decided that information about the annual index of book prices it suspected Trevor was suppressing should be taken into account in drafting the library budget, something best assured by having the Assistant Librarian, David Cooper, attend meetings of the committee. By now, however, Trevor's relations with David Cooper were bad: he saw him as a traitor and an enemy. On 15 February 1985 he wrote to Dover resigning his Fellowship, but then wrote again at 3.30 a.m. on the 16th withdrawing that resignation. On 20 February, however, he resigned from the librarianship rather than accept the committee's requirement.[25]

Neither what I have read, nor my memory, tells me how Trevor divided his time between then and August, whether in Corpus, in London, or in his recently acquired house in Spain. For various reasons I was spending much less time in college than in the 1970s. So it is only from James Howard-Johnston's 'Chronicle' that I know the next act in Trevor's tragedy. On the evening of Wednesday 14 August, he behaved violently to his wife Judith; on Thursday 15 he had to be forcibly ejected from the hospital where she worked; on Friday 16 took an overdose in the taxi driving him to Oxford, collapsing in his rooms on arrival: he was then pumped out in the John Radcliffe Infirmary. After a terrible Saturday (17) he agreed, on the morning of Sunday 18, to go to the Warneford Hospital; by Monday 19 he was planning to rearrange the furniture in his ward. On Tuesday 20 (I quote James Howard-Johnston's 'Chronicle') 'Judith had an injunction served on Trevor, giving notice of divorce proceedings and banning him from their flat (in London) and her place of work. He made a first bolt for freedom at midday [i.e. from the Warneford], but was forcibly taken back as he waited for a taxi on Old Road'.

It was thus a seriously disturbed Aston with whom Dover had to deal on returning from a trip to South Africa in September 1985 (*MC* 226). He had spent some of the days since 20 August in the Warneford, some in college, and sometimes seemed to be coming to terms with the prospect of divorce, though in college on the night of September 24 he got very drunk, and on Wednesday 25 shouted in public at several people, including college staff.[26] These events were mentioned in a letter Dover wrote to Trevor on 30 September, where he also referred Trevor's letter of resignation from his Fellowship written on the black day Tuesday 20 August, and they were the subject of a meeting early in October during which Trevor discussed his 'history of mental illness' with an increasingly unsympathetic Dover (*MC* 228). Nevertheless, it seems that he got noticeably better over the next two weeks. He was well-shaven; he lunched, dined and conversed; he attended parties in London on 10 and 11 October.

On Monday 14, however, the library's annual Visitation discovered that a valuable book was missing; recollections conflict as to whether it was Loggan's *Oxonia Illustrata* (1675) or a volume of Ackermann's prints of Oxford. Trevor had indeed borrowed it to have an illustration copied but could not produce it. Instead of letting Charles Webster, now Fellow Librarian, handle the issue, Dover took it over himself, telling Charles he proposed to have a disciplinary hearing before a panel of senior Fellows, something he apparently communicated to Trevor by letter, though no such letter exists in the college archives.[27] At the Governing Body meeting on Wednesday 16 October the missing book was mentioned in the report of the Visitors, which said that the president was 'pursuing an enquiry into the matter', and that report was accepted: the minutes do not record whether it was discussed. That same day, divorce papers arrived, and Trevor's frantic conversation with a common friend led her to telephone Dover: he communicated with Trevor's doctor,[28] but it seems that that doctor did not come to see Trevor (*MC* 230). The last person to talk to him, asked to call on him in his rooms at 8.45 pm, was the Tutorial Fellow in ancient history, Elizabeth Rawson, who also had rooms in the Fellows' Building. She was worried he might have drunk too much and taken pills, but his repeated assurance that he had not done so allayed her worries – and she was unaware of at least one of the two crises Trevor had faced that day.[29] He died in the early hours of Thursday 17 October.

Dover's account in *Marginal Comment* both presents himself as welcoming a cumulation of pressures on Trevor that might drive him to suicide and suggests that, when he talked to the doctor, they decided that they must respect Trevor's stated wishes and not force his locked door to secure his safety (e.g. by getting him yet again to the Warneford). To my mind, only the first of these attitudes explains the second. The common friend who telephoned had lost her own husband to suicide, knew Trevor well, and would have been heeded by somebody who wanted to prevent Trevor killing himself. At a number of points, either what Dover said then or his account in *Marginal Comment* fall short of the precise accuracy for which he always strove. When he told Trevor 'of the embarrassing occasion on which his Fellowship was renewed [in 1982] by a narrow margin'[30] – which provoked Trevor's response 'You're trying to push me out of the College!' – this was not strictly true: Fellows were apparently slow to raise their hands, but none voted against Trevor's renewal. Furthermore, when Dover recounts that he 'called an informal meeting of six other Fellows, in order of seniority after Aston',[31] this squares neither with my recollection nor with the account in Charles-Edwards and Reid 2017.[32] Neither I nor Dick Hare was among the Fellows consulted, but we were both senior to the bursar, and I was senior to Brian Harrison. The term 'six Fellows in order of seniority after Aston' is perhaps ambiguous: Dover may have meant seniority by age, and Brian Harrison and Brian Campbell were indeed older than me, though junior to me by date of election; but neither was older than Dick Hare. Dover may well have thought that I, once close to Trevor, fell amongst those in the Governing Body whom he feared might be 'irrationally hopeful or indiscriminately compassionate', and that Dick Hare would strongly express and compellingly argue for a very different view of the morality of pushing Trevor towards suicide. Furthermore, *Marginal Comment* says nothing of a letter Dover sent to Trevor concerning the missing book.[33]

There are, then, two strands in the account in *Marginal Comment*. On the one hand Dover represents himself as rationally reaching the decision that it would be best for the college if Trevor killed himself, and as giving Trevor the impression that his colleagues might well vote to deprive him of his Fellowship. But on the other, he gives readers the impression that his handling of the events was legitimized by his consultation of senior Fellows 'in order of seniority after Trevor'.[34] As he makes clear in his letters, his patience with Trevor had worn thin: the president who once gave importance to communal decision-making now hesitated to allow a decision about depriving Trevor of his Fellowship to be taken by the Governing Body as a whole.[35] It is also remarkable that Dover did not allow the matter of the missing book to be handled by the senior and

Ewen Bowie

experienced Charles Webster, whom the Governing Body had appointed as Fellow Librarian when Trevor resigned that office, but insisted on dealing with it himself. Dover's part in Trevor's death may have lost him the respect of only a few Fellows in 1985: his account of it in 1994 lost him the respect of many more.

Appendix 1:
Dover's letter to Trevor Aston after his resignation of his office of librarian

24 February 1985

T.H. Aston, Esq.,
C.C.C.

Dear Trevor

When I wrote to you to convey the Governing Body's thanks, my carping over details would have been uncouth. Since, however, your letter of 20 Feb.[36] comments on my conduct of the last Library Committee meeting, I propose to reply; and I am particularly impelled to do so by the fact that your letter is a strikingly complete exemplification of all that has gone wrong.

You told me earlier in the year that a pathological inhibition prevents you from opening letters from me, and that in consequence you ask Judith to open them at the weekend and give you the 'gist' of them (an expression which, I note, you used also with reference to a letter from me in MT 1980). Such a disability naturally evokes compassion, and I agreed to communicate with you orally instead of writing. Compassion, however, inevitably wears thin when it becomes apparent that your recollection of what has been said viva voce or on the telephone is also unreliable, and we seem to have reached a point at which you select, from oral and written communication alike, only those ingredients which make tenable a standpoint untenable once the other ingredients are added.

For example, you commented on a paper of mine (8 Feb.) which had actually been cancelled in part by a second paper (dated 16 Feb., sent to you on the morning of the 18th) rendering part of your comment unnecessary.

However, to go back to January: I told you by telephone that a majority of members of the Library Committee (including me) wished the Assistant Librarian to be invited to attend meetings of the Committee. You replied that this was 'unprecedented'. You added that you would have a word with me about it, which you didn't. I said that the matter was 'bound to be raised', emphasising the word 'bound' rather heavily, at the next meeting. Having chosen not to put the matter on the Agenda, you now criticise me for allowing it to be raised when it was not on the Agenda!

Val Cunningham's intervention in the discussion rested on his mistaken belief that you had had no notice of the matter. When I told him the facts after the meeting, his attitude changed completely.

As you will recall, you told the Committee that if Cooper were invited, you would leave. After discussion and some reflection on my part, I said: 'My priority is to transact this afternoon's business. If the Librarian leaves, that will impede the transaction of business. For that reason I am not / going to put the matter to the vote, but it must be reported fully to Governing Body, and I shall ask for a ruling'. After that, you make the extraordinary statement, in your letter of 20 Feb.: 'Obviously I have no idea what your reason or reasons were'.

Your statement could be true only if your memory were a complete blank in regard to that part of the meeting. Or, of course, if it were occupied by non-facts, which is a possibility. When I rang you – before circulating my note of 8 Feb. – to say that the report of the Committee could all be Unreserved Business, minus the Cooper question, and I would put that question on a separate paper as Reserved, you said 'I thought that was deferred'. I reminded you then of what I had said at the meeting.

On a wider front, you complain that Scott and others have not approached you directly about Library matters. The reason they, and also other Fellows who are not now members of the Committee, ceased to approach you directly was that they felt that when they did they were fobbed off. I sympathise with them because, frankly, I felt I was fobbed off too. Several attempts on my part to discuss accessions lists with you produced nothing but two feeble arguments against them – one, indeed, so feeble that you recognised its nature yourself as soon as you uttered it. Only constant pressure, enlivened by the occasional ultimatum, induced you in the end to operate the Library in the way the College wishes it to be operated. I found the whole process both exhausting and demoralising, and all the more so because it should never have been necessary to pursue it. For me, the opposition you put up to Cooper's attendance was the signal that our troubles were not over, and it forced me to recognise that I could not conceivably propose you for re-election as Librarian this summer (a matter on which I had, in fact, sought advice from senior colleagues who are not on the Committee).

I have no doubt at all – and I know many go along with me in this – that the kind of arbitrium you exercised over Library purchases was the right answer in the late sixties and early seventies. But things which are the right answer at one time do not necessarily remain so indefinitely; the Hertford Matriculation Offer scheme is a striking case in point.[37]

Yours
Kenneth

Appendix 2:
Two paragraphs of Charles-Edwards and Reid 2017 (pp. 415–16)

He asked six Fellows of the College to come to a meeting on 27 September: the outgoing Vice-President, Peter Hodgson, his successor, Christopher Taylor, Brian Harrison, who was Senior Tutor, Professor Nisbet, the Bursar, and Dr Hill. After this meeting, Dover wrote to Aston on 30 September and reported back to the six Fellows: he had talked to Lord Bullock, Chairman of the Committee overseeing the History of the University, who told him that the committee were not minded to take any steps to remove Aston from the general editorship, and that they were not dissatisfied with progress. Dover had also had 'long conversations with Dr Hall & Dr Solomon at the Warneford, & have learned a lot about our patient from the clinical point of view, & a good deal else. Dr Hall's opinion is that a real threat now could precipitate suicide.' He had written to Aston to express 'my personal exasperation at his behaviour, and to tell him that I expect him to take the medical advice that he is unstintingly given, but I have not suggested to him that Fellows may set Statute III 26 (a) in motion'. But he then added 'If five Fellows do set it in motion, I am bound to call a Governing Body meeting.'

Statute III 26 (a) defined the procedure whereby a Fellow might be deprived of his Fellowship. In Dover's mind, it seems clear, if the possibility of invoking that statute were suggested to Aston, that would constitute the 'real threat' to which Dr Hall referred. At this stage, he would not make the suggestion himself but offered it as a possibility for five of the six Fellows. In Dover's mind there were huge difficulties over instituting such proceedings in the Governing Body: 'others, especially among the younger Fellows, might be irrationally hopeful or indiscriminately compassionate'. Yet, if the threat precipitated suicide, there would be no need to institute such proceedings. In one of the conversations between Dover and Aston, Dover seems to have revealed the threat by implication: 'I told him of the embarrassing occasion on which his Fellowship was renewed by a small margin.' Yet, there was never a vote on that occasion: the embarrassment to which Dover refers was a pause before someone took it upon himself or herself to propose, and another to second, renewal. If Dover did indeed represent the occasion to Aston in the way he describes in *Marginal Comment*, he gave the descent towards suicide a hefty push.

Notes

1. Among holders of the White's chair (attached to Corpus) J.L. Austin (1948–60), W.C. Kneale (1960–6), R.M. Hare (1966–90), and Bernard Williams (1990–6).
2. Similarly, Brian Harrison in an email to Chris Stray on 5 December 2020: 'when Dover's name came up as a possible President, Dick Hare (I think the only other Balliol man present apart from Christopher Taylor) who seldom intervened in Governing Body, piped up and said (without any explanation) that he didn't think Dover a suitable person for President. He never intervened to that effect in the later processes of appointment, but my impression was that he had some moral delinquency in mind, perhaps from his Balliol days as a tutor'. I doubt that any *specific* delinquency need be supposed, nor that Dover's reservations about philosophy (as SH suggested to me) were a factor: I think it was a judgement on Dover's character and personality.
3. Both Dover and Trevor Aston had military careers in the war as officers in command of troops.
4. From a letter (never sent) by Dover to Trevor Aston, 29 June 1982, prompted by his violent reaction to the refusal of the Estates and Finance Committee to agree to his request for a rent

rebate on 3 Merton Street, but expanding into wider observations on his treatment of the college and his colleagues.

5. Email from Ford Weiskittel (MCR President 1975–8) to ELB, 1 March 2021.
6. See *MC* 192. I am no longer sure Corpus was 'among the first colleges to have junior member representation on Committees and on Governing Body', as I wrote in *The Pelican Record* 2010, 54.
7. I have some memories of this debate, which have been reinforced by James Howard-Johnston's 'Chronicle'.
8. Patrick 2019.
9. A little later I benefited as editor of the *Journal of Hellenic Studies* from Dover's knowledge of the evidence from vases when deciding whether to publish his pupil Martin Kilmer's article 'Genital phobia and depilation' in *JHS* 102 (1982) 104–12. It was in this context that he disclosed how his researches had led him to investigate the artistic trimming of pubic hair by dancers (female) in the *Crazy Horse Saloon*, Paris.
10. As suggested to me by Simon Sadler, the undergraduate in question, it is possible that Dover was influenced by lack of confidence in the course then used by the university, developed at McGill.
11. Email from Nick Denyer to ELB, 20 February 2021.
12. Email from Ross Leckie to ELB, 2 November 2020. Relations between Ross and Dover deteriorated when Dover sent him several pages listing errors of fact in Leckie 1989; they went further downhill when Ross published a harsh review of *MC* in which he questioned Dover's treatment of Trevor Aston.
13. Email from Judith Mossman to ELB, 10 November 2020.
14. Probably 1983/4.
15. Harrison 1994a, responding to Cunningham 1994. James Howard-Johnston had already reacted to *MC* in the *Independent*, 29 November 1994, 19.
16. Bowie 1985. For an assessment of Dover's *Theocritus*, see Hunter's chapter in this volume.
17. I say 'seemed' because, as the editors point out, Dover did refer at *MC* 38 to 'the unforgettable Greek landscape'.
18. Howard-Johnston, 'Chronicle'. In fact, he made two trips as a schoolboy and one later trip to inspect the terrain that related to his Thucydides commentary; his visits to Greece and Italy for the BBC 1980 series 'The Greeks' were after 1975.
19. A letter written by Dover to his parents, 9–10 April 1937, on board SS *Cairo City* between Athens and Santorini. I owe knowledge of this letter to Christopher Stray.
20. I assume the chief immediate cause was distress at his divorce from his first wife, Margaret Bridges, which became final in 1969.
21. On 10 December 1973, see Charles-Edwards and Reid 2017, 407–8.
22. Also referred to above, n. 4.
23. *MC* 224.
24. *MC* 225, with the addition from Dover's notes on *MC* in the College Archives that the individual accused of jealousy was Thomas Charles-Edwards. The decision to allocate Trevor Fellows' Building 1. 10 was taken at the Governing Body meeting of 15 February 1984.
25. Letters of Trevor dated 20 February and Dover dated 24 February: the second of these is Appendix 1.

26. The dates are those of Howard-Johnston, 'Chronicle': *MC* assigns these incidents to the 26/27.
27. For this communication to Trevor see James Howard-Johnston's 'letter' to Dover in the *Independent*, 29 November 1994, and Dover's addendum to the 2nd impression (1995) of *MC*, 264–5: 'I learn from Charles Webster ... that I wrote Trevor a letter about the book in the last few days before his death, and that I insisted on treating the loss as justifying a special enquiry by senior Fellows. As I don't remember writing the letter, and I am informed that no file copy of it has so far been found in the college, I cannot say any more about its content or tone. Yet I must have sent it, because I do remember a telephone conversation with Trevor about the loss, which must have been on 15th or 16th October, and I don't think he would have rung me then unless he had had some communication to answer. The anxiety in his voice persuaded me that he had no idea where the book had gone'.
28. I understand this to be Trevor's doctor in the Warneford, though James Howard-Johnston's 'Chronicle' has his GP involved.
29. *Pace* Howard-Johnston, 'Chronicle', she will have known about the missing book from the Library Visitors' report, which was on the Governing Body agenda.
30. *MC* 229, referring to a meeting with Trevor some days before 15 October.
31. *MC* 227, on 27 September (Charles-Edwards and Reid 2017). By 'other' is meant other than the seven Fellows or lecturers who had gone to see Dover (or in one case telephoned) on 27th or 28th September to let him know in how bad a state Trevor was.
32. This lists the Fellows as Peter Hodgson (outgoing Vice-President), Christopher Taylor (incoming Vice-President), Brian Harrison (Senior Tutor), Robin Nisbet, Brian Campbell (Bursar) and Ron Hill (Tutorial Fellow in Physics and the college's first Fellow in the Natural Sciences).
33. See n. 27 above.
34. In a letter to the *Times* on 16 December 1994, 17, Christopher Taylor states firmly that discussion at that meeting of how to deal with Trevor was not framed in terms of life or death, a statement endorsed by Dover in his *Addenda* to *MC* in the revised impression of 1995, 284.
35. *MC* 227.
36. The letter in which Trevor Aston resigned his office of Librarian.
37. In the competition between colleges to attract good applicants for undergraduate places Hertford College initiated a scheme whereby on the basis of performance in the entrance procedures in December an offer might be made to an applicant on condition of attaining grades in the following summer no lower than E in three 'A' level subjects, i.e. both college and applicant could be virtually certain the condition would be met. Dover thought this unilateral move should not be perpetuated after the great simplification of the Oxford admissions system introduced by the committee that he chaired: cf. *MC*, ch. 27.

CHAPTER 5
DOVER, BLUNT AND THE BRITISH ACADEMY[1]
Robin Osborne

No reader of *Marginal Comment* can be left in much doubt as to the profound influence that his parents had on Kenneth Dover's attitude to life. Dover himself acknowledges this of his mother, Dorothy, both implicitly, in the epigraph from something she wrote in 1948 (*MC* 9) with which he starts the chapter on his early life, and explicitly: 'She treated every opinion and argument on its merits, regardless of who said it or hrs motives for saying it. In these respects I have tried to live up to her standards' (*MC* 10). But the shadow cast by his father is clear too: 'He was, I think, scared of the portrayal of profound emotion' (*MC* 9). By contrast, it is much harder to see the influence of any of Dover's teachers as equally profound, for all that Dover acknowledges that writing a commentary on the Cassandra scene for Fraenkel's *Agamemnon* seminar set him on the road to his 'professional career', and that Meiggs taught him to prioritize contemporary evidence and remember that the people of history are real people (*MC* 40, 59).

When it comes to how to chair a meeting, it is doubtful whether anyone ever explicitly taught Dover how one should do this, but the parental influence undoubtedly bulks large. Dover's own first experiences were of A.D. Lindsay as Master of Balliol, for just a single year, and then his successor David Keir, a man for whom Dover had little admiration: 'in his social, political and moral attitudes he was more profoundly conservative than any of us had realised. It would have been better if he had expressed his own predilections more robustly, but he went to great lengths to avoid any confrontation with a tutor, and the transparency of his occasional subterfuges invited disrespect' (*MC* 82). Dover did not perhaps learn as much as he might from this negative example; he may have learned more from Sir Malcolm Knox, Principal of St Andrews and the man who had a significant part to play in persuading Dover to take up the chair of Greek there. Dover notes that he 'had several occasions, when matters of academic standard[s] were at issue, to welcome his ability to deflate pretentiousness with a question of deadly simplicity' (*MC* 94 n. 1).

Soon after his arrival in St Andrews, Dover began to acquire significant experience of chairing committees himself. Expansion of the university dominated discussion in both the university and the town. Dover was made Chair of the St Salvator's College Council Committee on New Residences. He took the role seriously, going to see new residences at Hull, Leicester, Newcastle and Southampton. The new residences were not uncontroversial, and Dover noted that his experience of having to field hours of often hostile questions from the College Council with patience and good humour put him 'through a much more advanced course in chairmanship than at any time in my life up to then' (*MC* 98).

Dover served as Dean of the Faculty of Arts from 1960 to 1963, a period from which he recalls the pleasure that came from the opportunities 'to manipulate or circumvent regulations in order to rescue people from predicaments not altogether of their own making' – a pleasure he notably did not indulge later in life.[2] When he was offered a second, two-year stint as Dean in 1973, Dover agreed because of his desire to use his chairmanship of the Faculty Council and the Faculty Planning Committee 'to attempt a thorough overhaul of the examination system in Arts' (*MC* 149). By that time, he had begun to be sought after as a chairman elsewhere – as President of the Hellenic Society (1971–4), Chairman of the Classical Journals Board (1975–8), and as President of Corpus, Oxford, from 1976.

As a chairman Dover was, on his own admission, keen that everyone should have their chance to put their arguments forward, even at the cost of meetings going on for five hours (*MC* 185). He records that at Corpus, even when he decided to circulate a memorandum before a meeting, he only once declared his own opinion: he describes his role as 'a combination of . . . seducer and midwife' (*MC* 186). His reluctance to express an opinion as Chair meant that he found the Staff-Student Joint Committee at Corpus problematic, since he was expected both to represent the Fellows and to be Chair, so that he explicitly told the Fellowship that the job of representation would have to be taken by other Fellows on that committee (*MC* 193). Even when he favoured one side in an argument, he made no attempt to force the issue: the representation of students on Governing Body was something which he favoured, but although he wrote the paper on the topic which set out the advantages and disadvantages, he saw the proposal twice defeated (*MC* 192). What caused Dover despair was not failing to persuade a committee of his own view, but failing to find a way to structure a decision into a linear sequential argument: 'what, after all, are chairmen *for*?'[3]

When Dover was approached in 1978 by Isaiah Berlin to consider becoming President of the British Academy there were obvious problems to be sorted out – in particular the question of the Academy's own premises.[4] But such questions were unlikely to put the chair of the discussions on the spot, either in terms of their complexity or their divisiveness. And so, when on 15 November 1979 Blunt was unmasked as a former Soviet spy and J.H. (Jack) Plumb, Master of Christ's College, Cambridge, wrote that he hoped 'immediate action will be taken to expel Anthony Blunt from the Academy. I do not think we should harbour traitors', Dover was faced with a situation he had not anticipated, and of a kind for which he was not prepared.

Blunt

Born in 1907 and partly brought up in Paris, where his father, the Rev. Stanley Vaughan Blunt, had served the British Embassy Chapel, Anthony Blunt was a Marlborough College contemporary and friend of Louis MacNeice, with whom he shared a study in their final year and who wrote of him: 'In my own house the dominant intellectual was Anthony Blunt, who had a precocious knowledge of art and an habitual contempt for conservative authorities'.⁵ Blunt's was a well-connected family; he not only had the poet Wilfred Scawen Blunt as a great uncle but his mother was second cousin of Claude Bowes-Lyon, father of Elizabeth the Queen Mother, and he was a relative of Oswald Mosley. He went up to Trinity College, Cambridge, in 1926 to read Mathematics, moving directly to read Part II in two years and then changing to Modern Languages (French). Graduating in 1930, he taught French for two years before being elected a Fellow of Trinity in 1932. His Fellowship dissertation was published in 1940 as *Artistic Theory in Italy, 1450–1600*.

Blunt had been recruited to the Cambridge Apostles, as would be his younger Trinity contemporaries Guy Burgess, to whom he dedicated *Artistic Theory in Italy*, and Michael Straight. It seems to have been Burgess who introduced Blunt in 1937, as the threat of Fascism became ever more apparent and the responses of European governments ever more feeble, to an agent for the Soviet Interior Ministry (NKVD), and Blunt played a part in recruiting three further Trinity students: Michael Straight, Leo Long and John Cairncross. Blunt's own activities in passing classified information to the Russians came when, after his early involvement in the Dunkirk evacuation, he was recruited by MI5 and gained access to the information deciphered by the Enigma machine. He passed on intelligence about German spy-rings in Russia and about Wehrmacht plans. In all he passed on some 1700 documents.

In 1945 Blunt was appointed Surveyor of the King's Pictures in succession to Kenneth Clark, and two years later, aged 40, he was appointed Professor of the History of Art and Director of the Courtauld Institute. He would hold both posts concurrently, and both for twenty-seven years, and in both positions, he served with great distinction. He was the chief architect of the opening of the Queen's Gallery at Buckingham Palace, to show off the Royal Collection, in 1962, and he was largely responsible for the pre-eminence that the Courtauld Institute attained in the study of the history of art. In 1950 he was elected a Fellow of the British Academy.

In 1951 Blunt collected Guy Burgess from Southampton when he returned from the British Embassy in Washington after his spying activity had begun to be detected, and he put him up in his flat in London, effectively assisting his and Maclean's flight to the USSR. He notes in his unpublished memoirs that he was himself also encouraged to leave for the Soviet Union by the KGB, but preferred danger in the UK to life in Stalin's Russia. From 1952 Blunt was interviewed on some eleven occasions about his activities, but he revealed nothing. After Michael Straight, as part of a background check for government employment in Washington in 1963, had revealed his own activities in the 1930s along with those of Blunt, the FBI passed this information to MI5. Blunt was interviewed again, first by Arthur Martin and then by Peter Wright of MI5 and, following a promise of lifelong immunity from prosecution and that the information he gave would be kept secret for fifteen years, admitted in April 1964 that he had spied for Soviet Russia.

The background to Blunt being offered immunity from prosecution and that his information would be kept secret is complex and muddied by the subsequent frustrations of Peter Wright and the allegations he made, in particular against the head of MI5, Roger

Hollis, when he published *Spycatcher* in 1987. The intelligence that Blunt had been a Soviet spy was given to the then Home Secretary, Henry Brooke, who had been four years above Blunt at Marlborough, and to the Queen, but not to the prime minister of the time, Alec Douglas-Home. The 'escape' of Kim Philby, along with the Profumo scandal, meant that MI5 were particularly sensitive about intelligence failures, and any revelation that a figure as well established as Blunt had been engaged in espionage might have had very serious consequences. Although Blunt in his memoirs classifies it as naïve, his belief 'that the security service would see to it, partly in its own interest, that the story would never become public' was arguably well-calculated.

For fifteen years, Blunt's life continued effectively unchanged – barring a significant increase in his alcohol consumption – by his confession. Despite the Queen's knowledge of his activity, he was not required to cease being Surveyor of the Queen's Pictures and he did not step back from any positions of responsibility. It was indeed during these years that Dover got to know Blunt as they served together on the Leverhulme Research Awards Committee during the 1970s.[6] Blunt published his catalogue raisonné of Poussin's paintings in 1966 and a general monograph on Poussin in 1967 – the year in which he was himself honoured with a Festschrift for his sixtieth birthday.[7] He expanded his Italian interests into baroque architecture, with books on Sicily, Naples and baroque architecture more generally. He also wrote further on Picasso, on whom he had first published with Phoebe Pool, a Courtauld student whom he had unmasked as also a Soviet spy in his confession.[8]

During those fifteen years, talk of Blunt as 'the Fourth Man' had not ceased. In particular, Goronwy Rees, who had been a Fellow of All Souls in the 1930s, and himself passed information to the NKVD, and to whom in 1951 Blunt had admitted his own activities, published a memoir in which Blunt and his activities were referred to, but Blunt was not named. This made little impression, partly perhaps because Rees had himself been forced to resign from being Principal of the University College of Wales at Aberystwyth after publishing anonymous articles in the *Sunday People* in 1956 in which he made various revelations about Burgess and Maclean. In 1979, however, the public revelation that Blunt had been a spy was precipitated by the publication by Andrew Boyle of a book, *Climate of Treason*, heavily based on evidence from Rees, in which Blunt's identity was hidden behind the veil of the pseudonym 'Maurice', a veil promptly removed by *Private Eye*.[9] Challenged in Question Time to reveal the name, the new prime minister, Margaret Thatcher, named Blunt on November 15 and then gave a fuller statement six days later. Jack Plumb's two-sentence letter to Dover followed on November 16.

The British Academy

In *Marginal Comment*, Dover admits that neither Thatcher's announcement on November 15 nor the subsequent revocation of Blunt's knighthood prompted him to question Blunt's status as a Fellow of the British Academy, and that he was therefore surprised by the arrival of Plumb's letter (*MC* 212). In this, Dover was arguably not alone.

No institution that had given Blunt an honorary degree revoked it in the wake of the revelation, and his French membership of the Legion of Honour was not taken away (though he avoided the removal of his Honorary Fellowship at Trinity and of his Fellowship of the Society of Antiquaries only by resignation).[10] Dover's surprise arguably influenced his reaction. He wrote back to Plumb on 19 November: 'I fully share your sentiments about traitors, but no "immediate" action of any kind is possible' because Council could neither itself expel a Fellow nor summon a General Meeting to do so except in June/July. He went on to say: 'You may find that many Fellows will be sympathetic (as I am not) to E.M. Forster's declaration, "If I were ever forced to choose whether to betray a friend or to betray my country, I hope I would have the guts to betray my country".'[11] This quotation had been used by Blunt to Goronwy Rees in 1951 à propos of not denouncing Burgess. It is used by Dover in *Marginal Comment* to express what he took to have been Blunt's motivation were it true that he had tipped off Burgess and Maclean and enabled them to flee the country (*MC* 212).

At the first meeting of the Academy sections after the November announcement, the Art History section did not formally discuss the question of Blunt's membership. Its chairman, William Watson, wrote to Dover on 7 February 1980, after the meeting, to say that, outside the meeting, six Fellows had expressed the view, which he shared, that it would not be proper to exclude Blunt or require his resignation, since Fellowships of the Academy were awarded for contributions to knowledge, though a seventh had admitted that he would be relieved were Blunt to resign.[12]

The Academy Council met on 15 February. Item 7 was a 'proposal for Council Action under Bye-Law 11' and Plumb, a member of Council, proposed that Council should act under the Bye-Law to remove Blunt's name from the list of Fellows. Plumb had replied to Dover's earlier message by saying that he hoped that Dover would 'give the Academy a strong lead'. Dover remarks in *Marginal Comment*:

> I was certainly not going to do that; my job as chairman was to ensure that all members of Council had their say and that the outcome truly represented the considered view of the majority. The only 'lead' I proposed to give was – as in the business of my College – an insistence that everything which called for decision was decided clearly and in good time.
>
> *MC* 212

In the discussion everyone was certainly heard (all but one member present spoke at length). The lines of division were clear: the wording of the Bye-Law gave 'that he or she is not a fit and proper person to be a Fellow'; some considered that Blunt's passing of official secrets to Soviet Russia showed he was not a fit or proper person, others either that, since it was 'distinction in some one or more of the branches of scientific study which it is the object of the Academy to promote' that made one a 'fit and proper person' for election in the first place, misconduct irrelevant to that distinction should not bring expulsion, or that whatever the situation in theory, in practice too much time had passed for Blunt's misconduct to be taken into account in his old age.[13]

Dover's own considerations are laid out in a document entitled 'Retrospect' which he wrote on 12 May 1981 and deposited with the rest of the relevant papers at the Academy and elaborated in *Marginal Comment*. 'Retrospect' starts with three statements: 'that a nation which fails to tear a traitor to pieces is doomed'; 'that a nation which gives precedence to the word of the law over irrational feelings deserves respect and is likely to receive it'; and that 'There was only one justification for expelling Blunt: that he had worked treacherously for the supremacy of a totalitarian nation which has consistently frustrated and persecuted scholarship, and by so doing he tried to defeat the purposes for which the Academy exists'.[14]

There is much that is curious about these statements and how they are expressed. The first is the distinction he makes between what he has 'always felt, and still feel[s]' about traitors (where his use of 'feel' is meant as an acknowledgement of irrationality), and what he has 'always believed, and still believe[s]' about the precedence of law (where 'believe' implies a background of reasoning).[15] It is hard to see why one might not find reasons for thinking that harbouring traitors is a bad idea, as much as one can find reasons for preferring law to irrational feelings. The second curious feature is the violence involved in 'tearing to pieces' traitors, which is echoed by the sentiment expressed in *Marginal Comment* that 'So far as my feelings went, I would cheerfully have assisted Blunt to fall from a top-floor window'.[16] One might think that action should be taken against all treachery, but *sparagmos*? The third curiosity is the emphasis on the 'word of the law'. This is doubly odd since in this case the relevant 'law' is the Academy's own statute, not a law of the nation, and since the emphasis on *word* seems to imply 'as opposed to spirit'. Dover himself, in *Marginal Comment*, is well aware that understanding the wording of the statutes is both a complex and a disputed matter and that the word alone is not adequate: he is insistent that Bye-Law 11 must be read in the light of Bye-Law 27(1)(b) and Article 6 – that is, that the words 'fit and proper' must be understood in terms of the requirement for distinction in 'scientific study' (*MC* 213); and he acknowledged that at least one legal scholar, F.A. Mann, took a different view of how to interpret 'fit and proper', arguing that had his treachery been known at the moment of his election, Blunt would not then have been thought 'fit and proper' for election, and that its subsequent discovery meant that he ceased to be 'fit and proper'.[17] The final curious aspect is how Dover presents Soviet Russia. Since Blunt's espionage took place in the context of war, what was at stake was something very much bigger than 'frustrating and persecuting scholarship'. The (admittedly complicated) context in which Blunt passed documentation to Soviet Russia – something to which the art historian John Beckwith had drawn Dover's attention as early as March 1980[18] – is simply by-passed. At no point did Dover, or any Fellow of the Academy, make any attempt to ascertain exactly what Blunt had passed on when, and to what effect. Espionage was treated by all as a black and white matter; the context was either ignored or presented in highly generalized terms.

None of this, however, is as curious as what follows. 'Retrospect' continues: 'This justification was not mentioned either on Council or at the AGM. I did not think it right to reveal even on Council, let alone at the AGM, that I myself considered it a justification.'[19] That the justification was unmentioned is in fact untrue; as we will see, Dover's own briefing document for the second Council meeting lays out this justification. Nevertheless, *Marginal Comment* expands, in relation to the first Council meeting:

> to my astonishment, not a word was said about it ['the only justification'] in the Council meeting. During the last twenty minutes of the discussion I fought against the temptation to raise the point myself; at the end of the meeting both Vice-presidents and the Secretary told me that they had no idea which side I was on, and I went home satisfied that I had done my job as chairman.
>
> MC 213

Dover's 'doing his job as chairman' resulted in Council voting by a single vote, with Dover himself not voting, to expel Blunt. That Dover thought that a decision taken by the narrowest of majorities, and without what he regarded as 'the only justification' for expulsion having been aired, showed a job well done suggests that he had a somewhat curious view of what that job was.

Council's decision provoked a flurry of letters to Dover from those who opposed Blunt's expulsion, including the first threats of resignation from Richard Wollheim and A.J.P. Taylor.[20] The longest letter came from Eric Hobsbawm and focused on the discredit that would fall on the Academy were Blunt expelled, citing as a parallel the case of Jacques Soustelle, who tried to overthrow De Gaulle's government and was exiled for seven years for attempting to undermine the authority of the French state, but who was not deprived of his post at the École des Hautes Études (and indeed was subsequently, in 1983, elected to the Académie française).[21]

Since anyone whom the Academy intended to expel had a right to appear before Council before it made a recommendation for expulsion, Dover wrote to Blunt after the 15 February Council meeting, but Blunt declined to attend, saying that he had nothing to add to what he had earlier said (in a press conference on 20 November) 'except perhaps to re-emphasize my regrets at what I did, which I am frequently accused of not having expressed'.[22] Dover wrote, and then, at the suggestion of his vice-presidents, Michael Howard and Owen Chadwick, rewrote, a briefing paper for the next Council meeting on 18 March. In this paper he picked up on others' arguments, expressed in the earlier meeting and in letters to him, first dismissing some claims and then laying down three particular questions that Council had to address. The claims he dismissed were that 'integrity is indivisible' and that 'moral delinquency justifies expulsion', pointing out that the first was disproved by Blunt himself, the second raised questions about Council turning 'its attention to (e.g.) adulterers'. The questions he prioritized were: whether treason was *sui generis*, on which he suggested Fellows would individually decide their moral priorities; whether Blunt realized that he was helping a totalitarian regime inimical to the purposes for which the Academy exists; whether, had his behaviour been known in 1950, he would have been thought a fit and proper person to be elected.[23]

The minutes of the 18 March meeting lay out some of the main points of the discussion, which include that Blunt's behaviour 'could be characterized as treachery' and continued after his election as a Fellow; that fitness for election and fitness to continue in the Fellowship could be distinguished; that scholarly values could be distinguished from other values but that the Academy was a public institution; that the offences had ceased many years before, but that there was no time limit on the responsibility for 'offences of this kind, especially when they had been concealed'; that holding particular opinions or committing a criminal offence did not render a person unfit to be a Fellow. Nine of those present voted that Blunt was not fit to be a Fellow, with three voting that he was fit, and three abstentions, without Dover voting. There was then a vote of eight to seven for the proposal for Blunt's expulsion to be taken to the AGM, but only after Blunt had been invited to resign and the result of that invitation reported to Council.[24]

It is a notable feature of Dover's conduct throughout the affair that he was reluctant to talk personally with Blunt. He had not done so when the news of Blunt's espionage broke, and he had not done so at any subsequent stage. Faced with Council's desire to secure Blunt's resignation, he went through an intermediary, Peter Lasko, Blunt's successor as Director of the Courtauld. In a letter to Lasko written on the day of the Council meeting he set out the situation. He noted that Council would recommend expulsion, that it was likely that the AGM would reject the recommendation, but that the consequence would be 'that a fair amount of sensational and inaccurate publicity will descend on the Academy – which matters a great deal'. By comparison he predicted that were Blunt to resign, some of his strongest supporters would resign in sympathy, 'but the acrimony and consequent publicity will be less'. Dover excused himself from suggesting resignation to Blunt on the grounds that he was the Chairman of Council and official spokesman of the Academy, and therefore in a position of authority, and on the grounds that he would feel a fool asking Blunt to do something for his (Dover's) and the Academy's benefit.[25]

Dover repeated this view of the possibility of his asking Blunt to resign in *Marginal Comment*, but it sits oddly with his view, clearly stated in 'Retrospect', that 'My job as President was to take whatever course of action seemed most likely to be to the advantage of the Academy'.[26] Why should a man who thought that the Academy's advantage should be put first fail to act because 'feeling a fool'? And did Dover not see that in concluding his letter to Lasko with the statement that were he ever required to give a casting vote he would give the 'vote of Athena' for acquittal, he was undermining his earlier stress on the importance for the Academy of Blunt's resignation? There can be no surprise that five days later Dover received from Lasko a reply reporting that Blunt 'felt most strongly that he did not wish to resign'.[27]

Dover reported Blunt's response to Council on 16 May 1980 and Council reaffirmed, nem. con., its decision to propose the removal of his name from the list of Fellows.[28] When this became known, Lionel Robbins and Isaiah Berlin, both former Presidents of the Academy, formulated an amendment, in the end put over the names of Robbins and Helen Gardner.[29] Initially, the formula was 'While not in any way condoning the conduct of Professor Anthony Blunt, [the AGM] decides not to proceed further in the matter', but, without Gardner being consulted, this was changed before the agenda paper was circulated to 'deplores the conduct of Professor Anthony Blunt and decides not to proceed further in the matter'.[30] No paper or guidance document was circulated in support of Council's motion, or in support of the amendment. Although this is understandable, since any such paper would have been a hostage to fortune and could not have been prevented from leaking to the press, the consequence was that the AGM was offered no lead from the measured discussions of Council. Procedure at the AGM was to discuss first the Robbins amendment and only if this were not passed to discuss Council's recommendation. In fact, after speeches from Robbins and Gardner for their amendment, from T.B. Smith against, and from a number of other Fellows, L.C.B. Gower proposed that the meeting should pass to the next item on the agenda. Robbins withdrew his amendment, and a vote on Gower's proposal took place: it was passed on a show of hands by 120 votes to 42 with 25 abstentions.[31]

Dover had prepared to report on one of three options – expelling Blunt; deploring Blunt's conduct but not expelling him; or the decision neither to deplore nor to expel. He was now faced with having to report a decision not to decide. His press release noted that 'those who voted may well have had more than one good reason for voting as they did', but ended by noting that 'The scale and distinction of Professor Blunt's contributions, as scholar and teacher, to the history of art are a fact which cannot be unmade by any other facts... The implication of the decision is that the Academy is an inappropriate body to pass judgement on conduct in matters other than scholarship'.[32]

That implication was found unacceptable to three Fellows of the Academy, Theodore Skeat, Colin Roberts and John Crook. The grounds of resignation were put most eloquently by Crook in a letter of July 6:

> I cannot bring myself to believe that the Academy is, or should be, an ivory tower of nothing but scholarship. I recognise the intensity with which people fear the consequences of allowing politics to touch scholarship, but for my own part I fear more intensely the danger of scholars just standing aside. I further believe that, while open expression of political opposition is honourable and necessary and ought not to be persecuted in any nation or by any body, secret gnawing at the foundations of the state damages the whole of society, including, ultimately, its scholarship.[33]

'That, I thought, was that', Dover writes (*MC* 216). As far as the formal procedures of the Academy were concerned it was. But at this point the discussion escaped formal procedures – just at the moment when Dover himself escaped back to St Andrews.

The Press

What was expressed politely by Crook was expressed in other terms by other Fellows of the Academy who found themselves in the minority in the vote – and not simply in letters to Dover. An attempt by Ian Christie to gain publicity for the case against the Academy decision in the *Times* was unsuccessful, but following a letter from George Huxley, Professor of Greek at Queen's University Belfast, and not a member of the Academy, published in the *Daily Telegraph* on 26 July, Christie and others published a succession of letters there.³⁴ This caused Blunt himself to write to Dover on 8 August to express his distress at how the *Daily Telegraph* was using him 'as a stick with which to beat the Academy'.³⁵ On the same day the *Daily Mail* published an article by Lord Blake, Provost of Queen's College, Oxford, under the headline 'British Academy of cowards. If they won't expel this traitor, who will they ever kick out?' – an article suggesting that a double standard of morality was being exercised by the Fellows of the Academy and that they would have had no truck with a supporter of a right-wing regime.³⁶

At this point a new tactic was introduced by those who still wished Blunt to be removed. The tactic was first suggested by W. Sidney Allen, Professor of Comparative Philology at Cambridge, who wrote to Dover on 7 August to say that he would resign at the end of the calendar year had Blunt not resigned or the AGM decision not been rescinded.³⁷ Allen copied this letter to a group of Fellows he expected to be sympathetic, and Plumb, another of the group, wrote to Dover on 11 August saying that he would follow Allen's line and urging Dover: 'I do hope that you personally will see Blunt rather than dealing with him through intermediaries and tell him how his conduct has caused strife and despair in the Academy and that his continued membership is doing untold harm'.³⁸ Plumb sent copies of his letter to Allen, Blake, Christie, John Ehrman and Norman Gash, with covering notes urging them to follow suit in order to pressurize 'the Academy into thinking again' and 'create uproar': 'I think it is very important that we should not be over-discreet about what we intend to do because the Academy loves to hide, and certainly Dover does, behind confidentiality' (an allusion, perhaps, to Dover's first and minuted instructions to the Academy Council that their proceedings were to be entirely confidential).³⁹ Accordingly, Plumb also sent copies of his letter to Dover to the *Times* and *Daily Telegraph*. Ian Christie, meanwhile, penned an article for *Encounter* and wrote to Dover on 12 August about it, not only threatening his own resignation at the end of the year had Blunt not resigned, but calling for an 'Extraordinary General Meeting or a Referendum'.⁴⁰ On the morning of 13 August Norman Gash, who was Professor of History at St Andrews, met with Dover there, and urged him to urge Blunt to resign. That same afternoon Dover was telephoned by the *Daily Telegraph*.⁴¹

At this point Dover wrote to Blunt, while at the same time writing back to Plumb at some length and with obvious irritation, objecting that Plumb's publicizing his demand that Dover ask Blunt to resign was likely to prevent Blunt resigning.⁴² Meanwhile John Ehrman wrote to Dover proposing a variation on the referendum – that there should be a postal vote on the Robbins amendment, and if that were not to pass, a postal vote on Council's original recommendation.⁴³ This was reported in the *Sunday Telegraph* on 17 August, but by then Blunt had telephoned Dover on 15 August, on receipt of his letter, saying that he would resign if it were to do any good, but that if he resigned others would resign too, objecting to the pressure put on him to resign. Nevertheless, on 17 August Blunt wrote to Dover to resign 'in the hope that my resignation will reduce the dissension within the Academy about my membership', telephoning Dover again to say that he had persuaded his friends not to resign in sympathy.⁴⁴ Dover quickly passed the news to the Fellows who had been in correspondence with him and went away to stay with his son, cutting himself off from all communication.⁴⁵

The news that Dover had suggested to Blunt that he resign, and Blunt's agreement to do so, enraged a number of Fellows of the Academy. James Joll wrote to Dover from the LSE immediately on 17 August to note that 'it will appear to the outside world as the direct result of a press campaign started by the statements and articles (one of them in the cheap press) of the two or three fellows unwilling to accept a clear decision . . .' and to say 'how deeply I deplore that the decision to suggest to Blunt that he should resign was taken in these circumstances'.[46] Two days later John Mackie wrote more directly to say that if the implication of a report in the *Times* that Dover had suggested that Blunt resign was correct 'then I wish to express strong disapproval of your action, which is inconsistent with the intention of a clear majority of members present at the Annual General Meeting'.[47] A.J.P Taylor wrote on the same day to the same effect: 'you have revived the controversy and enabled a small group of Fellows to thwart the wishes of a substantial majority'. Taylor resigned as a Fellow of the Academy.[48]

On 22 August Dover circulated the Fellows of the Academy with his account of the sequence of events, denying that he had brought any pressure to bear on Blunt: 'After 3 July . . . [i]t seemed to me that there was now no threat, overt or covert, which I could possibly bring to bear on Professor Blunt even if I wanted to'. Dover claimed that he only mentioned the possibility of resignation to Blunt because he was writing to him anyway to thank him for his earlier letter: 'It was in the light of the public controversy as a whole that I concluded that in replying to him I ought to ask him to consider resignation.'[49] Not everyone was satisfied. The most interesting reaction came from 'Jim' Gower, who had moved the motion that the AGM should pass to the next item of business. Gower wrote a letter of resignation but sent it only to Lionel Robbins for comment and decided not to act upon it. But in the draft Gower lays out two grounds for dissatisfaction:

(a) The way that this matter has been handled throughout by the Council has sapped my confidence in them. (b) The conduct of certain Senior Fellows in seeking to achieve their aims by whipping up press publicity and threatening to resign if they don't get their way seems to me to be deplorable. I have always understood that seeking to influence the decisions of a body of which one is a member by threatening to resign is quite improper; yet, in this case, it seems to have achieved the aim of one faction by securing Professor Blunt's resignation despite the clearly expressed view of the meeting that he should not be asked to do so.[50]

In 'Retrospect' Dover finds himself 'guilty of an error of judgment in (a) failing to realize that my suggestion to Blunt possessed a certain *auctoritas*, and consequently (b) underestimating the reactions which the resignation would provoke'.[51] The first of these realizations had been urged on Dover by Tony Andrewes, who had written to him to that effect after the 22 August note had been circulated to Fellows.[52] The second seems to indicate how far Dover was from understanding what had happened: far more significant than his underestimating the reactions which followed Blunt's resignation was, arguably, his overestimating the force of those who desired that resignation. In *Marginal Comment*,

Dover states that: 'My real feeling about the Allen-Christie-Gash-Plumb combination was the indignant resentment which one feels towards terrorists who threaten to blow up innocent passengers if they do not get everything they want' (*MC* 216). Dover had already used the terrorist analogy in 'Retrospect', but there to note that faced with the threat 'to kill a planeful of hostages' 'we usually yield, attaching some value to the lives of the hostages. This is not a condonation of terrorism, but a consequence of weighing the alternatives'.[53] He goes on to cite the resolution of 'the Plumb faction', a letter from Oliver Gurney asking whether 'if a large number of signatures could be obtained to some sort of manifesto, there would be any possibility of overturning the decision of the A.G.M.', the resignation of Charles Bawden three weeks after the AGM, and his judgement that 'the number of resignations by 1 January 1981 might be well into two figures'.[54] Dover is explicit in 'Retrospect' that 'The threats of resignation made by Plumb, Gash, Allen and Christie were disgraceful and inexcusable, and if they have earned the hostility and contempt of many other Fellows they have only themselves to blame'. But nevertheless, it seems to have been the activities of Plumb, Gash, and Christie (Allen behaved rather differently) that led Dover significantly to overestimate the number of 'terrorists' (already at the time of the AGM, Geoffrey de Ste. Croix had identified a group of 'nasties' – ironically in the context of wishing that they had indeed threatened to resign at that point).[55] More than that, what exactly did Dover regard as the equivalent of the 'planeful of hostages'?

Dover suggests in *Marginal Comment* 'that there was no clear correlation between division of opinion on this issue and the political division between Right and Left, for some lifelong Conservatives thought that Blunt's treason should be forgiven and forgotten, while many Socialists (including at least two ex-Communists) were merciless'.[56] That may have been true of attitudes in the run up to the AGM, but the group of 'terrorists' who sought to use the press to counter the AGM decision were firmly from the Right: Lord Blake, biographer of Disraeli, historian of the Conservative party, made a life peer by Edward Heath and taking the Conservative whip in the Lords; Ian Christie, while a strong defender of the need to have fought against fascism, devoted much of his work to understanding conservatism (with a small c), arguing (e.g.) that in eighteenth-century Britain 'oligarchical government stood foursquare on its foundations in the tacit consent of the people';[57] Norman Gash, best known for his biographical work on Sir Robert Peel; Jack Plumb, one time communist who turned increasingly to the right, desperate for establishment recognition, was an eighteenth-century historian whose work included a biography of Sir Robert Walpole and adviser for a 1977 television series *Royal Heritage*. Gash had tried to tell Dover that the AGM had been packed by University of London supporters of Blunt: Dover had no truck with that – in *Marginal Comment* he notes that only 48 of the 187 present were from London and that this included eleven whom he knew to favour expulsion (*MC* 216). What Dover does not seem to have fully realized is the particular politics of the rump who sought publicity for their opposition to the AGM decision.

The total number of Fellows of the Academy in 1980 was 409.[58] Even this, the best attended of any AGM, was attended by fewer than fifty per cent of the Fellows. The proportion of Fellows who had resigned or indicated any intention of resigning over the failure to expel Blunt was under ten. The noise deliberately created by those who disapproved of the AGM decision was disproportionate to their number. Yet Dover, who had, when first approached by Plumb, been so insistent on the formal rules of procedure, abandoned those rules under this pressure.

In the response that he wrote to Christie's article in *Encounter* and in the concluding paragraph of 'Retrospect' Dover insisted that 'an important determinant of the AGM's decision' was 'forgiveness'.[59] In *Marginal Comment*, he begins his chapter on 'The Blunt Affair' with an epigraph from Luke 17.3 ('If your brother wrongs you, rebuke him. If he repents, forgive him'), and he goes on to recount that 'One Fellow told me privately that his vote against expulsion was determined by a Christian duty to forgive the repentant, but he "did not have the courage" to say so in the debate'. He continues: 'People find religion so embarrassing a topic that we shall never know how large a part was played by the duty to forgive, but among those who voted against expulsion I certainly recognised many whom I knew to be of strong Christian faith' (*MC* 219). In 'Retrospect', Dover's final comment is that he could have defended with pride an AGM which 'had said firmly and openly that it forgave Blunt' but that 'To disguise the will to forgive under vulnerable reasons is not good enough'.[60]

Marginal Comment

Dover's conduct of the Academy discussions about Blunt variously drew admiration, sympathy and criticism at the time. Could a different approach to the role and responsibilities of either the President of such an institution or the chairman of its Council and AGM have led to a different result? It was never hard to predict that the public discussion at an AGM of the fitness for membership of a national institution of a person with a very high public profile who had confessed to actions universally disapproved would serve little useful purpose. How could taking Blunt's membership of the Academy to the AGM have ever seemed like a good idea? What could Blunt conceivably gain by continued membership of the Academy?

Dover's decision to look to the rule book, when challenged by Plumb in November 1979, was decisive. In any dispute where something less than criminal behaviour is at issue, informal modes of dispute settlement are invariably to be preferred. Yet Dover made no attempt to discuss the matter with either Plumb or with Blunt, let alone with both together. Equally important was the matter of timing. Since, as he saw it, the final decision could not be taken until July 1980, Dover saw no reason for summoning Council before its scheduled meeting in the middle of February. By adhering to the standard timetable Dover ensured that the discussions dominated the whole year.[61] The 15 February meeting minutes give no indication of the nature of the discussion; Dover regarded the arguments brought at that meeting for expulsion to be poor, but he refrained from offering what he considered the stronger argument. Had he given a steer, it would have been to reinforce the decision, rather than to go against it, but a more far-sighted president might have directed the Council's attention to the likely longer-term consequences of such action. And even at this stage, and the next, Dover could reasonably have been expected (Plumb was surely correct in this) to have talked directly to Blunt.

In 'Retrospect', Dover declares that 'By July 3 I was indifferent to the outcome, aware that I could not defend Council's proposal on grounds of which I approved, very well aware that the proposal to expel Blunt stood no chance at all, and suspecting that even Robbins' motion would not command a majority'.[62] The problem that Dover faced was extremely difficult, but that he had let himself get into this position was certainly in part a product of the view that he took of chairmanship. Indeed, nothing in 'Retrospect' or *Marginal Comment* suggests that he ever thought that this was an inappropriate position for the President of the British Academy to be in. We might expect that a responsible chair of a Council would fight hard to prevent that Council from proposing something which he or she knew to stand 'no chance at all'. Yet, as the correspondence with Peter Lasko shows, at the time of the decisive 18 March Council Dover already held the view that the AGM would 'probably (but not certainly) reject the recommendation' of Council to expel Blunt.[63] Yet Dover seems either never to have considered that to have Council make a proposal that would be decisively rejected was in effect to have the AGM pass a vote of no confidence in Council, or if he saw it, not to have been bothered by this.[64]

It is unclear whether Dover had a hand in changing the Robbins amendment from 'not condone' to 'deplore', but that decision arguably decisively changed the nature of the AGM discussion and practically invited the creation on the spot of an alternative proposal, with various of those speaking – A.J.P. Taylor, Michael Dummett, Richard Southern – wishing to dissociate themselves from deploring. But the alternative proposal, when it came, left the question of Blunt's status formally unresolved; neither had he been removed from the membership, nor had a decision been taken not to proceed further than an expression of censure, the matter had simply been left to one side. Leaving it to one side allowed those who desired to do so to treat Blunt's status at the Academy as still open business.

It is difficult to imagine any future circumstances in which the Academy or any similar academic institution faces a comparable question to that of whether it should expel a retired academic of distinction whose early acts of treachery have remained concealed for more than thirty years. But the incident remains instructive with regard to the appropriate roles and responsibilities of those responsible for the conduct of an institution and its governing bodies. The points at which a chair's impartiality becomes inappropriate, when insistence on following the rules creates serious problems, and when fear of seeming foolish stands in the way of exercising emotional intelligence are well illustrated by this case. Even more, the case shows the importance of establishing the facts. It remains a remarkable aspect of a remarkable case that the assumption made throughout was that judgement could be passed without the need to establish exactly what it was that Blunt did and to what effect.

How does Dover the flawed chairman relate to Dover the scholar? There are clear links between Dover's obsession with impartiality and his scholarly desire to call a spade a spade, and not consider what it might look like when viewed from another angle or through different filters. Dover was used to following the scholarly argument, wherever it took him, as most obviously in *Greek Homosexuality*, and that meant that he was quite unused to looking ahead to what the conclusion might be and what impact it might have. So too, there is something of Dover the philologist, and indeed of Dover's positivism, in his actions as chairman; his insistence that 'words mean, at any given time, what the people who use them *intend* them to mean' is certainly reflected in his insistence on following the letter of the law with regard to Academy statutes.[65] Those who have undertaken the enlightening exercise of reading Dover on Greek homosexuality and then reading what Foucault made of reading Dover on Greek homosexuality, in *The History of Sexuality* vol. 2 (*The Use of Pleasure*), will recognize Dover's ability to write informal power out of the equation. David Cannadine, complaining that the 'Retrospect' is rather jumbled, suggests that this is 'perhaps a sign that Dover had been ill-served by his lifelong lack of interest in ancient Greek philosophy', but the problem is rather, as Russell and Halliwell note in their memoir of Dover, his 'outlook on life (which he summed up by calling himself "an English empiricist to the core")'.[66]

What would not be predictable from the scholarship, however, is Dover's shame. Given that Dover presents himself in the Preface to *Greek Homosexuality* as 'fortunate in not experiencing moral shock or disgust at any genital act whatsoever, provided that it is welcome and agreeable to all the participants', and his own willingness to use sexually explicit 'vulgar' words (e.g. 'We do not normally interpret instances of modern colloquial usage, e.g. "wanker", or "motherfucker", as conveying precise charges of sexual deviation') and dislike of euphemism, we might expect him to be relatively impervious to shame.[67] But his actions in this case reveal a rather different man as he excuses himself, in his letter to Peter Lasko of 18 March 1980, from approaching Blunt about resignation on the grounds that 'I would feel a fool in asking any man to be so kind as to consult the convenience of his executioners and put them in a better light'.[68] But perhaps this does precisely repeat, and help us to see the shortcomings of, a feature of Dover's scholarship – his tendency to treat issues, including moral issues, that have many components as merely intellectual problems.[69] Ironically, this tendency closely mirrored the view conveyed by the majority vote at the AGM on 3 July 1980. My predecessor John Crook's verdict on the majority that day bears repeating with regard to Dover himself: 'I recognise', he writes, 'the intensity with which people fear the consequences of allowing politics to touch scholarship, but for my part I fear more intensely the danger of scholars just standing aside'; to do so, he thought, was to hold 'an untenable view of the nature of the institution and of its necessary relationship to the life of the nation in general'.[70]

Notes

1. I did not know Dover personally, though I heard him speak at a schools event when I was an A level student; nor did I ever meet Anthony Blunt, although his work on Poussin figured significantly in my sixth-form studies on the history of art. This paper makes no claim to original archival research. All the information used here comes from publicly available sources; the great majority of it can be found in Cannadine ed. 2020 [referred to subsequently as *Retribution*] or in Dover 1994 [referred to subsequently as *MC*]. What I have

tried to do is to understand both why Dover handled 'the Blunt affair' as he did, and to what extent his handling was responsible for the course of events. I am very grateful to the editors both for the unexpected invitation and for their helpful critical reading of an earlier draft.

2. *MC* 99. Stephen Halliwell kindly drew my attention to a letter that Dover wrote to his parents about the deanship on 17 October 1959, in which he said, 'Some interesting rows are brewing, which will ripen into maturity under my chairmanship'. For some recollections of Dover as a decanal chairman, see Craik in this volume.
3. *MC* 235, concerned with the review of Oxford admissions which he chaired in the 1980s and which led to the end of the Oxford Entrance Examination.
4. *MC* 167–8, 169–70.
5. MacNeice 1965, 95 (quotation), 96 (shared study). This section on Blunt is otherwise drawn from information contained in *Retribution* 4–6, Carter 2001, and a particularly helpful online biography at https://en.wikipedia.org/wiki/Anthony_Blunt.
6. *MC* 212 and fig. 20.
7. Blunt 1966, 1967; Kitson and Shearman 1967.
8. Blunt 1968, 1975, 1978; Blunt 1969; Blunt and Pool 1962.
9. Boyle 1979.
10. *Retribution* 1.
11. *Retribution* 13.
12. *Retribution* 15.
13. *Retribution* 16.
14. *Retribution* 86; compare *MC* 212–13.
15. On Dover's distinction between 'feel' and 'believe', see *MC* 2.
16. *MC* 212. Cf. Dover's view later in 'Retrospect' (*Retribution* 86) that 'no degree of harshness towards him [Blunt] was unjust'.
17. *MC* 213 alludes to Mann's view, which was set out in a letter of 19 June 1980 (*Retribution* 42). It is worth noting that the wording of Bye-Law 27(1)(b) requiring that those proposing Fellows should state that they are fit and proper on the basis of 'knowledge of the person proposed or of his or her work' makes it very hard to think that the 'word' of the law here excludes 'misconduct which lies outside the "scientific study which it is the object of the Academy to promote"', as Dover maintains (*MC* 213).
18. *Retribution* 36.
19. *Retribution* 86.
20. *Retribution* 20 (Wollheim), 21 (Taylor).
21. *Retribution* 21.
22. *Retribution* 19.
23. *Retribution* 23.
24. *Retribution* 29.
25. *Retribution* 34.
26. *Retribution* 86.
27. *Retribution* 35.
28. *Retribution* 37.
29. *Retribution* 38, 40–1.

30. *Retribution* 76.
31. *Retribution* 44–6, *MC* 215–16.
32. *Retribution* 47.
33. *Retribution* 54–5.
34. *Retribution* 56.
35. *Retribution* 60.
36. *Retribution* 62.
37. *Retribution* 61.
38. *Retribution* 64.
39. *Retribution* 65.
40. *Retribution* 66.
41. *Retribution* 68–9, *MC* 216–17.
42. *MC* 217, *Retribution* 69.
43. *Retribution* 70.
44. *Retribution* 71, *MC* 217–18.
45. *Retribution* 72–3, *MC* 218.
46. *Retribution* 73.
47. *Retribution* 74.
48. *Retribution* 75.
49. *Retribution* 79.
50. *Retribution* 84. When Dover wrote to John Crook on 2 September asking him whether he wished to rescind his resignation in the light of Blunt's resignation, Crook responded 'I think the answer is "thank you warmly, but no"', going on: 'I should like it to be on record that I do not believe it was right for Fellows of the Academy, after the decision of the Academy, to attempt to secure the reversal of the decision by threats of resignation, and I would not have been one of such Fellows' (*Retribution* 85).
51. *Retribution* 87.
52. *MC* 218: 'Tony Andrewes, whose judgement I could never fail to respect, asked whether it is ever safe for a President to ask anyone to 'consider' anything, because the source of the suggestion necessarily lends it weight'.
53. *Retribution* 86.
54. *Retribution* 87.
55. 5 July 1980 letter of Geoffrey de Ste. Croix to Dover, cited at *Retribution* 56 n. 32; 'disgraceful', *Retribution* 86.
56. *MC* 213, echoed by Cannadine in *Retribution* 90.
57. Christie 1984, 33.
58. *Retribution* 44.
59. *Retribution* 87.
60. *Retribution* 87.
61. The importance of this emerges from Helen Gardner's letter of 20 August 1980, *Retribution* 76.
62. *Retribution* 86.

63. *Retrospect* 34.
64. Cf. Helen Gardner's letter to Dover of 20 August 1980 (*Retribution* 76): 'I hoped the size of the majority at the meeting would lay the matter to rest. I regarded it as fundamentally a vote of no confidence by the membership in the judgement of the Council. I felt this very strongly myself when I first heard of the Council's recommendation'; and cf. L.C.B. Gower's draft letter to Dover of 30 August 1980 (*Retribution* 84), quoted above at p. 91.
65. *MC* 126. Instructive here is a comparison of Dover's discussion of χρηστός at Dover 1993a, 212, with Goldhill 1991, 203–4.
66. Cannadine, *Retribution* 89; Russell and Halliwell 2012, 161, quoting *MC* 146.
67. Dover 1978, viii, 17; cf. *MC* 3, 'I applaud Bernard Levin's dictum, "Every euphemism is a lie", and I prefer nasty truths to silly lies'.
68. *Retribution* 34, essentially repeated at *MC* 213. Dover's shame appears otherwise in *MC* largely in connection with his own body (e.g. *MC* 56, 242), but n.b. *MC* 43.
69. Arguably it is this that enabled Dover to write *Greek Popular Morality*. The problems are nicely revealed in Dover 1978, 109–10, where on successive pages he is able to claim 'that the evaluative judgements implicit in Greek law and openly expressed by individual writers and speakers often took little note of the extent to which a morally good disposition or intention is warped or frustrated by circumstances outside one's own control', and that 'On the whole the Greeks attached more importance to the effect of practice and habituation than to genetically determined qualities and dispositions'. Both statements are supported by references to Dover 1974 (144–6, 296–8 and 88–95 respectively) but there is clear tension between them. Both statements are themselves the product of taking texts that are argumentative and tendentious and treating them as texts that are capturing agreed truths. On *GPM*'s methodology, cf. Carey in this volume.
70. *Retribution* 54.

CHAPTER 6
MARGINAL COMMENT: COMPOSITION, PUBLICATION AND RECEPTION
Christopher Stray

The latter part of Kenneth Dover's life was marked by three controversies. The first concerned his treatment of Trevor Aston while president of Corpus (1976–86) and is dealt with in Bowie's chapter. The second centred on attempts to expel Anthony Blunt from the British Academy while Dover was president of the Academy (1978–81); this is discussed in Osborne's chapter. The third and final controversy was associated with the writing, publication and reception of Dover's autobiographical memoir *Marginal Comment*, published by Duckworth in 1994.

When Dover's memoir was offered to Oxford University Press, one of the Press's readers referred to it as an 'academic autobiography', a characterization rejected by Dover, who insisted that it was 'an autobiography *simpliciter* . . . academics are non-academic for much of their waking lives'.[1] Of the two dozen or so autobiographies of classical scholars published in Britain since 1800, a few stand out, but for different reasons. For sheer literary quality E.R. Dodds' *Missing Persons* (1977) takes the blue riband, followed by his friend and pupil Louis MacNeice's *The Strings are False* (1965). Both men, we should note, were poets as well as scholars, and had wide-ranging literary connections.[2] Some scholarly autobiographies are useful as sources of information on particular periods or institutions: for Oxford, for example, that of George Grundy, for Cambridge, that of William Heitland.[3] We should also take account of a related genre, the biographical memoir. In the nineteenth century, it was common for scholars to be the subject of substantial biographical memoirs after their deaths; in some their letters were also published. Benjamin Jowett received both, as did Samuel Butler.[4] Some projects of memorialization were frustrated, as in the case of Benjamin Kennedy: his pupil Thomas Ethelbert Page agreed to assemble a volume but found that life as a busy Charterhouse housemaster made the task impossible. Others were memorialized, but not as originally planned. After his death in 1905, Richard Jebb's widow could not find a scholar willing to write a memoir, Arthur Benson having rejected the task as being beyond his scholarly resources. In the end, she wrote it herself, but added a long account of Jebb's scholarship written by his colleague and ex-pupil Arthur Verrall.[5] The problem was especially severe in the case of polymaths, such as the last great universalist, William Whewell. A plan to memorialize him in three books fell apart, and what eventually emerged was a study of his academic work by a fellow-mathematician, and a 'domestic memoir' by his niece.[6]

Dover's memoir can usefully be contrasted with those of two earlier Oxford classical scholars, both of them holders of the Greek chair that he was offered in 1960: Gilbert Murray and E.R. Dodds. Murray wrote an incomplete autobiography ending with his marriage to Lady Mary Howard in 1889; after his death in 1957 he was the subject of two biographies.[7] Dodds' autobiography *Missing Persons* is perhaps the most impressive of its genre, though its subject remains in some ways elusive.[8] Dover's own memoir thus belongs to a line, though it is strikingly different in some ways from its two predecessors. An obvious point of comparison relates to the three men's sexual activity. As might be expected of a man born in 1866, Murray makes no mention of this. We know that he flirted with some of the actresses he worked with, and that when Lady Mary challenged him on this, he responded that 'I behave all right, but of course I do become charmed by a certain kind of beauty... these rather emotional friendships do come drifting across my heart'.[9] Murray's pupil and successor Eric Dodds included some sexual references in his own memoir, but they were on a small scale. In 1908, the teenaged Dodds encountered a woman on a country walk and had an erection. His account is circumspect: 'At that moment, something happened. After the woman had passed, I inspected my organ carefully. Could I be stricken with elephantiasis?' (Dodds 1977, 10). In 1923 Dodds and his then fiancée went on a 'trial pre-honeymoon' at an inn in the Austrian Alps. The weather was very bad, they had neither books nor cards, and 'love-making apart, we had nothing to do but talk' (ibid. 81). To a Victorian, 'love-making' would have meant little more than holding hands, but we can assume that it meant more than that to Dodds. Both these passages would have been alien to Murray's generation, but it is significant that they occur at all. With Dover, we move not only into a later period, but to a writer determined to reveal all about himself. He is unsparing in his account of his own sexual experience and that of others, and those who read his typescript for Oxford University Press agreed that this was one of the aspects of the book that made it unpublishable. A passage that attracted particular attention from reviewers described how he responded to the beauty of an Italian landscape by masturbating:

> At one point in lecturing on the *Symposium* I remembered a strange occasion in 1944 when I had gone to the top of a hill a few miles south of Mignano. It was an absolutely still day, with a blue sky from one horizon to the other, and the Matese massif was covered from end to end with snow. The scene struck directly at my penis, so I sat down on a log and masturbated; it seemed the appropriate response.
>
> *MC* 114

Dover later told one of his reviewers that

> The incident was actually elicited from my memory of *Phaedrus* 250D. I didn't think a precise reference would go well with the general reader ... but at any rate I did say that the memory came up when I was working on the *Symposium* (work which necessitates reading *Phaedrus* as well). The whole point of bringing up the matter in the book was the *interrelation of the academic and the personal*.[10]

The passage in question has to do with the primacy of sight in the appreciation of beauty. 'The general reader' might not have made the connection between the *Symposium* and the *Phaedrus*, but Dover did so explicitly (*MC* 114).

Marginal Comment and OUP

In November 1993 Dover sent his completed typescript to Hilary O'Shea, the Classics editor at Oxford University Press, having earlier on promised the Press first refusal. On 7 January 1994 she sent him two readers' reports, with a covering note in which she remarked diplomatically that they were 'not unreservedly in favour of publication'. The report by Jasper Griffin ('Reader A') began, 'This is not an easy book to report on'.[11] The text was 'rather long', and had too many harsh quotations attributed to other people, but Griffin's major objection was to Dover's 'aggressively outspoken sexual content ... which certainly startled and caused distress in this reader ... Such material, in such a tone, will completely eclipse the discussion of the Melanesian languages or of the authenticity of the speeches of Lysias'. Griffin concluded, 'the Press would be prudent not to accept it without requiring important changes'. Dover responded to O'Shea: 'Considering the part played in the lives of most of us by our genitals, 1.2% [of the text] does not seem to me too much'.[12]

The report by Henry Chadwick ('Reader B') began, 'This book is likely to be of interest primarily to readers in Oxford or St Andrews with some concern for classical studies'.[13] He described the book as 'A self-portrait of an outstandingly clever man ... Dover is no coward in either body or mind'. Yet he thought the text limited in scope, too critical of contemporaries, and the 'emphatic descriptions of ... sexual experiences ... take frankness to the point where a good many readers will think him deficient in decent good taste'. Chadwick also thought the text was too long, said too little about Dover's real areas of expertise, showed anti-Christian bias, and might give a distorted impression of Corpus to those unfamiliar with the college. The passages on Trevor Aston, however, which later excited comment, simply 'show how patient and skilful Dover could be'. A more particular concern was Dover's portrait of his colleague Robert Ogilvie, which exhibited 'a lack of compassion, a quality he evidently admires in others'.[14] Chadwick used the phrase 'lively local history' to describe Dover's descriptions of Trevor Aston, the admissions system, and the rejection of an honorary degree for Margaret Thatcher.[15] He recognized Dover's 'natural streak of coarseness' but claimed that 'He identifies his values, in broad terms, as stoic' [Dover commented in the margin, 'No, I don't think I do']. An ordained clergyman, Chadwick deeply disliked what he saw as Dover's anti-Christian stance: 'Religion is one of the few subjects on which he allows himself sarcasm'. Dover responded, 'No. I allow myself sarcasm twice, and neither time is the target religion'. Chadwick: 'Colleagues if unsatisfactory or delinquent are candidly portrayed'. Dover's characteristically forensic response was, 'I praise 77 named individuals unreservedly, and condemn only 7 outright'. As for Robert Ogilvie, Dover stressed his concern not to add to the family's grief: 'But I have learnt a lot about him since his death from people who knew him well, and I can only say that he does not deserve compassion'. In summary, Chadwick thought the text would 'diminish [Dover's] honour and standing' and harm Oxford's reputation among those unfamiliar with the university. He concluded that if the Delegates were to think it publishable, it should be shortened.

Hilary O'Shea's covering letter echoed the referees' concerns, singling out as problems Dover's harsh comments on other people and the 'very explicit and possibly obtrusive nature' of his sexual comments. She suggested that the book was 'rather long for leisurely reading' and asked if he would consider making cuts. Normally only two referees would have been asked to report, but in this case, presumably because of Dover's status and the negative consensus of the first two reports, O'Shea asked Fergus Millar to provide a third opinion.[16] His report, dated 18 January, was even more negative than those of Griffin and Chadwick; in fact, it contained no positive comments at all.

> As you know, I was already very apprehensive about this book, fearing that it would probably damage its author's reputation, even before I found that it had been offered to the Press. In the event I find it a far more daunting prospect even than I had feared.... my view is categorically that the Press should not publish it. Indeed I believe that it should not be published.... the book is simply not interesting. The life he has led, though highly successful, has been wholly conventional. As for the personal side... the effect is simply embarrassing and naïve, as is his painfully self-conscious use of four-letter words.... I got to the end of it feeling depressed and embarrassed.

Millar was concerned that O'Shea might receive a furious response if she shared his conclusions with Dover and suggested that she consult the Secretary to the Delegates.[17] Understandably, given its unrelentingly dismissive nature, O'Shea did not share Millar's report with Dover. She and Dover met on 2 February; soon after this, she sent him a short report from another reader, with whom she had discussed the proposal by telephone, and whom Dover called 'Reader C' in his response. Reader C declared that 'the question is whether what might, in another context, be seen as soft porn or libel, is compatible with the stance of a person delivering himself of an academic autobiography'. He also described parts of Dover's text as 'a verbal equivalent of indecent exposure: i.e. of behaviour acceptable in a specialized private context being brought forward in a public one'. In his response, as we have seen, Dover insisted that his book was not an 'academic autobiography', but 'an autobiography *simpliciter*'. Who was Reader C? He referred to Dover as 'K' rather than 'D' and quoted a statement by Pliny the Elder; he also stated that his and Dover's careers had run in parallel, and declined to go into details about Dover's text, in case they revealed his identity. All this evidence suggests that Reader C was Dover's long-term friend and colleague Donald Russell.

On 21 February a diary entry appeared in the *Evening Standard* under the heading 'Oxford don takes memoirs in hand':

> Dover, 73, has just sent the Oxford University Press memoirs of a rare candour, describing his experiences of the solitary pleasures of Onan. 'Dover's prospective publishers don't quite know what to do,' reveals an Oxford insider. 'He's hugely grand - the ex-President of Corpus Christi College. The OUP's governors, the Delegates, are in a terrible state. Just to make it more embarrassing, a senior

Delegate, Sir Keith Thomas, is Dover's successor at Corpus.' 'I have put in one or two things which I think they found a bit shocking,' concedes Sir Kenneth. This is, I suspect, a forgivable reaction, given that at one point the Professor reveals that, as a young man, his weakness for physical self-indulgence was on one occasion set off by no more than the beauty of the view from an Italian hill. Sir Kenneth, I am happy to discover, is quite unabashed. 'I was merely recording a moment of insight into the philosophy of Plato,' he tells me.

On 24 February O'Shea told Dover that though the book was 160,000 words long rather than the 300,000 she had originally estimated, it was still over-long, and that it would be helpful to cut passages which gave an unduly pessimistic picture of 'university life'. She also expressed her horror at the leak to the *Evening Standard*, and assured him that nobody at OUP had spoken to the press.[18] Dover replied on 25 February saying that (1) he believed the leak must have come from an OUP Delegate, (2) he was willing to look at his allegedly over-pessimistic view of the university if he could be told precisely what was objected to, (3) he was willing to consider 'a more compassionate treatment of dead villains, especially Ogilvie', but (4) he was not prepared to cut references to sexual incidents and (5) he was not willing to substitute euphemism for coarse words. This was a matter of style, 'not unconnected with some thoughts about "stylistic recipes" in my other book'.[19]

After some discussion about cuts, O'Shea wrote to Dover on 4 March suggesting that it would be best for him to find another publisher: 'As an academic publisher we would be particularly concerned about offence to relatives of the deceased (however "villainous" in your view they may or may not have been), and about your use of coarse sexual language.'

Dover replied on 5 March saying that he would now offer the book to Duckworth. His MS comment on the phrase 'As an academic publisher' was 'Non seq'. He appears not to have appreciated the particular sensitivities common to such presses. Hilary O'Shea later told me, 'We couldn't possibly publish it, of course'; and the reactions of the referees effectively blocked publication, especially as Dover had refused to compromise on crucial issues. On 7 March, Fergus Millar wrote to Dover saying that as one of the two classical Delegates of OUP he felt the book was not suitable for the Press. He told Dover that he did not want to hide behind O'Shea: Dover's MS comment was, 'Little did he know!'[20]

Marginal Comment at Duckworth

About four years earlier, an editor for the publisher Heinemann had expressed an interest in the book, but he was now retired, and his successor was interested in autobiographies only of the famous. In her covering letter to James Arnold-Baker, Hilary O'Shea had remarked, 'I am sure Duckworth would snap it up'.[21] On 5 February Dover had written to Colin Haycraft, part-owner and managing director of the publisher Duckworth since

1968, asking if he would like to publish the book if he and OUP could not come to an agreement about it. In his reply to O'Shea of 25 February, Dover had told her that Colin Haycraft was 'slavering after the book'; his own MS note on this was 'In conversation; no commitment'. After his negotiations with OUP collapsed, he sent his typescript to Haycraft, who told him that he was keen to take it: 'It is an excellent book, full of interest of various kinds, and we would love to publish it.'[22] Colin Haycraft was an Oxford Classics graduate: he entered Queen's College in 1949, and after National Service graduated with a first in Literae Humaniores in 1953. After buying Duckworth in 1968 he had built up a substantial classical list, including Hugh Lloyd-Jones' *Blood for the Ghosts* (1982), a collection of essays on the history of classical scholarship; he had also published books by Michael Dummett and Roy Harris.[23]

From this point on, Dover dealt with Duckworth's Classics editor, Deborah Blake.[24] Duckworth was then a small and unhierarchical firm with a congenial and friendly atmosphere. Deborah Blake remembered no cuts or changes but thought that 'it was unclear to us why exactly OUP had rejected it. [There was] speculation that it was because of the sexual revelations. But I don't think anyone was particularly concerned about the Trevor Aston business.'[25] The last comment perhaps shows the extent to which a London press did not feel troubled by issues that reverberated especially in Oxford.

Somewhat surprisingly, given his mastery of linguistic minutiae in Greek, Dover was not a good proof-reader of his own text; the first printing contained a number of errors, many of them spotted by Paul Cartledge, who sent him a long list of corrections. A few addenda were squeezed into this printing ('Epimetron 1994', pp. 263–4); a second printing appeared in 1995, in which Dover was able to add some additional corrections and afterthoughts (pp. 263–5).

At some point, Dover composed a long list of supplementary notes to the book, enlarging on brief comments, identifying individuals and so on.[26] This substantial text (33 pages) probably incorporates the portions of text rumoured to have been preserved separately, but not found in that form. For example, the two pages on Robert Ogilvie which Dover noted that he had excised (*MC* 173 n.1) are probably those included in the supplementary notes at that point.[27] Some of the material in these notes remains sensitive, and Dover's decision to sequester it there reflects his concern to avoid pain or embarrassment to individuals. For example, he gives the full name of the teenage girl with whom he had an affair in north Italy in 1945, and who appears in his book under a pseudonym (*MC* 57–8). In 1994 she will have been in her mid-sixties, and they had had no contact for over forty years; the care Dover took to conceal her identity is an indication of how scrupulous he was in such matters.

Reception

Marginal Comment was published by Duckworth in November 1994. The leaking of comments on the Aston affair in February of that year made it inevitable that when the book was published later that year, it would attract interest from the press. The ancient historian Mark Humphries remembers that

> I was in St Andrews when Dover's *Marginal Comment* was published, and the place was infested by press looking for stories. At the time the editor of the student newspaper was in my Greek history seminar group, and I congratulated him on having the guts to publish an edition which had on its front page a photo of Dover and a headline, referring to the Trevor Aston business, that read 'Chancellor's Death Plot'; he alleged that an earlier version had been 'The White Stiffs of Dover', but that the student union legal people had said that was a no-no.[28]

When the book was published, a copy was acquired for the Joint Library of the Hellenic and Roman Societies at the Institute of Classical Studies in London, then in Gordon Square in Bloomsbury. It was given the shelf-mark 'Room 508' (the library office); borrowing was not restricted, but it had to be signed out for use in the library. The Room 508 books were mostly on sex (class mark 152J.3), but also included material that had gone missing in the recent past. The controversy about the book presumably played a part in its classification.[29]

Dover's files contain a tabulated list of responses to his book: his count is 107 positive, one mixed and 11 hostile. One of the hostile ones is an anonymous handwritten letter. It begins,

> Sir
>
> After reading your psychopathic admission of driving your colleague to his death Mr Trevor Aston I find your intellectual pose akin to Reginald Kray. He too is divorced from his emotions. No hatred you say motivated your murderous intent. I disagree. Your pathetic and sadistic act was one of extreme hatred, anger and jealousy. You will Sir be repaid ... I await news of your demise with anticipation.

A welcome contrast is provided by anecdotes of old times, among them a recollection of a Fraenkel seminar:

> Fraenkel: what metre is this?
>
> Student: a telesillean.
>
> Fraenkel: you will have to speak up.
>
> Student: A TELESILLEAN.
>
> Fraenkel: No! it is a telesillean.[30]

A review by Ross Leckie, who as president of the Corpus JCR during Dover's presidency had known him quite well, contained less praise than criticism, and ended:

> *Marginal Comment* advances our understanding of nothing but the strangeness of man.... OUP were right to decline to publish this sad book. As a bizarre curiosity, like its hideous cover, it has merit. But it will puzzle and offend many who, like me, preferred the Kenneth Dover we used to think we knew and loved, the Dover who taught us so much.

Leckie sent a copy of his review to Dover, whose response began, 'Well, it's certainly an antidote for swollen head.'[31] Another review, sent in advance of publication, brought a constructive response from Dover from which I shall quote only the opening: 'Many thanks for sending me a copy of your review. I greatly appreciate your recognition that it is an "experimental" work.'[32]

Comment on the book also came from friends, family and colleagues. Donald Russell, whom Dover had known since they were undergraduates at Balliol in the late 1930s, was very unhappy with it. He told Dover that, 'I found the book fascinating ... but not really *you*, or worthy of you. What I mean is that the qualities your friends love in you ... don't seem to come through ... the text does not reflect your goodness and humanity.'[33] In the notes for the British Academy memoir he wrote with Stephen Halliwell, Russell stated that he had told Dover that he did not like the book for that reason; Dover found this hard to take, but Russell had felt bound to make the point.[34] A similar comment came from Dover's Corpus colleague Brian Harrison. He had admired Dover's work as president of the college, but was shocked by his account of the Aston affair, and felt that the Dover portrayed there was not the man he knew: 'if some think that Dover and others have traduced Aston, Dover the autobiographer obliges by traducing himself – as a cold and calculating man with stunted emotions, biding his time playing cat to Aston's rather formidable mouse.'[35] The American classicist and philosopher Martha Nussbaum, who had been collaborating with Dover over a legal submission for a court case about homosexuality, stayed with the Dovers in June 1994. When she read *Marginal Comment*, she was very enthusiastic about it, finding the combination of the personal and the professional very well done, and very powerful from a literary point of view. She was however surprised by Dover's account of his funnel chest; she saw him as an attractive man with an imposing physique.[36] Dover's cousin Ana Healey thought *Marginal Comment* 'All round, a marvellous book'. She knew about his funnel chest (she and her mother also had the condition) but was shocked to find how blighted his early life had been by it. Her letter of thanks for the book made no mention of the issues which aroused so much public criticism: masturbation, criticism of colleagues, the Aston affair.[37] I hope these examples give some idea of the value of Dover's papers as a source for the history of the book and its reception.

Notes

1. Donald Russell to Hilary O'Shea, Kenneth Dover to O'Shea, February 1994. See further in my text at p. 102.

2. Dodds 1977, MacNeice 1965.
3. Grundy 1945, Heitland 1926.
4. The intertwining of education and religion meant that some of those biographized were not just scholars but also headmasters and/or bishops: Samuel Butler was all three.
5. Jebb 1907; Verrall's 'The scholar and critic' is at pp. 427–87. A similar strategy was adopted by Norman Page for his biography of A.E. Housman, in which the chapter on Housman's scholarship drew heavily on the memoir published by Housman's friend and pupil A.S.F. Gow.
6. Todhunter 1876, Douglas 1881. On the memorialists' problems, see Stray 2023.
7. Smith and Toynbee 1960: Murray's fragment is at pp. 23–103. West 1984, Wilson 1987; cf. Stray 2007b.
8. Dodds 1977; Stray, Pelling and Harrison 2019. Dodds' memoir was awarded the Duff Cooper literary prize.
9. Murray to Lady Mary Murray, 25 June 1908: Wilson 1987, 144.
10. Dover to Ross Leckie, 19 December 1994. The passage in question has to do with the primacy of sight in the appreciation of beauty. In his response to Jasper Griffin's report on the book (see p. 101), Dover had stated that his masturbation 'contributed to my understanding of Plato's *Phaedrus* and *Symposium*'.
11. Jasper Griffin (1937–2019), FBA 1986, was tutorial fellow of Balliol 1963–2004 and Professor of Classics at Oxford 1992–2004. The identities of Readers A and B have been confirmed from internally circulated copies of their reports. My thanks to the OUP archivist, Dr Martin Maw, for information about the relevant editorial file (OP2693/19078), and to Sir Keith Thomas, a former Delegate to the Press, for discussion of the reports of the readers, and for the loan of his copy of Dover's original typescript.
12. The referees' reports (without attribution) are held in Dover's papers in the Corpus Christi archive.
13. Henry Chadwick (1920–2008), FBA 1960, Regius Professor of Divinity at Oxford 1959–79, Dean of Christ Church 1969–79, Regius Professor of Divinity at Cambridge 1979–83, Master of Peterhouse 1987–93. 'Chadwick always loved footnotes' (Mayr-Harting 2012); I dedicate this footnote to his memory. The geographical limits Chadwick refers to (Oxford and St Andrews) are hardly convincing, given Dover's global reputation: he was described by his successor as president of Corpus, Sir Keith Thomas, as 'the world's leading Hellenist'.
14. On Ogilvie, see Meiggs 1982. Ogilvie had succeeded Dover as tutor in Classics at Balliol in 1955; he was Professor of Humanity at St Andrews from 1975 until 1981, when he committed suicide. Dover cut most of what he had written about Ogilvie in order to avoid causing pain to his widow.
15. Dover chaired a committee which proposed changes in Oxford's admissions system (the Dover Report, 1983). He was the only head of house to vote against the award of an honorary degree to Margaret Thatcher in 1985. For these two matters, see *MC* chs 27 and 30.
16. Fergus Millar (1935–2019): Camden Professor of Ancient History 1984–2002; knighted 2010; an OUP Delegate from 1992 to 1995. The other classical Delegate was Anna Morpurgo Davies, Professor of Comparative Philology 1971–2004, who though technically a linguistics Delegate (1992–2004) was sent the papers for classical books, and often advised on them.
17. The Secretary was the administrative head of the Press; James Arnold-Baker was Secretary from 1993 to 1998.

18. The source of the leak was probably Jasper Griffin. (Dover was told by Hugh Lloyd-Jones that Griffin had read his typescript, though apparently he did not know Griffin had been a referee for his book.)
19. The 'other book' was Dover 1997a: on p. 55 Dover compares stylistic recipes with food combinations, giving examples of combinations his parents would never have countenanced but which he was happy to try himself. Cf. p. 87, 'The idiolects of two authors may be so similar that we can regard them both as using the same recipe, but differing in the seasoning'; p. 88, 'The trouble is that it [α > ε before O-vowels] is by no means common in epic, and is therefore recherché as an epic condiment'.
20. This may suggest that Dover already knew that Millar had acted as a referee for the book.
21. This letter is preserved in the OUP editorial file, OP2693/19078.
22. Haycraft to Dover, 11 April 1994.
23. Dummett was Wykeham Professor of Logic 1979–92; Harris was Professor of General Linguistics 1978–86; both could be described, as could Haycraft himself, as mavericks. I was once told that Haycraft's aim was to create 'a one-man university press'; his intellectual elan was unfortunately not accompanied by financial skills, and the firm's history was punctuated by a series of financial crises. See Martin 1995. During the 1973 oil crisis, several books accepted by Duckworth were sent back to their authors without explanation. Among them was *Reading the Classical Page*, a collaborative volume I had organized and edited whose contributors included Arthur Adkins, Robert Coleman, Donald Earl, Pat Easterling, Ted Kenney and Niall Rudd. At a dinner for contributors given by Haycraft, he was asked about contracts, and replied breezily that he thought a gentleman's agreement would be sufficient. When I mentioned this to my friend Tim Rix, then chairman of the Longman Group, he commented that a written contract would not protect me from Colin Haycraft on a dark night.
24. Having dealt with her myself on many occasions, I can record that he was lucky to work with her. Deborah Blake had an Oxford degree in history; her father, the historian Robert Blake (life peer 1971), was Provost of Queen's College, Oxford, 1968–87.
25. Blake to Stray, 10 December 2020.
26. These supplementary notes, held in Dover's papers at Corpus Christi College, Oxford, have been drawn on in the reissue of *Marginal Comment* with annotations by the editors of the present volume (Dover 2023).
27. This is confirmed by the markings in the copy of the book Dover gave to Stephen Halliwell; the marginal marks correspond exactly to the entries in the supplementary notes.
28. My thanks to Mark Humphries, Professor of Classics, Swansea University, for sharing this memory.
29. Most of these books were put back on the ordinary shelves in 1997, when the library moved to Senate House. (Thanks to Paul Jackson, Deputy Librarian, for information.)
30. Thomas Brown to Dover, 2 January 1995.
31. A review was commissioned from Nicholas Horsfall for the Corpus Christi magazine *The Pelican* but was cancelled by the editor to avoid controversy within the college.
32. Dover to C.A. Stray, 12 August 1995; the published review is Stray 1996.
33. Russell to Dover, 7 December 1994.
34. Russell, autobiographical memoir at British Academy, 37pp.
35. Harrison 1994a, which responded to Valentine Cunningham's discussion of Dover's account of 'the Aston affair' in Cunningham 1994.

36. Nussbaum's admiration for both Dover and his memoir was made plain in her *Arion* review (Nussbaum 1997).
37. Anastasia Healey to Dover, 9 November 1994. Healey was Librarian of the Joint Library of the Hellenic and Roman Societies at the Institute of Classical Studies in London, 1971–89; cf. Craik, this volume, p. 58. She had therefore retired before the publication of *Marginal Comment* but may have had an informal say in its restricted classification.

PART II
THE WORK

CHAPTER 7
DOVER ON THUCYDIDES
Christopher Pelling

Thucydides, Dover said, was the author on whom he had spent most time;[1] he was also the author, others have said,[2] with whom he felt the closest intellectual affinity – all that rationalism, all that search for ἀκρίβεια, all that impatience with humbug, all that justified pride in his diligence in gathering materials (think of the laboriously compiled statistical tables in *The Evolution of Greek Prose Style* and his early construction of an index to 'the phonological and morphological features of the inscriptions which predated the mid-fifth century');[3] and perhaps also, shall we say, a certain tendency to pontificate. Composing the long second appendix to volume 5 of the Gomme, Andrewes, Dover *Historical Commentary on Thucydides*[4] was the work, he said, that 'gave me more lasting satisfaction than anything else that I had written' (*MC* 76). That volume, published in 1981, brought to a conclusion what was clearly his most monumental Thucydidean work; he had earlier contributed the commentary on Books 6 and 7 in *HCT* vol. iv, published in 1970. But there was a good deal more as well: school commentaries on those same two books in 1965,[5] put out at a time when there is reason to think he was frustrated at the slow progress made by his co-contributor Tony Andrewes;[6] the *Greece and Rome* New Survey of 1973;[7] a stream of articles starting in the early fifties, a fair number more than those he chose to include in *The Greeks and their Legacy*; the chapter on classical historiography in his *Ancient Greek Literature*;[8] and there is a good deal on Thucydides also in *The Evolution of Greek Prose Style*, where Thucydides is the author providing comfortably the most examples. There had been rather less in *Greek Word Order*, and perhaps Thucydides' practice was just too maverick to serve his purposes there.[9] To disagree with any of his notes is to stick one's neck out a long way, especially on any matter of language, topography, chronology, or the simple question of what actually happened. Supplementing rather than contradicting is another matter, perhaps; and perhaps also the few cases where he does seem to go astray may be where he assumes that the intellectual affinity is even closer than it is. More on that later.

In *Marginal Comment* Dover talks about the exhilarating experience of Thucydides tutorials with Russell Meiggs just after Gomme's first volume had appeared.[10] One can understand that. Meiggs was an inspiring tutor (I caught his last year myself), not reluctant to live up to his own dictum that Dover so admired, 'teaching is a branch of the acting profession' (*MC* 147), and Gomme's is a great book. It is interesting, though, how Dover puts it: he learned from Meiggs to remember that these people were *real*, and that he must make every effort to put himself into their place; and always to go to inscriptions first and only then to literature.[11] In a way, fair enough, even with the second of those lessons; as he says, *ATL* was beginning to come out,[12] and there is a lot of engagement with its first volume in Gomme's treatment of the *pentêkontaetia*; and nobody knew more about inscriptions than Meiggs. But that stress on the inscriptions is not the one that most people, myself included, would give to their memories of Meiggs talking about Thucydides. Dover was usually paired with Donald Russell, and Russell wrote later about the 'humbling' experience of listening to his 'lucid, elegant, and cogent essays';[13] one can believe it, though also that Dover would have his humbling moments too. Meiggs told him that Donald 'had a better brain' than he had but would 'never be as good a historian', and to his credit Dover records that in *Marginal Comment*, adding that Donald always had a literary sensitivity that Dover himself knew he lacked (*MC* 65). This, I suspect, is quite telling. In later life Dover several times said that he had never tried to be a literary critic and would prefer to be described as a historian of literature;[14] when we reach the commentaries, we will see that he rarely ventures anything that we might call 'literary', even at times when such considerations closely affected matters that he did comment on. Is he shying away from areas where he knew he was not at his best, and others could do better, perhaps Russell in particular, though Hugh Lloyd-Jones and some more senior figures like E.R. Dodds may be relevant too?

When he began as a don, he took over from Dorothea Gray the lectures on Thucydides 6–7 for Classical Mods. Thucydides 6 was then a 'special book', and 7 a 'general book': that meant that students needed to know 6 in great detail, extending to intricate textual criticism, and be able to exploit 7 as well for essays – not that essays figured all that much in either the week-to-week tutorial work or in the examination. The books were extensively lectured on, and from 1950 to 1955 Dover gave three lectures a week in Trinity term and continued into Michaelmas. In cases where there was no good commentary, that meant taking students slowly and in uncompromising detail through the text after, doubtless, some general introductory lectures. As Dover says, the essence of the job was 'to produce a better commentary on them than anyone had done hitherto' (*MC* 72). Unsurprisingly, lectures like that often led to commentaries in print, and Barrett's *Hippolytos* and Ogilvie's *Livy* both had a similar genesis.[15] It has been remarked that books by Oxford authors often have eight chapters just as lecture courses have eight weeks: might those two facts be in some way related? Something similar is true of those commentaries. Students who had no taste for getting up in the mornings could always opt for the books where those commentaries had already appeared. Fifteen years later I was one of them: I still have those battered copies of Barrett's *Hippolytos* and Ogilvie's *Livy*.

Not that Dover could have anticipated that his own lectures would end like that. In 1950 Gomme was in his early sixties, in good health and well advanced on what was still expected to be the second volume of three; with his retirement looming, everyone thought that he would finish the job himself, and even after he retired in 1957 Gomme expected that he would have enough years left to allow him to work first on the Menander commentary that he co-authored with Sandbach.[16] The thousand hours that Dover reckoned he put into preparing those lectures did produce some spin-off articles – five of them between 1953 and 1955, one of them still a classic;[17] still, he thought of his major projects as different, OCTs of Antiphon and Andocides, a grammar of Attic inscriptions, and, first, his preparation of Denniston's *Greek Particles* for the press.[18] Then Aristophanes took centre stage, and towards the end of the fifties he turned to *Greek Word Order*.[19]

Gomme, though, died in January 1959, and within days the Press asked Andrewes and Dover to finish the work. They immediately agreed, though at the start Dover did not expect it to supersede his Aristophanes schedule: he had been working on the *Clouds* since 1955. He wrote about it in a letter home on 4 February: 'I did after all lecture on Thuc. VI–VII for five years,[20] have put an immense amount of work into it, and could pretty certainly do a better commentary on those particular books than anyone alive.' Well, you are allowed to say that sort of thing to your mum and dad, and it was true. A week or so later he agreed with the Press that he would move this up his priorities and set about it before returning to Aristophanes. With those thousand hours already under his belt and lectures already tailored to a commentary format, it is not surprising that he made quick progress. By October 1959 he had about twenty chapters in final form, and about a third of the whole work in something close to it;[21] in November he reported that he was moving at a rate of about a chapter a day (there are 192 chapters).[22] In *Marginal Comment* he says that he made particularly good progress at Harvard between September 1960 and January 1961, and by then he had already done his tramping around Epipolae and the environs of Syracuse in spring or summer 1960. By the end of 1961 he was free to get back to Aristophanes.[23] Things, though, did not go as quickly with the commentary as was hoped. Andrewes had a smaller quantity of text in Book 5 to cover than Dover, but he was setting about it from a standing start and, given the strong assumption at the time that 5 and 8 raised indivisible questions of composition and completion, he clearly had to do a lot of the work on Book 8 as well.[24] Also, it is fair to say, on some bits Andrewes simply found more to say than Dover would have done; his commentary on the Melian Dialogue is fuller and I think richer than any of Dover's, or indeed Gomme's, commentary on the speeches in their sections. So it was not till 1970 that the next volume appeared. Nothing, though, prevented Dover from cashing in at least some of the work he had done before then, and his school commentaries, described as 'abridged' from the longer work, appeared in 1965.

Before we get into the commentaries I shall jump forward to a relatively late article, first published in 1983, on 'Thucydides "as history" and "as literature"',[25] as this is where he makes his own views clearest on what he envisaged as his job. Could one write a 'literary' commentary on Thucydides at all? For the full *HCT*, he reasonably says, his rubric excluded this, at least as a priority: it was a *Historical Commentary*, after all. But he is sceptical anyway about the whole idea. One could write a linguistic commentary, he says, as one could on any author; but to write a solely literary commentary would ignore the question 'what sort of writer was he?', and the fact that a historical writer is writing about things that actually happened. (There is a prefiguring there of a much later debate of the 2010s about intertextuality: does its subject matter make historiographic intertextuality significantly different from intertextuality in other genres?[26]) Nobody, Dover says, has denied or would deny that historians were most of the time doing their best to say what they thought was best reconcilable with the evidence they knew;[27] this can be glossed as 'telling the truth', as the rest of the paper makes clear, and he is particularly hard on Virginia Hunter for making Thucydides a 'liar' for tweaking his account of Pylos to exaggerate the degree of chance.[28] He would doubtless have said the same a year later when Bob Connor suggested that Thucydides moulded his picture of the topography of Pylos to make it closer to that of the Harbour of Syracuse, part of the mirroring of the two episodes that was so important to him.[29]

There is a lot there that needs unpacking, and even if one accepts that Thucydides always tried to 'tell the truth' (and I would, at least broadly, though five years later Tony Woodman would have his doubts about how historiographic 'truth-telling' ought to be defined[30]), Dover does not dwell on the question whether there might have been other assumptions, ones we would not share, on the best way to get at that truth; that is, whether 'the evidence they knew' ought to be interpreted more broadly than what they had heard or read. If Thucydides genuinely thought that individual historical events might suggest more universal insights (and Dover does stress Thucydides' belief in these 'constants in human history'[31]), those insights might in their turn cast light on individual events: it is a two-way street. If he thought, as so many experienced soldiers have thought, that fighting often develops in ways that belie the best-laid plans and luck plays a large part – and Hans-Peter Stahl had already made a strong case for that in 1966[32] – then that insight would itself affect how he interpreted and would tell the tale of Pylos. That, indeed, is part of 'what sort of author this is'.

The article ends with a plea for pluralism, a let-a-thousand-flowers-bloom approach; he acknowledges that there may be all sorts of reasons, apparently including literary ones, why a Thucydidean passage might be 'unsatisfactory and perplexing'.[33] But his main emphasis rests on why the literary critic needs to bear in mind that this is a historical text, and he is much less precise on why the historian needs to keep an eye on literary aspects, what Thucydides might be doing with the evidence to construct his sort of narrative. John Davies did exactly that in a much later paper,[34] arguing that Greek historians have so little information that they need to squeeze every orange they can lay their hands on: fair enough. To an extent Dover does it himself; he comments, for instance, on Thucydides' tendency not to give his readers all the information at once but to distribute it through widely separated passages (*HCT* iv. 382 = 7.2.2 n.), or alternatively to collect together material that belongs together logically but not chronologically (*HCT* iv. 403 = 7.27–28 n.), and he several times acknowledges that his author has a tendency to exaggerate for effect.[35] He certainly has a very clear view, right or wrong, of how far the speeches are attempts to reconstruct what was really said. But he does not go much further, and this is not where his heart is. One recalls those comments that he has never tried or claimed to be a literary critic himself.

Let us move on to the commentaries themselves, and continue this back-to-front journey in time by starting at the end, for many typical features are visible in the second appendix to the last volume, *HCT* v (1981). This deals with 'strata of composition' after Andrewes has dealt with 'indications of incompleteness' in Appendix 1. It is interesting that these compositional questions are the only ones they thought needed addressing in the Appendices which Gomme several times promised to include at the end of the commentary, and to which he was postponing many of the questions traditionally treated in an introduction. I have written elsewhere about that idiosyncratic choice of Gomme.[36]

The Appendices' length as well as that focus reflect how that compositional issue – THE *Thukydidesfrage*, as it was sometimes called – had dominated earlier scholarship, and in some ways this can be seen as its last hurrah. One can only admire the way in which Dover trenchantly dismantles and sometimes just discards a hundred years and more of mighty scholarship – Ullrich, Krüger, Eduard Meyer, and especially Schwartz – before finally turning his guns on Canfora and his then very recent ideas about Xenophon as an 'editor' of Books 5 and 8.[37] There in particular he shows himself one of the earliest to sense the statistical possibilities opened by digital computing, using this to generate some strong arguments about linguistic usage;[38] he would exploit it much more in *The Evolution of Greek Prose Style* (1997).

There is precious little to argue with in terms of approach.[39] He reasonably says that there is no reason to think that the burden of proof should always fall on the 'analyst' rather than the 'unitarian' ('analyst' here in the sense of identifying different strata of composition rather than different authorship): there are some pretty incontrovertible indications that some passages were written after 404 and others some time before, and there is nothing in principle to exclude the likelihood that Thucydides changed his mind on some issues and revised some passages but had not yet got around to revising others.[40] But in fact the bulk of the argument is concerned with addressing analytic arguments that in almost every case he thinks do not hold up: he is very much in prosecuting counsel mode, with the shades of the 'analysts' cowering in the dock. The effect is really to be a unitarian in each case until proved differently, and so the burden of proof is thrown on to the analyst after all; still, it does matter that incomplete revision or a change of mind is there at the end as an acceptable inference if a unitarian defence fails to convince. That seems to me spot-on. He does draw those inferences on only a very few occasions; we might now think that even those were mostly unnecessary – for instance, that Thucydides changed his mind on Alcibiades, or that he had not satisfactorily made up his mind on the Megarian Decree, or that the verdict on the Sicilian expedition in Book 2 does not sit comfortably with the narrative in Books 6 and 7. But many readers at the time would probably have been surprised that there were not more. I especially admire the genteel way in which he steers around a case where Andrewes had argued that Thucydides had changed his mind on the causes of the war: was it all Corinth's fault?[41] Andrewes had thought too that he knew when the change of mind had come: some time during the Peace of Nicias, for those years demonstrated how little influence Corinth could really exert on Sparta. Dover produces all the arguments to show that there is very little reason to think like this (pp. 416–21), but he makes a few polite nods towards Andrewes' article on points of detail, and ends by saying that perhaps 'such disquiet as we may feel' about the balance of Book 1 might still be justifiable; then he swiftly shifts to an unusually convoluted and speculative paragraph about the Megarian Decree (pp. 421–23) – and so perhaps there *is* after all a detectable change of mind. I do not think so myself in that case either, but it is a neat *pas de deux* to avoid trampling on his partner's feet.

One often has a more indirect sense of 'Dover at work', as there is a fair amount of 'this is how I would have done it myself'. He indeed defends the principle (pp. 402–3): 'if I am not to start from myself, whence am I to start?', and says something similar about some of his other books in *Marginal Comment*.⁴² Most of the time, this works reasonably well: thus

> Anyone who has taken many years to write a book knows from his own experience that he revises some parts of it thoroughly and often and other parts very little, with the result that eventually one paragraph which has been recast a dozen times may stand, in the form which it assumed in year n, between two others which have been barely touched since they were first drafted in year $n - 10$.
>
> HCT v.401

And he adds a footnote giving a learned reference to 'the anonymous author of a nineteenth-century sexual autobiography': *das Doverische im Dover*.⁴³ He might have paid more attention there to the differences between making adjustments in a papyrus roll or even a codex and those in the late twentieth century, even before word-processing (he makes a gesture in that direction, p. 400, but does not really engage); but, still, on the whole, this is reasonable. 'Introspection' – he uses the word – is also used as a guide to the reason why Thucydides might have cut down his usual end-of-year signing-off formula to a shorter version during the years of the Peace (p. 391 n. 1). He encourages a similar 'how would you do it yourself?' approach in his readers: just try boiling down a Demosthenes speech to give yourself an idea of how much of the original would be lost during the sort of condensation process that Thucydides must have carried out (p. 397 n. 1).⁴⁴ I am reminded of Simon Schama's response after a TV lecture, in that case to a know-all questioner who implied that writing narrative was something of a let-down for a serious historian: 'just try it, buster'.

All that, I think, is fair, but there are also times when he posits a Thucydides who is just a little too much of an alter ego, a Dover-twin before his time. He is convinced, as he so often is in the commentary, that Thucydides would avoid any ambiguity, and that will particularly be so when an important statement of principle is at stake.⁴⁵ Thus nobody would be in any doubt of what 1.22 meant on the speeches – it is 'quite obvious' that Thucydides intended to give as accurate a version as he could, and it is only the speeches themselves that cause us to wonder if he has done what he had said he would do (p. 394).⁴⁶ 1.22 itself for Dover can only mean that he aimed for the greatest fidelity possible, given the need for condensation.⁴⁷ He does not allow the possibility that there were positive advantages in a certain looseness there, allowing Thucydides to strike a different balance between fidelity and creative reconstruction in different cases while always paying some respect to both; he must have had very different amounts of remembered detail for the Plataean debate or Nicias' last speech, both with very few surviving witnesses, from say the *Epitaphios*. Dover is clearly troubled, too, by Thucydides' taste for superlatives – 'the greatest in the war' and so on: 'we' do not have the same expectations of a historian as of a journalist (p. 407), an anachronism and indeed a 'we' that might start alarm bells ringing.⁴⁸ He does expect a historian to be precise. Thucydides' famous fantasy – if anyone in future generations saw the remains of Sparta they would never guess that they are leaders of the whole Peloponnese and many outside allies, whereas they would think Athens had double the power that it has (1.10.2) – only fits if written 'soon after the battle of Mantinea' in 418, and that allows a similar dating of the whole Archaeology. Doubts might be felt about both those steps.

Some of his more intemperate statements show his impatience with more 'literary' approaches. 'The Greeks in general had more sense than to call a pretentious kind of falsehood "ideal truth", "true historical objectivity", etc.' (p. 396 n. 2). He is using that footnote to wave away a straw-man opponent who claims the speeches are 'simply fiction'; but should one be so clear that the debate of the generals at 6.47–49, say, took place just like that, on arrival in Sicily? Would they not have talked it over earlier during a quiet evening in Corcyra, and might Thucydides not then for clarity's sake formalize the views into a structured debate? 'All his speakers talk the same language, irrespective of nationality and cultural milieu, and it is *his* language ...' (p. 395), something he had already said in 1965 and again in 1980;[49] but 1981 was nine years after Dan Tompkins had published an article that has become a classic, showing how distinctive is the style of Nicias and Alcibiades,[50] and it is not difficult to do the same for Hermocrates or indeed for Pericles.[51] Dover even doubles down on it, comparing 'the virtual absence of individualization in the language of characters in epic, tragedy, or comedy' (p. 397): does Achilles really talk like Hector,[52] or Sophocles' Ajax like his Odysseus?[53]

All this is of course over-carping; one is still bowled over by the penetrating intelligence and grateful for all the application of the stiletto to so much earlier work. Many a Thucydidean scholar will have given a huge sigh of relief that due diligence might not after all demand a painstaking work-through of Ullrich and Schwartz. The magisterial and confident tone is certainly striking, another feature that he shares with Thucydides himself. If one says that nobody else could have written it quite like this the compliment is genuine even if there is also a barb.

Let us go now to the commentary itself in *HCT* iv, with an eye too to the earlier school commentaries. Unsurprisingly, many of the same features are there: of course the lucidity, vital for instance in the way he disentangles the various strands of ambiguity in the enigmatically phrased final sentence on Nicias, 'the least deserving of Greeks, at least in my time, to arrive at such a pitch of misfortune, in view of the way he had ordered his behaviour according to every virtue' (7.86.5) – if that is what it means, and here Dover seems to have changed his mind on one point between the school edition and 1970.[54] His note in *HCT* is exemplary too in setting out what is at stake, not at all unequivocal approval of Nicias' leadership – on that he has already not minced his words, as we shall see – but simply that he did not deserve to die like this given his ἐπιτήδευσις, the way he had led his life. The firm clarity with which he makes linguistic points will also have saved many scholars from misinterpretation, for instance when he insists on the importance of the indicatives at 7.42.3: Demosthenes' verdict that it had been a mistake in 415 not to march directly on Syracuse is not just what Demosthenes thought or said, it is a view on which Thucydides bestows authorial approval as well,[55] though that in itself raises further issues about how precisely that analysis maps on to Thucydides' own account in Book 6.[56] The care with which he handles topographical issues is very clear, and he had certainly put in many days and many miles tramping around Epipolae; his is still the go-to authority there. The historical and particularly epigraphic notes are magisterial,[57] and here too his close attention to the intricacies of the Greek often pays dividends.[58]

There is also the no-beating-about-the-bush trenchancy: 'Nikias' pride and consequent cowardice in the face of personal disgrace leads him to put forward as disgraceful a proposition as any general in history: rather than risk execution, he will throw away the fleet and many thousands of other people's lives, and put his country in mortal peril' (*HCT* iv.426 on 7.48.4). Or: 'If Hermokrates' proposal had been adopted, and if there had been time (as there was not) to put it into effect, the probable outcome was the annihilation of the Sikeliot fleets and the rapid imposition of Athenian rule on Sicily and South Italy' (*HCT* iv.299 on 6.34.4). Or again: 'During the critical period when [Nikias] was left in sole command he was inept, dilatory, and querulous' (*HCT* iv.462 on 7.86.5). Issue has been taken with, especially, the first two of these;[59] I would personally quarrel at least with 'cowardice' in the first, as Nicias was concerned with honour, something that would resonate with an ancient audience, and he had good reason for thinking that the position was not yet hopeless. But you certainly know where you are with Dover, and one feels professional gratitude to a scholar who provides you with so many lines to which you can just add 'discuss'.

As for introspection and self-reference, there is less of it explicitly than in *HCT* v. Perhaps, indeed, there might have been more, especially in the school commentaries of 1965: it is in *Marginal Comment*, not in a preface here, that he tells how his wartime experiences in Libya had helped him to understand the desperate 'if we can only get to that next ridge' feelings of the Athenians on their final retreat (*MC* 53); it is in *The Greeks* that he says that reading that narrative for the umpteenth time still made his hair stand on end.[60] I know that the sixth-former that I was myself in 1965 would have found such things intriguing and engaging, and they would have made that narrative even more vivid. But, especially in *HCT*, there are still times when one feels the cri-de-coeur of the practising scholar, and one remembers that point that he learned from Meiggs – always to remember that these are real people, and to put yourself in their shoes, in this case the very large shoes of Thucydides himself.[61] Why did Thucydides dilate on the end of the Peisistratid tyranny? 'The most plausible explanation is that he succumbed here to the temptation before which all historians and commentators are by their very nature weak, the temptation to correct historical error wherever they find it, regardless of its relevance to their immediate purpose' (*HCT* iv.329 on 6.54–9 = 1965a, 62).[62] And why does Thucydides seem to assume that an audience, without maps and typically without local knowledge, would know immediately what to make of names like 'Dascon' or 'the fig-tree'? 'Now, he cannot consciously have assumed that his readers ... were familiar with the environs of Syracuse ... His apparent assumption of our [i.e. his readers'] familiarity with places and objects rests on his own familiarity with them as recurrent elements in the many individual narratives on which he based his history ...' (*HCT* iv.467, from the Appendix on topography). I can confirm that from my own experience as a commentator: one spends so long trying to make sense of it all, in our case from the 'many individual narratives' in Thucydides himself, that it is hard to bear in mind what you have already made clear to your readers and what you have not.

Still, again there are times when he may make Thucydides *too* like himself. One must not overstate this: he knows Thucydides has a tendency to exaggerate, especially in those superlative 'greatest in this war' and 'greatest ever' statements,[63] and he is ready – more ready than Gomme, in fact – to slap Thucydides on the wrist when he thinks there are mistakes or signs of carelessness.[64] But I do wonder if his own taste for plain lucid expression can lead him astray. One of Thucydides' most delightful paradoxes comes when he is describing the Syracusan frustration when, at a point when the balance had tilted and things seemed to be going so well, the massive Athenian reinforcements suddenly appeared in the Great Harbour: they were seriously shaken εἰ πέρας μηδὲν ἔσται σφίσι τοῦ ἀπαλλαγῆναι τοῦ κινδύνου (7.42.2) – is there to be no end of this escaping from danger? They have heaved so many sighs of relief already, and now still another turnaround will be needed. It is the zigzagging of joyful release and renewed terror that is so hard to take. But Dover, along admittedly with other commentators, does not take it that way: he seems to take it as the more pedestrian 'if there is to be no end *consisting in* escape from danger', and he quotes a parallel from the orator Demosthenes (in fact pseudo-Demosthenes, 40.40: *HCT* iv.419). In fact, that Demosthenic passage makes the same paradoxical point. The speaker there has already had the issues dealt with, in his favour, in several previous arbitrations and cases: τί γὰρ ἂν ἦν πέρας ἡμῖν τοῦ διαλυθῆναι; How many more times does he need to be let off? How many more times before this is settled?[65]

Then there is the absence of literary comment. One cannot complain about that too much in *HCT* itself, though one can complain a little, and I shortly will. This is after all a *Historical Commentary*, and he makes it clear in the 'Thucydides as history and as literature' paper that '... in writing my portion of it I consistently regarded understanding Thucydides as a means and understanding the Peloponnesian War as an end' (1983a, 55–6 = 1988a, 55 = Rusten 2009, 47). That may be one reason why, at least in my view, the commentary on 6 is more successful than that on 7 as well as much longer (182 pages to 87, or 2.60 pages per OCT page to 1.28); commentators tend to be fuller on 6 than on 7, but not to this degree – Hornblower's figures are 279 to 205, or 3.99 per OCT page to 3.01, and my own 227 to 173, or 3.24 to 2.54.[66] Book 6 gave Dover the chance to dilate on the herms and the Mysteries, with juicy chronological puzzles and a major inscription to discuss (*HCT* iv.264–88), and there is also important epigraphic material illuminating the decision to sail (*HCT* iv. 223–7). These show Dover at the top of his game.[67] Book 6 has more speeches too than any other book, and their sometimes bewilderingly difficult sentences offer plenty of scope for his muscular linguistic wrestling.

The glories of Book 7, by contrast, are more literary. 'His emotions are rather more in evidence in Book VII than elsewhere' (Dover 1965b, 24, cf. *HCT* iv.410), and Dover finds less to say about such passages. He does not even mention the remarkable passage of 'Longinus' on the grimness at the Assinarus, with men fighting to drink the befouled bloody water (7.84): 'the best hyperboles are the ones that do not even seem hyperbolic' in the emotion of the moment (*On the Sublime* 38.3). On the pathetic fate of Mycalessus

(7.29–30) Dover emphasizes that it was the Athenian deployment of Thracian barbarians that might have aroused particularly bitter condemnation, and 'Interesting parallels are to be found in the use of Red Indians by British, French, and Americans in the late eighteenth and early nineteenth centuries' (*HCT* iv.410; 1965a, 24 is almost identical). True, no doubt, but a bit bloodless, and such passages do not show him at his best; in everyday life, as he admits in *Marginal Comment*, he was never comfortable with the emotional.[68] One reviewer – Westlake, on the whole a big fan – noted the absence of any signs of enthusiasm: 'Nevertheless, the virtual absence of acknowledgement, explicit or implicit, that the sixth and seventh books have any particular merit may lead less knowledgeable readers of this commentary to imagine that they have none' (Westlake 1972, 191).

If the rubric of a *Historical Commentary* gave him good reason to be light on the literary side, the same cannot be said of the school commentaries five years earlier. When one compares the introductions with what a commentator would offer today, one is struck by the points that are not there: there is nothing, for instance, on the relation of Book 6 to the Melian Dialogue; nothing on the structure of Book 7, with its three narrative climaxes of Night Battle, Battle in the Great Harbour, and the final retreat and slaughter; nothing on how the Sicilian books go together, with the end of 7 picking up many themes from the beginning of 6. The sections on 'language and style' are much more about language than style, or perhaps one should say that they concentrate on the narrowest features of style – the 'reference of demonstratives', 'the unemphatic anaphoric pronoun αὐτόν', 'the possessive adjective σφέτερος' and so on. There is nothing on how scenes are built up, how pace is varied, how historic presents or scene-setting imperfects are used. This is admittedly over fifty years ago, and these gaps would not have seemed so glaring at the time; in his review Westlake indeed commented that, despite their brevity, the introductions 'do not, it seems, leave out anything that the student needs to be told' (1966, 26), though N.G.L. Hammond did miss a section on 'narrative style' (1966, 186). This was very much the context when the Cambridge green-and-yellows were launched to meet a gap in the market for commentaries that dwelt on literary questions,[69] and they were sorely needed. But one does also recall that insistence that he had never tried to be a literary critic.

The notes in those school commentaries themselves are often miracles of concision, and his gift for lucidity is here of immense value;[70] even if sometimes the density pushes the limits of easy reading,[71] it is hard to think that on these points he could have made much better use of the space he was presumably allowed, and perhaps he can be forgiven, given the need to keep things simple, for giving clear-cut explanations of the Greek syntax when it is possible that different native speakers might not all have heard that syntax in the same way.[72] Clarifying the topography must have been particularly difficult to do as he was allowed only one small map, but he does it marvellously.[73] The economy with which he conveys the historical background, on a strictly need-to-know basis, is also remarkable. He certainly takes a fairly high facility with basic grammar for granted,[74] and in some of the real monster sentences – and they are not few in these books – even a gifted linguist could do with being led more gently through the whole thing, not just helped with the beastliest phrases; but he wisely often chooses just to translate literally to make the sentence structure clear.

There are however times when the shying away from literary comment and interpretation leads to silence on other points that his target readers need, or might at least want, to know.

The end of Alcibiades' first speech is a good example (6.18.3–7, with p. 31 of the school commentary [Figure 7.1] and pp. 254–5 of *HCT*): I will base most of what I say on the school commentary in the first instance but keep an eye on *HCT* as well.

DEBATE AT ATHENS 31

in this light, and Alkibiades will have been among those who shared his view.

3. **καὶ οὐκ ἔστιν ἡμῖν ... ἄρχοιμεν**: The danger of inactivity on the part of an imperial city is a recurrent theme in the speeches of Thucydides' Perikles. ἄρχειν is used here straightforwardly, and without apology, of Athens' relation to her Empire.

4. **τάδε ... ἐκεῖνα**: 'Our empire *here* ... our enemies in *Sicily*.'

εἰ δόξομεν: '(sc. as we shall) if it is seen (sc. as it will be) that we ...'

ἄρξομεν ... κακώσομεν: Although these words are co-ordinated with the final clause ἵνα ... στορέσωμεν, the mood (in both senses of the word) changes, the change being helped by εἰ δόξομεν; emendation to produce grammatical uniformity would spoil the rhetorical effect.

5. **τὸ δὲ ἀσφαλές κτλ.**: lit., 'safety, both for staying ... and for departing'. The infinitives simply amplify τὸ ἀσφαλές, and ἀσφαλές should not be regarded as an attributive adjective qualifying a substantival infinitive τὸ μένειν. Cf. X. *An.* i. 3. 13 ἀπορία ... καὶ μένειν καὶ ἀπιέναι.

6. **τοῖς νέοις**: Used instead of the expected objective genitive, for variation after Νικίου τῶν λόγων.

ἐς τάδε κτλ.: The sentiment is that of Thucydides' Perikles, i. 144. 4 οἱ γοῦν πατέρες ἡμῶν ... ἐς τάδε προήγαγον αὐτά, and immediately below we find another 'Periklean' phrase, ὥσπερ καὶ ἄλλο τι; cf. i. 142. 9 τέχνης ἐστί, ὥσπερ καὶ ἄλλο τι.

τό τε φαῦλον κτλ.: The idea that health in the body depends on the right 'mixture' (κρᾶσις) of unlike elements in its constitution is a commonplace in the earlier Greek medical works; and the ethical doctrine that right action is a mean between extremes is related to this.

ἐγγηράσεσθαι: 'The skill of all' is the subject, the point of ἐγ- being 'in the city', but with ἀγωνιζομένην we return to 'the city' as subject; for the succession of subjects A–B–A cf. 86. 2 n.

7. **γιγνώσκω ... δοκεῖν**: There is no tautology here; Alkibiades is delivering his γνώμη, i.e. his opinion on the matter under debate, and γιγνώσκω formally indicates that.

ἀπραγμοσύνης μεταβολῇ: 'By a change *to* inactivity'. The 'philosophy' of πολυπραγμοσύνη, advocated in § 3 on the grounds that any alternative is dangerous for a city that rules an empire, is defended also in 87. 2 (v. n.) and by Perikles in ii. 63. 2 f.

οἳ ἄν ... πολιτεύωσιν: Appeal to traditional practice and character was always rhetorically cogent; Kleon is represented as exploiting it in the debate on Mytilene, iii. 37. 3 f.

Figure 7.1 Commentary on Thucydides 6.18.3–7 from Dover 1965a, 31.

[18.3] καὶ οὐκ ἔστιν ἡμῖν ταμιεύεσθαι ἐς ὅσον βουλόμεθα ἄρχειν, ἀλλ' ἀνάγκη, ἐπειδήπερ ἐν τῶιδε καθέσταμεν, τοῖς μὲν ἐπιβουλεύειν, τοὺς δὲ μὴ ἀνιέναι, διὰ τὸ ἀρχθῆναι ἂν ὑφ' ἑτέρων αὐτοῖς κίνδυνον εἶναι, εἰ μὴ αὐτοὶ ἄλλων ἄρχοιμεν. καὶ οὐκ ἐκ τοῦ αὐτοῦ ἐπισκεπτέον ὑμῖν τοῖς ἄλλοις τὸ ἥσυχον, εἰ μὴ καὶ τὰ ἐπιτηδεύματα ἐς τὸ ὁμοῖον μεταλήψεσθε. [18.4] Λογισάμενοι οὖν τάδε μᾶλλον αὐξήσειν, ἐπ' ἐκεῖνα ἢν ἴωμεν, ποιώμεθα τὸν πλοῦν, ἵνα Πελοποννησίων τε στορέσωμεν τὸ φρόνημα, εἰ δόξομεν ὑπεριδόντες τὴν ἐν τῶι παρόντι ἡσυχίαν καὶ ἐπὶ Σικελίαν πλεῦσαι· καὶ ἅμα ἢ τῆς Ἑλλάδος τῶν ἐκεῖ προσγενομένων πάσης τῶι εἰκότι ἄρξομεν, ἢ κακώσομέν γε Συρακοσίους, ἐν ὧι καὶ αὐτοὶ καὶ οἱ ξύμμαχοι ὠφελησόμεθα. [18.5] τὸ δὲ ἀσφαλές, καὶ μένειν, ἤν τι προχωρῆι, καὶ ἀπελθεῖν, αἱ νῆες παρέξουσιν· ναυκράτορες γὰρ ἐσόμεθα καὶ ξυμπάντων Σικελιωτῶν. [18.6] καὶ μὴ ὑμᾶς ἡ Νικίου τῶν λόγων ἀπραγμοσύνη καὶ διάστασις τοῖς νέοις ἐς τοὺς πρεσβυτέρους ἀποτρέψῃ, τῶι δὲ εἰωθότι κόσμωι, ὥσπερ καὶ οἱ πατέρες ἡμῶν ἅμα νέοι γεραιτέροις βουλεύοντες ἐς τάδε ἦραν αὐτά, καὶ νῦν τῶι αὐτῶι τρόπωι πειρᾶσθε προαγαγεῖν τὴν πόλιν, καὶ νομίσατε νεότητα μὲν καὶ γῆρας ἄνευ ἀλλήλων μηδὲν δύνασθαι, ὁμοῦ δὲ τό τε φαῦλον καὶ τὸ μέσον καὶ τὸ πάνυ ἀκριβὲς ἂν ξυγκραθὲν μάλιστ' ἂν ἰσχύειν, καὶ τὴν πόλιν, ἐὰν μὲν ἡσυχάζῃ, τρίψεσθαί τε αὐτὴν περὶ αὑτὴν ὥσπερ καὶ ἄλλο τι, καὶ πάντων τὴν ἐπιστήμην ἐγγηράσεσθαι, ἀγωνιζομένην δὲ αἰεὶ προσλήψεσθαί τε τὴν ἐμπειρίαν καὶ τὸ ἀμύνεσθαι οὐ λόγωι ἀλλ' ἔργωι μᾶλλον ξύνηθες ἕξειν. [18.7] παράπαν τε γιγνώσκω πόλιν μὴ ἀπράγμονα τάχιστ' ἄν μοι δοκεῖν ἀπραγμοσύνης μεταβολῆι διαφθαρῆναι, καὶ τῶν ἀνθρώπων ἀσφαλέστατα τούτους οἰκεῖν οἳ ἂν τοῖς παροῦσιν ἤθεσι καὶ νόμοις, ἢν καὶ χείρω ἦι, ἥκιστα διαφόρως πολιτεύωσιν.

Syntactic difficulties are concisely explained; there are also a few parallels with the rhetorical technique in Pericles' or Cleon's speeches, though today we might want to say more about the point of, particularly, those Periclean echoes. But he does not comment on some startling figures of speech: 'we cannot be stewards (ταμιεύεσθαι) of how far we wish to be rulers'; 'to lay low the spirit of the Peloponnesians' (where a scholion comments that 'this is the harshest figure in Thucydides but in keeping for Alcibiades'); the body does best with a mix of τό τε φαῦλον καὶ τὸ μέσον καὶ τὸ πάνυ ἀκριβές; the best way for a city to ward off senescence (ἐγγηράσεσθαι) of its skill is by constant contending (ἀγωνιζομένην), a suitably athletic image in the mouth of this Olympic victor and one that ties into a subtly developed motif that culminates in the rousing Syracusan cry of καλὸς ὁ ἀγών before the Great Battle (7.68.3). Dover's target reader might not merely be struck by these, but also wonder what several actually mean. Does στορέσωμεν mean 'lay flat' rather than 'cast to the winds'? (Yes, probably.) Why should including anything φαῦλον be good for a mixture? What is meant by τὸ πάνυ ἀκριβές? What exactly would a fifth-century 'steward' do that is so comparable, given that sixth-formers in 1965 did not come across many stewards in the everyday run of life? Dover does note the importance of medical works in the background of the 'mixture' idea and says a little more in *HCT*, but there are other medical tinges here too (the dangers of a μεταβολή, the notion of a body's senescence), and there might also be some link with Nicias' earlier call to the presiding chairman to be an ἰατρός of the city (14). It is not that Dover does not know the difficulties, though the equivalent pages of *HCT* are also pretty thin on these points; still, he would later give over three pages of discussion to στορέσωμεν in *EGPS* 119–23. Of course, he had very little space, though he could have allowed himself more in *HCT*. But interesting choices are made here.

Let us finally go back to *HCT* and remember that scholion comment on the boldness of the figure being 'in keeping for Alcibiades': Dover does quote that in *HCT*, though not in the school version. That, then, is the sort of 'characterization by style' that Dover would still be flatly denying in 1980 and 1981 (above, p. 119) and also explicitly rejected in 1965 and 1970.[75] This affects some of his textual choices. At 6.38.4, for instance, he implies a preference for Weil's κολάζειν rather than the manuscripts' κολάζων. That preference has the effect of making Athenagoras promise 'to persuade' the people to punish any plotters whereas the MSS text makes Athenagoras do the punishing himself; but is not such an anticipatory brag in character for the loud-mouthed blusterer? There are other 'literary' points too that pass Dover by. His comments on the reasons for the Peisistratid digression (partly quoted above, p. 120) are rather reductionist, and later critics have found much more to say about its resonance with the events of 415 than Dover allowed when he dismissed such approaches rather sniffily ('to discover such similarities . . . we have to adopt a standpoint far removed from that of the candid reader', *HCT* iv.328–9; similarly 1965a, 62).[76] And he is surely over-hasty in dismissing the Herodotean allusion in the πανωλεθρίαι of Thucydides' final words at 7.87.6.[77]

All this might seem over-negative about what is undeniably one of the great books of our time, and under-grateful to a work which, along with Hornblower 2008, has been always on my desk and usually open for the last two years. (Full tribute to Oxford University Press, incidentally, that it is not falling physically to pieces, which is more than can be said for my Thucydides OCTs.) Doubtless, as a literary type, I am over-emphasizing what he does not do and have not said enough about the value of what he did do; a professional ancient historian would put the stress differently. And most certainly it is better to work on an author to whom you feel temperamentally close, and perhaps that mattered particularly with Dover. He after all made his coolness about Plato clear in the preface to his *Symposium*,[78] and many have felt that that commentary falls short of his others (see Sheffield in this volume). The 'Informal History' of the Press commented on the first volume of Gomme that it would prove to be 'of the enduring kind',[79] and his continuators lived up to the standard he had set. Dover was quite right in what he said to his parents: nobody in the world could have done it better.[80]

Notes

1. Russell and Halliwell 2012, 156.
2. Russell and Halliwell 2012, 158, 'an author with whose fastidious rationality he undoubtedly felt a close affinity'. Similarly, 160. He is not the only modern scholar of whom this has been said: so also Crawford 2009, 68 on Peter Brunt.

3. *MC* 72.
4. Gomme, Andrewes, Dover 1945–81 (henceforth *HCT*).
5. Dover 1965a and b. 'School commentaries' is what they will be called here for convenient discrimination from *HCT*, though the prefaces define the target audience more broadly as 'senior pupils in schools and students in universities'. The idea of a school edition had earlier been put to Gomme by Oxford University Press (letter of 7 February 1956: OUP file BACKB00549), but evidently did not appeal.
6. Dover is tactful about this at *MC* 76–7, but some impatience is visible in correspondence in the OUP files and may be sensed at *MC* 137. But Andrewes made a reasonably sprightly start: see n. 24 below.
7. Dover 1973b.
8. Dover 1997b, 88–104.
9. Dover 1960, 10, explaining why he has paid particular attention to Herodotus: 'He does not try, as Thucydides constantly tries, to say too much in too few words'.
10. *MC* 58–9. Two books of Thucydides had already figured among his extensive classical reading at St Paul's.
11. For Dover's interest in inscriptions from a linguistic point of view, see Prauscello, this volume.
12. Meritt, Wade-Gery, McGregor 1939–51.
13. Russell and Halliwell 2012, 154.
14. *MC* 208; 1988a, 308; and most elaborately in the preface to *EGPS* v. This disavowal should be seen in the context of Dover's broader tendency to regard all humanities as essentially historical: see Halliwell in this volume. In the preface to his *Theocritus* (Dover 1971) Dover similarly disavows any pretence to have contributed to 'the study of Hellenistic poetry at the level to which the experts in that field have accustomed us'. Thanks to Simon Hornblower for reminding me of this, and cf. Hunter in this volume.
15. Barrett 1964, Ogilvie 1965.
16. *MC* 75–6.
17. Dover 1953.
18. *MC* 72.
19. *MC* 72–5.
20. These may include the lectures on Thucydides 6 and 7 that he went on to give at St Andrews (Craik in this volume, p. 54).
21. Letter home, 19 October 1959.
22. Letter home, 14 November 1959.
23. *MC* 77.
24. In October 1960 Andrewes reported that he had about a quarter of the commentary on Book 8 in draft, but there was much still to do on Book 5 (letter to Dan Davin of OUP, 3.10.60: OUP file BACKB00549).
25. Dover 1983a.
26. The debate was triggered by important remarks of Levene 2010, 84–6 and Damon 2010: see then the working papers from two conferences in 2011 and 2013 collected at https://research.ncl.ac.uk/histos/Histos_WorkingPapers.html. My own paper was published as Pelling 2013.

27. Dover 1983a, 55 = 1988a, 54 = Rusten 2009, 46.
28. 1983a, 61–2 = 1988a, 62–3 = Rusten 2009, 56–7, criticizing Hunter 1973. Hunter's suggested reasons for Thucydides' tweaking are admittedly not those that I go on to offer here. The uncompromising 'liar' prefigures W.K. Pritchett's similar call-a-spade-a-spade *The Liar School of Herodotus* (Pritchett 1993).
29. Connor 1984a, 197 n. 33.
30. Woodman 1988.
31. 1983a, 59–60 = 1988a, 60 = Rusten 2009, 53–4. On what both Dover and Thucydides might have meant by this, see Halliwell, this volume, pp. 295–6 and 312 n. 42.
32. Stahl 1966.
33. 1983a, 63 = 1988a, 64 = Rusten 2009, 59.
34. Davies 2016.
35. *HCT* iv.274 (μετοίκων at 6.28.1), 328 and 331 (aspects of the Peisistratid digression).
36. Pelling 2021, 231–5.
37. Canfora replied at length in a particularly lavish review (Canfora 1983).
38. Cf. in particular *HCT* v.434 n. 2.
39. Much of what follows, especially in terms of approach, could also be said about Jacqueline de Romilly's much earlier *Thucydide et l'impérialisme athénien*, published in 1947. A great deal of that book is concerned with questions of strata and the criteria for distinguishing them, and she argues for some changes of emphasis and signs of revision while insisting that the general view of imperialism remains constant until 404 (e.g. p. 171 of the translation, 'his opinions have not altered, but his preoccupations are no longer the same', of a contrast she sees between 2.65 written after the war and the Mytilenean Debate which she takes to have been written much earlier; cf. pp. 228–9). Still, most of the argument with her predecessors is negative, and (e.g.) 'it is therefore expedient to call a halt when confronted by so carefully finished a result that the process leaves no trace' (p. 154). Much ground is thereby cleared for further discussion of the other interesting aspects covered in de Romilly's book and her later *Histoire et Raison* (1956). Dover, we should notice, quite often quotes de Romilly generously in *HCT* and in his 1973 *New Survey*.
40. Cf. Rhodes' summary of the upshot in his review (1984, 204): 'it would be good if one could think that no one will ever again return to a crudely unitarian approach'.
41. Andrewes 1959.
42. Esp. *MC* 201, on *EGPS*: 'I began, as always, with my own experience'; in the case of *Greek Popular Morality* (1974), 'Introspective analysis', 161, and on this as a feature of that book see Carey in this volume, p. 151; also Cartlidge, p. 281, on the link between Dover's understanding of style and his own experience of agonizing over a single sentence (*MC* 201). Dover 1983a begins with several pages on his own experience in compiling an account of the Blunt affair. On this self-referential tendency see also Halliwell in this volume, p. 292; Sheffield, pp. 141–2 similarly notes his tendency to over-generalize from his own response to *Symposium*.
43. Dover's citation of Marcus 1966, 87 makes clear that this was *My Secret Life* (anonymous, but the author sometimes refers to himself as 'Walter'), an eleven-volume work that appeared over several years towards the end of Victoria's reign: see 'Walter' 1972.
44. This expands the similar point he had already made in Dover 1973b, 24.
45. Here we can contrast his successor-commentator Hornblower, who suggested that Thucydides' language can be deliberately evasive when profound political issues are involved (Hornblower 2004, 368).

46. Thus 404 n. 2 may come closer to home than he would have found comfortable: 'It may well be that what Thucydides says in i. 22 about his aims and methods creates in his readers the unconscious expectation that he will always live up to the standards which they would have in mind if they formulated those standards in his words.' There was a similar warning against unconscious transfer of expectations already in Dover 1953, 19 = 1968, 367.
47. Cf. Dover 1973b, 22. A different approach: Pelling 2000, 114–22 = Rusten 2009, 176–87.
48. For a similar 'we' in the commentary itself cf. *HCT* iv.198, on the Sicilian 'archaeology': 'We might have expected Thucydides to amplify his judgement (1. 1), that the Athenians did not realize the magnitude of their task, by giving us an account of the population and resources of Sicily as they were in 415.' This then seems, though he is not quite explicit on this, to be one of the reasons why he favours a large debt to an earlier source, he thinks Antiochus of Syracuse. He does not consider the literary advantages of feeding material to his readers/listeners gradually, just as it would have all become clearer and clearer at the time to the public and the participants themselves; nor the possibility that (for instance) those Odyssean 'Cyclopes' and 'Laestrygonians' (6.2.1) could reinforce the idea of a plunge into a world very different from contemporary Athens. Nor does he wonder whether the Ionic flavour of the language may be a gesture towards the typically Ionic texture of earlier ethnography rather than drawn mechanically from the diction of that single posited source. The treatment of these chapters' chronological puzzles is however authoritative.
49. See p. 125; cf. Dover 1997b, 98. In the *Greece & Rome* New Survey he puts it less absolutely: 'there is very little individual characterization of speakers' (1973b, 23).
50. Tompkins 1972. Stephen Halliwell points out to me the equally startling silence concerning the first few Thucydides papers of Colin Macleod; in particular, the treatment of Alcibiades' speech at Thuc. 6.16–18 (Macleod 1983, 68–87, first published in 1975) has much to say about both style and content.
51. As Tompkins has now done for both (2013 and 2015). I say more about Nicias' style at Pelling 2022a, 126, 251–2 and 2022b, 109, 203, 234–5; about Alcibiades' at Pelling 2022a, 146, and 290–1; and about Hermocrates' at Pelling 2022a, 186 and 285–6.
52. See esp. Griffin 1986.
53. Dover may similarly have underplayed the differences between different parts of the narrative: Connor's review observes that he neglects the possibility, already aired by Wade-Gery in *OCD*, that Thucydides could have played with different narrative techniques for different stretches, and that the variations need not be due to incomplete revision (1984, 231).
54. The question whether πᾶσαν qualifies ἀρετήν or ἐπιτήδευσιν. In 1965 Dover favoured ἐπιτήδευσιν; the discussion in 1970 tilted, so it seems, towards ἀρετήν.
55. Not that this was a novel view: the point had been made strongly by Donini in 1964, as Dover acknowledges. In his 1981 paper (next n.) he adds that Donini's article, like his own contribution, originated in a seminar during his time at Harvard in 1960.
56. These particularly concern (a) the relation to Lamachus' opinion at 6.49 (not a total match, but a similarity of mindset), and (b) exactly when Demosthenes is implying such an attack should have taken place. One might still wonder if Demosthenes would really have bothered to refight mentally that campaign and sort out which of several missed opportunities mattered most. Dover tends to presume, both in *HCT* and in his later revisiting of the issue in Dover 1981a, that he would. This may therefore be a further case where he assumed that people were closer to his own temper and mindset than they necessarily were.
57. It would be surprising if everything survived unscathed after fifty years. To take just two examples, (a) he seems to have been wrong in assuming that Athenian ships were largely rowed by non-citizens (he thought mercenaries, *HCT* iv.442) and non-slaves (*HCT* iv.388),

with the Athenians themselves contributing only the officer class. It is now thought that both citizens and slaves rowed as well (Graham 1992 and 1998); cf. Hornblower 2008 on 7.13.2, a passage where this affects a textual decision that Dover made. (b) At 6.14 he seems wrong to take λύειν τοὺς νόμους as 'abolishing our established procedure' rather than the seemingly more obvious 'break the laws': Harris 2014 here has the better of the argument.

58. For instance, at 6.30.1 it is important that θέρους μεσοῦντος ἤδη means, not 'at the time of the summer solstice', but 'after the middle period of the summer had begun' (*HCT* iv.271), and at 7.2.1 he teases from the phrasing several points that illuminate Gylippus' status and authority in Syracuse, drawing attention *inter alia* to the importance of a choice of reading at 7.22.1.

59. On the first, see Hornblower 2008 on 7.48.5; on the viability of Hermocrates' plan see Bloedow 1993 and Stahl 2003, 195–8.

60. Dover 1982, 41.

61. Cf. *HCT* v.405, 'That Thucydides was a real person and that caprice, inconsistency, inattention, and blind spots are normal ingredients of human personality are also facts.'

62. See also p. 125.

63. Above, p. 118.

64. E.g. *HCT* iv.247, 'no doubt there was sometimes a slight discrepancy between what Thucydides had actually written and his mental picture of what he had written'; iv.319, 'he does not always take enough trouble to put himself in the reader's place (cf. 4.1 n., 15.3f. n.) and our difficulty in identifying the subjects of verbs is one consequence of his negligence (cf. 18.6 n., 73.2, vii.18.3)'; *HCT* iv.328, 'Thucydides, not for the first time, has misled us in a way in which an author most commonly misleads his readers: by forgetting that we do not know what he knows'; *HCT* iv.420, outlining two views neither of which 'absolves Thucydides from a charge of rhetorical distortion'; *HCT* iv.456, 'Thucydides' characteristic lack of precision in his account of the fighting'. Westlake's review (1972, 191) notes the contrast with Gomme.

65. I am grateful here to Stephen Halliwell for alerting me to some of the complexities.

66. Fuller tables in Pelling 2021, 227.

67. Not that all his argument is beyond reproach, especially in the herms and Mysteries digression. A good deal of the detailed chronology depends on the assumption that the Salaminia must have returned from Sicily before the Panathenaea, as Andromachus and Teucer would not have received their rewards at that festival unless the guilt of those they had denounced was by then regarded as established (*HCT* iv.274, cf. 276). But Alcibiades and others in Sicily were not the only ones they had denounced (Andoc. 1.12, 15, 34–5); it may easily be that the guilt of enough people was regarded as sufficiently clear well before the Salaminia returned. For criticism of further aspects cf. e.g. Furley 1996, 28 n. 87, 47 n. 26; Pelling 2000, 36; and Dover himself later withdrew one minor tentative suggestion (1974, 8 n. 1). But these carpings are minor, and most has stood up extraordinarily well. In particular, his mastery of the intricacies of the Athenian calendar and his disentangling of the sequence of denunciations remain deeply impressive: 'a *tour de force* of thoroughness, independence . . . and acumen' (Hornblower 2008, 368, in agreement with Lewis 1977, 74).

68. 'If I call someone "emotional", I imply: unreasonable, impatient, bad-tempered, unreliable, to be avoided if possible' (*MC* 28).

69. On this series see Gibson 2021.

70. Good examples are his notes on 6.23.1, 62.2, 7.10–15 (introductory n.), 7.36.2, 7.69.2, and 7.78.2. In some cases Dover is clearer or fuller in these commentaries than in *HCT*:

Hornblower 2008 notes cases at 6.15.4, 7.28.3, 7.48.5, 7.47–59.1, 7.71.4, 7.79.3, and 7.84.2; one could add e.g. 6.56.1 (shift from singular to plural), 6.66.2 (reasons for retaining ἔρυμά τι), 7.48.3 (reference of σφῶν αὐτῶν), 7.63.3 (Athenians contributing only officers rather than oarsmen, though he is probably wrong about this: cf. n. 57).

71. e.g. the 1965 notes on 6.34.9, 6.77.2 (misnumbered as 77.1), 6.82.4, 7.28.3, 7.57.4, and 7.68.1.
72. Examples: the Syracusans press the Spartans to renew the war more energetically 'so that either they ἀπαγάγωσιν them or that they should be less able to send reinforcements to the army in Sicily' (6.73.2). The second 'they' is clearly the Athenians, but is the first 'they' the Spartans, forcing the Athenians out, or the Athenians, deciding to withdraw'? It could be either, but Dover is clear: it is the Athenians (1965a, 78). Nicias tells the Athenians how bad things have become – why, they are virtually under siege themselves: οὐδὲ γάρ the surrounding countryside is accessible to them because of the Syracusan cavalry (7.11.4). 'Not even' the countryside, or 'we cannot venture into the countryside either'? For Dover, the second (1965b, 8, HCT iv.387). Demosthenes, newly arrived in Sicily, presses forward with his troops ὅπως τῆι παρούσηι ὁρμῆι τοῦ περαίνεσθαι ὧν ἕνεκα ἦλθον μὴ βραδεῖς γένωνται (7.43.5). Is the genitive τοῦ περαίνεσθαι to be construed with βραδεῖς – an unusual construction, but possible for 'slow in the accomplishment' – or with ὁρμῆι, 'momentum towards the accomplishment'? For Dover, the first (1965b, 36, HCT iv.422). Equally, there are times when his decisiveness is welcome. He is almost certainly right to insist that at 6.6.2 Λεοντίνων must be taken with ξυμμαχίαν rather than with πολέμου ('the Leontini war'), even though Osborne and Rhodes 2017, 96–7 prefer the second interpretation.
73. e.g. 1965a on 6.96.1, 'There are few places where the edges of the plateau present any difficulty to a man picking his way up or down, but even fewer where a body of troops could move straight up in formation'; also the notes on 6.99.3 and 6.101.4.
74. Westlake 1966, 27: 'Dover is not disposed to make much concession to the frailties of less advanced students …'.
75. 1965a and b, p. xi in both volumes. Cf. HCT iv.229 on the debate as a whole, 'he casts their arguments into his own peculiar language'.
76. And not just later ones: Stahl had already found much to say in 1966 (his ch. 1). Subsequently cf. *inter alia* Hunter 1973, 174 n. 28, Connor 1984, 176–80, Tsakmakis 1995, 176–225 and 1996, Rood 1998, 180–1. Kallet 2006, 340–4, Pothou 2009, 144–51, and Hornblower 2008 and Pelling 2022a ad loc.
77. Cf. Kallet 2001, 114–5. The allusion would be to Hdt. 2.120.5 on the fall of Troy, and Dover notes Strasburger's suggestion (1958, 39 n. 3 = Herter 1968, 529–30 n. 83 = Rusten 2009, 216 n. 82) to that effect. He thinks it 'refuted' by the phrasing 'in utter ruin, *as they say*' (πανωλεθρίαι δὴ τὸ λεγόμενον); hardly. It is true, as he says, that Thucydides might have had difficulty in subscribing to Herodotus' theology in that important passage, but that again might be the point (so e.g. Grethlein 2008, 137–8).
78. Dover 1980a, viii.
79. Sutcliffe 1978, 257.
80. Many thanks to the Secretary to the Delegates of Oxford University Press for permission to reproduce Figure 7.1 (p. 123) and to quote from the Thucydides commentaries, and to Charlotte Loveridge and Martin Maw for facilitating access to their files; and to Stephen Halliwell, Simon Hornblower, Tim Rood, Richard Rutherford, Chris Stray and Dan Tompkins for helpful comments on an earlier draft.

CHAPTER 8
DOVER AND PLATO'S *SYMPOSIUM*: ATTRACTION, AVERSION AND INTEMPERANCE
Frisbee C.C. Sheffield

Dover spent many years working on Plato's *Symposium*, which resulted in what is still held to be one of the best editions of the text, and which motivated groundbreaking work on Greek homosexuality.[1] Such sustained engagement with Plato might seem surprising, however, since Dover by his own admission was not philosophically inclined and seemed averse to Plato. What, then, explains the appeal of the *Symposium*? Dover's later reflections refer to the fact that when he was prompted to lecture on a Platonic text the attraction of the *Symposium* was that 'it is devoted to a series of encomia, delivered at an imaginary party, in honour of Eros, the god who is the personification of sexual love'; he was also drawn to its 'treatment of homosexual eros as eros *par excellence*' (*MC* 111). Much of Dover's interest in homosexuality was in fact stimulated by study of the *Symposium*, rather than the other way round, and the work's literary artistry does not suffice to explain why Dover engages with the *Symposium* rather than, say, the *Phaedrus*, which arguably provides equal interest to those interested both in Greek prose style and in Greek homosexuality.[2] Taking my lead from Dover's self-characterization in the autobiography, where he explains that he was 'an English empiricist to the core' (*MC* 146), I will argue that if one were to take a Platonic work and sanitize it for the empirically minded, there may be no better choice than the *Symposium*. It is not just the content, but also the distinctive form that may have sustained his interest; the *Symposium* is the most multivocal of Plato's works, and its structure resists the dogmatic tone that Dover found so irritating in works where 'politicians and litigants' are 'criticised so articulately' (1980a, viii). Dover's aversion to Plato's philosophy remains conspicuous, however, in the commentary; this chapter will explore its basis in the empirical orientation identified above, along with how this shaped the questions he identified as central for this text. But since this hostility is targeted towards Socrates and Diotima, the work still leaves a distinctive content and form to satisfy Dover, allowing the commentary to develop its dominant concerns with Greek homosexuality and prose style. This is Plato for the empirically minded literary historian.

Dover and philosophy

Dover's distaste for Plato is so apparent in the *Symposium* commentary that he was urged to moderate his views for the second printing on the grounds that they appeared 'intemperate'.³ He confesses that he was not philosophically inclined, and 'had never previously tackled any philosophical text more advanced than the *Apology*' (*MC* 111) before being prompted to lecture on a Platonic text. Given Dover's disinclination for philosophy, and the distaste for Plato in particular, why did the *Symposium* appeal?

The aversion to Plato cannot be explained away as an aversion to philosophy period.⁴ Dover confesses to being 'an English empiricist to the core', aligning himself with a tradition whose major figurehead was John Locke.⁵ This allows us to appreciate why the *Symposium* may have been an appealing choice. A central point of contention in Locke's *Essay on Human Understanding* (Chapter I) is the doctrine of innate ideas, together with the metaphysical speculation and justification of certain principles this doctrine entailed. One of the issues that motivated Locke in this polemic was the supposition that we know innately certain maxims, including religious and moral principles such as that the soul is immortal and that god exists. This was a contentious issue in the seventeenth century when clerics and philosophers saw the foundations of morality and Christianity to be under threat and attempted to justify their principles by appealing to innate a priori ideas: if these were stamped on the minds of all humans, then they cannot be doubted and must be assented to.⁶ Central to Locke's work is an aversion to speculative metaphysics, rationalist epistemology, and the authoritarianism that can follow from both. Basing one's thinking on observable empirical facts was designed to liberate one from religious superstition, faith and dogma – all three elements which Dover identifies in Plato.

Evidently Dover and Plato will not be natural allies if one takes Plato to be someone who supposed that there exist intelligible forms which are implanted in the soul before birth and whose truth no rational agent can fail to appreciate. That Dover held in view Plato the metaphysician, the dogmatist, and even the proponent of a 'faith' masquerading as rational argument, is evident from the hypotheses which guide his commentary and are repeated elsewhere too. Consider the following from the Introduction to the *Symposium*:

> I do not find [Plato's] philosophical arguments even marginally persuasive. Much that is written about him is marked, in my view, by uncritical *enthusiasm for the abstract and immutable, as if such an enthusiasm always and necessarily afforded better access to the truth about man, nature and divinity than is afforded by a love of the particular, material and perishable* [my itals]. One consequence of this is that Plato is sometimes welcomed as an ally by people who would not like what they found if they attended less selectively and more precisely to what he actually says.⁷

The abstract and immutable need not come with the metaphysical determination Plato brought to them, of course; but Dover substantiates the basis of his failure to be persuaded by Plato in the autobiography as follows:

> 'It seemed to me that [Plato's] metaphysical arguments make sense only if one adopts, with the fervent faith patently characteristic of his Socrates, three axioms.

First, that since what we perceive of the world is subject to change and decay, *there must be something which is eternal and immutable*. Secondly, that since opinions and inferences founded on our experience of the world are corrigible, *there must be something which is understandable by incorrigible reasoning* [i.e. the theory of forms]. And thirdly, that if we follow the path of reason to the end, *we must perceive that ultimate reality is good*, and since love is necessarily our reaction to good, reason and love converge and fuse in the experience of that perception' [all itals D.'s].[8]

Here we have the key characteristics of Dover's Plato: speculative metaphysics, bolstered by faith, a rejection of experience as a guide to truth, and love as its crowning glory.[9]

This view of Plato, coupled with his own philosophical orientation, infuses Dover's suspicion of Plato at every turn, and shapes his work on the *Symposium*. Dover saw the 'most congenial' view in the dialogue to be the 'popular' view of *erôs* expressed by Aristophanes. As he states in one of three published papers on the work, one of the reasons for this is that 'we would rather accept *observed facts*, however mysterious, than close our eyes to them in order to construct a coherent metaphysical doctrine' (Dover 1966, 48, my itals); 'observed facts', 'respect for evidence' and 'observable realities' recur time and again in the commentary.[10] This orientation brings into sharper focus why the *Symposium* was the right text, if any, from amongst the Platonic canon. The *Symposium* dances tentatively between the so-called 'twin pillars of Platonism', the forms and the immortality of the soul; the doctrine of *anamnêsis* does not make an explicit appearance (see below), and the *Phaedo*-like notion of the immortality of the soul is eclipsed from view. Further, the one and only form mentioned is something that many, perhaps even Dover himself, would tolerate being discussed in transcendent terms. If one were to take a Platonic work and sanitize it for the empirically minded, there may be no better choice than the *Symposium*.

There is something decidedly pagan about the *Symposium*. It is not just that what are often taken to be key Platonic 'doctrines', along with the Socratic 'methodology' in which such ideas are often expressed, do not take centre stage; the treatment of those themes and practices is highly unorthodox when compared to other works. Consider *anamnêsis* first. If it is seen at all in this work, it is to be found in the claim that the characteristic activity of *erôs* is reproduction in the presence of beauty (206c). All human beings, we are told, are pregnant in both body and soul; within the soul this pregnancy consists in 'wisdom and the rest of virtue' (207c). This may be taken to suggest that there are 'embryonic truths' held innately in the soul.[11] This earthly, human model of innate ideas (*if* one accepts that it gestures towards such a notion, at least) 'forestalls' any questions about how the soul became pregnant in the first place, and with it any metaphysical speculation about previously acquired knowledge during incarnate existence.[12] Take the discussion of immortality next. This is not defended on rationalist grounds, or within an account of what must be true if something is to be a cause, followed by reflection on the essential properties of the soul as cause of life (for which see the final argument of Plato's *Phaedo*); immortality in the *Symposium* is a doctrine introduced *by observation* of the natural and animal worlds. We are given no account of forms as causes, or the *Phaedo*'s 'essential bearers' (102a–5d), from which arguments for immortality are launched in that text, but are told instead *to observe*: 'Do you not perceive, Socrates,' (ἢ οὐκ αἰσθάνῃ), Diotima begins, as she relays her account of immortality, how all animals alike are disposed by *erôs* for intercourse, reproduction and the nurture of their young (207a–b). This observation is then extended to gain further grounding in the natural cycles of birth, growth and death observed in the world around, all of which are exposed as carrying a deeper truth about the cause of *erôs*; human beings here are seen as part of nature and subject to its rhythms. As Dover summarizes Diotima's views: 'We see in animals the strength of the impulse to reproduce, rear and protect offspring; this proves that mortal nature strives after immortality. During a creature's life every element in the body perishes and is replaced; the same is true of the soul, wherein thoughts, emotions and knowledge are constantly renewed' (Dover 1980a, p. 149). Mortality, as he puts it (ibid.), is 'exalted' by the natural reproductive process, a view grounded in Dover's privileged triad of the 'particular, material and perishable' (Dover 1980a, p. viii). Even if, as Dover suggests, this model is no evidence that Plato dropped the immortality of the soul, the *Phaedo*-like formulation of that idea is eclipsed from view in favour of an account of immortality that has three characteristics Dover applauds elsewhere: 'the individual, the particular and the familiar'.[13] Desiring agents seek to reproduce what they value in their particular lives, be it 'laying up a name for themselves' via offspring, securing honour through heroic deeds, lawgiving, or creating virtue. This is far from the impersonal, abstract and unfamiliar account of the *Phaedo*.[14]

Though Dover may have been relieved by the absence of such distinctively 'Platonic' elements, by which I mean features such as transcendent forms and immortality, it is not as if the Platonic 'Socrates' fares any better in Dover's view; but he, too, is sanitized here. Dover dislikes Socrates on two counts: first, for his savage critiques of his fellow Athenians, those 'politicians and litigants' who are 'criticised so articulately', reduced to yes-men and compelled to a state of *aporia*; second, for 'the fervent faith patently characteristic of [Plato's] Socrates' (*MC* 117), which gave rise to implausible arguments fervently expressed.[15] These features, too, are moderated, by the encomiastic form of the *Symposium*. Socrates' distinctive philosophical mode is given unorthodox treatment; dialectic makes a meagre appearance in a work dominated by a literary form that Plato critiques (199d–201c; cf. *Lysis* 210e). Socrates is thwarted from his 'habitual' mode of speech (194d), and when it *is* integrated into his positive account with Diotima this seems to take the unusual form of didactic dialectic. There is no demolition job done on Socrates' peers, followed by *aporia*; the speeches, on the whole, escape the explicit critiques that so irked Dover (with the exception of the elenchus of Agathon: 199c–201d). Socrates appears as one speaker amongst many, all of whom seem to have roughly equal 'air-time', if not (to me at least) equal substance. Even those who are inclined to privilege Socrates' speech as the heart of the work must wrestle with the disruptive presence of Alcibiades, who thwarts any straightforward attempt to absorb the authoritative pronouncements of Socrates and Diotima. The *Symposium* is the most multivocal of Plato's works, allowing many voices from the Greek world to be heard in rich detail. This not only enables the text to be a valuable resource for the literary historian, but crucially resists that authoritarian tone that Dover found so irksome. For the clerics and philosophers versus Locke, understand Plato and Socrates versus 'politicians and litigants' – a contest now tempered to achieve plurality of a kind.

Even those who argue in favour of reading the speech of Socrates and Diotima as the climactic centre-piece (which Dover would doubtless resist) have to acknowledge how that speech works by incorporation and revision of previous views, in a manner reminiscent of the more empirically minded Aristotle.[16] Elements of many of the speakers' ideas are appropriated in Socrates' account, which professes to 'speak the truth'. For example, the claim that *erôs* desires what it lacks (191a); that *erôs* is of beauty (197b); that *erôs* for the soul is more valuable than *erôs* for the body (184a); that good things arise from the love of beautiful things (197b); that *erôs* aims at virtue (178c, 179a, 180b, 188d), the good (188d), and happiness (180b, 188d); that *erôs* must be governed by knowledge (188d; cf. 184d-e), or at the very least, that it has some intimate relationship to *phronesis* (182b-c, 184d), *episteme* (187c), *sophia* (196d), and that *erôs* brings together the human and the divine (188d). All the speakers, including Socrates, supplement and build on their predecessors in various ways, which lends itself to reading the speeches as one 'intertextual web',[17] a characteristic feature of sympotic discourse.

From the perspective of Socrates' distinctive philosophical goals as he states them here (199a-b), the previous speakers do not have an adequate grasp of *erôs*, so their opinions need modification and amplification; but there is enough continuity to lead one to wonder whether Socrates is using these earlier opinions in a more Aristotelian sense to guide inquiry.[18] These opinions are not taken by Socrates to be authoritative (previous speakers show no concern for truth, 198a-9a), and nor does Socrates try to preserve as many of them as possible in the final account (so much differs, perhaps, from Aristotle's 'endoxic method'); even when false, though, their underlying puzzles guide the inquiry in a productive direction. It is this continuity between the earlier opinions and Socrates' account that Dover embraces when he writes that in this text, we see Plato as 'an heir to the tradition of didactic poetry, a nursling of Attic drama and a product, no less than the politicians and litigants whom he criticised so articulately, of a culture'.[19] Philosophical views are embedded within their cultural traditions more vividly here perhaps than anywhere else. Situating the philosophical within the popular more explicitly may well have appealed to Dover's sense that there was much to be gleaned from studying 'popular' thought (which held a greater connection to his cherished 'observed facts'),[20] though as Adkins pointed out in his critical review of *Greek Popular Morality*, there is also more continuity between the 'popular' and the 'philosophical' than Dover appreciated.[21]

The fact that philosophical views are situated within Plato's cultural traditions so vividly in this work might suggest that this is something the topic of *erôs* demands. Perhaps *erôs*, as opposed to 'knowledge' or 'Being' as a topic, had a longer literary tradition, of which one could make use in an inquiry; but the point is surely not that *erôs* is a topic that would, by its very nature, somehow be free of the 'twin pillars of Platonism'. One need only compare the *Phaedrus*, which deploys forms and a robust argument for an impersonal immortality, grounded in an account of soul as a self-mover (245c-6a). It is for that reason that I have resisted focusing on the appeal of the topic too quickly. For it is not obvious why *erôs*, as opposed to knowledge or justice, for example, would by its very nature lend itself to treatment that shows not only that Plato was 'heir to a tradition' but also that he can free himself from what Dover considers to be metaphysical speculation (e.g. *anamnêsis* and *Phaedo*-like immortality), as the *Phaedrus* shows. The topic alone does not explain why someone averse to 'Platonism' would choose this text for such sustained work; it is rather the distinctive treatment of that topic in the *Symposium* that sugars the pill of Platonism for Dover, i.e. the dialogue's sanitized Platonic content and its tempered Socratic form.[22]

Dover, philosophy and *erôs*

The *Symposium*'s distinctive form allowed Dover to engage in the kind of multidisciplinary approach of which he gave such a virtuoso performance in *Greek Homosexuality*, where he created a beautiful synthesis of evidence from literature, oratory, visual art, mythology, religion and philosophy. The speakers seem to be representatives of a wide variety of Greek literary and cultural traditions and to reflect the intellectual currents at work in the fifth and fourth centuries. This medley enabled Dover to mine a variety of traditions for those norms of Greek homosexuality, in order to substantiate his sense that 'practically everything said during the last few centuries about the psychology, ethics and sociology of Greek homosexuality was confused and misleading' (*MC* 111). Here Pausanias' speech took centre stage, as it did in his 1964 paper, 'Eros and Nomos', reactions to which prompted Dover to decide to write *Greek Homosexuality* (*MC* 114), and which laid much of the groundwork for the book. The order of topics in the Introduction to Dover's edition shows his preferences: first *erôs*, then homosexuality, and after that we may do a bit of philosophy as required; the weight of the commentary falls very much in line with that order.

So how did this approach shape Dover's treatment of those topics? First, it enabled him to downplay the novelty of homosexual *erôs* in Plato's philosophy and locate its central point of interest for Plato by situating the topic within its literary and historical context. In answer to the question why Plato 'exploit[ed] exclusively homosexual emotion for his philosophical theory of *erôs*', Dover (1964a, 39) writes:

> The answer might be that he had no real alternative, that when men in his own milieu spoke of *erôs* and *eran* their reference was almost always homosexual, and that he accepted the fact that men pursued boys when leisure and wealth made them free to choose their pursuits. It must, however, be observed that even if he did have alternatives homosexual *erôs* still provided the most useful starting-point for his own theory ... The *pedagogic relation* is central to Plato's theory of *erôs* (cf. *Symp.* 211b–c; emphasis mine).

In other words, erotic relationships with young boys (of the sort that typically took place at symposia such as this one), were relatively standard practice in elite social circles and had an important educational dimension. Appreciating this allows one to shift the focus (rightly, I believe) away from speculation about Plato's own inclinations towards Plato's concern with the moral education of the young.[23]

Plato's account of *orthôs paiderastein* ('loving boys correctly', 211b) is deeply disappointing to Dover, of course. Here, aversion to the metaphysical guides Dover's critique and shapes what he takes to be *the* central contrast in the work: a clash between *homo Aristophaneus*, identified with the common man, committed to the 'individual, particular and familiar', and *homo Platonicus*, identified with the abstract, impersonal and formal. Plato, writes Dover (1964a, 40), claims that: 'a desire for a perishable object must necessarily be either a step on an upward path, so long as it is recognised as a step (*Symp.* 211c), or an error, if it is not recognised as a step.' Here he refers to the so-called 'ladder of love', where *erôs* for a beautiful individual is a step towards a grasp of the form of beauty. Leave aside for the moment the metaphysical determination that Plato will give to the end of that process and focus first on the notion of the 'upward path'. If the focus of the *Symposium* is the moral education of the young, and (as Dover rightly saw) homosexual *erôs* is the *context* for that account, it is not clear why Dover takes umbrage at the thought that Plato is advocating an 'upward path'; that is what education is supposed to be, and the pederastic institution of which Dover gave us such good evidence would have had little justification without it. This much at least is not Platonic invention, but Plato as 'heir to a tradition'.

This focus on the 'upward path' is indicated by the encomiastic format. Evidently, the speakers are aware that there is a longstanding literary tradition about *erôs*, so when Phaedrus remarks that *erôs* has never been properly *praised* (177c), we are to take that with emphasis; this is about the beneficial effects of *erôs* on human life, in other words, its educational import and how to do *orthôs paiderastein* (211b). *Erôs* was the subject of much poetry and prose (as Dover brings out so well in his commentary), so the emphasis falls on showing that *erôs* is a good thing and does good things. Neither the ode to *erôs* in the *Antigone* (781–801), nor the ode in Euripides' *Hippolytus* (525–64) could be seen as so focused.[24] This is the gap Phaedrus proposes to fill with encomia.[25] This perhaps explains why there is so little about the pleasures of *erôs* and such a lot about virtue and happiness (an 'upward path' if ever there was one).[26] This is conceived differently by different speakers, of course; but the point is that for *all* the speakers, *erôs* is a step on an upward path, be it honour on the battlefield for Phaedrus, the acquisition of virtue for Pausanias, medical balance and harmony for Eryximachus, or poetic creativity for Agathon.[27] Even Aristophanes suggests that lovers are aspiring to *something* beyond the interpersonal: the lovers who strive for each other are not aware of what they are really looking for (192d); their hidden aim is being fused with each other for ever, so that they can return to a former state of unity where they were closer to the divine (190b–c). Even if Aristophanes' speech is read as championing the individual in a blissful state of sexual union, this would make him the outlier within this pederastic, educational context; indeed, neither Eryximachus nor Agathon refers explicitly to ἐραστής– ἐρώμενος relationships or mentions gendered erotic pairings at all.

What explains Dover's emphasis on this contrast between *homo Aristophaneus* and *homo Platonicus* is shaped by his preference for the empirical over the metaphysical.

Consider some memorable passages. After Aristophanes' speech, Dover writes the following: 'Having composed for Aristophanes the only speech in *Smp.* which strikes a modern reader as founded *on observable realities*, Plato later makes Diotima reject and condemn its central theme' (Dover 1980a, 113; emphasis mine). Further, 'Plato believed', writes Dover, 'that popular values, as assumed and exemplified in comedy and folklore, were committed to the individual, the particular and the familiar, and that such a morality was irreconcilable with the practice of philosophy' (Dover 1966, 50). Consider also, the following: 'What becomes, on Diotima's theory, of the observed facts of what I have called "preference", and what is it *right* for A to do if he finds that he has preferred someone who, as his intelligence tells him, is an inferior medium? Is "preference" no more than an error?' (Dover 1966, 49). As if it is a sort of clincher in the argument between Aristophanes and Diotima, Dover argues that 'we would rather accept observed facts, however mysterious, than close our eyes to them in order to construct a coherent metaphysical doctrine; and the facts afford us a secure base from which we can assess the issue between Aristophanes and Diotima' (Dover 1966, 48). The most memorable remark to that effect in the commentary must be the following observation made with reference to Alcibiades' attempted seduction of, but rejection by, Socrates: 'Plato undoubtedly wishes to suggest that physical relations are inimical to the pursuit of metaphysical truth with the same partner on other occasions. This may not be true, and even if it is true not everyone will regard it as a good advertisement for metaphysics' (1980a, 165). If there is a clash between sex and metaphysics, then sex wins the day – on the apparent basis that it is an observed fact that human beings prefer it.[28] Why Plato entertains that 'clash', has little to do with any aversion on Plato's part to *sex* (which Plato probably considered to be a mere appetite like the desire for a bit of cake) and everything to do with *erôs* as a specific form of desire, and the obsessional focus and aspirational potential *that* drive brings with it. *Erôs* is an aspiration for happiness (205d), of which sexual *erôs* is but a mere example, and if Alcibiades wants happiness and supposes that 'nothing is more important to [him] than to become as good a person as possible' (218d), then he needs to think harder about how that is achieved, and where his *erôs* is, ultimately, directed. Surely Dover's privileged experience tells us that the aspiration for happiness must look beyond the bedroom, however much one hopes it may include it – and regardless of whether metaphysical satisfaction is the ultimate prize.[29]

Dover is surely right that Aristophanes' speech is one that strikes 'a modern reader' as founded on observable realities, but surely not those historically sensitive readers who owe so much to Dover. For if it is right to say, with Dover, that the pederastic focus in Plato's text had a central pedagogic dimension, and the encomiastic focus lends itself to emphasis on an 'upward path', then – with this historical hat on – there is no expectation that the central clash is between *homo Aristophaneus* and *homo Platonicus*. That is to say, if one is aware of the educational context, and the orientation towards virtue and *eudaimonia* adopted by the speakers and theorized by Socrates (205d, even though Pausanias does not use the vocabulary of *eudaimonia*), then Aristophanes' speech, surprise, surprise, is *funny*. Who but the most committed romantic would entertain the thought that our aspirations for a life worth living can be satisfied in the arms of another, in a constant state of sexual union? Even Aristophanes *denies* that what lovers most want is ἡ τῶν ἀφροδισίων συνουσία (192c), though being physically fused together is the means by which we achieve the desired state of unity on his view. What kind of praise, let alone justification, for the institutionalized practice of pederasty would it be if its prize were to champion rolling around together forever? Can that do justice to the expansive, creative and life-changing force of *erôs* that has formed part of the 'observable realities' of the human experience of love for centuries? Dover seems to anticipate that criticism, arguing that 'Modern sympathy for Aristophanes' attitude may be a product of romanticism, but the speech which expresses the attitude is not a modern interpolation in <an> ancient text'.[30] And yet it is *only* the speech of Aristophanes that speaks so strongly to this romantic theme; that we continue to obsess about it says rather more about us than about the Greek notions of *erôs* at play in this work. It may be objected that Diotima's talk of union (συνεῖναι) between contemplator and object of contemplation (212a) suggests in turn a kind of metaphysical, or spiritual 'romanticism'; the point is only that this moves beyond the interpersonal in a way that is in accord with Phaedrus, Pausanias, Eryximachus and Agathon, all of whom look to an aim beyond interpersonal union (as even Aristophanes intimates, 192d), when *praising* the aspirational benefits of love. Dover's greatest legacy, perhaps, is the work which persuaded us that human sexuality has a history shaped by cultural factors and yet here he seems averse to considering how his cherished 'observable realities' are shaped by his own. Perhaps this is related to his conviction that understanding of the past had to proceed via an understanding of one's own experience (see e.g. *MC* 261);[31] but here Dover's experience seems to be at odds not just with the symposiasts, but with the aspirational potential of *erôs* cherished by humans for centuries, with which Diotima's (no doubt highly specific) expression thereof is not out of step.

Dover, philosophy and faith

The real engine of this dispute, for Dover, resides in resistance to Plato's axioms, which comes to fruition when the *telos* of that upward path – in the so-called, 'ascent of *erôs*' – is specified as a form and presented (for Dover, at least) in the manner of faith and dogma. 'Having parted company with love [by which he means the individual and personal], Platonic eros now takes wing' (Dover 1980a, 155). It is as if there are no arguments for why one might reject the 'observed facts' of (what Dover calls) 'preference' (see p. 138 above). This is reflected in Dover's lack of attention to any argumentation in the commentary.[32] Clearly the *Symposium* does not proceed by means of the *elenchus*, but one has to have a very narrow sense of what counts as an argument to see no argument here at all. Dover writes in the Preface, as we have seen, that Plato writes 'from first to last as an *advocate*, an *heir* to the tradition of didactic poetry, a nursling of Attic drama and *a product*, no less than the politicians and litigants he criticised so articulately, of a culture which admired the art of the persuader' (emphasis mine). 'Advocacy' and 'persuasion' are not incompatible with rational argument.[33] There is no doubt that persuasion is a theme of this text, indicated by Socrates' remarks about how he was persuaded by Diotima and now tries to persuade others (212b), and Socrates is clearly an advocate for the philosophical life. 'Product' is clearly meant to bite, as if Plato was deluding himself as to the extent to which he was steeped in previous traditions; but given that Socrates' advocacy and persuasion proceed on rational grounds, and not by reference to what the poets or legislators say (as in so many of the other speeches), the work is not reduced to being a mere product of its time, nor advocated on the basis of 'faith'. Dover's 'hypothesis' is that Plato has his axioms, fervently and faithfully promoted by his Socrates, and since the arguments rely on (or, better, 'lead to') these supposedly implausible axioms they render the arguments a matter of *mere* advocacy and persuasion. That hypothesis informs Dover's neglect of Plato's arguments and shapes his task as commentator, which is to alert us to the extent to which 'Plato employed the same artfulness' as was 'employed by forensic speakers in seeking to implant assumptions and attitudes in the mind of a jury'; he fashions himself, by implication, as our 'guard' when such Platonic artfulness is 'in the service of metaphysics' (Dover 1980a, 8).

Dover's fervent aversion to Plato's supposed 'axioms' encouraged a dismissive attitude to *most* of Socrates' speech, which makes no reference to metaphysics, or at least the theory of forms, at all; forms, at least, appear only at its end. Consider when and how these 'axioms' actually enter the account. As has been noted, Socrates builds on many of the ideas of his peers. Central is the idea that *erôs* has beauty as its object, which is taken as axiomatic by most of the speakers (though Aristophanes does not use any καλός terms and Agathon calls Eros himself, *qua* a god, κάλλιστος, 195a).[34] Socrates attempts to *explain* why it is the case that human beings are so relentless in their pursuit of beauty. He considers it obvious that if you ask any rational agent what they ultimately desire, the answer will be good things and *eudaimonia* (205d). Nothing strangely metaphysical here and many of Dover's exponents of 'popular' morality, as they are presented here, evidently agree.[35] Since we are mortal, and cannot possess anything in any straightforward way, mortal beings must be productive to secure such things, and this explains the pursuit of beauty, which inspires us to creative work. True enough: there is a metaphysical distinction being deployed here between a mortal world of flux and change, and a divine one characterized by stability; if the mention of the divine is removed that seems to be no more than a distinction made on the basis of the observation of change and decay, of the sort we might well find in Homer, e.g. *Il.* 6.146–9. The next thought is that a beautiful object holds out the promise of good things and happiness (variously specified), which explains why human beings pursue it so relentlessly and so productively, as they try to capture the value of their beloved object in a variety of reproductive practices ranging from child-bearing to law-making and philosophy. This is how they make a life worth living for themselves as parents, poets or legislators. There is nothing so far that relies on any implausible metaphysical axioms. More to the point, even *this* much is enough to reject an exclusive and obsessive focus (characteristic of *erôs*) on an individual; for if *erôs* seeks possession of an object that makes life worth living, then that is surely a heavy burden for any individual to carry. Dover himself clearly had broader aspirations than that, since he confessed that friendships came second to his work, and his towering achievements in the field are evidence of his creative ambitions. If there is anything in Dover's dispute with Plato up to this point, it must only be a semantic one, namely that Plato expanded the sense of *erôs* beyond the interpersonal; but then so did the other speakers. As Dover himself notes in the very first page of his Introduction: '"Love" in general is *philia* in Greek ...; it can denote non-belligerency between nations, the affection we may feel for a colleague and the great love which we commonly feel for a parent, child, close friend or (combined with sexual desire) for a spouse or lover'; *erôs*, by contrast 'can denote *any very strong desire*' (emphasis mine), and is most strongly associated with a response to beauty.[36] Unless one wants to suppose that the desire for beauty is restricted to individual persons (and Dover's famous reaction to a beautiful landscape in Italy, recounted at *MC* 114, provides an obvious counter-example to that), then one needs no Platonic metaphysics to get on board with the idea that there are a variety of objects people desire as beautiful, and a variety of creative ways to respond to those beautiful objects, which move beyond the interpersonal.[37]

Metaphysical assumptions enter the account *at the final stage*, where Socrates attempts to explain the nature of the creative work in beauty that can deliver the end in question – a stable and lasting state of happiness. The argument for why someone should avoid an 'inferior medium', as Dover puts it (p. 138 above), comes about because as lovers we are trying to secure a lasting good, something that makes *a life* worth living (211d), which can only happen through reproductive means. The question, then, is what kinds of beautiful media are such as to deliver that end? This question is not one that requires any metaphysical axioms, and it is one which naturally leads most reflective people, including Dover himself, to become creative beyond the production of children in beautiful individual others to secure that end. The point is simply this: suppose one accepts that we all desire happiness and this involves securing a lasting good to make central to the life you deem worth living, what is so implausible – even in the face of Dover's 'observable realities' – about the thought that one looks to something more permanent than physical attraction, or even beyond something as unstable as honour, to secure that end? One might even accept (by which I mean Dover himself) that wisdom is a more lasting basis for *eudaimonia* than making a name for oneself in one's children, or securing honour, and so seek beautiful media, such as Classical literature, to secure that end. What one is resisting, then, is surely not the move to the imperishable, nor to the intelligible; one is simply resisting the metaphysical determination Plato *eventually* gives to that end.[38]

My task here is not to defend Plato against Dover's charges. It is rather to show how his distinctive view of Plato as a dogmatic metaphysician so dominated his view of the *Symposium* that it rendered Socrates' entire speech no more than the product of a 'psychopathological symptom' which 'Plato yielded to', namely that rejection of experience which Dover held to be an 'intellectual failure'.[39] 'If we do not share [Plato's] assumptions, we may not find any part of his account even momentarily plausible' (Dover 1980a, 8). I see no evidence that these assumptions inform *all* parts of Plato's account. Dover's aversion to the metaphysical determination Plato eventually gives to beauty was doubtless driven by the fact that metaphysics was almost a dirty word in Oxford in Dover's time, but this eclipses how much of the *Symposium* may have been congenial to him, and which quite possibly drew him to this text in the first instance. The *Symposium*, taken as a whole, and to some extent at least, incorporates three empirical 'axioms': observation, memory and experience. Plato is here observing his culture, bearing witness to 'the many and varied things' (193e) said on the subject, noting explicitly that these things are 'worthy of remembrance' (178a) and using those observations and memories of Homer, Hippocrates and Aristophanes to reflect on the human experience of beauty and desire. That is surely why this text, above all other Platonic works, appealed to Dover.

Conclusion

I have taken two features that struck me about Dover: his being 'an English empiricist to the core' and his identification with 'popular values'. These features may explain the attraction of the *Symposium*, as well as Dover's aversion at numerous points. Dover was writing at a reactionary time in Platonic studies, when Jowett's vision of Plato shaping a new world order, spread by Empire, was long since past, and Crossman's *Plato Today* (1937) and Popper's *The Open Society and Its Enemies, Volume I: The Spell of Plato* (1945) had exposed a darker side of Platonism, which made that 'uncritical enthusiasm' to which Dover referred disparagingly in his edition of the *Symposium*, increasingly difficult.[40] The 'spirit of the age' which Dover (*MC* 63) referred to as captured by Ayer's *Language, Truth and Logic* rejected metaphysical speculation, while the narrative of aesthetic homosexual self-discovery, of which Wilde had earlier taken Plato to be the figurehead, and which was entwined with narratives of Empire, was wearing thin.[41] Dover's frank approach to homosexuality was a riposte to such sanitizing and idealizing narratives, and his deflationary, empirical approach to Plato's philosophy prompts a healthy scepticism in those of us who remain under 'the spell of Plato'. But Dover's aversion seems to go beyond sceptical restraint and to have a fervour of its own, perhaps acknowledged when Dover accepted that some of his remarks in the first edition 'look[ed] intemperate'. I can think of no better illustration of this fervour than an unforgettable detail in Dover's autobiography that many of us would rather not have known. It is not the fact that Dover masturbated in the face of a beautiful Italian landscape, but how he tells the tale. Surely this is not just an 'assault on prudery',[42] for Dover embeds the recollection in the context of his thinking about the *Symposium* and the *Phaedrus* and the idea that our response to the stimulus of beauty 'seemed to Plato the strongest hint we have of the existence of abstract, immutable Beauty' (*MC* 114); for Dover, by contrast, 'the scene struck directly at my penis'. For so great a scholar of the Classical world to leave us with an image that is so decidedly popular, ordinary and familiar – positively *Aristophanic* – can be seen as the ultimate 'screw you' to any idealizing, Platonic interpretation of beauty, and perhaps of any overly reverential responses to Sir Kenneth Dover himself. The experience of beauty, he seems to be telling us, may very well be a 'step on a short flight which led nowhere'; and so what?[43]

Notes

1. Dover's edition has sold almost 17,000 in total and is the bestselling in the series to date; it still sells approximately 200 copies per year. Many thanks to Michael Sharp at Cambridge University Press for this information.
2. *MC* 111 does, however, explain that when prompted to take on some Plato lectures to give Ian Kidd 'a rest from that' he did not suppose he could compete with Kidd's *Phaedrus* lectures, in addition to its being 'wasteful' for both of them to prepare Honours lectures on the same text.
3. See the short 'Preface to 1982 reprint' added at the bottom of p. viii. *MC* 117 writes that he was sorry to have upset a good friend when he received a 'reproachful letter' from Gerrit De Vries for suggesting in the commentary that 'modern interpretation of Plato has tended to underrate the extent to which, as an evangelist for his metaphysical faith, [Plato] sometimes found rhetorical techniques a more serviceable instrument of persuasion (all in a good cause) than cool reason, and I went so far as to compare him in this respect with the forensic orators'. Though De Vries had 'incomparably detailed knowledge of the Platonic corpus', this did not lead Dover to recant, since the letter was based more on 'sentiment than scholarly argument' – as if the same quality of passionate fervour Dover identified in Plato also applied to De Vries! Sandbach 1981, 126 said in his review that the commentary 'bears the stamp of its editor's personality'.
4. In *MC* 63–4, when discussing his future wife Audrey (who had studied Maths and Physics), he wrote admiringly that she was 'strongly reductionist'; though she had never read Ayer's *Language, Truth and Logic*, 'the spirit of the age works in many people at many levels'. Dover's engagement with her prompted him to re-work two years of philosophy material 'in quite a different way' and 'condensing' it served him well in his two philosophy papers in Greats (Moral Philosophy and Logic and Metaphysics).
5. *MC* 146; cf. 261, 'Anglo-Saxon empiricist'.
6. See Scott 1987, 346.
7. Dover 1980a, viii; cf. ibid. 6, which discusses Plato's theory of forms and the idea that 'the human soul is able to attain firm and certain knowledge of real unchanging entities'. This is explicitly contrasted with an empirical worldview, 'In the light of experience . . .'.
8. *MC* 116–17. Dover sees the role of faith as central to Platonic philosophy. Cf., for example, Dover 1982, 115, on Plato's Socrates as 'wholly devoid of the genuine curiosity which makes a scientist or a historian'.
9. Dover's suspicion of these principles may well have been fuelled by the climate of Oxford philosophy at the time; so-called 'ordinary language philosophy' held sway, so an aversion to speculative metaphysics came with the territory (see n. 4 above for the 'spirit of the age' captured by Ayer). Popper's *The Open Society and Its Enemies* (1945) had decidedly sullied the waters of unabashed Plato enthusiasm. Note Dover's remark that 'Plato and (before insanity supervened) Mao would have understood each other' (*MC* 118).
10. Compare Dover 1980a, 113, on Aristophanes' speech as the only one 'which strikes a modern reader as founded on observable realities' (cf. p. 133); 138, Diotima's statements 'irreconcilable with observed fact'; 149, 'philosophers and moralists generalising about the animal world have seldom shown respect for evidence'.
11. On the relationship between the image of the pregnant soul and *anamnêsis*, see Sheffield 2001.
12. On the strange reversal of pregnancy and procreation which 'forestalls' such issues, see Burnyeat 1997.

13. On the individual, particular and familiar, see Dover 1966, 50, quoted on p. 138; as will become clear, Dover himself identifies with the position of popular morality he sees Plato to be rejecting. For Dover's cautious remarks on immortality, see 1980a, 149: 'If Plato did not think it would enter his readers' heads that he disbelieved in the immortality of the soul, it is understandable that he did not take more trouble to guard against misinterpretation'.
14. I leave aside the controversial issue of whether the account of immortality in the final portion of Socrates' speech in the ascent also satisfies these conditions or gives intimations of a different form of immortality. The point still holds insofar as the model in general terms – and for most of the account – is personal and familiar, whether Socrates eventually departs from those characteristics in the Highest Mysteries or not.
15. Dover 1980a, viii, discusses what he perceives to be the 'uncritical enthusiasm' that marks much of what is written about Plato, including the fact that 'the Platonic Socrates is taken, in all seriousness, as if he were a man with a genuinely open and enquiring mind, and the quality of other Greek intellectuals, some of whom are best known to us through Plato's portrayal of them, is underrated'. Note, too 1980a, 133, where Dover is dismissive about Socrates' trademark use of dialogue.
16. See Halliwell 2016a, 3–13, who addresses those philosophers who pay lip-service to textual 'polyphony' but proceed to read everything in the light of Socrates-Diotima.
17. See Stehle 1997, 222, from whom I take the phrase. Commenting on sympotic discourse more generally, Stehle argues: 'All of the forms that this might take, the singing in turn, the new turn on the known song, are designed to keep the discourse collective, while at the same time highlighting each person's contribution. The participants must constantly respond to one another, but the full forms ... require the work of more than one contributor. One could say that ideally the symposium should create one intertextual web.'
18. For an exploration of this view, see Sheffield 2006.
19. The full passage (Dover 1980a, viii) is: 'The working hypothesis adopted in my commentary and introduction is that Plato writes not as a scholar or scientist but from first to last as an advocate, an heir to the tradition of didactic poetry, a nursling of Attic drama and a product, no less than the politicians and litigants whom he criticised so articulately, of a culture which admired the art of the persuader.'
20. On which see Dover 1966, 41–50 (with quotation on p. 133).
21. Adkins 1978; Dover's response is 1983b. Cf. Carey's chapter in the present volume.
22. Why Plato gives two such different treatments of *erôs*, one of which makes more use of the 'twin pillars of Platonism' and the other of which downplays these, is a different question, which is more pressing for someone like Dover, who reads Plato as a dogmatic philosopher with a coherent body of doctrine. For those so inclined, appeal can be made to the different dialectical contexts of each work to explain discrepancies in terms of a difference of emphasis (for a sustained argument in favour of this interpretative strategy, see Rowe 2007).
23. For those who speculate on Plato's own sexual proclivities, which seem impossible to substantiate, see for example Plass 1978, Wender 1973. That pederasty was an important social institution in classical Athens is now a scholarly commonplace; see e.g. Foucault 1985, Bremmer 1990, Calame 1999.
24. See, however, Euripides fr. 897, with Halliwell 2016a, 3–4. The start of the fragment (παίδευμα δ' Ἔρως σοφίας ἀρετῆς / πλεῖστον ὑπάρχει, ...) contains a textual problem that is relevant here: ἀρετῆς which is in the mss of Athenaeus and makes good sense as being governed by ὑπάρχει ('has a share in virtue') is emended into ἐρατῆς ('lovely' [sc. wisdom]) by most modern editors. But it is ἀρετῆς that really puts this fragment close to Diotima's view of *erôs*. On this reading, *erôs* is not just to be controlled and 'educated' by wisdom

(παίδευμα σοφίας) but is directly conducive to virtue; *erôs* is the key incentive for education and virtue (ἀρετῆς ὑπάρχει). See also the use of initiation language later on in the fragment (τοῖς δ' ἀτελέστοις), and the requirement to 'use (*erôs*) rightly' (χρῆσθαι δ' ὀρθῶς), which puts this fragment close to Diotima's account. I thank Christian Keime for these comments.

25. Dover 1980a, 12, cites the later treatise *Rhetorica ad Alexandrum* (35) as prescribing the following order for encomia: external blessings (e.g. wealth, beauty, good birth), virtue proper (divisible into the traditional four cardinal virtues), ancestry, achievements. It is not clear whether the speakers in the *Symposium* follow this procedure exactly; as Hunter 2004, 35, puts it with subtlety: 'To a greater or lesser extent, all the speeches in the *Symposium* show elements of these formal patterns, though none simply reproduces a scholastic formula'; for example, how many of them focus on external blessings? As Christian Keime remarks, when Phaedrus quotes Hesiod at 178b (ἠδ' Ἔρος . . .) he stops just at the point where the poet proceeded to describe such external qualities (. . . ὃς κάλλιστος ἐν ἀθανάτοισι θεοῖσι, *Theog.* 120), as if Plato wanted to focus only on the virtues and the achievements of *erôs* (with a little on the ancestry).

26. Pleasure was considered by some prominent thinkers at the time as the key to excellence and happiness, and as perfectly compatible with *paideia* (see Diog. Laert. 2.87–90 on Aristippus), so the emphasis here should fall on marginalizing the physical pleasures *of erôs* in the *Symposium*.

27. Dover, however, took the last two of these speeches to be parodic and satirical.

28. Dover thinks that *Plato's* preferred position is due to his psychology and a *Republic*-style division of the soul into parts: the appetitive and spirited parts must be controlled for reason to do its work; but there is little indication that the soul is divided into parts in the *Symposium*.

29. Within the logic of the text, Alcibiades seeks to exchange his body as an instrumental tool: 'because by gratifying Socrates I could hear everything he knew' (217a). Here physical relations are disdained partly on the grounds that wisdom is not the sort of thing that flows from what is fuller into something emptier 'if only we touch each other' (175d–e), and even if it were such a thing this would be an exchange of 'gold for bronze' (219a). None of this speaks to a disdain for physical relations as such; it is their role in a dynamic of exchange which is criticized here. Whatever Plato's views on physical relations, it is clear that Socrates and Alcibiades had a longstanding interpersonal relationship and as Rowe 1998, 204 argues, 213c ff. suggests that Socrates sees himself as still being in love with Alcibiades and it becomes evident during Alcibiades' speech that the feeling is mutual.

30. Dover 1966, 49–50.

31. This is related to what Nussbaum 1997, 157 identifies as the central feature of *Marginal Comment*: 'the desire to show the scholarly life as growing out of a particular set of personal experiences'.

32. Compare Nussbaum 1997, 154: 'His 1980 commentary on the *Symposium* seems to me unduly dismissive of Plato's arguments, unduly disposed to see all the interesting results as dependent on unstated and implausible metaphysical assumptions'.

33. As Dover evidently sees when he adds in a note to the 1982 reprint (p. viii) that '"from first to last as an advocate" does not mean that Plato discarded reason in favour of advocacy when reasoning seemed to him cogent in itself'; the real issue is that Dover 'does not find [Plato's] philosophical arguments even marginally persuasive' (ibid., in the original Preface).

34. Compare Sappho fr. 16.3–4: 'Whatever one loves is most beautiful (*kalon*)'.

35. Dover gives this little comment, attending instead to the further claim that we desire to have good things always, which 'does not rest on reasoning at all' (1980a, 144). Indeed, Dover takes

this as evidence of sophistry: 'Plato uses the art of rhetoric more subtly than when he is caricaturing the verbal sophistries of others (e.g. 196c3-d4; *Euthd.* 276ab), but no more honestly' (145). The sophism in question, I take it, is the slippage of 'always': *erôs* always desires to have good things is taken (without argument) as the claim that *erôs* desires to have good things always, which introduces the claim that *erôs* desires immortality with the good. Dover is right that there is no argument here, but this need not be the kind of verbal trickery characteristic of sophistry. The idea may rather be that lasting possession of the good is built into the Greek conception of the *eudaimôn* life, which characterized the gods.

36. In 1994, 113, however, Dover writes that *erôs* denotes 'love' in the sense 'which it has in the English phrases "to be in love (with ...)" and "fall in love (with...)", not just simple lust (for which Greek has other words) but the exclusive and obsessive lust which one feels for a particular person'.

37. Indeed, when commenting on the final vision of beauty at 210e, Dover 1980a, 157, writes that 'the notion that a vision of overwhelming beauty is the reward of long toil (e6) may make us think of the view from a summit after a long ascent, but mountaineering was not a Greek sport, and a closer analogy would be the excitement of glimpsing a wonderfully simple, comprehensive answer to a problem after a process of reasoning which was full of difficulties and discouragements'. Compare 1980a, 5, when commenting on Plato's view that our response to visual beauty is 'the clearest glimpse of eternity that our senses afford us', he makes reference to a Beethoven symphony and a Highland landscape.

38. Even though the axioms to which Dover refers only make an appearance towards the very end of the speech, many Platonists would resist the thought that they are 'axioms' at all. They are hypotheses (explicitly flagged as such in the text which makes the most use of them, the *Phaedo*), whose truth (and Dover is right about this much) Plato *persuades* us of by showing their explanatory power (and also criticizes in the *Parmenides*). And whether one finds them persuasive or not, there are *arguments* for these axioms. One argument is captured by Aristotle (*Met.* A6 987b): 1. Sensible things are in flux; 2. Whatever is in flux is unknowable; 3. Therefore sensible things are unknowable; 4. There is some knowledge; 5. Knowledge is of something; 6. Therefore there are objects that are different from sensible things, that are the objects of knowledge and definition; 7. Therefore there are non-sensible objects of knowledge; 8. Therefore there are forms. The relationship between reason and the good is explored in *Republic* Book VI: for a sober assessment of that argument, see Denyer 2007.

39. 'In life we encounter many things, people and events. Each of these "particulars" is limited in time and space: it comes into being, it exists here or there, it changes, it ceases to be. Since we do not encounter anything which is wholly unlike everything else, we can form and use "universal" concepts, generalising, exemplifying, defining, deducing and predicting. In the light of experience, and in accordance with our needs in trying to understand and affect our environment, we correct our generalisations, modify our definitions, replace our axioms. To many people this situation is wholly acceptable. Others, of whom Plato was one, believe that there is something more, something which "really exists", unchanging, independent of our indefinitely adjustable generalisations and pragmatic definitions. Whether this belief happens to be right, happens to be wrong, or is insufficiently meaningful to be called either, it is at any rate not dictated by reasoned reflection on experience; it is engendered by a kind of craving, which may itself be an operation of divine grace, a psychopathological symptom, the product of an intellectual failure ... Whatever it is, Plato yielded to it' (Dover 1980a, 6).

40. On Jowett, Plato and Empire, see Dowling 1994, xiv, Goldhill 2011, 6, 8.

41. For Wilde's use of Plato and discussion of those who used Hellenism to 'cast a veil of respectability over ... a hitherto unmentionable vice or crime', see Dowling 1994, Chapter I, 'Aesthete and Effeminatus', at 28, who throughout the chapter explores the 'legitimating

counter-discourse' of erotic identity found in Hellenism (36). Compare Evangelista 2006. *MC* 115 writes that 'some homosexuals did not like to be told that much of their wilful idealisation of "Greek love" was wide of the mark'. The tide has turned away from Dover's attempt to bring homosexuality down from its idealizing heights; see Davidson 2007, 101, who is opposed to Dover's reductionist focus on sex acts, with the review of Davidson by Blanshard 2009. For how homosexuality was deployed in an imperial context, see Orrells 2012 and Aldrich 2003.

42. An option explored by Nussbaum 1997, 158.
43. I would like to thank participants at the conference in Oxford 2021 in honour of Dover, especially Stephen Halliwell for detailed written comments, Christopher Stray and Jaś Elsner. I would also like to thank Christian Keime for written comments.

CHAPTER 9
DOVER AND GREEK POPULAR MORALITY
Christopher Carey

Kenneth Dover's *Greek Popular Morality in the Time of Plato and Aristotle* (1974) was one of a clutch of publications appearing in rapid succession in the second half of the twentieth century which vastly enriched the resources available for the study of Greek social history. It appeared just a year earlier than Pomeroy's *Goddesses, Whores, Wives and Slaves*, four years earlier than MacDowell's *The Law in Classical Athens*, and two years earlier than the seminal debate on *hybris* in *Greece and Rome* between Nick Fisher and Douglas MacDowell. Since that period, monographs have appeared, sometimes multiple monographs, on every aspect of the value system discussed in Dover's book. But for anyone looking to locate creative literature within an historical context and try to get a sense of how the original audience might have responded, this work filled a lacuna. It was also one of four ambitious mid- to late-twentieth-century books on Greek thought by distinguished anglophone classicists at the peak of their intellectual power, the others being E.R. Dodds' *The Greeks and the Irrational*, Arthur Adkins' *Merit and Responsibility* and Hugh Lloyd-Jones' *The Justice of Zeus*.

The lacuna which Dover identified in his justification for the project was the absence (despite a large number of scholarly works dealing with the origins and evolution of Greek moral concepts drawing on epic, tragedy and philosophy) of attempts to explore Greek morality as represented explicitly and implicitly in works aimed at a mass audience.[1] This is probably about as close as we get to a definition of 'popular morality' in the book, which never fully defines its theme. The Contents page assigns seven and a half pages to the question 'What is popular morality?' But very little of the discussion actually consists of definition.[2] The definition *is* fleshed out to some degree in the detailed argument for the choice of material, though it requires a little reading between the lines. Popular morality is emphatically not moral philosophy, which Dover defines (*GPM* 1) as 'rational, systematic thinking about the relationship between morality and reason'. What popular morality does share with moral philosophy both in the scoping pages and in the body of the book is that it consists of thinking and talking about morality; it deals with principles. It concerns the beliefs about right and wrong which people espouse or claim to espouse for one reason or another, the standards according to which people describe and evaluate their own character and behaviour and that of others, though not necessarily those by which any one person lived.[3] What the term 'popular' does not mean, though this is never stated, is 'the morality espoused by the common people' as distinct from the views and practices of a socio-economic elite. The issue for Dover is cognition, not status; the antithesis at the heart of the term is between public and purely personal, between shared and individual, between conventional and idiosyncratic. If one were to express the fundamental concept in terms meaningful to an Athenian in the fifth or fourth century (a test Dover once put to me when I was trying to articulate some thoughts on Aristophanes), one might use the term *idiôtês*, the 'ordinary person' or 'layman'; that is, 'popular morality' is the shared morality of the non-specialist population as distinct from the *sophistês*, the person who makes a special study of such matters. In defining its exclusion zone as it does, the book presents a continuum of beliefs which stretches across the social and economic spectrum.[4] To see what is at issue here one only has to flick through E.R. Dodds' monumental *The Greeks and the Irrational*, where the phrases 'popular belief' and 'popular religion' regularly appear in opposition to a more privileged perspective, whether poetic, social or intellectual.[5] Dover's Athens is in contrast a homogeneous culture, at least in its address to moral values. His approach is for a classical scholar of his generation remarkably egalitarian. Though the question of the relationship between intellect, education and status on the one hand and moral thinking on the other is never theorized as a cross-cultural issue in the book, his view of classical Athens in this respect probably does reflect a broader belief of Dover's about thinking, including moral thinking, in his own contemporary society. It is consistent with the view he took of the modern academic as just another professional rather than a caste apart. When one press reader of *Marginal Comment* described it as an 'academic autobiography', he dismissed the description with the words: 'academics are non-academic for much of their waking lives.'[6]

For anyone who has not encountered the book, or has not re-read it recently, a brief summary may be useful. *Greek Popular Morality* falls roughly into two halves. The first deals with sources and problems. Over three chapters Dover discusses, first, the various sources available to the researcher and the generic features of each, justifying his decisions about what to include and exclude; then, the moral vocabulary of the Greeks; and, thirdly, the factors which in Greek sources are believed to affect the moral capacity of the individual: nature and nurture, sex, age, socio-economic status and location, intellect, divine intervention. The third chapter is the longest and most discursive of his methodological chapters. It finishes with a section entitled 'moral responsibility', which looks rather odd in context but makes a kind of sense as an attempt to pre-empt any impression that the factors at work in Greek moral decision-making are in some sense deterministic. This chapter is for me one of the most enjoyable sections of the book, since the author's own voice emerges almost uninterrupted. It also occupies a rather ambiguous place, since it has one foot in the book's second half: it is difficult to separate out the way in which people think about psychological, social and economic determinants of conduct from their expectations about behaviour and the way in which they respond to the realization or frustration of those expectations. The second half of the book examines numerous categories of behaviour with their related contexts and the way these are evaluated, dealing first with relations between the individual and others under various heads, then the range of sanctions which constrain and punish individual conduct, and finally the various social structures within which behaviour takes place and is evaluated.

The book is a little more informative about method than about definitions. One obvious way to phrase the research questions would be to start from 'Greek terminology and the ancient classification of virtues and vices' (*GPM* xii). This Dover firmly rejects in favour of an approach which formulates questions prompted by his 'own moral experience' (ibid.). The sense of the researcher's own experience as the basis for the research questions recurs repeatedly in the way Dover appears in the book either as a source of anecdote or as a hypothetical example, most notably in his dismissal of Adkins' appeal to the universal application of the Kantian concept of 'duty':

> I cannot recall experiencing a temptation to use the word "duty" in its Kantian sense (except, of course, when talking about Kant) and, at least in the course of the last six years, I do not think I have heard the word so used. Unless I am seriously deceiving myself, I and most of the people I know well find the Greeks of the Classical period easier to understand than Kantians.[7]

This sense is accentuated by the way Dover often projects himself into the hypothetical position of an imaginary moral agent.[8] There are risks in this approach and I return to them below. Here I note only the self-awareness about what the researcher is doing and how. There is a recognition that in writing about the past we are always to some degree writing about the present; and there is none of the illusory objectivity generated by the avoidance of the first person common in academic publications.[9] This personal experience is, however, offered as something less individual and idiosyncratic than the use of the first person might suggest. As he goes on to explain: 'To understand Greek morality it is certainly necessary to become capable of looking at morality through Greek eyes, but it is necessary also to switch off and become ourselves again whenever we want to know what, if anything, they thought about issues which are important to us.' (*GPM* 2). So 'my own moral experience' is at least to some degree offered as anecdotal evidence for collective contemporary experience rather than as something purely personal and this is about using that modern experience to frame questions about the ancient world. This use of the first person does however sit oddly alongside the analogy Dover employs for the framing of those research questions, which is the field worker formulating a questionnaire which will allow comparison between the moralities of different cultures.[10] Though the point is not developed, the model is clearly that of the social sciences. Elsewhere in his writing Dover views the role of the classical scholar in broadly anthropological terms, as Stephen Halliwell observes in his chapter,[11] and that understanding of the nature of the research project seems to lie behind the terse statement of method here. But he shows no interest in any contemporary or cross-cultural research available which might help to provide a more objective external frame for the project.

In expressing reservations about the lexical approach, Dover does not mean that vocabulary is unimportant, as Adkins objected,[12] merely that it cannot be the sole basis for any attempt to reconstruct the moral experience of a culture. Dover's suspicion of simple word hunting is fundamentally sound. There has to be room for a range of elliptical modes of expression which are too fine-grained to be caught in a lexical net – periphrasis, metaphor, allusion, presentation through negation. In fact, there is no way of escaping the role of vocabulary, and accordingly a substantial section in the first half of the book (about 8 per cent of the volume as a whole) is devoted to the evaluative terminology of the Greeks. But Dover is firm that starting from a lexical search will tell us only a limited amount about what the Greeks valued (or not) in terms of behaviour and why. And he rightly insists that implicit judgment which does not use immediately recognizable evaluative terminology can tell us as much as descriptive moral vocabulary.

Since our access to ancient Greek moral thinking (as distinct from material culture and social and economic history) is through the written word, and primarily through literary texts, the question of the value of the sources available is of critical importance. Dover's address to this issue shows a crisp and clear sense of genre and context and the ways in which these shape the topics which can be discussed and in what kind of language. In this the book is a product of its time, since at this point genre was beginning to impact significantly on classical scholarship.[13] The book wears this influence relatively lightly. Genre is a constraint, but the constraint is generated by the interaction with the audience, not by firm rules. It is not the straitjacket it was for some of his more formalist contemporaries.

Genre is central to the most fundamental of the methodological decisions, the choice of primary sources and the related justification. The purpose of the book is to examine what 'ordinary and unphilosophical'[14] Athenians thought about morality. This focus on the non-specialist leads Dover to reject moral philosophy as a source. Moral philosophy represents a conscious attempt to systematize, which shared morality does not. The result is, almost uniquely in the literature on Greek intellectual history, a discussion of Greek ethics which marginalizes philosophy. The Presocratics, Plato and Aristotle get only an occasional mention. Plato and Aristotle are in fact more of a presence in the book than a glance at the index might suggest. Aristotle there gets three mentions, Plato just one. But the index does give a sense of where they stand in the book's priorities. Aristotle pops up far more frequently in footnotes than among the primary sources in the main text, and both Plato and Aristotle tend to be used more for contextualization than as primary evidence for shared ethics. Not only are views of morality articulated in philosophical texts rejected as a reliable source of information but also statements about and allusions to commonly held beliefs found in these sources.[15] The rationale for this is cursory at best. Dover moves rapidly from caution about the reliability of statements by philosophers about generally held beliefs, based on questionable assertions of this kind in modern sources, to a dismissal of the value of such evidence altogether.[16] From a purely practical point of view this has an enormous advantage in making the material manageable. Any attempt to combine even a fraction of the works of Plato and Aristotle with his selected sources would have made the book unwieldy, at least in the omnivorous form in which Dover realized the project, or it would have necessitated far more authorial narrative and far more selective use of primary texts. But in methodological terms the exclusion is highly questionable. Plato may be 'atypical' (to use Moses Finley's term, quoted by Dover at *GPM* 2 n. 1). And Aristotle's uniquely penetrating intellect should invite caution before we make him the spokesman for what his Greek contemporaries thought, as scholars long did and to a surprising extent still do. But both philosophers lived in Athens (and Plato belonged to the citizen elite) in the periods covered by the book, a fact advertised in the full title – *Greek Popular Morality in the Time of Plato and Aristotle*. We may feel on occasion that they exaggerate for their own rhetorical purposes, that Plato's idiosyncratic views on ontology and epistemology make him an outlier in any attempt to map mainstream Greek thought, at least on those issues. We may also feel that Aristotle's desire for clarity and system sharpens boundaries which were far less sharp for many of his contemporaries. But in practice it is not difficult to test for distortions in either source by a process of comparison and contrast. In practice this is what one has to do for any of the sources Dover favours. It is also in effect what Dover does in juxtaposing different perspectives and contexts in the second half of the book.[17] Plato cannot be allowed out unchaperoned; but nor can Aristophanes, Aeschines or Demosthenes.

A discussion which begins by ruling the evidence of the philosophers out of court inevitably suffers. Any treatment of enmity and revenge for instance has to take account of the remarkable exchange in Plato's *Crito* (49a–c) where Socrates leads Crito from the idea that one should not requite injustice with injustice to the startling notion that one should never requite harm with harm. Socrates may exaggerate when he says that 'the many' believe that it is right to repay injustice with injustice. Some, perhaps many, Athenians or Greeks more generally might bridle at the use of the word injustice (*antadikein*). They might also object to the tendentious way in which reciprocal harm is represented (literally) as reciprocal wrongdoing (*antikakourgein*, where the more neutral *antiblaptein* was available, if less rhetorically useful for Socrates' purposes). And he misleads us if we conclude that the approval of revenge was unconditional, since both tragic and oratorical texts make clear that there are limits and conditions, however subjective, shifting and context-specific. Revenge was neither an unconditional good nor an inescapable duty. But the striking uniqueness of Socrates' position in our sources for the classical period in rejecting outright the idea of harm for harm is one of the most dramatic indicators of the gulf which separates pagan Greek from Christian and post-Christian ethics in some areas. The exclusion of Aristotle is especially problematic, since in his ethical and political works he explicitly starts from *ta legomena*, what people say, not from abstracts or ideals. And for anyone working with the orators, the *Rhetoric* is potentially an important source. And reviewers rightly questioned the desirability, indeed the possibility, of drawing the firm line which Dover wanted between the philosopher and the layman.[18] In his response to Adkins almost a decade later Dover was dismissive of the possibility that moral philosophy could seriously affect the views of society at large. But both comedy and tragedy attest to the seepage of ideas from contemporary thinkers into the public domain, which opens up the possibility that popular thought was still more diverse than *GPM* suggests.

Ironically, given the exclusion of Aristotle from the discussion, the figure who most comes to mind especially when I read the section on method is Aristotle. As with Aristotle, one gets the exhilarating sense of someone approaching a subject by clearing away the brushwood of reflex action, impulse and intuition in order to get a clearer view of the matter under discussion. It is a comparison which has often struck me when reading Dover. It is especially visible in the third chapter, where one is brought back to the discussion of determinants of character and the implications for the orator in Aristotle's *Rhetoric*.

The other important dimension to the choice of sources is the question of delivery. This is almost synonymous with performance; but not quite, since the analysis in the second half draws not just on literary texts but also on inscriptions,[19] especially on epitaphs, which in describing the merits of the dead illustrate both the qualities which earn praise and the terminology which expresses that praise. And almost by definition, epitaphs must achieve their effect by communicating with language and concepts (however implicit) which will generate a positive reception. But for the most part the texts chosen for inclusion are performed texts, particularly oratory and drama, though in practice tragedy is largely confined to the background, leaving oratory and to a much lesser extent comedy as the core material for study.[20] The key point is that the text should be aimed at a public rather than destined for private reading. The rationale is that the private reader is assumed to be sympathetic to the text, as someone who elects to read it. In contrast, utterances aimed at a public have to win over their audience. Though the book has little to say about theory, Dover was familiar with the early work on pragmatics, as we know from passing comments in earlier publications. This reading almost certainly lies behind his observation that 'evaluative words hardly ever have a purely descriptive role' (*GPM* 50) and the following account of the interpersonal dimension of moral utterance in live communication. It is important here to note the word 'purely'. He is not denying descriptive force (as Adkins seemed to feel in his thoughtful but largely hostile review),[21] merely arguing that context impacts on content in more than one way and *vice versa*; there are other dimensions to value judgments general and specific than articulating ethics. In insisting on the importance of public and performed texts Dover offers a valid means of testing for convergence of opinion. The criterion can only ever be imperfect, when there is disagreement over the composition of the audiences for some of these texts. But the emphasis on the importance of texts written for delivery is rational and defensible.

The problems begin with Dover's insistence on the exclusive reliance on such texts and his dismissal of texts aimed at a reader. Dover notes (*GPM* 5) that whereas the seriousness of the consequences of failure mean that the speaker in court or the Assembly has to locate what he says within the shared values of a large collective, a text written for a sympathetic reader can espouse minority or aberrant beliefs. The example offered is Xenophon's discussion of civil conflict in Sikyon (*Hell*. 7.3.4), which contrasts 'the best men' with 'the people'. The consequence of the dismissal of texts aimed at the reader is that historiography like philosophy is largely absent from the book. Thucydides and Xenophon appear infrequently, Herodotos only slightly more often. Again, the basis for the exclusion is open to question. Whether one can treat any of the classical Greek historians solely as a text for reading is contentious. Even Thucydides does not actually deny that he ever delivered any of his text via oral performance; he merely asserts (1.22) that elements in his work may make it less appealing as a delivered text. And though individual statements and even the presentation of narrative episodes by a historian may betray a particular bias, it is a large step to dismiss whole texts on that basis. But even if one excludes authorial statements, the speeches still have a good claim to be included, since by definition they are offered as something addressed to a public audience. Thucydides' speeches may be idiosyncratic, and they may betray a passion for abstract generalization (*GPM* 8); but again, the leap from demurrer to ejection is too rapid. Even if we doubt the fidelity of Thucydides' speeches to what was said, either *en bloc* or intermittently, the sentiments are offered as things which could plausibly be said in a formal public context, and they are offered as such to a Greek audience who were in a position to evaluate them.[22] And as with the philosophers, we have a control in the presence of texts which were undoubtedly composed in order to be publicly performed, which allows the reader to cross-check speeches in historiography for divergence or eccentricity.

It is worth dwelling a little longer on these exclusions. The tendentious reasoning, from a writer so capable of pellucid argumentation, leads one to suspect that, though Dover regarded himself as 'an English empiricist to the core',[23] the foundation of the book was more intuitive than his introduction would suggest. In his autobiography, when discussing the decision to write *Greek Popular Morality* and its relationship to previous work on Greek shared values and ethics, Dover notes: 'None of the books I have mentioned started from what I was now convinced ... was the right point: forensic oratory' (*MC* 156). It is difficult to escape the impression that the decision to explore the orators as a source for Greek moral thinking was the starting point for the project, while the rationale for exclusion was a secondary consideration. Armed (as the first generation of readers of *GPM* was not) with the autobiography, one is also struck by the fact that from his undergraduate years Dover found philosophy uncongenial,[24] which inclines one to wonder how far the decision to exclude moral philosophy was born of an impatience with the texts in question rather than the carefully reasoned process of evaluation which *GPM* seems to suggest.

So far, I have mostly looked at Dover's account of his sources and methods. I have said little about how the project is realized. As noted above, the book sets out a number of broad headings for the discussion of morality, each occupying a chapter. Each of these is then subdivided into narrower categories of varying size and number which form the basis of detailed illustration. Chapter IV (pages 161–216) will serve as a useful example, though one could take any of the analytical chapters. It takes as its overarching theme 'Oneself and others'. This is then broken down into a number of sections, each of which is further subdivided into subsections (either linked by transitional sentences or simply juxtaposed) to allow for a more precise focus. The first section deals with death, pain and grief. The detailed analysis starts with a subsection on physical danger (IV.A.1), which begins with a scene-setting paragraph on the importance of the citizen-soldier for the survival of the *polis* as the background to the positive evaluation of the readiness to face risk and to sacrifice oneself for others. The discussion then moves by a formal link (the qualities required of the soldier) to the value attached to exertion to benefit others or to achieve one's goals, both in war and in life more generally (IV.A.2). Both these subsections include not just translations of the primary sources for the evaluations in question but also paraphrase of the particular terminology used. The language used to express commendation in these cases is taken up in the next subsection (*Terminology*, IV.A.3), which treats the terminology used to evaluate courage and its overlap with other positive qualities and finishes with a brief paragraph on the sarcastic use of such language in comedy and (in passing) the extension of the terminology in Plato to apply to the 'courageous' pursuit of an argument. The following subsection (IV.A.4) is devoted to attitudes to the endurance of misfortune. It begins by noting the readiness of the Greeks 'to express grief noisily and extravagantly, weeping when disappointed or humiliated or when asking for clemency' (*GPM* 167), then illustrates the positive evaluation of the refusal to give way to emotion and the value attached to endurance of life's vicissitudes as a sign of manliness. Finally, it notes that the emphasis on the value of endurance of misfortune does not lead (as it might have) to a negative evaluation of suicide as flight from suffering but that suicide itself could be seen as a courageous act. The last subsection under this heading (IV.A.5, *Appropriateness of fear and aggression*) deals briefly with the relationship between fear, aggression and courage and more specifically the inappropriateness of the use of force against the vulnerable or the dead.

The second section of the chapter (IV.B) deals with 'Money and property'. This has just two subsections: acquisition and expenditure. The first of these explores the range of attitudes to the acquisition of money, beginning with the obvious fact that acquiring or withholding money which was considered to belong to someone else was held to be *adikos* together with the positive evaluation of a refusal to act dishonestly when in need, before moving to more nuanced discussion of the shifting and subjective nature of reactions to perfectly honest acquisition of money, and finishing with the relationship between money and luck in the collective imagination. The second subsection, on expenditure, examines the positive and negative evaluation of different ways of spending money, with expenditure on the polis and on generous benefaction to friends commended on the one hand and hedonistic and extravagant consumption condemned. The third section is entitled 'Advantage'. Under this heading he treats firstly friendship and enmity (IV.C.1). Here he amasses passages which demonstrate the familiar idea that one should help friends and harm enemies, including the longevity (even over generations) of feuds, the explicitness and intensity with which Athenians acknowledge and express their enmity and the pleasure to be derived from and justifications for retaliation for perceived wrong. The treatment of enmity leads organically to the next subsection (IV.C.2, *Law, custom and sentiment*), which looks at the range in usage of the terms *dikaios* and *adikos* and the relationship between the concept and terminology of justice and those of legality. This leads by a natural progression to the next subsection (IV.C.3) on litigation, which examines the way in which the decision to litigate is evaluated. This subsection is actually more interested in the disincentives to litigation and the figure of the *apragmôn*, the person who seeks a 'quiet' life, than in litigation as such. The final subsection under the heading 'Advantage', *Magnanimity* (IV.C.4), emerges naturally from the discussion of litigation, since it addresses qualities such as *epieikeia*, where the decision of the agent to forgo his or her entitlement under strict *dikaiosyne* is expected to elicit approval.

The fourth section, 'Sensibility', has just two subsections. Its first subsection (IV.D.1, *Compassion*) follows naturally from the discussion of magnanimity. Like the preceding, it addresses the potential divergence between strict entitlement under law and justice and, on the other hand, pity for the implications of punishment. It then moves to the relationship between pity and the merit of its object and the pity accorded to the weak. It also notes (following Lattimore) that in epitaphs *eleein* and *oiktirein* can refer 'less to sentiment than to formal acts or utterances which maintain the approved relationship between the world of the living and that of the dead' (*GPM* 197). The second subsection under this heading (IV.D.2), *Friendliness*, again follows naturally from what precedes, since it addresses the often-elusive concept of *philanthrôpia*. The fifth and final section is 'Sexual behaviour'. This section begins with a discussion of inhibition (IV.E.1) whose purpose is largely to remove any notion that the Greeks lived in a world of uninhibited sexuality; he argues instead that inhibitions increased over time. The next subsection (IV.E.2) deals very briefly with the positive evaluation of resistance to desire based both on ethical considerations (the general approval of qualities of restraint and endurance) and the potential conflict between excessive sexual desire and the law. The third subsection (IV.E.3, *Segregation*) is more substantial. It shows an awareness (rare for its time) that the restricted nature of our evidence gives us a skewed impression of the extent of female segregation in Athenian society by masking more extensive opportunities for contact between the sexes among less well-off people. It also notes that the emphasis on the continuance of the family and on inheritance in our forensic sources obscures the existence and value of affection between husband and wife. But Dover (reasonably) accepts the existence of restrictions on contact of females with unrelated males for the better-off and argues (as later in *Greek Homosexuality*) that one result was the channelling of desire into homoerotic relationships. A second consequence he finds is a tendency to devalue women. This leads us fluently to the final subsection, IV.E.4, *Homosexuality*, which rehearses briefly themes later explored in depth in *Greek Homosexuality*. He begins with the acceptance of homosexual desire as natural, even by the Aristophanic hero, then notes that the image of homosexual relationships provided by Plato and Aeschines underplays the physical dimension. He proceeds to note the double standards imposed by society on the *erastês* and on the *erômenos*, and finally observes the penalties attached to homosexual prostitution by citizens.

This brisk survey does not really do justice to the level of detail and nuance in the discussion. It also over-compartmentalizes the material, since Dover himself regularly cross-references his discussions, creating additional links between different sections. But it does give a sense of the range of material and topics discussed within a short compass. It also illustrates graphically that in organization and presentation *GPM* is very different from other ambitious works on Greek thought such as Dodds' earlier *The Greeks and the Irrational*, Adkins' *Merit and Responsibility* and Lloyd-Jones' contemporary *The Justice of Zeus*, which address a more sharply defined subject and argue a thesis, using primary sources to sustain the argument. *Greek Popular Morality* lacks this precise focus; it attempts instead to give an overview of the moral thinking of the Athenians. And it does not really have a discursive argument. Overarching argument if there is any is partly formulated in the discussion of method and still more embedded in the presentation. Part of that argument is about the sources to use and the way to interrogate them, if one wants to understand shared Greek morality rather than potentially peripheral views. My use of the word 'interrogate' here is only partly metaphorical. Dover speaks hypothetically, as we saw earlier, of the prospect of compiling a questionnaire on morality to put to different cultures (*GPM* 2). The second half of the book is in some respects a proxy for the results of such a questionnaire. Instead of offering an argument, *Greek Popular Morality* gives centre stage to the primary evidence, not to an authorial thesis. One can quibble with the translation of individual terms or the potential distorting effect of cropping passages from the texts in individual cases, as one reviewer did at some length.[25] But the emphasis throughout is on what Athenian speakers say on various moral issues, as though one had shoved a microphone under their noses. This is one of the strengths of the book. It gives us a kind of textual vox pop, with distinct voices compared, contrasted and contextualized. We should not overstate this. The views are not unmediated, since they come filtered through Dover's selection, organized according to his categories and framed by his presentation. Authorial comment is there throughout. And these statements by different speakers on different occasions are juxtaposed in a way they never were in real life in order to place them in dialogue with each other (another important methodological principle left implicit in the book) and so give a rounded picture. But these are words addressed by Athenian speakers to their Athenian audience or in dialogue or monologue in texts meant for an Athenian audience; they are not Dover's paraphrase. Not only is the primary evidence foregrounded; it is present in vast quantities. So although Dover is constantly leading the reader, the primary evidence is made available to offer the reader a degree of autonomy. The scale and breadth of the knowledge in play here is quite remarkable; it is easily missed in the age of *Thesaurus Linguae Graecae*, *JSTOR* and *Google Books*, when anyone can access almost any piece of data, almost anywhere, with little effort. *GPM* is all the fruit of primary reading.[26] The result is not an easy read. Or rather, it is not a fluent read. This is not really a book to sit down and read through, unless you are charged with the task of reviewing it. Again, this is unlike a book such as *The Justice of Zeus*, where to appreciate the book (whether to agree or disagree) one has to follow the argument. *Greek Popular Morality* in contrast is a dipping book.

Another tacit element in the embedded argumentation resides in the static nature of the analysis.[27] Modern political and intellectual historians would differ on the question of continuity and change in Greek thinking in general and Athenian thinking in particular. In combining fifth and fourth century texts within a single hermeneutic framework and combining them in individual cases to demonstrate specific points, Dover tacitly accepts a fundamental continuity in the value system across the life cycle of the democracy. On most of the issues at stake in this book I think he is essentially correct, though the (understandable) decision to focus on a circumscribed period and place means that larger continuities and developments between classical Athens and archaic Greece and across the boundaries between *poleis* go undiscussed.

There is a second major difference between this book and other explorations of Greek morality or intellectual history. Not only is there no single coherent argument, but there is also no narrative of coherence. Implicit in Dover's decision to foreground oratory as a source and explicit in his discussion of the way in which communication functions is a recognition that moral positions are conditioned by communicative contexts. Diversity is ingrained in the project. There is a gap, potentially a vast gap, between abstract principle and moral judgment in particular cases. He wryly remarks:

> We should not imagine that we shall discover the Athenians to have lived, any more than we do, by an internally consistent set of moral principles. If a philosopher builds logical contradictions into a theory, he will lose his reputation as a philosopher; equally, if a man persists in an attempt to live by principles of such a kind that their practical applications are constantly and conspicuously irreconcilable, he is likely to lose his friends and may lose his reason. But it would be quite untrue to say that we *cannot* hold contradictory moral beliefs or apply contradictory principles.
>
> GPM 3, Dover's italics

The analysis in the second half of the book systematically notes the way different situations open space for different perspectives on, and consequently different evaluations of, human behaviour. Even where the starting position is one which would command widespread or universal assent, Dover draws attention to the way in which context colours the precise formulation and practical application. So for instance on priorities in duty and responsibility: 'It may be said in broad terms – but as we shall see, refinement of that statement introduces complications – that an Athenian felt that his first duty was to his parents . . ., his second to his kinsman, and his third to friends and benefactors . . .' (*GPM* 273). The exposition in the main sections of the book is as much about moral judgment in action as about moral values in the abstract. The relentless emphasis on divergence is invaluable as a corrective to some theoretically more sophisticated but tendentious approaches to the same phenomena. The result is that there are few absolutes in the book. A strong and surprisingly long-lasting approach to Greek social history sees Greek society as relentlessly competitive. There is a fundamental truth to this. Our Greek sources show not only that an element of competition was at work in socio-political interaction, but also that such competition was collectively introduced into contexts which to us are quite alien, most notably religion. It is a fundamental truth, but it is also a limited truth. The competition becomes the basis of social interaction. To achieve this understanding one has to jettison a lot of the available evidence. In contrast, Dover matter-of-factly notes both the undeniable and explicit presence of competition in Athenian society and the ability of the Athenians both to collaborate and to value collaboration in others (*GPM* 82–3, 232–4).

One sympathetic reviewer complained that Dover's contrast between popular morality and the attempt by moral philosophy to achieve a consistent understanding of moral issues understated the degree of the coherence in popular morality.[28] Dover remained unapologetic on this point. In his later paper on moral evaluation in Greek poetry he cheerfully repeats his assertion of 'the inconsistent, incoherent and unsystematic nature of Greek (or any other) popular morality'.[29] It is however worth asking if Dover's research supports this contention, at least in the terms in which he formulates it. The material he offers demonstrates enormous gaps between agreed general principle and the way that principle is understood and applied by individuals in the shifting circumstances of everyday life. The term 'unsystematic' is entirely justified. Popular morality is not a unitary code but the product of evolutionary and largely organic processes.[30] I am sure that he is right that any collective morality contains contradictions, then and now. It then becomes a question of *how* inconsistent, *how* incoherent one finds collective morality to be. This is not a binary division.

One casualty of the way in which Dover sets out his material is that the breadth of learning and the depth of analysis underpinning the book are easily missed. One cannot really begin to describe the moral presuppositions of any society without having a sense of the *Realia* of the world in which its inhabitants live, in the widest possible sense. This is a great strength of the book, which rests on a deep foundation of his own previous and ongoing work combining historical and literary research. Questions of historical context are never addressed at length, since that is not the focus of the book. But there is always a carefully articulated frame. A good example is the question of class consciousness (*GPM* 37–41). A question which exercised Dover, and not just Dover, was the surprising coherence (surprising to us at least) between ordinary Athenians and members of the elite on matters which in our world invite very different responses which are often split along socio-economic lines. Comic theatre ridicules as lowborn, and even servile, people who are undoubtedly Athenian and are far wealthier than most of the audience. Speakers in court expect the audience to share their hostility to sycophants who would exploit the legal system to soak the rich. It would be a mistake to suppose that there was no room for resentment of the rich by poorer people in Athens. The Greeks in general (not just the Athenians) were alert to the inevitable tendency of wealth, beauty and success to invite *phthonos*. But texts addressing mass audiences make relatively little use of the opportunity to excite *phthonos* against the rich as a rhetorical ploy to gain advantage.[31] There seems to be no ideological base for a reflex hostility to the elite which might be exploited in court or in the Assembly. And there was never serious pressure for radical redistribution of wealth. In this respect democratic Athens was a remarkably conservative culture. This is not the unambiguous good it might seem to be at first sight, as Dover was well aware. Dover clearly respected the Greeks and was fascinated by Greek culture; but he had no romantic belief in the superiority of ancient Athens over the modern world. Like Moses Finley, Dover notes the significance of chattel slavery for the sense of solidarity between the richest and poorest of the elite citizen group.[32] Only by drawing strict exclusive boundaries between citizen and foreigner, slave and free, could the Athenians generate the sense of identity which sustained the (largely successful) democratic consensus. I would also single out Dover's exemplary discussion of the Athenian juries. The modern reader of the orators is struck by the presence of explicit statements which seem quite out of place in a court of law – references to character, attempts to malign the opponent, often irrelevant (in terms of modern jurisprudence) appeals to past services by the speaker and promises of future gains for the jury, appeals to prejudices about social groups or other nations. This has led some readers to conclude that trials are largely a competition for favour and that Athenian juries have no interest in the facts at issue.[33] Not so Dover:

> When these passages are taken in conjunction with others in which the litigant or defendant seems to be offering the community a bribe ... it is tempting to believe that an Athenian jury was normally concerned less with the facts of the case than with calculation of communal profit and loss. Such a conclusion, however, would not do justice to the complexity of the issue.
>
> *GPM* 293

The other, more important, downside to the breadth of the treatment is that some important issues receive only limited cover. The book could have taken an aspect of the value system such as friendship and enmity (as Blundell did later[34]) and explored this in depth either in an author or genre or across the board in Greek society. Or it could, like David Konstan or Douglas Cairns, have taken an emotion, or like Nick Fisher a sociopsychological phenomenon, and treated it at length and in depth.[35] Instead, it strives for breadth of cover. The positive outcome is a rich tapestry of information about Athenian attitudes. But the collateral result noted by John Gould is that some features which mark a vast gulf between ancient Athens and modern Christian or post-Christian cultures, such as the right and even duty to help friends and harm enemies, lose their salience, so that the alienness of some aspects of Athenian morality (though never ignored by Dover) is reduced.[36] The same could probably be said about religion. This is not of course a book about religion. But the gods receive only limited attention (they have a short section in the chapter on sanctions, 15 pages). Dover personally saw no necessary link between religion and ethics (*MC* 164). And he was writing in an age when organized religion across much of the western world was in decline. But the gods are more prominent in Greek thought than the space they occupy in the book would suggest. The result of the attempt to give equal cover to all issues overall is that Athenians become a lot more like us than they probably were. This is reinforced by the fact, noted earlier, that the starting point is explicitly the author's own questions about morality, not data from Athens, which carries with it the risk that we will look for and find ourselves. The problem here is a familiar one, that of negotiating the intellectual and cultural distance between us and any other time or place. It is a problem to which there is no single and simple solution. The problem can also be seen in the terminology used in Chapter VI, which addresses moral priorities; one section is entitled 'The state and the individual', another 'The state as moral agent'. Dover makes explicit that the Athenian political system was very different in structure from anything encountered in the modern world. But the notion of the state is a modern concept, and the terminology carries a risk of distorting the way in which one views Athenian attitudes toward the relationship between the individual and the organized society around him or her.

What then of the enduring value of the book? Though we would probably all like to think otherwise, everything we do as researchers is a product of its own time and place. It is influenced by trends in theory or method, by intellectual fashion, by the academic *Zeitgeist*, by the gaps on the shelves and our desire to fill them, and more generally it is shaped by larger social and political trends and interests, as well as by the author's personal experience and individual ambition. It is also in consequence provisional, since subsequent research will test and either validate or refute what we say. Ultimately, we are footnotes in the work of later researchers. But if we are lucky, we also have the chance to frame some at least of the questions of the next generation. For my generation (certainly for me) Dover's work was profoundly important. A significant part of the legacy of *Greek Popular Morality* is that it was one of the works which (in the anglophone world) helped to bring the orators out of the shadows and established them as authors worthy of study in their own right. In one respect they had never gone away. You cannot study fourth-century Athenian political history without Demosthenes and Aeschines, and if you want to discuss the regime changes at the end of the fifth century you cannot ignore Lysias. But interest in the orators as literature worthy of serious study among anglophone (especially British) scholars was fairly limited for much of the twentieth century. So too was interest in their potential for an understanding of the collective value system and for Athenian social history. And since curricula in secondary and tertiary education rely on the scholarly support of published works, higher education syllabuses likewise had little interest in the oratorical corpus. They did not figure in my undergraduate or even postgraduate education at Cambridge, beyond the off-piste reading I chose to do. I did not encounter oratory as part of a syllabus until I arrived in St Andrews and found myself teaching it. Now the study of the orators is part of the teaching mainstream at undergraduate and postgraduate level and forms the subject of scores of MA and PhD theses. There is a further, collateral, benefit. The orators are the most important underpinning for the serious study of Athenian law. In helping to bring the orators into focus, the book contributed (in tandem with MacDowell's more precisely focused work) to the emergence (again in the anglophone world) of interest in Greek law both at research level and in undergraduate and graduate courses.

It would be difficult to claim that the book has the same value for anyone commencing research now. On all the subjects addressed in the book the discussion has moved on. Subsequent scholarship has covered the same topics but in greater depth. It has also drawn more overtly on theoretical models to explain the phenomena, though not always to better effect. In this respect *Greek Popular Morality* has not weathered as well as *Greek Homosexuality*, which is the starting point for any attempt to understand this aspect of Greek culture, even for those who disagree with it fundamentally. Nor has it weathered as well as Dover's commentaries; commentaries by definition have a longer shelf-life than monographs, since they are replaced less frequently and (if rarely read in their entirety) are regularly raided by puzzled readers of the primary text.

There are however (at least in my opinion) three major elements of the book which are of lasting value. The first is the sheer volume of data. Dover observed that his approach of letting the Greeks do the talking meant that the book might look like 'a rampage through an epitome of Stobaeus' (*GPM* 12). That is one way of putting it. A more positive appraisal of the range and diversity of content is that it gives us a vast array of material on almost all areas of Athenian morality and what conditioned their workings. So it is still an excellent entry point for anyone wishing to access ancient Athenian views on all areas covered by the book. A second aspect is the explicit address to source and method. Dover was well aware of theoretical approaches current in his lifetime. But as Stephen Halliwell notes,[37] Dover was largely suspicious of theoretical approaches and his corpus taken as a whole does not foreground theory. He was however scrupulous in his address to method, including in *GPM* the selection and careful evaluation of the sources to be used and the problems presented to the researcher by any particular category of evidence. A careful evaluation of the raw material available is indispensable for any serious attempt to mine a corpus for facts or ideas or values. His discussion of the relative value and the nature of different sources remains exemplary, irrespective of the view one takes of the selection he makes. This explicit address to questions of source and method is something I have over the years impressed on my research students. The researcher has to be explicit about what they are doing, what evidence they are using and how they are using that evidence. The third aspect I would foreground is the refusal to impose consistency on the voices emerging from the texts, a collateral benefit of Dover's disinclination to work from a theoretical base. This openness to disharmony or divergence within the primary sources is again something I have stressed with research students as a useful antidote to the all-too-common desire for neatness. Discord is hard-wired into the oratorical texts by the adversarial context, the diversity of situation and agents, the issues at stake, the inevitably conflicting accounts and the need to locate individual acts within a moral framework acceptable to the audience. But in any field, it is unusual for the evidence available to present no discrepancies. Nothing in life is neat and nothing in scholarship should be, and this again is something I have tried to impress on my students. In general, if it looks too neat, it is.

Notes

1. *GPM* xi. Though he does not spell it out in the book, Dover was responding in particular to the rigidity of Adkins 1960, as he subsequently made clear in his rejoinder to Adkins' review of *GPM* (Dover 1983b) and later still in *MC* 155. His rejection of philosophical writing both as a source for collective morality and as an influence on societal thinking represents a deliberate attempt to distance the work from the enormous weight which Adkins placed on the significance of Kantian philosophy for collective modern western moral thought. The other issue on which Dover radically distanced himself from Adkins was in the role played by terminology, both in the focus on and interpretation of individual terms and in the socio-rhetorical force ascribed to particular lexical items.
2. Contrast more recently Morgan 2007, 1–22, whose introduction offers an explicit (though still brief) account of what the term means; this is of course three decades later.
3. *GPM* 4: 'It cannot, of course, be claimed that we can discover much of importance about the extent to which the Greeks actually lived by any of the moral standards which their utterances imply.'
4. This is made explicit in the section on social class, *GPM* 34–45.
5. Poetic, Dodds 1951, 30 (Homer *vs* popular superstitions); intellectual, ibid. 52 (Plato *vs* popular belief), 192 (the Greek Enlightenment *vs* popular religion). The distinction is most visible in Chapter VI, 'Rationalism and reaction', where it forms part of his presentation of what he sees as the ultimate failure of the Greek rationalist agenda at the societal level.
6. Cited by Stray in this volume (p. 99). Dover's account of the genesis of *GPM* decades later at *MC* 156 suggests that his attitude to the relation between the intellectual and the larger

society was probably shaped to some degree by his wartime experience. Though he does not dwell on it, Dover himself saw his 'five years absence from academic life' (on military service in the Second World War) as part of his justification for what might seem an arrogant claim to understand the minds of 'ordinary people'. He presents his wartime experience there as an important part of the foundation for *GPM*, and he draws particular attention to the exposure which his period as an officer gave him to people from social and educational backgrounds remote from his own and to his realization that education and social class were an inadequate guide to ability and intelligence (*MC* 52–3). This may have been a fairly common phenomenon, at least for those with a mind open to new experiences and ideas; exposure to people from social backgrounds far removed from his own through National Service had a similar shaping effect on Douglas MacDowell (Carey 2011, 235). The shaping influence of the war probably also lies behind Dover's discomfort with the rigid divide between town and gown in Oxford and the pleasure he took in the easier social relations he found in St Andrews (*MC* 88).

7. *GPM* 2 n. 3. Cf. *GPM* 43 n. 21: 'I once heard the information "He is a member of the Communist Party of Great Britain" conveyed by the words "He's a *very* nice man", spoken slowly and deliberately by one party member to another.'

8. e.g. *GPM* 183: 'If I realize my own wishes in opposition to the wishes of someone who has previously realized his in despite of mine, I am *dikaios* in restoring the boundary; if, acting in my own interest, I deceive, deprive, worry, sadden or insult or injure someone who has not so treated me – and that, after all, means most people – I am *adikos*.'

9. Cf. Donna Zuckerberg (with explicit reference to Dover's use of the first person in his *Clouds* commentary): 'The suppression of the authorial "I" in scholarship is a rhetorical trick that allows us to assume a position of speaking objective truth. But this forced separation between scholar and scholarship is necessarily artificial, because our backgrounds *always* inform what we write.' https://medium.com/@donnazuckerberg/the-authorial-lie-how-scholars-fabricate-authority-by-erasing-their-identities-fb453bee386f, accessed 07/05/22.

10. *GPM* 2. This point was impressed on me by Stephen Halliwell in comments on the first draft.

11. Halliwell, this volume, pp. 292, 301, 304.

12. Cf. Adkins 1978, 157–8: 'For, in general, this work gives the impression of having been written by two authors not always in perfect harmony with one another. One decries the lexical approach; the other compiles page after page of material which could well have been derived from lexica.'

13. Most notably in the work of Elroy Bundy on Pindar (Bundy 1962), most extensively (at that date) in Cairns 1972.

14. *GPM* 2.

15. *GPM* 7.

16. The exclusion is the more striking for the fact that Dover re-read these texts as part of his preparation for the book, n. 26 below.

17. See further at p. 158.

18. The dismissal of philosophical texts is lamented by de Romilly 1976, 209 in an otherwise sympathetic review on the ground that the division between moralizing texts and moral philosophy as a genre is less precise in classical Greece; the oddness of the failure to include Aristotle's *Rhetoric* was noted by Donald Russell in his obituary of Dover in *The Times* (Russell 2010).

19. Inscriptions had long been a particular interest of Dover's, though previously from a linguistic perspective, *MC* 72, 73–4; see Prauscello, this volume.

20. On tragedy and *GPM*, see Güthenke, this volume.
21. Adkins 1978, 148–9.
22. Ironically, Dover makes use of Antiphon's *Tetralogies*, which were never delivered in an Athenian court, and which share Thucydides' penchant for abstract generalization. On Dover and Thucydides' speeches, compare Pelling's chapter in this volume.
23. *MC* 146; cf. the discussion of this self-description in Sheffield's chapter in this volume.
24. *MC* 60–1; cf., again, Sheffield's chapter.
25. Adkins 1978, 150–7.
26. *MC* 158: 'Once they [sc. the commentary on Theokritos and *Aristophanic Comedy*] were published in the winter of 1971/2 I made good progress, reading the relevant corpus of Greek literature again, more carefully and reflectively, plus Xenophon, Aristotle's *Ethics*, and whatever Plato said or implied about the popular moral attitudes which his Socrates found unsatisfactory.'
27. This statement needs to be qualified a little. The book does recognize change over time. Thus e.g. at *GPM* 206–7 Dover finds an 'increasingly rigorous confinement of uninhibited sexual expression to "privileged" compartments of progressively narrowed artistic, literary and ritual practice.' Cf. p. 157 above. But in general, the book does not emphasize chronological development.
28. Gould 1978, 287.
29. Dover 1983b, 46–7.
30. Or geological, consisting of layers superimposed upon but never quite replacing what goes before; Dodds following Gilbert Murray uses the term 'inherited conglomerate' for the accretion of beliefs which builds up over time (Dodds 1951, 179).
31. Sanders 2014, ch. 5.
32. *GPM* 39: 'The very extensive use of slaves for the work now done by unionized wage-earners, combined with the existence at Athens of a very large category of resident aliens who were debarred from participation in the processes of political decision and subject to great legal disabilities... allowed even the poorest Athenian citizen to be conscious that he was a member of an elite...' (citing Finley 1959). See on this now the excellent book of Lape 2010, esp. ch.1.
33. For an extreme example of this approach, see Cohen 1995.
34. Blundell 1989.
35. Cairns 1993, Fisher 1992, Konstan 1997 (inter alia).
36. Gould 1978, 287.
37. In this volume, p. 292; cf. *MC* 146.

CHAPTER 10
DOVER AND GREEK DRAMA
Constanze Güthenke

'I have no poetical humbug about me' – these are not Kenneth Dover's words, though they could well be. They belong to Lord Byron, apparently uttered to an acquaintance who inquired about the poet's stay on the island of Ithaca and his 'classical recollections' as he experienced the *genius loci*. Dover quotes the anecdote in an undated manuscript of a conference talk entitled 'Byron on the Ancient Greeks'.[1] The talk is in many ways characteristic of its author. It relishes an oblique take-down of the idealization of Byron, or rather of the short-sighted frequent re-use of his poetry as ready philhellenic quotation ('The isles of Greece, the isles of Greece / Where burning Sappho loved and sang . . .'); it offers some well-researched down-to-earth contextualization of Byron's schooling, his library and his command of ancient languages (not great); and it discusses with equal relish the erotic and homosocial coding as much as the actual encounters that shaped or would or could or should have shaped the motivation and outlook of Byron apropos Greece and in Greece.

Dover's opening gambit is to remind the reader of the 'intentional fallacy' – although this is not a term he uses.[2] In fact, the vocabulary of the New Criticism, whether in its British or American version, is notably absent from Dover's writings on ancient literature, as are explicit references to contemporary literary criticism generally, despite the fact that this was in many ways probably the most easily accessible idiom of the field of literary studies for a good part of his writing life.[3] By pointing out that one should not mistake the sentiments expressed in poetry for a direct representation of those of the author, Dover makes room for the mediation of literary form and the inflections it carries, and he acknowledges that historical contextualization and reading texts as historical sources always need to take account of mediation through the art form as such.[4]

That he attributes this attitude to Byron himself is reflected in the anecdote Dover quotes apropos Ithaca, when we see it in full: 'Yet when he was asked later by a friend if he was not "gratified by the classical recollections" of Ithaca, he replied, "You quite mistake me. I have no poetical humbug about me. I am too old for that. Ideas of that sort are confined to rhyme"'.[5] That he, at the same time, considers this a generally valid form of interpretation is clear from the opening passage of his lecture. Here he spells out a warning about the intentional fallacy with specific reference to drama: 'We naturally tend to assume that a poem cast in direct and passionate language expresses the poet's own emotion at the time of writing, though we grant a special exemption to the dramatists, declining to identify Shakespeare with Iago or to assume that Wolsey's heartfelt repudiation of ambition was necessarily felt by Shakespeare's heart.'[6]

Even though his chosen example here is Shakespeare, the point serves as an indication of Dover's attitude to ancient drama as well, and especially comedy, and of the tensions or ambivalences of this attitude. On the one hand, there is a firm belief in a contextualist-historicist approach, and in the value of reading dramatic texts and performances in light of their contemporary environment, which includes and reflects significant historical events. On the other hand, there is ready acknowledgement about the limitations of assuming causal relationships, and an insistence that fictionality plays a large part in drama. We see at work the same 'obsession with realism' (Jaś Elsner's term in the present volume, apropos Dover's approach to art) or his 'fundamentalist realism' (as Tim Whitmarsh put it in a review of the 2016 reissue of *Greek Homosexuality*).[7] Such realism allows the double game of highlighting the intervening medium, but also insisting on its transparency and accessibility. In this context, one may wonder whether it was particularly Attic comedy as an art form that both confirmed but also continued to destabilize Dover's certainties about the representation and functionality of classical texts and that therefore kept challenging and simultaneously affirming Dover's premises.

This is not to say that Greek tragedy would have stood outside those structures, quite the contrary. It would be easy to follow Dover's own pattern of invocation followed by swift side-lining when it comes to discussing tragedy. Thus, the present essay on Dover's approach to Greek drama will deliberately not try to simply replicate his priorities and understand drama as mostly synonymous with comedy, with the occasional nod towards tragedy. Instead, I will first of all enquire what kind of reader of tragic texts Dover is, and what continuities and differences between tragic genres and their interpretation may have impacted his preferences.

A good example of Dover's assumption about the fundamental accessibility and cognitive compatibility of Greek drama *tout court* is the reading he offers of Aeschylus' *Agamemnon* and the question of Agamemnon's ethical dilemma and its representation.[8] Here, he highlights contrast and difference between ancient and modern moral preconceptions: 'The Classical Greek offers a strong contrast with Christian and modern attitudes alike.'[9] At the same time, he insists on the ostensibly clear grounds on which those differences can be mapped and drama can thus be fully apprehended: 'In the meantime, it may be useful to see how many passages in Greek drama are explicable without residue as realistic portrayal of irrational processes, familiar to us from introspection and observation, working upon matter furnished by Greek beliefs and values and expressing themselves in Greek terms.'[10] Or, as he lays out in a companion piece on the *Agamemnon* and the significance of the red fabric, 'When I speak of "psychology", I do not mean modern theories designed to trace psycho-dynamic mechanisms, but ways of speaking and acting which, when we have observed them in ourselves, we can find everywhere in Greek tragedy, conspicuous even on the surface, not hidden in the darkness of the unconscious.'[11]

Dover's engagement with tragedy, such as it is, also indexes his otherwise well-known misgivings about philosophy, or rather about expectations regarding metaphysical import.[12] The piece on Agamemnon's dilemma is, again, a good case in point. As Dover argues, referencing Albin Lesky's opinion that 'with all the powers of his mind' Aeschylus 'wrestled with the problem arising from the conflict between human existence and divine rule', there is no need to evaluate Aeschylus only by the parameter of how sustained or consistent his own theological and intellectual worldview are:

> I [do not] take the view that a dramatist passionately involved in metaphysics and theology is a wiser and greater man than one who devotes the powers of his mind to concrete problems of poetic and theatrical technique. The scale of values adopted by interpreters of early Greek tragedy has certainly been affected, and has perhaps been somewhat distorted, by the dominant position of philosophy in European culture and education.[13]

In the article that follows from this opening salvo, Dover argues that in the 'dilemma' over the killing of his daughter on apparently divine orders Agamemnon's actions need to be understood as part of the artistic narrative with its structural and dramatic needs, but also as part of a complex and contextual calculation about right and wrong action in light of the gods' uncertain wishes, which are mediated only through a seer's authority.[14] However justified an emotional response to this situation is, as shown by the chorus for example, it would be wrong to extrapolate from a comprehensible psychological appreciation to a transcendental or transhistorical truth about either the human condition or about characteristics of the divine. This would mean, though Dover does not spell this out or push it further, that no readings that postulate fundamental compatibility between ancient and modern human understanding should be taken as self-evident but that they equally need subtle calibration, whether they are in an idealist vein (what he had referred to as 'the dominant position of philosophy in European culture and education') or whether they reflect a psychological and common-sensical viewpoint such as his own. In this way, Dover's reflections are a further excellent example of the characterization of Dover's cast of mind identified in Stephen Halliwell's epilogue to this volume: that a strong self-referential and self-reflective tendency goes hand in hand with 'a marked aversion to sustained theorization of his practices or his values as a scholar'.[15]

By extension from this observation, Dover's sibling pieces on the *Agamemnon*, published within a few years of each other in the 1970s, are also a good example of the openness of his readings of tragic texts as artistic and literary texts in theory (or in potential), and of a more restricted approach, or even entrenchment, in practice. In his article on the significance of the red fabric, Dover suggests a wide range of possible reasons that would or could make it appear justified and persuasive for Agamemnon to follow his wife's plea to step on the precious material. After invoking possible explanations with components from the study of structural anthropology or religion (destroying something valuable in one's possession acts as a form of self-abasement before the gods, rather than a form of over-reach), the ace up Dover's sleeve rests ultimately on a historical parallel: that of the Spartan statesman Pausanias, whose example of alienating his allies in 478 through his own adoption of a lavish Persian style Dover draws in from the textual record in Thucydides and Herodotus. Again, Dover is careful not to be seen as turning a historical analogy into a claim about causation, and he does so with a nod to other forms of literary interpretation that are equally possible: 'There is no doubt of the utility of subjecting Greek tragedy to structural criticism which discovers identical schemes in different parts of the same play, but it must also be recognized that there are structures and schemata common to certain historical events and the dramatic themes of a poet influenced by those events'.[16] Apropos 'structural criticism', he adds a footnote to Anne Lebeck's then still fairly recently published *The Oresteia: a Study in Language and Structure* (1971), itself in many ways a ground-breaking and seminal study of the complex networks of imagery created across the trilogy. In citing the work of a young female scholar, an American, an outsider in her own right, and one with very explicit literary and structuralist objectives, Dover shows himself to be casting his net quite widely, though just how open or critical his line 'there is no doubt of the utility' is – damning with faint praise or genuine possibility? – is arguable.[17] What is clear, regardless, is that Dover takes pride in making explicit links between literary and historical study:

> The fact that no commentator on the *Agamemnon* has mentioned Pausanias may be due to a decision on the part of commentators that the difference between the fate of Pausanias and the fate of Agamemnon are more important than the resemblances. It may, on the other hand, simply be due to the fact that Greek literature and Greek history are commonly studied in separate compartments, and a fortunate combination of circumstances has enabled me to study and teach both at the same time, so that I very readily treat as historical events both the political vicissitudes of a Spartan regent and the creative process which went on in the mind of an Athenian poet of genius.[18]

This neatly sums up Dover's approach to Greek drama – understanding it and its particular creativity as a historical event – and it equally neatly expresses his self-positioning as a scholar. It also describes what would, with course reform at Oxford around 1970 when Dover was publishing this piece, become the orthodoxy certainly at Oxford, namely the closeness of historical and literary study and the expectation that linguistic and historical skills were in essence a mutual extension of each other.

If I have treated some of Dover's writings on tragedy in more detail, Dover's overall engagement with Attic tragedy is of course, unlike that with comedy, compact in size. Besides the two pieces on Aeschylus' *Agamemnon* already mentioned, there is another article, from twenty years earlier, on the political aspects of the *Eumenides*, namely the reforms of the Areopagus and the question of whether Aeschylus' play suggests a positive or negative response to them;[19] a short note on Aeschylus, fr. 248M;[20] a piece on a passage of Sophocles' *Trachiniae*, which was Dover's contribution to a Festschrift for Jan Kamerbeek;[21] and some short reviews, one a fairly scathing one of Robert Lowell's translation of Aeschylus, and one a reading of Brooks Otis's *Cosmos and Tragedy* (1982), in which Dover makes short shrift of Otis's quite holistic and metaphysical reading of Aeschylus.[22]

In his *Greek Popular Morality* (1974), tragic texts are clearly within purview, but are then also rather side-lined. Again, there is ready acknowledgement – or rather an acknowledgement by way of a caveat – about the fictionality of the tragic world and, generally, the dramatic contextualization of any utterance in a play, tragic or comic: 'The chief obstacle to the identification of elements of popular morality in drama of any kind is the simple fact that drama consist of the utterances of fictitious persons in fictitious circumstances.'[23] Tragedy is mentioned as the first example of available source material for *Greek Popular Morality*, though it reads a little as if it needed to be gotten out of the way before Dover can move grand-scale to comedy and oratory, and their affinities.[24] In *Marginal Comment*, Dover gives a fairly good outline of the method employed in *Greek Popular Morality*, which signals well the slightly ambivalent status tragedy holds there. Included for reasons of comprehensiveness, and to maintain an eye on drama as a whole, tragedy quickly takes a back seat to oratory, towards which the project gravitates, and to comedy, which is its second area of emphasis, and which offers more clues to its own reception by an (implied) audience:

> My first task, therefore, was to re-read the whole of Attic oratory, noting and classifying relevant passages. The second was to re-read the whole of comedy and late fifth-century tragedy in search of passages which conformed – or, more interestingly, did not conform – with the scheme of values which I drafted after reading the orators. Playwrights competed for prizes, and winning mattered a lot to them, but they did not risk their lives and property as a man in court did, and they could afford to put into the mouths of characters on stage ideas which it would have been extremely imprudent to voice to a jury. We do not know what the playwright himself thought, because he gave a character words which *that* character would have uttered in *that* situation (though often rhetorically formal and intellectualised to a highly unrealistic degree), but dramatic form (especially in comedy) gives us plenty of clues to what was acceptable in sentiment to the audience.
>
> MC 157–8

To probe the silences about tragedy it is especially instructive to compare Dover's approach to that of one of his one-time students, the (classically trained) philosopher Bernard Williams. In her review of *Marginal Comment*, Mary Beard pointed out how little we get to hear from Dover about his pupils or about ways in which his teaching and research created genealogies, or constellations, of interests and orientations – what she calls an 'intellectual descent group'.[25] Beard acknowledges that one of the rare exceptions is indeed Bernard Williams, who does get a look-in, though brief and for the most part in passing. Aside from mentioning him as a notably bright undergraduate, Dover recounts his attempt, the day after Williams had taken Greats, to get him to acknowledge that 'philosophy was a branch of English lexicography'.[26] Tellingly, he also mentions Williams in the context of narrating the background to the event that prompted the writing of *Greek Popular Morality* itself. Asked by the American Council of Philosophical Studies to take part in a seminar in Colorado Springs, in 1970, for early career scholars in Greek philosophy, Dover provocatively turned to 'popular morality' as a way of discussing morality beyond philosophy in the age of Plato and Aristotle, not least since 'it was far beyond me to provide adequate philosophical fare for people who would also be having seminars with – among others – Gregory Vlastos, Bernard Williams and Gwil Owen' (*MC* 155). There is not only relative silence on Williams as a (former) student, or regarding philosophy, but it is also clear that Dover's own approach to tragedy in terms of the possibilities of reading and the parameters of interpretation were radically different. While both he and Williams seem to agree on an awareness of tragedy's fictional and artistic character, Williams reads analogously rather than trans-historically and with a view to making 'structural substitutions'.[27] Williams is markedly sceptical about an easy transferability between ancient and modern culture or thought, and thus he seeks to establish a dialectical relationship between modern moral problems and ancient textual sources that stays attuned to a kind of double fiction, a double *as if*: there is the fictionality of the art form of drama itself, but there is also the suspension implicit in the attempt to read ancient texts through an inevitably modern lens.

With all that said, tragedy does, at the same time, hold a place of origin for Dover, both in his academic (auto-)biography, but also by extension in his own drawing up of a genealogy and hierarchy of academic practices, something that renders his silences and choices arguably all the more deliberate and/or revealing. Regarding his undergraduate training at Oxford, it is clear that the literature teaching he received was, at Mods and thus for the first half of the course, barely what we would now expect of an introduction to literary analysis, though it was entirely in line with Classics teaching in Oxford at the time.[28] The work was mostly an extension from school, with several compositions (i.e. translation from English into Latin and Greek) per week, and a good deal of lectures available. Dover recounts that he did not write a single essay on a literary subject, or any classical subject for that matter, for Mods, though he was assigned a couple of essays on general topics by the Master of Balliol and by some of his tutors (*MC* 39). He does, elsewhere, mention E.R. Dodds as a lecturer who left an impression,[29] and of course he invoked the lack of structural change and flexibility, especially regarding the study of Greek literature as such, as one of his reasons for declining the invitation to become Regius Professor of Greek at Oxford in 1960 (*MC* 90–1); indeed, it was not before 1970 that ancient literature as such became an official part of Greats, beyond or beside history and philosophy. It is, however, not Dodds but the refugee scholar Eduard Fraenkel whom Dover singles out as the most influential scholar of literary texts and the one with the longest reach regarding Dover's early understanding of professional scholarship. Like many of his contemporaries, Dover was marked by the experience of Fraenkel's *Agamemnon* seminar that ran from 1936 to 1942 after Fraenkel's arrival and his subsequent and (for a German refugee scholar) unusually prominent appointment as Corpus Professor of Latin. Like many of his contemporaries, he was equally marked by the pull of the charismatic, even if not unproblematic, *persona* of the scholar that Fraenkel embodied and by the conceptualization and image of German scholarship that accompanied it.[30] Dover's reflections on this encounter are worth quoting in detail:

> What mattered most at Oxford was Eduard Fraenkel's seminar on the *Agamemnon* of Aeschylus, which was attended by some dons and a select number of undergraduates recommended by their tutors. We took turns at presenting our

expositions of successive portions of the play. My portion was part of the Kassandra scene, which I treated as if it were a newly discovered text and we were looking at it with innocent eyes. Fraenkel had an immense influence on me (too much; it was twenty years before I came to acknowledge his limitations), but it was hard to explain the nature of the spell which he cast. Not long ago I put the question to a friend who had attended his seminars some years after me, and on reflection she said, 'It was his *seriousness*.' She didn't mean that he was gloomy or portentous, but that he acknowledged the Greeks and Romans as real people, who did not write *for us*, but for and within a culture which we can come to understand if we work at it. I felt that the older generation of Oxford scholars, for the most part, had not worked at it hard enough, but thought of the Classical poets as interesting neighbours who called in at the vicarage for tea and entertained the company by quoting from their poems. This is an arrogant judgement, and if I had been called on to justify it I don't think I could have done so, but, looking back, I can see what provoked it; Fraenkel understood and explained to us the constants and the variables in Greek and Latin literature, the interplay of tradition and innovation, and that was an aspect of literature which did not seem to interest many British scholars. The younger generation – notably Bill Watt, Spencer Barrett and Frederick Wells – understood it well, and cared about it; so, among their elders, did Dodds, who had succeeded Gilbert Murray as Regius Professor of Greek in 1936.[31]

Dover thinks it important to mention Fraenkel's own account of his filiations and his reminiscences of the seminar of his own *Doktorvater* Wilamowitz. What mattered for admission to the seminar, he quotes Fraenkel as saying, 'was not how learned you were, but how much you cared about the subject and how hard you were prepared to work' (*MC* 40).[32] With hindsight, Dover is explicitly acknowledging and also resisting Fraenkel's autocratic streak, as a charismatic scholar who was felt by others to pay exceptional and uncustomary attention to the intellectual standards of Oxford undergraduates, but was in doing so also seeking reaffirmation of his own views in and through his seminarians. For all his critique of Fraenkel, though, Dover concludes that:

All the same, in setting me the task, within a few months of my arrival in Oxford, of expounding the Kassandra scene to the seminar, he was saying in effect, "Go away on your own, compose a *good commentary* on this portion of the play, and come back and tell us all about it." In saying that he was starting me on my professional career.

ibid.

In saying that, Fraenkel may also have inculcated in Dover a strong expectation (and he was likely not the only one to do so) that a good commentary constitutes the clearest exemplification and materialization of a professional career. With his commentaries on Thucydides, on Aristophanes' *Clouds* and *Frogs*, and even on the *Symposium*, Dover both followed and sidestepped Fraenkel's precept – not least by never attempting a commentary on a tragic text, whether out of respect, complementation or avoidance. One small, but quite striking area in which Fraenkel might shine through as a model is Dover's own predilection for the extensive reconstruction (or, arguably, construction) of stage directions.[33] The commentary on *Clouds* begins with a page and a half of single-spaced, small-print scene-setting, which draws together social, historical, narrative, and performative information in a mutually reinforcing way. In his less specialist *Aristophanic Comedy* (1972), Dover includes an explicit section on the reconstruction of stage directions.[34] Here, he argues for the value of the scholia in doing so, but he also acknowledges frankly that in the absence of ancient information or testimonia, writing new ones is justified as a means of explication or disambiguation, quoting as an ostensibly self-evident example the final scene of *Lysistrata* (with its multiple inferred comings and goings).[35]

There is another way in which Fraenkel's strong *persona*, and Dover's willing reflection on the complex interplay of power and intellectual creativity, may offer an analogy for his own approach to drama and especially to Aristophanes. Just as, arguably, Fraenkel's Aeschylus was an image of Fraenkel himself, Dover's Aristophanes is, unsurprisingly, also very much an image of Dover himself.[36] Dover did, of course, consider Aristophanes along the lines of inquiry that had been shaping British scholarship since the nineteenth century, namely how Aristophanic comedy related to Athenian politics, what its use as a historical source was, what Aristophanes' political views were, and what kind of representational calculus was at play in translating those into the form of comedy.[37] In this context, Dover's own repeated self-assertion in the face of authority, his life-long scholarly command of technique and canonical material combined with an appreciation of paths less well trodden, of kicking against the goad, of calling a spade a spade, and of his readiness to acknowledge this programmatically and explicitly, reads like an embodied commentary itself on the description of Aristophanes which he puts forward in *Aristophanic Comedy*.

In a section entitled 'Self-Assertion', he states firmly that Aristophanes' treatment of religion and politics are two sides of the same coin and continuous with each other. Both show Aristophanes to be pushing back against authority and they show his criticism as a form of self-assertion in the face of real existing power. For Dover, this does away with the surface paradox of conservatism and insurrection, since both can co-exist. In other words, Dover does not come down on the side of treating or classifying Aristophanes as either a political conservative or a revolutionary, since comedic insurrection is contained within existing structures of power. Also, for Dover, Aristophanes is not questioning the constituency of Athens: in terms of his support or lack of support for any specific political orientation, democracy remains a basic assumption that is firmly baked into his understanding. If there is any threat of actual political revolution, it inevitably arises in Dover's reading from the conservative or reactionary end of the spectrum (as embodied, for example, in the oligarchic coups in 411 and 404).[38]

Dover is characteristically assured in stating his opinions. As Chris Pelling points out in his contribution to this volume, apropos Dover's attitude to Thucydides, he did not recognize ambiguity as a value. This does, of course, on some level also mean that comedy, which celebrates ambiguity, will continue to put pressure on such categorizations, or throw a spanner into the works of the assured scholar. In a review of Victor Ehrenberg's study *The People of Aristophanes: A Sociology of Old Attic Comedy*, Dover is quite clear that comedy cannot easily be used as a historical source, in the sense that it does not accurately reflect and reflect on event history or social history; instead, it ought to be considered as something that exceeds the status of a source of historical information, seeing that it is implicated in changing combinations of fantasy and parody, imagination and fiction.[39] At the same time, Dover reaches the limit of responding to literariness and of conceptualizing form beyond imagining it as a set of conventions that contain and at times deform or reform content. A telling example in this context is his treatment of Aristophanes' speech in Plato's *Symposium*. As Frisbee Sheffield mentions in her chapter in this volume, Dover published a separate piece on Aristophanes' speech in which he focussed on the folkloric aspects of Aristophanes' tale of the severed half bodies in search of their missing counterparts, a choice in keeping with his contextualist, historicizing approach, but also with his assumptions about literary form and its possibilities.[40] Aristophanes' inset narrative of the primordial bodies rent asunder by Zeus is a deeply Aristophanic move that combines the concrete and the abstract to great and striking effect and enables the important transition to greater abstraction in the dialogue, away from real bodies and real communities. Dover locates the narrative core of the speech simply and squarely in the realm of 'fable'. By extension, and in response to Aristophanes' narrative in the *Symposium*, he concludes that 'Plato believed that popular values, as assumed and exemplified in comedy and folklore, were committed to the individual, the particular and the familiar, and that such a morality was irreconcilable with the practice of philosophy'.[41] As well as supposedly elucidating the nature of Plato's work, this reflects Dover's own preference for comedy over any other dramatic form. For him, Aristophanes' fantastic art and comedic form sit, like fable, on the side of moral realism, and are thus not compatible with the abstraction of philosophy; at the same time, fiction, fable and literary form emerge as optional and detachable additions to reality, as if they did not inhabit a much wider, stranger and more elusively efficacious place, one that is continuous with reality rather than staking a claim to be its opposite.[42] Maybe it was also this paradox of dramatic art and how to describe and judge its artifice in the first place that made comedy, at least in Dover's conceptualization of it, a clearer fit for his priorities as a reader and interpreter than tragedy did or would have done.

Dover had no trouble reading Greek drama from a declared vantage point of common sense, whether the rationality of that common sense was understood to be psychological or historical. 'Obvious' is a favourite word in his writing. And yet, an analysis of Doverian hermeneutics may be better served by not simply reacting to strong opinion with equally strong counter-opinion. Despite his lack of appreciation for ambiguity, might there not also be evidence in turn for a highly ambivalent relationship with drama on his part and with the ambivalence of dramatic language and form itself, an insight, however disavowed, which kept Aristophanes dynamically present in his thinking? For every historical argument, there is an acknowledgement of the elusiveness of dramatic form. In order to describe and capture such elusiveness in scholarly, interpretive terms, Aristophanic irreverence may have appealed more strongly to him as a paradigm than something like tragic genius. Comic, personalized, historically grounded irreverence was a textual model in which overdetermination and proliferation of meaning could find a place.

In *Marginal Comment*, Dover reiterated his fundamental commitment to the intelligibility of Greek writing and drama, when he stated: 'When a contemporary audience sees a Greek tragedy, it may find a great many of the ingredients, taken one at a time, alien; it is the structure, the interrelation of the ingredients, which makes the complex intelligible' (*MC* 125). Significantly, this comes right after a long discussion of his varied and at times rather fraught relationship with the maverick French-Romanian scholar George Devereux, whom he had at some point recommended for a visiting fellowship at All Souls College in Oxford, with whom he considered working on Greek homosexuality, and whose work on dreams in Greek tragedy he had successfully promoted to publishers.[43]

Dover had clearly been drawn to some of Devereux's work on ethnopsychology, anthropology and psychoanalysis, and he appreciated, or in his own turn read, his work for the possibility of seeing tragic poetry as a transformation of the same impulses, drives and pathologies that Freudian analysis was interested in – but, to Dover's mind at least, captured less persuasively. His own account of his acquaintance with Devereux is characteristic: much initial expression of misgivings about easy and reductive psychoanalytical literary criticism is followed by a *volte-face* and considerable mellowing when Dover is able to make greater sense of Devereux's approach to tragedy, first by connecting it with a dream about one of his own childhood experiences, and then later by recounting how a dream about a social event during which his skills in scansion are discussed sheds new light for him on an issue he had recently been grappling with apropos a passage in Thucydides.[44] Dover's vacillation is not my main point. Instead, it is the readiness with which he seems to suggest that reading Greek tragedy could become an analogous expression of the therapist's analytical work.[45] May it be that an alternative to 'reality' or 'fantasy' emerges here in studying the 'pathological', where his interests in anthropology, self-analysis and historical and linguistic analysis could coalesce?

The fundamental intelligibility of antiquity to which Dover held so firmly is captured, as Mary Beard astutely pointed out, in a footnote in which he seems slightly to misquote, but does not attribute, Louis MacNeice's lines from the long poem *Autumn Journal*, originally published in 1939: 'It was all so unimaginably different / And all so long ago.'[46] Dover ostensibly alludes to those lines, which conclude a self-consciously modern imagination of ancient scenes, as representing the view of a 'scholar' quite different from his own, namely that Greek civilization is 'similar enough to ours to be intelligible'.[47] Beard takes this elision of MacNeice as a prompt to reflect on how Dover – unlike E.R. Dodds, for example – did not cultivate the networks that both linked the spheres of academia and art and fostered the contiguities of Greek literature and modern poetry, certainly in that mid-century moment.[48] Dover is thus symptomatic of a professionalization that rendered the scholarly and artistic worlds much less mutually permeable. But beyond that, Dover's use of the quotation and his description of it as reflecting a 'scholarly view' elides (as does Beard) that MacNeice, as a scholar-poet, deals in *Autumn Journal* also with the challenges and the moral and personal deformations which a traditional

Classics education could (and can) wreak, on its students and its teachers alike. After all, a slightly earlier section of *Autumn Journal*, XIII, which describes MacNeice's experience as an Oxford undergraduate, reads: 'Not everyone here having had / The privilege of learning a language / That is incontrovertibly dead.'[49] MacNeice initially went from Oxford to the University of Birmingham as a young instructor (hired by Dodds), and *Autumn Journal* is, aside from capturing the vertigo of the immediate pre-war atmosphere, also a poem about the range of conflicting and complicated affects marking the classical scholar, about his sharp recognition of the false nostalgia and complacency of Oxford, including the comfort of disinterested reading, and about the labour of academia and the analogous demands of labour outside academia.

MacNeice ultimately left the academic world, and the lines from *Autumn Journal*, 'It was all so unimaginably different / And all so long ago', reflect the disorientation that ultimately led to his radical decision about the separation of scholar from poet. His conclusions about the unsustainability and absurdity of Classics in moral, political and aesthetic terms, despite its considerable pull, certainly went far beyond Dover's own views. Yet Classics as it was taught to MacNeice and practised by him was nonetheless familiar to Dover. Dover may have had a keen eye for deformity, institutional as much as personal, intentional as much as accidentally grown. As a stylistic and narrative choice, he could recognize and appreciate it especially in the work of Aristophanes, and still maintain a belief in its transparency and accessibility. Ultimately, though, Dover diverged from MacNeice and instead sided more readily with the Byron he selected from the anecdotal evidence of the poet's own testimony: 'I have no poetical humbug about me. I am too old for that. Ideas of that sort are confined to rhyme.'

Notes

1. Dover 1988a, 299. Stephen Halliwell points out to me that Dover lectured on Byron for the British Council in Japan in 1982, though the relationship of that lecture to the piece printed in *G&L* cannot now be ascertained.
2. The term was coined by Wimsatt and Beardsley 1946, in the context of a discussion of Romantic poetry.
3. The English Faculty in Oxford was in its outlook for the most part very historicist, rather than invested in forms of close reading and associated new-critical forms, both during Dover's tutorial fellowship and during his tenure as Corpus President. There would, tellingly, have been not much need during either period of Dover's time in Oxford for a classicist to profess interaction with modern literary criticism for the better study of ancient literature.
4. A point he makes in other writings, too. See, for example, his essay on 'The poetry of Archilochos', Dover 1964b (reprinted in 1987, 97–121). Here he pushes back against (auto-) biographical readings assumed to apply to the Greek iambic poet.
5. Dover 1988a, 299.
6. Dover 1988a, 292. At the same time, Dover confidently described himself as an 'intentionalist' when it came to hermeneutics (Dover 1997a, 13 n. 15), or expressed impatience with the idea of the intentional fallacy, *MC* 258–9. My thanks to Stephen Halliwell for those further references.

7. Whitmarsh 2016.
8. Dover 1973c, reprinted in Dover 1987, 135–50.
9. Dover 1987, 137.
10. Dover 1987, 150.
11. Dover 1987, 155 (originally in Italian as Dover 1977).
12. For Dover's attitude to philosophy, see especially Frisbee Sheffield's contribution in this volume.
13. Dover 1973 = Dover 1987, 135. Dover here quotes Lesky 1966, 85.
14. Dover's interest in tragic dilemmas is pointed, yet select, and it may owe something to his self-declared experience about the world of decision-making in war; with regard to Fraenkel's (war-time) *Agamemnon* commentary he emphasizes Fraenkel's own comments on war, and he appreciatively references N.G.L. Hammond's view that Agamemnon's dilemma is 'very familiar to those who are engaged in a war and exercise command' (Dover 1987, 144 n. 12).
15. Halliwell in this volume, p. 292. For the argument that Idealist traditions of reading and defining Greek tragedy have remained integral to modern scholarship yet underestimated in their implications, see Billings 2014.
16. Dover 1987, 157.
17. Ewen Bowie rightly points out to me that new American work on tragedy would quite naturally have appeared on Dover's horizon and on that of his colleagues, but the reference here still seems pointed.
18. Dover 1987, 157.
19. Dover 1957, reprinted in Dover 1987, 161–75.
20. Dover 1964c, reprinted in Dover 1987, 184–5.
21. Dover 1987, 186–9; originally Dover 1976b (misdated as 1977 in the Contents of Dover 1987, vi).
22. Dover 1980c (reprinted in Dover 1987, 176–81) and Dover 1983c (reprinted in Dover 1987, 182–3). He also reviewed Bernard Knox's *Word and Action*, Oliver Taplin's *Greek Tragedy in Action*, both in 1981, and the English translation of Albin Lesky's *Greek Tragic Poetry* in 1984, but none of them in specialist Classics journals: for further bibliographical details, see Craik ed. 1990, 408.
23. Dover 1974, 14.
24. The section on 'Special Characteristics of Greek Tragedy' in the first chapter ('Interpretation of the Sources') takes up four pages, 14–18. *Ad hoc* references to tragedy are for the most part to Euripides (the tragedian with the closest overlap to Aristophanes), though even those are brief and do not receive detailed discussion. For *GPM*'s selection and use of sources, see Carey in this volume.
25. Beard 1995; Dover may of course have been resistant to the idea of exercising direct influence on students, even though he was clearly conscious of how well they did, especially in the competitive environment of Oxford.
26. See, respectively, *MC* 68 and 61 (where, despite what he says, it seems unlikely that Williams really agreed with this view of philosophy).
27. For 'structural substitutions', see Williams 1993, 19 and 164 ff.
28. For the syllabus and course structure at the time, see Tim Rood's contribution in this volume.
29. See Stray's chapter on 'Dover at school and university' in this volume.
30. On Fraenkel, see Stray 2016, Elsner 2021.

31. *MC* 39: the friend referred to was Stephanie West.
32. Ibid., 40.
33. My thanks to Jaś Elsner for pointing this out to me.
34. The book, as he says in the Preface, 'began to take shape during a course of lectures which I gave at Berkeley in 1967 to a class which included scientists and social scientists as well as classicists.' That year, Dover primarily gave the Sather Lectures at Berkeley, on a different topic, Lysias and the Corpus Lysiacum, published under that title in 1968.
35. Dover 1972a, 10–12. This is not to deny that Dover was also unusual for scholarship of his time in his readiness to pay new and sustained attention to questions of stagecraft and the imagination of theatrical space.
36. Cf., again, the two essays by Stray 2016 and Elsner 2021 for the self-projection of the scholar in Fraenkel's *Agamemnon*.
37. For an account of some of those continuing preoccupations and their history, see Walsh 2009.
38. Dover 1972a, 31–41.
39. Dover 1952. Ehrenberg's book was originally published in 1942, its second edition in 1951.
40. Dover 1966, reprinted in Dover 1988a, 102–14.
41. Dover 1988a, 114.
42. Compare Carol Atack's observations, in her contribution to this volume, on Dover's dependence in *GH* 'on the interpretation of literary texts which themselves may present an ideologically inflected distortion of observable realia': 'only with Attic comedy did he accept that it contained "fairy tale" elements'.
43. Blackwell published Devereux's *Dreams in Greek Tragedy* in 1976; Bernard Knox's acerbic review in the *Times Literary Supplement* (10 December 1976) is fairly representative of the critical reception it received from classicists.
44. *MC* 122–5.
45. 'The remarkable aspect of the dream was that my unconscious mind perceived and abstracted a structure, a relationship, from a memory not accessible to me and constructed a new complex of events which exhibited that structure. It seems to me that this kind of perception is highly relevant to the appreciation of one culture of the art and literature produced by another. When a contemporary audience sees a Greek tragedy, it may find a great many of the ingredients, taken one at a time, alien; it is the structure, the interrelation of the ingredients, which makes the complex intelligible' (*MC* 125). Note the choice of the term 'complex'. Even so, at least in *MC*, Dover emphasizes the examples of self-analysis much more than those of reading Greek tragedy.
46. MacNeice 1966, 119.
47. *MC* 126 (the start of the chapter which immediately follows his discussion of tragedy and analysis just discussed in my text). See, however, the editors' note on this passage in Dover 2023 for Dover's own claim that what he was half-recalling was not (only) MacNeice's poem but a similar phrase of Ruth Padel's.
48. On the close connection between MacNeice and Dodds, see Walker 2019 and McDonald 2019.
49. MacNeice 2012, 42; on MacNeice's career and circumstances, McDonald 1991.

CHAPTER 11
AFTER *GREEK HOMOSEXUALITY*
Carol Atack

In his memoir *Marginal Comment*, Kenneth Dover wrote:

> My ambition in 1945 had been: to marry a congenial wife, and with her to bring up children who would become good people; to get a tutorial fellowship at an Oxford or Cambridge college, preferably Balliol; and to write at least one book which would be well regarded by people in my own subject and would be of lasting value to them. I felt by 1950 that I had not done too badly so far. I leave aside wilder ambitions, such as writing a good novel or becoming Regius Professor of Greek at Oxford, and fantasies, such as growing a prehensile tail covered with dense fur.[1]

Greek Homosexuality, published in 1978, became that book. It stands as 'the most widely-known and controversial' achievement of Dover's long and productive career, according to his British Academy memoirists Donald Russell and Stephen Halliwell.[2] David Halperin wrote in 1990, 'It would be difficult to exaggerate the importance, within the field of classical studies, of Dover's long-awaited monograph on homosexual behaviour in ancient Greece.' For Halperin and others, the importance of *Greek Homosexuality* rested not just on its scholarly content, but on the status associated with its distinguished author's eminent positions as head of an Oxford college and President of the British Academy. They suggested that his disinterested status as a heterosexual observer rendered the book free from bias, although this claim is suggestive of a continuing societal background of homophobia.[3] From a perspective of decades of further transformation in the social and legal status of homosexuality, Dover's authorial standpoint seems less generous now than it did in 1978, but continuing waves of anti-LGBT backlash offer a reminder that even an imperfect act of allyship can be significant.[4]

Greek Homosexuality now appears more clearly as the product of a specific moment, in which the medical conceptualization of homosexuality persisted along with outbreaks of 'homosexual panic'.[5] Since then, the academic discussion of sexual behaviour has evolved with fast-moving developments in gender studies and the emergence of queer studies.[6] Early responses to the book exemplified the fierce disputes of the time between constructionist and essentialist approaches to sexual identity, the opposing views that a person's sexual preferences are socially acquired or innate.[7] Such binaries have themselves been disrupted by further developments in queer theory.[8]

This chapter offers a contextualist and critical account of *Greek Homosexuality*. It first situates Dover's work in its post-war historical, social and intellectual context, then examines its argument and presentation, considering methodological questions about

Dover's handling of the relationships between past and present, and between language and reality. It then traces the reception and influence of the book, exploring its huge personal impact on scholars and students.[9]

Text and context

Greek Homosexuality has many antecedents in Dover's work, dating back to long before its 1978 publication, to his inter-war childhood as well as to the post-war social and political context. After WWII, homosexuality became part of a broader public discourse on changing values, affecting its legal and cultural status. The contemporary valorization of the 'pure relationship' of equal, consenting and empowered partners, in all human personal relationships rather than just heterosexual ones, makes the asymmetries Dover identified within ancient relationships more problematic.[10]

While these social changes were taking place, sexuality and gender emerged as topics of study across the humanities, accompanied by new methodologies. The post-war environment was one of social change and restructuring, changes which Dover, rejecting his father's conservatism, appears to have supported, and which offer an immediate historical context for academic interest in sexuality.[11] This was part of a broader reconsideration of private life in the post-war period. A parallel but related discourse saw an increased emphasis on the production of children within companionate marriage, one of Dover's own personal aims, as noted above; this can be situated within a broader post-war reconstruction of masculinity.[12]

It is not clear how closely Dover followed these developments, but he read two significant studies while preparing one of his first publications on ancient sexuality, 'Eros and nomos' (1964a). These were the Kinsey reports of 1948 and 1953, sociological surveys which provided data on the sexual lives and preferences of American men and women, and Donald West's 1960 *Homosexuality*, a Pelican paperback which introduced its topic and made a plea for tolerance to a popular readership.[13] One aspect of the recognition of homosexuality as an identity at this time was its pathologization as a disability or aberration through the 'medical model'.[14]

Homosexuality had become a political and social issue in the post-war years, which saw a growing number of middle-class men incarcerated for sexual offences. Growing visibility of homosexuality went along with intensified public and media homophobia, and an increase in prosecutions and imprisonments of men for same-sex acts.[15] Eventually the government established a committee to investigate attitudes to homosexuality and prostitution, chaired by Lord Wolfenden, in 1954, and the publication of the Wolfenden Report in 1957 marked the beginning of a slow change in the UK establishment's engagement with homosexuality.[16] The resulting Sexual Offences Act of 1967 decriminalized homosexual sexual activity between consenting adults over the age of twenty-one in private, at least in England and Wales, although this limited act of liberalization left gay men still liable to police harassment and prosecution outside their homes.[17] Jeffrey Weeks argued that the Wolfenden Report 'conjured the modern homosexual fully into being' (2012, 314); before the publication of the report, homosexuality was seen in terms of outlawed acts, but it was now reconceptualized as a 'sexual identity' and 'a legitimate way of being', albeit one that was still treated negatively.

Dover can hardly have been ignorant of the lives of homosexual colleagues and students – for example, he endorses 'from personal knowledge' another scholar's view that some existing work on the subject constituted interested 'apologetics' (*GH* vii).[18] He had consulted a range of sociological literature, notably Michael Schofield's pseudonymously published sociological survey, *A Minority: A Report on the Life of the Male Homosexual in Great Britain*, which provided a wealth of detail of the experiences of homosexual men.[19] Other studies in the bibliography for *GH* include the updated version of West's book, *Homosexuality Re-examined*, and Arlo Karlen's *Sexuality and Homosexuality*.[20] But in St Andrews, in Scotland, where decriminalization took place only in 1980, Dover may have had less direct experience of the gay liberation movement and of cultural changes more evident in London and English university cities. However, he makes no comment about the social and political context of the writing of *Greek Homosexuality*, only its academic context.

Dover's interest in ancient Greek homosexuality began in Oxford in 1954, when he perceived deficiencies in the existing scholarship as he prepared lectures on the Greek elegiac poet Theognis, whose corpus includes same-sex love poetry.[21] In his memoir, he presents this as a sudden recognition that immediately formed into a replacement model, but as James Davidson notes, the evidence from Dover's publications of the 1960s and 1970s is of a more gradual development of his ideas.[22]

In 1962, some years after moving to St Andrews in 1955, Dover taught Plato's *Symposium*, perhaps the most iconic text in the reception history of Greek homosexuality; this too reinforced the need for an exploration of Athenian pederasty as a social practice.[23] In a series of lectures given in London, one of which was published as 'Eros and nomos' (1964a), Dover developed his analysis of the kind of pederastic relationship the character Pausanias describes. This article begins his campaign against the then prevailing model of the 'Dorian' origin of pederasty, together with other points which would later be expanded in *Greek Homosexuality*.[24] These include the difference between acts and identities, the relation to a modern 'double standard', and the role of prostitution. The article also uses literary sources vital to the book: beyond Plato's *Symposium*, Aeschines' *Against Timarchus*, and Aristophanic comedy, especially the *Clouds*.[25] A favourable reception for this first article encouraged Dover to continue his research.

Dover's interest in Athenian society and its ethical structures also intersected with the arrival of the 'second wave' of feminism, and the development of feminist approaches to social history and the new discipline of Women's Studies.[26] This focus on popular morality, and criticism of the use of elite sources such as Plato's dialogues, might be seen as broadly congruent with the 'history from below' approach of UK socialist and feminist historians of the 1960s.[27] The early 1970s saw feminist approaches work their way into Classics with the development of a new focus on women in antiquity; Dover contributed 'Classical Greek attitudes to sexual behaviour' to the ground-breaking 1973 issue of *Arethusa*, which acted as a manifesto for feminist approaches to Classics.[28] This paper explores topics that would play an important part in *Greek Homosexuality*, such as inhibition, resistance to desire, and the effects of sex segregation.[29] A related section appeared in *GPM*, where Dover wrote: 'homosexual relations provided a youth, for whom marriage lay some years ahead, with the opportunity for the seduction of a partner on the same social plane as himself, an opportunity of the kind which exists in modern heterosexual societies which neither own slaves nor segregate the sexes' (Dover 1974, 213). Dover's analysis suggests a complicated relationship between the past and present, in which the difference between the Greek world and the modern world is emphasized, while an attempt to parallel the two complicates that separation. Note too the emphasis on the 'situational' nature of pederastic relationships involving older and younger youths, explored below.

These earlier publications also exemplify another theme which recurs in *Greek Homosexuality*, the idea that a homosexual relationship or act is somehow a 'pseudo' imitation of the (implicitly and sometime explicitly heterosexual) real thing, a view which Dover appears to have taken from the French psychoanalyst George Devereux, and the Freudian tradition more broadly, and which Stephen Halliwell has described as 'regrettable'.[30] Dover had supported Devereux's application to come to Oxford as a visiting scholar at All Souls College, after reading his work on classical subjects.[31] But Devereux's 1968 article 'Greek pseudo-homosexuality and the "Greek miracle"' now seems 'profoundly homophobic', as Konstantinos Kapparis notes, with its focus on same-sex attraction as a 'perversion', a view perhaps explicable in the context of the medical model of homosexuality as aberration.[32] Its positive conclusion is that Greek culture's prolongation of adolescence through same-sex relationships was responsible for the 'Greek miracle'.

While the societal transformations of the post-war era made the examination of sexuality an approachable and timely topic, Dover's published research owed more to older strands in the study of sexual behaviour as well as to the methods of classical philology. *Greek Homosexuality* is, typically for Dover, a traditional philological work of cataloguing examples and developing typologies.[33] This is a further significant part of the work's context; in it, scholarly debates seem more evident than broader social changes. Dover's Oxford 'Greats' education included a great deal of philosophy, and his experience as an Oxford tutor brought him into contact with developments in philosophy. His antipathy to these contributes to *GH* appearing as an anti-philosophical work. His antipathy to the specific form of academic philosophy which developed at Oxford in the post-war years perhaps made it a more enticing target for his arguments. Oxford philosophers developed a focus on the relationships between language and the world it describes, and between language and morality.[34] One attempt to link that work to a classical context was Arthur Adkins' *Merit and Responsibility*, an exploration of Greek ethics through philosophical texts which Dover countered in his *Greek Popular Morality*.[35] Dover himself sought to assert philology's priority over philosophy; he recounts asking Bernard Williams, whom he had taught and who had just taken Greats, 'whether he would agree that philosophy was a branch of English lexicography' (*MC* 61). But Dover, using philological methods to explore the culture of classical Greece, could not avoid engaging with philosophical approaches so closely allied to the study of language, even as he presented his work as an empirical alternative to its methods and conclusions.

Re-reading *Greek Homosexuality*

Re-reading *Greek Homosexuality* now raises questions about Dover's methodology: his insistence on an active/passive binary, his related focus on penetrative sex, and the presentism in his transpositions of examples between ancient and modern and across genders and sexualities. Despite the title, and an initial definition of homosexuality as 'the disposition to seek sensory pleasure through bodily contact with persons of one's own sex in preference to contact with the other sex' (*GH* 1), Dover often discusses acts rather than identities. In doing so, he identifies the Greeks as displaying a 'disposition' toward same-sex relationships as a temporary diversion from the permanent heterosexual relationships entered by most citizens during mature adulthood; other scholars would label such temporary behaviours 'situational'. Jeffrey Weeks points to 'schoolboy homosexuality in public schools' as a classic example of 'situational' homosexuality, in which participation in same-sex relationships or acts does not construct a stable homosexual identity.[36] Dover stated that he regarded homosexual sex as 'pseudo' sex: 'Established linguistic usage compels me to treat "heterosexual" and "homosexual" as antithetical, but if I followed my inclination I would replace "heterosexual" by "sexual" and treat what is called "homosexuality" as a subdivision of the "quasi-sexual" (or "pseudo-sexual"; not "parasexual")' (*GH* vii–viii). This claim situates the work within the discourse of sexology, and its search for names and definitions from a heteronormative standpoint. Despite Dover's claim of disinterest, a view standard for his time but now exposed by, for example, feminist standpoint ethics, his work reflects a personal standpoint.[37] Dover responded to criticism by restating this view in the second edition: 'we have the word "sex" because there is more than one sex, definable in terms of reproductive function, and I accordingly use "sexual" to mean "having to do with (difference of) sex"' (Dover 1989, 206). This, perhaps unfortunately, reinforces the homophobic and conservative idea that only heterosexual reproductive intercourse is the real thing.[38] In framing heterosexuality as a transhistorical norm, Dover's account of sexuality is not proleptically Foucauldian. But his definition also exemplifies his resistance to established structures, even of language, and desire for precision.

Dover explicitly stands back from any emotional commitment to the material and to the human interactions it depicts, while demonstrating 'candour unprecedented in serious classical scholarship'.[39] He experiences no 'moral shock or disgust at any genital act whatsoever' (*GH* viii), but the acts he enumerates are not, for him, really sex. The assumption of disinterest brought authority to the discussion according to the academic practices of the time but feels jarring now when scholars in this field make their own situatedness explicit.

A recurring strain in philosophers' readings of *Greek Homosexuality* is that the book is empirical and unphilosophical, even anti-philosophical.[40] But that is an insufficient description of Dover's methodology, and his claim to empiricism should be challenged because of his dependence on the interpretation of literary texts which themselves may present an ideologically inflected distortion of observable realia. Dover's source texts do not permit us to grasp the realia of Athenian life, but rather the language the Athenians used to describe their lives, and sometimes to evade frank description. Dover also goes beyond the actual language of his sources, such as the speech ascribed to Lysias in Plato's *Phaedrus* (233d–e), to argue that their language masks more explicit accounts of sexual intercourse; 'there is no room for doubt about the nature of the "favour"' which the speaker requests (*GH* 44), using the verb *charizesthai*, 'to grant a favour'. Davidson argues that Dover is here interpreting his sources generously to produce the evidence he seeks for his model, rather than straightforwardly cataloguing data, although elsewhere Dover does point to a broader range of possible senses for *charizesthai*, which should not be limited to a single sex act.[41] Such interpretative processes complicate Dover's claim to empiricism.

A comparative example will demonstrate the limits of the evidence available to Dover from Athens, in both quantity and quality. Michael Rocke's exploration of the homosexual culture of Renaissance Florence tabulates much more documentary data to support his model of a system of 'age-graded homoerotic relations', which, he argues, shares a Mediterranean heritage with the Greek and Roman past.[42] There are significant differences between Renaissance Florence and classical Athens; in the former, Christian morality had identified sodomy as a crime, and Rocke's evidence comes from court documents of the 'Office of the Night', which operated from 1432 to 1502, as well as from literary and artistic sources. But both Athens and Florence represent cultures where men's sexual interactions might at any point be either or both an expression of power hierarchies and an expression of interpersonal affection. Dover sometimes downplays the latter in identifying the former.[43] While Dover's key forensic source, Aeschines' *Against Timarchus*, is a courtroom speech, it is a retrospective work of politicized rhetoric and not a documentary text like the records Rocke analyses, and one which cannot be fully separated from the philosophical and intellectual context Dover is keen to escape.[44] As Andrew Lear has noted, because Dover only considers in detail evidence from classical Athens, he misses the way in which the texts he explores constitute a new and changed discourse on pederasty, in which it is both idealized in a past form and problematized in the present.[45]

This leads to a second methodological question about evaluating the real versus the imaginary, and gradations and slippages between them, perhaps more messy than Dover's binaries admit. In *Greek Popular Morality* he had emphasized that courtroom rhetoric provided access to everyday thought, with speakers' arguments appealing to the common sense of fellow citizen jurors and aiming to avoid offending them (*GPM* 2). Dover distinguishes between rhetoric and philosophical dialogue, imagining a modern reader of Plato's *Phaedrus* and *Symposium*, 'which they may well have seen in the pornography section of a bookshop', believing that the anti-democratic and elitist views of Plato were representative of those of Athenians more broadly (*GH* 13). Dover notes that texts such as Plato's dialogues and objects such as sympotic pottery may transmit ideas, aspirations and whims rather than the actuality of everyday life, and considers the differences between them.⁴⁶ However, he sometimes fails to acknowledge the appeal to the imaginary and idealized in his sources. Aeschines' *Against Timarchus*, which Dover presents as a more representative guide to Athens (*GH* 13–14), contains a manicured confection of laws attributed to ancient lawgivers, as well as an idealized account of pederasty to set against the degraded version claimed to be embodied by Timarchus.⁴⁷ Dover argued that 'it is to be presumed that a speaker could not expect to get away with plain misrepresentation of the law's actual words' (*GH* 24), but subsequent scholarship on *Against Timarchus* has identified misrepresentations of the law within it, and suggested that the speech constructs a highly idealized picture of Athens, set against the titillating details of the debauchery of the defendant and his associates.⁴⁸

There is an uneasy relationship between ancient and modern in *Greek Homosexuality*. Dover's presentation of his work, often retrojecting the present into the past, and interpreting the past through the frames of the near-present, is prone to both presentism and anachronism. However, presentism is rarely absent from scholarship on ancient sexuality and especially homosexuality, because of the entanglement of Classics and classicists with continuing controversy over the manifestations of same-sex relationships and actions in antiquity, pederasty as a practice within their own societies and institutions, and the continuing fascination with the topos of 'Greek love'.⁴⁹ Queer theorists such as Valerie Rohy have also argued that a non-normative temporality is inherent in the social construction of homosexuality, through the negative perception of homosexuality as a state of failed personal development through the stages of heterosexual reproductive adulthood.⁵⁰ However, the presentist connections Dover draws between the worlds of Greek love and contemporary identity may enable a more positive anachronism, in Loraux's sense.⁵¹ So his temporal collapses may be both inevitable and useful, rather than inherently vicious.

Sometimes Dover seems to connect uneasy aspects of modern discourses of homosexuality to the past, such as the division of male homosexuality into socially acceptable and unacceptable forms, the 'good' discreet and restrained, and the 'bad' excessive in desire and behaviour.⁵² The figure of the *kinaidos* offered by Plato's Socrates as the embodiment of shamelessness in his relentless quest to satisfy his physical desires (*Grg.* 494e), and underlying Aeschines' presentation of Timarchus, is echoed in modern homophobic tropes. Dover notes that 'homosexual taste was by no means uniform', using Schofield's survey findings on the rejection of effeminacy by gay men to support his assessment of the ancient material.⁵³

Dover finds modern parallels for the Greek use of hunting as a metaphor for erotic pursuit (*GH* 87, citing Aeschines, *In Tim.* 195 and numerous passages from Plato, including *Phdr.* 241d); he also cites West, who noted that the dominant partner in homosexual prison encounters ('desperate fights for sexual supremacy') was known as the 'wolf', just as, Dover notes, Plato's Socrates describes the *erastês* (*Phdr.* 241d).⁵⁴ Dover easily drew an analogy between the agonistic brutality of modern incarceration and the formal reciprocities of the classical Athenian elite. The idea of the agonistic society of Athens as one of 'zero-sum' competition between citizens has a long history going back to Jacob Burckhardt, and was emphasized by the French structuralists, but its further pre-eminence in the scholarship of the 1980s and early 1990s might owe something to the context of the rise of free-market economics and its supporting ideologies under the leadership of Ronald Reagan in the USA and Margaret Thatcher in the UK.[55] Dover's account of processes of domination among citizen men provides a component helpful to such a model.

This results in a version of Athens where popular morality appears 'analogous to the sexual double standard of Victorian England', as Jeffrey Carnes noted.[56] Dover compares Athens with the 1930s England of his own teenage years, equating the situation of the young Athenian citizen male to his own experiences: 'No great knowledge of the world is needed to perceive the analogy between homosexual pursuit in classical Athens and heterosexual pursuit in (say) British society in the nineteen-thirties' (*GH* 88). He goes on to identify a similar double standard in both societies, where 'parents are ... apt to issue different commands (explicit or implicit) to their sons and to their daughters', imagining an Athenian father guarding his fourteen-year-old son from pursuers while being pleased that his twenty-year-old son 'had "caught" the fourteen-year-old boy next door' (*GH* 88–9). Dover himself had vividly experienced double standards between his experience in the repressed worlds of school and Oxford and, on the other hand, life on military service during the Second World War; Russell and Halliwell observe that Dover appeared to regard the latter experience as instructive for his studies of popular morality.[57]

Dover rarely wavers from assuming that his reader is a heterosexual male, and obligingly translates homoerotic moments from his texts into heterosexual ones (usually with the man assumed to be the senior partner), making perhaps unwarranted assumptions about the male gaze. Even the brief discussion of women and homosexuality starts from the viewpoint that women, whether *hetairai* (*GH* 171) or wives, might object to their male partners' current or former male lovers.

Dover's focus on and perhaps even anxiety about anal penetration and intercourse, expressed throughout *GH*, has a modern context too. This anxiety may have been magnified by concerns expressed during the 'homosexual panic' that flared across newspapers during the 1950s and 1960s, as liberalization drew close.[58] Jokes about the anus and anal penetration in Attic comedy suggest that similar panic was present in fifth-century Athens. Cleon in Aristophanes' *Knights* is praised for 'monitoring arseholes' (πρωκτοτηρεῖν) and keeping 'men who are fucked' (τοὺς βινουμένους) out of politics (*Eq.* 878–80), but at the same time his motivation is shown to be reducing competition from other orators and politicians. In fourth-century sources, intercourse is not always the primary concern.[59] For Xenophon, pederasty was problematic because it exemplified the loss of self-mastery caused by pursuing any physical appetite to extremes (*Mem.* 1.2.29–31, 1.3.8–14). While Dover claims that Socrates in both Xenophon's and Plato's work 'condemn[s] homosexual copulation' (*GH* 160), Davidson countered that the Greek writers' concern lay more with the broader pursuit of appetite.[60]

Dover's phallocentric focus on penetrative sex is most clear in the section 'Dominant and subordinate roles' (*GH* 100–9), in which he developed a typology of homosexual acts separated between active and passive roles, which are not negotiated between the parties but socially determined through their age and status. This distinction, rather than that between sex involving free citizen partners and that involving non-citizen sex workers, dominates his reading of *Against Timarchus* and is then applied more broadly.[61]

In this discussion of active and passive roles, Dover himself turns frequently to modern comparators and sociological research to justify his argument, collapsing the idea that ancient Greek and modern sexual behaviours should be seen as distinct. This section contains more frequent references to modern psychological and social studies, as well as to diachronic surveys of sexual behaviour, than other parts of the book, and assumes a universalism and continuity in human behaviour.[62] In particular, the idea of dominance and submission is drawn from Karlen, who in turn draws on the work of Ivan Maslow, but in both cases their consideration of what Karlen labels 'phallic aggression' goes beyond sexual contact.[63] Perhaps Dover's long-term fascination with monkeys led him to grant authority to the evocation of animal behaviour in psychological studies.

Dover's standardization of the terms *erastês* and *erômenos* to describe the two parties in pederastic relationships emphasizes this active-passive distinction (*GH* 16–17), drawing on the grammatical structures of Greek, in which those with sexual agency have their actions expressed with active verbs, those without, passive verbs (*GH* 140). It is less clear in the contrast between *erastês* and *paidika*. Dover notes the use of both *erômenos* and *paidika*, both standard terms, and retains the latter when it appears in his sources; both Plato and Xenophon use *paidika* more frequently than *erômenos*.[64] But in emphasizing the term *erômenos* for the younger partner, Dover leans on the participle's grammatical passivity and risks transforming a linguistic structure into a social one, over-emphasizing the passivity of the younger partner.[65]

In Dover's model, passivity provides a social constraint which protect the *erômenos* from the negative social consequences attached to being penetrated. The appropriate action for the *erômenos* is to evade the advances of lovers, and should he permit any form of intercourse, not to experience any pleasure from it, like the good woman of Victorian fiction (*GH* 90). Another option which Dover suggests got around the taboo on the penetration of citizen males was non-penetrative 'intercrural sex', which he identified with the verb διαμηρίζειν.[66] Dover identified this sexual practice from vase paintings, but this interpretation has been criticized.[67] Robin Osborne argued that Dover's construction, in which the partners face each other and the *erastês* inserts his penis between the youth's thighs (*GH* 98–9) 'has no basis in historic Greek sexual behaviour' and is 'an entirely fantastic construction of Greek sexuality', although Davidson suggests a ritual context far removed from Athenian pederasty for the vase scenes.[68] Dover does concede that vase paintings might not be a reliable guide (*GH* 100 n. 81), but also connects them to modern pornography (*GH* 102 n. 83, on the practicalities of threesomes).

The Dover-Foucault paradigm which emerged from Foucault's use of *GH* in his *History of Sexuality* (see section III below) presents sexual behaviour in antiquity as a matter of acts, not identities. But this is not quite what Dover argued. He recognized that Athenians saw sexual preference as a *prohairesis*, a matter of choice but a choice that could become embedded in identity as a stable part of individual character (*GH* 32, 62).[69] The term is more familiar from its later use to denote adherence to a philosophical or religious sect, and in the fourth century is coming into use to mean 'preferred style of life', as Dover notes (*GPM* 151–2), citing Demosthenes' *Against Aristocrates* and the *Erotic Essay*, both of which use it explicitly in this way (τῇ προαιρέσει τοῦ βίου, Dem. 23.141).[70] However, Dover does not explore the possibility of stable or later-life same-sex relationships, such as that of Pausanias and Agathon, depicted by Plato in the *Symposium*.[71]

Rather than pursue what a *prohairesis* might permit, Dover focused on a form of homosexual interaction that was specific to citizens at a particular point in their lives. Because the socially accepted form of pederasty had a limited term, it can be seen as an act not an identity and separate from the kind of *prohairesis* which might be satisfied in later life through encounters with male prostitutes, as envisaged by Aeschines (*In Tim.* 195, *GH* 32). Dover avoids the question of whether Athenian pederasty can stand in for all of Greek homosexuality, or even that of the limited context of Athens. Rather than an empirical survey, he produces an abstract model. This model of zero-sum competition was exactly what Foucault needed, but its simplifications overlook the social context in which citizens have access to non-citizen as well as citizen sexual partners.

Dover rationalizes pederasty on utilitarian grounds: in classical Athens, men marry many years after reaching sexual maturity, and have no legitimate outlet for their desire for a companionate sexual relationship during their early adult life. This provokes further presentism, as he conflates the ancient society with modern middle-class Britain. Yet he identifies a desire for companionship, not simply for intercourse: 'the need in question was a need for personal relationships of an intensity not commonly found within marriage or in the relations between parents and children or in those between the individual and the community as a whole' (*GH* 201). In this concluding section, Dover rests his argument on some rather general and unreferenced sociobiological claims about the status of 'the fighter, the adult male citizen' in polis society.

Athenian citizen men married much younger women who lacked the advanced education enjoyed by the male citizen elite (Xen. *Oec.* 7.5–10); marriage even to the best of women did not offer the opportunity for a 'pure relationship' in Giddens' terms.[72] The kind of companionate marriage that Dover wanted for himself was not on offer in classical Athens. But, as Alain Schnapp observed in his review, what about the courtesan?[73] Athenians could purchase sophisticated and congenial company along with sexual services from both male and female sex workers; intercourse with citizen youths, even within the constraints of pederasty, was a high-stakes alternative. Dover is aware of sex workers in the Greek city, and that prostitution is a theme of *Against Timarchus* (*GH* 19–23). Yet his focus on penetration within citizen relationships, and relative neglect of prostitution, caused him to lose sight of pederasty's place within a network of interpersonal and potentially sexual relationships and interactions beyond those involving citizen males. An alternative model of 'homosociality' is offered by Eve Kosofsky Sedgwick, who drew on *Greek Homosexuality* to present Athens as a society in which male homosociality extends from friendship to sexual partnerships structured by the conventions of pederasty, and without homophobia.[74]

In his earlier papers on sexuality, Dover had tended to transpose same-sex and heterosexual attraction, when moving between ancient and modern. In 'Eros and nomos', he wrote:

> These Aristophanic jokes could be converted into heterosexual jokes of the type which is the stock-in-trade of vulgar comedy today. A similar transposition would be possible in many passages of Plato, notably Alcibiades' account of his desperate attempts to seduce Socrates (*Smp.* 217a2-219d2) and the well-known passage of *Charmides* (155b9–e2) which, if we turned Charmides into a girl and changed the gender of the pronouns, would pass in a modern context as a light-hearted description of the effect which the proximity of a very pretty girl may have on a courteous, middle-aged, rather nervous bachelor.
>
> Dover 1964a, 35

It is apparently unthinkable that a 'rather nervous bachelor' might be as moved by the presence of a boy as a girl (although 'middle-aged' might alert the reader to the then current euphemism of the 'confirmed bachelor'). Dover does not envisage homosexual humour from a modern Aristophanes, nor, in this paper, that a reader might not require any such translation. Perhaps the illegality of homosexuality at the time of publication made transposition necessary. In *GH*, the same passage of Plato provokes another, more sexualized, past-present gender transposition: 'If we translate this scene into heterosexual terms, so that Socrates' glimpse inside the cloak of Kharmides becomes a glimpse of the breasts of a young woman of extraordinary beauty, as she leans forward to ask an unaffected question, we come as close to seeing through ancient Greek eyes as we are likely to come' (*GH* 156). Dover does acknowledge that there might be homosexual readers who do not need this transposition, and who 'may see clearly enough through Greek eyes already' (*GH* 156 n. 6), although this rare acknowledgement of the possible gay reader suggests that homosexuality offers some mysterious and privileged connection to the classical past.[75]

By focusing on Athenian texts and images, Dover sidelined a major strand in the previous scholarship on pederasty, and made a radical claim about its origins, placing it in the archaic polis rather than in pre-polis society (*GH* 1–4). Much previous scholarship on Greek pederasty had followed ancient sources in identifying it as an inheritance from early Greek society, the Dorian culture of Sparta and Crete, rather than a novel development within the classical polis. Dover's preface begins by rejecting Erich Bethe's Dorian model (*GH* vii), instead suggesting that the origin of Greek pederasty is 'an interesting subject for speculation' (*GH* 1).[76] He addresses the non-Athenian material only in his final chapter (*GH* 185–96), separately from his main material. Here he admits that the idea of a Dorian origin for Greek homosexuality 'is not refutable' (185) but goes on to conclude, after considering the complexities of the literary and non-literary evidence, that 'there can be no question of tracing the diffusion of homosexual eros from Sparta or other Dorian states' (196). However, this leaves unexplained the cultural association in Athens of pederasty with societies valorized for their antiquity. Dover's analysis of Ephorus' fragment on pederasty as citizen initiation in Crete (*FGrH* 70 F149) is rather thin; he dismisses it as 'irrelevant' to 'the problem of the origins of the homosexual ethos' (*GH* 190).[77]

Dover's careful readings of texts tease out many insights; yet his handling of language often invokes a scientism and factitious certainty that the messy realities of language do not support. The binary oppositions he developed would lead to *GH* being incorporated into the structuralism-influenced work of Michel Foucault, perhaps the most significant moment in the work's reception.

Reception: domination and historicism

Greek Homosexuality inspired an unusually intense critical response, perhaps because of the personal commitment of scholars to matters of identity, and the continuing context of homophobia in a backlash to decriminalization and the growing visibility of gay culture, amid the arrival of the AIDS pandemic of the 1980s.[78] Dover's own tendency to robust criticism provoked responses in kind; his memoir *Marginal Comment*, with its disquieting personal revelations, fuelled later *ad hominem* critiques. These illuminate and power, for example, James Davidson's criticisms of Dover.[79] Responses to Davidson, such as David Halperin's retrospective reassessment from 2015, continue the argument in personal terms.[80]

Michel Foucault's use of *GH* in the second volume of his *History of Sexuality* (*L'usage des plaisirs*, 1984) was transformative; Dover's research provided the evidence for 'a whole social game', and offered a 'partage radical entre activité et passivité', a dichotomy congenial to his own structuralism.[81] Foucault incorporated Dover's model into his *History of Sexuality* much more substantially than his few explicit references suggest.[82] He had previously praised Dover's 'grande alacrité intellectuale', 'drôlerie', and his 'amoralisme acide, savant et oxfordien de la pensée'.[83] James Davidson observed that Foucault and Dover 'achieved together far more than either could have achieved on his own', even though 'it is hard to imagine two men more different' than 'the sophisticated Frenchman' and 'the Oxford empiricist'.[84] Martha Nussbaum suggested that Foucault retheorized Dover's model, transforming an empirical observation back into a structuralist model largely built of binary oppositions.[85] However, as noted above, Dover's linguistic analysis is primed for incorporation into a structuralist model, and less empirical or untheoretical than Nussbaum suggests, as well as prone to *a priori* argument.

After encountering Dover's work, Foucault reconceptualized the grand project of his *History*, identifying classical Greece as the site of sexual behaviours distinct from those of the later Christian era. Dover had written: 'the Greeks neither inherited nor developed a belief that a divine power had revealed to mankind a code of laws for the regulation of sexual behaviour' (*GH* 203). Foucault's volume 1, *The Will to Knowledge*, first published before *GH* in 1976 as *La volonté de savoir*, posited the emergence over historical time of a systematic and repressive social control of sexual activity. After the appearance of *GH*, Foucault now decided that the world depicted in the texts of fourth-century BCE Greece predated the emergence of repression with the advent of Christianity.[86] Foucault rejigged his masterplan to incorporate material from this period, further in the past than his previous explorations in intellectual archaeology and genealogy.[87] He recognized that he needed to recover the 'genealogy' of the development of sexuality, and to investigate 'the slow formation, in antiquity, of a hermeneutics of the self'.[88] He found this in the changing understanding of relations between citizen men in the societies of classical antiquity. Dover's influence becomes clear in Part 4 of *The Usage of Pleasure*, 'Erotics', which opens: 'The use of pleasure in the relationship with boys was a theme of anxiety for Greek thought – which is paradoxical in a society that is believed to have "tolerated" what we call "homosexuality"' (Foucault 1985, 187). Foucault brings in Dover uncritically – he writes that Dover has 'amply documented' the 'reality' of Athenian pederasty (ibid. 196). He uses him to support his account of the 'courtship practices' which ensured that pederastic relationships had a 'beautiful form'; Foucault emphasizes the interlinked ethics and aesthetics of pederasty. However, he emphasizes other texts, foregrounding the pseudo-Demosthenic *Erotic Essay*, whose language Dover had thought to be non-standard (e.g. *GH* 50, 197 n. 2). Mark Poster criticized Foucault's uncritical adoption of Dover's work, complaining that he failed to ask questions of either the ancient sources or the modern historians about the presumed stability of the association of activity and passivity with the older and younger lovers.[89] Like Davidson, he expressed concern over the downplaying of emotion in favour of power dynamics within the Dover-Foucault model.[90]

The development of the Dover-Foucault model and its application back to the study of Classics intersected with the growing interest in male sexuality and gender in the discipline, building on earlier feminist projects such as the rediscovery of women's voices and lives, and understanding the ancient city as a community constituted by more than its male citizens. Dover and Foucault's work became foundational to a new wave of work on ancient sexuality in Classics, with a significant wave of publications in 1990–1, which offered a dramatic reframing of ideas of ancient masculinity and at the same time moved the discussion of gender and sexuality away from a singular focus on women and back towards a 'new cultural history' (Cohen 1992) of citizen-status men, at a point when the emerging discipline of Women's Studies was being transformed into Gender Studies.[91] Some feminist critique of the Dover-Foucault paradigm responds to this change of direction and criticizes the return of a focus on male citizens rather than previously overlooked women and non-citizens.[92] Lin Foxhall's critique is focused on Foucault's methodology and the exclusion of women as subjects from his analysis; her brief discussion of pederasty as part of the social development and acculturation of male citizens beyond their own household offers a telling beginning of an alternative model.[93]

Two significant contributions to the study of masculinity in classical Athens demonstrate the significance of the Dover-Foucault paradigm. Papers by John J. Winkler and David Halperin used it to explore Athenian systems of social control, competition between citizens, and particularly the interface between prostitution and citizenship. Their work historicized the model more effectively, within the specific context of Athenian history, and with some changes of emphasis, developing the idea of 'zero-sum' competition between citizens. Winkler summarized the model: 'Sex ... was basically a way for men to establish their social identities in the intensely competitive, zero-sum formats of public culture' (Winkler 1990, 11). Both Winkler and Halperin cite Dover positively ('excellent', Halperin 1990, 56), although each re-examines the sources and brings his own perspective.[94] Winkler's 'Laying down the law' studied the legal frameworks which governed relationships between male citizens.⁹⁵ He concluded that: 'the content assigned to standards of proper sexual behaviour ... is dramatically different from our modern conventions ... The calculus of correctness operated not on the sameness/difference of the genders but on the dominance/submission of the persons involved' (Winkler 1990, 70). Within this framework, he explored 'the cultural images of right and wrong manhood', moving the focus away from understanding an idealized pederasty. He opens up the question whether the *kinaidos* may represent an identity, rather than an act, noting Plato's invocation of the 'life of the *kinaidoi*' as something shameful (*Grg.* 494c–e) and turning to the pseudo-Aristotelian *Physiognomonics* for a portrait of the *kinaidos*, which affirms that this was an identity rather than an act (*Physiog.* 808a12–16). The *kinaidos* represents a form of 'wrong manhood' attached as an identity to a person, a man who 'desires to lose' in the zero-sum competition of masculinity, and so is opposed to the hoplite masculine ideal, and risks being deprived of citizenship through democratic scrutiny.⁹⁶

David Halperin's 'The democratic body: prostitution and citizenship in classical Athens' re-read Aeschines' *Against Timarchus* with a greater emphasis on its account of commercial rather than pederastic sex and included women sex workers within his model.⁹⁷ Halperin concluded that: 'Democracy at Athens ... was not what we might call a purely "political" system; it was a system of sex and gender as well' (1990, 104). For Halperin, the sex lives of male citizens could not be understood in isolation from those of married citizen women, non-citizen and enslaved women sex workers, and male sex workers; his analysis makes steps towards an intersectional account of Athenian sexualities (1990, 104–12).

We have Dover's response to these developments of the model. He noted connections between Halperin's and Winkler's arguments and their attempt to generate a broader model drawing on his own book.⁹⁸ Others have criticized aspects of this model. Matthew Fox critiques the idea of the Athenian citizen as a 'constrained man', arguing that Winkler fails to note the irony in Socrates' use of the *kinaidos* and that he finds social norms expressed in texts which are not straightforwardly normative.⁹⁹ This criticism could be referred back to Dover's own reading of his literary sources, as argued above; only with Attic comedy did he accept the presence of 'fairy tale' elements (*GH* 11).

Another critique challenged the model's emphasis on the agonistic nature of Athenian society, arguing that in respect of pederasty it misplaces that competition. Such critiques often draw on Eve Kosofsky Sedgwick's model of homosociality.¹⁰⁰ The ancient literary sources support such a reading; in Plato's *Euthydemus*, for example, Ctesippus the *erastês* and Cleinias his *paidika* are not locked in conflict for dominance, but support each other in agonistic encounters with others.¹⁰¹ Velvet Yates has argued that it is the *erastai* who are in competition with each other, for the social advantage of connection with a widely admired *paidika*.¹⁰² One might also see pederastic relationships as a broadening of the social networks of elite citizens seeking to make their mark in public life. This approach is used by Craig Williams and Mark Masterson to explore men's relationships in classical Rome and later antiquity.¹⁰³

Another thread is criticism from cultural historians such as Paul Cartledge and Jan Bremmer, reasserting a diachronic account which reincorporates the Greeks' own idea of pederasty as a surviving initiation practice from earlier societies.[104] Harald Patzer, in a strong critique of Dover and his focus on Athens, offered in its place cross-cultural anthropological accounts of initiation rites, particularly those observed among indigenous peoples of the Pacific islands.[105] Paul Cartledge offered a careful examination of Spartan pederasty; his 1981 paper fills the gap left by Dover's focus on Athens.[106] Cartledge identifies the place of pederasty within the Spartan education system as a means of integrating young citizen males into military and social organizations and establishing their position in the social hierarchy. Drawing on a range of anthropological evidence, he argues that Spartan pederasty was a rite of passage, and that pederastic relationships had a significant social function in Spartan politics, establishing networks of influence. For example, Sphodrias, an elite Spartan accused of treason by the highest court, was acquitted thanks to the patronal influence of king Agesilaus II (Xen. *Hell.* 5.4.20–33; Cartledge 1981, 29). Thus Agesilaus appears to have been alert to the possibilities of using pederastic networks for political ends. Plato's depiction of Athenian pederasty leaves open the possibility that elite networking among the wealthy and powerful was part of its function, in terms both of individual connections between lovers and the establishment of the public profile of young men as they entered adulthood and full citizenship; given the Laconophilia of the Athenian elite, this is not surprising.

Dover responded to the reassertion of the Dorian hypothesis in turn with a lecture on 'Greek homosexuality and initiation', later published in his collected papers, which constructs a laboured argument to dismiss claims that pederasty in the classical polis represented a survival of initiation rituals, in which older men transmitted community values to younger men along with their semen.[107] Dover wonders whether a 'false analogy' has been made between anthropological and philological argument (120–1), but he uses the latter to dismiss the former (132), arguing that the initiation model is irrelevant to Athens. He concludes that historical argument from the minutiae of evidence is as vulnerable to new data as arguments in the physical sciences from experimental results, but his own argument rests on argument from silence, such as the absence of explicit pederasty in the surviving texts of early Greek epic.

Foucault, with his preoccupation with the structure and exercise of power, has been presented as an anti-humanist; the Dover-Foucault model, on this analysis, can be subjected to a humanist critique.[108] Such a model may underlie James Davidson's criticism of the model's focus on power dynamics, first in his *Courtesans and Fishcakes* (1997), then in a 2001 *Past and Present* review article, and finally at much greater length in his 2007 monograph *The Greeks and Greek Love*.[109] Davidson sets out the development of both Dover and Foucault's thought, with some sharp observations on changes in Dover's views on Athenian homosexuality between 1964 ('Eros and nomos') and the publication of *Greek Homosexuality* in 1978. For Davidson, Dover's increased emphasis on the differentiation of active and passive roles had led to an even greater error on Foucault's part, the idea of 'ethical passivity' (1997, 175). While Davidson's later version of male same-sex relationships in Athens, consensual and conducted between those who are all safely over eighteen, has not found much favour, his plea not to discount the emotional and social aspect of 'Greek love' is an important one.[110] The evidence from

Socratic dialogue is that pederastic relationships operated at a public and collective level, in the evaluation and incorporation of youths into the networks of civic society. This might especially be the case among the Laconophile elite, eager to imitate and participate in institutions recalling those of the ancient customs of Sparta and Crete. Another space in which such a critique might be placed is within the 'affective turn' of queer theory, which responded to Foucault by placing greater emphasis on personal emotion.[111] But it could also be incorporated within Sedgwick's model of homosociality.

Conclusion

The publication of *Greek Homosexuality* was a significant moment for the study of the cultural and social history of classical Athens. Dover's painstaking tabulation of literary and visual sources was a major service to scholarship, and the production of a monograph on this subject by an eminent and established scholar was a significant milestone in Anglophone classical scholarship. *Greek Homosexuality* contributed a model long influential for the understanding of the sexual behaviour of citizen men in the classical city, a model refined and extended by its incorporation into Foucault's work and by the great wave of work on ancient sexuality and gender in the decades which followed. The subsequent emergence of new models and perspectives makes work from the 1970s across the field of studies in gender and sexuality seem dated and even problematic in its use of language and concepts, and perhaps renders works like *Greek Homosexuality* of increasingly historical interest.

Dover's narrow chronological and geographical focus, in a work which claimed only a 'modest and limited aim' (*GH* vii), his treatment of his literary sources, and the occasionally stealthy transformation of linguistic structures into argumentative structures, left some questions unexplored. But it also created space for others to both build on and to challenge his work, and to expand into, for example, the role of women and non-citizen men in the complex social structures that enabled pederasty as an elite social practice.[112] Despite these critiques, *Greek Homosexuality* continues to stand at the head of any list of key works on the subject, and to influence work on same-sex relationships and pederastic cultures in other pre-modern societies.

Notes

1. Dover 1994, 69; cf. Brooke 2002. Note the heteronormative ordering of Dover's ambitions, and the persistence of his childhood fascination with monkeys (on which see Chris Stray's chapter on Dover's school days, and Dover's own diagram of his interests through his life, reproduced at the end of Halliwell 2011). The latter may have fed into the way he interpreted psychological studies on primates in his research for *GH*.
2. Russell and Halliwell 2012, 164.
3. Halperin 1990, 4–5 ('a maddening book to read'); also Nussbaum 2010, xi, Demand 1980, 124.

4. Whitmarsh 2016, 15.
5. Halperin 1990, Orrells 2015, Kapparis 2022.
6. Demand 1980, Schnapp 1980, Boardman 1980, and others. Full overview in Davidson 2001.
7. See Thorp 1992. Halperin 1990 and Davidson 2007 exemplify the two positions. Greenberg 1988 offers a constructionist account of the history of homosexuality; see also Sedgwick 1990, 40–4.
8. See Butler 1993 and 2004.
9. See Halliwell 2016b, Masterson and Robson 2016, Whitmarsh 2016.
10. Weeks 2007, 137–8, citing Giddens 1993.
11. *MC* 29–30, 42.
12. Giddens 1993, 49–64, Weeks 2012, 301–6.
13. Dover 1964a, 40 n. 2; Kinsey et al. 1948, West 1960. The Kinsey Report introduced the claim that around ten per cent of adults were predominantly homosexual, with sexual identity treated as a scale between homosexuality and heterosexuality. West's introductory work was later criticized by gay rights activists for its cautious approach (see Davidson 2007, 132–4); Dover *GH* cites a revised version of West (1977, cf. n. 20), published like *GH* by Duckworth.
14. Weeks 1990, 23–32.
15. On homophobia in the UK during this period, see Weeks 2007, 156–64, 2012, 307–9, Lewis 2016, 3–6, and the reflective memoir of Duncan 2005, especially 131–4.
16. See Lewis 2016 for a detailed history of the report and its context.
17. Weeks 2012, 306–14, Lewis 2016, 261–4. The 1967 act left gay men and venues still subject to arbitrary police harassment.
18. All references to *GH* are to the first edition (1978) unless otherwise indicated. See Duncan 2005, 241–5 on gay experience in 1950s Oxford.
19. The report's chapter on 'Early experiences' (Schofield 1960, 24–39, published pseudonymously under the name Gordon Westwood) compares with Dover's account of his own experiences as a schoolboy, particularly the occasion when he thought a boy demonstrating masturbation to him was asking him to be the receptive partner in anal intercourse (*MC* 18–19). Dover's response resembles the 'homosexual panic' characteristic of the era.
20. West 1977, Schofield 1960, Karlen 1971, and also Vanggaard 1972 on phallic domination. See Waters 2012.
21. Russell and Halliwell 2012, Halliwell 2016b, viii.
22. *MC* 111–12, Davidson 2001, 7–8.
23. Halliwell 2016b, ix; Dover 1980. On Dover on Plato, see Frisbee Sheffield's chapter in this volume.
24. Dover 1964a.
25. Dover's work on Aristophanes includes Dover 1968a, 1972a, 1993a; see also Dover 1978, 135–53, on 'comic exploitation'.
26. The development of women's history and its evolution into gender history is surveyed in Des Jardins 2011.
27. Bentley 2011.
28. Dover 1973a; later republished in Peradotto and Sullivan, eds, 1984.

29. Dover 1974, 213–16.
30. Halliwell 2016b, xi.
31. *MC* 122–3. Malcolm Schofield, then a research fellow at Balliol, recalls hearing Dover and Devereux discuss homosexuality at dinner at All Souls during this visit.
32. Devereux 1968, *passim*; Kapparis 2022, 28.
33. Halliwell 2011 offers perceptive comments on the strengths and limitations of Dover's philological method.
34. Key publications include Ryle 1949, Austin 1962, and Hare 1952; for context, see Lipscomb 2021, 83–6 and Mac Cumhaill and Wiseman 2022, 138–43, 165–74. Hare was a near contemporary, and a Balliol colleague, mentioned only in passing in *MC* 64; cf. Bowie, this volume, p. 61. Thanks to Sophie-Grace Chappell for alerting me to this important context.
35. Adkins 1960.
36. See *MC* 123–4, with Weeks 2012, 135, Halperin 2002, 114–15; cf. Schofield 1960.
37. See, for example, Hartsock 1983. A charitable interpretation would be that Dover explicitly uses his own status to legitimize the object of his research.
38. Edelman 2004, 1–31.
39. Russell and Halliwell 2012, 164.
40. Nussbaum 1997. See also Frisbee Sheffield's chapter in this volume.
41. See *GH* 54, with Davidson 2001, 20–7; 2007, 116, 131–2. David Halperin defends Dover's interpretation (and Foucault's), differentiating 'giving favours' from being the 'gender-deviant male' represented by the *kinaidos* (Halperin 2002, 71–3). On practices of *charis* and *charizesthai*, see Azoulay 2004; Xenophon, *Hiero* 1.37 paraphrases *charizesthai* as the indefinite τι ὑπουργῇ ('renders some favour').
42. Rocke 1996, 88, citing Dover at n. 8. Rocke has enough primary source material to provide statistical tables (243–52), although his data has been criticized (Halperin 2002, 190 n. 24). On Greek homosexuality in Renaissance Italy, see also Blanshard 2010, 124–35.
43. Dover explores the relationship between *erôs* and love at *GH* 49–54.
44. Commentators have connected Plato's portrait of the tyrannical character, with its excessive appetite (*Resp.* 9.571a–76d), to Aeschines' portrayal of Timarchus: Fisher 2001, 350–1.
45. Lear 2015, 116–17, cf. Félix Buffière's diachronic approach, which situates changing practices in pederastic culture in the fourth century in a historical context (Buffière 1980).
46. Noted in Boardman 1980; see Foucault 1982, Demand 1980. Dover drew on Sir John Beazley's typology of same-sex interactions in vase painting (Beazley 1989). See Jaś Elsner's chapter in this volume, and Osborne 2018a.
47. Fisher 2001, 126–7.
48. Fisher 2001; see also Lape 2006, Spatharas 2006, Worman 2008, 240–7, and Westwood 2020, 197–222, on Aeschines' manipulation of an idealized Athenian past.
49. The role of the classical past in the development of the idea of homosexuality is complex: see Matzner 2010 and 2015, Halperin 1990, 15–40, Blanshard 2010, 143–9. So, reciprocally, is the role of homosexuality in the development of Classics as an academic discipline: see Orrells 2011, and on Corpus Christi College and E.P. Warren, Rutherford 2020, 136–50. On the disinclination to consider pederasty within accounts of the history of homosexuality, see Amin 2017.
50. Rohy 2009.

51. Loraux 1993; see also Matzner 2016 and Freeman 2010.
52. On this phenomenon in modern times, see Weeks 2007 and Buckle 2015. On the multiplicity of phenomena incorporated within the concept of homosexuality, see Halperin 2002, 104–37.
53. *GH* 81 n. 35, citing Schofield 1960, 88–91 and 155–65 (on 'proselytism').
54. West 1960, 234. Hackforth 1952, 46 n. 3, notes a Homeric antecedent (*Il.* 22.263) cited by the scholiast Hermeias of Alexandria for Socrates' striking image.
55. That is not to identify these scholars with those ideologies, but to note that the interest in and identification of 'zero-sum' competition between Athenian citizens, present within and critiqued by authors such as Thucydides and Plato, may correlate with the rise of *homo economicus* as a default model of human behaviour, as well as looking back to Burckhardt's model (Burckhardt 1998).
56. Carnes 1998, 106 n. 9.
57. Russell and Halliwell 2012, 154.
58. *MC* 111–12, Davidson 2001; see also Waters 2012, Salter 2019 and 2022, 50.
59. Dover cites this passage as evidence for the law against citizen prostitution on which Aeschines depends (*GH* 34; cf. Fisher 2001, 47); but Aeschines' argument may be tendentious, and Plato's *erômenos* need not equate to Aristophanes' *binoumenos*.
60. Davidson 1997, 167–82, and Kapparis 2022, 27–31.
61. See Davidson 2001, 11–13, commenting on Dover's attitude.
62. Dover might well be expected to draw on Thucydides' methodological observation on the continuity of 'the human', 1.22.4.
63. Karlen 1971, 414, cited at *GH* 105 n. 91, draws on primate studies to illustrate the concept of 'phallic aggression' and responses to it: 'The connection of rump and anus with conquest and submission persists in our idioms ... Old primate rear-approach patterns probably exist as a substratum in our behavior and imagination.' Compare Maslow 1937.
64. Cartledge 1981, 19–20, discussing Xenophon, *Lac. pol.* 2. Davidson 2007, 27, and also 120–1, suggests that *paidika* refers to a more personal relationship.
65. Plato uses both terms carefully in Socrates' two speeches in the *Phaedrus*.
66. Dover argues (*GH* 98) that διαμηρίζειν ('to part the thighs') was 'almost certainly' the term used, citing Aristophanes, *Birds* 669, 706, 1254. The word also appears in scholia to Aristophanes, where it is interpreted as meaning sex with male and female partners, as it explicitly does in a saying of Zeno cited at Sextus Empiricus, *Math.* 11.190.
67. Schofield's survey (1960) shows that non-penetrative sexual contact was a typical practice among his subjects and preferred by some; Dover cites his study as correcting the view that 'homosexual anal copulation' was 'the most characteristic mode of homosexual consummation', *GH* 99.
68. Osborne 2018a, 318, 321–2; Davidson is both critical of Dover (2007, 477–90) and yet accepts Dover's sense of the verb (2007, 116 and 251); see also Lear and Cantarella 2008 and Elsner's chapter in this volume.
69. Dover 1966 also notes the possibility of sexual preference.
70. Also cited here: Dem. 48.56, 61.2.
71. Halliwell 2016b, x.
72. One companionate relationship in classical Athens, that between Pericles and Aspasia, was mocked by the comic poets, who presented the non-citizen Aspasia as a sex worker: Henry 1995.

73. Schnapp 1980; however, note the mythologization of the courtesan (*hetaira*) in both ancient literature and modern scholarship.
74. Sedgwick 1985, 4.
75. This would appear to acknowledge the presence of a classical aesthetic in modern gay imagery, rather than making a serious suggestion that homosexuality necessitated participation in a culturally specific presentism. But it is interestingly suggestive of the role of queer temporalities in classical reception. Nussbaum 1997, 152, finds Dover's cross-gender comparisons 'deft'.
76. Bethe 1907; see the next section for responses to *GH* that reassert the Dorian hypothesis.
77. Demand 1980 notes this.
78. Buckle 2015, Halperin 2002, with further bibliography on the recent history of homosexuality.
79. Davidson 2007.
80. Halperin 2015, 318–19.
81. Foucault 1982 (= 1994, 316), 1985, 196.
82. Jarratt 2014, Poster 1986, with Foucault 1985, 196–7, 252.
83. Foucault 1982.
84. Davidson 2007, 152.
85. Nussbaum 2010, xii.
86. Poster 1986, 209.
87. Jarratt 2014, Elden 2016, 62–71, 164–90.
88. Foucault 1985, 6.
89. Poster 1986, 213–14.
90. The later 'affective turn' in queer theory perhaps reacts against the Foucauldian model.
91. See Foxhall 1994, Richlin 1991, Cohen 1992.
92. Richlin 1991, Halperin 2002, 165–7.
93. Foxhall 1994, reprinted in Larmour et al., eds, 1998.
94. Stephen Halliwell reports that Dover and Winkler met during Dover's visits to Stanford in the late 1980s.
95. Winkler 1990, 45–70, at 45; also published in Halperin et al., eds, 1990, 171–209.
96. On the *kinaidos/cinaedus* as a personal identity in antiquity, see Sapsford 2015 and 2022.
97. Halperin 1990, 88–112; cf. Lape 2006 and Kapparis 2022.
98. Dover 1991, 162.
99. Fox 1998, 7–10.
100. Sedgwick 1985, 1–5.
101. The pleasure-seeking lover of Socrates' first speech in the *Phaedrus* does, however, seek to dominate and control his beloved (*Phdr.* 238e–9c); Dover cites this passage at *GH* 79 n. 32 for its suggestion that the *erastês* would prefer a beloved whose susceptibility to domination was marked in his self-presentation.
102. Yates 2005.
103. Williams 2010, Masterson 2014.

104. Bremmer 1980, Cartledge 1981, Patzer 1982. See also Buffière 1980. On the problematic anthropological concept of 'anachronistic survivals', see Rood et al. 2020, 119–43.
105. Patzer 1982; see Halperin 1990, 54–71 for a partisan comparison of Patzer and Foucault.
106. Cartledge 1981, reprinted as Cartledge 2001, 91–105. Cartledge, unlike Dover, acknowledges the situationality of both homosexual and heterosexual acts governed by age-specific norms within ancient Greek societies (17–18).
107. Dover 1988.
108. Bevir 1999, Thorp 1992.
109. Davidson 1997, 169–76, 2001, 2007. Ormand and Blondell (2015, 1–14) identify Davidson's position as humanist.
110. Davidson 2007, 68–98.
111. Love 2007, Sedgwick 2003.
112. Thanks to the organizers and participants for helpful comments and suggestions, to Christopher Stray, Emily Rutherford and Frisbee Sheffield for sharing unpublished work, and to Chris Brooke, Paul Cartledge, Sophie-Grace Chappell, Jennifer Ingleheart, Malcolm Schofield and Luke Syson for helpful discussions.

CHAPTER 12
DOVER'S 'INCH': REFLECTIONS ON THE ART-HISTORICAL METHOD IN *GREEK HOMOSEXUALITY*

Jaś Elsner

Kenneth Dover was by any standards a brave scholar. To write the cultural history of human sexuality in a far away moment, having already attempted that of popular morality, was bold, and it remains a fraught topic.[1] To focus on homosexuality, which in the year of publication (1978) had only been legal for eleven years, since 1967, in England and Wales, and had yet to be legalized in Scotland (where Dover began his work on this topic), again reflects his courage (legalization eventually took place in Scotland in 1980 and in Northern Ireland in 1982).[2] The book caught the spirit of the times: in June 1977 his most brilliant Balliol student, Bernard Williams,[3] was appointed by the Labour Government to chair a committee on obscenity, which published a liberalizing report in 1979.[4] Dover's work thus stood within a revolution in attitudes in Britain, between the late 1950s and the early 1980s,[5] and at the heart of changes within the scholarly community. Such changes included freeing-up of the censorship laws, especially in the 1960s.[6] The timeliness of Dover's inquiry in the 1970s goes alongside the discovery, for instance in the work of Masters and Johnson, that one could speak about sex and sexuality in the current moment,[7] which liberated the historian to ask questions about the 'unspeakable' in the past. In the transforming popular culture, it went side by side with the Women's Liberation movement of the same period (Germaine Greer's *Female Eunuch* was published in 1970), itself not unrelated to the licensing of the contraceptive pill in 1960 in America and 1961 in Britain.[8]

To do justice to Greek homosexuality, Dover saw he had to extend his command of the relevant material to areas well beyond his normal expertise – an acute perception,[9] although the history of ancient sex had earlier already turned to the visual.[10] By Dover's art history, I mean specifically his attempt to use the visual evidence of Greek painted pottery in order to write *Greek Homosexuality* – an evidential base that was empirically essential to the project, and has become a fundamental underpinning of the many histories of ancient sexuality that have been founded on his book. That these should include the work of Foucault as well as that of numerous classicists,[11] has meant that Dover's project stands at the epicentre of some of the most important work in the humanities in the last half century, across all disciplines. Dover's art history stands at the empirical base of the entirety of that collective project, which makes the topic significant well beyond a centenary celebration of his scholarly achievements.

Dover rightly saw that literary evidence was insufficient to his theme and the visual materials were key.[12] Note that by 'visual' I mean 'iconographical' since it is purely by means of their pictorial subjects that Dover selected his evidence (not for example in relation to kinds of vases and their functions or to their excavation histories and findspots). He also saw that you could not do this project in a simple chronological manner, since the empirical materials were not equally spread across the period of archaic and classical Greece. He wrote at the outset: 'The chapters which follow do not take the evidence in chronological order; they begin not at the beginning but in the centre of things, where the evidence is most abundant and detailed.'[13] That centre is Aeschines' prosecution of Timarchus in 346 BC (Chapter II, pp. 19–109) and as the culmination of that, in a section entitled 'Nature and Society', he lays out his visual evidence synchronically in a series of subsections named 'Male and female physique', 'Masculine and feminine styles', 'Pursuit and flight', 'Courtship and copulation', 'Dominant and subordinate roles' (pp. 68–109). The discussion is supplemented by – or perhaps its persuasive force predicated upon – the list of 535 vases placed at the back of the book (Dover 1978, 205–25; Dover 1989, 207–27), a number that has risen to 647 examples in more recent catalogues.[14]

Several historical points are worth emphasizing about this structural conception of the project. First, the images are made to offer *supplementary* evidence that the textual materials do not supply. As Dover admits in a chronological complication for his alignment of Aeschines and the arguments from pottery: 'Most of the vases which portray homosexual relations ... were made between 570 and 470 BC; the great age of erotic vase-painting was therefore at an end half a century before the birth of Plato and the earliest plays of Aristophanes.'[15] Second, Dover is not given to explaining or adjusting for the differences between, and the individual complexities of, the genres he is dealing with – notably polemical legal speeches and comic abuse among his key elite texts and the very different symposiastic playfulness of relatively low-level, quite possibly non-elite, visual materials created in quantities for a mass market.[16] He conflates these kinds of evidence and avoids examining the problems for ascertaining conclusions about what realities may lie behind the representations. Third, the placement of the list of vases before the bibliography and index at the end is a marvellous means of implying an overwhelming quantity of evidence that serves to make the whole case convincing. But that is a rhetorical and persuasive device. If there are – on the most recent estimates – between 30,000 and over 100,000 surviving Athenian pots and fragments from the period of Dover's focus,[17] then there are (on the most generous count) a good deal fewer than 2 per cent of surviving pots that make any reference to sex, let alone homosexuality (excluding mythological material) – a tiny proportion and one that is statistically close to insignificant when it comes to assessing the attitudes and desires, let alone the realities, that governed a whole culture.[18] Dover, it should be said, makes no statistical claims.

My caveat about mythology is significant. The real-life obsession of too many of those concerned with documenting apparent facts about ancient Greek sexuality (or, more correctly, sex life), however much they may concede that painted images are not direct reflections of real life, means that the selective sample of chosen objects, not only Dover's but several after him,[19] often excludes or underplays sexually explicit imagery with mythological actors.[20] Yet such material (by the same artists, sometimes on the same vases, made at the same times, for pottery used in the same contexts) was equally

Art-Historical Method in *Greek Homosexuality*

susceptible to erotic fantasy in ancient Greek life and usage, though the imagery of the cavortings of satyrs cannot determine anything 'real'.[21] Dover himself in fact does discuss mythological images (though he hardly illustrates them), notably pots with imagery of Ganymede and of Dionysus, blurring the line between what may be imagined as belonging to the real world and what may be imagined as mythical fantasy.[22] The reason for avoiding myth in most of the Greek sexuality project that followed Dover is the empirical obsession with realism.[23] But, as Dover implicitly saw, the occlusion of mythology has no basis.[24]

Let me begin by laying my cards on the table, before we go into specific art-historical details, as opposed to these more broadly historical points. Dover was a terrible art historian with no eye, no training and absolutely no reflex to questioning the problems of his evidence beyond what he wanted it to do. The results of this naïveté, for which he has not been sufficiently condemned, were disastrous for the field of the history of sexualities, and have only begun to be explored with critical acuity very recently.[25] In what follows, I lay out some of the problems of Dover's use of art-historical materials – important, as I have suggested, beyond his own work because they underlie the procedural practices of the entire field of ancient sexualities in the more than forty years since *Greek Homosexuality* was published. Then I will examine some conceptual underpinnings behind his project, in respect of the problems of representation, which have disturbing consequences for the practice of art history beyond Classical antiquity.

Dover's painted pottery

Dover undertook assiduous research in looking at the visual material: 'In the course of working on this book I have looked at most of the published photographs of Greek vases.'[26]

It appears that this was largely work in two dimensions, mediated through photography.[27] Dover's published work shows no grasp of materiality (objects in the round, images over a curved surface, the sides of pots or their interiors and exteriors in dialogue and often in ironic relation to each other, sometimes several cups in series potentially utilized in relation to each other),[28] and reveals no real effort at contextualizing the uses, functions or viewings of vases in their social world.[29] He makes no reference to looking at the originals in museums or handling them (although Stephen Halliwell tells me Dover mentioned looking at actual pots on one occasion), quite unlike John Beazley, the inspiration for how an Oxford philologist could also be an art historian and author of the article on which Dover's work on homosexuality in vases was predicated.[30] Dover is not interested in the objects or iconography per se but in the generalizations which he can extract from the mass of empirical data for his theme: 'the really interesting job' was 'relating the visual representation to the literary representation' (*MC* 115).[31] He claimed: 'My generalisations may need to be modified in the light of new material or by rectification of errors caused by negligence and inexperience on my part in the interpretation of existing material, but I should be surprised if any of them can actually be replaced by contrary generalisations.'[32] The reliance on really quite bad photographs and the impulse to generalization make him an extremely crude reader of the individual image in its rich specificity. Let us begin with Dover's B65. This is the black figure amphora in Nicosia that prompted Beazley's catalogue of vases with imagery of homosexual courtship, on which Dover's project depends (Figures 12.1 and 12.2).[33] Dover only shows one side (Beazley's 'A', Figure 12.1) and only includes that side in his

Figure 12.1 Dover's B65. Lydos Painter, black-figure belly amphora, c. 540 BC, found in Tamassos, Cyprus. Cyprus Museum, Nicosia C440. Side A. Dover's caption: 'A man courts a youth who shields his own genitals with his hand'. Photograph: By permission of the Department of Antiquities, Cyprus.

Art-Historical Method in *Greek Homosexuality*

catalogue, discussing it with his usual brevity.³⁴ But the picture on the other side is, as Beazley puts it, 'the same with variations'.³⁵ The key variation is that – at any rate from what can be seen in Beazley's 1947 photograph – the erastes is not ithyphallic on side B (something Beazley takes care not to mention),³⁶ from which may be inferred to follow Beazley's comment that the action of the eromenos' left hand, which Beazley characterized

Figure 12.2 Dover's B65. Side B (which Dover neither cites nor illustrates). Photograph: By permission of the Department of Antiquities, Cyprus.

as protective on side A, 'is less marked'.[37] Recent photographs show the erastes aroused on both sides but his penis delineated in a weaker shade of black than the rest of the imagery and now something of a shadow (Figure 12.2). But my point is that swift judgments from old photographs and the lack of Beazley's impeccable drive for autopsy of the vast majority of the vases he studied, mean Dover does not assess the entirety of a pot that shows *almost* the same thing twice but with interesting differences. The eromenos on side B holds a wreath out towards his erastes, and the two flanking dancers look away to left and right leaving the central pair in intimate isolation, while on side A the left dancer looks round at them, opening the thematic of voyeurism. On that side the three figures to the left (the lovers and the voyeur) are united by having garlands hanging from one forearm, unlike the dancer to the right. On side B only the central pair have garlands. Dover never looks at any pot closely enough to unravel the kinds of commentarial complexities it might offer to his theme, since he is concerned only to get on with illustrating various sexual acts – in this case the 'hand over [the] genitals as a shield'.[38]

To put it crudely, Dover's characteristic model of exploration of the grainy black-and-white photographs of sexual imagery which he was able to consult is to focalize on the sex acts. The procedure is not unlike the perusal of pornographic photographs,[39] passed between children in avoidance of the adult gaze, before the internet and the near-universal availability of pornography at the touch of an iPhone.[40] It has hardly been discussed in the literature that much of the sexual activity performed on pots includes images of spectators or observing non-participants, whose presence may comment on the response of the handler or viewer of the pot in which such themes occur.[41] The spectatorship issue is substantial in another black-figure amphora of the mid sixth century, Dover's B64 (Figures 12.3 and 12.4).[42] Here the courtship scene between two nude males takes place flanked by two pairs of figures looking on, two beardless to the left, two bearded to the right, the outer pair dressed and the inner pair naked. Here handling the pot, and interrogating its full materiality, makes a substantial difference: the other side (Figure 12.4), using the same framing devices above and below, shows the nude Heracles fighting the lion also flanked by spectators, two to the left (the outer one nude, the inner one clothed) and one clothed to the right. The pot offers a play of spectatorial confrontations but also a juxtaposition of kinds of aggression. In other words, Attic pottery is self-conscious about the complex conditions of its spectatorship in relation both to material forms and issues of handling; its visual commentary is often wry and potentially humorous. But such issues are never raised by Dover.[43] Any qualities of self-reflection, sophistication or irony in the vase-evidence Dover adduces are never discussed.

Dover's B76 demonstrates his reductive simplification in reading images (Figure 12.5). What is interesting here, apart from the lack of erection – indeed the lack of a penis – in the erastes (which does not discourage Dover in this case), is the magnificent and ironic ambivalence of the tail. Does it belong to the dog, whose interest in the youth's genitals seems no less marked than that of the erastes, or to the erastes, who thus becomes a category mistake for a satyr? Of course, if the erastes is a satyr without a penis (erect or not) then he is a most peculiar construct. Or is there an oblique and humorous reference to anal penetration by the dog's tail?[44] The pot plays on these issues jokingly, its black-figure

Figure 12.3 Dover's B64. Lydos Painter, black-figure belly amphora, *c*. 540 BC, found in Vulci, Etruria. Cabinet des médailles Paris, no. 206. Side A (which Dover cites but does not illustrate). Photograph: Bibliothèque nationale de France.

technique allowing the ambivalence of tails and opening the potential to visual commentary on what is depicted. Again, Dover shows no awareness of this kind of subtlety, although it is normal in Greek painted pottery. Nor does he make anything of the Amazonomachy with Heracles on the other side, which places the erotics against a mythical battlefield.[45]

Despite his disclaimers,[46] at the root of Dover's art-historical method is a model of realism whereby what can be 'generalized' from the imagery on painted vases becomes a

Jaś Elsner

Figure 12.4 Dover's B64. Side B (which Dover neither cites nor illustrates). Photograph: Bibliothèque nationale de France.

fact about ancient Greek sex.[47] Realism is high in Dover's values for historical scholarship.[48] In his autobiography he reserves highest praise for his teachers who emphasized the real. He defines Fraenkel's *'seriousness'* by the fact 'that he acknowledged Greeks and Romans as real people', while 'I learned from Meiggs ... never for a moment to forget that the people whose activities I was studying were *real*'.[49] In his classification of homoerotic courtship scenes (Types α, β and γ) Beazley introduced the last by saying 'the moment depicted is later than in Types α and β, and the two figures are interlocked'.[50] The reading

210

Figure 12.5 Dover's B76. Painter from Beazley's 'Group E', black-figure belly amphora, *c.* 550 BC, found in Vulci, Etruria. Vatican, Museo Gregoriano Etrusco 352, renumbered as 17829. Dover's caption: 'A man courts a youth with massive physique'. Photograph: Copyright of the Governorate of the Vatican City-State Directorate of the Vatican Museums.

of temporal progression, moving towards the clinch of climax – entirely an interpretative choice, with no evidential basis in the material[51] – reveals the realism underlying Beazley's readings,[52] no less than the identification of artists, workshops and schools (which he believed to be real) underpins his connoisseurship. Incidentally, one might ask why we need classify all the gift scenes (Type β) as images that evoke sex or the build-up to it through courtship; Beazley's motive is to maximize his evidential base. Dover entirely followed the model in the section of his discussion entitled 'courtship and copulation', as if the narrative pattern invented by Beazley were the equivalent of a nineteenth-century novel culminating in marriage.[53]

Typically, he spares no blushes in his description of what is an ideal type and not any particular pot (e.g. Figure 12.6): 'When courtship has been successful, the erastes and eromenos stand facing one another; the erastes grasps the eromenos round the torso, bows his head on to or even below the shoulder of the eromenos, bends his knees and thrusts his penis between the eromenos's thighs just below the scrotum.'[54] What this has done, however, is to deduce a general set of behavioural principles about real sexual activity on the basis of a relatively small corpus of images.[55]

In his captions to the illustrations from actual pots, Dover's realism allows indulgence in some spectacular 'reading-in'. He is very certain in determining (whatever artists may have intended or viewers may have seen) that 'penetration is clearly anal, not vaginal' (caption to B51, cf. R543, R545, where he decides 'that portrayal of vaginal copulation is intended', and R577). He sees subtleties of emotion or response even in small fragments that may be argued to require significant faith and conviction in one's judgments. At B53 he comments, 'the odd man out entreats a youth, who rejects him'; the extent to which this is rejection, or anything else, is in the beholder's eyes. At B598 Dover sees affection in the boy's responses (cf. R27, R59). He identifies enough with the scenes depicted to read all kinds of motivations, so at R223, for instance, 'The youth on the left, perhaps impatient at having to queue, importunes another youth'. At B342 'a muscular youth *resists* [my itals.] a man's attempt to touch his genitals' (Figure 12.7) – but the resistance is only in the clasped hands (while the youth might well be directing the man's hand, cf. B65, CE33, R196a).

The main text itself is full of such interpretative interventions. On p. 102 'there can be no doubt of the woman's enjoyment of intercourse in (e.g.) B49 and R506 …'. The interpretative reflex here is entirely dependent on so powerful a belief in the reality of what is depicted that one has no option but intuitively to identify with the various emotions such scenes may evoke in their actors. Despite the disclaimers, Dover really believed in the real. Let us take B250, an example of a black-figure amphora dated to the mid sixth century which has the merit of depicting all three Beazleyan stages of courtship (α, β and γ), not in that order.[56] Dover only discusses and illustrates one side (Figure 12.8), despite the fact that the two sides replicate the theme, with slight differences as usual.

Both sides of the pot have seven male figures (Figures 12.8 and 12.9). The two on the left approach the centre, both bearing garlands on one side. The figure on the far left is an older bearded male on both sides of the pot, ithyphallic only on the 'front' side (Figure 12.8), the youth having longer hair.[57] On both faces, the younger man looks back at the older (who touches his chin on the 'front') holding a love-gift (a stag on the 'front' and a cockerel on the 'back'). These are versions of Beazley's love-gift theme (β). In the centre on both sides are three figures. The two on the left of the centre, a youth on the left and a bearded man on the right, are 'interlocked' in Beazley's chaste terminology for his third stage (Type γ), or copulating, according to Dover,[58] in the intercrural position. Next to

Figure 12.6 Dover's B114. Taleides Painter, black-figure Lekythos, *c.* 530 BC, provenance unknown. Princeton University Art Museum 86.53. Dover's caption: 'A man and a youth copulate intercrurally'. Photograph: Princeton University Art Museum/ Art Resource NY.

these is a single older figure, dancing, in a cloak, with his head turned back to the amorous couple on one side, fully naked and looking forwards on the other. To the far right are two figures at the foreplay stage (a version of Beazley's Type α), eromenos at the left and erastes to the right, the youth holding a garland and the older man a cockerel love-gift on the one side, while on the other, the youth holds the cockerel and the older man appears to have taken the garland. There are many complexities here – notably whether one reads

Jaś Elsner

Figure 12.7 Dover's B342. Fragment from an incense burner by a 'Painter akin to that of the Nicosia Olpe', c. 530 BC, provenance unknown. Boston Museum of Fine Arts 08.31i. Dover's caption: 'A muscular youth resists a man's attempt to touch his genitals'. Photograph: Boston Museum of Fine Arts.

a narrative at all, how one relates the near-replicated imagery, whether one sees the three couples on each side as the same couples at different stages, whether one flips between the sides (so in the pair on the right one might see the difference between 'front' and 'back' as the exchange of love-gifts – cockerel for garland). There are multiple levels of ithyphallicism, including no penis at all in the older figure holding a garland to the far

Art-Historical Method in *Greek Homosexuality*

left of the one side, his equivalent on the other side being ithyphallic. There are similar but slightly different framing borders at the tops of the two sides, and the 'front' has two extra animals – a hare hanging between the 'intercrural' couple and the dancer above the garland that is apparently being held out to the dancer by the eromenos, and what looks like a dog against the right-hand side, not really arranged in the same dimension as the human figures but surely not dead like the hanging hare. Dover explores none of the peculiarities of all this, or its stylized and repetitive formalism, but he does emphasize realism. He notably focuses on revelry: 'Since copulation is naturally associated with festivity and the brighter side of life, both partners in a sexual approach or embrace may

Figure 12.8 Dover's B250. The Painter of Berlin 1686, black-figure amphora, *c*. 540 BC, from Vulci, Etruria. British Museum 1865,1118.39. Dover's caption: 'Men court youths and one pair copulates'. Photograph: British Museum.

215

Jaś Elsner

Figure 12.9 Dover's B250. The side Dover neither cites nor illustrates. Photograph: British Museum.

be shown holding garlands: B250'.⁵⁹ Of the couple to the right on the 'front' (Figure 12.8) he writes: 'One youth in B250 expostulates [I do not see how we can know this: JE], but does not protect his genitals from the touch of the man's fingers or from the man's (horizontal) erection hovering an inch away'.⁶⁰ The spatial distance is extremely interesting here since 'an inch' does not define the space on the black-figure image but in the implied reality of the sexual event taking place: Dover has put himself in the picture and describes not it but the imagined process of approaching intercourse ... His own reading into the image, a product of fantasy, has created his reality, and hence his scholarly construction of ancient Greek sexual behaviour.

Dover's development of Beazley's three stages of courtship serves to deliver the realities of intercrural sex,[61] which is evidenced only by the visual material and for which no textual support exists. To be sure, Dover's philology enabled him to find a single set of passages from Aristophanes using the word *diamêrizein* to ground his art history in textual fact.[62] It is worth remarking that this is the reverse of his normal method in *Greek Homosexuality*, which grounds the textual discourse of literatures of sexual polemic and abuse in what he imagined was visual fact. It has been argued that there is no basis for *diamêrizein* meaning intercrural sex, which means there is no basis in the category at all,[63] save his own fantasy-driven reading-into the images: where Beazley saw 'two figures interlocked', Dover, as noted above, saw 'copulation'. In part the problem is Dover's weird philological exactitude, famously evident in his reading of *Clouds* 973–8 where he gives a medically precise definition of the particular seminal fluid he imagines the word *drosos* to mean in the context.[64] But sexual terminology – especially in contexts of abuse or humour – is not precise: hearers or readers are given space to imagine their own personal versions of the activities (transgressive to some) that are being evoked. Moreover, slang terms for sex change over time – in some cultures very swiftly, as anyone who has kids will know if they compare the terms used in the playgrounds of their childhood with those used a generation later or earlier. Lexical precision is not what is called for in writing this kind of history. The bigger problem is that one must worry if the empirical evidence for a whole category of social behaviour, presented by many scholars as certainly true of ancient Athenian homosexuality, rests on the controversial interpretation of a single word in a passage of comedy alongside a group of pictures on Greek pots that have been aligned with it on not very strong grounds by modern scholarship.

Let us summarize. Effectively Dover borrowed Beazley's classification, removed it from its careful closeting and reframed it with much more robust language. He placed Beazley's pattern in a big range of literary contexts, reformulated his 'interlocked' clinch as 'intercrural' intercourse and presented this as the respectable way to consummate homosexual passion by contrast to the degrading model of anal penetration, in what he assumed to be an older/younger pattern of sexual partners with the former active and the latter passive. As has been shown by James Davidson, the drive behind Dover's account was an obsession with penetration as the model for ancient Greek anxieties about sex, which has been key to the later literature including Foucault.[65] The realism of this and its focus on the penis is the subject of the section of Chapter III entitled 'Predilections and Fantasies',[66] which Dover concludes by announcing that 'Greek art and cult were extremely interested in the penis'.[67]

Not only does the penetration model deserve serious circumspection, but its empirical basis lies in intercrural sex (which may well never have existed) as a respectable fig-leaf for the penetrative that dare not risk representation. The realist instinct has dominated the approaches of almost all Dover's followers, who have continued to read actual practices out of ancient visual fantasy.[68]

It is worth reflecting on Dover's terminology, since the ekphrastic language used by any writer in the intermedial translation of visual material into a rhetorical argument is inevitably tendentious.[69] By marked contrast with the emotive discourses of 'love' in same-sex writing about both art history and Classics in earlier generations (notably by such Oxford-connected aesthetes as Walter Pater, John Addington Symonds, Oscar Wilde and Edward Perry Warren),[70] Dover's language for sex is strikingly instrumental, unaffectionate, arguably violent. One might cite such terms as 'copulation' (for what Beazley called 'two figures … interlocked'),[71] 'mauling and hauling',[72] 'resistance' and 'non-resistance',[73] 'penetrate',[74] 'dominant' and 'subordinate',[75] 'surrender',[76] 'sexual cravings',[77] not to speak of his turn to animal and anthropological comparisons at p. 105 with 'mounting', 'buggered' and 'fucked' or his – to a modern ear particularly unsuccessful – schoolboy joke at p. 96 ('respond willy-nilly'). Despite his protests about 'not experiencing shock or disgust at any genital act',[78] and his anti-discriminatory agenda on the liberalization of legal restrictions on sexual acts, this is in keeping with what Carol Atack elsewhere in this volume suggests may be read in terms that contemporary society would see as homophobic, or perhaps a repulsion-coupled-with-attraction for all forms of sexuality.

If we were to seek a personal cause for the anxieties in play here, then the closeted homosexual culture of British boys' public schools (and notably in relation to the dominance of Classics in the curriculum) from at least the later nineteenth century,[79] coupled with the long history of paedophilia and child abuse in the same institutions, including St Paul's which Dover himself attended, may serve.[80] The recent revelations of systemic sexual abuse across that sector have been appalling, with St Paul's among the prime culprits in ways well-documented since the 1970s (when Dover was writing) and very plausibly in the thirties, when he was there.[81] The issues are about a culture in which such assaults from masters or older boys were normal and feared, but unspeakable. This offers a complicated take on the ancestralism of Classics as a discipline in Britain and the ways that the ancient world could be used to justify attitudes and activities of abuse that are simply wrong; it involves the playing out of problematic identifications through the prism of scholarship, in ways that make a parody of any attempt at objective historicism. Questions of paedophilia hugely complicate the generally celebratory story of the development of British gay culture in relation to Classical education (normally a narrative of consensual sexual orientations and decisions for people after school age, straightforward by modern standards) with ethically problematic imbrications from a contemporary perspective.[82] Is Dover here projecting his own unresolved anxieties about the threat of penetration onto the ancient past, presented as history, and onto his privileged cultural model of archaic and Classical Athens, as if they could thus be allayed? The fact that the most notorious revealer of his most private thoughts and actions in his memoir, *Marginal Comment*, makes no mention of abuse at school may intimate not that the fear of this did not arise, but that (like *Greek Homosexuality* itself) his autobiography may have closeted the secrets of the cruel formation of a child's identity through a culture of abuse at school . . .[83]

Dover's 'inch': the problems of realism

The realist model for understanding how images work has been central to classical art as a history of the development of mimesis, the rise of techniques of illusion and ever more realistic representation.[84] But, in the context of our subject here, and in particular in relation to human sexual activity in the past, realism is essential not only to Dover's aim of inferring social history and sexual behaviour from images, but also to two other 'technologies' on which his project depends. These are, first, the pre-digital assumption that photography is realist because it in some sense records reality (something that has been fundamentally destabilized by the ways artificial intelligence generates virtual realities entirely independent of any 'real' referent, such as 'deepfakes');[85] and, second, the practices of pornography, especially photographic pornography, in the pre-digital modern world, Dover's world.

While dictionary definitions of pornography emphasize explicitness and sexual arousal,[86] both legal and philosophical accounts have made the issue of realism – or transparency between representation and its *causal* referent – key to the effects of arousal.[87] The focus on sex acts that characterizes Dover's approach to Greek pots, largely as represented by photographs, is at once governed by the historical drive to exploiting their evidence of sexual behaviours in the past (one kind of realism) and the pornographic gaze that seeks transparency between the image and its referent (something particularly enmeshed in the claims to realism in photography). This expectation of photographic transparency is hugely dated by our moment, when the first thing we must say of any such image is that it may have been sophisticatedly faked: it is not real but only real-*ist*. The issues are well encapsulated by what we may call Dover's 'inch' – the remarkable description, as noted above, of the 'youth in B250' who 'expostulates, but does not protect his genitals from the touch of the man's fingers or from the man's (horizontal) erection hovering an inch away'.[88] The analytic move is towards acts and organs; the inch is not a spatial measurement of the imagery on the pot but refers to the pornographic fantasy of the writer in imagining a situation in which the distance, yet the closeness, defined by 'an inch', can only have a narrative thrust as inch moves towards clinch ...

Pornographic photography (in still or moving form) could, in the analogue era, plausibly claim to be a record of the real, detailing and recording acts committed between real persons, which were causal of the given representation. In the pre-digital age before photoshop, the Williams Committee affirmed (with a certainty that now seems quaint) that pornographic 'photographs ... must inevitably be *records* of sexual activity with the usual human limitations' (my itals).[89] Drawings – adhering to a variety of pictorial conventions – are always a matter of artists' fantasies to some extent, and of course particularly so in erotic subjects. When such drawn imagery occupies complex curving surfaces on three-dimensional objects like painted pots, it is subject to significant contextual functions and needs to be assessed with some sensitivity to its social usage, conditions of viewing and formal constraints. Moreover, Greek sexual imagery is very often socialized in groups or with non-participant observers witnessing the scene, again complicating analysis. Discussion of the functions of such erotic subject-matter on

Greek pots in their contexts of use has been less decisive than, for instance, that of Japanese erotic prints (*Shunga*) between the eighteenth and twentieth centuries, where the conclusion has been that fantasies of sexual activity, often fantastically represented, were for purposes of solitary satisfaction: '*Shunga* were largely for those who had sex alone'.[90] Admittedly we have a richer and more recent range of contextualizing social history for the Japanese example, including poetry referring to masturbation; and prints or books of prints are perused in entirely different and perhaps more private ways than the imagery on pots made for the symposium,[91] even if these were subsequently reused for funerary or dedication purposes.

Pictorial representations of sexual activity on Greek vases are, in other words, very far from being transparent and are certainly not causally-derived depictions of anything actually done between Greek individuals. This is a point frequently made in critiques of Dover,[92] and one to which he himself responded in *MC* 116. But one issue, which may in part help to explain the strange phenomenon of Dover's 'inch' in turning visual signs into a real-life fantasy, is the way art historians have tended to use *photographs* of works of art – including focalized details of iconography – to represent the real *objects* to which their discussion refers. Often the photograph comes to stand for the object, and to prove the truth-status of the claims made through illustration. This is normal in the history of art and has been since the advent of photography at the end of the nineteenth century; it invests the disciplinary practice of art history with an extraordinary confidence in the photograph of a given work of art as its direct and realistic reflection, a touchstone to verity that supplies cognitive reliability to any argument from images. There is, in other words, a profound commitment to the realism of photographs in the behaviour of the discipline. This is misconceived (since it is obviously the case that a black-and-white photograph of a Greek vase from any chosen angle is at best a partial and limited representation of the original object, disguising at least as much as it may reveal), but it is normal practice in the disciplinary genre which Dover appropriated.

That disciplinary practice of photographic realism underpins Dover's method. Of R196 (Figures 12.10–12.12), a famous pot with images of courtship which he illustrates twice but in very poor and partial photographs,[93] Dover writes:

> The pairs of youths and boys in R196 [Figure 12.10 here] illustrate different stages of seduction admirably. In one pair, the boy tries to restrain the arm of the youth which has stolen tentatively to the back of his head. In another, the boy is close to surrender; he gazes up into the face of the youth and satisfies honour by taking hold of the youth's right arm above the elbow, which does nothing to interrupt the dandling of his penis by the youth's fingers. The most dramatic pair stands between those other two; here the youth sags at the knees, looking up in abject entreaty, his penis swollen and the fingers of his right hand spread despairingly, while the boy, chin high in a defiant pose, grips the arm of the youth hard and keeps it from its goal. What gives this picture its peculiar interest is that it is matched on the other side of the vessel by heterosexual pairs [Figure 12.11 here] where the atmosphere is quite different, though in an unexpected way: the youths and women do not

Figure 12.10 Dover's R196. Red-figure cup signed by 'Peithinos' as painter, *c.* 500 BC, from Vulci Etruria. Berlin Antikensammlung, no. F2272. Side A. Dover's caption: 'Youths court boys whose degree of resistance varies. Note that some are dark-haired and others blond'. Photograph: Antikensammlung/Johannes Laurentius/Art Resource NY.

Figure 12.11 Dover's R196. Side B. Dover's caption: 'Youths court women'. Photograph: Antikensammlung/Johannes Laurentius/Art Resource NY.

touch each other at all, but seem immersed in a patient, wary conversation, in which a slight gesture or an inflexion of the voice conveys as much as the straining of an arm in the other scene.[94]

This is a highly interpretative description – a serious case of 'reading-into' what Dover revealingly calls 'a picture'. His account – full of emotive colour in such comments as 'stolen tentatively', 'satisfies honour', and 'defiant pose' – allows the pot to perform a narrative of 'different stages of seduction',[95] presented as 'an illustration' of those stages as if referring back to a prior reality. That narrative is much more than a series of stages schematically listed: it is a pornographic fantasy of sexual feelings – moving via sagging knees and 'abject entreaty' to a 'penis swollen' and 'the fingers of his hand spread despairingly'. There are no facts in all this, but just the identifications and projections of the scholar's fantasy, as revealed through the choice of adjectives and adverbs, occupying the same virtual and voyeuristic space we saw earlier in Dover's 'inch' between penis and groin.

My point is that, following normal (if unreflective) art-historical practice, Dover has taken a photograph to be the true representation, or index, of the image on the pot and effectively of the pot itself (and thereby transparently of the reality of what the image represents). By omitting consideration of the pot's totality and the relation of its iconography as aligned to its material structure and usage, it is a partial and one-sided reading. The other side represents heterosexual courtship, which Dover mentions only as an aside in relation to flowers and garlands and to *kalos* inscriptions,[96] in this case ignoring the interplay between the two sides in relation to seduction. The interior plays on the courtship theme from a mythological point of view in its tondo of Peleus and Thetis (Figure 12.12, which Dover does not mention).

Dover's account is massively reductive; and by virtue of the focalized photographic angle in which his illustration presents the pot, he massively distorts the vase's actuality as well as ignoring its functions as a drinking cup. He then subjects his 'picture', which he takes to reveal the real pot, to the heady ekphrasis I have quoted, geared to prove his interpretative extrapolation of sexual activities from imagery, but filled with his effusive relation of feelings characteristic of twentieth-century people (and their pornographic fantasies).[97] All the while he makes a move that is entirely unwarranted philosophically or methodologically, and never signalled overtly in his writing, but on which the entire procedure has been predicated. That is, he takes the 'reality' of what is on a pot (as indexed by what is on the photograph he is describing and has illustrated) as an index of the realities of sexual life, notably the complex game of courting and seduction, as it actually took place in Athens where the pot was made and where he imagines its use (rather than in Etruria, where it was found). This slide, from the photograph as reflecting the real pot, to the pot's imagery as reflecting real life, is catastrophic scholarly method. But it is the result of the pornographic process that seeks the real behind or transparently through the image (however much the image has been staged or distorted), and simultaneously of the historical process that seeks ancient reality behind or through the fragments that remain to us.

Figure 12.12 Dover's R196. Interior with Peleus and Thetis, which Dover neither cites nor illustrates. Photograph: Antikensammlung/Johannes Laurentius/Art Resource NY.

If these problems – above all philosophical issues in relation to representation and methodological matters in relation to how we press images to offer empirical evidence for history – were confined only to Dover's work, then the point would be trivial. But, alas, Dover's method – including the overreach into the real – has been the normal model for writing the history of ancient sexuality ever since. Things may be more judiciously phrased or tentatively suggested than in Dover's writing, and the need to separate ideology from lived reality has been recognized,[98] but the thrust from photographic representations of pots to the representations on those pots as somehow testimony of the real world remains in place and is unavoidable.[99] At issue is the trickiness of academic method in the writing of both history and art history. Not only is it misguided in its use of photographs as the standard proof of the cognitive reliability of empirical data in the case of works of art (and indeed often as if they were empirical data, in place of autopsy of the original objects), but also in the intermedial problematics that translate three-dimensional objects into two-dimensional photographs, that translate two-dimensional pictures into textual descriptions, and that use descriptions of such imagery alongside rhetorically similar descriptions of 'reality' to create something that passes for 'history'. By this method, ancient Greek sexuality – and a number of other fantasies that currently pass for historical truth – have been created.

Dover's 'inch' between penis and genitals is not a distance on any actual picture on any actual pot. Nor is it a distance in ancient reality. It exists, like so much of what passes for the 'real' in Dover's account of Greek homosexuality, in a projective fantasy from the imagery on the pots, alongside a deep knowledge of the literary texts. The spatial fantasy in its pornographic context becomes, as I have implied, a form of narrative: not only an imagined distance but also a process by which the distance is bridged ... The distance bridged is simultaneously that between eromenos and erastes in the vase painting Dover purports to describe, and that between modern scholar-viewer and the ancient reality as indexed by the picture on the pot. The fantasies derived from Dover's pots, described in robust, sometimes sober but sometimes highly fanciful prose, are mapped onto fantasies of ancient reality derived from other sources, and the entirety is packaged as if it were ancient reality. I fear we need to start again.

Coda: If not reality . . .

The solution to the problems of constructing an ancient sexual *reality* out of the visual evidence of Athenian vases, alongside a selection of texts, has been to call what we find in the pots and what underlies their imagery '*ideology*'.[100] But the question – vast beyond the issue of sexuality – is: whose ideology? The issues include the extraction of our own cultural perspectives (whether on visual materials in the age of so much virtual media or on sexualities in an era of astonishing change in attitudes to sexual practices, orientations and preferences over the last six decades), so that we are clear that the ideologies elicited are ancient and not modern projections. We also need clarity on what we are doing in relation to the empirical evidence in creating a construct by which to explain that evidence. The constraints include whether to insist on Athenian elite consumption for Dover's pots in order to enable ideological inferences about how their iconography reveals attitudes to personal intimacy in the world which our literary texts also evoke;[101] or to distinguish, however awkwardly, between 'elite' and 'middling' ideologies, presumably with equivalent levels of consumption;[102] or to allow the ideology to extend to the 'popular audience'.[103] Yet how certain, historical or likely are such assumptions, and how does 'ideology' translate into the images painted on ancient pottery?

Most fundamentally, *ideology* – like Pierre Bourdieu's *habitus*,[104] or Erwin Panofsky's 'intrinsic meaning' (which constitutes the ultimate level of his 'Iconology'),[105] or Alois Riegl's *Kunstwollen*[106] – is a modern concept, hypothesized to inform the totalities of how culture manifests itself. The concept is posited by generalist scholars in order to make sense of a vast arena of cultural epiphenomena (notably the range of material and visual production) within the world of their creation and consumption. Finding a convenient formulation of desires, wills, structures and conceptual frames that define how a culture presents itself and can explain it, is obviously attractive. But is any such formulation fully true? To what extent, in the lived experience of the reader of this chapter, do the variety of ideologies of our own times conflict and contradict each other between groups and across generations? Moreover, the positing of an ideology (or *habitus* or intrinsic meaning or *Kunstwollen*) is circular, because we derive what that ideology (or *habitus* or intrinsic meaning or *Kunstwollen*) is on the basis of the variety of data that it is intended to explain.

That circularity in itself need not be so vicious as to destroy the entire project, but it requires caution because of the exclusions necessarily conducted in order to enable it. In the case of Attic pottery, we have the problem of its viewership within the city (an issue foregrounded in the spectators presented on the imagery of so many pots). How can we be certain they were made for the elite (given the quantities that survive and the vast numbers that must have been made), or that their ideology is fully compatible with what we derive from texts? What about the women and slaves who also used, looked at, maybe owned painted pots, who are largely excluded from our text-derived accounts of elite ideology?[107] Did everyone in Athens who used such materials share similar views of their iconography? What did the female half of the population think about male homoerotics?

Beyond that lies the problem of the market. A large quantity of surviving Attic pottery was found in Etruria (including most examples discussed in this paper), exported there in antiquity and buried in tombs.[108] That includes a significant proportion of the corpus from which Dover made his specifically Hellenocentric, actually Athenocentric, arguments.[109] I have taken those examples from Dover's lists to which he gives a reference in Beazley's corpora of painted pottery and collated them against Beazley's reports of findspots (see the Appendix to this chapter). Of 376 pots in this category, 136 (36 per cent) have no archaeological provenance (not surprising in material that combines objects excavated long-ago alongside illicit finds, some recent, for which the market necessitates the obscuring of findspots); but the majority of these in older European collections were certainly found in Italy. Of the 239 pots with likely provenance given by Beazley, 20 are from Attica (5.3 per cent of the total of 376), 31 from Greece as a whole including Attica (8.25 per cent), 12 from the eastern Mediterranean (including the Black Sea, the Islands, Asia Minor and Naucratis in Egypt), and 197, well over 50 per cent, from Italy. The Italian figure rises significantly if we consider that most of the unprovenanced pots are probably from there. The figures are of course extremely rough and skewed by the likelihood that Italian burial practices were more conducive to the survival of complete vases than Greek ones. The issues include how one extrapolates from such figures to what might have been likely in the sixth and fifth centuries, and what are the ethics of doing so – that is, working not with our actual empirical data-set but with the ways we adjust for it to suit our designs.[110]

But we may ask, do the pots that landed in Italy (perhaps made for and only ever used in that market) represent Athenian attitudes or ones targeted to their purchasers, especially in Etruria and South Italy? Does the intended non-Attic consumer-base make a difference to how we should understand the ideologies and unspoken assumptions depicted? The argument has raged.[111] Our problem, however, is not the intent of the market, but the appropriateness of deducing 'ideology' from evidence that is at best problematic when it comes to attesting purely Athenian or Greek attitudes. If we think of contemporary cultural productions designed for global markets (for instance, Netflix series, made in various countries globally) it is not obvious that they always reflect the attitudes or ideologies of the place of manufacture and filming ...

The list of vases Dover supplies (pp. 205–25 in the first edition) are effectively selected on iconographic grounds (on a 'real-life' basis, eschewing sex between mythological figures), with some eccentricity to which he admits: 'By no means all of them portray homosexual behaviour or bear erotic inscriptions; a great many vases which do portray such behaviour or do bear such inscriptions are not listed' (205). He then orders them chronologically, black-figure followed by red-figure, effectively following Beazley's model, which dates pots by their makers and hypothetical schools of artists, and implicitly assuming that chronology delivers history.[112] Others make their lists from the same material (with some variations and some extension of the database) and then taxonomize differently – for instance by sexual position and number of participants involved in any given act, effectively assuming a synchronic model of some kind of essential Athenian sexuality over a long period.[113] In all cases the governing axiom is that the place of production (Athens) and the moment of making (rather than the long period of reception) determines our ability to derive 'ideology' from the corpus, alongside other Athenian productions such as texts.[114] One glance at my recalibration of Dover's list in terms of archaeological provenance throws doubt on the apparently straightforward juxtaposition of Athenian images and Athenian texts. The texts were produced and initially received in Athens. The images may have been produced there but the vast majority were not consumed there and may well have been exported immediately on manufacture, never to be seen by anyone in Athens outside the potter's workshop and the shipper's packing crew (the issue of whether and what percentage of pots moved after primary use in Athens is another vast unknowable). The question is how selective iconography derived from material of which a great deal was probably not intended to be seen in Athens can be used to determine Athenian ideology.

I raise these questions at the end because, although they are not precisely Dover's issues, they illustrate the tremendous and unsolved problems of how to place and understand the nature of the iconographic evidence he collected in relation to ancient experience, realities and desires. I do think none of the questions has been resolved.[115]

Appendix: Dover's List of Vases Collated Against Beazley's Corpora by Provenance.

Abbreviations:

ABV: J.D. Beazley, *Attic Black-Figure Vase Painters*, 1956, Oxford

ARV: J.D. Beazley, *Attic Red-Figure Vase Painters*, 2nd edn, 2 vols, 1963, Oxford

Par: J.D. Beazley, *Paralipomena: Additions to Attic Black-Figure Vase Painters and to Attic Red-Figure Vase Painters*, 2nd edn, Oxford 1971

Art-Historical Method in *Greek Homosexuality*

Athens and Attica: 20

B28 (ABV 82); B31 (ABV 83); B109 (ABV 175); B134 (ABV 198); B330 (ABV 186); B370 (ABV 505); B406 (ABV 664); R31 (ARV 1559); R164 (ARV 91); R219 (ARV 130); R585 (ARV 447); R655 (ARV 479); R729 (ARV 566); R752 (ARV 587); R847 (ARV 890); R913 (ARV 1050); R994 (ARV 1561); R1005 (ARV 1001); R1006 (ARV 1001); R1007 (ARV 1001).

Greece: 11

B6 (ABV 39, Pharsalus); B20 (ABV 70); B107 (Par 72); R27 (ARV 20, Kolias, Corfu); R48 (ARV 45, Tanagra); R144 (ARV 80); R168 (ARV 95, Corinth); R476 (ARV 331); R699 (ARV 554, Boeotia); R887 (ARV 995, Eretria); R894 (ARV 998, Eretria).

Eastern Mediterranean, the Islands, the Black Sea: 12

B12 (ABV 67, Naucratis); B 16 (ABV 69, Camiros); B 65 (ABV 109, Tamassos); B 84 (ABV 156, Camiros); B98 (ABV 162, Ialysos); B120 (ABV 186); R132 (ARV 75, Berezan, Black Sea); R462 (Par 360, Turkey); R502 (ARV 362, Delos); R741 (ARV 579, Camiros); R 774 (ARV 652, Camiros); R997 (ARV 1579, Odessa).

Italy: 197 (all together)

Various: 24

B262 (ABV 314, Ferento); B334 (Par 179); R50 (ARV 1602, Taranto); R90 (ARV 54, Campagnano); R344 (ARV 204); R358 (ARV 221); R405 (ARV 275, Telese); R480 (ARV 335, Pomaricio); R680 (ARV 505, Adria); R733 (ARV 566, Ruvo); R754 (ARV 601, Altamura); R783 (ARV 741, Vari); R833 (ARV 880, Spina); R837 (ARV 882, Spina); R841 (ARV 887, Suessula), R863 (ARV 911, Populonia); R867 (ARV 953, Cortona); R902 (ARV 1045, Vico Equense); R904 (ARV 1045, Sorrento); R918 (ARV 1052, Vico Equense); R930 (ARV 1111, Cortona); R958 (ARV 1171, Egnatia); R970 (ARV 1208, Locri); R1017 (ARV 1607, Mastrillo).

Bologna: 4

R6 (ARV 4); R112 (ARV 65); R851 (ARV 903); R926 (ARV 1089).

Capua: 8

B152 (ABV 203); B378 (ABV 707); R414 (ARV 279); R422 (ARV 286); R567 (ARV 434); R663 (ARV 488); R762 (ARV 637); R954 (ARV 1154).

Cerveteri: 16

B295 (ABV 380); R12 (ARV 10); R16 (ARV 14); R20 (ARV 16); R200 (ARV 118); R263 (ARV 167); R279 (ARV 173); R283 (ARV 173); R322 (ARV 189); R406 (ARV 275); R446 (ARV 320); R545 (ARV 408); R555 (ARV 429); R581 (ARV 446); R603 (ARV 1570); R634 (ARV 471).

Chiusi: 91

B24 (ABV 76); R148 (ARV 85); R303 (ARV 177); R305 (ARV 177); R438 (ARV 316); R456 (ARV 324); R471 (ARV 329); R 478 (ARV 1559); R496 (ARV 357); R875 (ARV 974); R1015 (ARV 1601).

Cumae: 3

B434 (ABV 678); R693 (ARV 550); R845 (ARV 890).

Etruria: 6

B79 (ABV 151); B130 (ABV 198); B190 (ABV 245); B283 (ABV 332); R695 (ARV 551); R813 (ARV 822).

Falerii: 4

B287 (ABV 375); B362 (ABV 495); R638 (ARV 471); R853 (ARV 904).

Orvieto: 9

R251 (ARV 153); R291 (ARV 174); R391 (ARV 260); R450 (ARV 321); R465 (ARV 327); R486 (ARV 339); R531 (ARV 404); R569 (ARV 438); R651 (ARV 478).

Nola: 16

R317 (ARV 188); R340 (ARV 202); R377 (ARV 246); R430 (ARV 309); R521 (ARV 380); R659 (ARV 484); R671 (ARV 500); R690 (ARV 530); R691 (ARV 530); R692 (ARV 530); R766 (ARV 646); R770 (ARV 647); R778 (ARV 653); R817 (ARV 832); R938 (ARV 1128); R942 (ARV 1139).

'Rome market': 2

B53 (ABV 102); R 177 (ARV 108).

Sicily: 6

B94 (ABV 675, Selinus); R527 (ARV 384, Gela); R701 (ARV 556, Agrigento); R705 (ARV 557, Gela); R712 (ARV Agrigento); R950 (ARV 1145, Gela).

Tarquinia: 10

B178 (ABV 226); R102 (ARV 60); R313 (ARV 183); R361 (ARV 224); R373 (ARV 236); R506 (ARV 367); R507 (ARV 367); R543 (ARV 408); R574 (ARV 443); R805 (ARV 821).

Vulci: 78

B49 (ABV 102); B51 (ABV 102); B 64 (ABV 109); B 76 (ABV 134); B80 (ABV 151); B118 (ABV 181); B138 (ABV 199); B202 (ABV 256); B218 (ABV 264); B 220 (ABV 266); B222 (ABV 266); B226 (ABV 273); B 242 (ABV 285); B 250 (ABV 297); B 254 (ABV 308); B 267 (ABV 321); B 271 (ABV 315); B322 (ABV 425); B326 (ABV 426); B422 (ABV 674); R4 (ARV 3); R23 (ARV 16); R39 (ARV 21); R52 (ARV 26); R55 (ARV 27); R57 (ARV 28); R62 (ARV 31); R78 (ARV 1594); R82 (ARV 36); R110 (ARV 65); R114 (ARV 66); R125 (ARV 72); R140 (ARV 78); R192 (ARV 113); R196 (ARV 115); R212 (ARV 125); R216 (ARV 129); R223 (ARV 132); R227 (ARV 135); R 235 (ARV 137); R239 (ARV 138); R261 (ARV 166); R267 (ARV 169); R275 (ARV 170); R309 (ARV 181); R315 (ARV 187); R326 (ARV 197); R328 (ARV 197); R329 (ARV 197); R332 (ARV 198); R336 (ARV 199); R351 (ARV 208); R352 (ARV 220); R365 (ARV 225); R369 (ARV 231); R381 (ARV 248); R385 (ARV 256); R387 (ARV 257); R434 (ARV 315); R472 (ARV 329); R474 (ARV 329); R514 (ARV 371); R519 (ARV 372); R520 (ARV 378); R 539 (ARV 407); R589 (ARV 449); R627 (ARV 468);

R628 (ARV 468); R630 (ARV 469); R636 (ARV 471); R637 (ARV 471); R667 (ARV 495); R742 (ARV 580); R801 (ARV 816); R912 (ARV 1050); R917 (ARV 1051); R946 (ARV 1143); R978 (ARV 1275).

No Provenance: 136

B35 (Par 35); B39 (ABV 96); B60 (Par 41); B90 (ABV 157); B102 (ABV 169); B108 (ABV 174); B114 (Par 73); B 122 (Par 78); B126 (ABV 188); B142 (Par 82); B146 (Par 82); B154 (ABV 206); B158 (ABV 208); B166 (Par 82, probably Italy); B170 (Par 82); B 176 (ARV 122); B186 (ABV 239); B194 (ABV 247); B214 (ABV 263); B258 (ABV 313); B266 (ABV 321); B299 (ABV 280); B302 (ABV 384); B310 (Par 171); B318 (ABV 423); B336 (Par 192); B 342 (ABV 454); B 346 (Par 198); B 354 (ABV 469); B358 (Par 220); B366 (Par 241); B382 (Par 289); B386 (Par 241); B394 (ABV 631); B398 (ABV 646); B410 (ABV 664); B418 (ABV 671); B426 (ABV 676); B 430 (ABV 677); B422 (ABV 674); R8 (ARV 4); R 35 (ARV 20); R44 (ARV 23); R46 (ARV 23); R59 (ARV 31); R70 (Par 508); R86 (ARV 48); R94 (ARV 56); R136 (ARV 76); R152 (ARV 85); R156 (ARV 86); R160 (ARV 89); R169 (ARV 95); R 171 (Par 330); R 173 (ARV 97); R189 (ARV 113); R204 (ARV 1577); R207 (Par 333, probably Italy); R208 (ARV 120); R231 (ARV 1628); R243 (ARV 150); R247 (Par 336); R255 (ARV 154); R259 (ARV 157); R265 (ARV 169); R295 (ARV 175); R299 (ARV 1570); R311 (ARV 183); R348 (ARV 206); R356 (ARV 220); R367 (Par 347); R383 (ARV 250); R418 (ARV 284); R426 (ARV 306); R442 (ARV 317); R454 (ARV 322); R458 (ARV 325); R463 (Par 360); R 467 (ARV 329); R484 (ARV 339); R490 (ARV 339); R494 (ARV 356); R.498 (ARV 359); R518 (ARV 372); R525 (ARV 382); R528 (ARV 402); R529 (ARV 403); R546 (Par 373); R547 (ARV 421); R551 (ARV 1566); R559 (ARV 1567); R563 (ARV 431); R565 (ARV 432); R571 (ARV 441); R573 (ARV 443); R577 (ARV 444); R593 (ARV 450); R 595 (ARV 450); R 607 (ARV 1565); R619 (ARV 463); R623 (ARV 467); R632 (ARV 469); R675 (ARV 504); R682 (ARV 505); R684 (ARV 506); R688 (ARV 516); R716 (ARV 564); R720 (ARV 564); R728 (ARV 566); R 737 (ARV 571); R750 (ARV 586); R758 (ARV 636); R779 (ARV 653); R789 (ARV 784); R791 (ARV 785); R795 (ARV 792); R797 (ARV 792); R821 (ARV 861); R825 (ARV 872); R829 (ARV 874); R843 (ARV 889); R861 (ARV 911); R871 (ARV 971); R879 (ARV 976); R898 (ARV 1029); R922 (ARV 1083); R928 (ARV 1101); R932 (ARV 1112); R934 (Par 453); R962 (ARV 1172); R966 (ARV 1174); R990 (ARV 1560); R999 (ARV 1593); R1000 (ARV 1593); R1019 (ARV 1610); R1023 (Par 523).

Total: 376

Notes

1. Dover 1974 and 1978, with his own discussions, respectively, in *MC* 155–66 and 111–18.
2. *The Sexual Offences Act* (1967): http://www.legislation.gov.uk/ukpga/1967/60/pdfs/ukpga_19670060_en.pdf; *Criminal Justice (Scotland) Act* (1980): https://webarchive.

nationalarchives.gov.uk/20090516181457/http://www.legislation.gov.uk/acts/acts1980/pdf/ukpga_19800062_en.pdf; *Homosexual Offences (Northern Ireland) Order* (1982): https://web.archive.org/web/20100130103644/http://www.statutelaw.gov.uk/content.aspx?activeTextDocId=1007455.

3. Mentioned in *MC* 61 and 68; cf. Güthenke in this volume, pp. 171–2.
4. Williams 1979, with Hilliard 2021, 188–213.
5. A key British context was the Wolfenden Report to Parliament (1957), which recommended the legalization of homosexual acts between adults, although it took ten years to bring this recommendation into law: Wolfenden 1957 with Willett 2019. On homosexual lives between the *Criminal Law Amendment Act* (1885), which made male homosexual activity illegal, and the *Sexual Offences Act* (1967), which initiated liberalization: Porter and Weeks 1991.
6. One might cite the *Obscene Publications Act* (1959, https://www.legislation.gov.uk/ukpga/Eliz2/7-8/66/contents, revised 1964 http://www.legislation.gov.uk/ukpga/1964/74, following the Chatterley Trial, 1960); or the abolition of theatre censorship (1968, https://www.legislation.gov.uk/ukpga/1968/54).
7. Before Dover published: Masters and Johnson 1966, 1970, 1974. Their book on homosexuality was not available to Dover when conducting his research: Masters and Johnson 1979. Dover had read the American Kinsey reports of 1948 and 1953 by 1964 (Halliwell 2016b, ix).
8. On the context, what we know of Dover's reading in it and the development of his thought on homosexuality, see Atack's chapter in the present volume.
9. Dover 1974, 214, the significance of imagery on pots for the problems of sexuality; Dover 1978, 4–9, the evidential importance of the 'visual arts'; *MC* 115, 'Literary texts ... only tell half the story. The other half is to be sought in the many hundreds of painted vases ...'
10. Notably Licht 1925–8, Vorberg 1926, Vorberg 1928.
11. Foucault 1976–2018, Vol. 2 (*L'usage des plaisirs*, 1984), is significantly indebted to Dover: see Foucault 1985, 196, 218, 252, with Davidson 2001, Meyer 2018, Kapparis 2022, 27–31.
12. Parker 2015, 40, Meyer 2018, 148.
13. Dover 1978, 15.
14. See Meyer 2018, 152, discussing Lear and Cantarella 2008, xvii and Parker 2015, 106–26.
15. Dover 1978, 7. Discussion of some of the problems: Osborne 2018a, 318, 334–5, and esp. with relation to Aeschines, Kapparis 2022, 29–41.
16. Low value of Greek pottery: Vickers and Gill 1994, 85–101, Chankowski 2013, Osborne 2018b, 30.
17. Over 100,000: Bresson and de Callataÿ 2013, 21 and Meyer 2018, 152. Over 30,000: Webster 1972, 3 and Osborne 2018b, 40.
18. How we extrapolate from survivals to numbers actually produced is fraught. Webster 1972, 3–4 makes a sane case for a little over 1 per cent of Attic Panathenaic prize amphorae surviving; if correct and also for other classes of painted pottery (both big assumptions), and extrapolated to his total of about 45,000 survivals, we get 4.5 million pots between the early sixth and the late fourth century, rising to 10 million on the survival figures estimated by Meyer 2018. How surviving genres of shape and iconography might relate to lost reality is anyone's guess. For more (large) estimates see Bundrick 2019, 26.
19. e.g. Kilmer 1993, 237–64, Lear and Cantarella 2008, 195–233, Parker 2015, 106–26.
20. Some extension into mythology: Sourvinou-Inwood 1991, 29–98, Stewart 1997, 167–70, Lissarrague 2013, 73–96, Osborne 2018b, 124.

21. Dionysiac sexualities: Lissarrague 2013, 73–96, Heinemann 2016, 161–222, Osborne 2018b, 188–204.
22. See e.g. Dover 1978, 70, 71, 72, 78, 79, 92, 93, 94, 98.
23. The obsession with discovering *Realien* from vases is not restricted to sexuality: on religion see Gaifman 2015, 51–66, Gaifman 2018, 1–15.
24. Against the realist distinction of mythological from 'real life' imagery: Bažant 1980, Bažant 1981, 13–22, Sourvinou-Inwood 1991, 63–4, Ferrari 2002, 11–60, Ferrari 2003, Topper 2012, 2–5.
25. Notably Meyer 2018 and Osborne 2018a.
26. Dover 1978, 4 n. 5. Cf. *MC* 115.
27. Reproduction in the study of Greek painted pottery: Meyer and Petsalis-Diomidis forthcoming.
28. Sympotic vessels in archaeological context: Lynch 2011, 75–146. Embodiment and usage: Gaifman and Platt 2018.
29. Meyer 2018, 156–63.
30. Beazley 1947.
31. Dover 1994, 115.
32. Dover 1978, 4 n. 5.
33. Beazley 1947, 198–9 and 1956, 109, no. 28; Lear and Cantarella 2008, app. 2.2.
34. Dover 1978, 95 and 208.
35. Beazley 1947, 198.
36. No one has discussed the difference between courting scenes with ithyphallic erastes (as in Dover's B65 or R520) *vs* flaccid (e.g. B76, B271, B598, R196a). I follow Dover's own practice (1978, 16) in anglicizing, without italics, the Greek nouns erastes and eromenos.
37. The reissue of Beazley 1947 as Beazley 1989 fails to illustrate side B, mistakenly using before- and after-restoration shots of side A in its plates 4 and 5. Dover used a before-restoration photograph.
38. Dover 1978, 95.
39. Deborah Blake, who worked for Colin Haycraft, Dover's publisher, wrote to Stephen Halliwell (pers. comm.): 'I arrived at Duckworth in January 78 and ... remember being sent to the British Museum to collect images for the book, and also being told that some of them could not be sent through the post as if the package was opened they would be regarded as pornographic. How serious this was I really don't know. Colin certainly enjoyed telling people about it and we all thought it was rather ridiculous, if true. There was a sort of portacabin at the back of the BM where I was handed the photographs in a brown envelope.' Black-and-white photography and gay pornography: Evangelista 2010.
40. Studies of ancient erotica avoid the term 'pornography' as too modern or derogatory: Sutton 1992, Shapiro 1992, 53–72, Kilmer 1993, 170, 199–200; cf. Clarke 2003, 11–13. Dover 1978, 102 n. 83 draws a comparison between vase painting and 'ancient and modern pornography'.
41. Only three inconclusive pages in Stansbury-O'Donnell 2006, 180–3.
42. See Steiner 2007, 58–60.
43. He does however occasionally detect humour: e.g. Dover 1978, 96, 106 (n. 100), 128.
44. Ormand 2018, 139: 'goosing'.
45. For the reverse: Beazley Archive no. 301064: https://www.beazley.ox.ac.uk/xdb/ASP/recordDetails.asp?newwindow=true&id={0E145C4D-F6C0-4A77-87AD-9BE3D10546D3}.

46. Dover 1978, 7: 'we must not imagine ... that the vase-paintings directly "illustrate" the literature available to us, or that the literature is any kind of "commentary" on the vase paintings'; Dover 1989, 204: 'I was (and remain) well aware that there may have been considerable differences between representation and reality'; *MC* 116: 'It was clear from some reviews that I was thought not to have understood (but I did understand and fancied I had said so) how greatly the way Greeks actually behaved may have differed from the way their behaviour was conventionally represented'.
47. Clarke 1998, 20.
48. Davidson 2007, 107: 'one of the most muscular champions of truth in the whole field of the humanities'; for the field following his realism: Meyer 2018, 152–4.
49. Respectively, *MC* 39 and 59 (his italics).
50. Beazley 1947, 216.
51. Why Type β – the presentation of love gifts – should implicitly be placed after Type α, a kind of initial foreplay, is beyond me.
52. Osborne 2018a, 316–17.
53. Dover 1978, 91–100. The charter for reading progression into such scenes lies in archaic lyric and its emphases on creating narratives of courtship: see Neer 2002, 9–23, Blanshard 2015, Lear 2015, 120.
54. Dover 1978, 98.
55. See Meyer 2018, 150–1.
56. See Osborne 2018b, 126–8, with critique of Dover at n. 17.
57. Dover 1978, 78.
58. Dover 1978, 92, 98 (caption).
59. Dover 1978, 92.
60. Dover 1978, 95.
61. Parker 2015, 32 n. 32 prefers 'interfemoral' as 'more accurate', followed by Ormand 2018. Even Davidson 2007, 116 and 251 – despite his extensive polemic against Dover – accepts intercrural sex as a reality.
62. Dover 1978, 98 with Aristophanes, *Birds* 706, and a different sense for heterosexual intercourse at 669 and 1254; see Osborne 2018a, 320–3.
63. Osborne 2018a, 317–18, 328. This dismissal may be contestable, but that argument needs to be made. Stephen Halliwell (pers. comm.) defends the potential intercrural meaning of *diamêrizein* in a homosexual context on the grounds that the *prima facie* semantics of the verb at *Birds* 706 imply 'between' or 'parting' the thighs, and not anal penetration (as suggested by Osborne 2018a, 322). Against this, the comic context of the chorus of birds commenting on human sexuality certainly offers the option of a much less philologically lexical meaning for the passage in question to signify something like 'get between their thighs' (i.e. 'fuck'). In that case, deriving a whole category of intercrural sexual behaviour from the word is extremely problematic.
64. See Dover 1968a, 216–17, partially retracted at Dover 1978, 125 n. 1.
65. See Davidson 2001, 7–14, Davidson 2007, 120–1, Meyer 2018, 147–8, and Atack in this volume. A key passage is Dover 1978, 103.
66. Dover 1978, 124–35.
67. Dover 1978, 134. More on the penis: Dover 1978, 126–30 (pots) and 1994, 20–1 (personal).

68. Osborne 2018a, 327: 'The temptation to read these scenes as somehow, often in defiance of human anatomy, snapshots of life has proved irresistible'; also Osborne 2018a, 317–18, Meyer 2018, 153–4. Doubters of the realism of intercrural sex: Lear and Cantarella 2008, 106 ('visual euphemism'), Lear 2014, 107, Ormand 2018, 141, 154–5. Parker 2015, 23–4 is ambivalent but commits to the real 'with due caution' at 53–4.
69. Elsner 2010, 11–16.
70. e.g. Pater 1877 (especially on Winckelmann and Michelangelo's poetry), Symonds 1908, Raile 1928–30.
71. The term is ubiquitous: Dover 1978, 91–100 (section title and many times in the text); captions: B51, B114, B486, B538, B634, R502, R520, R543, R545, R573, R577, R970, R1127.
72. Dover 1978, 93.
73. Dover 1978, 95.
74. Frequent: e.g. Dover 1978, 93, 100, 101, 102, 104.
75. Dover 1978, 100–9 (section title).
76. Dover 1978, 95.
77. Dover 1978, 102.
78. Dover 1978, viii, cf. *MC* 114.
79. e.g. on E.M. Forster's *Maurice* (drafted 1913–14): Ingleheart 2015, 3–5; also Hickson 1995, Ingleheart 2018, 15–32, 49–74 on Classics and homosexuality in schools in the generation of Dover's teachers.
80. Trauma may be closer to home: *MC* 7 is a disturbing passage where issues of 'secretiveness' and 'concealment' applied to himself, his father, and his father's father, as well as language like 'sick', 'fuck', 'hatred', 'rage', 'trauma' and 'primal scene', hint potentially at complex and deeply unresolved issues within the family.
81. The Serious Case Review of the school going back to the 1970s but not before: https://kingstonandrichmondsafeguardingchildrenpartnership.org.uk/media/upload/fck/file/RSCB%20Serious%20Case%20Review%20St%20Paul's%20School%20Report%20for%20publication%2013_01_2020.pdf.
82. Celebratory: e.g. Halperin 1990, Evangelista 2009, Blanshard 2010, Orrells 2011 and 2015, Ingleheart 2018. But the story of paedophilic abuse in schools, perfumed by fantasies of unproblematic pederastic antiquity, has yet to be told. For the issues in relation to medieval sexuality: Elliott 2020.
83. *MC* 28 n. 2: 'in the whole of my six years at St Paul's, there were only two occasions on which I saw a boy beaten, and one on which I knew someone was beaten behind closed doors'.
84. e.g. Gombrich 1960, 99–125, with Osborne 2018b, 11–22. For the realist attitude still: e.g. Oakley 2020.
85. Photography and 'mechanical objectivity': Daston and Galison 2010, 125–61.
86. *OED* online: 'The explicit description or exhibition of sexual subjects or activity in literature, painting, films, etc., in a manner intended to stimulate erotic rather than aesthetic feelings; printed or visual material containing this'.
87. Hence the code for Crown Prosecutors advises, 'An image is pornographic if it is of such a nature that it must reasonably be assumed to have been produced solely or principally for the purpose of sexual arousal ... Section 63(6) of the Act states that an extreme image must be explicit and realistic; both those terms take their ordinary dictionary definition.': https://www.cps.gov.uk/legal-guidance/extreme-pornography. Realism in philosophical accounts:

Mag Uidhuir and Pratt 2012, 138–40. Transparency: Levinson 2005, 232–3, 239, Todd 2012, 96–102.

88. Dover 1978, 95.
89. Williams 1979, 97.
90. Screech 2009, 14–41, 299–315 (quote from 300).
91. Pederasty and sympotic vases: Catoni 2010, 70–84.
92. e.g. Boardman 1980, 245.
93. Signed by Peithinos (a jokey pseudonym meaning 'Persuader' or 'Seducer'?). See Davidson 2007, 528–46, Hedreen 2016, 280–93.
94. Dover 1978, 95. Dover (followed by Kilmer 1993, 13–14, 19) ignores the interior, which has Peleus grasping Thetis, a mythological take on courtship that complicates interpretation of the exterior: Osborne 2018b, 128–31.
95. Narrative as temporal progression constructing realism: Osborne 2018a, 316–17.
96. Dover 1978, 96, 120.
97. For the descriptive problems, see Baxandall 1979, Elsner 2010.
98. e.g. Shapiro 2000, 15.
99. e.g. Keuls 1985, 274–99, Kilmer 1993, 74, Lear and Cantarella 2008, xv, 189, Parker 2015, 53–4.
100. e.g. Sutton 1992, 34, Stewart 1997, 162, Osborne 1998, 20–1, Shapiro 2000, 15, Neer 2012, 210, Parker 2015, 102, Osborne 2018a, 327, Osborne 2018b, 146–8, 150, 217.
101. Hence the elevation of sympotic pottery (assuming it was for symposia like that described by Plato): Lissarrague 1990, Neer 2002, 9–26, 87–132.
102. Hobden 2013, 11–13, Osborne 2018b, 209–12.
103. Parker 2011, 129–31, Topper 2012, 9, Shapiro 2015.
104. e.g. Bourdieu 1977, 72–95, Bourdieu 2020.
105. e.g. Panofsky 1939, 3–17, Panofsky 1955, 26–41, with Elsner and Lorenz 2012.
106. e.g. Riegl 1901, 209–17 (translated in Wood 2000, 87–103), with Olin 1992, 129–53 and Elsner 2006. These pre-ideology models for formulating culture are interlinked through Panofsky's critique of Riegl and Bourdieu's appropriation of Panofsky, whom he translated into French.
107. Lewis 1998/9, Lewis 2002, 130–71.
108. Spivey 1991, Osborne 1996, Osborne 2001, Reusser 2002, Bentz and Reusser 2004, Osborne 2007, and Bundrick 2019, 20–50 on the vase trade, 51–92 on Etruscan consumption.
109. Of the lists of pots with sexual iconography, neither Dover 1978, 205–25 nor Lear and Cantarella 2008, 196–233 give archaeological provenance, contra Parker 2015, 106–26. This skews interpretation towards assuming Athenian contexts and meanings: cf Kapparis 2022, 28.
110. For the corpus of the 'Harrow Painter' understood through finds: Bundrick 2012, 25–8, arguing that the artist had no idea where his pots might be shipped and that his subjects therefore needed generic appeal.
111. Etruscan consumption of erotic Athenian pottery: Lewis 1997, 141–54, Vickers and Briggs 2007, 47–50, de la Genière 2009, Lynch 2009 and 2017, 136–7. Contra: Topper 2012, 11–12, 101–4, Osborne 2018, 46–8. Discussion: Bundrick 2019, 50–7.

112. Followed by Lear and Cantarella 2008, 196–233, who expand the corpus.
113. As with Parker 2015, 106–26, or the catalogue of type γ courtship scenes (Dover's 'copulation') in Sutton 2014, 331–3.
114. Writing of Athenian material with different subject matter discovered in Italy, Marconi and Osborne disagree which way the ideologies face – towards Italy or Athens: Marconi 2004b, Osborne 2004 with Lynch 2017, 135–6. Osborne 2004, 52 puts the Athenocentric reading: 'the range of imagery from which purchasers elsewhere chose was determined by interests and demands at Athens itself rather than by any second-guessing by Athenian painters of the tastes or needs of the export market', a position which allows the assumption of the normative ideology of the imagery of Greek homosexuality.
115. My thanks to the Editors, Carol Atack, Ewen Bowie, Paul Cartledge, James Davidson, Milette Gaifman, Constanze Güthenke, John Ma, Caspar Meyer, Helen Moore, Richard Neer, Robin Osborne, Alexia Petsalis-Diomidis, Adrian Rifkin, Michael Squire and John Watts.

CHAPTER 13
DOVER AND THEOCRITUS*
Richard Hunter

Kenneth Dover's commentary on Theocritus, published by Macmillan in 1971, stands out in the present context in a number of ways. It is mentioned once *en passant* in *Marginal Comment* (158), but Theocritus the poet is entirely absent from the book's index, despite the fact that we learn on p. 37 that Dover read 'most of Theokritos' while at school at St Paul's.[1] Theocritus has not here been singled out for special non-treatment. On the same page of *Marginal Comment* we learn that Dover read some 'Vergil' at St Paul's, but Vergil also is missing from where we would have expected to find it in the index, immediately below 'venereal disease'.[2] The two absences may not be unconnected.

It is presumably connected to the first phenomenon I have mentioned that *Theocritus* was Dover's only real 'foray' (his term: 1971, vi) into Hellenistic poetry or, indeed, into Hellenistic literature *tout court*; the great poets of the third century play only the smallest of walk-on-walk-off parts in the two volumes of his collected papers. Dover of course had more than enough interests to fill more than one scholarly life – Greek comedy and oratory, Greek morality and ethics, Greek history and historiography, Greek linguistics – and it is hardly surprising if he left some fields for others to plough. Nevertheless, the reasons for his neglect of Hellenistic poetry may be worth brief exploration. On the one hand, his academic and teaching duties may, in fact, have conspired with any natural lack of enthusiasm. Hellenistic poetry remained, until perhaps the last three decades or so, a rare bird on university syllabuses. It is unlikely that Dover in fact taught much, or had much to do with, Hellenistic poetry during his Balliol years; Theocritus was regularly available as a possible Mods choice, both in General Books and Special Books, while Dover was at Balliol, but teaching on these books was by university lectures and was offered by others.[3] Rudolf Pfeiffer (nowhere mentioned in *MC*), an Oxonian by adoption, had put Callimachus firmly back on the scholarly map during Dover's early years as a Fellow of Balliol, but most of Callimachus was still very rarefied and difficult fare, and was not set before Mods undergraduates; even the *Hymns* made only a brief appearance.[4] Apollonius was easier to get hold of, and there were serviceable commentaries, but although Book 3 did appear for a while on the Mods syllabus alongside Theocritus, there is little sign that the *Argonautica* was widely read or taught.[5]

I was formally introduced to Hellenistic poetry through a course with Alan James in my last year as an undergraduate at the University of Sydney in 1974; no doubt Dover's *Theocritus*, which made Theocritus far more accessible at every level and deserves high recognition for that, was often in my hands.[6] My interest was aroused and persisted, but as far as I can remember, when I was a graduate student at Cambridge (1975–8), the few people who were keen to discuss Hellenistic poetry with me were other graduate students studying Latin poetry. These were in fact heady days for the study of Latin poetry in the UK. Francis Cairns' *Generic Composition in Greek and Roman Poetry*, in which Theocritus is given considerable attention, appeared in 1972 and his Liverpool (later Leeds) Latin Seminars became a venue where it was accepted that the 'literary criticism' of Latin (and Greek, including Hellenistic) poetry could be seriously practised. So too, in 1970 Robin Nisbet and Margaret Hubbard published their commentary on Book 1 of Horace's *Odes*; this remarkable book, with its extraordinarily rich information (*inter alia*) about the Greek background of the *Odes*, combined with its (presumably provocative and teasing) dismissal of 'literary criticism' (p. v), acted as a further spur to Latinists to take the *whole* range of Greek poetry seriously. As it happened, I did not approach Hellenistic poetry through Latin poetry – I was lucky enough to have both interests, originally (sort-of) independently – but many people did,[7] and there is at least some truth in the notion that in those decades it was not just such as Rudolf Pfeiffer and Francis Vian who kept serious appreciation of Hellenistic poetry alive, but also Latinists. There was, of course, the danger, not always avoided at the time, that Hellenistic poetry was made to seem like Latin poetry written in Greek, but the great upswing in Hellenistic studies from the 1980s much weakened the spread of that particular misreading.

Virgil's *Eclogues*, of course, make Theocritus a special case. No student of the *Eclogues* needs a special reason to be interested in Theocritus, but does the reverse apply? My own view is very clearly 'yes', if only (and this is the very least of reasons) because seeing what Virgil, or indeed Theocritus' Greek successors, did with the tradition is one way of allowing us to see what is important (and what is not) in Theocritus; I take it as a given that Virgil was an incomparably better reader of Theocritus than I am, and my experience is that reading the *Eclogues* always reveals things about Theocritus which I had not seen before. Virgil (or 'Vergil') does not appear in the index of *Theocritus*, any more than of *Marginal Comment*; the *Eclogues* in fact appear at least twice in the commentary (pp. 91, 98), but even if I have a missed the odd citation – I have not checked thoroughly – they are anything but prominent. Dover's reader is given, for example, no hint of the Virgilian *Nachleben* of the name Amaryllis from *Idyll* 3 (cf. *Ecl.* 1.5, 2.52),[8] nor that vv. 3–5 of the same poem are adapted/translated as a fragment of 'Menalcas' at Virgil, *Ecl.* 9.23–5 and that the differences between the Greek and Latin are interestingly discussed by Aulus Gellius at *NA* 9.9.7–11.[9] Dover might have pleaded that 'the learner' does not *need* these Virgilian adaptations, or indeed any passage of the *Eclogues* where Theocritus resonates, in order 'to understand what the Greek *means*' (Dover's italics: 1971, v), but that case might be thought much weakened by how Dover then adds 'not only in terms of translation from one language into another but also in terms of literary, mythological, ethical and sensory associations'. One might also imagine that the banishment of the *Eclogues* was an attempt to ensure that Theocritus was indeed approached on his own terms, by readers as uncluttered as possible by misleading notions of what came after; it is, after all, very likely that most of the 'learners' whom Dover had in mind would have already known some Latin before facing Theocritus, and that would make the danger all that more acute.

It is in fact striking that the still very helpful section of the Introduction on 'Bucolic Poetry', a quite original discussion with no real precedent in Gow's edition,[10] makes absolutely no mention of the post-Theocritean tradition. It is now a standard move, and rightly so, to seek to distinguish 'bucolic' from the 'pastoral' poetry which was the invention (as it were) not of Theocritus, but of Theocritus' imitators and of Virgil; attention to 'pastoral' can (again) shed light on what Theocritean 'bucolic' is and is not. Dover of course was well aware of the distinction; he thanks Thomas Rosenmeyer for an advance copy of the latter's 'book on pastoral poetry' (1971, vi),[11] though I think it fair to say that it is not obvious, at least from *Theocritus*, that Dover actually read it with any attention.[12] Dover's concern here is entirely on 'bucolic elements' in Greek literature and culture before Theocritus, with – as one would expect from Dover – due attention given to popular culture and the behaviour of 'real' herdsmen. The starting-point for Dover's focus is perhaps revealed by the opening sentence of the 'Bucolic Poetry' section: 'Theokritos's claim to recognition as an original genius rests primarily upon the poems in which he portrays herdsmen and other countrymen in a rural setting' (liv). If the search for 'originality' in a poet, that search which took Dover backwards rather than forwards in time, is still very high on the critical agenda, though the decades of literary theory which separate us from *Theocritus* might be thought to have changed the meaning of the term almost out of recognition, I doubt that many would now write that sentence as Dover wrote it. This is not only because we have become more sceptical of the supply of 'original geniuses' (or, perhaps rather, because the terms have become debased through overuse in the media), nor even (I think) because many are now wary of the cult of the author rather than of the text, but more simply because such language now seems both outdatedly romantic and (more importantly) unhelpful: it does not explain anything – it is just a pat on the back (or, rather, head) – and certainly does not describe what students of ancient literature 'do'. Dover, however, here breathes the same spirit which infused the (now discontinued) British Academy Master-Mind lectures, which were intended (so the Academy's website) 'to be an appreciation of an individual of "genius".[13] The classical (broadly understood) figures so celebrated were (in chronological order of lecture) Aristotle, Plotinus, Virgil, Cicero, St Paul, Origen, Lucretius, Thucydides, Eratosthenes, Pindar, Socrates and Plato; both Peter Fraser (Eratosthenes) and Hugh Lloyd-Jones (Pindar) began their lectures by worrying whether their subject qualified as a 'Master-Mind' or how one would tell if a poet deserved the label. Like 'genius', 'Mastermind' itself is now associated with achievement of a very different kind than we would ascribe to any of those whom the Academy's lecture series celebrated, but if Dover had been giving such a lecture on Theocritus (which he would not have done), he might well have begun with such a sentence as cited above.

The treatment (or rather non-treatment) of Virgil's *Eclogues* in *Theocritus* must, however, also have roots in Dover's broader intellectual and academic interests. In his first term at St Paul's, so Dover tells us, 'I became competent in Latin, and I fell in love with Greek' (*MC* 15), and he further reports that Virgil is the only Latin author whom he can be sure he read at school, though there were of course many others (37). Latin seems to have been for Dover not second to Greek, but not even really in the race; Pacific languages absorbed him far more (*MC* 22-6).[14] The organization of academia did nothing to endanger this position. Both at Balliol and at St Andrews Latin was the business of other people (cf. *MC* 87-8), and Dover would never have had to sully his hands with the Romans.[15] This is one way in which Eduard Fraenkel, who brought to Oxford the European (though not just European) model of the scholar who worked at the highest level in both Greek and Latin and who had 'immense influence' on Dover, failed to cast his spell (*MC* 39). Volume II of Dover's collected papers is entitled *The Greeks and their Legacy*, and one of the subjects of the papers listed in the sub-heading is 'influence'. There is, as far as I can see, absolutely nothing about Rome and Latin literature in the volume; no Roman poet makes it to the index, nor does Tacitus, to whom one might have thought Dover would be attracted. Rome was simply one part of the Greek legacy in which Dover appears to have been not much interested.[16] It is perhaps telling that Dover never published on Menander;[17] it is very hard to have a serious interest in Greek New Comedy and not spend time with Plautus and Terence.

I have already suggested that Dover's apparent twin avoidances of Hellenistic and Latin poetry were connected in various ways. For the reasons for the former, however, we have more solid evidence in *Theocritus* itself. The very opening sentence of the Preface leaves us in no doubt where we are: 'The scenes and events which Theokritos portrays are not as a rule complicated or obscure, nor are the sentiments which he expresses profound' (v). The 'p-word' recurs in one of the better known sections of *Theocritus*, as Dover is rehearsing both the 'great virtues' of the Hellenistic poets and the qualities which, in his opinion, they lacked: 'they did not bring their intelligence to bear upon profound issues which excite the intellect and the emotions simultaneously, and they treated poetry as if its province had been defined at some date in the past and it had been forbidden to advance in certain directions or to penetrate below a certain phenomenological level' (lxix).[18] Dover's view that 'post-classical' writers and artists were inhibited by their canonization of a 'classical' past, which they felt could not be surpassed or even emulated, is more fully expressed elsewhere,[19] although one might wonder whether Theocritus himself was not in fact proof that poets did *not* regard the province of poetry as 'defined at some date in the past'. In the present context it is the repeated assertion that Hellenistic poetry does not deal in 'profound' issues which attracts attention. There seems little point in arguing about the meaning of the term, or wondering whether some of the implications of, say, Callimachus' *Hymns* to Athena and Demeter or the fourth book of Apollonius' *Argonautica* might not deserve the label. What, rather, is striking is Dover's simple 'statement of fact'; what he means, of course, is 'which excite [my] intellect and [my] emotions simultaneously', but 'the learner' is in fact being presented not with an opinion but a 'fact', and 'the learner' is likely to add that fact to the store of what s/he (thinks s/he) 'knows'.[20] It is true that most of us (thankfully) do not add 'in my opinion' to every sentence we write; we trust readers, particularly experienced readers of academic prose, to understand that. The rhetoric of *Theocritus*, however, suggests that something rather different from that is going on, and not just because Dover claims to write with 'the learner' in mind and not to have made 'a serious contribution to the study of Hellenistic poetry' (v). We are, of course, being offered Dover's opinion, but that is presented as a self-evident truth which all readers, 'learners' or otherwise, inevitably share.

Dover proceeds to set Hellenistic literature against the Athens of the late fifth century BC, 'a period in which philosophical, political, religious and scientific thinking were developing at an almost explosive pace' (lxix), before suggesting – in what might be the most influential claim of the book – that Hellenistic poetry began 'with the deaths of Euripides and Sophokles' (lxxi). What is clear, I think, is that here lies a principal reason why Dover had little time for Hellenistic poetry throughout his career.[21] Put simply, it did not 'turn him on'. Behind these pages lies of course a real difference between the fifth and the third centuries BC; the much clearer institutional and disciplinary boundaries of the third century seemed to Dover to inhibit the kind of free-floating interplay between forms of both thought and expression which seemed to characterize the earlier period (that freedom which allowed questions such as 'Was Aeschylus a Presocratic?' etc. etc.). One of the reasons why the search for 'philosophy' in Hellenistic poetry is marked by a string of journal articles which, speaking broadly, have failed to carry any widespread conviction is that we can say with some precision, for the third century, what 'philosophy' actually was. It is notoriously much harder, and much more debated, for the fifth century, and this clearly appealed to Dover, who kept his distance, as is well known, from what ancient philosophers and modern students of ancient philosophy do.[22] The reasons which *Theocritus* allows us to infer for Dover's lack of interest in Hellenistic poetry point in fact to very important issues of cultural and intellectual history, some of which are indeed admirably sketched in *Theocritus*, pp. lxx–lxxii. There is no reason to doubt that Dover's relative neglect of the poetry of the third century was indeed built upon both an 'intellectual' consideration of what seemed to him to be the evidence and an 'emotional' pull in other directions; what might surprise, but should not I think, is that this at least partly 'rational', as Dover would have seen it, view, is presented as a truth about which the possibility of dissenting views is not even mentioned. To be fair, Dover may well never have encountered such a dissenting view, either in Oxford or St Andrews.[23]

It is very hard to overestimate the change which A.S.F. Gow's 1950 edition and commentary on Theocritus brought to the serious study of the poet; a glance at Gow's list of the commentaries preceding his own (Vol. II, 563–4) offers a quick index to the scale of his own achievement. Dover, very rightly, drew on Gow on practically every page of the commentary and very graciously acknowledges the debt (1971, vi).[24] The debt extends, of course, well beyond the commentary, and some of it might be thought to fall into the 'unconscious' category, familiar to anyone who knows the work of a predecessor very well. Thus, for example, even the very opening of Dover's Preface (cf. above) which then passes on to the 'difficulties' which Theocritus presents looks like a rewriting of Gow: 'Theocritus is not a difficult author in the sense that Pindar or Aeschylus is difficult. His thought is for the most part simple and straightforward ... In most Greek poets however the precise sense of a word or phrase is often difficult to determine, and in Theocritus such difficulties are often increased' (Gow 1952, I ix–x). Little profit would be gained by pursuing further the extent of Dover's debt to Gow. Rather, I want briefly to try to capture some of the particular character of *Theocritus* by a few brief test-probes. Almost inevitably, it will be absences, rather than visible strengths, which are highlighted, but one strength cannot be passed by in silence. As one would expect from Dover, the handling of linguistic and dialectal matters is throughout both helpfully full and often genuinely illuminating. Clearly, the 'learner' today would expect much more linguistic help than Dover actually offers, but the commentary is shot through with intelligent observations on things such as word order, tense and the use of particles. We are all 'learners' from Dover in this respect.

Dover himself clearly had his favourite poems, though he does not quite put it like this. He recommends 'a learner' short on time to 'give priority' to *Idylls* 1, 2, 5, 7, 11 and 15 (vi), and with the possible exception of 5, I think that is a list of 'greatest hits' which many readers of Theocritus would still endorse. It is a priority which, I think, it fair to say matches Dover's own.[25] Without question, *Idyll* 7 takes top spot; 'No other poem of Theokritos poses problems of interpretation so numerous and interesting as this' (145). Very many would agree, and Dover's introduction to that poem is a very helpful presentation of the evidence and a well-judged discussion of it, even if (unsurprisingly) it does not anticipate all the interpretations of the *Thalysia* which the subsequent years have called forth. This clearly was a poem which 'interested' Dover and over which he had mulled. The same is not true, I think, for every poem. The unevenness of the commentary, and hence by implication of Dover's 'interest', even within the 'select' poems, is in fact one of its most marked features. The contrast, for example, between the introduction to *Idyll* 7 and that to *Idyll* 1, which could fairly be described as 'thin', even allowing for the fact that the myth of Daphnis is discussed elsewhere (lxiv–lxv), is very striking, although to some extent already anticipated by Gow's variable treatment of the two poems. Some of that thinness, as it now seems, perhaps derives from Dover's belief that 'we do not know . . . the order in which [Theocritus] would have liked us to read [the poems]' (xvii); that belief must be correct, particularly if we give emphasis to 'know'. Many more recent readers of Theocritus have, however, felt that *Idyll* 1, which there are good reasons for thinking was indeed placed first in ancient collections of the βουκολικά,[26] has powerful proemial and 'programmatic' elements, regardless of whether Theocritus collected his own poems. Virgil imitated the sound of the opening of *Idyll* 1 at the opening of *Eclogue* 1, which does not 'prove' that it was first in the edition of Theocritus known to him, but it is something . . .; there is of course (see above) not a word of this in Dover.

It is perhaps this sense of variability of response, and hence of personal engagement, which most marks the style of *Theocritus*. On *Idyll* 15, for example, the mime about two Syracusan women, who are resident in Alexandria, visiting the Ptolemaic palace, Dover is clearly 'interested' in the representation of the characters and their language: 'The clichés of which the women's conversation is composed, and the attitudes and values which underlie everything they say, give them an extraordinary resemblance to their modern counterparts, but the spiteful element in their characters is sharpened for comic effect' (197). It is probably just as well, even in 1971, that Dover did not spell out who exactly these 'modern counterparts' are, and whether he is referring to 'real women' or to characters from, e.g., sitcoms, but it is not difficult to guess that he means the former; why it should be only the spitefulness which is 'sharpened' is never explained. As is typical of him, Dover is always looking in texts for reflections of what he considered 'real' human nature and its foibles. When Gorgo asks Praxinoa how much her dress cost, Dover notes that 'the British are shyer than Mediterranean peoples of asking directly, "What did it cost you?"' (202); whether that is actually true of one British woman speaking in private to another about clothes, whether in 1971 or 2022, I for one have no idea. When Praxinoa tells the baby that she will not take him with her, we have 'an interesting indication that even in a family which owned female slaves it is the mother, not the nursemaid, who is the focus of the baby's emotional interest' (ibid.); however rash the conclusion, Dover's constant search for patterns in human behaviour shines through.

One area, however, where Dover was less than curious is with the Ptolemaic background of *Idyll* 15 and some other poems. At the palace, the women listen to a song in honour of Adonis, during which the singer refers to the apotheosis of Berenice:

Κύπρι Διωναία, τὺ μὲν ἀθανάταν ἀπὸ θνατᾶς,
ἀνθρώπων ὡς μῦθος, ἐποίησας Βερενίκαν,
ἀμβροσίαν ἐς στῆθος ἀποστάξασα γυναικός·
τὶν δὲ χαριζομένα, πολυώνυμε καὶ πολύναε,
ἁ Βερενικεία θυγάτηρ Ἑλένᾳ εἰκυῖα   110
Ἀρσινόα πάντεσσι καλοῖς ἀτιτάλλει Ἄδωνιν.

Theocritus 15.106–11

Cypris, Dione's child, you made mortal Berenice an immortal, so men say, sprinkling ambrosia on to her woman's breast. And so in your honour, many-named and many-shrined goddess, Arsinoa, daughter of Berenice, who resembles Helen, now pampers Adonis with delights of every kind.

trans. A. Verity, adapted

On ἀνθρώπων ὡς μῦθος, Dover has a helpful note (filling out Gow's rather laconic assertion); for Dover the phrase opens issues such as 'concepts of evidence' and the whole nature of Greek religion, as 'concerned with the establishment of the right forms of human intercourse with the supernatural' (211).[27] The 'facile' comparison of Arsinoe to Helen, however, brings forth merely a semi-joke: 'It is to be hoped that Arsinoe was at any rate attractive enough to prevent the comparison from sounding absurd' (ibid.). One of the several things which one might say about this observation is that here Dover reveals a striking lack of curiosity about *why* a figure of the royal house might be likened to Helen; it is true that much more has been written about Helen in Ptolemaic self-representation after, than before, Dover,[28] but the subject was hardly *terra incognita* while Dover was at work on *Theocritus*. Two things have here, I suspect, conspired in Dover's silence. One is (again) his distaste for anything which he would regard as 'flattery' of the great, and secondly there is no note of any kind on Ἑλένᾳ εἰκυῖα in Gow; that pattern of repeated silence is a very common phenomenon.

Helen is also the subject of a poem which sheds light both upon the nature of *Theocritus* and upon how the ground has shifted since then. *Idyll* 18 purports to be an *epithalamion* sung by twelve young Spartan women outside the wedding-chamber on the night of Helen's marriage to Menelaos; it is introduced by a short narrative frame which sets the scene. There is in *Theocritus* a helpful account of the form and standard themes of such songs (230–1), with proper attention to Sappho, and the puzzling initial ἄρα of the poem shows Dover's razor-sharp feel for Greek in a very brief space. There are some typically Doverian touches: talk of young Spartan women and athletics turns Dover's mind not to Alcman but to Lampito in Aristophanes' *Lysistrata* (230, 234, 236), even though Lampito is a married woman and the resonance of her physique and physical exercise might be thought to be far from that of maiden-song. There are, however, also silences at which the learner might despair. The women praise Helen's weaving:

οὐδέ τις ἐκ ταλάρω πανίσδεται ἔργα τοιαῦτα,
οὐδ' ἐνὶ δαιδαλέῳ πυκινώτερον ἄτριον ἱστῷ
κερκίδι συμπλέξασα μακρῶν ἔταμ' ἐκ κελεόντων.

Theocritus 18.32–4

No woman spins a subtler thread and winds it from her basket on to her spool, or, as she moves the shuttle at her inlaid loom, weaves and then shears a finer cloth from the long crossbar.

trans. A. Verity

Most readers, even experienced weavers, would, I think, find these verses difficult; Gow discusses them at length and fully sets out the (in parts somewhat contradictory) evidence. Dover has two notes on the verses:

32. ἔργα: ἔργον is not 'work' in the abstract, but a product of work, e.g. a tilled field, a statue or a cloak.

34. ἔταμ': The freedom with which the aorist can be used in generalizing statements is strikingly apparent from the sequence πανίσδεται – ἔταμε – ἐπίσταται.

Of these brief notes, the first is misleading at best; the Vocabulary at the back of *Theocritus* translates πανίζομαι as 'wind (thread)', and Gow had understood ἔργα here as indeed 'yarn/thread', which is certainly not what Dover's note on line 32 suggests. Dover of course is far from the only classicist who has faltered in front of descriptions of the details of weaving, but if you write a commentary, there is a duty at least to try. If, on the other hand, Dover really thought that the learner would find no difficulty in these verses, then that too is very instructive.

Rather, however, than cherry-pick individual notes, I want to consider the nature of the poem as a whole. The surviving *argumentum* to the poem asserts that 'some things in the poem have been taken from the first [book] of the *Helen* of Stesichorus'; this is not much to go on, but it is at least not *prima facie* improbable, although Gow, for one, found it easy to resist the invitation to speculation (Gow 1952, II 348). Unless I am mistaken, there is no word in *Theocritus* of this ancient (or Byzantine) note, and no user of the book would even know that Stesichorus might have something to do with *Idyll* 18. I can only guess at the cause of this omission; Dover records the ancient evidence that Theocritus borrowed from Sophron in *Idyll* 2 (p. 97, though missing from the index) and *Idyll* 15 (p. 198),[29] and Stesichorus appears elsewhere in *Theocritus* as a potential source for Theocritus. Perhaps (again) Dover was just not that interested in the poem.

More recent criticism of *Idyll* 18 has focused principally on two (perhaps related) issues, namely whether there is a Ptolemaic background to the poem and whether or how *any* wedding-poem for Menelaos and Helen must inevitably be 'ironic' (to oversimplify a great range of possibilities), given what was to happen. Of all of this there is again not a single word in *Theocritus*, even when the chorus wish 'equal love' for the 'happy couple' (vv. 51–2). When the chorus praise Helen as 'such as no other Achaian maiden treads the earth' (v. 20), this is, as Dover (following Gow) notes, an imitation of *Odyssey* 21.107 where Telemachus describes his mother to the suitors as 'such as no woman now exists in the Achaean land', but neither Gow nor Dover seem to think that the possible implications of a compliment to Helen in a wedding-song which makes her 'another Penelope' deserve a note. Dover in fact offers no indication of what he thinks the poem is 'for', no attempt at contextualization or explanation as to why Theocritus might have written this poem. By comparison, the retelling of the fate of Pentheus in *Idyll* 26, where a thick debt to Euripides' *Bacchae* is normally acknowledged, receives a much fuller Introduction and attempt at contextualization and discussion of literary form. I have already noted Dover's antipathy to the Ptolemaic side of Theocritus' poetry (above p. 243), but the apparent lack of curiosity about *Idyll* 18, which goes much deeper than whether or not Helen was an important Ptolemaic figure, puzzles. It is tempting again to seek one answer at least in Gow's edition. Gow too has no discussion of these matters in his commentary ('the purpose and occasion of the poem remain unknown'), though he does note that some indications might point to Alexandria (II 348). Helen's future does in fact peep through once in Gow's commentary. When the chorus pray that Menelaos and Helen will have children to carry forward the prosperity of the house, Gow (II 360) notes 'this is not the only respect in which the maidens' high hopes for the marriage were doomed to disappointment'. That, I think, is Gow's only nod to what every reader of the poem must know; to what extent that knowledge should be used in our reading is precisely the issue of so much modern discussion.[30] Dover was very well placed to make an important contribution here, but the matter, at least as far as it concerned Theocritus 18, clearly did not interest him.

To speculate further about this lack of interest may be idle, but the genre of the present essay (and the volume in which it is embedded) invites such speculation. One (unsurprising) thing which emerges very clearly from *Theocritus* is that Dover constantly sought in the text things which it could teach him and us about 'real' Greek life and religion. *Idyll* 18 had very little to offer Dover in this regard, except perhaps evidence on Greek wedding-songs and the aetiology of a Spartan cult; even apart from the fact that it was not one of the poems upon which Theocritus' 'claim to recognition as an original genius' lay (cf. above), there was otherwise nothing here which shed light (for Dover) on real Greek experience. It is tempting to think that this might in fact apply more widely, say to the poetry of Callimachus and Apollonius. Did Dover in fact ever habitually read Greek literature 'for pleasure' or, to put it equally banally, just for its own sake? On p. 67 of *Marginal Comment* he observes of his experience as a Mods Tutor: 'I myself had always found that six hours or more spent on a composition [of English into Greek or Latin] (and I sometimes spent twelve) taught me more about the language than the same amount of time spent on reading texts'. There is much that one could say about this staggering (to me) sentence, but the final part does set one thinking; of course, Dover does not mean that 6–12 hours reading ancient texts would be wasted, even if it would teach him less about the ancient languages than the same amount of time doing compositions, and of course he does not mean that he would read the texts during those hours *only* to learn about the language, but something of his priorities does, I think, here emerge, and it can perhaps shed a bit of light on why *Theocritus* is so uneven. I suspect that no professional scholar of Greek reads Greek texts 'just' to pass the time – there is always half an eye or half a mind on learning something or noticing something you have not noticed before – but I wonder whether Dover in fact was a rather extreme case in this regard, as in others. Alternatively (or, rather, as a complement to that), we may say (and this too is no secret) that his interests and his instincts were those of the historian, epigraphist and linguist, not those of the critic of literature.

Be that as it may, this constant search to move from the text to the 'real life' of 'real people' leads to a further blurring of the boundary, inevitably itself constantly re-negotiated, between 'literature' and 'life'; the text may be interrogated as though it were (almost) a documentary, but partial, record which invites us to fill in the gaps. Sometimes – and this too seems typical of Dover – he allows us to believe that it is his own experience which is used to illustrate the text. In *Idyll* 2 (cf. further below), an abandoned woman recalls how her lover used to visit her 'three or four times a day' and 'often he left his Dorian oil-flask with me' (vv. 155–6). On the oil-flask Dover notes (111): 'A silent pledge of return is often more tasteful than verbal assurances'. Was this Dover's experience in dealing with women, and why 'tasteful'? What is 'the learner' to take away from this note?

The commentary on *Idyll* 2, in which Simaitha uses magic to try to win back the lover who has abandoned her and recounts the story of the unhappy affair, offers intriguing examples of both the advantages and the drawbacks of Dover's pursuit of the historical and 'real'. There is, for example, an excellent survey of our (largely literary) evidence for Greek magical practice (98–100) and a full and helpful note on the 'identification' of Artemis and Hecate (100–1) and how such syncretism can throw light upon Greek religion generally. Here Dover is engaged in using the text on which he is commenting as a jumping-off point to teach his reader about Greek culture.[31] So too, Dover pursues at (for him) unusual length the question of Simaitha's position, social station and family ('perhaps we are meant to imagine that Simaitha's father was abroad, that her mother was dead, and that no officious uncle was to hand', 96); Dover here may be elaborating Gow's comparison of Simaitha's position to that of 'several young women in the New Comedy' (Gow 1952, II 33), which would suit the otherwise unexpected 'officious uncle', but in fact

Dover, like many a reader of a modern novel, is seeing Simaitha, 'a suburban Medeia' (95), as a 'real' person and is trying to fill in the gaps in her life and situation which Theocritus' silence has both concealed and laid bare.

One aspect of his Simaitha's situation particularly interested Dover:

> The modern reader wonders whether Simaitha is pregnant – he must, indeed, wonder why, after making love so often (155), she does not say that she is pregnant and worry about this. Possibly Greek contraceptive and abortifacient techniques were more advanced than we know; more probably, since Greek society regarded infanticide by exposure as respectable and was so constructed that an unmarried mother did not face the same economic problems as nowadays, the risk of pregnancy is nothing like as important, even to Simaitha herself, as we might have expected. But maybe Simaitha's apparent indifference to pregnancy is attributable to the fact that Theokritos, like most Greek writers, was male.
>
> Dover 1971, 96

Here Dover certainly goes his own way; perhaps 'the modern reader' is intended precisely as a marker of distance between himself and Gow, who does not seem to have been very interested (here or elsewhere) in the possibility of pregnancy. We have, however, met this Doverian rhetoric before: the 'modern reader' who 'must ... wonder' about pregnancy and the use of contraception is, of course, Dover himself. Here again the text is being used as a jumping-off point for the pursuit of 'the real' (and of Dover's own interests). There is, I suspect, a very great deal one could say about Dover's 'rational' conclusion that pregnancy was not a big deal, socially and economically, for a Greek woman 'in Simaitha's position' (whatever that was), but what is also striking in the present context is the final sentence. Suddenly, almost as an afterthought, there is indeed a poet who intrudes between us and the reconstruction of 'what really happened', but even this intrusion is not there to allow Dover to make the point that this poem is not in fact a record of what could be 'real events'; rather, the intrusion itself is accommodated to the pursuit of 'the real', in this case male indifference to the consequences of male libidinousness: if Theocritus had been female, her Simaitha would almost certainly have worried about being pregnant.

Although this constant desire to contextualize the poems within Greek life is partly responsible for Dover's apparent lack of consistent attention to poems which simply seem to float free in the realm of 'literature', it is also one of the principal reasons why every reader has much to learn from Dover's *Theocritus*; fifty years is in fact rather a good innings for an avowedly small-scale commentary, and for many of Theocritus' poems *Theocritus* remains the most accessible and serviceable 'way in', particularly for Anglophone readers. Dover himself clearly did not rate it high in the ranks of his output, and we may well agree, but only someone of Dover's magisterial command of Greek language and culture could have written it. Despite the veil of silence which *Marginal Comment* draws over *Theocritus*, it has very rightly not been forgotten, and it can help us to understand the extraordinary scholar whom the present volume celebrates.

Richard Hunter

Notes

* I am grateful to Stephen Halliwell and Christopher Stray for their invitation to contribute this short essay, for their reasoned responses to my hesitations, and for much help along the way; many thanks also to Tim Rood, Philip Hardie and Cédric Scheidegger Laemmle. It is, I think, still worth putting on record the source of my principal doubt about contributing on this subject to this volume. The fifty years which have passed since Dover's *Theocritus* was published have seen a complete revolution in our understanding and appreciation of Hellenistic poetry, and it is almost inevitable that any account of *Theocritus*, a volume which Dover himself may have done his best to conceal from public examination, is bound to focus on absences, rather than on the very many merits of a book which has contributed very significantly to the widespread appreciation of Theocritus' poetry. I did not want to write a piece which simply took easy shots, particularly of course as I myself have written two books (and more) on Theocritus, including a commentary (Hunter 1999) which in part overlaps with Dover's; I fear, however, that there probably are easy shots here, and I apologize for them. I very much hope that no one will interpret this essay as suggesting that I have anything but boundless θαῦμα for Dover as a scholar.

1. This may be one reason (there were probably others) why the undergraduate Dover wrote to his parents from Oxford on 1 March 1939: 'I am doing Theocritus for end-of-term collections – not a very tall bill' (information from Christopher Stray). The new edition of *Marginal Comment* (Dover 2023), edited by the same scholars as this volume, has a much-improved index.

2. Dover uses the spelling 'Vergil' at *MC* 37 though he had earlier written 'Virgil' (ibid. 18); in *Theocritus*, the abbreviation 'Verg.' occurs. In what follows I myself prefer the form Virgil, in part to celebrate the memory of Ted Kenney, who had very strong views on the subject.

3. Cf. *MC* 67. Among those who did lecture on Theocritus were Frank Geary, Maurice Platnauer and Constantine Trypanis; Dover may of course have set practice tests etc. for any of his pupils who chose Theocritus. I am very grateful to Tim Rood for his help and his research here.

4. In 1932–5, just before Dover's time, 'Alexandrian Poetry' was an optional Mods Special Subject; *Argonautica* 3 and some of Callimachus' *Hymns* were the prescribed texts.

5. A very distinguished Oxford Hellenist told me in the 1980s that s/he had never read the *Argonautica*. What I most remember is that this was said without any apparent embarrassment or regret, as though s/he was just observing over a drink that s/he had never seen a particular French arthouse movie.

6. The copy of the original 'Macmillan red' edition of Dover's *Theocritus* on the table in front of me now was purchased (presumably in 1973 or 1974) from the University of Sydney 'Co-op. Bookshop' for A$12.

7. The informatively named 'Alexandrian Poetry (with special reference to Roman Poetry)' was in fact available as a Special Subject in Greats during Dover's Balliol years, but such Special Subjects were hardly ever taken up.

8. Dover in fact offers no note on the name and never considers the possibility that Amaryllis is a figment of the goatherd's imagination. *Idyll* 3 is not on Dover's priority list of poems (see my text at p. 242); I suspect that (*inter alia*) he did not care for what he saw as 'the poet's tone ... of patronising humour' (113).

9. Cf. Hunter 2021, 231–3.

10. The closest Gow comes to any general discussion is in the introduction to the commentary on *Idyll* 7, but nowhere does he really deal with the Greek precedents to Theocritus, as Dover does.

11. Rosenmeyer 1969.
12. Chapter 2 of Rosenmeyer 1969 on 'Beginnings' naturally has some overlap with Dover's section on 'Bucolic Poetry', but that lies more in the evidence which is discussed than in the nature of the evidence.
13. The inverted commas are those of the website statement.
14. Cf. also Russell and Halliwell 2012, 155, 'He [i.e. Dover at Balliol after the war] was not so keen on Latin (and it may be that this indifference persisted)'. For the young Dover's liking of the *Aeneid*, however, cf. Stray, this volume, p. 18.
15. This institutional separation of the languages and the necessity it imposes upon young scholars to present themselves as 'one or the other' persisted, of course, long after this, and in many ways still (unfortunately) does. When I was an undergraduate at Sydney, it was at least believed by the happy few studying these subjects that lecturers in the Department of Greek were not permitted to lecture in the Department of Latin and *vice versa*; whatever the truth, they were two utterly separate worlds, and in his memoir Dover makes Greek and Latin at St Andrews sound a bit like that.
16. Dover, ed., 1992 does contain a chapter by Elizabeth Rawson on Roman perceptions of the Greeks.
17. Menander is, of course, cited on a number of occasions in *Greek Popular Morality*, and Elizabeth Craik (this volume) reports that Dover taught some Menander, alongside Aristophanes, at St Andrews.
18. I have had my say on some aspects of this discussion and some of the examples with which Dover illustrates these claims in Hunter 2008, 15–24.
19. Cf., e.g., Dover, ed., 1997b, 3–4; further discussion in Halliwell's chapter in this volume.
20. Dover is adept at various versions of this projection of his own views. At *Theocritus* p. 217 (in connection with *Idyll* 16) we are told that 'Modern readers are commonly repelled by an ancient poet's flattery of a patron or potential patron'; '*Which* modern readers?', we may be tempted to ask. The omission of *Idyll* 17 (the 'Encomium of Ptolemy') from *Theocritus* might be thought evidence pointing towards the answer.
21. The chapter by Jasper Griffin on Hellenistic literature in Dover, ed., 1997b is, as would have been expected, graceful and (mostly) sympathetic to its subject.
22. Cf. Sheffield, this volume.
23. One of Dover's appointments (in 1968) to a position in Greek at St Andrews was Malcolm Campbell, a very learned scholar of Hellenistic and imperial poetry; Dover thanks him in the Preface of *Theocritus* (vii) for his 'acute and helpful criticisms' on a draft of the Introduction and Commentary. Stephen Halliwell points out to me that *MC* 158 suggests that *Theocritus* was not finished by the autumn of 1970, but the Preface is dated December 1969. There is clearly some error and/or confusion here.
24. Gow appears once in *MC* (40) as Dover's host at dinner in Trinity College, Cambridge 'about 1958', a dinner also attended by Kurt Latte; the occasion was presumably in the context of a Triennial Conference of the Hellenic and Roman Societies. The subject of the anecdote is a discussion at dinner about whether or not Wilamowitz would ever brook disagreement from a student (Gow appears to have been corrected by Latte on the matter). It would be nice to know whether Theocritus was also discussed over dinner; I would guess not, or at least not at any rate by Gow and Dover. In a letter to his parents of that summer (kindly drawn to my attention by Christopher Stray), Dover refers to the 'lavish' entertainment offered by 'Cambridge friends'.

25. The representation of low life, the references to buggery and the social and anthropological aspects of *Idyll* 5, clearly appealed to Dover (cf. pp. 127–9, 133–4). For the sake of fairness, let me put on record that my biggest regret about Hunter 1999 is the failure to include *Idyll* 5; there were perfectly good reasons of word-count for this decision, but it would be disingenuous not to admit that it has also never been one of my 'favourites'.
26. The most important discussion since Dover is Gutzwiller 1996.
27. On these verses see further Hunter 1996, 131–2.
28. For some guidance cf. Hunter 1996, 163.
29. Dover in fact misrepresents the situation with regard to *Idyll* 2: despite what is said on p. 97, the ancient scholium does not name the mime from which Theocritus is alleged to have borrowed; on *Idyll* 15, Dover does not let his reader know that there is an ancient assertion of indebtedness to Sophron in the case of *Idyll* 15, but merely reports our knowledge of Sophron's mime. On the scholiastic evidence for the three poems, cf. Hunter 2015, 152–3.
30. Cf. Hunter 2015, 162–3.
31. Cf. Dover's own description of a seminar he organized at Wadham on Lysias' *Epitaphios*, 'a peg on which I could hang many different explorations of Greek literary form and ethos' (*MC* 68).

CHAPTER 14
NO STONE UNTURNED: DOVER AS HISTORIAN OF GREEK LANGUAGE BETWEEN EPIGRAPHY AND LITERATURE

Lucia Prauscello

Dover's work on Greek language in general and Attic comic language in particular has proved foundational in establishing some of the most successful directions of international scholarship in these areas. This is most apparent when one considers *Greek Word Order*: though not the first to move beyond the grammar of the sentence to that of discourse, Dover's attention to larger discourse structures (subordination, discourse particles, the connectedness between the different parts of the text perceived as a unified entity), together with his focus on the category of 'logical' (*vs* syntactical) determinants, made him a pragmatist *avant la lettre* at a time when functional grammar was only beginning to be fully theorized.[1] Dover's sustained forays into the study of register variation (colloquialism, technical languages, vocabulary of sex and scatology, etc.) and of stylistics, by identifying patterns across different linguistic *corpora* (comedy, oratory, historiography, to mention only some of his favourite subjects), have been equally inspirational for future generations.[2] In this sense, the recent burgeoning of sociolinguistic studies on Greek comic language is much indebted to Dover's previous work on the subject.[3] Likewise, contemporary studies on fifth-century Attic dialect still take as a starting-point his influential papers on colloquial strata in classical Attic prose (Dover 1981c = *G&G* 16–30), the language of Attic documentary inscriptions (Dover 1981d = *G&G* 31–41), and the ever elusive relationship of early Attic with Ionic prose (Dover 1950, 56–60 = *G&L* 29–34 and *EGPS* ch. 5).[4] His readiness to harness typological parallels from anthropological and sociolinguistic research outside Classics to investigate various aspects of Greek culture and language has also proved to be farsighted and ahead of its time.[5]

The unifying thread of this extraordinarily diverse scholarly production is Dover's unrelenting interest in the inner workings of Greek language *as* language, from both a synchronic and a diachronic perspective, and his deep conviction that it is the fullest possible understanding of these workings that must provide the basis for the further historical and/or literary interpretation of the texts and their contexts. A self-professed 'historian of words',[6] Dover could proudly take delight in the most technical and forbidding aspects of the subject, but was always aware that what matters is the bigger picture, that is, how linguistic choices align with communicative goals and intentions.[7] It is within this framework that the present chapter will consider Dover's engagement with both literary and documentary evidence in mapping out the trajectory of two long-standing and favourite interests of his: the colloquial levels of Attic language and register variation. The first part of the paper will briefly sketch Dover's own lifelong fascination with the value of inscriptional evidence as the primary medium by means of which to gain insight into the inner dynamics of Greek language and culture. In the second part, a number of case-studies will be analysed in more detail. Both parts will be necessarily selective and no doubt influenced by the personal interests of the writer; it is nevertheless hoped that the selection, however idiosyncratic, may serve to highlight Dover's overall approach to the study of Greek as a rewarding field in the history of human behaviour.

'A history man': Language, inscriptions and the human past

Throughout his career Dover always defined himself as a historian, with a constant emphasis on history as a form of enquiry into human behaviour in its multiform manifestations.[8] His view of history was an all-encompassing one:[9] 'The good reason for studying Greek is that it is a peculiarly interesting and worthwhile compartment of human history; and I use "history" in its broadest sense, to cover linguistic behaviour as well as artistic, religious, social, economic, political, scientific and philosophical behaviour' (*MC* 127); 'I suppose that I could be most accurately described as a historian of Greek behaviour, and what happened to me in the late nineteen-seventies was a decisive shift from political, social, moral and sexual behaviour to linguistic and literary behaviour' (*MC* 200). What is deeply characteristic of Dover's intellectual attitude is his view of language as a form, if not *the* most important form, of human behaviour in and through time. To study ancient Greek was for Dover tantamount to reconstructing part of a shared human experience. In this sense the triggering point was always very personal and at the same time empirical: as, in his own words, 'an Anglo-Saxon empiricist hospitable to ideas but hostile to any theory which boasts of its own comprehensive power', Dover always staunchly defended his 'considered *refusal to separate interpretation of my own experience from the recovery of the experience of others*, no matter how remote in time and place' (*MC* 261; my italics).[10]

He firmly believed that a scholar worth his/her name should first collect the available data and then 'formulate demonstrable hypotheses' (*MC* 259), where the emphasis is very much on the 'testable' nature of such hypotheses. Though perfectly aware that in some cases certainty may well be beyond our grasp given the nature of the available evidence,[11] Dover never doubted the existence of a historically determined answer. This also explains why he was an unashamed intentionalist and saw language above all as a vehicle of purposively intelligible communication:

> It is the authors who matter; what were they trying to do, and what were the expectations of their original audiences? Critics for whom 'intentionalist' is a naughty word will not think much of those questions, but I can't say that that worries me. I have paid attention to such critics, but my attention has not been

rewarded by insights which have been of the slightest use in answering the questions which interest me. I do not consent to being told by other people what *ought* to interest me, and I have no patience with literary critics whose writings resemble incantation rather than rational communication. Perhaps this is because I consider that it is people who 'mean', and words are only the instrument by which they do so.

MC 258–9[12]

This conviction ('it is people who "mean", and words are only the instrument by which they do so') lays bare the overwhelming influence of the ancient rhetorical tradition on Dover's approach to language. It is not by chance (even if Dover would have liked us to think otherwise)[13] that his first monograph was *Greek Word Order*. Ancient rhetoric and modern pragmatics share an important point of convergence: they both regard language first and foremost as an instrument of communication.[14] What we now call text-cohesion (attention to the composition and structure of the text as a whole) belonged in antiquity to the field of rhetorical studies. Another interesting consonance between the ancient rhetorical tradition and Dover's attitude as a historian of language is that both perceive *style* as a central element. The overriding principle governing style is, for both, the *effectiveness* of its communicative function between speaker and addressee in a given context. This, in its turn, brings us very close to the reason why Dover so highly valued documentary evidence (above all, but not only, inscriptions). He himself traced the origin of this lifelong attitude back to the legacy of Russell Meiggs, his tutor in ancient history during his undergraduate years at Oxford:

The seed of two habits was planted in me by Meiggs more firmly than either of us realised at the time. One was: on any question in Greek history or the Greek language, *go first to inscriptions* and only after that to literature. The general practice among ancient historians in the English-speaking world had been to treat Herodotus, Thucydides and Xenophon as 'authorities' and inscriptions as an optional side-dish. *I preferred to begin with the inscriptions*, construct historical hypotheses to account for *this* stone, bearing *these* words, found *here*, and then to see how the historiography of the time fitted. Students of the Greek language mostly ignored the existence of inscriptions, and even in my own time good scholars have made untrue statements through failure to look in the right places.[15]

MC 59

Because of its inherently practical purposes, the language of documentary evidence (public decrees, stones demarcating boundaries, but also private letters, vase inscriptions, graffiti, etc.) exhibits better than literary texts, on Dover's view, the essential purpose of verbal communication: its intended intelligibility. Though well aware of peculiarities of the documentary corpus as such (its formularity, archaizing tendency, lexical niches, etc.), Dover chose to start his study of Greek word order not with literary texts but with inscriptions (a field that contemporary pragmatics often blindly ignores, notwithstanding all its theoretical sophistication):[16]

> As for inscriptions, it must be admitted that Greek documentary inscriptions exhibit, at certain times and places, positive characteristics of their own, and that we cannot assume without qualification that their language is 'basic' or 'natural' Greek. Nevertheless, these characteristics are few and easily identifiable; [...] and there are several other considerations which make inscriptions of prime importance to students of word order. First, [...] an inscription may be presumed to be only one stage removed from an autograph and slips of the chisel are likely to be rarer than slips of the pen. Secondly, the composition of documentary inscriptions is motivated by a desire to *communicate clearly* and not invite admiration as a work of art.
>
> GWO 11 (my italics)

Some of Dover's assumptions quoted above are debatable, indeed still hotly debated.[17] It is however significant that Dover chose to put the emphasis on the *intended clarity of information* of documentary texts: once again his intentionalism comes to the surface. And so much so that Dover regarded inscriptions as the necessary point of departure for any linguistic investigation: 'There is some value in applying to word order, and to all problems in the history of the Greek language, a principle which was applied on a famous occasion to a matter of higher importance [Plato, *Resp.* 369a]: πρῶτον ἐν ταῖς πόλεσιν ζητήσωμεν ποῖόν τί ἐστι' (*GWO* 11).[18] At the basis of Dover's conviction is the very modern inclination to see 'literariness' not as an absolute peak but rather as a discrete point on a much broader continuum constantly subject to renegotiation.[19] Within this continuum the evidence provided by documentary texts is for Dover as important as that glimpsed from literary works when it comes to understanding the workings of a language in its diachronic and regional variations. In the next section I shall take a closer look at some examples of this intersection between literary language and documentary texts.

No stone unturned

In his attempt at identifying existing clusters of usage through time and in different genres, Dover was always aware that any single linguistic category, be it morphological, syntactical, lexical or dialectal, does not stand on its own. Hence the need to look always *across different corpora* of evidence when searching for an answer. Dover also bore constantly in mind that '[s]ince every dialect of every language is in process of change at any given moment, no dialect is ever wholly consistent' (Dover 1963, 17 = *G&G* 298). Hence dialectology can show us 'changes in the distribution of alternative forms *up to* a given time, but it never provides a complete explanation of their distribution *at* a given time. There are always phenomena of which the geographical distribution is at variance with their putative history' (ibid., Dover's italics). This insight has been particularly fruitful in Dover's investigation of the elusive *Sprachgut* common to Ionic and early Attic (on which see below). Similarly, and notwithstanding his positivistic inclinations, Dover was ready to recognize that just as linguistic innovation in a language may happen at different times in different places and spread at a different pace also within a substantially homogeneous linguistic area, so also the language of a given author is not bound to absolute consistency when it comes to choosing between linguistic allomorphs.[20] With these caveats in mind, Dover repeatedly emphasized the importance of going back to documentary evidence to properly assess the literary evidence, and *vice versa*, especially as far as classical Attic is concerned: 'I am persuaded that not poetry but documents should be the starting-point for the study of Greek vocabulary of the fifth century; indeed, these documents reveal an aspect of the Attic vocabulary which has nearly always, wrongly, been overlooked' (*G&G* 226 ~ Dover 1970, 9); similarly, 'One thing at least is certain: documentary language never became strong enough to exclude intrusions from literature and the vernacular' (Dover 1981d, 5 = *G&G* 35).

Among Dover's favourite *pièces de résistance* to illustrate this tenet is his contention that the origin of the widespread extension of the adjectival suffix -ικός in fifth-century literature cannot be entirely explained as due to sophistic influence. Literature is not the only place where one must look:[21]

> By the late fifth century it [i.e. the suffix -ικός] had already become characteristic of the language of technology and administration, as is clear from a glance at the index of *IG* i², where we find (e.g.) ἀγαλματοποιϊκός, δημιουργικός, ἐπιβατικός, ληξιαρχικός, λιθοκομικός, τεκτονικός, etc. In the fourth century it continues to extend its domain, e.g. ἀρτοπωλικός, ἐγκτητικός, ὀργεωνικός, πρυτανικός, τειχοποιϊκός. It was not just the sophists or the poets who created the widespread use of the morphemes by which Greek literature was enriched.
>
> *G&G* 229 ~ Dover 1970, 13–14[22]

The same also applies to the increasing diffusion, both in early Attic prose but also in Attic tragedy,[23] of various other phenomena:

> I have suggested elsewhere that the rich and versatile vocabulary of Antiphon and Thucydides was not an autonomous development of a literary and intellectual tradition; its growth was stimulated by the example of technology and administration. A run through the index of *sermo Atticus* in *IG* i² yields an extraordinary crop of agent-nouns in -της, abstracts in -σις, neuter nouns in -μα, adjectives in -ικός and -τος and in alpha privative with -τος. Some in this last category are technical, ..., while others are administrative, e.g. ἀπρόσκλητος (39.10) and ἀχορήγητος (187.4).
>
> Dover 1981d, 9 = *G&G* 39–40

Thus, to select just one particular example, Dover argued that the verbal adjective ἀψήφιστος at Aristophanes, *Vesp.* 753,[24] a term that occurs again only once in literary texts up to the second century CE (Secund. *Sent.* 17 Perry)²⁵ and is absent in extant documentary papyri and inscriptions, 'may fairly be judged, on this analogy, to offer us a genuine formula rather than a poet's invention', allowing us to recover a piece of fifth-century BC Athenian administrative language otherwise lost.²⁶

As Dover himself makes clear, parallel development of linguistic innovations in both literary and administrative/technical writings and the possibility of reciprocal interaction need not necessarily be seen as mutually exclusive phenomena:

> To make this observation is not (I hope) to derogate from the magnitude of the achievement of the poets in the centuries preceding the earliest surviving Greek prose literature. It was their inventiveness, more than anything, which made the Greeks responsive and sensitive to language as an art-form. It is only necessary to remember also that the need for public written utterance in the fields of technology, law, administration and politics made its own contribution to the παιδεία of the Athenians, and that interaction between different genres of utterance was continuous.
>
> Dover 1981d, 12 = *G&G* 40

As he explains further in his last book, 'It is not that technological and administrative languages imitated poetry and literary prose, or that the learning process was the reverse, but simply that from the very beginning *all* genres of utterance in Greek exploited *in parallel* the creative potential of word-formation and *also* interacted' (*EGPS* 117; Dover's italics).

A good example is provided by the distribution of the verbal adjective παλιναίρετος, which at first sight might strike us as a poetic lexeme (a compound adjective with a prepositional first constituent). Dover *EGPS* 117 n. 44 quotes Pindar fr. 84 S-M (= Harpoc. p. 231.7-16 Dindorf = Keaney p. 199 (Π 3)), from a Dithyramb, where the adjective is said to refer to 'buildings pulled down and rebuilt' (ἐπὶ δὲ τῶν καθαιρεθέντων οἰκοδομημάτων καὶ ἀνοικοδομηθέντων Πίνδαρος Διθυράμβοις),²⁷ and *IG* I³ 386.131 (408/7 BC), where we find the mention of two talents of 'reconstituted iron' (σιδέρο παλινhαιρέτο)²⁸ as part of the collection of a fee for the cult of Demeter and Kore at Eleusis. This, however, is only part of the story. The entry of Harpocration from which Pindar's usage is taken tells us a broader tale: παλιναίρετος was used by the orator Dinarchus in his *Writ of indictment against Polyeuktos* (= Din. *Or.* 2 fr. 4 Conomis) of the said Polyeuktos 'after he was voted out' of the Athenian boule (Δείναρχος ἐν τῇ κατὰ Πολυεύκτου ἐκφυλλοφορηθέντος ἐνδείξει). Harpocration then goes on to say that Eupolis in his *Baptai* (fr. 98 K-A) and Archippos in his *Ichthyes* (fr. 14 K-A) also used παλιναίρετος to designate 'those who were voted out of office and then re-elected'.²⁹ The adjective παλιναίρετος, therefore, was, among other possible usages, a specifically Athenian legal term which, though attested only thanks to the lexicographical tradition (Harpocration ≈ Photius, *Lex.* π 79 Theodoridis, *Suda* π 99 Adler), must have been quite a common term in the administrative jargon of Athenian political life in the fifth and fourth century BC.³⁰ At the same time, what Dover defined as the 'creative potential of word-formation' is such that in the *Timaeus* Plato could use παλιναίρετος to indicate the reverse process by which secondary bodily substances are literally 'taken backwards' in their physical receptacles, thus causing disease, rather than flowing in their natural direction.³¹

Documentary texts, for Dover, not only help us to recover single, isolated words which must have been common currency at a given time but are nevertheless poorly attested either because of the limited survival of ancient literature or because of the semantics of the word itself. They also allow us to notice stylistic features which have a counterpart in the literary tradition, thus reinforcing each other. Dover, for instance, did not hesitate to defend the textual soundness, at Lysias 1.17, of the repetition καὶ πάντα μου εἰς τὴν γνώμην εἰσῄει, καὶ μεστὸς ἦν ὑποψίας ('and everything came back to my mind and I was filled with suspicion') ... ταῦτά μου πάντα εἰς τὴν γνώμην εἰσῄει, καὶ μεστὸς ἦν ὑποψίας ('All these things came back to my mind and I was filled with suspicion') by quoting the comparably clumsy repetitiousness of a private letter on a lead sheet from Berezan (Olbia, dated *c.* 550–500 BC):

ὁ δὲ ἀναβῶι τε | καὶ οὔ φησιν ἔναι οὐδὲν ἑωυτῶι τε καὶ Ματάσ<υι> | καί φησιν ἔναι ἐλεόθερος καὶ οὐδὲν ἔναι ἑωυτ<ῶ>ι | καὶ Ματάσυ<ι>. ἒ δέ τι αὐτῶι τε κἀναξαγόρηι, αὐτοὶ | οἴδασι κατὰ σφᾶς αὐτός

IGDOlbia 23.6–10

('But he disputes it and denies that there is anything between him and Matasys and says that he is free and there is nothing between him and Matasys. But what there is between him (sc. Matasys) and Anaxagoras, they alone know.' Translation after Ceccarelli 2013, 335.)

The first occurrence of καὶ πάντα μου εἰς τὴν γνώμην εἰσῄει, καὶ μεστὸς ἦν ὑποψίας at Lysias 1.17 had been deleted by Dobree because of the general aversion of Attic prose for repetitions,³² but, as Dover rightly saw, 'the Berezan letter simultaneously justifies the retention of the words by modern editors and alerts us to the possibility of deliberate naivety of style in other part of Lys., i' (Dover 1981c, 21 = *G&G* 24). Similarly, to explain *and* contextualize the repetition of the protasis as a characteristic feature of early Greek prose, Dover boldly compared Anaxagoras' claim that Nous is an unlimited, unmixed thing, and thus 'alone itself by itself' (Anax. B12 DK, εἰ μὴ γὰρ ἐφ' ἑαυτοῦ ἦν, ἀλλά τεῳ ἐμέμεικτο ἄλλῳ, μετεῖχεν ἂν ἁπάντων χρημάτων, εἰ ἐμέμεικτό τεῳ)³³ with a 'strikingly vulgar message from the first century AD', that is, P.Oxy. 3070.4–8, where a certain Apion and Epimas tell Epaphroditos that 'if he let them bugger him (ἢ διδῦς ἡμεῖν τὸ πυγίσαι) and this is fine by him (καὶ καλῶς σοί ἐστι)', he 'must not fear that they will skin him (οὐκέτι οὐ μὴ δείρομέν σε) if he allows them to bugger him (ἐὰν δώσῃς ἡμεῖν τὸ ποιγίσαι)'. Both examples, as Dover puts it, let us recover 'a glimmer of affinity between the sentence-structure of non-literary utterance and the sentence-structure of prose literature in its emergent stage or in a deliberately unsophisticated style' (Dover 1981c, 21 = *G&G* 25).

Dover's search for 'affinity' between documentary and literary texts could, of course, also backfire.³⁴ Always keen to clarify procedural details, while commenting on Aristophanes, *Thesm.* 431–2 (... ταῦτα μὲν φανερῶς λέγω. / τὰ δ' ἄλλα μετὰ τῆς γραμματέως συγγράψομαι), Dover acutely observed that it takes three persons to 'publish' a decree: the proposer of the measure, the secretary of the council and the under-secretary.[35] Dover also remarked that notwithstanding (or perhaps because of) this collaborative effort, the secretary and the under-secretary, within the constraints imposed by formulaic diction, could nevertheless find occasion to show some 'sensitivity to style'. One of the examples he quotes is *IG* I² 154.13-14 (= *SEG* X 98, now *IG* I³ 169.27-28), dated to *c.* 430-10 BC. It is an honorary decree bestowing proxeny on two non-Athenians. Among the protective measures granted them by the Athenian state there is a clause that if they meet a violent death, or are imprisoned and abducted, the penalty for the wrongdoers will be the same as that decreed for Athenian citizens. Then follow the highly lacunose lines that concern us (as supplemented by Wilhelm and read by Dover): κα[ὶ ἐὰν βλαβõσι, τὲν] | [βλάβε]ν ἰᾶσθαι δ[ιπλε̃ν.[36] Dover observed that this usage of τὴν βλάβην ἰᾶσθαι 'does not occur in any passages of the orators concerning βλάβη ... but surfaces in Pl. *Lg.* 933e μέχριπερ ἂν ἰάσηται τὸ βλαβέν: a figure of speech which occurred independently to the composer of *SEG* x 98 and to Plato, or an ingredient of the traditional language of Attic law?' (*G&G* 40) The correct answer is neither of those alternatives. Given the extremely fragmentary state of the lines, editors of *IG* I³ 169.27-8 more cautiously print κα[ὶ ....10....]| [...8....]ν ἰᾶσθαι δ[....11.....], relegating Wilhelm's supplement to the apparatus. It is also more reasonable to see in ἰᾶσθαι a reference not to a metaphorical expression but to the actual profession of the two honorands.[37] And this with good reason: the Platonic passage adduced by Dover is highly idiosyncratic in its language. At *Laws* 933e[38] the Athenian Stranger is saying that in cases of damage caused by an act of robbery or violence 'one shall in every case pay a sum equal to the damage done <u>up to the point at which the harm done is cured</u>' (παρὰ πάντα δὲ τοσαύτην ἡλίκα ἂν ἑκάστοτε ζημιώσῃ τίς τινα, <u>μέχριπερ ἂν ἰάσηται τὸ βλαβέν</u>). As scholars have recognized, Plato's 'penology' is self-consciously medical:[39] one must first cure (ἰᾶσθαι) the soul of the offender (cf. e.g. 862c, τὰς τοίνυν ἀδίκους αὖ βλάβας τούτων ὁπόσα μὲν ἰατά, ὡς οὐσῶν ἐν ψυχῇ νόσων, ἰᾶσθαι· τὸ δὲ τῆς ἰάσεως ἡμῖν τῆς ἀδικίας τῇδε ῥέπειν χρὴ φάναι). It is no surprise, then, that Plato recurs here to standard medical phraseology: the polarity ἰάομαι/βλάπτω is omnipresent in medical writings (cf. e.g. [Hipp.] *De morb. sacro* 53.1, ἀλλὰ τὰ ἐδέσματα τὰ ἰώμενά ἐστι καὶ τὰ βλάπτοντα, or Galen, *De meth. medendi* 10.514.17 Kühn, ῥᾷστον δὲ δή που τὴν τοιαύτην ἰάσασθαι βλάβην). *IG* I³ 169.27-28 and Pl. *Laws* 933e thus do not attest independently to 'an ingredient of the traditional language of Attic law' otherwise lost: in the former, the verb ἰᾶσθαι probably, though not certainly, refers to the actual medical profession of the honorands, while Plato's singular expression μέχριπερ ἂν ἰάσηται τὸ βλαβέν must be understood within the *Laws*' broader programme of curative punishment.

Dialect and register

As already mentioned, one of Dover's lifelong interests was the evolution of the Attic dialect (its phonology, morphology, syntax and lexicon) and its relationship to early

Ionic prose.⁴⁰ Throughout his work Dover repeatedly emphasized that the common lexical *Sprachgut* between Ionic and early Attic might have been much more extensive than we are now inclined to think,⁴¹ exhorting caution before we declare a lexeme 'poetic' simply on the basis of its absence from later (i.e. mainly fourth-century BC) Attic prose.⁴² In particular Dover showed that the distinction between technical and poetical vocabulary may not always be a useful analytical tool for the first part of the fifth century. In this sense he was very conscious that as readers we may apply biased criteria to our sources: 'This at once raises the question: was Ionic prose influenced by poetic vocabulary? Or is our notion of prose vocabulary fundamentally distorted by the fact that we read prose through the eyes of a fourth-century Athenian?' (*G&G* 225 ~ Dover 1970, 9). Dover's magisterial linguistic analysis of Ion of Chios, *FGrHist* 392 F 6 at *EGPS* 92-5 shows us how misleading it may be to automatically equate words shared by poetry (mainly Homer, but also the elegiac and iambic tradition) and Ionic prose (mainly but not only Herodotus) as quintessentially 'poetic'. He demonstrated how 'a significant proportion' of such lexemes 'appear also in documents, and there are some shared by poetry with documents but not yet attested in prose literature' (*EGPS* 93). This evidence strongly suggested to him that such words should not be mechanically traced back to the influence of poetry but that they might instead be examples of the 'Ionic vernacular' of the time.⁴³ And there is always the possibility that what looks to us like 'Ionic vernacular' may at a certain point have been part of the common stock of early Attic and Ionic. Dover was aware that this common stock was not limited to semantics, yet he also allowed for the possibility that some phonological and morphological developments usually ascribed to the influence of Ionic may simply be due to independent intradialectal diachronic developments and that authors could also make personal choices from coexisting variant forms, mainly genre-dictated.⁴⁴

To search for a common stock of vocabulary shared by Ionic and early Attic is a difficult and slippery enterprise because it necessarily relies almost uniquely on the (for us) *attested* geographical distribution of a given lexeme, which is often random.⁴⁵ As Thumb already saw more than a century ago, words in Attic prose that at first sight may appear 'Ionic' or 'tragic' could just as well have been originally 'Altattisch',⁴⁶ and there is no certain way to settle the question one way or the other. Or, to rephrase it in Dover's own words, 'archaism, whether or not it was ever actualized, remained a potential stylistic feature' available to an author choosing to write in Attic (*EGPS* 81). With this warning in mind, it may be profitable to look afresh at the famous bidialectal inscription of Phanodicus of Proconnesus, from the Sigeum (Troad), that is, *IG* I³ 1508, datable to the mid-sixth century BC.⁴⁷ The stone, an approximately 2 metre high marble pillar, presents two texts, both written boustrophedon, the first (text I) in Ionic dialect and East Ionic alphabet, the second (text II) in Attic dialect and alphabet. This is the text as printed by Threatte, followed by his translation (slightly modified):⁴⁸

(I)   Φανοδίκο
        ἐμὶ τὀρμοκ-
        ράτεος τô

	Προκοννη-	4
	σίο· κρητῆρ-	
	α δὲ : καὶ ὑποκ-	
	ρητήριον : κ-	
	αὶ ἠ<θ>μὸν : ἐς π-	8
	ρυτανήϊον	
	ἔδωκεν : Συκε-	
	εῦσιν.	
	vacat	
(II)	Φανοδίκο : εἰμὶ : τō h-	12
	ερμοκράτος : τō Προκο-	
	νεσίο : κἀγὸ ⋮ κρατέρα	
	κἀπίστατον ⋮ καὶ ℎεθμ-	
	ὸν ⋮ ἐς πρυτανεῖον ⋮ ἔ-	16
	δοκα ⋮ μνêμα ⋮ Σιγει-	
	εῦσι ⋮ ἐὰν δέ τι πάσχ-	
	ο, μελεδαίνεν ⋮ με, ō̂	
	Σιγειε̂ς ⋮ καί μ' ἐπο-	20
	<ίε>σεν ⋮ ℎαίσοπος : καὶ	
	⋮ ℎἀδελφοί.	
	vacat	

(I) I belong to Phanodicus, the son of Hermocrates, from Proconnesus. He gave to the people of Sigeum a crater and a stand and a strainer for (use in) the prytaneion.

(II) I belong to Phanodicus, the son of Hermocrates, from Proconnesus. And I gave as a memorial to the people of Sigeum a crater and a stand and a strainer for (use in) the prytaneion. And if anything happens to me, take care of me, you people of the Sigeum! And (H)aisopos and his brothers made me.

A votive or funeral monument (more probably the latter),[49] the Ionic text (I) records that the stele is dedicated to Phanodicus of Proconnesus and that he made a gift of a krater, a stand and a strainer to the prytaneion of Sigeum. The Attic text (II) repeats as much, though with a shift from the third to the first person singular, and adds important new information: it expresses the wish that the citizens of Sigeum will take proper care of the monument if it suffers harm (ll. 18–20, ἐὰν δέ τι πάσχ|ο, μελεδαίνεν με, ō̂| Σιγειε̂ς) and it mentions (H)aisopos[50] and his brothers as the carvers of the stele (ll. 20–22). Very much remains elusive, including whether the two texts are written by the same hand or not and whether the Ionic and Attic versions were copied simultaneously or, if not, which version was inscribed first.[51] What is, however, beyond doubt is that the Attic 'enlarged version' of the Ionic text was not motivated by any need of intelligibility: whoever could understand one of the two dialects would have been able to understand the other without any difficulty; enabling linguistic comprehension was not the issue.[52] Rather, what was at stake was a political factor: the Attic text, written in Attic alphabet *and* dialect, was necessary because it was a statement of Athenian identity, recording the city's gratitude to one of its benefactors.[53] That is, it would have made no sense to 'translate' the Ionic version into Attic if the stele had not been erected at a time at which the Sigeum was under Athenian domination.[54]

Despite that, commentators continue to puzzle over the presence, in the Attic version, of what is commonly labelled as an 'Ionism': the verb μελεδαίνειν at line 19.[55] Take, for instance, Threatte 2015, 120: 'The occurrence of the Ionic μελεδαίνω in the Attic version is of some interest, for in prose it is an Ionic, not an Attic word; it occurs in Ionic poetry, Herodotus and the Hippocratic Corpus'.[56] Minon too takes for granted the 'Ionic' nature of μελεδαίνω,[57] so much so that she asks herself whether we should read at ll. 19–20 μελεδαίνεν μεο, Σιγειές ('[If I happen to suffer some harm], take care of me, citizens of Sigeum!') rather than μελεδαίνεν με, ὁ Σιγειές; that is, Minon would have μελεδαίνω + the genitive μεο (another Ionism), and Σιγειές as vocative without ὦ or as nominative *pro* vocative.[58] Syntactically, μελεδαίνω can take both the direct object (e.g. Archil. fr. 14.1 W, δήμου μὲν ἐπίρρησιν μελεδαίνων) or the genitive (e.g. Theogn. 1129 W, πενίης θυμοφθόρου οὐ μελεδαίνω, / οὐδ' ἀνδρῶν ἐχθρῶν, Theocr. 9.12, τῶ δὲ θέρευς φρύγοντος ἐγὼ τόσσον μελεδαίνω; epigraphically, a sixth-century BC *lex sacra* from Argos, SEG XI, 314.12, has *ho* δ' ἀμφίπολος ⋮ μελεταινέτō (*sic*) ⋮ τοῦτōν). Threatte discards Minon's reading, objecting to μελεδαίνω + genitive as a later use; this objection can be dismissed without too much difficulty since SEG XI 314 just mentioned above (not quoted by Threatte) clearly shows that the use with genitive is already at home in the sixth century BC. More weight attaches to Threatte's reluctance to accept the introduction of a morphological Ionism like μεο into the Attic version (text II).[59] In defence of Minon's ingenious μεο, one might argue that at ll. 17–20 ἐὰν δέ τι πάσχ|ο, μελεδαίνεν μεο| Σιγειές, the stone is speaking *pro parte Phanodici*, an Ionian from Proconnesus, and hence mimetically representing his native tongue (East Ionic). This, though, will not do: apart from the fact that it presupposes a remarkably sophisticated mimetic *Spiel* for a prose inscription of this period, the protasis is introduced by the Attic ἐάν and not by the Ionic ἤν. How, then, should we explain the supposedly Ionic μελεδαίνειν in the Attic part of the inscription, that is in a part of the stele programmatically affirming the Athenian political presence in Sigeum? To adopt Dover's explanation (not mentioned by Threatte, Minon or Luraghi) seems to me much more economical: μελεδαίνω must have belonged to those words 'originally shared by Ionic and Attic but discarded in Attic' at a later stage (*EGPS* 81). That is, 'μελεδαίνειν, "to take care of", found in archaic poetry and Herodotus, seems to have been in ordinary use in sixth-century Attic' (Dover 1973b, 12).[60] Alternatively, the use of μελεδαίνω in the Attic version might be explained as an intentional Attic archaism in that part of the stele (the Attic text) which looked much more like an 'official' rather than a private statement.[61] In this sense, we modern readers seem to share the prejudice of an imagined fourth-century BC Athenian audience: 'Some words which would have sounded to Isaeus and Demosthenes poetic, alien, dialectal, archaic, or affected were part of a common Attic-Ionic stock in the language spoken by

Thucydides and his contemporaries during the first half (at least) of his life' (Dover 1973b, 12).[62]

Another interesting example is the verb ἐπιόψασθαι in *IG* I³ 3.4, a decree datable to 490–80 BC regulating the establishment, by the games-masters (ἀθλοθέται, cf. ll. 2–3),[63] of a competitive festival (ἀγών) in honour of Heracles at Marathon. I give here the text and translation of *IG* I³ 3.1–8 as printed by Stephen Lambert in *Attic Inscriptions Online*:[64]

[Μ]αρ[αθο͂ν]ι hερακλείο[ις τὸ]-
[ν] ἀγο͂ν[α] τιθέναι τὸς ἀ[θλοθ]-
έτας· τριάκοντα ἄνδρ[ας δὲ]
τὸν ἀγο͂να ἐπιόφσασθ[αι ἐκ]
το͂ν ἐπιδέμομ, τρε͂ς ἐκ [φυλε͂]-   5
ς hεκάστες, hυποσχομ[ένος]
ἐν το͂ι hιερο͂ι hός ἂν οἶ[όν τ' ε͂]-
ι χσυνδιαθέσεν τὸν ἀ[γο͂να]

'The games-masters shall put on the competitions in Marathon at the Herakleia. Thirty men shall oversee the competitions, (selected) from those present, three from each tribe. They shall undertake in the sanctuary jointly to arrange the contest in the best possible manner …'

translation by S. Lambert and J. Schneider

In surviving literary texts, the defective ἐπιόψομαι is attested twice in Homer (*Il.* 9.167, εἰ δ' ἄγε τοὺς ἂν ἐγὼ ἐπιόψομαι, οἳ δὲ πιθέσθων, and *Od.* 2.294, τάων μέν τοι ἐγὼν ἐπιόψομαι ἥ τις ἀρίστη), always with the sense of 'I will select', as explained by the relevant scholia.[65] We find it then in Pl. *Leg.* 947c, where we are told that the highest officials of the second-best city, 'the examiners', once dead, will be carried to the tomb by a procession of one hundred young men 'selected by the relatives of the dead' (φέρειν αὐτὴν μὲν τὴν κλίνην ἑκατὸν τῶν νέων τῶν ἐν τοῖς γυμνασίοις, οὓς ἂν οἱ προσήκοντες τοῦ τελευτήσαντος ἐπιόψωνται),[66] and in an anonymous fragment quoted by Phot. *Lex.* ε 1815 Theodoridis = *Suda* ε 2504 Adler (ἐπιώψατο· κατέλεξεν, ἐξελέξατο. ἔστιν δὲ Ἀττικόν· "ὁ βασιλεὺς ἐπιώψατο ἀρρηφόρους", οἷον κατέλεξεν, ἐξελέξατο. Πλάτων ἐν Νόμοις), with reference to the King archon selecting the young girls to carry Athena Polias' symbols in the procession.[67] Both the Platonic passage and the anonymous fragment transmitted by Photius and *Suda* make clear that we are dealing with a word belonging to the language of cult. This is matched by our extant epigraphic evidence: ἐπιόψομαι is attested also in two fourth-century BC sacred inscriptions from Eleusis in connection with the duties of the hierophant (*IG* II² 1933.1, τούσδε ἐπιώψ[ατ]ο ὁ ἱεροφάντης κτλ., and *IG* II² 1934.1–2, ἱεροφάν]της … ἀνέ[[γρ]α[ψεν] τοὺς ἐπιοφθ[έ]ντας ὑφ' ἑαυτοῦ κτλ.).[68] On the basis of these occurrences Wackernagel, more than one hundred years ago, convincingly argued that Greek ἐπιόψομαι does not derive from ἐφοράω 'to oversee' but from an 'uraltes' root ὀπ-, cognate with Latin *op*- of *optare*, 'to choose, to select'.[69] According to Dover (who does not quote Wackernagel), in the text of *IG* I³ 3.3–4 as reconstructed by

Lewis (τριάκοντα ἄνδρ[ας δὲ]|τὸν ἀγῶνα ἐπιόφσασθ[αι) we should apparently take ἐπιόψομαι to mean 'to select for' (i.e. the contest), that is, 'to oversee the contest', and not the traditional meaning of 'select' (*EGPS* 79).[70] Hence ἐπιόψομαι would belong to the 'list of changes which occurred in the language of Attic prose between the sixth century and the mid-fourth' (ibid.).

This interpretation of *IG* I³ 3.3–4 has found widespread acceptance,[71] yet Vanderpool had already proposed the right solution, integrating the end of line 3 not with [... δὲ]|τὸν ἀγῶνα ἐπιόφσασθ[αι but with ἐς]|τὸν ἀγῶνα ἐπιόφσασθ[αι: that is, the board of game-commissioners had to select thirty men for the practical organization of the competition.[72] With Vanderpool's solution we have asyndeton between ἀγῶν[α] τιθέναι τὸς ἀ[θλοθ]|έτας and τριάκοντα ἄνδρ[ας ἐς]|τὸν ἀγῶνα ἐπιόφσασθ[αι, yet the continuity of subject (the 'game-commissioners') makes the transition quite seamless; from this perspective asyndeton seems to me a very minor price to pay in order to make the syntax acceptable without having to postulate an unattested meaning of ἐπιόψασθαι. In this way the sense of ἐπιόψομαι in *IG* I³ 3 does not testify to any semantic shift in fourth-century Attic: as already seen by Wackernagel, the fact that ἐπιόψομαι is attested both in Homer and Attic dialect simply means that Attic had preserved in its cultic language an *archaism* used *also* by Homer (though in a 'secular' way).[73] In this sense the 'Attic nature' of ἐπιόψομαι attested by Σ in *Od.* β 294b1 Pontani = Slater 1986, 194 (ἐπιόψομαι) Ἀττικὸν λίαν φησὶν ὁ Ἀριστοφάνης τὸ "ἐπιόψομαι" ἀντὶ τοῦ ἐποπτεύσομαι, περιβλέψω)[74] and by Phot. *Lex.* ε 1815 Theodoridis (ἐπιώψατο· κατέλεξεν, ἐξελέξατο· ἔστιν δὲ Ἀττικόν κτλ.) is only partially correct: ἐπιόψομαι can be said to be specifically Attic (Ἀττικὸν λίαν) only inasmuch as it was part of the early common *Sprachgut* between Ionic and Attic so dear to Dover's linguistic research.

This of course does not mean that a lexeme must carry the same nuance or belong to the same stylistic register across dialectal boundaries. A good example adduced by Dover is the verb τελέθω. In his introduction to Theocritus' *Idylls* Dover rightly noted that τελέθω, usually perceived by readers of Homer and tragic poetry as pertaining to an elevated register, may have had quite different stylistic connotations for Doric speakers and readers:

> [F]or example, when in [Theocritus' *Idyll*] V.28 the South Italian goatherd prays that the Nymphs may be (τελέθοιεν) gracious to him, he uses a verb which to an Athenian would have been associated with elevated poetry, especially epic. But this verb occurs in a documentary inscription of a Dorian city in South Italy, Herakleia (ὅτι κα τελέθει ψαφισθέν, 'whatever has been voted' [= *Tab. Her.* 1.111]); Xenophon in the *Anabasis* twice puts it into the mouth of a Spartan speaker [Xen. *An.* 3.2.3, 6.6.36]; and Epicharmos uses it (fr. 170.17 [= 276 K–A]) in a passage of dialogue. We have enough inscriptions to show us that different localities differed significantly in vocabulary even in the third century BC, and it would be prudent to assume that perhaps as many as half the words in Theokritos which seem to us 'poetic' when we consider them from an Attic standpoint were not so from a Dorian standpoint.
>
> Dover 1971, xxxix

The *tabula Heracleensis* (*IG* XIV 645, late 4th cent. BC) deals with regulations for the administration by civic authorities of the estates of two temples, one of Dionysus and one of Athena: given the prose nature of the text and its legislative content, the presence of τελέθω as synonym for the verb 'to be' (interestingly in a periphrastic construction) strongly supports Dover's claim that in a Doric speaking area the verb τελέθω did not have a 'poetic' association but was part and parcel of the current spoken language at the time. The case of Epicharmus 276 K–A is, however, less straightforward than it may seem. In this fragment (in catalectic trochaic tetrameters) a person tries to persuade his interlocutor that everything, human beings included, is subject to constant change: tomorrow we shall be a different person from what we are today. The lines which concern us are ll. 11–12:

καὶ τὺ δὴ κἠγὼ χθὲς ἄλλοι καὶ νὺν ἄλλοι τελέθομες,
καὖθις ἄλλοι κοὔποχ' ωὑτοὶ κὰτ τὸν <αὐτὸν αὖ> λόγον

12: <αὐτὸν αὖ> Cobet

(And you and I yesterday were different and we are different now and then different again and never the same according to this same argument)

As remarked in detail by Favi 2020, 223–31, the context of this fragment (for us the first attestation of a way of argumentation known later in the philosophical tradition as the αὐξόμενος λόγος, i.e. 'the growing argument') was most probably parodic: an insolvent person was trying to avoid paying his share for a common meal by resorting to the presocratic (specifically Heraclitean) doctrine of constant flux, thus indirectly lampooning philosophical ideas and language. Epicharmus, an early fifth-century Sicilian playwright, wrote in what is usually described as a literary version of a Syracusan dialect with an admixture of Ionic features of various origins and Italic words.[75] Given that in our lines Epicharmus is parodying Ionic presocratic philosophy, the use of τελέθομες remains ambiguous: it may well be just a Doric word commonly used in Syracusan everyday life as a synonym for the verb 'to be', but the suspicion of parody of Ionic philosophical language by means of an Ionic/Homeric tessera (τελέθω) cannot be ruled out.

Yet Dover was nevertheless right in the broader picture he sketched, as confirmed by one of the most exciting epigraphic discoveries of the last twenty years. Among the oracular *lamellae* from Dodona, we find the following text (Lhôte 2006, no. 2, dated to *c*. 350–300 BC):

[θ]εός. ἐπικοινῶνται τοὶ Κορκυ-
ραῖοι καὶ τοὶ Ὠρίκιοι τῶι Διὶ τῶι Ναί-
ωι καὶ τᾶι Διώναι τίνι κα θεῶν ἢ ἡ-
ρώων θύοντες καὶ εὐχόμενοι τὰ-
ν πόλιν κάλλιστα οἰκεῦεγ καὶ ἀσφα-   5
λέστατα καὶ εὐκαρπία σφιν καὶ πο-

λυκαρπία **τελέθοι** καὶ κατόνασις παν-
τὸς τὠγαθοῦ καρποῦ.

(God. The citizens of Corcyra and Orikos consult Zeus Naios and Diona, asking by sacrificing and praying to which god or hero they might govern their polity in the best and safest way and might have a good and prosperous harvest and enjoy the profit of all the good harvest.)

This tablet, a public consultation by the συμπολιτεία of the cities of Corcyra (a Corinthian colony) and Orikos (Northern Epirus), presents a linguistic profile clearly marked as Doric: retention of ᾱ, nominative plural of the definite article τοί, modal particle κα (though it is impossible to specify whether the redaction is in Corinthian or Epirotic dialect).[76] As Lhôte observes, the verb τελέθω is mainly poetic yet its occurrence in the *tabula Heracleensis* strongly suggests that 'l'emploi inattendu de ce verbe dans la lamelle relève donc plutôt du dialecte dorien de Corcyre que de la tradition poétique' (2006, 32).

Conclusion

This very partial and inevitably subjective survey has not attempted to do justice to Dover's outstanding achievements as a historian of the Greek language. Dover's lifelong interest in the dynamics of interaction and mutual exchanges between literary and documentary texts continues to show us how important it is not to see the language of high-brow literature as totally severed from other, less elevated but not less 'visible' linguistic strata, if we are willing to search beyond the narrow limits imposed by canonical literature. Dover's legacy points us to the benefits and advantages of incorporating inscriptions more systematically into a lexicographical study of Greek which also aspires to be a cultural history of words.

Notes

My sincerest thanks to A.C. Cassio, G. D'Alessio, E. Dettori and O. Tribulato for having read a draft of this paper. Needless to say, I alone am responsible for what I have written.

1. For Dover's role in promoting a discourse-oriented linguistic approach to Greek word order, see Dik 1995, 261–5 and Scheppers 2011, 36–7; see also Cartlidge, this volume. On Dover's enduring fondness for his first monograph, see *MC* 73–4 (esp. 74: 'If I were to be remembered for just one contribution to the subject, I would rather be remembered for *Greek Word Order* than anything else'). Dover 1985 (= *G&G* 43–66) remains to date the standard point of reference for the study of 'abnormal' word order in Greek comedy.
2. For a balanced assessment of the present state of art of studies on colloquialism in Greek, see Collard 2018, 24–30. Register variation in Greek comedy: Dover 1970 (= *G&G* 224–36) and 1976c (= *G&G* 237–48); technical languages: *EGPS*, ch. 6; stylistic features and syntactic patterns in Ionic and Attic prose (literary and documentary): *EGPS* chs 4–5 and 7; for Lysias see esp. Dover 1968b, chs 6–7 (cf. Bers 1984, 5 with n. 16: 'forensic narrative has been shown

to differ from comic narrative in ways that went unrecognized until Dover's research on the Lysianic corpus'). The still unsurpassed importance of Dover's studies on Attic oratory and its 'oral' aspect is clearly recognized by Vatri 2017, ch. 1.

3. Cf. e.g. Willi ed. 2002 and Willi 2003, Colvin 1999b and López Eire 1991, 1996 and 2004.
4. Cf. e.g. López Eire 1994, 1998, 1999a and 1998b, Willi 2010.
5. Cf. Dover 1964b (= *G&G* 95–121) on Archilochus' fictional *persona* (cf. *MC* 78) and 1979 (= *G&G* 1–15) on oral poetic language in Oceanic pre-literate cultures; see also *EGPS* 69–73 on the emergence of oral-like narrative style in Greek prose (the 'additive' style of traditional storytelling), where he draws parallels with Papuan languages that do not have participles, infinitives and subordinate clauses (cf. Dover 1981c, 22–5 = *G&G* 26–8).
6. See Dover 1981d, 7 (= *G&G* 36).
7. This larger preoccupation is already visible in Dover's otherwise fairly technical study of the diction of Antiphon's tetralogies: cf. Dover 1950, 34 (= *G&L* 34), 'Was Antiphon's linguistic development purely his own, or was it in response to changes in general taste in a period of intense linguistic self-consciousness? ... A detailed analysis of the language not only of early speeches, but of dated tragedies and comedies also, would yield beginnings of an answer ... That matters more than Antiphon'.
8. See *MC* 60, 'By the end of my first year back at Oxford I felt sure that I wanted to be a Greek historian, but I did not draw any sharp distinction in my mind between different kinds of history: of politics, of society, of literature, of language'; cf. *MC* 200, 'I have never tried to be a literary critic, but always to be a historian of language and literature', and *EGPS* v, 'I do not profess to be a literary critic at all, but a historian of literature and language'.
9. For Dover's conceptualization of history, see the illuminating remarks by Halliwell, this volume.
10. Cf. also *MC* 59: 'The second thing I learned from Meiggs was never for a moment to forget that the people whose activities I was studying were *real*, and that *I must make every possible effort to put myself into their place*. This I have found an invaluable principle in textual criticism' (my itals).
11. See e.g. Dover 1981d, 14 = *G&G* 41: 'We are dealing here with suspicions and possibilities, not demonstrations, but with suspicions which must be voiced and tested repeatedly if the history of Attic Greek is to be understood'.
12. Cf. *EGPS* 13 n. 15. On Dover and intentionalism, see Güthenke, this volume, pp. 167–8.
13. Cf. *MC* 72–4.
14. See de Jonge 2007, esp. 219–20.
15. The first two sets of italics are mine, the last three Dover's.
16. A choice Dover continued to defend thirty years later in *MC* 74: 'But I do not repent of starting from inscriptions rather than literature.'
17. See already the caveats by Rosenkranz 1930, 130–4. For the existence of a 'natural' word order in ancient Greek rhetorical thought, see de Jonge 2007, 2008 ch. 5 and 2019.
18. Cf. esp. Dover's use of Attic boundary-inscriptions of the late fifth century BC in discussing logical determinants (*GWO* 53–4), of lists of payments in Athenian tribute lists for the analysis of 'multinuclear clauses' (*GWO* 55–6), and of formulae in decrees (esp. prescripts) at *GWO* 56–60; on the complex intradialectal diffusion of lexical and syntactical phraseology in decrees and public documents, see Morpurgo Davies 1999.
19. On contemporary stylistics and literariness, see Jeffries 2019, 674 and Jeffries and McIntyre 2010, 61–5.

20. See *EGPS* 86–7, esp. 87 n. 32, 'Much harm has been done to the study of Greek by the strange notion that consistency in choosing between linguistic alternatives is a virtue and to impute caprice to a great writer is an insult to his memory'. The study by Rosenkranz 1930 remains fundamental.

21. Cf. Dover 1955, 207 and *EGPS* 118–19 on this issue. Instructive also is Dover 1981d, 14 n. 17 (= *G&G* 39 n. 17): 'It seems to me that when λευκωτής, λιθοπριστής and λογιστής are not to be found among the c. 1700 entries in the index of G. Redard, *Les Noms grecs en -της, -τις* (Paris, 1949), nor ληξιαρχικός and λιθουργικός in the index of P. Chantraine, *Études sur le vocabulaire grec* (Paris, 1956), 75 pages of which are devoted to -ικός, something has gone wrong with our approach to the history of fifth-century Attic'.

22. For a recent appraisal of Dover's position, see Willi 2003, 142–5: while recognizing the plausibility that '-ικός spread first in the domain of economics because it was firmly established in ethnic adjectives and the transfer from e.g. Ἰωνικὸς φόρος "Ionian tributes" to ξυμμαχικὸς φόρος was particularly easy', Willi emphasizes how 'the linguistic fashion depicted by Aristophanes went beyond the traditional applications of the suffix -ικός in administrative usage' (2003, 143 and 144). This is certainly true, yet Dover never stated the opposite.

23. For examples from Attic tragedy see *EGPS* 116–17.

24. Ar. *Vesp.* 752–3, κεῖθι γενοίμαν / ἵν' ὁ κῆρυξ φησί 'τίς ἀψήφιστος; ἀνιστάσθω' (Philocleon expressing his desire to be in the law-court 'where the herald says: "Who has not voted? Let him stand up."').

25. Secundus defines poverty as ἀψήφιστον κέρδος, translated by Perry as 'profit not to be reckoned in terms of cash' (Perry 1964, 89 with n. 13, following Holstenius' Latin rendition *divitiae non supputandae calculis*); ἀψήφιστος would mean here, literally, 'uncountable' (cf. LSJ s.v. ψηφίζω A 'to count'). The language of transaction and commerce does indeed permeate some of Secundus' oxymoronic expressions defining poverty (e.g. ἄφθονος πραγματεία, ἀσκόπευτος οὐσία, ἀζημίωτος ἐμπορία, ἀσυκοφάντητον κτῆμα). Yet the Armenian version (Perry p. 116) has, in roughly the same sequence where we would expect the equivalent of the Greek ἀψήφιστον κέρδος, 'a prosperity that no one runs after', which may suggest that poverty is a 'profit not voted for', that is not willingly chosen by anyone. It is curious to note that in early Christian literature (patristic and monastic texts) ἀψήφιστος comes to mean 'humble', 'not worth reckoning in one's own eyes', see Lampe 1971, s.v. For the verbal adjective suffix -τός, capable of conveying both active and passive meanings, see Wackernagel 2009, 177.

26. See Biles and Olson 2015, *ad loc.*, with explicit reference to Dover 1981d, 12. That τίς ἀψήφιστος; ἀνιστάσθω may have been part of the actual formula used by the herald in a law-court had been previously suggested by other commentators for metrical reasons (already Dindorf had noted that the lack of diaeresis in the anapaest may be due to Aristophanes' unwillingness to disrupt a formulaic expression: cf. MacDowell 1971, 234–5), but it is Dover who strengthened the argument by looking at patterns of word-formation.

27. Cf. also Hesych. π 194 Cunningham and Phryn. *Praep. Soph.* p. 102 l. 10 de Borries.

28. Klaus Hallof translates 'wiederverwendbares Eisen' at http://telota.bbaw.de/ig/digitale-edition/inschrift/IG%20I%C2%B3%20386.

29. ὅτι γὰρ τοὺς τοιούτους ἐκάλουν παλιναιρέτους, καὶ τοὺς ἀποχειροτονηθέντας τὴν ἀρχὴν καὶ πάλιν χειροτονηθέντας. The adjective occurs also in Nicostratus, fr. 24 K–A (= Phot. *Lex.* s.v. ο 494 Theod., ὅρμενα· . . . Νικοστράτῳ Ῥήτορι "ἐξωρμενικότες, δυσχερεῖς, παλιναίρετοι", where παλιναίρετοι is Meinecke's correction for the transmitted πάλιν αἱρετοί).

30. Casella 2018, 194–5 includes Harpocration's entry among his juridical glosses.

31. Pl. *Tim.* 82e, παλιναίρετα γὰρ καὶ διεφθαρμένα τό τε αἷμα αὐτὸ πρῶτον διόλλυσι κτλ.; cf. 82c, ὅταν ἀνάπαλιν ἡ γένεσις τούτων πορεύηται, τότε ταῦτα διαφθείρεται. See also Tim. Soph. *Lex. Pl.* π 3 Valente παλιναίρετα· φευκτά, ἔκκλιτα, τὸ ἐναντίον {πρὸς} αὐτῇ τῇ αἱρέσει πάθος ἐμποιοῦντα. σημαίνει δὲ καὶ τὰ †πάλιν αὐτά†· ἐν Τιμαίῳ (82e)· "παλιναίρετα γάρ" φησι "γεγονότα πάντα καὶ διεφθαρμένα".

32. Dobree 1874, 174.

33. 'For if Nous were not by itself, but had been mixed with anything else, then it would partake of all things, if it had been mixed with anything' (transl. after Curd 2007, 23).

34. When aware, he always corrected himself: see e.g. Dover 1981d, 14 n. 20 = *G&G* 40 n. 20 in the case of the false reading ῥ[υ]θμέσει in *SEG* X 142.8 (on which see Dover 1973b, 12). The first editors of the inscription (J.H. Oliver and S. Dow, in *Hesperia* 4 [1935] 1, 15) thought they could read ὅτι ἂν ῥυθμήσῃ τὸ δικαστήριον, 'whatever sum the court determines', thus providing a surprising example in an Attic decree (c. 406 BC) of a metaphorical use of ῥυθμέω, so far unattested. On the basis of a new autopsy of the stele by H.A. Thompson, Handley 1976 showed the correct reading to be the more conventional ὅτι ἂν τιμήσῃ τὸ δικαστήριον.

35. Dover 1981d, 1–2 = *G&G* 31–2; on συγγράφεσθαι, 'to copy down someone else's utterance', see Austin and Olson 2004, 188 (with reference to Dover).

36. Wilhelm's supplement is printed also by Walbank 1978, 302 and Reiter 1991, 272; Walbank 1970, 413 admitted that he could find no adequate parallel for this supplement.

37. Klaus Hallof, at http://telota.bbaw.de/ig/digitale-edition/inschrift/IG%20I%C2%B3%20164, translates ἰᾶσθαι 'als Arzt arbeiten'.

38. *Laws* 933e, ὅσα τις ἂν ἕτερος ἄλλον πημήνῃ κλέπτων ἢ βιαζόμενος, ἂν μὲν μείζω, μείζονα τὴν ἔκτισιν τῷ πημανθέντι τινέτω, ἐλάττω δὲ ζημιώσας σμικροτέραν, παρὰ πάντα δὲ τοσαύτην ἡλίκα ἂν ἑκάστοτε ζημιώσῃ τίς τινα, μέχριπερ ἂν ἰάσηται τὸ βλαβέν ('In all cases where one man causes damage to another by acts of robbery or violence, if the damage be great, he shall pay a large sum as compensation to the damaged party, and a small sum if the damage be small; and above all, every man shall in every case pay a sum equal to the damage done, until the loss is made good', Bury 1926, II 457, slightly modified). Part of the text of the passage is uncertain: I have followed England 1921, II 556.

39. See Saunders 1991, ch. 5.

40. See above, pp. 251, 254–5.

41. In this same direction cf. Bers 1984, 8–9, Willi 2010, 106–8. Rosenkranz 1930 is still the most detailed treatment of the matter (though his focus is more on phonetics, morphology and syntax than on lexicon).

42. Cf. Dover 1970, 8–9 = *G&G* 125–6; 1973b, 12–13; *EGPS* ch. 5.

43. See Dover *EGPS* 91 with n. 58.

44. Cf. e.g. Dover 1981d, 3–5 = *G&G* 33–4; most of the time Dover relied on the fundamental work by Rosenkranz 1930. See more recently Willi 2010, 106–8.

45. Cf. Dover 1963, 17 = *G&G* 298, quoted above at p. 254. See also the methodological difficulties of such a task already identified by Rosenkranz 1930, 129–30.

46. Thumb 1909, 374 with reference to the language of Thucydides.

47. For the dating see Threatte 2015, 108; Guarducci 1961, 167 favoured a dating of c. 550–540 BC (cf. below n. 54).

48. Threatte 2015, 106–7.

49. See Minon 2009, 4–6 and Threatte 2015, 110–11.

50. Either an incorrect spelling of Aisopos with improper aspiration (so initially Threatte 1980, 501) or crasis of *ho* Αἴσοπος (Minon 2009, 102, followed now by Threatte 2015, 118).
51. For a balanced survey of these difficulties, see Threatte 2015, 113–16.
52. Cf. Luraghi N. 2010, 77: 'There is no question that whoever could read one of the two texts could read the other one as well: facilitating understanding was clearly not the purpose of inscribing the text twice.'
53. Cf. Minon 2009, 6, 'la seconde inscription, par le seul fait qu'elle a été écrite dans la langue des bénéficiaires du don et destinataires du monument lui-même, rend manifeste la reconnaissance qu'ils éprouvaient envers leur évergète', and Luraghi 2010, 77 on how in our inscription 'the appropriate local alphabet was a necessary component of such a statement of political identity'. More generally, on alphabets politically exploited to emphasize boundaries, see Luraghi 2021.
54. Guarducci 1961, 167: 'The "translation" of the Ionic text into Attic shows in fact that the Athenians had by then established a stable dominion over the conquered territory and had begun to amalgamate with the local population.'
55. Thus already Fraenkel 1906, 27, who classifies μελεδαίνειν among those denominative verbal formations that '[n]icht attisch, dagegen ionisch, entweder aus alter Zeit überkommen oder aber erst neuionisch sind'.
56. With the exception of late lexicographical sources (Hesych. μ 667 Cunningham, *Suda* μ 472 Adler), μελεδαίνω is attested once in Archilochus (fr. 14.1 W), twice in Theognis (185, 1129), once in Herodotus (8.115), fifty-one times in the *Corpus Hippocraticum* (and three times in later medical writings), twice in Theocritus (9.12 and 10.52) and once in Greg. Naz., *Carm. de se ipso* 975.9 Migne.
57. Minon 2009, 5, 'le verbe μελεδαίνεν ... représente la seule intrusion assurée d'un ionisme non attique en B [i.e., the Attic text]'. At 13–14 Minon explicitly puts μελεδαίνειν among the 'dialectismes lexicaux' together with ὑποκρητήριον (= Att. ἐπίστατον).
58. Minon 2009, 14.
59. Threatte 2015, 119: 'Although μελεδαίνω appears to be an Ionic word, the introduction of an East Ionic pronominal form into the Attic version seems much harsher than the use of a non-Attic vocabulary item and I therefore think it most unlikely'.
60. For other examples by Dover of words originally belonging to the common Ionic-Attic stock, see *EGPS* 79–80.
61. Cf. Guarducci 1961, 166: 'Thus the first inscription considers Phanodikos as a private person, while the second is more concerned with the city in which the stele was set up and can be regarded, to some extent, as an official record'. A further possibility, not explored by Dover and suggested to me by Albio Cesare Cassio, is that, if the Argive μελεταίνω is a conflation of μελεδαίνω with μελέτη, then μελεδαίνω might have been a very old formation shared not only by Attic and Ionic but also by the Argive dialect. That is, there is the possibility that μελεδαίνω might originally have been 'gemeingriechisch'.
62. It is singular that Dover 1950 (= *G&L* 13–35) did not seem to entertain this possibility to explain some of the supposed Ionic lexemes in Antiphon's *Tetralogies*. Cf. Willi's observation on the allegedly Ionic καταδοκέω ('to suspect') otherwise attested in Herodotus: 'If it is true that not every word found in Antiphon is necessarily "good" Attic, why should every word found in Herodotus be "good" Ionic? And how could we ever exclude that καταδοκεῖν was not also used in early Attic, thus merely constituting an "archaism" in Antiphon?' (Willi 2010, 108).
63. On the plausibility of identifying the ἀθλοθέται of *IG* I³ 3 with the Athenian board of ten officials charged with the administration of the Great Panathenaia as detailed in [Arist.] *Ath.*

Pol. 60, see Vanderpool 1984, 296 and Van Effenterre and Ruzé 1994, 24. More sceptical, however, is Lambert, n. 2 at https://www.atticinscriptions.com/inscription/IGI3/3: 'It is unclear how the *athlothetai* mentioned here relate to the Panathenaic ones and whether they are identifiable with the officials for whose appointment provision is made in ll. 3 ff.'

64. https://www.atticinscriptions.com/inscription/IGI3/3?text_type=greek. This is basically the same text as that published by Lewis in *IG* I³ (the text used by Dover), with the only difference that for ll. 1–2 Lambert accepts, rightly in my view, Vanderpool's new readings (Vanderpool 1984, 295–6). The text printed by Lambert in *AIO* is also that of *IG* I³ online (http://telota.bbaw.de/ig/digitale-edition/inschrift/IG%20I%C2%B3%203).

65. Cf. Σ on *Il.* 9.167b Erbse, where the verb is glossed with ἐπικρινῶ, 'I shall select', and Σ on *Od.* β 294b1-c Pontani, where it is variously explained as a synonym for ἐποπτεύσομαι 'I shall oversee' by Aristophanes of Byzantium (on which see n. 74 below), for περιβλέψ-ω/-ομαι 'I shall look around for', for ἐπικρίνω (*sic*) and for ἐκ- and ἐπιλέξομαι 'I shall select'.

66. The Platonic mss have ἐπόψονται: ἐπιόψωνται is Buttmann's correction; Pseudo-Didymus already read ἐπιόψωνται, see [Did.] *De dubiis apud Platonem lectionibus* s.v. ο 19 Valente.

67. In the lexicographical tradition the verb is recorded also by Hesych. ε 5035–36 Cunningham, and *Et.Gen.* AB s.v. ἐπιόψομαι.

68. On the technical, i.e. religious, nature of ἐπιόψομαι, see Burkert 1966, 4.

69. Wackernagel 1913, 261–2 (= Wackernagel 1953–79, II 1238–9); cf. also Wackernagel 1916, 153. Wackernagel could not know of the existence of *IG* I³ 3, first published by Vanderpool in 1942. Kölligan 2007, 256 with n. 727, still derives ἐπιόψομαι from ἐφοράω, ignoring Wackernagel's argumentation to the contrary.

70. Dover *EGPS* 79 n. 2 acknowledges that this is dependent on Lewis's restoration and that there are alternatives.

71. Cf. the incorrect translations by Lambert and Schneider in *AIO* ('Thirty men shall oversee the competitions'), Koerner 1995, 5 ('Dreißig Männer [...] sollen den Wettkampf beaufsichtigen'), and Klaus Hallof ('... dass dreißig Männer den Wettkampf beaufsichtigen') at http://telota.bbaw.de/ig/digitale-edition/inschrift/IG%20I%C2%B3%203.

72. Vanderpool 1984, 296; his translation runs '[t]hirty men are to be chosen (i.e. by the *athlothetai*) for the contest' as if ἐπιόφσασθ[αι were passive, which it is not. Vanderpool 1942, 334–5 had initially proposed a different (and erroneous) reconstruction of these lines.

73. Wackernagel 1916, 153, 'Die Übereinstimmung des Attischen mit Homer beruht also in diesem Falle einfach darauf, daß jenes in seiner Kultsprache eine auch bei Homer vertretene Altertümlichkeit bewahrt hat'. See also Burkert 1966, 4.

74. On Aristophanes of Byzantium's incorrect interpretation of ἐπιόψομαι as ἐποπτεύσομαι 'to oversee', as if derived from ἐφοράω, see Wackernagel 1916, 153.

75. For a most illuminating analysis of Epicharmus' language, see Cassio 2002.

76. See Lhôte 2006, 371 §112. As to the optative οἰκεῦεγ at l. 5, probably from ϝοικεοιεν, see Lhôte 2006, 391 §135.

CHAPTER 15
DOVER ON STYLE
Ben Cartlidge

When I was invited to contribute something to this project about Dover's study of Greek prose, I instinctively reached for a copy of *Marginal Comment* (1994). But *The Evolution of Greek Prose Style* postdates that book, and so we lack the benefit – or constraint? – of Dover's own reflections on the work. Nonetheless, we do learn a lot of importance about Dover's conception of the subject (which *MC* portrays as rather static over time). Another part of my brief was to reflect on Dover's position in modern teaching of Greek prose (and prose composition) at Oxford. Is there a link between scholarship on Greek style and the teaching of prose composition? Anyone who still teaches Greek prose composition today (and there are vastly fewer of us than in Dover's time) is more likely to be concerned that words are inflected correctly; that rules of grammatical agreement are observed; that vocabulary is accurate; and that a range of basic constructions has been used correctly. Prose composition at its most advanced is likely to be an exercise in 'hitting all the targets': every prose should have a purpose clause, a result clause, a number of participles of various kinds, particles at (or near) the start of each sentence, etc. This conception of the practice turns composition into a test of *grammar* (roughly, morphology and syntax). Style, if the question arises, is most likely to be an afterthought – an optional extra.

It was not, however, always thus. Shortly after Dover's election to the Balliol fellowship in 1948, a circle of Oxford dons (including J.D. Denniston, Maurice Platnauer, and Maurice Bowra) brought out *Some Oxford Compositions*, a selection of versions in Latin and Greek prose and verse. In the preface, Tommy Higham states that composition is '*a test* of knowledge gained by reading'.[1] So it is; and therefore we should begin from Dover's account of his own formative reading, ancillary to composition, at St Paul's School. The scale of the school curriculum is almost incredible in comparison with even university syllabuses today: 'three plays of Aeschylus, three of Sophokles, two books of Thucydides, two of Plato's *Republic* ..., most of Theokritos, much of Pindar, and so on ... We also learned by heart half of Euripides' *Hecuba* and most of Vergil's first and fourth *Georgics*'.[2] Around twenty years ago, at a school not dissimilar from St Paul's, we read about fifteen pages of Thucydides (from, of course, Dover's edition of Book 7), the same of Plato, under a book of Homer (absent from Dover's account – or taken as read?) and dialogue portions of under half a Sophocles play. (Enterprises to read more were supported but certainly not demanded.) Prose composition was still a key ingredient, the ambitious among us asking for verse composition and the rules for Greek accents. This detour into autobiography reveals an already archaic-looking syllabus. But it also illustrates a crucial difference between Dover's days and my own in the relationship between composition and reading. Composition, at my school, was the trick of mastering rules that were communicated in the abstract ('ἵνα or ὅπως plus the subjunctive') and being creative in the absence of firm knowledge in a spirit of grammatical entrepreneurship. Far from being a test of reading, composition had little reading to test (and fifteen pages of Thucydides did not always turn up the kind of features useful for the proses we were asked to produce).[3] My experience as a teacher suggests that a common approach to overcome this sort of gap is simply to assume that Greek and Latin are rather similar to English, and to translate as literally as possible in the hope that misplaced exactitude in mapping version to original will be rewarded as much as, or more than, virtuous knowledge. In reality, the exercise requires a further step: to recast the English into a form that can be expressed using Greek syntactic resources.

What might be done to fill the vacuum left by an absence of wide reading, that mysterious source of nebulous insight into what is 'really Greek'? The answer can be sought in scholarship designed to expound by rational means what is otherwise acquired unconsciously by exposure. By refining rules that can be learned and applied regularly, you obviate the need for a process of osmosis that is by definition inexact. In other words, you attempt to define 'style'; furthermore, you attempt to reduce style to a series of principles that can be easily grasped. A distant avatar of this approach is the 'tip', the phrase guaranteed to make stylish versions of wooden ones.[4] The hypothesis of this paper is that something of this sort represents the link between Dover's studies of word order and style and his interest in the teaching of Greek.

Greek Word Order and early studies

The Dover of *Marginal Comment* sets the period of his life when he was concerned with this question of 'style' as 1977–1994 (*MC* 199–204); of course, his other activities have to be supplied from other chapters. But the chapter covers a long period, and the composition of a range of different works. In fact, however, the choice of chronological starting-point is a series of lectures delivered biennially 1977–1985: didactic concerns therefore lie at the root of Dover's conception of what these investigations were for. A number of additional considerations might be brought to bear here. First, Dover may simply have cast around for a subject to lecture on while President of Corpus Christi. On the other hand, these lectures were not simple orations: they were classes designed to provoke discussion and active participation.[5] Furthermore, in a 'stemma' of intellectual interests drawn up by Dover himself in 1993, style has a unique position: not only is the line representing it one of the thickest on the page, but it is fed by more contributing interests than any other subject.[6] 'Epigraphy', 'Thucydides', 'chronology (of the orators)', 'stylometry', 'syntax' and 'Plato's *Symposium*' are part of this nexus. Further didactic concerns of Dover's came out in the first edition of the popular textbook *Reading Greek*, published in 1978.[7] 'Style', then, seems to have involved Dover in a confrontation with more than purely technical aspects of classical scholarship; yet the investigation was calculated to appeal to the combination of technical and historical interests that marked his work generally. The preface to *EGPS* gives a further explicit clue: 'My preaching is confined to the field of method'.[8] If *EGPS* has importance, it seems Dover saw it as an experiment designed to teach us how to investigate these questions. Didactic concerns and 'pure research' are linked by an interest in method: a method that results in testable or falsifiable results is similar in kind to a method that a learner can use to acquire knowledge. If style was a didactic question as well as a research question, methodology was the tool that linked both together.

However, even before 1977, we see some traces of the later preoccupation with prose style. The small school editions of Thucydides 6 and 7 contain a synopsis of Thucydidean stylistic habits; beside orthographical matters, these pay a great deal of attention to syntactic figures, to particles, and to antitheses.[9] However, there is also a clear indication that Dover was thinking in methodological terms, even from his vantage point as an 'historian':[10]

> The inadequacy of our evidence for Thucydides' contemporaries leaves us uncertain how far words which we find in him and in poetry, but not in fourth-century prose, really were at the time recognizably 'poetic'.

That interest in structured difference between text types is a clear forerunner of the remarks in *EGPS*.[11]

Still earlier than the Thucydides editions, Dover had prepared much of this ground in his book *Greek Word Order*.[12] Dover himself names *Greek Word Order* as a predecessor to the later work. Halliwell concurs:[13] 'The nature of linguistic style, both literary and sub-literary, was always a prime interest of Dover's (it forms a thread of connection, for one thing, between his first book, *Greek Word Order*, and his last, *The Evolution of Greek Prose Style*).' Furthermore, *Greek Word Order* shared with *EGPS* an interest in the establishment of 'rules'. In the earlier work we read in the preface that previous scholarship was unsatisfactory, because 'the "rules" which it offers prove inadequate'; in the next sentence: 'Sometimes the rules admit neither of proof nor of disproof'.[14] The sudden disappearance of 'scare-quotes' around 'rules' is significant; indeed, although Dover does not consider the possibility that there simply are no rules of Greek word order 'unscholarly or disreputable', it is plain that his book is written with a conviction that there *are* rules of some kind or other.[15] The same challenge to produce exact statements based on data lies at the root of *EGPS*: 'if the validity of all statements about them [stylistic differences] were founded on the requisite quantification'.[16] Dover is interested in *proofs*, not in intuition; but the stress on data also in effect subordinates literary to historical approaches.[17]

To what extent did Dover break new ground? The idea of dividing Greek words by their possible positions is found in Schwyzer.[18] Earlier, Frisk had already applied a statistical approach to the study of Greek word order, in an attempt to find syntactic conditions.[19] Loepfe, in a study boldly using the recently discovered fragments of Menander,[20] had also made use of statistically founded generalizations alongside close reading of continuous texts. Furthermore, Loepfe had realized that genre – in a rather general sense – was a crucial factor in determining the 'rules' of Greek word order.[21] Loepfe's terminology, distinguishing *Thema* (or *Start*, or 'psychological subject'; in modern terms often 'topic') from *Rhema* (or *Ziel*, or 'psychological predicate'; in modern terms often 'comment'), is discarded by Dover – a position which he later recanted.[22] The most helpful indication, however, of what a scholar in 1960 might have published on Greek word order[23] can be found in the third edition of Humbert's *Syntaxe grecque*.[24] The approach taken by Humbert is, in fact, remarkably similar to the kind of thing Loepfe (1941) already did: a number of sentences are excerpted from Plato's *Gorgias* and studied for their word-order features, usually with an eye on their 'affect'.[25] All the same, Humbert scotches a number of common misconceptions about word order. Relevantly for Dover, Humbert notices that sentence-initial position is often not especially 'emphatic' (being reserved for words such as καί, ἀλλά, etc.).[26] Dover's systematic application of this insight in creating his class of 'prepositives' shows how close he is to contemporary thought on word order, despite the austere manner of presentation. Even if its approach was less revolutionary than might be thought, and even if it did not perhaps make the impression which Dover had hoped for it,[27] there is no doubt that it stimulated further research, and that Dover remained a key figure in the subject's development: he records correspondence with Helma Dik, who published two works on word order.[28] Debate over Greek word order for a time focussed on the distinction between 'non-configurationality' ('free' word order) and 'discourse configurationality' (word order determined by pragmatic considerations); the problems of Greek can now be fitted into ever more wide-ranging accounts of word order in linguistic typology.[29]

It may have been the rise of a new generation of scholars, such as Dik, that refocussed Dover's attention on this kind of subject in the mid-90s and stimulated afresh his interest in problems of style and word order. But in fact the roots of *EGPS* go back much further. A crucial 'absent presence' in a most literal sense is the work of Sophie Trenkner.[30] Trenkner was born in Poland in 1908; her academic career proceeded along rather conventional lines until 1938 brought the disruption of war. Trenkner joined the resistance and was imprisoned. After liberation, she produced a doctoral thesis in Brussels on the Greek 'novella', a further book (on καί) in French and Polish, and a series of reviews for the Belgian journal *L'Antiquité Classique*. Receipt of a grant to study Greek parataxis and prose style brought her to Girton College, Cambridge in 1948, and thence in 1955 to Oxford to work on the *Oxford Latin Dictionary*. During this period, one assumes, she had amassed the materials referred to in *EGPS* vii; Dover records collecting this documentation from Alison Duke at Girton (*MC* 104). But Trenkner's Oxford links were obviously well-established and of personal importance: she credits the influence of Mary Denniston (J.D. Denniston's wife) in finishing the composition of Trenkner 1958. In *EGPS*, Dover acknowledges an initial glance through Trenkner's material in the 70s, and an intention to return to it in the 80s.

EGPS, like *Greek Word Order* many years previously, was stimulated by lecturing on Greek prose style in alternate years between 1977 and 1985, as well as additional performances elsewhere (*MC* 199). This, one can assume, accounts for the inspection of Trenkner's archive, as well as the delay in attending to it in more detail. Presumably, then,

Dover inspected Trenkner's archive shortly before 1977, and had intended to study it more intently after his return from one of his winter visits to Stanford (1988–1992).[31] In the meantime, however, this archive of material had disappeared. It can only remain the subject of frustrated speculation what the possession of these materials might have done for *EGPS*; what is clear from Fehling's notice in *Gnomon* is that Dover's treatment was conducted in complete independence.[32] Nonetheless, the mere presence of this mass of information may have stimulated Dover to take on the project of studying Greek prose by assembling data. And this brings us back round to statistics.

The purpose of statistics

Dover was not the first classicist to present statistical information on the subject of word order, or linguistic subjects generally: Frisk's important book had already done this for word order; even further back, Groot's studies of prose rhythm were full of statistical tables.[33] In *Greek Word Order*, the tables presented words organized according to classifications based on their positions in the sentence. The phenomena in *EGPS* are obviously more varied in keeping with the book's wider scope.[34]

What are Dover's statistical generalizations for? One answer, I suggest, is found in the considerations with which I began my chapter. The statistical generalizations found in Dover's books amount to a way of 'testing reading' without requiring osmosis. Dover – and his students – have at the least a basis on which to say what a 'normal' word order might be, given certain parameters. But *Greek Word Order* also takes the opportunity to call our attention to potential for personal biases even in a matter like this:[35] 'but because most of us who know Greek at all began to learn it as children, and became accustomed to it gradually, we fail to see that the fundamental differences in order between Plato's language and ours are at least as great as that between Sitting Bull's[36] and ours.' Furthermore, Dover's approach can be contrasted with those of his elders and contemporaries.[37] Perhaps the greatest assemblage of classical knowledge and learning from this time was Denniston's *Greek Particles* – itself viewed as a contribution, not to linguistics, but to literature, and a book with which Dover had deeply engaged in the preparation (from Denniston's materials) of the second edition.[38] Denniston wishes the reader 'to *bathe* in examples', to engage not in 'hours of anxious thought' but in 'semi-quiescent immersion', and to exercise 'instinctive judgement'.[39] Denniston's seminal work – probably the most widely cited twentieth-century work on Greek linguistics – has come in for certain criticism on precisely this head.[40] Rijksbaron's *New Approaches to Greek Particles* sneered at Denniston's assumption that intuition and bath-loads of examples added up to secure knowledge.[41] Even if *Greek Word Order*'s statistical approach might be taken as an index of a greater technicality than Denniston had employed in *Greek Particles*, the mastery of exacting linguistic detail is a typical product of a scholar with the kinds of career ambitions Dover had at this time.[42]

Dover's technical approach might be contrasted with the work of his exact contemporary Donald Russell, who in the late 80s and early 90s produced his *Anthology of Greek Prose* and the parallel volume of *Latin Prose*.⁴³ The basis for these books was curriculum reform at Oxford, in particular the construction of an alternative examination to prose composition.⁴⁴ The atmosphere of the *Anthology* and *EGPS* could not be more different, and yet the books in a sense aim for the same goal. Russell works, a little like Denniston, by illustration – allowing the reader to absorb the history of Greek prose style by giving selected examples with some notes to orient the reader in cultural and (particularly) linguistic matters.⁴⁵ After the long introduction to the history of Greek prose, Russell's notes are laconic: a bare reference to a paragraph of a grammar is not unusual; the work's centre of gravity is its Greek texts, not its notes. Russell's two volumes could serve as a kind of textual companion to somebody reading Norden's *Antike Kunstprosa* (on which more below) – the full range of periods and genres is represented, unlike the more concentrated focus of *EGPS*. Russell's reverence for Norden is palpable.⁴⁶ *EGPS* is clearly the more innovative book methodologically, much of which Dover has thought out from first principles;⁴⁷ but it remains true that Russell's *Anthology* is a unique work.

Dover and Russell, however, were in an important respect engaged on a similar mission: how should adult learners be encouraged to read more, and more widely? Russell's answer was to devise a way of making substantial passages of Greek accessible even to the inexperienced.⁴⁸ Dover's was to attempt to specify with ever greater precision what the 'rules' of Greek were, thus obviating the need to rely on a vague sense of 'intuition' or 'how things are done'. Plainly, books such as *Greek Word Order* and *EGPS* are rather too technical for complete beginners; they are however useful for a teacher or textbook-writer wishing to relate his or her teaching to the actual practice of Greek texts – *in usu sociorum*, in an Oxford context. Dover relates two cases in *MC* in which he is exposed to this issue. The first is an encounter with Robin Nisbet, in which Dover can only give *Sprachgefühl* as a reason for preferring one word order over another.⁴⁹ The second is the planning and execution of a new Greek course for use at St Andrews, and ultimately his contribution to the textbook *Reading Greek*.⁵⁰ This was an issue crucial enough to make a significant appearance in the inaugural lecture of Dover's successor as Professor of Greek at St Andrews, Ian Kidd.⁵¹ Time is the premium here. Dover's own course, he estimated confidently, 'would teach first-year university students, in one-third of their time, more Greek than most of them would have known if they had done Greek at school.'⁵² This course depended, not on osmosis from wide reading over a long period, but on actively deriving the rules of the Greek language – including word order, expression and style – from a series of specially devised sentences. These can of course only be devised to begin with on the basis of a study such as Dover (1960), or indeed *EGPS*. In other words, Dover had to begin by really knowing some empirically derived facts, which could then be fed back into his students via his examples. There is thus a unity of purpose between Dover's didactic aims and his research goals in writing about Greek prose style.⁵³ It must be stressed, however, that this does not make his stylistic work *equivalent* either in design or content to his didactic work: the explicit setting out of rules (or, rather, of methods by which to arrive at those rules) was done, as it were, away from student eyes. What the textbooks might then contain draws on those principles and allows the reader to deduce them for her- or himself.

This perhaps comes into clearest focus in Dover's work on *Reading Greek*, for which he composed the texts with Eric Handley.⁵⁴ Here, to produce reasonably authentic texts will have relied on the instincts of two first-rate Hellenists; in Dover's case, this is then tempered by his stylistic researches. Like Russell's *Anthologies*, *Reading Greek* is a textbook linked to curriculum reform – the need to produce a work for adult learners of classical Greek. Dover's earlier attempt at writing a textbook for his St Andrews pupils no doubt informed this experience. But for our purposes, we can see *Reading Greek* as a didactic application of his research into Greek stylistics.

The evolution of *The Evolution of Greek Prose Style*

EGPS sets questions about Greek style into an explicitly diachronic framework. That should not suggest that the book is an annalistic approach to Greek prose; rather, the different sections are individual historical essays about stylistic features: mini histories, if you will. Furthermore, *EGPS* is chronologically rather restricted – not unhelpfully;⁵⁵ but nonetheless this marks out rather clearly what the book is *not* about. Plainly the book is no history on the scale of Norden's *Antike Kunstprosa*.⁵⁶ Norden's project was conceived on a monumental scale, covering ancient prose literature from the beginnings to the Middle Ages. Norden is interested in defining the literary qualities of prose texts; in theory, it could just as well have been entitled 'the evolution of ancient prose'. Norden, however, takes the emic viewpoint: ancient Greek prose literature is described in the terms that the ancients (at least in the rhetorical tradition represented in most detail by Aristotle and Cicero) themselves used. Thus the 'beginnings' of ancient prose are described according to a trio of criteria – Gorgianic figures; poetic prose; rhythmic prose – all of which are motivated by their description in Aristotle.⁵⁷ Dover's approach, quite differently, takes Greek prose as a sample of human language susceptible in principle to the same sorts of analysis as any sample might be – a version of the 'uniformitarian hypothesis' more or less explicitly accepted by modern historical linguists.⁵⁸

Denniston's earlier *Greek Prose Style* is another important touchstone for the scope of *EGPS*, particularly in seeking to understand its diachronic framework.⁵⁹ In general, Dover avoided topics to which Denniston had devoted space.⁶⁰ Nevertheless there is one interesting point of contact in the study of repetition.⁶¹ From the outset, it is clear how Denniston's book differs from Dover's: 'In general, I think, the orators avoid such antitheses as καλός... οὐ καλός.'⁶² This kind of cautious statement of an intuition gained by experience would have been replaced in Dover with a table of instances. Denniston starts from a particular example and does not tell us what other examples 'such antitheses' might cover. Dover, admittedly, begins his chapter with a close reading of a passage of text – characteristically a papyrus text – but then immediately points out that 'it is not simply the recurrence of a lexeme within a passage (how is "passage" to be defined?) that matters, but the size of the interval between occurrences.'⁶³ Denniston's example presumably requires us simply to intuit when a καλός (etc.) is related to an οὐ καλός; for Dover this is too imprecise. In any case, there is a significant difference in how 'repetition' is even understood: for

Denniston, the question is an aesthetic one,[64] and subsequently defined in relation to syntactic and rhetorical categories; for Dover, the question is how repetition should be measured in the first place. Even though some aesthetic categories are canvassed ('the anaphora in Antiphon v. 12 ... is not just a formal pattern, but strengthens the indignation which the speaker hopes to provoke'), Dover's statistical tables are hard to relate to the appearance of such phenomena.[65] One feels Denniston's observations can still be valid without the proofs being advanced by Dover. But we get the sense that 'style' itself is for Dover a problematic category that he must define (perhaps particularly after his rather circumscribed comments in *Greek Word Order*): the 'historian of language and literature' takes 'style' to mean something empirically measurable.[66] As a result, 'style' is a diachronic problem for Dover – changes over time and between texts are the path to illuminating it. Denniston's approach, by contrast, could be termed 'synchronic'.[67]

We can now consider *EGPS* as a work with some kind of research programme: what are its research questions, and what is it trying to establish? In *Marginal Comment*, Dover is apparently dissatisfied with aspects of the theoretical scholarship with which he engages: 'nothing at all which had not already occurred to me' is his dispiriting account of the secondary literature.[68] What were these works? Luckily, he is explicit, naming Nils Erik Enkvist and Roman Jakobson. Enkvist (1925–2009) was a Finland-Swede who established applied linguistics as a discipline in Finland, as well as making seminal contributions to the nascent discipline of discourse analysis.[69] Interestingly, it is now hard to find information about Enkvist other than in Finnish. By contrast, Jakobson remains a major figure in linguistic scholarship; as an illustration, the recent *Bloomsbury Companion to Stylistics* has thirty-five entries for Jakobson in the index, but has no explicit discussion of Enkvist at all.[70] Tellingly, however, another textbook calls attention to Enkvist's application of stylistic methods beyond literary texts; Dover's interest in inscriptions may have found a kindred spirit in this sort of approach.[71] Jakobson was with Nicolai Trubetzkoy a founding member of the Prague School, and thence acquired enormous influence over linguistics as a discipline, especially after his move to New York in 1941.[72] Structuralism needs less introduction than the linguists who pioneered it; but it is worth recalling that Jakobson himself exploited structuralist insights far more widely than only in linguistics.[73] Enkvist, Jakobson and Dover, are, moreover, a group of European scholars with links to the US.[74]

Is there an overall argument in *EGPS*? In fact the book is somewhat loosely structured in form, and very little attempt is made to link the chapters together. The opening chapters give a sense of the problems at issue: the relationship of form and content, and a principle of dividing text into sections.[75] This leads Dover onto the issue of quantification – broadly speaking, the ways in which he will prove his assertions. The remainder is then the meat of the book, thinking about the oral component of literature; the setting; register; and what one might call 'literary embellishment' (variation; prose rhythm). In principle, the book's conclusion could have been that Greek prose did not in fact show any particular 'evolution' in respect of any of these five subjects. Despite the word *Evolution* in the title, this is not a continuous diachronic account, but rather a series of case studies. Of course, if genre is a determining factor for stylistic features, and if the features of a genre are slow to evolve, then it would in principle be unexpected for diachrony to be a crucial factor in the development of prose. Rather the question would be one of different functions of Greek prose style, and whether or not these vary over time. In what follows, I trace some of the subsequent developments in scholarship on these issues, particularly those problems which were foreshadowed in *Greek Word Order*.

Thinking about units of utterance fits Dover into a long history of research on what constitutes a 'unit' in an ancient text. Modern linguists will also happily tell you that defining even something as basic as a 'word' is full of problems. Dover's own approach is rather unique: Greek words belong to one of the classes 'declinable', 'conjugable', 'infinitives' and 'uninflected' lexemes.[76] This is an odd mix: on the one hand, it involves an unusual division of two things a modern linguist might lump together (e.g. by describing declination and conjugation in terms of affixes); on the other it adds a single morphosyntactic category (infinitives) as a separate entity (presumably because infinitives as a category exist on a continuum between substantives and predicates). In grappling with the definition of 'sentence', Dover introduces the term 'MCF' ('main-clause finite-verb unit'); given the agreement (rather uncritical agreement at that) with Fraenkel's methods (though criticisms of Fraenkel's results must have been known to him),[77] it seems peculiar that Dover does not make more use of 'colon' as a unit of analysis, instead preferring to follow the punctuation put in by editors.[78] Dover's linguistic work suffers sometimes from the use of his private technical vocabulary: the introduction of '=S' (presumably to mean 'anything equivalent in syntactic structure to a substantive') is extremely unhappy when the notation NP ('noun phrase') familiar from general linguistics would have done just as well.[79] All this, with less terminological upheaval, is now well-served by work emanating from the Netherlands; one thinks especially of a recent volume on discourse organization.[80] Dover's definitions are perhaps hammers used to crack nuts: by using pragmatic and functional frameworks to think about information structure, rather than about individual lexemes, much of the worry about defining these categories can be avoided. It is in any case not entirely clear what Dover means to achieve by '=S' and 'MCF' – perhaps a kind of grammatical *Verfremdung* from everyday language (and indeed the language of existing grammars of Greek).

A closer approximation to later approaches can be found in chapter 4 ('Speeches, Stories, and Talk') – at least in the final section in which he tries further to quantify Trenkner's 'style καί'. But the chapter as a whole has the curious disjointed character of the book: the thought experiment about what sort of things the earliest prose writers had to say is abruptly abandoned in the search for colloquialism, and thus for speech, which leads us to the quantification of sentences (MCFs) linked by καί. Dover's graphs here are a spectacular reminder of the role that choice played in the composition of literary texts: Herodotus and Thucydides were not bound by laws of necessity to write the way they did. This kind of observation shows that Dover's literary interests are, in a way, applied history.[81] And once again we can see the interest in particles which is part of understanding discourse organization in Greek. Furthermore, Dover's study of colloquial (and non-colloquial) features points to the later interest in register, in recent years particularly stimulated by Andreas Willi;[82] the application of sociolinguistic methodology to Greek comedy is in fact foreseen by Dover: 'the boundary between stylistics and sociolinguistics is – or if it is not, should be made – a fuzzy one.'[83]

Ben Cartlidge

The reception of *The Evolution of Greek Prose Style*

At the beginning of this paper, I stressed the fact that *EGPS* appeared after *Marginal Comment*. In dealing with the reception of the book, it is once again important to recall this. Some of the book's early fate, I suggest, may have been in part coloured by the furore over *Marginal Comment*. Even if the scandal-mongering headlines had died down by 1997, it is fair to record a muted response to the book. I have traced three reviews (only one of which is recorded by *L'Année philologique*).[84] The judgement of one reviewer is decidedly cool: *EGPS* is a 'useful book to own but a difficult one to summarize', has a 'slightly misleading' title, and in sum is called 'a slim volume of *Essays on Greek Language and Style*'. Perhaps most telling is the summary: 'interesting and characteristically unconventional'.[85] The other reviewers are much more lavish with explicit praise: *EGPS* is a book whose 'contribution to an accurate understanding of Greek literature can hardly be exaggerated',[86] and 'a wonderful book.'[87]

Dover's presentation of *EGPS* perhaps obscures his aims: 'evolution' makes it sound like a history, rather than a series of more or less independent studies. The result is perhaps to obscure the usefulness of the book to the commentator. As a control, I have surveyed the volumes dealing with Greek prose in the 'Green and Yellow' series published at Cambridge since 1997:

Author	Date	Title	*EGPS* cited?
A. Bowie	2007	Herodotus 8	n
Hopkinson	2008	Lucian	n
Denyer	2008	Plato, *Protagoras*	n
Hunter / Russell	2011	Plutarch, *How to Study Poetry*	y
Yunis	2011	Plato, *Phaedrus*	y
Hornblower	2014	Herodotus 5	n
Hornblower / Pelling	2017	Herodotus 6	n
E. Bowie	2019	Longus	n
Sansone	2019	Plato, *Menexenus*	y
Herrman	2019	Demosthenes	y
Whitmarsh	2020	Achilles Tatius i-ii	n
Denyer	2019	Plato / Xenophon, *Apology*	n
Huitink / Rood	2019	Xenophon, *Anabasis* 3	y
Pelling	2022	Thucydides 6 and 7 (2 vols)	y

Broadly this selection has ten texts of the 'classical' period and four of Imperial prose. Only six texts in total refer to Dover (five 'classical', one Imperial); since Dover deliberately excluded the Imperial period from his book, the fact that books on Imperial prose have neglected the book is perhaps not surprising. Still, this brief survey suggests that we might, on the whole, have made more use of this book than we have. Commentators have perhaps taken Dover too literally at his word when he states that his aims are methodological.

If commentators did not exploit the book, who did?[88] In 1998, Garrity's paper on Thucydides includes reference to Dover, but one has the impression that the references were added rather late.[89] Part of Garrity's solution to the problems of Thucydides 1.22 (the infamous method chapter) is a comparison to a passage of the *Republic* with similar language – rather a Doverian operation; indeed, Garrity inserts a reference to Dover at exactly this point.[90] The book has not yet been synthesized however.[91] By 2000, things seem to have changed, and Pickering's paper on the *Prometheus Bound* was able to exploit Dover's book methodologically.[92]

Where would a modern scholar begin who wished to investigate stylistics in ancient texts? Dover's labour-intensive start would be obviated by the existence of tools he no doubt welcomed – alongside the *Thesaurus Linguae Graecae*,[93] *Diogenes*, *Perseus*, *Logeion* etc. Perhaps he would now consider that our capacity to search so easily has diminished our *Sitzfleisch*, as well as the importance which we attach to these things. He would perhaps also point out that one cannot search for places where a phenomenon is *absent*, and that careful 'long-hand' reading of a text (or number of texts) is not an obsolete practice.[94] Indeed, it is interesting that Dover's analysis of style begins with self-reflection (*MC* 201) – taking five minutes over a sentence just as he had taken six to twelve hours over a prose composition.[95] Would a modern scholar see his own writing as a matter of stylistics? Perhaps less so. The modern condition of writing in an era of blogs, online posts, and (dare I say) Twitter – rapidly being superseded by the non-textual TikTok as a means of communicative self-expression – is that writing is ephemeral; and in a post-truth age it is more than usually easy to discount what one has said, and particularly the manner in which one said it.[96] Where I suppose a modern scholar might find most interest is in style's interactions with identity – style as a component of identity, or perhaps a style that is imposed by unwelcome societal or cultural constraint.

Future – Tense?

'What was venerated as style was nothing more than an imperfection or flaw that revealed a guilty hand.' Thus Orhan Pamuk, in a chapter of *My Name is Red* significantly entitled 'I will be a murderer', reflects on the dual nature of style: it can reveal more than we bargain for. Is it too glib to suggest that Dover's own rational and statistical approach to Greek style, designed to improve upon what could be gleaned by instinct (*Sprachgefühl*), paradoxically reveals more of his cast of mind than he (or we) might expect? Dover's cool rationalism in linguistics is at least in correlation with a certain dispassionate *froideur* on other issues – at least in his self-portrayal.[97] This may be a conclusion too easily won.

A more difficult and perhaps more optimistic conclusion might be sought by looking to the future. Will prose composition survive, and if so, what for? Entropy applies to grammar teaching as to everything else: I seem to know less grammar than my teachers did, and have little confidence that I manage to inculcate even that much in my students. But on the other hand, any foreign language is a useful code; an ancient language can be still more secure. And in parallel with such an observation, a great deal of recent work in Greek grammar has been distinctively functionalist in nature. An approach that stresses Greek as a communicative system – used by real people in their literature and talk – rather than a baffling and varying rule book,[98] will allow us to rearticulate prose composition as a way of recasting communications, and thereby explore the ways in which Greek texts do the job of communicating.[99]

More recent curriculum reform at Oxford has turned away from the short and varied prose passages of Russell's *Anthologies*, now setting extended pieces of prose (Caesar and Cicero in Latin, Lysias and Xenophon in Greek) for detailed study. In a sense, this looks more like the approach of Humbert (1960) or even Loepfe (1940) to word order discussed above; it is also the kind of approach for which Dover's techniques are helpful. Since students now read a pair of writers in both languages, it should in principle be possible to quantify differences between them. In a recent exercise, my students investigated syntactic (temporal clauses) and morphological topics (comparatives) in Lysias and Xenophon using a comparative approach; the advantage is less of an emphasis on translation and more of a direct journey to the basic meaning of the text, with a concomitant increase in confidence that such an approach is possible. A last glimmer of hope, perhaps: *EGPS* may finally be coming into its own.[100]

Notes

1. Higham 1949, xxxiv (emphasis in original). For similar reflections, see Sargent and Dallin 1900, v: 'All composition in a dead language must be by imitation of forms already, as it were, stereotyped; but that is the best which insensibly recalls the tone of a classical author without either travestying his peculiarities or borrowing his phrases'. In France, something similar seems to apply to J. Carrière, *Stylistique grecque pratique. La phrase de la prose classique* (Paris 1960); see Hudson-Williams 1962.

2. *MC* 37; I am unsure what governed the variation between Dover's transliterations of Greek kappa with *c* and with *k*. An 'Advanced Greek' course at a modern university (Liverpool, for instance, to cite an example from personal experience) would almost certainly envisage covering a single Greek tragedy at most in a semester, with perhaps some prose passages as 'unseens' and for variation.

3. I remember an extremely Doverian discussion about the relative position of ἄν and the verb.

4. Higham 1949, xxx amuses with the relative merits of *utpote qui* and *quippe qui* in the composition of award-winning proses.

5. I owe this information to Stephen Harrison.

6. The stemmatic diagram, reproduced at the end of Halliwell 2011, was a handout for an autobiographical lecture given in Rome and is therefore labelled in Italian; I translate the terms used. It is curious to note that the only line of corresponding thickness to 'style' (or is it merely doubled?) is that of 'Lysias' but that 'Lysias' and 'style' represent different branches of 'stylometry'.
7. For Dover's contribution, see Jones 2007, x.
8. Dover 1997a, v. Compare Poultney on *Greek Word Order*: 'it is a sort of prolegomena to the whole problem of Greek word-order' (1962, 325).
9. Dover 1965a, xiii–xviii; Dover 1965b, xiii–xvii. There is considerable but not total overlap between the two, and the examples are taken from the relevant book in each case.
10. Dover 1965b, xvi. Similar remarks, though much more impressionistically presented, in Dover 1973b, 9–13. The *Greece & Rome* survey on Thucydides is a good counterbalance to a view of Dover that sees him *only* deal in dry quantification.
11. Dover 1997a, 98–9.
12. Dover 1960.
13. Halliwell 2011, 2. But notice that in Dover's 'stemmatic' diagram of his research interests (n. 6 above), *Greek Word Order* is assigned to 'syntax'; 'syntax' in turn feeds the later interest, 'style'.
14. Dover 1960, 1.
15. Dover 1960, 1; an interesting list of possible criteria is given at Dover 1960, 3–4.
16. Dover 1997a, vi.
17. *MC* 200.
18. 'Abgesehen von den satztonlosen (enklitischen, proklitischen) Wörtern, einzelnen Konjunktionen, dem bestimmten Artikel kann jeder Satzteil seine Stelle verändern'; Schwyzer and Debrunner 1950, 691–2.
19. Frisk 1933.
20. Loepfe's work on Menander was taken up later by Svensson 1986, which uses a still subtler (though less convincing) psychological apparatus to explain word-order variation.
21. Loepfe 1940, 13–14.
22. *MC* 74.
23. It is intriguing that a study very similar in scope and technique to Dover's appeared two years after *Greek Word Order* treating word-order variations in Middle English: Świeczkowski 1962 (not widely cited, but see discussion in Bech 2001, 16; Bech's thesis and subsequent work show clearly how far things have come in this area). Its themes – the relative position of subject and predicate; the predicate's position in the clause; the position of the object – are highly reminiscent of Dover's interests, as is its relatively compact scope. It also uses a complex series of notations and is even richer in statistical tests than Dover. One interesting point of difference is the adoption of an *a priori* definition of 'emphasis' (Świeczkowski 1962, 8) quite different from the sceptical presentation at Dover 1960, 32–4. Świeczkowski does not cite Dover, but the two works plainly arise from a similar attitude towards scholarship on word order.
24. First published in 1944; the edition of 1960 was the third edition but had seen very little change since the second.
25. Humbert 1960, 92–9, e.g. 94: 'l'indicatif dans la phrase: Λείπεται δὴ ἐκεῖνος μόνος ἄξιος λόγου doit être traduit en soulignant la place *insolite* du verb' (emphasis in original).
26. Humbert 1960, 93.

27. *MC* 74. My own sense is that *Greek Homosexuality* eclipsed *Greek Word Order* in determining Dover's subsequent reputation. The *TLS* review calling the book 'meagre and gritty' (*MC* 74) seems simply not to exist; the *TLS* for 10 February 1961 has a brief factual summary of the work's scope (a notice in 'books received' rather than a review). The *TLS* reviewer was identified by Dover (in supplementary notes to his memoir: I owe this information to the Editors) as W.B. Stanford, but his review appeared in *Hermathena* 96 (1962) 112 and termed the book 'far-reaching and valuable, though some may wish that it was less condensed and formulaic' (was it 'condensed and formulaic' that Dover, always sensitive to criticism, 'reworked' in his memory as 'meagre and gritty'?). Beattie 1962 is a balanced account of the work's novelty.

28. Dik 1995 on Herodotus, on which see Matić 2003; and Dik 2007, on which see Probert 2010 with an interesting comparison to the study of Baechle 2007. The study of Greek word order, it seems, is alive and well.

29. For (non-)configurationality in Greek, see Luraghi (S.) 2010, and compare Humbert 1960, 92. For a recent overview of problems in word-order typology, see Dryer 2004; to read this chapter while considering its applicability to ancient Greek is an instructive exercise in some of the problems faced by anyone attempting to describe ancient Greek word order in detail.

30. On Trenkner's life, see Gałęzowski 2008; I owe this reference to Graham Whitaker, whose forthcoming work on female classical scholars will be a further key source.

31. *MC* 199; in the event the spell at Stanford, alongside graduate teaching, was mostly spent in preparing the edition of *Frogs*.

32. Fehling 1972 gives the subjects of the data as 'Asyndeton, Satzverbindung (besonders καί), Wiederholung, Gnomik und Oxymoron'. For asyndeton, see Denniston 1952, 99–123; Dover 1997a, 44 refers the reader to Denniston's treatment. For repetition, see Dover 1997a, 131–43 and Fehling 1969; Denniston's work on repetition is discussed further in my text at pp. 277–8. *Satzverbindung* is the subject of Trenkner's own posthumous work (Trenkner 1960). *Gnomik* and *Oxymoron* take us out of stylistics into rather more literary territory. At the very least, this must have been a considerable mass of material.

33. Frisk 1933; de Groot 1921. An even earlier statistical approach can be found in Zieliński's study of Latin prose rhythm (1904). Both Frisk and Dover were influences on Lilja 1968, 52–72, whose work, while solid, selected an intractable corpus of quotations of early prose; Dover 1997a, 86 addresses some of the problems.

34. They are moreover useful bases for comparison. Cartlidge 2014, 218 applied Dover's methods for studying deictic -ί (Dover 1997a, 63–4) to Menander; the result established that Menander used the forms less frequently than Aristophanes, but more than the fourth-century prose authors studied by Dover.

35. Dover 1960, 6.

36. The point of comparison in the previous sentence was between Native American languages and European ones.

37. For the contemporary interest in this kind of inquiry, it is curious to note that the hero of the David Lodge novel *The British Museum is Falling Down* (1965) is a linguist engaged on a study of 'long sentences' in English literature, involving a great deal of collection and tabulation. Lodge's character, inspired by his experience as an academic, may reflect something of the spirit of research in this period; it is tempting to speculate that this played a role in Dover's selection of the book to demonstrate a point about style at Dover 1997a, 2–3.

38. Dover, 'Preface', in Denniston 1954, iv.

39. Denniston 1954, vi.

40. Knight's review ended prophetically: 'There are, however, likely to be few, if any, greater works of scholarship in our generation' (Knight 1938, 494).

41. Rijksbaron 1997, 2–3. See already Bolling 1935, 260: 'Denniston's interests are frankly literary … [H]e has had to treat a linguistic problem. Its treatment would have gained had it been handled as a scientific task, rather than as a literary adventure.'
42. Dover declined the Regius chair at Oxford in the same year *Greek Word Order* appeared; it is just about safe to assume however that when he wrote the lectures, he still had a move back to Oxford in mind: see *MC* 84–5.
43. Russell 1991. It is worth underlining the production of the Latin book, as this was an area of Russell's expertise that Dover was keenly aware he could not match.
44. Stephen Harrison (p.c.) reminds me of this. When I was an undergraduate, the alternative to prose composition – linguistic commentaries on passages of prose – was still simply known as 'the Russell paper'.
45. The same could also be said of Denniston 1952, which gives long prose extracts in illustration of its points. It is telling for changes in Classics that Denniston (or his amanuensis) did not translate the examples, while Rutherford 2012, which also quotes extensively, does.
46. Richard Rutherford (p.c.) drew my attention to this.
47. Sansone 1998 gives a particularly valuable account of this.
48. Russell's preface to his edition of Dio Chrysostom (1992) has a similar readership in mind; on the *Euboicus* he remarks (vii): 'I recall using it many years ago as a confidence-building text with first- and second-year undergraduates'.
49. *MC* 73; Dover 1960, v. For Nisbet, see Harrison 2014.
50. *MC* 128–30.
51. Kidd in Ayres 1995, 3: 'Each new incumbent faces different problems, and one of the most pressing which did not tax my predecessors arises form [*sic*] the now rather precarious existence of Greek in the schools … I consider it of prime importance that we at University should teach beginners and persuade students that they will lose little and gain much by starting Greek studies at University.'
52. *MC* 129. See Craik, this volume, for the challenges of this course.
53. Cf. *MC* 79 for the synergy of his teaching and research. One might entertain a doubt about whether the 'pedagogic zeal' to reply to Adkins' criticism of *Greek Popular Morality* (*MC* 165) is reported in entirely good faith; *MC* 164 (!) reports his desire always to have the last word.
54. See Jones 2007, x.
55. Richard Rutherford suggests to me (p.c.) that Dover kept away from Plutarch (1997a, vi) in deference to Russell – a tempting hypothesis.
56. Norden 1958, first published in 1898. For a brief assessment see Schröder 1999, 16–17; for the influence of this work in Italy, see Calboli 1994; for a contextualization of Norden's career see Lebrecht Schmidt 1995 (useful bibliography at 134–5 n. 85), and for a study of the rhetoric of Norden's history, see Zanker 2014. Dover does not name Norden as such, but his remarks on the genesis of *EGPS* (*MC* 199: 'not attempt to follow the entire history of the genre down to the end of the Eastern Roman Empire') make it plain that the model exerted some weight on his mind.
57. For Norden's use of terms from the ancient rhetorical tradition, see Cancik and Cancik-Lindemaier 1994. Russell 1991, xxiii–xxix takes a very similar approach.
58. For an explicit statement, see e.g. Ringe and Eska 2013, 30–1.
59. Denniston 1952.
60. Dover 1997a, vi.

61. Denniston 1952, 78–98; Dover 1997a, 131–59.
62. Denniston 1952, 78.
63. Dover 1997a, 133.
64. Denniston's first subheading in the chapter is 'Effectiveness of repetition' (1952, 79).
65. Dover 1997a, 135–7.
66. *MC* 200. See Bowie, this volume, for an illuminating reminiscence by Nick Denyer on this subject. Dover's approach to literature more generally reflects a similar problem: 'literature' must somehow be related to some specific set of features, as for instance when Aristophanes' speech in *Symposium* is turned into a 'folk-tale'.
67. Rutherford 2012 in some respects is also a 'synchronic' examination of tragedy, taking the genre as a whole and reading individual passages in detail rather than quantifying distinctions between individual tragedians.
68. *MC* 199; related wording in Dover 1997a, vi.
69. Enkvist 1967 and particularly 1973 (cited in *EGPS* along with a further paper, 1 n. 2) are probably the works most relevant for Dover.
70. Sotirova 2016. Jeffries and MacIntyre 2010 do refer occasionally to Enkvist.
71. See Jeffries and MacIntyre 2010, 1, with Prauscello, this volume, for the importance of Dover's interest in inscriptions.
72. On the Prague School, Raynaud 1990; for some of Jakobson's influence on linguistic scholarship in the UK, see contributions by Aitchison, Quirk and Smith in Brown and Law 2002; other contributions to that volume show the importance of other members of the Prague School, particularly André Martinet and Nicolai Trubetzkoy.
73. The voluminous *Selected Writings* (1966–90) have volumes on language and poetry (vol. III) and comparative mythology (vol. VII) as well as more standard linguistic applications.
74. Jakobson emigrated to America in 1941; Enkvist was associated with Purdue University, Indiana, from 1985, and was in 1994 to receive an honorary degree from Indiana University (https://honorsandawards.iu.edu/awards/honoree/424.html accessed 20/7/21). *Marginal Comment* records a host of speaker engagements and job opportunities offered him from America (the Sather Professorship, of course, but many others also).
75. Dover is curiously unengaged with Fraenkel's famous series of papers beginning with *Kolon und Satz* in 1932, best accessed in Fraenkel 1964, i 73–139 (see a note of approval at 1997a, 40 n. 37). Turner's paper on questions in Menander faced a similar issue, which Turner solved with the claim that 'if a piece of Greek can be taken as a question, it *should* be taken as a question' (Turner 1980, 5); unfortunately this stricture is both impossible in principle and disregarded in practice; it is however an instructive indication of some of the problems inherent in attempting to define a 'unit' in a Greek text.
76. Dover 1997a, 26–7.
77. Dover 1997a, 40 n. 37.
78. Fraenkel 1965, 71–2 presents some examples of editorial failings in this regard. On the development of 'colon'-theory in Greek syntax, see Scheppers 2011.
79. Since an NP can be further defined with reference to its constituents, Dover cannot claim that the peculiarity of Greek noun phrases (e.g. complex articular infinitives such as τὸ πάντας τοὺς ἀνθρώπους τἀληθῆ μὴ εἰδέναι) renders the term unworkable. In my copy of *EGPS* I have several times had to remind myself in a marginal note that '=S = NP'.
80. Wakker and Bakker, eds, 2009.

81. See *MC* 200.
82. Willi 2003; and see Dover 2002.
83. *MC* 203.
84. By contrast, *Greek Word Order* has some twenty reviews recorded by *APh*. The lack of notice of *EGPS* in *Greece and Rome* is striking, given the general audience targeted by that journal (and given that Dover's other productions in this period, such as the *Frogs* commentary, are reviewed there).
85. Colvin 1999a, 177.
86. Engel 2000, 229.
87. Sansone 1998.
88. In what follows I consider some papers which a Google Scholar search turned up as engaging with Dover. I have selected those which reveal something about the book's scholarly reception. No scholar is obligated to cite any other scholar, and if I puzzle over omissions, these should not be read as criticisms of these pieces of scholarship in the round.
89. Garrity 1998. One wonders, frankly, whether Dover had been a referee for the journal, particularly as he is not in the acknowledgements. But Garrity may simply have come across the book late in the process as 'the state-of-the-art'.
90. Garrity 1998, 370–2, and see 372 n. 21; compare Dover 1997a, 5–10, still a wonderfully instructive passage for undergraduates to examine.
91. A surprising omission in the literature review at Garrity 1998, 377 n. 26.
92. Pickering 2000, 81, see Dover 1997a, 133–4. The fact that Richard Janko supervised this work (see Pickering's acknowledgements) may be significant, as Janko has also exploited statistical reasoning in his research; see Janko 2012, 21–5 for some discussion.
93. *MC* 120, with 119–22 for Dover's own experiments in computer processing. The preface to Dover 1968b strikes a much more sceptical note about the value of computers for this kind of work. This may account for the absence of reference to Dover's work in Ledger 1989; see also Usher and Najok 1982 for criticism.
94. For an application of this principle, see Dover 1997a, 98–9.
95. *MC* 67. On introspection in linguistic studies, see Dickey 1996, 34.
96. See Oborne 2021 for a recent study of this.
97. The notorious passage on his impotence at *MC* 242–3 is only one of many.
98. My Greek teacher, Tim Reader, used to recall an occasion on which he asked a colleague τίνες εἰσὶν αἵδε αἱ γυναῖκες; – thereby eliciting the information without needing to whisper.
99. Stephen Halliwell reminds me of Dover's interest in the 'reality' of ancient Greeks (e.g. *MC* 39, 59; interestingly in both passages the insight is communicated from an inspiring teacher: Russell Meiggs and Eduard Fraenkel). I do not mean to suggest that functional approaches would have been antagonistic to Dover.
100. My thanks to Richard Rutherford, Chris Stray and Stephen Halliwell, who patiently read a first (and far from camera-ready) draft, and offered a great deal of encouragement, information and feedback. Richard Rutherford allowed me to see a copy of Dover's 1977 handout on Greek prose style; I am grateful for this, and for his support as a colleague at Christ Church, Oxford, where this was written. More specific acknowledgments are made in footnotes in the relevant places.

EPILOGUE

CHAPTER 16
DOVER AND THE PUBLIC FACE OF CLASSICS
Stephen Halliwell

I suppose that up to the first World War British upper-class and middle-class society was extraordinarily confident of its own values. It knew what it wanted from the Classics, and it exploited them in order to sustain its values. Now, especially since the Second World War, this self-assurance has given way to self-doubt, humility and guilt; we do not now 'exploit' the Classics, because we are not agreed on the ends to which the study of Classics is a means.[1]

This epilogue offers some critical reflections on the way in which Kenneth Dover's distinctive intellectual values informed his (evolving) conception of Classics as a discipline in an age of transition. My material will be drawn principally from a series of pieces which Dover wrote at the height of his academic career, in the 1970s and 80s, for non-specialist audiences, or at any rate on occasions which called for something other than exercises in primary research:[2] his Presidential address to the Classical Association in 1976; a lecture to the 7th Congress of the International Federation of the Societies of Classical Studies (FIEC) in Budapest in 1979 (but not published till 1984); a 1985 lecture, 'What are the "two cultures"?', delivered at Rougemont School in Wales;[3] and a short article for an Italian magazine in 1988, 'Il valore degli studi classici' (translated here in an appendix), which borrows from the 1979 and 1985 lectures but contains a few revealing details of its own. The first and third of these items were reprinted in *The Greeks and their Legacy*. The second lecture supplied (or, rather, given the chronology of composition, it incorporated) some passages which are also to be found in the introductory chapter to *The Greeks*, the book which accompanied the ill-fated 1980 series of BBC TV programmes of the same title.[4] Finally, some of the formulations adopted in the Italian article found their way into *Marginal Comment*, which itself provides a certain amount of additional material pertinent to my argument.

The four pieces I have selected were not, of course, Dover's only writings for non-specialist audiences. In fact, it is important to remember that he thought of several of his books (with whatever degree of hopefulness) in that same light, including *Aristophanic Comedy*, *Greek Popular Morality*, and, not least, *Greek Homosexuality*. But my focus on these four items will allow especially close attention to some of his more carefully calculated pronouncements in his role as a high-profile spokesman (probably not a term he himself would have used) for the discipline of Classics. It will also enable me to probe certain salient features, including points of tension, in Dover's self-presentation as a classical scholar. These features include his unequivocal repudiation of any exceptionalist justification for the educational and cultural value of Classics, a type of justification to which he was exposed in his education at St Paul's and which was prevalent in the subject's public self-image in the first half of the twentieth century; his consistent avoidance, in contrast to, for example, Eduard Fraenkel and E.R. Dodds, both of whom Dover greatly admired (if with eventual reservations in the case of the former), of a defence of Classics as a normative vehicle of humanism[5] (a term nowhere employed with endorsement in Dover's entire *oeuvre*); his attraction to a compound model of research in the humanities (a term Dover *was* happy to use, but without the idealizing force of 'humanism'), partly quasi-scientific, partly anthropological, partly comparatist; and, finally, his determination, in the wake of the debates triggered by C.P. Snow's Two Cultures thesis, to make 'history', in a deliberately expanded sense, into the master-concept of the humanities.

Bearing those points in mind from the outset will help us to negotiate a recurrent trait of Dover's work, namely its somewhat paradoxical combination of methodological self-reflectiveness with a marked aversion to sustained theorization of his practices or his values as a scholar. Dover saw 'theory' as conflicting with empiricism, though there is no shortage of those who perceive such conflict the other way round.[6] His aversion applied equally to abstract reasoning insufficiently anchored in documented experience and to wholesale theoretical systems – those boasting a 'comprehensive power' – such as Marxism, structuralism, and (despite some peculiarly personal interest in it on Dover's part) psychoanalysis.[7] What he allows himself, by contrast, are limited, local formulations of the methodological principles he brings to bear on specific problems. The result is a body of writings which stands self-consciously at a distance from the proliferation of 'theory' of various kinds which became general in the humanities, and not least Classics, in the later decades of the twentieth century. Dover's habit of offering discrete, unintegrated statements about his presuppositions, aims, and modus operandi might now strike us as frustratingly curt and under-elaborated, though I hasten to add that how things strike us now does not constitute a definitive viewpoint from which to consider the matter. To take just one token instance, it is remarkable to read in the Preface to *Greek Popular Morality* that rather than organize his material on the basis of a systematic treatment of Greek terminology or categories, he has taken 'a quite deliberate decision . . . to formulate such questions about morality as were prompted by my own moral experience'.[8] What rationale of historical scholarship could explain this ostensibly back-to-front decision, which goes beyond a mere acknowledgement that his own experience has (inevitably) impinged on his thinking and appears to give it a formative function in the entire project? In the immediate context, we are simply not told, though informed readers would at least recognize the implicit divergence from the model of the history of moral ideas (a model which posits a gulf between ancient and modern thinking) promoted by Arthur Adkins, a *bête noire* for this part of Dover's work.[9] By focussing here on a group of pieces in which Dover allowed himself to ponder his guiding intellectual principles at more discursive length than in his major research publications, I hope to be able to clarify this aspect of Dover's cast of mind.

Dover's standing as a prominent spokesman for Classics did not, of course, come into being overnight. It emerged gradually from the reputation he acquired within the discipline, and in due course from the institutional positions that followed from that reputation, including his presidencies of the Hellenic Society (1971–4), the Classical Association (1975–6), Corpus Christi College, Oxford (1976–86), the British Academy (1978–81), and JACT, the Joint Association of Classical Teachers (1985–7). How far Dover sought such a status, how far it was 'thrust upon' him, is a nice question which must be sidestepped here. But it is worth reflecting that when Dover left Balliol in 1955 to take up the chair of Greek at St Andrews, he was aware that he was moving to an educational and cultural environment where Classics in general and Greek in particular held a less privileged, safeguarded position than they did in Oxford. It was not the case, for sure, that their position in Oxford itself was impregnable. The percentage of all Oxford finalists represented by Literae Humaniores in 1948 was only half what it had been twenty-five years earlier, not least as the result of a diminishing role for Classics in the (public) school system.[10] Donald Russell, who became a fellow of St John's in the same year in which Dover became a fellow of Balliol (1948), recalled that in the post-war context there were even those who expected Classics soon to become a small fringe subject; anxieties on those lines were shared, among others, by Dodds.[11] Nonetheless, any classical scholar who had wanted to find as sheltered an academic home as possible would not have chosen to leave Oxford in 1955, still less to decline the opportunity to return there as Regius Professor of Greek in 1960. So there is an important sense in which Dover was ready to face the challenge in 1955 of moving to a more exposed part of the landscape of classical education in Britain. This is borne out by his subsequent involvement in initiatives to widen access to Classics at university level, including his introduction of an *ab initio* Greek stream (for which he wrote his own coursebook) at St Andrews in 1967, and his active membership of the advisory panel for the JACT *Reading Greek* project from 1974 onwards.[12]

By the time, then, of his appointment as President of the Classical Association for 1975–6, Dover not only had an international reputation as a philologist – he had given the Sather Lectures at Berkeley (which also offered him a chair) in 1967, and had already published ten books – but occupied a position which gave him the potential for considerable influence in shaping public perceptions of Classics. He called his Presidential address, delivered at Aberystwyth in April 1976, 'On writing for the general reader'. The title signals a concern about how Classics could sustain a significant function in the wider culture at a time when school and university enrolments in the subject's traditional degrees were continuing to fall. Since Dover starts by noting that the falling numbers of students in language-based programmes were offset both by rising numbers on Classical Civilization, translation-based degrees, and by the increasing popularity of books about the ancient world for the 'general reader', one might have expected him to mount a defiantly positive case for the resilience, adaptability and even the buoyancy of the subject in its various manifestations. One might also have expected at least an acknowledgement of the importance of translation, a subject which Dover pondered in other contexts but scarcely mentions here.[13] Instead, he strikes a somewhat defensive and, to my mind, unusually awkward posture.[14] This was probably in part because he was aware of stubborn resistance to change in certain quarters; hence his willingness to confront the hypothetical objection, 'why should we change at all?', together with a caustic suggestion that some classicists' anxieties about the writing of 'amateurs' might reflect an instinct of threat towards their 'social and cultural privilege'. For all his academic experience, and indeed the attention he had already paid, as both author and reviewer,[15] to the challenges of writing for the general reader, this was the first time Dover had had to nail his colours to the mast in a public forum. At this stage, he seems to be feeling his way towards the formulation of principles with which to build a bridge from the technicalities of specialist scholarship to the maintenance of a reading public interested in serious writing about classical antiquity. And just beneath the surface of the uncertainty of tone in this Presidential address is actually, I suspect, a lack of confidence in the extent of that reading public.[16]

Having posed the overarching question of what professional classicists should do in the prevailing climate, and having introduced a distinction between prudential or instrumental considerations in defence of historical study (as 'means to an end') and the more personal 'value' of such study to individuals,[17] Dover frames most of his argument as a matter of 'problems' to which practical solutions need to be found. What emerges from his wrestling with these problems is the following series of contentions: first, that it is vital not to misrepresent antiquity as in agreement with modern attitudes and concerns, nor to assume complacently that 'the present knows better than the past' (one version of presentism); second, that while stereotypes of the aridities of classical scholarship are sometimes justified, they often reveal misunderstanding of the significance of small (linguistic) details for the construction of larger explanatory hypotheses; third, good writing for the general reader should aspire to promote an improved understanding of the relationship between what Dover calls scholarly 'process' and 'product'; fourth, and finally, that there is no escaping the importance in Classics of 'the precise and subtle interpretation of language', a claim not to be reduced to a pedantically linguistic credo but which carries with it a weightier conception of historical and literary hermeneutics, as confirmed by Dover's passing remark (a criticism, by implication, of narrow *Wortphilologie*) that it is possible even for a 'good grammarian' to 'disastrously misinterpret' texts.[18]

There is the skeleton here of convictions that we will see developed and modified in later publications. But there is also, as I have noted, a general air of defensiveness, including the admission that Dover feels an 'unusual degree of agitation and indignation' (rather atypical vocabulary for his professional writings) over 'amateur' distortions of antiquity, of which, however, he gives no immediate examples.[19] This defensiveness is compounded by the fact that Dover's formulation of the 'prudential' importance of historical study, a tenet so crucial to his later intellectual stance, employs an infelicitous metaphor of history as a 'feed-pipe' from past to present, with historians themselves as the 'pipes' conveying information, or at any rate 'hypotheses', about a changing body of 'data' (in Dover's quasi-scientific lexicon, though here offset by the concluding insistence that history, including Classics, 'is not a science').[20] This ostensibly mechanical model not only lacks the enrichment of anthropological and comparatist dimensions which Dover will later stress; it is also difficult to square with his eventual attempt to make 'history' embrace everything in the humanities, including interpretation of art, literature, and systems of cultural values. At the same time, the reductive 'feed-pipe' model is partly counterbalanced by an eloquent statement of personal motivation: 'To value linguistic phenomena not for their utility as means to a non-linguistic end but precisely for their self-sufficient particularity, as one might value a tropical beetle or the movement of a bear, is one way of loving life'.[21] This passion for language remains distinct from, though it might well underpin, that need for 'precise and subtle interpretation of language', cited above, which Dover regards as an indispensable instrument of historical (including literary) study. But it is also said to be something that the 'general public' mostly does *not* share, so that it counts as part of the problem of how to satisfy Dover's desideratum of making good scholarly writing for the latter convey a sense of how 'process' contributes to 'product'. On one reading, then, the lecture might be thought to leave us with the paradoxical subtext that Dover's most precious intellectual value is a barrier to his hope of communicating effectively, as a classicist, with a wider audience.

*

If the 1976 Classical Association address betrayed a degree of unease in its view of how professional classicists should conceive of their relationship to society in a period of major cultural changes, Dover evidently continued to ponder such issues. In the following year, while completing *Greek Homosexuality*,[22] he started planning a popular book on the Greeks to accompany the BBC TV series mentioned earlier. He drew on some of the material for that book when he lectured at the 7th FIEC Congress in Budapest in 1979. Although his title, 'Archaic Greece and the continuity of ancient civilization', does not indicate a concern with contemporary issues, his lecture actually starts from what he describes as an increasing tendency, even among the educated, to question the use, value and justification of Classics. He immediately states his own preference for a short, 'deictic' answer – in effect, look at how good Greek literature and art are – though he is careful not to say (and he did not believe) 'how much *better*' than anything else.[23] This answer, as he admits, depends on a higher-order premise about the value of literature and art in general, but a premise he does not attempt to defend. Instead, he spells out two further justifications. The first is that it is possible to 'learn directly' even from a culture remote in time, and to apply what one learns to one's own life. This proposition, reinforced with the semi-confessional remark that 'some of us' have found that 'acquaintance with distinctively Greek attitudes ... has helped us to live', is not elaborated any further at this juncture. It might seem superficially tempting, given Dover's lifelong fascination with Thucydides, to call this a personalized Thucydidean justification for history. But it remains acutely uncertain whether the 'usefulness' Thucydides famously ascribes to history (1.22.4) is really a matter of 'learning lessons' at all (in a pragmatically positive sense), rather than the acquisition of a deeper understanding of why human affairs go so badly wrong in similar ways in different historical settings.[24] When we come later on to examine Dover's most mature thinking about the rationale for the study of history, we shall see that while he retains some form of the idea of learning from history, he also adopts an arguably unthucydidean view of the latter as consisting of unique particulars, not event-types that can be observed to recur in different contexts.

The second reason Dover advances for (part of) the value of Classics stems from a familiar-looking claim that ancient Greek culture was the first – at any rate, he is careful to add, the first in the Mediterranean and Near East – to exhibit certain phenomena, including democracy, critical historiography, religious scepticism, and drama. The remainder of the lecture is taken up with a selective attempt not just to fill out this claim by a series of comparisons between Greek attitudes and practices and those of the Near East, especially Egypt and Mesopotamia, but to characterize an explanatory factor he thinks common to all the Greek phenomena in question, a factor he identifies (with an acknowledgement of simplification) as an 'unprecedented *irreverence towards authority*' [his itals] in religion, politics, art, historiography, and science.[25] It is this defining cultural mentality of anti-authoritarian, heterodox scepticism, rather than simply being 'the first' in a chronological sense (something which would not in itself, he thinks, justify continuing to study the Greeks), that forms the nub of Dover's case. Furthermore, since he is explicit that the common factor of sceptical anti-authoritarianism is the thing 'from which we have most to learn', his second justification is actually an extension of the first. This may be the closest Dover ever comes to suggesting that studying the values of the Greeks can provide us with values to follow in our own lives, though he makes the point ever plainer in the overlapping material from *The Greeks* than in the FIEC lecture: 'One argument of this book', as he puts it there, 'is that . . . we *can* learn and profit directly from the Greek example' (1982, 15). Yet even in the book, so clearly aimed at the (putative) 'general readership' Dover had made his subject in the 1976 Classical Association lecture, he never actually translates this idea of a Greek 'example' into terms that would match the first part of his bipartite justification, namely the provision of values that can 'help us to live'. To do so would, I think, have gone against the grain in more ways than one, and that semi-confessional reference to what 'some of us' have learned by studying the Greeks remains a kind of personal protection against the pressure to assert for everyone else just what they stand to learn. The result is an unbridged gap between intensity of personal experience and the guiding principles of professional scholarship.

As a final observation on the FIEC lecture, it is well worth noticing Dover's intriguing use of a counterfactual thought-experiment. This occurs at the point where his argument loops back to form a connection with its initial statement of the quality of Greek literature as sufficient justification for the study of the language. Dover presents 'a passage of poetry' which at first glance appears to be Greek but turns out to be part of the Old Babylonian version of *Gilgamesh* with the original names replaced by Greek ones taken from Pindar's *Fourth Pythian*. The aim is to produce a sort of momentary alienation effect – a reaction on the part of someone familiar with Greek poetry to the effect that 'Unless it is quite extraordinarily distorted in translation, it is not Greek … and on *stylistic* grounds it could not conceivably be Greek'.[26] This intriguing exercise is designed to prompt reflection on the criteria by which certain literary features might be deemed peculiarly Greek (or patently *un*Greek). And this leads Dover to his concluding thesis that one vital aspect of Greek originality which, unlike democracy and the rest, has *not* been properly investigated is the culture's distinctive development of language 'as an art-form', shaping forms of stylistic expressiveness that have proved immensely influential in the history of literature.[27] The passage points forward to Dover's own later work on style, and affirms his conviction that stylistics cannot dispense with aesthetic criteria. It also provides a compact but forceful statement of the thesis that language itself is fundamental to a conception of the character of ancient Greek culture. Yet, significantly, Dover never repeated this type of comparison between Greek and Near-Eastern literature anywhere else in his work.[28]

Why not? One reason may be that the limited, provisional nature of his quasi-comparative exercise was overtaken by the more detailed and sophisticated forms of comparative work in this area undertaken by, above all, Walter Burkert and Martin West. It is unclear whether in 1979 Dover already knew of the emerging interests of Burkert, the most pertinent of whose publications, including those on Near-Eastern literature and Homer, did not start to appear till the early 1980s. Dover had, however, examined Martin West's edition of Hesiod's *Theogony* as a doctoral thesis in 1963 (see Stray in this volume, 20) and he re-read the whole book before publication (West 1966, vii), so he was undoubtedly aware of West's comparative interests even if he could not foresee the scope of their future trajectory. In any case, Dover (pardonably) underestimated just how far exceptional scholars like Burkert or West would be able to go in learning ancient Near-Eastern languages to a high level of competence.[29] Against that backdrop, one is left to wonder how Dover might have modified his view of the stylistic originality of Greek literature in the light of a possible challenge to it from West's *The East Face of Helicon* – but equally, perhaps, whether West's book itself takes sufficient account of the nuanced considerations sketched by Dover's miniature thought-experiment in his FIEC lecture.[30]

*

I have so far tried to show that both the Classical Association address of 1976 and the FIEC lecture of 1979 contain suggestive but, in part, elusive expressions of Dover's cast of mind and his conception of the values of Classics as a discipline. But, perhaps surprisingly, it was in a lecture delivered at a Welsh school in 1985, 'What are the "two cultures"?', that he produced the most sustained and wide-ranging explanation of his intellectual and educational principles.[31] Although Dover makes only minimal reference to the original 1959 Rede lecture by C.P. Snow (for whom he does not conceal his disdain),[32] and says nothing about the further details of the controversy it had sparked,[33] he nonetheless uses Snow's 'two cultures' thesis as one reference point for his own position. He contends, first, that several traditional reasons for the study of Classics (as well as some cognate reasons for the humanities in general) are bad reasons, even 'harmful'; secondly, that the humanities share with the natural sciences their basic methods of enquiry and analysis, so that in this essential respect the two cultures model is fatally flawed; thirdly, that Snow also conflated academic research in the humanities with artistic creativity, the latter being one vital object of study in the humanities but, in itself, a distinct kind of human activity; fourthly, that the humanities as a whole all belong to Dover's (expanded) category of 'history'; finally, that the relationship between present and past (and, therefore, any sophisticated notion of historical 'relevance') cannot be simply calibrated on a scale of temporal distance.

In starting his lecture (after a few autobiographical remarks) from a critique of traditional but 'bad' reasons for the study of Classics, Dover trenchantly repudiates stale orthodoxies in a way which was still rare among British classical scholars at this date; the closest comparandum I am aware of, written in a typically pugnacious style, is the contribution of Moses Finley to the 1964 collection *Crisis in the Humanities*.[34] Dover's critique is made all the more telling as a public pronouncement by the declaration that his scepticism about such reasons goes all the way back to his schooldays. In rebutting the premise that 'translation into Classical languages makes us think logically', he bluntly challenges a longstanding rationale for the practice of prose composition (and *a fortiori* verse composition) in which he himself had been intensively trained at St Paul's and which he taught with considerable commitment, though for more pragmatic pedagogical reasons, at Balliol, somewhat less so at St Andrews. His attitude to this conventional premise, which he actually calls an 'extraordinary notion', is not casually sceptical; it is grounded in his own demonstrably deep engagement with the workings of language, which he regards as too complex and fluid to be aligned with the requirements of logic.[35] His dismissal of the further argument that many influential figures of the past (he gives Karl Marx as a token example) were educated in Classics is easy to state ('they didn't have much choice', as he pithily puts it), but it is worth adding that even in the early twenty-first century, when Classics has supposedly moved away from its traditional self-vindicating tenets, one does not have to look far to find scholars still attempting to win a kind of kudos for the subject by citing the cases of Marx *et al.* The third of the 'bad reasons' dismissed by Dover involves more subtle and contentious considerations. This is the claim that classical Greek art and literature are 'canonical' (with classical here understood in its modern chronological sense). Dover here appears to be defining a double-sided position: he not only rejects the idea of a canon as a permanent, definitive standard of value; he also regards the classical-as-canonical mentality as an invention of ancient Greek civilization itself, its 'one fatal weakness', an 'inability, after a certain point in time, to comprehend and develop genuine innovation in the arts'.[36]

Dover's dismissal of the ideology of the canonical needs to be observed all the more carefully in the light of the fact, visible in some of my earlier citations from his work (including what his Budapest FIEC lecture calls his 'deictic' response to the question 'why study Greek?'), that his own preferred justification for the study of ancient Greece makes intrinsic appeal to criteria of artistic, literary and aesthetic value. Clearly, then, appeals to value need to avoid the trap of being converted into ideas of an authoritative canon. To adopt a slightly different formulation, qualitative judgements about the merits of ancient art and literature must avoid a presumption of exceptionalism. The study of Greek (or Roman) culture has, in Dover's mind, a strong rationale, but it cannot any longer lay claim to a (self-)privileged status; as regards such sense of privilege, he speaks sweepingly in the two cultures lecture of the (former) 'arrogance and complacency of classicists'.[37] At the same time, it is part-and-parcel of Dover's scheme of values as a Hellenist that, like many before him, he counts the chronologically classical (or, rather, the archaic and classical together) as superior in important respects to the post-classical, at any rate from the mid-Hellenistic age onwards, though he was scrupulous not to reduce this evaluative perspective to cheap disparagement of later periods of Greek culture.[38] What makes this familiar scheme of values notable in Dover's case is precisely that he subscribes to it without endorsement of the idea of a canon, indeed while making the historical judgement that it was notions of the canonical which proved deleterious to the evolution of Greek culture itself: far from the outstanding achievements of classical art and literature being some kind of unique miracle, inevitably followed by decline or degeneration, the relationship between classical and post-classical was itself the product, he maintained, of a contingent cultural psychology which inhibited continuing innovation. There is room, needless to say, to question the entwinement of evaluation and explanation in this position: among much else, what exactly counts as 'innovation'? and does innovation in any case trump other criteria of quality? Even so, we are dealing here not with mere adherence to a conventional scheme of values, but with a more intricate cluster of ideas – hence the paradox that such thinking, in the 1985 lecture, sits alongside an uncompromising critique of 'bad arguments' for the study of Classics.

Given the demotion of Classics by the 1980s from its earlier position of educational and cultural privilege to the standing of one among many of the humanities, Dover understandably spends most of his two cultures lecture outlining a defence of the latter in the round. He does so against the background of society's technologico-scientific priorities, for which he had considerable respect, but also of a political threat which should still strike us as all-too-present ('If everything is subject to market forces, how will the humanities fare?', as he summarizes the situation).[39] In seeking to validate the humanities *en bloc*, Dover again feels the need to clear out of the way some inadequate arguments: the teaching of foreign languages for practical purposes is best undertaken by specialist language teachers, not by university foreign language departments whose cultural and historical brief is much wider than that; the comparative financial cheapness of running humanities degrees is no argument of substance at all (there may still, in principle, be better things on which to spend the money); and the idea of academics as writers of works for a general readership, the very topic to which he had dedicated his Classical Association address a decade earlier, is here pushed aside with impatience as reducing scholars to 'tame jester[s]' in the service of 'the entertainment industry', together with the ironic *aperçu* – which might be thought to subvert the entire point of that 1976 lecture – that history, biography, etc., written by the 'ignorant' 'is even more entertaining ... than the truth'.[40]

And so we come to the crux: where *does* Dover locate the bedrock on which a general defence of the humanities can be built? The answer is linked to the lecture's specific point of engagement with Snow's two cultures thesis. Dover faults Snow, as already mentioned, both for neglecting the fact that the humanities share their core methods of enquiry, investigation, and analysis of evidence with the natural sciences, and for idly conflating humanities research with artistic creativity. On this basis Dover reconfigures the notion of two cultures (though he is hardly invested in retaining the label as such) in terms of a fundamental distinction between enquiry *tout court*, whose object is 'discovery', and artistic creativity.[41] His aim, however, is not to make the humanities as scientific as possible, since methods alone do not define the *raison d'être* of a practice, but to clear a space in which to position the humanities collectively as the pursuit of 'history'. Whereas science is taken to deal in universals, generating hypotheses testable by experiment, Dover regards all history, in a seemingly unthucydidean move, as a matter of unique particulars, thus making the study of history idiographic not nomothetic.[42] Moreover, he now defines history, in a deliberately expansionist spirit, as coextensive with the humanities, embracing the study of 'everything that human beings have done, said, written, thought or felt' (1988a, 320–1).

Leaving aside (to cite just one problem) the question of how philosophy, as opposed to the history of philosophy, is supposed to fit into this schema of the humanities as history, Dover's definitional equivalence between the two terms might still look at first sight as little more than a piece of terminological redescription.[43] It is the next step in his argument which carries more weight and brings with it more far-reaching consequences for his conception of Classics. This is the claim of 'smooth continuity', i.e. the absence of any kind of dividing-line, between historical research and the nature of 'everyday existence' in the present (1988a, 321–2). Both involve the same processes of interpretation and (attempted) understanding. Interpreting the distant past, the nearer past, and the present may have access to varying amounts of pertinent evidence, though there is no simple inverse ratio between the latter and the passage of time. But all, on Dover's account, are *au fond* one and the same activity of trying to make sense, in their full complexity, of human purposes, thought and behaviour.

History, then, is a potentially unlimited repository of human self-consciousness, the activity which makes a society's 'total, collective experience available to it', though Dover hesitates about applying to this the fuzzy concept of 'collective memory' (1988a, 323). Somewhat in tension with the idea of collective experience, which might in any case be thought to avoid the vexed issue of *competing* histories, is the metaphor from his 1976 address to the Classical Association to which he here returns, namely the historian as a 'pipe-line' (it was earlier a 'feed-pipe') acting as a conduit from particular parts of the past into the present. But that infelicitous metaphor makes little or no difference to the final stage of Dover's argument, which tackles head-on the issue of 'relevance', already in the mid-1980s a shibboleth of utilitarian and instrumentalist conceptions of higher education, yet also a criterion of educational value which defenders of the humanities often feel pressure to appropriate for their own cause. To take a conveniently cognate example, the 1964 essay by Moses Finley cited earlier states: 'If the past – any past, whether Graeco-Roman or nineteenth-century – is to enlighten and remain relevant to the present, it requires active interpretation and reinterpretation...'[44] Dover too wants to affirm the relevance of the humanities *qua* history, and as anyone who adopts such a stance must do, he has to attempt to disarm the prejudice that there is a negative correlation between relevance and distance from the present. It is entirely in keeping with his characteristic aversion to sustained 'theory', which I foregrounded near the start of this chapter, that he handles this task not with a piece of abstract reasoning but with a mixture of, first, anecdotal remarks on the relationship between the upbringing of his own grandmother and daughter; second, a pointedly counterintuitive comparison between certain ways of speaking in Homeric epic and on the part of modern committee chairmen; and, finally, some first-hand observations of cultural mentalities which he had made during a lecture trip to China and Japan (1988a, 323–5).

What emerges most strongly from these various considerations, all of them inevitably open to possible reservations, are the claims that 'anything to do with material conditions of life is comparatively superficial when we are talking about relevance' (323) and that the existence of 'extraordinary similarities' between some human phenomena in different cultures means that the availability of 'instructive examples', in literature and elsewhere, is not directly related to distance in time or place (324). These propositions, albeit anecdotally rather than theoretically supported (and this is, after all, a lecture for a general audience, not a treatise), take us into the realms of a historical anthropology. It is an anthropology that Dover elsewhere reinforces with the idea that historical distance itself is a relativistic concept: as he put it piquantly in *The Greeks*, in comparison to the entire history of *homo sapiens* 'Socrates was around only yesterday; he is virtually our contemporary'.[45] In the same vein of thought, when lecturing for the first-year undergraduate Classical Culture class in St Andrews, Dover used a handout which started with a chronological scale on which *homo erectus* was placed at one end, approximately (he indicated) a million years ago, while 'Homer, Plato, Newton, Marx, Freud, you, etc.' were squeezed together right at the other end of the line. So there is a sense in which the Doverian vision of the humanities can be thought of as compressing historical time for that whole stretch of history which covers the relationship of the present to classical antiquity. And it is a concomitant of this that Dover also appears to play down the sheer existence of cultural difference, making the Greeks of antiquity much less alien from us (whoever 'we' are) than it was already common among classicists in the 1980s (and earlier) to claim that they had been.

As it happens, however, Dover unsurprisingly wavered over how far we should think of ancient Greeks as 'alien' or as 'like us'. In *Marginal Comment*, he sarcastically criticizes older Oxford classicists who lazily assimilated ancient poets to their own small cultural world ('interesting neighbours who called in at the vicarage for tea ...'); he faults his former St Andrews colleague Douglas Young for having failed to understand 'the attitudes and presuppositions of an alien culture to the extent required'; he subtly observes that one might find individual elements in a Greek tragedy 'alien' yet the complex interrelations between them 'intelligible'; and at a later point he strikes a balance by describing Greek culture as 'similar enough to ours to be intelligible' yet 'different enough to make us reflect critically on ours'.[46] – this last formulation ostensibly akin to the position of Jean-Pierre Vernant, though Dover's style of scholarship shared little with Vernant's 'historical psychology' and its quasi-teleological account of the Greeks' invention of rationality, their discovery of the individual, and so forth.[47] But the descriptive, or, rather, evaluative, categories of similarity and difference as applied to cultural relationships across history are infinitely malleable, as Dover well knew. They are also perspectival, dependent for their perception and salience on the viewer's own background, interests and motivations. Dover encapsulated this very point, with a characteristically personal inflection as well as with a sideswipe at Arthur Adkins, when he wrote near the start of *Greek Popular Morality* that

'I and most of the people I know well find the Greeks of the Classical period easier to understand than Kantians.'[48] In a talk he gave in St Andrews in 2000 at a celebration of his 80th birthday, he remarked, in that same lightly ironic manner, that 'Personally I find [the Sophoclean] Ajax much more familiar and more intelligible than, say, Cardinal Newman.'[49]

But if judgements of historico-cultural similarity and difference are perspectively variable, so too must be judgements of 'relevance'. This represents a point of tension in Dover's attempted defence of the humanities in general as forms of history. Without a firm anchorage of relevance in a determinate set of concerns and motivations, a condition one can hardly expect to be met in the modern study of the humanities, the concept of relevance is likely to collapse into, at best, a subjectivist free-for-all, or, at worst, a perpetual and irresolvable clash of incompatible viewpoints. A cognate version of this principle applies to the basic notion of 'learning' from history, which we saw Dover subscribing to in his FIEC lecture of 1979 and which presumably underlies the notion of 'instructive examples' as found in the two cultures lecture (see above). But if one concludes, as I think one must, that Dover never fully came to terms with the problem of competing frameworks of interpretation and value through which history can be viewed (though he was less concerned about subjectivism than many would be),[50] that is a less damning verdict than it might seem: it arguably applies to all invocations of 'relevance' on the part of defenders of the humanities, which cannot, unfortunately, be cogently justified by any single criterion of value.[51] The problem in question has, moreover, been exacerbated by the presentist trends visible in much of the humanities in recent times. Presentism in an undiluted form, whatever else can be said about it, effectively short-circuits the challenge of facing up to the unquantifiable interpenetration of likeness and difference in the relationships which the present can construct with the past. Dover, as I noted earlier, was anxious not to succumb to presentism by judging the past from the standpoint of modern preoccupations, though it is an open and tricky question how far he compromised that point of principle, or his own methodological consistency, in yielding to what he admitted was a fondness for adducing 'modern parallels' sporadically in his work.[52] Presentism is a matter of degree on a spectrum on which all historians, whether consciously or otherwise, must position themselves.[53]

*

The final item for consideration here, an article which appeared in 1988 in the Italian cultural magazine *L'umana avventura* (and is translated in an appendix below), is also the shortest. But it provides a convenient summing up of themes and views which I have traced in various stages of emergence in three earlier pieces. Indeed, anyone who comes to it with knowledge of those pieces is bound to have a sense of *déjà vu*.

The Italian article, written explicitly against a background of anxiety that the teaching of classical languages was in danger of disappearing altogether from schools and universities, starts from Dover's conviction that most of the standard reasons for studying Classics do not hold water. He presses his case, with some irony, in a kind of miniature retrospective dialogue with those who had taught him at school. Of particular interest here is the fact that he mentions not only the bogus notion that Greek and Latin teach you to think logically, but two further arguments which he dismisses with some ridicule: one, that these languages teach you (i.e. via etymology) 'the real meaning' of words in various modern languages, a claim he rebuts bluntly in a related passage of *Marginal Comment* by saying that 'words do not have "real" meanings'; the other, the common contention that it is impossible to understand your own culture without understanding its roots.[54] This passage, which once again indicates Dover's rejection of any exceptionalist favouritism for the educational standing of Classics, is strikingly sceptical about arguments that attempt to derive evaluative conclusions from genetic premises (one form, therefore, of the genetic fallacy). Historical roots *per se*, he believes, have no authoritative claims on the attention of those interested in the forms of life which have grown from (or away from) those roots. Dover does not deny that the study of roots is one legitimate pursuit among many, or that it may play a distinctive role in specific instances of historical understanding. Nor is he questioning the validity of broader kinds of genealogical thinking that concern themselves with processes of influence and reception.[55] What he insists is that ideas of classical antiquity as the 'ancestor' of (certain aspects of) modern culture cannot underwrite a special status for Classics within the humanities, let alone be allowed to encourage a nostalgically classicizing mentality: the subject's fortunes must stand or fall, as he contended in the 1985 Rougemont lecture and now repeats, with those of the humanities as a whole.

With that premise in place, Dover proceeds to summarize his opposition to Snow's two cultures thesis (pointing out, as the 1985 lecture had not done, that Snow's dichotomy was drawn in terms of 'science' and 'literature', thereby neglecting the importance of history), briefly returns to the concerns of the 1976 Classical Association address about the dangers of popularizing works written by those who lack sufficient historical expertise, and challenges current demands for 'relevance' in the humanities as simplistic in their crude association of this concept with proximity in space or time – a valid complaint, though not one which does much to resolve the problem I identified earlier of how to give relevance a positive role to play in defence of the humanities. But the most significant feature of the article for my purposes is its attempt to refine Dover's conception of a dialectic between perceptions of similarity and difference in the study of history. We find here several new formulations. Dover now speaks of differences as being mostly easy to recognize, since they lie, so to speak, on the surface of cultural phenomena, while similarities or affinities may operate at a deeper, more structural level and need to be located by more active investigation. There is no question, he stresses, of appealing to an unchanging human nature; human nature has changed immensely since *homo erectus*, as he puts it (shades of the undergraduate handout I cited earlier), though only the thousandth part of that change has occurred in the last thousandth part, i.e. the last millennium, of the intervening period – a highly Doveresque framing of the point. For Dover as an individual classicist, the substrate of underlying similarities between ancient and modern matters far more than surface differences. To understand intuitively ('empatizzare') the clash between Antigone and Creon in Sophocles' play, he suggests, one does not need to worship Zeus or believe in omens, since one can tap into a modern awareness of what it means for arbitrary authority and basic 'human rights' to clash head-on. What is more, Dover has himself heard children arguing about issues akin to those in Sophocles' *Philoctetes* (he does not specify precisely which issues!), and, in a startling autobiographical reminiscence mentioned nowhere else in his work (including *Marginal Comment*), he recalls having once used Aeneas' morale-boosting speech in the first book of Vergil's *Aeneid* to help quell an incipient mutiny among troops.[56]

The brevity of these anecdotal examples suits a two-page magazine article but is also in keeping with Dover's characteristic belief that personal experience counts for more than abstract 'theory'. The examples themselves, which appear (no doubt partly because of their brevity) to peel away layers of cultural specificity in order to find a hard kernel of human intelligibility, speak to his view that cross-cultural historical understanding is possible on the basis of alignments not between discrete factors or elements but between structures of experience. At the same time, his stance remains conspicuously dialectical. Far from suggesting that such alignments lurk everywhere, or should dominate historical thought, he approaches the end of the article on an explicitly anthropological note. The vital differences between cultures, he maintains, reside in systems and hierarchies of value. But this in itself provides a good reason for historical study, a reason more compactly stated here than in any of the other pieces I have discussed. Dover regards history, in all its aspects, as a quasi-anthropological resource with which individuals and cultures can consciously and comparatively reassess their own values.[57] He remarks that it is ironic that Classics has fallen into decline during the very period in which social anthropology has become established in universities. Classics, he insists, has its own anthropological potential, its own mixture of 'exotic' and 'familiar', and it should work alongside anthropology as a disciplinary partner within the equal community of the humanities.[58]

So much Heraclitean water has flowed under the bridge in the decades since Dover expressed these thoughts that it is, or should be, difficult for anyone confidently to appraise his intellectual principles in relation to the flux of change in the subject, and all the more so for anyone who cares to contemplate the view in *both* directions, but without either presentist bias or arrogantly prescriptivist inclinations, from whatever position they occupy on the bridge in question. I hope, at least, that the present discussion has succeeded in clarifying some of the terms in which Dover not only came to understand the nature of his own work in relation to the parameters of his discipline, but also, in the process, made himself an instructive object of the kind of historical enquiry which he prized so highly.[59]

Appendix
Kenneth Dover, 'The value of Classics'[60]
(translated from the Italian by Stephen Halliwell)

When I was a schoolboy, the teachers used to give us bad reasons to entice us to study Latin and Greek. 'They teach you to think logically', they would say. But was that true? No language has ever been designed by a computer programmer; every language is a collection of behavioural patterns that is under continual modification, as proved by the fact that a translator has less need for logical acumen than for sensitive antennae and good experience of human irrationality. 'They make you understand the *true meaning* of the words we use today.' Alas, such an absurd misconception of the nature of language can only be a very poor advertisement for the classical culture of anyone who holds a view of this sort. 'You cannot understand our own culture if you do not understand its roots.' Really? Which problem relating to the actual operations of any element of our culture (unless it is an explicitly and precisely historical problem) *requires* a knowledge of the past that reaches back beyond the 19th century?

Fortunately, since I had always loved Latin and Greek simply because I found them extremely interesting, I have never needed any bad, independent reason for studying them. There will always be those who love them, just as there will always be those crazy about microbiology or Tibet or quasars. But to say no more than this is a lazy, selfish response, inadequate at a time when educational reforms threaten to eliminate even the possibility of enjoying a taste of the classical languages. Are there not perhaps good reasons for preserving that possibility, reasons intelligible to students, their parents and the Ministry of Education?

Let us be frank about practical usefulness: some academic subjects are more important than others; they are not all equal. If we need water and when we open the tap none comes out, we may even die. If we want to read Plato and cannot find him in bookshops, we may be upset or disappointed, but we don't die as a result. The sciences needed for the distribution of drinking water, the production of food and the building of shelter (as well as many other practical necessities) enjoy a specially privileged position, and rightly so, since life depends on them. The defence of Classics succeeds or fails with the defence of that whole field of studies we call the 'arts' or 'humanities', but which I actually prefer to group together under the heading of 'history', by which I understand the study of everything that humans have done, written, said, thought or felt.

The theory of the 'two cultures' popularized by C.P. Snow rests on the opposition between the physical sciences and technology, on the one hand, and literature, on the other. History has been left out: there is no place in this dichotomy for history as I have defined it and therefore for at least half the studies pursued in schools and universities. There are indeed two cultures, but they are not Snow's. One of them is the culture of analysis, inquiry and research; by its very nature this culture embraces every type of science and every kind of history: it is the study of what there is, what exists. The second culture is not science but art, a way of adding to reality, the creation of something that was not there before, that did not exist until we ourselves created it. The two cultures are not enemies. There may be some creative artists who fear and distrust history and science, but there are precious few historians or scientists who fear or despise art.

Within the genus 'history', the species 'Classics' must be able to compete on equal terms with all the other species belonging to the same genus. There is no special justification for creating a privileged position to give Classics a questionable advantage in this competition. No enthusiastic supporter of Classics will ever fear that without sufficient protection from special regulations classical literature and art may be forgotten. More than once in the last millennium the study of Greek has experienced periods of revival, not because someone thought it a key for solving practical problems, but always because it was recognized that there were things written in Greek which were worth reading.

There is, however, a danger. To set up a classical canon, to disseminate the idea that everything post-classical is decadent, involves a fatal error, an error committed by the Greeks themselves. Their 'classicism', which was both premature and nostalgic, ended by preventing and foreclosing a genuinely innovative impulse in the artistic domain. Nevertheless, the literature and art produced in the centuries when the Greeks were genuine innovators can stand comparison with the results of any other culture. We can and should enjoy this material on its own terms.

[p. 60] Numerous books are published these days about the ancient world (books on archaeology, biographies of famous individuals, translations of classical literature) which find a growing readership among a public whose working time is spent in other fields: industry or business, technology or finance. This tendency is starting to transform Classics into a minor branch of the entertainment industry or, at least, the leisure industry, but this does not mean that more people will start to study the classical languages. One must also consider the risk that, as time proceeds, the books which serve to entertain us and fill our leisure time might be written by authors increasingly less capable of distinguishing whether what they write has some relationship to historical truth or has turned into a kind of ignorant, fanciful work of fiction. And it is easy for books of precisely this kind to attract readers more than historical reconstructions.

One can be entertained without any need to study, as testified by the sale of some popular, best-selling books. One can also study without experiencing pleasure: discontented school and university students confirm this. If we are sufficiently curious to pose questions about the ancient world, and if we really want to answer our questions, then someone somewhere has important work to undertake: syntax, manuscripts, inscriptions, tax systems – thousands of things might prove important or fundamental to obtaining the answer we are looking for. There is in fact no way of knowing in advance, when one is committed to solving a problem, what will prove really important or fundamental in the process of research.

In this respect Classics is no different from any other type of historical study, and indeed no different from the study of the physical or biological sciences either. Establishing the text of a papyrus and using a microscope have the same status, both of them opposed to lazy or frivolous falsifications of the world, of the world as it is now or has been in the past. If Classics is put aside and deemed a useless ally in this battle, this can only be because it is considered of little relevance to our contemporary situation. The popular notion of relevance is absurdly simplistic, if not the result of outright ignorance. If B is nearer to A than C is in space and time, people assume that B has a closer connection with A. On this premise, medieval French would be a more suitable subject of study for English schools than classical Latin, not to mention that modern French would be the most interesting language in this context. In reality, every judgement on the relationship between A and B depends on the answer one wants to give to a double question: what experiences are shared by A and B, and in what respects do their experiences differ?

Normally, differences strike us before resemblances; they jump out at us because they exist on a more superficial level: e.g. the presence or absence of human sacrifice, emperor cult, television, computers. Similarities, however, must be looked for at a deeper level, in structures of personal relationships; they concern the ambitions and desires, the fears and frustrations, of individuals. To take account of this factor does not imply naive or complacent acceptance of the old popular adage that 'human nature never changes'. Human nature has certainly undergone substantial changes since the appearance of *homo erectus*, and it is an assumption that the last thousandth part of the intervening period has witnessed a thousandth of these changes, a tiny fraction that need not trouble us. It is a simple and widely observable fact that the substrate common to life in the ancient and modern world greatly exceeds the differences between them. To understand intuitively the conflict between Antigone and Creon we do not need to live in a city-state or worship Zeus or believe in omens; these are only superficial differences, whereas what makes an impression on us is the clash between arbitrary authority and what Antigone calls 'unwritten laws' and we call 'human rights'. I myself have seen this tragedy performed, with extraordinary conviction, by a group of Scottish schoolchildren who had scarcely heard of the Greeks before then. I have also had occasion to hear some boys, with scarcely a smattering of Greek culture, arguing passionately over problems and solutions highlighted by Sophocles' *Philoctetes*. And if I may be permitted a brief autobiographical digression, I once succeeded in quelling an incipient mutiny by quoting from memory some words used by Aeneas to raise the morale of his men in the first book of the *Aeneid*, in particular '*o passi graviora*' and '*forsan et haec olim meminisse iuvabit*'. One should not be surprised about this; Vergil knew much more than I do about war, defeat, hardship, and desperation.

The most important difference to be grasped between two cultures consists in differences in the range and hierarchy of their values, since these are profoundly reflected in individual choices and motivations. And this is important and significant because re-examining and reassessing our assumptions and values represents a vital necessity for the health of our own culture. Comparing ourselves with the assumptions and values of an alien culture constitutes the most effective stimulus to such a process.

There is a certain irony in the way in which Classics went out of fashion at the very time when social anthropology was becoming a fashionable subject. The latter is regarded as useful (and rightly so, in my view) because if we can grasp the basic elements common to the structure of Melanesian or Bantu society and the structure of our own, we have a good chance of understanding why one society chooses a certain path of development and another society a different path. But it remains to be asked whether from our point of view Melanesian or Bantu culture holds a real advantage as a subject of study over Greek or Roman culture. Why discard cultures which share many fundamental characteristics with ours in favour of cultures which have very few such characteristics? The study of these subjects belongs side by side. The modern classicist, whether consciously or not, is profoundly indebted to the valuable stimulus of data obtained by anthropology. We have also been able to benefit from being forced to recognize, if belatedly, that the *anthrôpoi* who form the subject of study of this -ology also include those who are white, literate and technologically advanced. For all these reasons, let us not neglect the Greeks and Romans. With them we find an exceptional mixture of the exotic and the familiar, constituting an extraordinarily rich field of research: sufficiently exotic to prompt a re-examination of ourselves, and sufficiently familiar to allow easy, immediate access to their territory.

Up to this point, I have simply advanced good reasons for the study of history in general: essentially, I have not said anything in favour of Classics in particular. I have done so deliberately, in keeping with my personal definition of 'history' and the strength of my conviction that history and science are complementary, a reason which entitles them to equal consideration and rights in our educational system. Bad science and bad history have contributed much to the tragedy of the human past, including the recent past. Given that, it remains for me to add just one thing, and this time in a defensive rather than assertive spirit: Classics can survive by basing itself exclusively on its own merits, provided that access to the subject is not barred. 'Let a thousand flowers bloom' and let Classics be one of these flowers.

Notes

1. Dover 1980b, 88 = 1988a, 290; the original publication is misdated as 1979 in the Contents of 1988a, vi.

2. Dover himself retrospectively, and oddly, categorizes the audience of his Classical Association address as 'non-Classical' (Dover 1988a, vii). This anomaly may reflect the fact that in the 1970s attendance at the Classical Association's AGMs included many – not least, schoolteachers and enthusiastic Classics graduates – who were not professional scholars; in the lecture itself, Dover alludes to the spectrum represented by his audience (Dover 1976a, 10–11 = 1988a, 305–6). For some thoughts on the 'genre' of CA Presidential addresses, see Schofield 2003, with Stray, ed., 2003 more generally for the CA's history.

3. The name of Rougemont School is misspelt in the Contents of *G&L* (Dover 1988a, vi), though it is correct in the Acknowledgements (viii).

4. Curiously, Clive James' scathing review of the TV series cited in *MC* 133 does not even mention Dover, targeting its fire solely against the presenter and producer, Christopher Burstall (James 1983, 121). But James' complaint that Burstall did not know how to 'fade into the background' implies that the programmes would have been better if the unmentioned Dover had been allowed more Burstall-free space.

5. The humanism of these two figures is prominent in their Oxford inaugural lectures, Fraenkel 1935 and Dodds 1936 (the latter treating humanism as an entire 'worldview' and advocating a 'new humanism'); note also Dodds' letter to Fraenkel of 31 July 1936, quoted in Stray 2019, 14. As early as 1920, Dodds complained that most classical scholars since the nineteenth century had ceased to be 'humanists', a class he equated, in a quasi-platonic idiom, with those who could recognize 'the True and the Beautiful' as 'infinite living values' (Dodds 1999, 347). On the extent to which modern conceptions of 'the humanities' depend on a conception of 'humanism', see Reitter and Wellmon 2021.

6. *MC* 261 (a passage he thought merited an index entry, s.v. theory); cf. ibid. 146, 'an English empiricist to the core and in politics more of a restless tinkerer than a revolutionary theorist'.

Dover does occasionally apply 'theory' to his own views: see his '"feed-pipe" theory of history' (cf. n. 20 below for context), though that is clearly a thin sense of the word. His general aversion to the heavily theoretical applied not least to linguistics: see *MC* 23 on theoretical versus comparative and historical linguistics; cf. ibid. 198.

7. For (unspecified) theories boasting 'comprehensive power', see, again, *MC* 261; cf. the passing reference, ibid. 248, to the potentially distorting effects of 'a theoretical schema drawn from sociology or metahistory'. Both a 'fundamental objection' to psychoanalysis (in the interpretation of literary texts) and a partial openness to its personal applicability can be seen in one and the same passage of *MC* 123.

8. Dover 1974, xii; cf. *MC* 261 on his 'considered refusal to separate interpretation of my own experience from the recovery of the experience of others, no matter how remote in time and place': it remains a difficult question how this refusal is to be reconciled with the quasi-anthropological approach to antiquity considered in the last part of the present chapter. For more on the methodology of *GPM*, see Carey's chapter in this volume.

9. Dover draws programmatic attention to his difference from Adkins in Dover 1983b, 35 = 1987, 77.

10. For the statistics, see Harrison, ed., 1994b, 142. But at the time Dover left Balliol, he himself felt 'no anxieties' about student numbers (*MC* 126); the 'downward plunge', in St Andrews at any rate, started in the mid-1960s (ibid.).

11. Russell 2007, 230–1; Dodds 1977, 172 dates the start of his own anxieties to the interwar years. In a longer vista, anxieties about the *raison d'être* of Classics in British education were already surfacing in the later nineteenth and early twentieth century: for various debates over values, see Stray 1998, 202–32.

12. Note also the introduction at St Andrews in 1975 of a first-year class in Classical Culture, based on texts read in translation, though Dover thought the subject unsuitable for a full degree programme (*MC* 130; cf. the similar reservations of Dodds 1964, 21–2 ~ 1977, 175–6).

13. The lecture mentions translation only as part of a suite of methods used by classical scholars (Dover 1976a, 14–15 = 1988a, 308–9); it does not discuss translations as free-standing publications. For some of Dover's thoughts elsewhere on the latter, see his review of several versions of the *Oresteia* in Dover 1980c = 1987, 176–81.

14. Philip Howard, reporting the lecture in *The Times*, picked up on this tone: see the main headline, 'Literacy on the defensive in a divided world of many cultures', *The Times*, 15 April 1976, p. 3.

15. *Qua* reviewer, his main contribution was a hard-hitting review of Peter Green's *Armada from Athens* (Dover 1972b = 1988a, 194–7, the latter including an additional note). His complaints about errors and shortcomings in Green's work are germane to parts of the CA lecture.

16. In his 1981 Presidential address to the British Academy's Council, Dover posited the existence of widespread philistinism in Britain, describing 'public opinion' as 'not particularly well-disposed to research in the humanities' (Dover 1981b, 80).

17. Dover's defence of history in general is called 'prudential' as a matter of utility for 'a given society as a whole' (Dover 1976a, 10 = 1988a, 305), yet this same passage goes on to refer to the 'value' of the past apparently on a more personal level ('for some'); certainly the latter appears later in the lecture as an explicitly non-utilitarian, self-sufficient value for individuals (1976, 16–17 = 1988a, 311, quoted in my text on p. 295).

18. Dover twice alludes to the potential failings of the 'good grammarian', the second time with the further phrase quoted: Dover 1976a, 15, 18 = 1988a, 310, 312. This is not, despite first appearances, at odds with his later admission of 'the power of syntax [and other technical

aspects of language] over my imagination and intellect' (Dover 1976a, 17 = 1988a, 311), since he relates this power to the aesthetic function of language 'as a medium of art'. On his conception of the aesthetics of language, cf. my text at p. 297.

19. Dover 1976a, 12 = 1988a, 307. Cf. n. 40 below for a related passage in the 1985 'two cultures' lecture.
20. 'Feed-pipe': Dover 1976a, 10 = 1988a, 305. 'Hypotheses' about 'data': Dover 1976a, 16 = 1988a, 310. History 'not a science': Dover 1976a, 19 = 1988a, 313. Dover's 'feed-pipe' model was repeated in the 1985 'two cultures' lecture (Dover 1988a, 323): see my text at p. 300.
21. Dover 1976a, 16–17 = 1988a, 311; cf. *MC* 200. In Halliwell 2011 I quoted a longer stretch of this passage (which expresses sympathy with Jane Harrison's 'tears of joy' on first making acquaintance with verbal aspect in the Russian language) as an especially telling specimen of Dover's writing. For Dover's attitudes to, and 'love' of, language in general, see Prauscello's chapter in this volume.
22. As already mentioned, the Classical Association address shows that Dover considered *Greek Homosexuality* itself a book for the general reader, a category he clearly conflates with the 'Greekless' reader (Dover 1976a, 10 = 1988a, 305). I wonder how many Greekless readers have actually read this book, as opposed to browsing it (and its images).
23. He is unambiguous about this judgement of value in *The Greeks*, asserting that Greek literature is not better than e.g. English or French literature but can 'stand comparison' with any other: Dover 1982, 9 (n.b. different pagination from the original 1980 BBC edition of *The Greeks*).
24. Cf. n. 42 below. On Dover's extensive dealings with Thucydides, see Pelling's contribution to the present volume.
25. Dover 1984, 27.
26. Dover 1984, 30–1.
27. Dover 1984, 31: there is something missing from Dover's text (either before or after 'expressions') in 'Greek innovations lay in expressions', but the thrust of the passage is not obscured by this blemish.
28. In the related/overlapping parts of *The Greeks*, Dover hints lightly at a comparative judgement on Greek and Mesopotamian or Egyptian literature, but leaves the matter hypothetical: Dover 1982, 12. In this connection, it is a pity that Dover nowhere mentions the famous comparative exercise, involving Homeric epic and the Hebrew Genesis, undertaken in the first chapter of Auerbach 1953: for all its arguable claims, Auerbach's comparison of Eurycleia's recognition of Odysseus' scar and Abraham's would-be sacrifice of Isaac poses questions akin to Dover's concerning the relation between individual linguistic features and a larger stylistic ethos.
29. Dover does allude (1984, 25) to the prospect of new kinds of comparative scholarship in this area, but he also records the existence of dismissive attitudes to comparatism among classicists, and it is evident that he was not able to anticipate the full potential of such work.
30. While West's book accumulates myriad examples of affinities/parallels between stylistically functional elements in Greek and certain NE literatures, it nowhere confronts the perspective opened by Dover's thought-experiment: in short, its preoccupation with similarity precludes attention to difference. Furthermore, although West uses the term 'style' in quite a few places (e.g. West 1997, 168–70), there is no attempt of the kind Dover thought important (e.g. Dover 1997a, 1–12) to clarify the concept of style itself.
31. Dover says in *MC* 258 that he started to form his view of the 'two cultures' controversy in the mid-1960s ('about thirty years ago'); was this linked to his personal (and less than admiring)

encounters with Snow when the latter was Rector in St Andrews (see n. 32)? There is, however, no explicit reference to the two cultures controversy in Dover's earlier publications: the earliest reference occurs in his British Academy Presidential address of 1981 (Dover 1981b, 81), where he combats Snow by positing 'three cultures' (i.e. scientific enquiry, enquiry in the humanities, artistic creativity): cf. n. 41 below.

32. Dover 1988a, 319. See also *MC* 172–3 (cf. 258) for Dover's personal dislike of Snow, who was Rector (a position in Scottish universities elected by the student body) at St Andrews 1961–4.

33. Collini 1998, esp. ix-xliii, provides a concise introduction to the controversy; for further reflections, see Small 2013, 30–47. Classicists should note that Rüegg, ed., 2003 includes a piece by Walter Burkert (91–102) which somewhat pessimistically stresses the challenges standing in the way of genuinely interdisciplinary thought, especially between the humanities and natural sciences.

34. Finley's argument, which Dover is likely to have read, has several points of contact with Dover's: the rejection of exceptionalist justifications for Classics (Finley 1964, 13 and 15), the 'fallacy' of appeals to distinguished products of classical education (ibid. 13–14), and the fallacy of thinking of language (Finley specifies Latin) as 'training the mind' to think logically *vel sim.* (18–19). It also stresses the need for expert scholars to write for the general public (21–2), thus anticipating the theme of Dover's 1976 Classical Association address, and identifies as a salient feature of ancient Greek culture the willingness to challenge 'inherited beliefs and authorities' (15), which Dover himself would later foreground in both his FIEC lecture and *The Greeks* (see the discussion in my text). But Finley, as an ancient historian with much less interest in ancient literature than Dover, is more sweepingly negative (19–20) about the centrality to Classics teaching of 'linguistic skills' (and not just the exercise of composition) than Dover would have found acceptable. On Dover's rather mixed views of Finley, see esp. *MC* 130 and 260 n. 3; but in a letter to his parents of 14 June 1956 he described Finley, with reference to *The World of Odysseus* (published 1954), as having 'a gift for asking simple questions which most professional scholars have completely overlooked, and he's not so bad at finding the answers to them'.

35. The same reason, together with other 'bad reasons' for studying Greek, reappears in the Italian article of 1988 (discussed at pp. 302–4) as well as in *MC* 126; cf. n. 54 below. In *The Greeks*, though not in the two cultures lecture, Dover also rejects the claim that ancient Greek 'was a uniquely subtle and expressive language' (Dover 1982, 8).

36. Dover 1988a, 316; contrast the position of Dodds 1964, 15–16 (repeated in Dodds 1977, 173–4), who, despite his careful qualifications, adumbrates a quasi-canonical conception of 'masterpieces'.

37. Dover 1988a, 316; cf. the related statement of his anti-exceptionalist stance at Dover 1982, 8–9.

38. Dover's presuppositions about the relative qualities of archaic/classical and post-classical literature and art are not spelt out in the two cultures lecture itself, but they are concisely explained, for literature, in Dover 1997b, 3–4, and, for the visual arts, in Dover 1982, 67–71. For his own principal foray into the post-classical, his 1971 edition of selected poems of Theocritus, see Hunter in this volume. The relatively restricted range (in chronological terms) of Dover's main interests was noted as a limitation in Russell 1989.

39. The government minister whose sneering attitude to anthropology is alluded to in this context (Dover 1988a, 316) was Norman Tebbit; cf. the related reference to Tebbit in *MC* 253.

40. Dover 1988a, 318. This passage illustrates the 'unusual degree of agitation and indignation' that Dover had said in 1976 was aroused in him by amateurish writing about antiquity

(see n. 19 above). But it remains curious that whereas in 1976 he had treated writing for the general reader as a topic meriting careful consideration, now in 1985 he gives it no more than this curt and jaundiced reference.

41. Dover 1988a, 319. Lloyd-Jones 1989, 372 garbles Dover's case by saying that it retains the status of 'two cultures' for science and history; this is incorrect, notwithstanding Dover's occasional reference elsewhere to 'three cultures' (see n. 31 above, with *MC* 258).
42. See Windelband 1980 for an English translation of the 1894 lecture in which he introduced this dichotomy; for some criticism of Windelband, see Collingwood 1946, 166–8 (a book known to Dover: 1983a, 57 = 1988a, 57). But to regard history as idiographic does not exclude the use of reasoning that incorporates generalizations and arguments from likelihood or probability ('general propositions are necessary at every stage of inquiry in the idiographic sciences', Windelband 1980, 182): Dover identifies these elements both in his own outlook (1988a, 323) and in that of Thucydides 1.22.4 (1973b, 43–4); cf. Dover 1983a, 62 = 1988a, 63. However, Dover 1973b, 43 also ascribes to Thucydides the stronger, nomothetic belief in 'general laws' of history, which seems at odds with his own denial in the two cultures lecture that history 'repeats itself' (1988a, 322). It remains an open question, therefore, just how Thucydidean Dover took his own view of history to be; cf. pp. 295–6.
43. For one perspective on philosophy as a humanistic discipline, see Dover's own undergraduate pupil Bernard Williams in Williams 2006, 180–99. But Dover's view of philosophy as confined to various kinds of abstract reasoning (esp. *MC* 60–1; cf. the definition of moral philosophy, ibid. 155) is harder to integrate into his conception of the humanities as history. Dover classed all philosophy as a form of 'theory' (see n. 6 above); cf. *MC* 161, 'philosophical theorising'.
44. Finley 1964, 22. Cf. n. 34 above.
45. Dover 1982, 5.
46. Phrases, in order, from *MC* 39, 87, 125, 126. At *MC* 126 n. 1 he dissents from the unattributed phrase 'unimaginably alien'; although this may be a half-remembered version of Louis MacNeice's 'unimaginably different' in his poem *Autumn Journal*, part IX (MacNeice 1966, 119; cf. Güthenke in this volume on the context and resonance of MacNeice's phrase) Dover himself subsequently thought he might (also) have had at the back of his mind 'astoundingly alien' in Padel 1992, 10. For a more basic reference to *any* culture other than our own as 'alien', see Dover 1983a, 62 = 1988a, 63. Richard Rutherford reminds me that Jones 1962, 17, describes Greek tragedy as 'desperately foreign' (cf. 277, 'very alien'); the phrase was used as the title of Moses Finley's review of the book (Finley 1972, 11–15), which partly modifies Jones' position by arguing that historical understanding always takes place 'in a contemporary way' (15) and is even, in the end, 'about the present'.
47. For a succinct statement of Vernant's position on the dialectic of cultural distance/closeness, strangeness/familiarity, in 'our' relationship to the Greeks, see Vernant 1996, 10 (= 2006, 14). Dover nowhere engages with the work of the French school of historical anthropology in Gernet, Detienne, Vernant, etc.: many of their ideas are likely to have struck him as too abstract, schematic, and 'theoretical' for his liking. There is a single passing reference to Vernant in *MC* 123.
48. Dover 1974, 2–3 n. 3. In reviewing *GPM*, John Gould criticized what he claimed was the book's consistent playing-down of the view of Greek attitudes as 'alien' to us (Gould 1978, 287).
49. From a copy of Dover's typescript in my possession.
50. Subjectivism, that is, in so far as Dover was never in any doubt that how interesting one finds ancient Greek culture (or anything else) is ultimately a matter of individual disposition:

token examples are Dover 1976a, 10 = 1988a, 305 ('If contemplation of a future society...'), Dover 1982, 146 ('if Greek ways of seeing and saying are congenial to you').

51. Small 2013 provides a helpful survey and analysis of arguments in defence of the humanities.
52. Dover 1983b, 48 (= 1987, 96) admitted, in response to criticism from Arthur Adkins, to a liking for 'modern parallels' when interpreting Greek moral attitudes. Russell 1989, 14 shrewdly notes that Dover's modern parallels sometimes sit alongside those from 'very remote cultures'.
53. Cf. Osborne 2017, esp. 218–19 and 226 (with 222–3 on what he considers the role of Dover's *GH* in a new wave of 'presentist' work on ancient sexuality).
54. Dover 1988b, 59; the related passage in *MC*, where the reasons in question are called 'bunk', is at 126. Compare Dover 1997a, 123–4, and 1988a, 45.
55. His most obvious acknowledgement of such interests was his editing of *Perceptions of the Ancient Greeks* (Dover, ed., 1992). Even so, it is notable that, as Donald Russell put it in his *Times* obituary, Dover 'never wrote or talked much about the continuities of European civilisation' (Russell 2010, 60).
56. Dover 1988b, 60: the speech in question is *Aen*. 1.199–208; Dover curiously implies that he quoted some lines in Latin, though most of the troops under his command cannot have had any knowledge of the language. Richard Rutherford points out to me that Aeneas is explicitly described as masking his own fears (1.209, *spem voltu simulat, premit altum corde dolorem*) and poses the intriguing question whether this could have (subliminally) influenced Dover's recourse to the passage.
57. Cf. the motivation for studying Greek moral attitudes in *GPM*: 'in order to conduct our own criticism... of our assumptions and principles, whether individual or collective' (Dover 1974, xiii).
58. In the stemmatic diagram of his intellectual formation originally produced as a handout for a lecture in Rome in 1993 (and reproduced at the end of Halliwell 2011), Dover marks anthropology as an interest which lasted from his mid-teenage years for the rest of his life.
59. This chapter has benefited from the comments of Ewen Bowie, Paul Cartledge, Jaś Elsner, Chris Pelling, Richard Rutherford, and Chris Stray.
60. Kenneth Dover, 'Il valore degli studi classici', appeared in the Italian magazine *L'umana avventura*, summer/autumn 1988, 59–60: I am very grateful to Dr Massimiliano Ornaghi for obtaining a copy of this article for me. Where it overlaps with some of Dover's English publications, both earlier and later, I have taken account of the forms of words used in those other places, though without thereby departing from the sense of the formulations employed in the Italian article itself.

CHAPTER 17
MEMORIES OF KENNETH DOVER

REBECCA DOVER
(with contributions from Wendy, Nicholas and Matthew Dover)

When the invitation arrived asking me if I'd like to write something about my grandparents I was, of course, delighted, but now the time has come to put pen to paper I'm actually finding it surprisingly difficult to find a point from which to start. My childhood memories seem to exist more as visual, tactile, dream-like sensory snapshots of the past rather than anything as concrete as being able to recount details of specific conversations. I have nothing but fond memories of both Kenneth and Audrey (Granny and Grandpa to me) and their house at Hepburn Gardens where we would visit as a family for Sunday lunch and spend afternoons with them. We would be shown round the garden with detailed commentary on the successes and failures, blooms and droops of the moment, and in late summer we would help to pick apples and blackberries. Kenneth was always very warm, welcoming and funny, appearing after lunch with a tray of freshly brewed coffee that we would have in the sitting room. I loved that room – the pale greens and creams were so relaxing after a big lunch, and I remember being fascinated by the eclectic artefacts that they had collected or been gifted from around the world. My favourite, though, was the Chinese cat with one paw waving by the telephone in the hall. They would come to visit us regularly in Glenfarg and joined us for Christmas Day every year, always dressed for the occasion – Audrey in her finest beads and a long skirt, finished with an exotic, otherworldly garment, never without a story; Kenneth would put together an incredible patterned shirt and tie ensemble, often with a brightly coloured jersey, and would regale us with hilarious stories around the Christmas dinner table.

I am not academic, my interests growing up were in art and music and I'm now a professional artist and work in community arts.* My Grandparents were always very interested in what I had been painting and were happy to hang my creations on their wall. They never made me feel as though I should be pursuing more academic subjects. My youngest brother Matthew remembers how good Kenneth was at finding just the right way to explain an idea or share his thoughts on a subject with his audience in mind, and as children if any of us got the wrong end of the stick he would always find such a lovely and neat way of correcting the misunderstanding so as to avoid any sense of embarrassment.

Kenneth wrote wonderful personal letters and funny notes on cards to all of us in the family. He exchanged news regularly with my brother Nicholas, where his letters often consisted of observations about normal everyday events (such as a boiler replacement), but he had a knack of making the most mundane of things sound interesting and amusing. If a funny observation concerned another party, it was tinged with kindness or fondness and he would also be quite happy to laugh at himself.

As Kenneth and Audrey reached their mid-eighties and their extensive garden became too much to manage, my Mum, Wendy Dover, took to going to St Andrews once a week, armed with flasks of homemade soup and cakes, to spend the day outside doing whatever jobs Kenneth saw fit. He would phone the evening before her visit with a shopping list, so she would arrive laden with the week's supplies, and the three of them would pass an enjoyable and productive day together. At the end of each visit Wendy left feeling elated at Kenneth's courage and determination in meeting old age and all of its difficulties head on with Audrey at his side.

SIR BRIAN HARRISON

J.S. Mill claimed in 1848 that 'a democratic constitution, not supported by democratic institutions in detail, but confined to the central government, not only is not political freedom, but often creates a spirit precisely the reverse, carrying down to the lowest grade in society the desire and ambition of political domination'.[1] In other words, radical Liberals were claiming at that time that democratic values must pervade not only central government, but also subordinate institutions; among these we would now include local authorities, business firms, trade unions and universities. Such a conviction influenced Kenneth Dover's approach to leading an Oxford college from 1976 to 1986. His career illustrates the ongoing capacity of liberal values to conquer new territory long after Labour had superseded the Liberals in national politics as the dominant party on the left. It also illustrates some of the difficulties, personal and institutional, experienced by a liberal located on the frontier of liberalism's late-twentieth-century evolution.

Dover had favoured women's advancement in universities well before 1975, the year he was interviewed for the presidency of Corpus. When asked on that occasion whether he favoured admitting women as undergraduates, he replied in just two words, 'Of course', with no further argument required and no certainty that this would advance his presidential chances. The Fellows' representatives offered him the post next day; a few days later he accepted it. In 1971 the Corpus Governing Body had debated whether to admit women as undergraduates, but the narrow majority of thirteen to twelve for the change did not suffice: a two-thirds majority was required to change the college statutes. Instead, a timid compromise proposal to admit women as postgraduates in an alliance with Somerville College was introduced. Thus did Corpus fail to join the first wave of five Oxford colleges admitting women as undergraduates in 1973; it decided to join the second wave in 1979, by which time Dover had been President for three years.[2] Very soon after he became President, his wife Audrey was shocked at the SCR rule that wives of Fellows could dine only on Tuesdays. Dover pointed out that the rule enabled him to bring in undesirable male guests and even 'an illiterate prostitute picked up in a bar, but not the person to whom I am married'. He used his presidential influence to get the rule abolished (*MC* 185).

Dover was liberal, too, on homosexuality. With characteristic frankness and directness, he declared in the preface to his *Greek Homosexuality* that 'I am fortunate in not experiencing moral shock or disgust at any genital act whatsoever, provided that it is ... agreeable to all the participants (whether they number one, two or more than two)'. It is difficult now, after the recently transformed outlook, to recall how radical such a statement was in the UK of 1978, coming as it did from so prominent a scholar. At the same time as pioneering new approaches to research in Classics, Dover was helping to open out a new area of public discussion with a new honesty and directness of language. It was testimony to the book's radicalism that some of his critics condemned him for exhibitionism. Yet to adopt such a position at such a time could hardly be effected by a shrinking violet.

The entire mood of this pioneering book – exhaustively analytic, every page riddled with in-text references – was far from exhibitionist. Asked to explain the source of his research ideas, Dover replied that 'my approach to my subject is ..., in origin at least, scientific rather than literary-aesthetic'.[3] 'And how!' the reader might reply. Nor do accusations of self-advertisement fit with Dover's conduct as President. When invited to sign the protest against Margaret Thatcher's honorary degree in 1985, he readily signed it without any consultation with the Fellows, with no flamboyant announcement, and (according to his own account) without realizing that he would be the sole Oxford head of house to do so. Having spent so much of his career in St Andrews he felt a certain loyalty to universities beyond Oxford, and 'it simply did not enter my head at the time that a head of house was in any different position from anyone else in this respect'.[4]

When the library needed to extend into the space hitherto allocated to the President, Dover moved to the floor below into a rather cramped and dim room in the front quad, badly furnished, and not at all of the quality a head of house requires and deserves.[5] Rightly or wrongly, the world judges a President by the quality of the accommodation that the college sees fit to provide for him. The shabbier the accommodation occupied by the head of house, the less respected the college will seem to visitors, including potential donors. It is no accident that Dover's five successors since 1986 have remained in the fine room which Keith Thomas (see below) in effect acquired for them.

Dover's presidency was liberal towards the young. His skill at defusing student unrest came with him from St Andrews. However, he found that Corpus's so-called 'Joint Committee' of senior and junior members was 'not a nice committee': it met twice a term, and fomented discord. 'There was no recurrent occasion which I dreaded more', Dover recalled. Senior members in the committee were often facetious or sarcastic, 'which made me curl up'. He had learned years before that such a response was counter-productive, and 'there were occasions when the patience and courtesy of the junior members earned my respect' (*MC* 193–4). I always regretted the reluctance of Corpus bursars to consult the young, given that they had knowledge and insights not available to their seniors. Dover's predecessor as President, Derek Hall, had been positively frightened of junior members.

On junior-member representation in Governing Body, already an issue in 1977, I was, however, in two minds: as I wrote in that year, 'I don't feel very strongly either way. There's a strong liberal case *for* their representation, and there is a certain case against on the ground of the amount of time it would consume, the boredom of it, the question of how competent they are to contribute'. My attitude owed much to student disruption of American universities in 1970 over the Cambodia war – disruption I had observed in its full force in 1970 when on leave for a semester at the University of Michigan (Ann Arbor). None the less, in the early 1980s Dover continuously edged the Fellows towards making the change – latterly in the knowledge, from the Master of Corpus Cambridge, that junior-member representation there 'had a very civilising effect on the Fellows' (*MC* 192). By then I opposed the change, but Dover ultimately prevailed, and (with hindsight) rightly. This change superseded the counter-productive 'Joint Committee', and I soon realized that I had chosen the wrong side: Corpus's junior members subsequently showed themselves sensible and valuable members of Governing Body, and relations with them were considerably improved by comparison with the 1970s. Dover's reform helped to perpetuate the closeness of the Corpus community which was one of its hallmarks.

I think I was right, though, to oppose conceding voting rights at Governing Body to junior-member representatives. 'Over the years . . .', Dover recalled, 'I had come to realise how much more strongly I sympathised with the young than with the old' (*MC* 178, cf. 197). He really liked young people. Once to my astonishment I heard him tell newly-arrived undergraduates that the day they first came up, a day viewed apprehensively by many overworked tutors, was for him 'the most exciting day of the year'. I think he meant it. In general, however, I felt that Dover went too far in deferring to the young, who in any one generation are sometimes right, sometimes wrong. I recall my surprise, when attending a plenary meeting on college matters, how Dover chose to sit with the undergraduates on the floor, whereas I (then Senior Tutor) was at least sitting on a chair.

As Senior Tutor of Corpus (1984–6, 1988–90) I straddled the presidencies of Kenneth Dover and Keith Thomas and can view Kenneth's comparatively. In his six years as twice Dean of Arts at St Andrews, he had aimed to avoid the combination of conspiracy and confrontation that as Fellow of Balliol (1948–55) he had observed in A.D. Lindsay at the end of his time as Master. Instead, Dover learned the arts of unobtrusive leadership. He planted his ideas with others, and was happy to advance them when they reappeared from colleagues who by then had appropriated them as their own. Dover was collegial and believed as President in working through mobilizing the aptitudes of colleagues. As Senior Tutor I found him very easy to work with, perhaps partly because by 1984 he seemed beset by something of an inertia, offering few ideas of his own. He usually encouraged me to do what I wanted, and backed me when I ran into trouble. Keith Thomas, after taking office in 1986, quite rightly took the initiative more frequently, leaving me less interestingly but more correctly out of the limelight.

There even seemed an element of weakness in Dover's liberal outlook, exemplified in a small but significant episode. In 1985 I was much involved in preparing a more inviting college prospectus, and at first proposed for its front cover a pleasantly atmospheric photograph of the Corpus front quad during term showing senior and junior members in gowns. Although I was content for the photograph to be moved off the front cover, I thought (and still think) that David Miliband, the junior members' representative on the relevant committee, was weakening liberal values by advocating a Corpus which opted for an intolerant junior-member uniformity. In wanting the photo thrown out altogether, he and his contemporaries seemed not to see that Oxford's formalities (including academic garb) attract some young people. The junior-member representatives seemed to be repudiating the diversity of intake that makes for a lively community. At this juncture Kenneth walked up and down in the room trying to make up his mind on where to jump, and even considered seeking the opinion of an absent member of the committee, who happened then to be in Italy. In the end, Kenneth came down on the side of uniformity, and so the photograph was rejected.

Then in 1986 came Governing Body's discussion of whether the college should cease to bank with Barclays; some claimed that British links in South Africa helped to advance liberal values there, others that such links propped up the apartheid regime. On the vote it was a draw, with eight on each side, including Dover's personal vote for withdrawal; he then also used his casting vote for withdrawal, in the full knowledge of the convention for casting votes to endorse no-change. He chose not to leave the issue for his successor; this, he thought, 'would have felt terribly pusillanimous'. Besides, he had met two vice-chancellors in South Africa who thought withdrawal advisable, and in the end he felt 'if I've got to vote, I really want to vote for what I think should be done'. The decision to withdraw reinforced his popularity with the junior members.

Was he a good President? Yes, said J.C.R. President Miliband, who wanted a large room in the college named 'The Dover Room'. As a previous President was still alive, however, this would have been embarrassing, and it was later named after John Rainolds (President 1598–1607). Dover was very popular with the undergraduates. Among the Fellows he had his critics, though I personally liked, respected and admired him throughout. He was accessible, considerate, conscientious and efficient as President, exemplifying the combined active and contemplative life. Some of his critics with long memories, however, came out against him in 1994 when his controversial autobiography brought trouble to the College. As for the old members, their importance was growing in the 1980s when government funding was at risk. Frank Hardie, Dover's predecessor-but-one, thought the old members very important, and gave much time to them in the 1950s and 1960s. This did not come naturally to Dover, but as a former Fellow of Balliol he was familiar with the cultivation of old members which reflected Balliol's relative poverty among Oxford colleges. He was, he said, 'surprised, after Balliol, to find – when I came to Corpus – that old members just didn't count at all with the Fellows'; they 'regarded old members as just rather a nuisance, and I thought this was rather short-sighted, and of course it was a tremendous contrast to Balliol'. Corpus Fellows didn't even take gaudies (reunions of old members) seriously, so Dover had to edge them tactfully into new priorities. Unfortunately, he was rather too academic in outlook for his addresses to go down well with them at gaudies – as was immediately apparent when his successor seemed consummately practised in this art-form.

I came increasingly and regretfully to think that Dover's popularity with junior members partly reflected his tendency to give them what they wanted at the tail end of the period when anti-Thatcher attitudes were rife among them. I also came to feel towards the end of his presidency that his liberalism encapsulated an element of weakness, of taking the easiest way out. Biographers, however, sometimes forget that their subjects inhabit bodies. Dover in his last three years was tired, less from old age as such, more from the demands being made upon him as President. In reluctantly agreeing to chair the University's committee on the admissions system (1982–3) Dover faced the 'unusually daunting remit' of securing unanimity on the subject, a prospect whose very idea initially occasioned laughter within the committee itself. In twenty-seven meetings, the last three of which lasted for more than six hours and ended only at midnight, requisite unanimity within the committee was attained, but the strain in securing this was one component of the exhaustion which Dover experienced in the last three years of his presidency (*MC* 232–43). 'I have felt pretty tired ever since 1983, actually', he told me in 1992: 'it's a curious business really of sort of stretching the mechanism so that it never really quite goes back. And that's the effect that the Dover Committee had on me. Because it involved an enormous amount of work, particularly at the end when I was writing the report. I think I had three nights running getting to bed between one and two in the morning, and so on'.

Liberalism is integrally linked with the pursuit of reason, and there Dover could not be faulted. In his internal struggles as a teenager, he had come to identify his ill-tempered father with unreason and his mother with reason. Feeling on this and on other grounds vulnerable, he decided as a teenager, as he puts it, 'to cultivate stoicism, to make myself live within a shell impermeable both to my emotions on the way out and to other people's on the way in' (*MC* 28). Dover's continuing exercise of reason in later life emerges from how he ran Governing Body as President. Oxford colleges are, or should be, miniature democracies, with the head of house persuading but not commanding. There was never any question of Dover's 'fixing' meetings by informal chats beforehand with prominent Fellows. He explained that he 'didn't want ever to be thought to be lobbying, and particularly I didn't want to be thought to be intriguing . . . I would never have gossiped to one Fellow about another Fellow, until it came to the Trevor [Aston] problem, really'. In Governing Body Dover was far from hierarchical. I had personal experience of this in summer 1981. As a relatively junior Fellow I was put on the College Visitation, a two-man committee to report to Governing Body about aspects of the College. After our report had been submitted, the Domestic Bursar adjusted it before Governing Body had seen it. The President was willing to go along with this, but I objected in Governing Body, and argued that it should first come to Governing Body without alteration, and I was much relieved to find President Dover supporting me rather than the Domestic Bursar.

Only once in his ten-year presidency did I see Dover lose his temper in Governing Body, and it was characteristic that at the end of the meeting, in full view of the Fellows, he apologized to the Fellow concerned. His approach to Corpus Governing Body, as with the British Academy when dealing as its President with the Blunt affair,[6] was privately and painstakingly to accumulate the relevant facts, to speculate beforehand about likely arguments, and then initiate discussion. His respect for the Fellows' rationality was such that he saw no need for a strong steer from the chair: he thought they could and should digest the facts for themselves, and through discussion decide on what to do. In the Barclays Bank debate, for example, he came to Governing Body with two lists: the arguments for and against withdrawing from Barclays, apparently assuming that this would suffice to launch the debate. 'For heaven's sake give us a *lead*' was the half-audible comment from the 'invariably sensible'[7] physics tutor Ron Hill.

Some Fellows questioned Dover's approach to resolving differences between himself, the Fellows and the bipolar history Fellow Trevor Aston. In the run-up to the contest for the Corpus presidency in 1985 Dover compiled at the Fellows' request an extraordinarily detailed and meticulous memorandum on how his presidential time had been expended. Only later did the Fellows realize how much energy he had for years been using up on preventing an explosion. He concealed this continuously wearing activity, but those who could read between the lines belatedly realized it from the statistics he supplied. Bulky files of Aston/Dover correspondence survive to record years and years of treating Aston's problems as rational: a monument that testifies to reason's dogged but unavailing assault on unreason. Reason may be integral to liberalism, and open discussion may be in principle desirable in collective and personal relations, but reason must be monitored by common sense and imagination. Bearing that in mind, reason's optimistic deployment in human affairs outclasses a flaccid and cynical acquiescence in its absence. If we behave as though reason were a little more prevalent than it really is, we have a slightly better chance of getting events within our control.

In discussing Dover, disproportionate attention has been given to the 'Aston affair', fuelled by media yearning for a touch of melodrama.[8] In truth, the 'affair' arose from the reluctant struggle by the Fellows of Corpus to carry out their statutory duty: to run the college's affairs in a proper manner when challenged by the talented individual who became over-mighty in their midst. At no stage in the 'Aston affair' was Dover acting as an individual: he acted as trustee for the welfare of a college. For the distinguished classicist Donald Russell, Dover's self-esteem, 'always great', had 'reached monstrous proportions'.[9] But this does not allow for the role of language in distorting Dover's autobiographical reflections. Languages greatly interested him: in *Who's Who* 'historical linguistics' was one of the two recreations he specified. He told me that the one occasion on which he had felt ashamed of the Corpus Governing Body was when it declined to secure a correction to a mis-rendering in the Latin wording of Lord Hailey's memorial plaque in the College cloisters. Much of the publicity surrounding the Aston affair paradoxically originated with problems posed by Dover's precise, almost pernickety, use of language, which sometimes led him to diverge from quotidian usage. Dover's comments in two interviews illustrate his tendency towards academic, or perhaps 'unworldly', phrasing. James Cox, in a BBC interview with Dover, asked him whether he felt he was 'behaving in a rather inhuman fashion . . . because you say quite openly that if you could have got away with it, you would have murdered him'. To this Dover replied, 'Yes, yes, I think "inhuman" is not a bad description of that. When one is responsible for others, one is pushed sometimes in the direction of the inhuman'. Cox then pressed him, 'you accept that you did in fact murder him?' Cox had been paraphrasing what Dover had written in his autobiography,[10] but Dover immediately corrected language which he knew would be misunderstood by listeners whose customary vocabulary differed: 'Oh, no. Good heavens no'. In the autobiography, Dover had used the word 'murder' only in the context of a piece of legal advice he received; for his own conduct, he chose the almost equally misleading word 'kill', but also (and more accurately, but still misleadingly) 'plan to cause the death of'.

In his interview with Anthony Clare, he said that 'against the advice of one or two people'[11] he had none the less retained the word 'kill' because he thought it 'awfully important that people should realise what they're doing when they're doing something and if, in fact, you're contemplating not saving a man from death when you've reason to think he's taken an overdose, well, that is killing him ... and then one should use brutal words to describe things. But of course I wasn't feeling "my God, I must get rid of this bastard", you see. I was thinking ... "is there any way in which the situation can be improved for the college? Is there any way in which I can bring about a situation in which this man is dead?"'[12] For a distinguished scholar concerned to be precise in his vocabulary, Dover's is an extraordinary comment. It is of course usually desirable not to be squeamish, and to call a spade a spade, but there should be no blurring of the clear distinction between killing a person and standing back to acknowledge people's right to kill themselves if they land in intolerable situations despite every effort to dissuade them. 'Thou shalt not kill; but needst not strive / Officiously to keep alive'.

The flames were fanned throughout this episode by Dover's deliberately publicizing fleeting thoughts that anyone might inwardly entertain: as Philip Howard pointed out in his *Times* review of *Marginal Comment*, 'many would have such thoughts about a troublesome colleague, few would dream of publishing them'. Dover was, wrote Howard, 'recklessly prodigal with the truth', whereas 'worldly men would be more diplomatic'. He was 'wonderfully indiscreet about his life, from scholarship to sex'.[13] The distinguished philologist Anna Davies told me, when discussing the fuss over Dover's autobiography, that 'Oxford dons don't like the truth'; and Dover told Clare that 'there's no *point* in writing an autobiography if one conceals things'. Both statements are only partially true. It was not so much that Dover's critics among Oxford dons did not like the truth, more that they disliked Dover's lack of reticence, and perhaps even thought that it was fine for Dover to record his honest thoughts, but not to publish them so bluntly, and perhaps also not to publish them during the lifetimes of people or institutions likely to be hurt or damaged by them.

Dover retired a year early, aged sixty-six, and according to his successor 'his handover of the Presidency was impeccable'.[14] On driving back to Scotland in summer 1986, Kenneth and Audrey 'did feel an extraordinary sense of liberation from obligations and responsibilities', privately reacting just as he had when Aston died, and in the same way as anyone else would in similar circumstances (*MC* 246, cf. 230). Kenneth was not happy with the regime that followed a contested presidential election. As President he had been content with his modest domestic and office accommodation in Corpus and failed to understand why Keith Thomas wanted more. He regarded Thomas's appointment as 'a devastating repudiation of my concept of the job and the style I have consistently tried to follow'. Dover was mistaken: Thomas was the continuity candidate.[15] On 1 April 1985 Dover even contemplated retiring two years early, rather than 'hang on for another whole year in which a feeling of humiliation will be the predominant element'.[16] He would have been even less happy in 1996 if he had known that some Fellows said they would sign off from dinner if they heard that Dover occasionally emerged from retirement to dine in Corpus. This did not seem to me the way for any college, least of all Corpus, to treat a distinguished scholar in retirement. After a Classics gathering in Balliol on 4 November 1995, Dover did not spend the night in Corpus but in a somewhat seedy hotel near the station. Ewen Bowie to his great credit wanted something better for him, and in November 1999 engineered his return to Corpus for a conference, after which he stayed overnight in the college. In December 1999 Ewen floated a project for Corpus to celebrate his eightieth birthday (11 March 2000), as had occurred for Frank Hardie, but some Fellows objected to the idea, and nothing came of it.

Kenneth hated old age, not surprisingly for an active scholar, distinguished in both appearance and achievements and accustomed to good physical health. I once asked him how, with all his commitments, he seemed never to be in a hurry when moving around Corpus: 'it's an act', he replied. On a Christmas card in 2004, when aged eighty-four, he told me, 'I finished by 1997 writing the books I had wanted to write', and now 'eyesight worse, senility oppressive . . . goodbye to my ambition to learn Hebrew and Sanskrit and grow exotic plants. I sleep instead'. When in Christmas cards I said I was enjoying retirement, he did not conceal from me the future that he thought I was in for. 'Retirement is OK until the aches start', he wrote. And on another occasion, more concisely: 'you wait!'

JAY PARINI

Sir Kenneth Dover was a figure in my life, an academic luminary who shaped a lot of my thinking about what it means to teach well and to take myself seriously as a writer and academic. He was a complex man: a brilliant linguist and historian of Greek culture whose literal-mindedness (combined with an almost childlike simplicity) at times worked against him, as in his compulsively readable yet infamous memoir, *Marginal Comment*, which did nothing to enhance his reputation, although it's a remarkable book that has been widely underestimated.

As a student and young member of the teaching staff at St Andrews between 1968 and 1975, I got to know Kenneth well and, over the years, spent a good deal of time in his company. When he became President of Corpus Christi College in 1976, I would go to stay with him whenever I could – he always let me stay with him at the President's Lodge. Once, in the mid-eighties, he and Audrey, his wife of many decades, came to stay with my wife and me in Vermont, and we went hiking together in the Green Mountains. His almost giddy delight in the woods, and his alertness to the flora and fauna of New England, stays with me. The last time I saw Kenneth was only a year before his death, when he had long returned to St Andrews, retaking possession of his beloved home in Hepburn Gardens, with its opulent garden – he was a fanatical gardener and relished putting his hands in the soil, as when at Corpus Christi College, as President, he claimed a portion of the garden, sharing the shed with the gardener. As one might expect of a scholar, the house also boasted countless bookshelves, which sagged with the whole of Western European literature and history arranged in neat categories.

On one visit to St Andrews in the early nineties, he asked me if I would read some chapters of his memoir, and I agreed with some anxiety, especially when he said, 'I've been very frank'. I remember sitting up in bed wide-eyed in his guest room, astonished by what I discovered. I liked his 'frankness' about his own sex life, for the most part. Who cares if, as a young soldier in Italy in 1944, he masturbated in the out-of-doors? And yet there was something inadvertently funny about his tone, as when he writes: 'It was an absolutely still day, with a blue sky from one horizon to the other, and the Matese massif was covered with snow. The scene struck directly at my penis, so I sat down on a log and masturbated; it seemed the appropriate response.'

I don't think he ever realized how odd this might sound to many ears. Nor did he think how readers might react to passages about problems with impotence in later life, a situation perhaps brought on by overwork and anxiety, and which led him seriously to consider suicide as a way of escape. Indeed, he mentions in one astonishing footnote that there were at least five earlier times when he considered suicide, usually as an 'escape from humiliation' (*MC* 242). Was this sharing too much, I wondered? And could the lack of an erection really lead one to such drastic measures?

I was quite startled when, at a later point, I read 'The Aston Affair', a chapter which deals with the period when Kenneth was President at Corpus. As it happened, he so came to dislike his (once estimable) colleague, the historian Trevor Aston, that – after half a dozen years of doing what he could to help the man – he gave up, welcoming his suicide. 'I had no qualms', Kenneth wrote, 'about causing the death of a Fellow from whose non-existence the College would benefit' (*MC* 229). This sentence troubled me, and it still does. Kenneth suggests that he actually wished to kill Aston if he could manage this without getting into trouble, even consulting a lawyer on the matter! As one might expect, this part of the memoir proved marvellous fodder for the press. The story of his wish to murder Aston was especially newsworthy, with shades of Agatha Christie, and lurid accounts of the incident appeared in *The New York Times*, *The Washington Post*, and elsewhere.

Was Kenneth being as honest about this 'affair' as he pretends? Observers who knew him at the time have suggested that a self-punitive tone crept into his memoir here, and that Kenneth exaggerated his hard-heartedness. Certainly I could never reconcile the kind and always compassionate man I knew with his account of himself in the Aston affair. I remember vividly how, in the early seventies, we talked at length about a research student we both knew well who had serious problems with depression. Kenneth went out of his way to support and counsel him.

When I sat with Dover over breakfast after reading part of his manuscript through the night, I tried, gently, to suggest that he might keep some of these revelations to himself.

Audrey (whom I liked very much) looked on, obviously worried, suggesting that frankness wasn't necessarily artful. Kenneth, as one might expect, was immoveable. 'I will tell the truth about myself', he said, 'and let the chips fall'.

The chips came crashing, and Kenneth nearly upended his mighty reputation as a classical scholar, head of an Oxford college, and President of the British Academy. Fortunately, nobody who has any knowledge of the field of Greek studies, or the humanities in general, could sweep away the mountain of great work he accomplished, from *Greek Word Order* (1960) through *Aristophanic Comedy* (1972), *Greek Popular Morality in the Time of Plato and Aristotle* (1974), to *Greek Homosexuality* (1978), his most famous book, which had an audience well beyond what is usual for classical studies. But this only skims the surface. His editions of specific works by Thucydides, Aristophanes, and others have few peers.

I first met Dover soon after my arrival in St Andrews. His reputation had spread throughout the university, his name whispered with awe. My friend Christopher Rathbone introduced us, in passing, on the street one afternoon. Another friend, a student in the Classics department, was attending a series of lectures he offered on Greek comedy, and I slipped into the back of the classroom out of curiosity. I found myself absorbed by this man who had an obvious gift for teaching. Indeed, he sometimes recorded his own lectures and played them back to himself to see what he might correct to make them more intelligible. Professor Dover, with his bright shock of hair and distinctive moustache, his noble bearing and brisk demeanour, was a commanding figure in the room, the embodiment of Greek rationality. As a lame student of ancient languages, I was impressed by how he could read a dense passage in Greek and translate it by sight. Every lecture by Dover was a piece of theatre, with dramatic pauses, wry smiles and authoritative asides. And his obvious passion for the subject rippled through the room.

Near the end of this term, I introduced myself again after one class, thanking him for letting me sit in on the lectures. 'No need to thank me. I never admitted you to the class, did I?' I froze, terrified. Then he burst into laughter. 'I'm teasing you, dear boy. Let's have a cup of tea in my room.'

I followed him back to the department, where we talked for a long time, as he kept pummelling me with questions. What did I like to read? How did I find university education in Scotland compared to the United States? What did I think of the Vietnam War? What kind of parents did I have? My answers seemed to prompt a mood of recollection, and he told me about his own childhood. He was the only son of 'a minor civil servant' named Percy (whom I later got to know, as the elderly Dover lived with Kenneth and Audrey at Corpus until his death). He told me about his father's 'mental instability' – this seemed like too much sharing at the time. I asked about his educational path, and he told me he'd won a place at St Paul's School in London, where he fell in love with the Greek language. The sound, the sheer physicality, of the language had possessed him, and he determined to devote himself to the subject, even to read as much as he could in Greek before he entered university. 'It was the whole world to me', he said, telling me about his undergraduate years at Balliol.

I asked if there had been a special teacher who influenced him. He sucked in a deep draft of his omnipresent cigarette. 'You've heard of Eduard Fraenkel?' I had not. He paused, then told me about the great German philologist, who had come to Oxford in the thirties, having been driven out of his homeland by the Nazis. Dover had been one of the privileged few (Iris Murdoch among them) admitted to his famous weekly seminars on the *Agamemnon* of Aeschylus. 'His intellectual rigour, his vast acquaintance with the secondary literature, but mostly his intense focus on the text changed me forever. It was his seriousness that stayed with me. For him, the ancient Greeks walked among us.'

In the years when I was a postgraduate student and tutorial fellow in St Andrews, I often had drinks or dinner with Kenneth. The friendship became a priority. I couldn't get enough of his conversation, and we often talked about projects in hand. To this day, I owe a lot to Kenneth for what he taught me about habits of work. He got up early and went to his desk every day, without fail, making use of spare periods that are usually lost in the shuffle. 'I get some of my best work done in those twenty-minute snatches of time that most people toss away', he said. When he worked, the rest of life fell away, and he could accomplish a good deal in a short stretch. He was expert at what people now call, rather painfully, 'multitasking'. He would edit a bit of a Greek text, make a phone call to a colleague in another department, read an article in a journal, skim a newspaper, then return to editing the passage in the text before him. He made notes on random scraps of paper, which he never seemed to lose. And he kept the broad picture in mind: 'I have one central project at a time, and that never moves too far out of focus', he once said to me, scolding, when I told him I was writing both a novel and a biography.

In my view, Kenneth was shy and self-isolated, even self-absorbed, highly aware of his reputation and determined to maintain it as best he could. He had a brisk public manner which he deployed as longtime chair of department and dean in St Andrews, as head of a house in Oxford, and as President of the British Academy; but this wasn't him, not really. He performed these demanding leadership roles with professional focus and characteristic energy, as with everything he did. And yet few people got to know him well. In St Andrews, he had a small circle of friends whom he could trust, such as Douglas Gifford or Terence Mitford. In later life he often socialized with Christopher Rathbone, mentioned above: a cosmopolitan former lecturer in Russian, with whom he shared a love of European and classical literature. But the circle remained small, and our particular friendship was possible, I suspect, because I was not a professional in his field.

Nobody who depends on *Marginal Comment* for understanding Dover will come away with a full appreciation of the man in his complexity. There's a bluntness and ferocity in this memoir – and an unmistakably naïve tone – that (to a degree) undermines its effectiveness and distracts readers from the inherent brilliance of the writing. His style, here and elsewhere, was modeled on Lysias, the fourth century rhetorician and master of the unadorned style who became the subject of his Sather Lectures at Berkeley. I suspect that the Trevor Aston and Anthony Blunt episodes in the book are meant to show off his management style, which had its strengths and obvious limitations. This was all part of the carefully constructed (if inadequate) public face of a man at pains to show himself a person of consequence, someone who took his role seriously, if not too seriously. In private, however, and among friends and family, he was modest, personable, even genial, and willing to extend himself.

Once, after sitting through a seminar with him, I asked him back to my house to listen to some music and have a drink. He seemed delighted, eagerly consuming my whisky, and – at least this was my impression – listening with keen attention as I played several albums by Bob Dylan, whose music I loved. 'I'm not a poet', Kenneth said to me, 'though I've tried my hand at writing poems, never with much success. But I recognize poetry when I hear it. This man is a poet.' He went away with a loan of my Dylan albums, which I didn't get back for several months. (In later life, he bestowed an honorary doctorate on Dylan in his role as Chancellor of St Andrews. He remembered that Dylan said almost nothing to him but wondered if he got to keep his colourful stole!)

One of Kenneth's colleagues at Balliol and in St Andrews was Gordon Williams, whose work on Horace and Latin poetry in general has been justly admired. I knew Gordon quite well, too – especially after he left St Andrews and moved to a chair at Yale. We shared a fascination with Dover, often talking about him. 'Kenneth is all mind', Gordon once said. 'When he turns sideways, you realize there is only half a man in the room, the profile of a man.' This was harsh, but it points to an aspect of Kenneth that, even fifty years later, is still hard for me to understand fully. Anyone who has read his books knows what intellectual pressure he brought to bear on the page. Reading him, one is aware of his massive learning and professionalism. He admired rationality and logic and hated all forms of what he regarded as 'superstition'. But there was always something missing.

When I told him that I attended the local Anglican church in St Andrews, he quickly gave me a copy of *An Atheist's Values* by Richard Robinson. 'Now here is what I believe', he said. 'Morality does not depend on some mythical figure in the sky.' He had very little interest in Christianity, and he found the Gospels 'oddly unreadable and certainly unreliable.' He said that miracles didn't happen and that our brains were an arrangement of chemical elements, nothing more. Mental illness, he told me, must be 'sorted out with chemicals'. He was a fan of electroshock therapy, too, as it had helped his wife, and he recommended this treatment to me when I told him that I'd been feeling gloomy. (Needless to say, I ran a mile from this prospect.)

The cool-headed rational approach to life that Dover admired could seem peculiar. Once in Oxford I attended a Greek play in the garden of Corpus with Kenneth and the former Regius Professor of Greek at the university, E.R. Dodds. We had dinner that night, and I mentioned to Dodds that I'd recently read and admired *The Greeks and the Irrational*. He pursed his lips, bemused, and said to Kenneth: 'I don't think you much liked the book, did you? Irrationality is always, to you, an evil thing.' 'I do my best to be rational', Kenneth said. 'But I fail, like most of us.' This was an honest response, and it was typical of a man who said what he thought, as best he could, in every situation. His legacy, as a classicist, is not for me to comment on. But his originality and presence as a scholar certainly made a deep impression on me, and I don't doubt the importance of his example. I go back to his books whenever I feel the need to brace myself, to take myself seriously. He was, as Henry James might say, the real distinguished thing.

DAVID STUTTARD

I matriculated just a year too late. As a schoolboy considering universities, part of the lure of St Andrews had been that there I would study under Kenneth Dover, and, while his migration to Corpus Christi did not lead me to change my plans, in my first few years as a student his absence was tangible. Older contemporaries would speak with nostalgic awe about their lectures or tutorials with him, and a cartoon by a gifted graduate, which showed their erstwhile professor in the guise of a bird (an eagle rather than a black swan) along with the legend 'rara avis in terris', prompted many a fond anecdote. (It now emblazons the cover of *Owls to Athens*, the collection of essays on classical culture presented to Kenneth, which was published by OUP in 1990.)

During my undergraduate and postgraduate years Kenneth did, of course, return occasionally to St Andrews both to fulfil his duties as Chancellor of the University (from 1981) and to give the occasional public lecture, and I experienced at first hand what I had only heard about from others – the precise yet elegant style; the inimitably cultured smoker's voice; the delivery which, though always measured, was never dull. As I listened, I was struck by how he always spoke in perfectly formed sentences – no hesitations; no discourse markers; no filler words – sentences that were so well-honed and so entirely discrete that at the end of each you could almost hear the full-stop. It was something that I noticed in my later conversations with him, too: no matter how informal the setting, his sentence structure, his choice of vocabulary, his ability to express the most complex ideas with limpid clarity and razor-sharp precision suggested that, before he said a word, each utterance was fully weighed and each idea was fully shaped and formed, like an Athena emerging from the head of Zeus.

Of course, some of those ideas were revolutionary. Like many at the time, I was intrigued by the depiction of Athenian life in his ground-breaking *Greek Homosexuality* – to such an extent that when it came time for me to choose a subject for my Latin (or Humanities) MA dissertation, I tackled homosexuality in the Roman world. Despite the advice and encouragement of my supervisor, Robert Ogilvie, my efforts were clearly less convincing than Kenneth's had been. At the *viva*, one member of the Latin department observed that in his opinion Romans neither fully accepted nor totally scorned homosexuality but thought it to be not quite the done thing, 'like eating peas with a knife'.

It was only after graduating, when I returned to St Andrews a few years later, that I came more regularly into contact with Kenneth. He had kept on the family house in Hepburn Gardens and, having just retired from his post at Oxford, had now returned to live there permanently. He had also accepted an invitation to become a member of the Board of Governors at St Leonards School, which as luck would have it was where I had gone to teach Classics. So, keen to do all I could to bolster my sixth form A level students' chances in the run-up to their exams, I wrote Kenneth a letter (something we still did in the late 80s) asking if he might be prepared to speak to them and answer any questions they might have. He did not hesitate, and it was now, observing as he gracefully addressed their queries and gently corrected their sometimes worrying misconceptions, that I first saw him as a person rather than simply a legend.

On several further occasions I invited him back, not just to speak to my classicists, but to address the entire sixth form. By now I had set up a General Studies programme at the school, part of which involved monthly Friday-evening lectures, which were also open to the wider town community. Kenneth's lectures were always packed – the great and good of St Andrews made a point of hearing him whenever they possibly could – and his passion for communicating his subject to a young audience was evident.

Then in 1992, after another of his seminars with my students, I plucked up the courage to ask if he would look at my translation of Euripides' *Hekabe*, which I was planning to stage the next year. (I had previously asked my headmistress to give me a month's sabbatical to let me mount a production with professional actors, to be performed at St Leonards before touring to other schools within the UK, and inexplicably she had agreed.) Kenneth said he would be delighted and next day with some trepidation I posted the translation. A week or so later I received an invitation to Hepburn Gardens. As I rang the bell, I was more nervous than I had been for years.

The door was opened by Kenneth's wife, Audrey, a delightful lady with a gentle smile, who could not have made me more welcome or tried harder to put me at ease. Now Kenneth appeared, too, and he led me through to his study, which I remember as a large high-ceilinged room full of books and redolent of the scent of cigarettes. On his desk were at least two Greek texts of *Hekabe* (Oxford and Teubner), a commentary, the Liddell and Scott Greek lexicon (ninth edition) – and my translation, which I could already see was heavily annotated. Audrey brought in a tray with tea and biscuits. Kenneth and I sat at his desk. And we began.

What followed was one of the most rigorous intellectual workouts I have ever experienced. Kenneth had been through the text with a fine-tooth comb, and not only did he correct my errors, he challenged many of my decisions, too – not in any hostile, overbearing way, but in order to be certain that I meant and understood what I had written. While my lasting memory of that afternoon is of being put through a benign wringer, two things especially stick in my mind. The first is Kenneth's antipathy to the word 'thing'. He thought it lazy, and whenever 'thing' appeared in the translation (underlined in his copy), he paused disapprovingly and suggested that I might find something better. The second is his reaction to my translation of lines 799–801, which I had rendered as 'the gods are strong, and our belief in them is stronger. It is that belief that makes us think the gods exist, and that is the law by which we live, by which we can tell right from wrong'. Literal or not, he liked it, and in fact said that he had never quite come to grips with Euripides' meaning in this passage, but that this translation had helped him to do so.

So, it was with a spring in my step that I invited Kenneth as guest of honour to the first performance by the company I had established and somewhat grandly named 'Actors of Dionysus'. I could not have been more delighted by his reaction. 'Splendid', he declared. 'One of the two best productions of a Greek tragedy that I have ever seen.' It was the start of a long association between Kenneth and Actors of Dionysus. That summer we invited him to a performance of *Hippolytus* at the Edinburgh Festival Fringe, and his arrival with Audrey at a dismal and an otherwise almost empty church hall on Princes Street lent stardust to the occasion. Luckily audience figures picked up; the company grew from strength to strength; and Kenneth continued to be generous with his time and support.

For many years I would run my translations by him, making my pilgrimage to his study whenever circumstances allowed – even after I had left St Andrews. In time the mugs on the tray were replaced by whisky glasses, and sometimes, after we were finished, Audrey would take me on a tour of her beloved garden. Actors of Dionysus launched an occasional pamphlet, *Dionysus*, which contained first essays about Greek drama (Kenneth, of course, contributed), then transcripts of talks given before performances. For, as we took our productions across the UK, we would invite scholars to give a brief introduction to whichever play we were performing, usually in the auditorium itself, to any audience members who might wish to attend. Whenever we appeared at St Andrews University's Crawford Arts Centre, Kenneth was the star turn. We could be certain of a sell-out audience. Once more the great and good would clamour for admission, and they relished his pre-performance talks to such an extent that for the actors who would soon perform their dramas Kenneth was, quite literally, a hard act to follow.

Because they were so carefully honed, we had no need to ask Kenneth for a written version of his talks. Instead, we would record them – first on a standard cassette machine, then on what was for its time a relatively sophisticated tape recorder, which could be worn in a pocket, from where a microphone snaked up to the lapel. While Kenneth's delivery was always impeccable, the technology invariably was not. The microphone seemed incapable of remaining plugged in, and several times, as I transcribed his utterances, I found myself listening to Kenneth's voice from the muffled perspective of his trouser pocket.

His live audience was more fortunate. They hung on his every word. Even those words which in other circumstances might cause the pillars of St Andrews society to blush. Kenneth, after all, was famous for never pulling his punches when describing bodily functions, genitalia or sex acts and, while the vocabulary he employed might seldom have been heard in the polite sitting rooms of Fife's East Neuk, he delivered it with such a scholarly mien that it seemed always to be appropriate to the context, and not a member of his audience ever took offence.

Nonetheless, it probably did amuse him to be provocative. In 1994 at the garden party on the last day of my final term at St Leonards School, he sought me out to bid farewell to that part of my life, and as pupils and their guests swirled around us, he regaled me with the episode from his soon-to-be-published autobiography, *Marginal Comment*, in which he described the effect that gazing on an Italian landscape had aroused in him during the Second World War. (When the book appeared soon afterwards, his account of the episode would excite some lurid headlines in the press.) Once more, his choice of vocabulary was appropriate to the story, but some of those parents milling close by, who caught a snippet of our conversation, were quick to usher daughters out of earshot.

In the years that followed I kept in sporadic contact with Kenneth, seeing him whenever Actors of Dionysus visited St Andrews and communicating by letter about chapters he would contribute to the company's booklets on individual tragedies. My last contact came when I was assembling a collection of essays which would be published by

Duckworth in 2010 as *Looking at Lysistrata*. Naturally I was keen for Kenneth to be involved. He was, after all, one of the world's leading authorities on Aristophanes. It was just up his street. But it was not to be. The last letter I received from him, written in an unsteady hand, told of his ill health and apologized that because of it he felt that he was simply no longer able to do the subject justice. The book must go on without him.

A few months later he was dead. Yet, as this present volume attests, not just his memory but something of his indomitable life force still lives on. What opinions of academic life he might have entertained just twelve years following his death, we cannot tell. Yet opinions he would most certainly have had, and he would have laid them out unswervingly and with unerring logic – and perhaps with a twinkle in his eye. For, despite his legendary rationalism and, at times, his ruthlessness, Kenneth could be warm and kind. For years he acted as my mentor, and I was privileged to know him.

Notes

* For examples of Rebecca's paintings see http://www.rebeccadover.com/ (Eds).

1. *Principles of Political Economy*, in Mill 1965, 944. I am most grateful to Ewen Bowie for constructive and painstaking scrutiny of an earlier draft of these memories of Dover.
2. Charles-Edwards and Reid 2017, 401–2.
3. Dover to Harrison, 27 October 1994.
4. Harrison interview with Dover, 25 August 1992; an audio recording has been deposited in the Corpus Dover archive. All further quotations not otherwise attributed are taken from this interview.
5. Cf. Bowie in this volume.
6. See Osborne's chapter in this volume.
7. Dover's phrase, *MC* 197.
8. See further discussion in Harrison 1994a.
9. Russell to Harrison, 24 December 1994.
10. The passage alluded to by Cox, on the BBC radio programme 'The World at One', 3 December 1994, is *MC* 228–9.
11. When he showed me the typescript of *MC* before publication, I was one of those who urged him to change the wording. We appeared in his 'Acknowledgements' but he did not take our advice. I also suggested he might wish to consult Aston's two widows before publishing, but again without success.
12. Dover's interview with Anthony Clare for the BBC radio programme 'In the Psychiatrist's Chair', originally broadcast 20 August 1995: published in Clare 1998, 81–115, the present passage at p. 98 (though the text above corrects some small inaccuracies in the printed version).
13. *The Times*, 1 December 1994, p. 40.
14. Keith Thomas to Brian Harrison, 22 June 2022.
15. Harrison to Dover and Dover to Harrison, 1 April 1985.
16. Dover to Harrison, 1 April 1985.

BIBLIOGRAPHY

Adkins, A.W.H. (1960), *Merit and Responsibility: A Study in Greek Values*, Oxford.
Adkins, A.W.H. (1978), 'Problems in Greek popular morality', review of Dover (1974), *Classical Philology* 73: 143–58.
Aldrich, R. (2003), *Colonialism and Homosexuality*, London.
Amin, K. (2017), *Disturbing Attachments: Genet, Modern Pederasty, and Queer History*, Durham NC.
Andrewes, A. (1959), 'Thucydides on the causes of the war', *Classical Quarterly* 9: 223–39.
Auerbach, E. (1953), *Mimesis: the Representation of Reality in Western Literature*, trans. W.R. Trask, Princeton.
Austin, C.F. and S.D. Olson (2004), *Aristophanes Thesmophoriazusae*, Oxford.
Austin, J.L. (1962), *How to Do Things with Words*, ed. J.O. Urmson, Oxford.
Ayer, A.J. (1936), *Language, Truth and Logic*, London.
Ayer, A.J. (1977), *Part of my Life*, London.
Ayres, L., ed. (1995), *The Passionate Intellect. Essays on the Transformation of Classical Wisdom Presented to Professor I.G. Kidd*, New Brunswick, NJ/London.
Azoulay, V. (2004), *Xénophon et les grâces du pouvoir: de la charis au charisme*, Paris.
Baechle, N. (2007), *Metrical Constraint and the Interpretation of Style in the Tragic Trimeter*, Lanham, MD.
Bailey, C. (1918–19), 'Honour Moderations in Classics, Part III', *Oxford Magazine* 37: 97–9.
Bakker, S.J. and G.C. Wakker, eds (2009), *Discourse Cohesion in Ancient Greek*, Leiden.
Barrett, W.S. (1964), *Euripides: Hippolytos*, Oxford.
Baxandall, M. (1979), 'The language of art history', *New Literary History* 10: 453–65.
Bažant, J (1980), 'Classical archaeology and French nineteenth-century realists', *Listy Filologické* 103: 193–201.
Bažant, J. (1981), *Studies on the Use and Decoration of Athenian Vases*, 13–22, Prague.
Beard, M. (1995), 'Straight talk', review of Dover (1994), *London Review of Books* 17.3, 9 February 1995, 12–13.
Beattie, A.J. (1962), review of Dover (1960), *Classical Review* 12: 234–8.
Beazley, J.D. (1947), 'Some Attic vases in the Cyprus museum', *Proceedings of the British Academy* 33: 195–244.
Beazley, J.D. (1956), *Attic Black-Figure Vase Painters*, Oxford.
Beazley, J.D. (1963), *Attic Red-Figure Vase-Painters*, 2nd edn, 3 vols, Oxford.
Beazley, J.D. (1989), *Some Attic Vases in the Cyprus Museum*, ed. D.C. Kurtz, Oxford.
Bech, K. (2001), *Word Order Patterns in Old and Middle English. A Syntactic and Pragmatic Study*, Diss. Bergen.
Beekes, R.S.P. (2010), *A Greek Etymological Dictionary*, 2 vols, Leiden.
Bentley, M. (2011), 'British historical writing', in A. Schneider and D.R. Woolf, eds, *The Oxford History of Historical Writing. Volume 5, Historical Writing since 1945*, 291–309, Oxford.
Bentz, M. and C. Reusser, eds (2004), *Attische Vasen in etruskischem Kontext. Funde aus Häusern und Heiligtümern*, Munich.
Bers, V. (1984), *Greek Poetic Syntax in the Classical Age*, New Haven.
Bethe, E. (1907), 'Die Dorische Knabenliebe: ihre Ethik und ihre Idee', *Rheinisches Museum für Philologie* 62: 438–75.

Bevir, M. (1999), 'Foucault, power, and institutions', *Political Studies* 47: 345–59.
Biles, Z.P. and S.D. Olson (2015), *Aristophanes Wasps*, Oxford.
Billings, J. (2014), *Genealogy of the Tragic: Greek Tragedy and German Philosophy*, Princeton.
Blanshard, A. (2009), review of Davidson (2007), *Journal of Hellenic Studies* 129: 179–80.
Blanshard, A. (2010), *Sex: Vice and Love from Antiquity to Modernity*, Oxford.
Blanshard, A. (2015), 'Fantasy and the homosexual orgy: unearthing the sexual scripts of ancient Athens', in Masterson, Rabinowitz and Robson, eds (2015), 99–114.
Bloedow, E. (1993), 'Hermocrates' strategy against the Athenians in 415 B.C.', *Ancient History Bulletin* 7: 115–24.
Blondell, R. and K. Ormand, eds (2015), *Ancient Sex: New Essays*, Columbus Ohio.
Blundell, M.W. (1989), *Helping Friends and Harming Enemies: A Study in Sophocles and Greek Ethics*, Cambridge.
Blunt, A. (1966), *The Paintings of Nicolas Poussin: A Critical Catalogue*, London.
Blunt, A. (1967), *Nicolas Poussin*, London.
Blunt, A. (1968), *Sicilian Baroque*, London
Blunt, A. (1969), *Picasso's 'Guernica'*, London.
Blunt, A. (1975), *Neapolitan Baroque and Rococo Architecture*, London.
Blunt, A. (1978), *Baroque and Rococo: Architecture and Decoration*, Ware.
Blunt, A. and P. Pool (1962), *Picasso, the Formative Years: A Study of his Sources*, London.
Boardman, J. (1980), review of Dover (1978), *Journal of Hellenic Studies* 100: 244–5.
Bolling, G.M. (1935), review of Denniston (1934), *Language* 11: 260–2.
Bourdieu, P. (1977), *Outline of a Theory of Practice*, Cambridge.
Bourdieu, P. (2020), *Habitus and Field: General Sociology. Volume 2, Lectures at the Collège de France (1981–1982)*, Cambridge.
Bowie, E.L. (1985), 'Theocritus' seventh Idyll, Philetas and Longus', *Classical Quarterly* 35: 67–91.
Bowie, E.L. (2010), 'Sir Kenneth Dover. Obituary', *The Pelican Record* 46: 53–5.
Bowie, J. and G. Popova (2019), 'Grammar and discourse', in B. Aarts, J. Bowie and G. Popova, eds, *The Oxford Handbook of English Grammar*, 554–78, Oxford.
Bowra, C.M. (1966), *Memories*, London.
Boyle, A. (1979), *The Climate of Treason: Five who Spied for Russia*, London.
Bremmer, J.M. (1980), 'An enigmatic Indo-European rite: Paederasty', *Arethusa* 13: 279–98.
Bremmer, J.M. (1990), 'Adolescents, symposion, and pederasty', in O. Murray, ed., *Sympotica: A Symposium on the Symposion*, 135–49, Oxford.
Bresson, A. and F. de Callataÿ (2013), 'The Greek vase trade: some reflections about scale, value and market', in Tsingarida and Viviers, eds, 21–4.
Brock, M.G. and M.C. Curthoys, eds (1997), *The History of the University of Oxford*, vol. 6: *Nineteenth-Century Oxford, Part 1*, Oxford.
Brock, M.G. and M.C. Curthoys, eds (2000), *The History of the University of Oxford*, vol. 7: *Nineteenth-Century Oxford, Part 2*, Oxford.
Brockliss, L.W.B. (2016), *The University of Oxford: A History*, Oxford.
Brooke, C. (2002), 'Marginal Comment', *The Virtual Stoa*, 2 April, at https://virtualstoa.net/2002/04/02/11381267/.
Brown, K. and V. Law, eds (2002), *Linguistics in Britain: Personal Histories*, London.
Buck, C.D. (1955), *The Greek Dialects*, 2nd edn, Chicago.
Buckle, S. (2015), *The Way Out: A History of Homosexuality in Modern Britain*, London.
Buffière, F. (1980), *Éros adolescent: la pédérastie dans la Grèce antique*, Paris.
Bundrick, S. (2012), 'Housewives, *hetairai* and the ambiguity of genre in Attic vase painting', *Phoenix* 66: 11–35.
Bundrick, S. (2019), *Athens, Etruria and the Many Lives of Greek Figured Pottery*, Madison, WI.
Bundy, E.L. (1962), *Studia Pindarica*, 2 vols, Berkeley.
Burckhardt, J. (1998), *The Greeks and Greek Civilization*, trans. S. Stern, London.

Burkert, W. (1966), 'Kekropidensage und Arrhephoria: vom Initiationsritus zum Panathenäenfest', *Hermes* 94: 1–25 (= *Kleine Schriften* v, 160–85).
Burnyeat, M.F. (1997), 'Socratic midwifery, Platonic inspiration', *Bulletin of the Institute of Classical Studies* 24: 7–16.
Bury, R.G. (1926), *Plato. Laws*, 2 vols, London.
Bush, G. (1990), *An Unsentimental Education and Other Musical Recollections*, London.
Butler, J.P. (1993), *Bodies That Matter: On the Discursive Limits of 'Sex'*, London.
Butler, J.P. (2004), *Undoing Gender*, London.
Cairns, D.L. (1993), *Aidōs: The Psychology and Ethics of Honour and Shame in Ancient Greek Literature*, Oxford.
Cairns, F. (1972), *Generic Composition in Greek and Roman Poetry*, Edinburgh.
Calame, C. (1999), *The Poetics of Eros in Ancient Greece*, Princeton.
Calboli, G. (1994), 'Die klassische Rhetorik-/Stil-Forschung in Italien und E. Norden', in Kytzler et al., eds, 25–46.
Cancik, H. and H. Cancik-Lindemaier (1994), 'Formbegriffe bei Eduard Norden', in Kytzler et al., eds, 47–68.
Canfora, L. (1983), review of Gomme, Andrewes, Dover (1945–81) vol. v, *Gnomon* 55: 396–410.
Cannadine, D., ed. (2020), *A Question of Retribution? The British Academy and the Matter of Anthony Blunt*, Oxford.
Cant, R.G. (1992), *The University of St Andrews: A Short History*, 3rd edn, St Andrews.
Carey, C. (2011), 'Douglas Maurice MacDowell', *Proceedings of the British Academy* 172: 233–48.
Carnes, J.S. (1998), 'This myth which is not one: construction of discourse in Plato's *Symposium*', in Larmour et al., eds, 104–21.
Carter, M. (2001), *Anthony Blunt: His Lives*, London.
Cartledge, P. (1981), 'The politics of Spartan pederasty', *Proceedings of the Cambridge Philological Society* 27: 17–36.
Cartledge, P. (2001), *Spartan Reflections*, London.
Cartledge, P. (2002), *The Greeks: A Portrait of Self and Others*, 2nd edn, Oxford.
Cartlidge, B. (2014), *The Language of Menander Comicus in its Relation to the Koiné*. Diss. Oxon.
Case, T. (1891), *Proposed Scheme of Literae Humaniores*, Oxford.
Casella, V. (2018), *I lemmi giuridici di Arpocrazione: introduzione, testo, traduzione e commento*, Alessandria.
Cassio, A.C., ed. (1999), *Kata dialekton: atti del III colloquio internazionale di dialettologia greca* (Napoli–Fiaiano d'Ischia, 25–28 settembre 1996), *AION*, Sez. Filologica-Letteraria 19, Naples.
Cassio, A.C. (2002), 'The language of Doric comedy', in Willi ed. (2002), 51–83.
Catoni, M.L. (2010), *Bere vino puro: immagini del simposio*, Milan.
Ceadel, M. (2007), 'Gilbert Murray and international politics', in Stray, ed. (2007b), 217–38.
Ceccarelli, P. (2013), *Ancient Greek Letter Writing: A Cultural History (600 BC – 150 BC)*, Oxford.
Chankowski, V. (2013), 'La céramique sur le marché: l'objet, sa valeur et son prix', in Tsingarida and Viviers, eds, 25–38.
Chantraine, P. (1933), *La formation des noms en grec ancien*, Paris.
Chantraine, P. (1999), *Dictionnaire étymologique de la langue grecque: histoire des mots, avec un supplément* sous la direction de A. Blanc, Ch. De Lamberterie, J.-L. Perpillou, Paris.
Chapman, R.W. (1922), *The Portrait of a Scholar, and Other Essays Written in Macedonia, 1916–1918*, Oxford.
Charles-Edwards, T.M.O. and J. Reid (2017), *Corpus Christi College: A History*, Oxford.
Christie, I.R. (1984), *Stress and Stability in Late Eighteenth-Century Britain: Reflections on the British Avoidance of Revolution* (The Ford Lectures delivered in the University of Oxford 1983–1984), Oxford.
Clare, A. (1998), *In the Psychiatrist's Chair III*, London.

Bibliography

Clarke, J. (1998), *Looking at Lovemaking*, Berkeley.
Clarke, J. (2003), *Roman Sex*, New York.
Cohen, D. (1992), 'Review article: sex, gender and sexuality in ancient Greece', *Classical Philology* 87: 145–60.
Cohen, D. (1995), *Law, Violence and Community in Classical Athens*, Cambridge.
Collard, C. (2018), *Colloquial Expressions in Greek Tragedy*. Revised and Enlarged Edition of P.T. Stevens, *Colloquial Expressions in Euripides*, Stuttgart.
Collingwood, R.G. (1946), *The Idea of History*, Oxford.
Collini, S. (1964), Introduction to Snow (1964), vii–lxxi.
Collini, S. (1999), *English Pasts: Essays in History and Culture*, Oxford.
Colvin, S. (1999a), review of Dover (1997a), *Journal of Hellenic Studies* 119: 177.
Colvin, S. (1999b), *Dialect in Aristophanes and the Politics of Language in Ancient Greek Literature*, Oxford.
Connor, W.R. (1984a), *Thucydides*, Princeton.
Connor, W.R. (1984b), review of Gomme, Andrewes, Dover (1945–81) vol. v, *Classical Philology* 79, 230–5.
Craik, E.M., ed. (1990), *'Owls to Athens': Essays on Classical Subjects Presented to Sir Kenneth Dover*, Oxford.
Crawford, M.H. (2009), 'Peter Astbury Brunt 1917–2015', *Proceedings of the British Academy* 161: 63–83.
Crocq, M.-A. (2013), 'Milestones in the history of personality disorders', *Dialogues in Clinical Neuroscience* 15: 147–53.
Crossman, R. (1937), *Plato Today*, London.
Cunningham, V. (1994), 'Contract terminated', *Times Higher Education Supplement*, 9 December: 15.
Curd, P. (2007), *Anaxagoras of Clazomenae: Fragments and Testimonia*, Toronto.
Currie, R. (1994), 'The arts and social studies, 1914–1939', in Harrison, ed. (1994b), 109–38.
Damon, C. (2010), 'Déjà vu or déjà lu? History as intertext', *Proceedings of the Langford Latin Seminar* 14: 375–88.
Daston, L. and P. Galison (2010), *Objectivity*, New York.
Davidson, J.N. (1997), *Courtesans and Fishcakes: the Consuming Passions of Classical Athens*, London.
Davidson, J.N. (2001), 'Dover, Foucault and Greek homosexuality: penetration and the truth of sex', *Past & Present* 170: 3–51.
Davidson, J.N. (2007), *The Greeks and Greek Love: A Radical Reappraisal of Homosexuality in Ancient Greece*, London.
Davies, J.K. (2016), 'The historical commentary', in C.S. Kraus and C.A. Stray, eds, *Classical Commentaries: Explorations in a Scholarly Genre*, 233–49, Oxford.
De Jonge, C.C. (2007), 'From Demetrius to Dik: ancient and modern views on Greek and Latin word order', in J. Allan and M. Buijs, eds, *The Language of Literature: Linguistic Approaches to Classical Texts*, 211–32, Leiden.
De Jonge, C.C. (2008), *Between Grammar and Rhetoric: Dionysius of Halicarnassus on Language, Linguistics and Literature*, Leiden.
De Jonge, C.C. (2019), 'Linguistic naturalism and natural style: from Varro and Cicero to Dionysius of Halicarnassus', in G. Pezzini and B. Taylor, eds, *Language and Nature in the Roman Classical World*, 171–90, Cambridge.
Demand, N.H. (1980), review of Dover (1978), *American Journal of Philology* 101: 121–4.
Denniston, J.D. (1919–20a), 'Honour Moderations and Literae Humaniores', *Oxford Magazine* 38: 147–9.
Denniston, J.D. (1919–20b), 'Classical Moderations and Literae Humaniores', *Oxford Magazine* 38: 225–6.

Denniston, J.D. (1934), *The Greek Particles*, Oxford.
Denniston, J.D. (1952), *Greek Prose Style*, Oxford.
Denniston, J.D. (1954), *The Greek Particles*, 2nd edn, Oxford.
Denniston, J.D. and D. Page (1957), *Aeschylus: Agamemnon*, Oxford.
Denyer, N. (2007), 'Sun and line: the role of the Good', in G.R.F. Ferrari, ed., *The Cambridge Companion to Plato's Republic*, 284–309, Cambridge.
De Romilly, J. (1947), *Thucydide et l'imperialisme athénien*, Paris; Engl. trans., P. Thody, *Thucydides and Athenian Imperialism*, Oxford 1963.
De Romilly, J. (1956), *Histoire et Raison*, Paris; Engl. trans., E.T. Rawlings, *The Mind of Thucydides*, Ithaca NY 2012.
De Romilly, J. (1976), review of Dover (1974), *Journal of Hellenic Studies* 96: 208–10.
Des Jardins, J. (2011), 'Women's and gender history', in A. Schneider and D.R. Woolf, eds, *The Oxford History of Historical Writing. Volume 5, Historical Writing Since 1945*, 136–58, Oxford.
Devereux, G. (1968), 'Greek pseudo-homosexuality and the "Greek miracle"', *Symbolae Osloenses* 42: 69–92.
Dickey, E. (1996), *Greek Forms of Address from Herodotus to Lucian*, Oxford.
Dik, H. (1995), *Word Order in Ancient Greek. A Pragmatic Account of Word Order Variation in Herodotus*, Amsterdam.
Dik, H. (2007), *Word Order in Greek Tragic Dialogue*, Oxford.
Dindorf, W. (1853), *Harpocrationis Lexicon in decem oratores Atticos*, 2 vols, Oxford.
Dobree, P.P. (1874), *Adversaria critica*, vol. I, Berlin.
Dodds, E.R. (1936), *Humanism and Technique in Greek Studies: Inaugural Lecture*, Oxford. [Repr. in *Arion* 7 (1968): 5–20.]
Dodds, E.R. (1951), *The Greeks and the Irrational*, Berkeley.
Dodds, E.R. (1964), 'Classical teaching in an altered climate', *Proceedings of the Classical Association* 61: 11–23.
Dodds, E.R. (1977), *Missing Persons: An Autobiography*, Oxford.
Dodds, E.R. (1999), 'The rediscovery of the Classics', *Classics Ireland* 6: 92–8. [Originally publ. in *The Irish Statesman* II.42, 10 April 1920: 346–7.]
Donaldson, J. (1911), *Essays and Addresses Delivered in the University of St Andrews*, St Andrews.
Donini, G. (1964), 'Thucydides vii 42.3: Does Thucydides agree with Demosthenes' view?', *Hermes* 92: 116–19.
Douglas, J.S. (1881), *The Life and Selections from the Correspondence of William Whewell, DD*, London.
Dover, K.J. (1950), 'The chronology of Antiphon's speeches', *Classical Quarterly* 44: 44–60.
Dover, K.J. (1952), review of V. Ehrenberg, *The People of Aristophanes*, *Cambridge Journal* 5: 636–8.
Dover, K.J. (1953), 'La colonizzazione della Sicilia in Tucidide', *Maia* n.s. 6: 1–20; German trans. in Herter 1968, 344–68.
Dover, K.J. (1955), review of A.N. Ammann, *-ΙΚΟΣ bei Platon. Ableitung und Bedeutung* (Freiburg, 1953), *Classical Review* 5: 206–7.
Dover, K.J. (1957) 'The political aspect of Aeschylus' *Eumenides*', *Journal of Hellenic Studies* 77: 230–7.
Dover, K.J. (1960), *Greek Word Order*, Cambridge.
Dover, K.J. (1963), 'Notes on Aristophanes' *Acharnians*', *Maia* 15: 6–25.
Dover, K.J. (1964a), 'Eros and nomos (Plato, *Symposium* 182A-185C)', *Bulletin of the Institute of Classical Studies* 11: 31–42.
Dover, K. J. (1964b), 'The poetry of Archilochos', in J. Pouilloux, ed., *Archiloque* (Fondation Hardt Entretiens X), 181–222, Geneva.
Dover, K.J. (1964c), 'Aeschylus, fragment 248M', *Classical Review* 14: 12.

Bibliography

Dover, K.J. (1965a), *Thucydides Book VI*, Oxford.
Dover, K.J. (1965b), *Thucydides Book VII*, Oxford.
Dover, K.J. (1966), 'Aristophanes' speech in Plato's *Symposium*', *Journal of Hellenic Studies* 86: 41–50.
Dover, K.J. (1968a), *Aristophanes Clouds*, Oxford.
Dover, K.J. (1968b), *Lysias and the 'Corpus Lysiacum'*, Berkeley and Los Angeles.
Dover, K.J. (1968c), 'Greek comedy', in M. Platnauer, ed., *Fifty Years (and Twelve) of Classical Scholarship*, 96–129, Oxford.
Dover, K.J. (1970), 'Lo stile di Aristofane', *Quaderni Urbinati di Cultura Classica* 9: 7–23.
Dover, K.J. (1971), *Theocritus: Select Poems*, Basingstoke and London.
Dover, K.J. (1972a), *Aristophanic Comedy*, London.
Dover, K.J. (1972b), review of P. Green, *Armada from Athens* (New York, 1970), *Phoenix* 26: 297–300.
Dover, K.J. (1973a), 'Classical Greek attitudes to sexual behaviour', *Arethusa* 6: 59–73.
Dover, K.J. (1973b), *Thucydides* (*Greece & Rome* New Surveys in the Classics, no. 7), Oxford.
Dover, K.J. (1973c), 'Some neglected aspects of Agamemnon's dilemma', *Journal of Hellenic Studies* 93: 58–69.
Dover, K.J. (1974), *Greek Popular Morality in the Time of Plato and Aristotle*, Oxford.
Dover, K.J. (1976a), 'On writing for the general reader', *Proceedings of the Classical Association* 73: 9–19.
Dover, K.J. (1976b), 'ΗΛΙΟΣ ΚΗΡΥΞ', in J. Bremer et al., eds, *Miscellanea tragica in honorem J. C. Kamerbeek*, 49–53, Amsterdam.
Dover, K.J. (1976c), 'Linguaggio e caratteri aristofanei', *Rivista di Cultura Classica e Medioevale* 18: 357–71.
Dover, K.J. (1977), 'I tessuti rossi dell'*Agamemnone*', *Dioniso* 48: 55–69.
Dover, K.J. (1978), *Greek Homosexuality*, London. [See also Dover (1989), (2016)]
Dover, K.J. (1979), 'Il linguaggio del canto nelle culture primitive', *Quaderni di Storia* 9: 225–45.
Dover, K.J. (1980a), *Plato Symposium*, Cambridge.
Dover, K.J. (1980b), 'Expurgation of Greek literature', in W. den Boer, ed., *Les études classiques aux XIXE et XXE siècles* (Fondation Hardt Entretiens XXVI), 55–89, Geneva.
Dover, K.J. (1980c), 'The speakable and the unspeakable', *Essays in Criticism* 30: 1–8.
Dover, K.J. (1981a), 'Thucydides' historical judgement: Athens and Sicily', *Proceedings of the Royal Irish Academy* 81c: 231–8, reprinted in Dover 1988a, 74–82.
Dover, K.J. (1981b), 'Presidential Address', *Proceedings of the British Academy* 67: 77–82.
Dover, K.J. (1981c), 'The colloquial stratum in classical Attic prose', in G.S. Shrimpton and D.J. McCargar, eds, *Classical Contributions: Studies in Honor of M.F. McGregor*, 15–25, Locust Valley NY.
Dover, K.J. (1981d), 'The language of classical Attic documentary inscriptions', *Transactions of the Philological Society* 79: 1–14.
Dover, K.J. (1982), *The Greeks*, 2nd edn, Oxford.
Dover, K.J. (1983a), 'Thucydides "as history" and "as literature"', *History and Theory* 22: 54–63 [reprinted in Dover 1988a, 53–63, and in Rusten 2009, 44–59].
Dover, K.J. (1983b), 'The portrayal of moral evaluation in Greek poetry', *Journal of Hellenic Studies* 103: 35–48.
Dover, K.J. (1983c), review of Brooks Otis, *Cosmos and Tragedy*, *Notes and Queries* 30: 242.
Dover, K.J. (1984), 'Archaic Greece and the continuity of ancient civilization', in J. Harmattan, ed., *Proceedings of the VIIth Congress of the International Federation of the Societies of Classical Studies*, vol. 1, 23–32, Budapest.
Dover, K.J. (1985), 'Some types of abnormal word-order in Attic comedy', *Classical Quarterly* 35: 321–43.

Bibliography

Dover, K.J. (1987), *Greek and the Greeks. Collected Papers Volume I: Language, Poetry, Drama*, Oxford.
Dover, K.J. (1988a), *The Greeks and their Legacy. Collected Papers Volume II: Prose Literature, History, Society, Transmission, Influence*, Oxford.
Dover, K.J. (1988b), 'Il valore degli studi classici', *L'umana avventura*, summer-autumn: 59-60. [Translated in an appendix to Halliwell's chapter in this volume.]
Dover, K.J. (1988c), 'A sharer of gifts', review of Wilson (1987), *Times Literary Supplement* 4447 (24-30 June): 700.
Dover, K.J. (1989), *Greek Homosexuality*, updated and with a new postscript, Cambridge Mass.
Dover, K.J. (1991), review of Halperin (1990), *Classical Review* 41: 161-2.
Dover, K.J., ed. (1992), *Perceptions of the Ancient Greeks*, Oxford.
Dover, K.J. (1993a), *Aristophanes Frogs*, Oxford.
Dover, K.J. (1993b), 'Russell Meiggs 1902-1989', *Proceedings of the British Academy* 80: 361-70.
Dover, K.J. (1994), *Marginal Comment: A Memoir*, London. [Second impression, 1995, contains enlarged Addenda on pp. 263-5. See also Dover (2023).]
Dover, K.J. (1997a), *The Evolution of Greek Prose Style*, Oxford.
Dover, K.J., ed. (1997b), *Ancient Greek Literature*, 2nd edn, Oxford.
Dover, K.J. (2002), 'Some evaluative terms in Aristophanes', in Willi, ed. (2002), 85-97.
Dover, K.J. (2016), *Greek Homosexuality*, reissue of Dover (1989) with Forewords by S. Halliwell, J. Masterson and J. Robson, London.
Dover, K.J. (2023), *Marginal Comment: A Memoir*, reissued with editorial material by S. Halliwell and C.A. Stray, London.
Dowling, L. (1994), *Hellenism and Homosexuality in Victorian Oxford*, Ithaca NY.
Dryer, M.S. (2004), 'Word order', in T. Shopen, ed., *Language Typology and Syntactic Description. Volume I: Clause Structure*, 61-131, Cambridge.
Duncan, B. (2005), *The Same Language*, ed. J. Howard, new edn, Tuscaloosa.
Edelman, L. (2004), *No Future: Queer Theory and the Death Drive*, Durham NC.
Elden, S. (2016), *Foucault's Last Decade*, Cambridge.
Elliott, D. (2020), *The Corruptor of Boys: Sodomy, Scandal, and the Medieval Clergy*. Philadelphia.
Ellis, H. (2012), *Generational Conflict and University Reform: Oxford in an Age of Revolution*, Leiden.
Elsner, J. (2006), 'From empirical evidence to the big picture: some reflections on Riegl's concept of *Kunstwollen*', *Critical Inquiry* 32: 741-66.
Elsner, J. (2010), 'Art history as ekphrasis', *Art History* 33: 10-27.
Elsner, J. and K. Lorenz (2012), 'The genesis of iconology', *Critical Inquiry* 38: 483-512.
Elsner, J. (2021), 'Room with a few: Eduard Fraenkel and the receptions of reception', in Harrison and Pelling, eds, 319-48.
Engel, D.M. (2000), review of Dover 1997a, *Mnemosyne* 53: 222-9.
England, E.B. (1921), *Plato: The Laws*, 2 vols, Manchester.
Enkvist, N.E. (1967), *Linguistics and Style*, London.
Enkvist, N.E. (1973), *Linguistic Stylistics*, The Hague/Paris.
Evangelista, S. (2006), 'Lovers and philosophers at once: aesthetic Platonism in the Victorian fin de siècle', *The Yearbook of English Studies* 36: 230-44.
Evangelista, S. (2009), *British Aestheticism and Ancient Greece: Hellenism, Reception, Gods in Exile*, Basingstoke.
Evangelista, S. (2010), 'Aesthetic encounters: the erotic visions of John Addington Symonds and Wilhelm von Gloeden', in L. Calè and P. Di Bello, eds, *Illustrations, Optics and Objects in Nineteenth-Century Literary and Visual Cultures*, 87-104, Basingstoke.
Farnell, L.R. (1898), *The Question of a Three-years' Classical Course and a Single Examination*, Oxford.

Bibliography

Farrar, A.S. (1856), *Hints to Students in Reading for Classical Honours in the University of Oxford*, Oxford.
Favi, F. (2020), *Epicarmo e pseudo-Epicarmo (frr.240–97). Introduzione, traduzione e commento*, Göttingen.
Fehling, D. (1969), *Die Wiederholungsfiguren und ihr Gebrauch bei den Griechen vor Gorgias*, Berlin.
Fehling, D. (1972), 'Nachlass Sophie Trenkner', *Gnomon* 44: 320.
Ferrari, G. (2002), *Figures of Speech: Men and Maidens in Ancient Greece*, Chicago.
Ferrari, G. (2003), 'Myth and genre on Athenian vases', *Classical Antiquity* 22: 37–54.
Finley, M.I. (1959), 'Was Greek civilisation based on slave labour', *Historia* 8: 145–64.
Finley, M.I. (1964), 'Crisis in the Classics', in J.H. Plumb, ed., *Crisis in the Humanities*, 11–23, Harmondsworth.
Finley, M.I. (1972), *Aspects of Antiquity: Discoveries and Controversies*, Harmondsworth.
Finley, M.I. (1973), *Democracy Ancient and Modern*, London.
Fisher, N.R.E. (1976), '*Hybris* and dishonour: I', *Greece and Rome* 23: 177–93.
Fisher, N.R.E. (1992), *Hybris: A Study in the Values of Honour and Shame in Ancient Greece*, Warminster.
Fisher, N.R.E. (2001), *Aeschines: Against Timarchos*, Oxford.
Foucault, M. (1976–2018), *Histoire de la sexualité*, 4 vols, Paris.
Foucault, M. (1982), 'Des caresses d'hommes considérées comme un art', *Libération*, 1 June 1982, 27.
Foucault, M. (1985), *The Use of Pleasure: Volume 2 of The History of Sexuality*, trans. R. Hurley, London.
Foucault, M. (1994), 'Des caresses d'hommes considérées comme un art', in D. Defert, F. Ewald, and J. Lagrange, eds, *Dits et écrits, 1954–1988: vol. 4, 1980–88*, 315–17, Paris.
Fowler, R.L. (1991), 'Gilbert Murray: four (five) stages of Greek religion', in W.M. Calder III, ed., *The Cambridge Ritualists Reconsidered*, 79–95, Atlanta.
Fowler, R.L. (1999), 'The authors named Pherecydes', *Mnemosyne* 52: 1–15.
Fox, M. (1998), 'The constrained man', in L. Foxhall and J.B. Salmon, eds, *Thinking Men: Masculinity and its Self-Representation in the Classical Tradition*, 6–22, London.
Foxhall, L. (1994), 'Pandora unbound: A feminist critique of Foucault's *History of Sexuality*', in A. Cornwall and N. Lindisfarne, eds, *Dislocating Masculinity: Comparative Ethnographies*, 133–46, London.
Fraenkel, Eduard (1935), *Rome and Greek Culture: Inaugural Lecture*, Oxford.
Fraenkel, Eduard (1964), *Kleine Beiträge zur klassischen Philologie*, Rome.
Fraenkel, Ernst (1906), *Griechische Denominativa in ihrer geschichtlichen Entwicklung und Verbreitung*, Göttingen.
Frazer, J.G. (1898), *Pausanias' Description of Greece, Translated with a Commentary*, 6 vols, London.
Frazer, J.G. (1890–1915), *The Golden Bough: A Study in Comparative Religion* (2 vols, 1890; 3 vols, 1900; 12 vols, 1906–15), London.
Freeman, E. (2010), *Time Binds: Queer Temporalities, Queer Histories*, Durham NC.
Frisk, H. (1932), *Studien zur griechischen Wortstellung*, Göteborg.
Furley, W.D. (1996), *Andokides and the Herms* (Bulletin of the Institute of Classical Studies Suppl. 65), London.
Gagarin, M. (2002), *Antiphon the Athenian: Oratory, Law, and Justice in the Age of the Sophists*, Austin.
Gaifman, M. (2015), 'Visual evidence', in E. Eidinow and J. Kindt, eds, *The Oxford Handbook of Ancient Greek Religion*, 51–66, Oxford.
Gaifman, M. (2018), *The Art of Libation in Classical Athens*, New Haven.
Gaifman, M. and V. Platt (2018), 'Introduction: from Grecian urn to embodied object', *Art History* 41: 402–19.

Gałęzowski, M. (2006), 'Zofia Trenkner (1908-1958)', *Meander* 3: 348-51.
Garrity, T.F. (1998), 'Thucydides 1.22.1: content and form in the speeches', *American Journal of Philology* 119: 361-84.
de la Genière, J. (2009), 'Les amateurs des scènes érotiques de l'archaïsme récent', in A. Tsingarida, ed., *Shapes and Uses of Greek Vases (7th-4th Centuries BC)*, Brussels.
Gibson, R. (2021), 'Fifty years of green and yellow: the Cambridge Greek and Latin series 1970-2020', in Harrison and Pelling, eds, 175-217.
Giddens, A. (1993), *The Transformation of Intimacy: Sexuality, Love and Eroticism in Modern Societies*, Cambridge.
Gilliver, P. (2016), *The Making of the Oxford English Dictionary*, Oxford.
Goldhill, S.D. (1991), *The Poet's Voice: Essays on Poetics and Greek Literature*, Cambridge.
Goldhill, S.D. (1998), 'The seductions of the gaze: Socrates and his girlfriends', in P. Cartledge, P. Millett, and S. von Reden, eds, *Kosmos: Essays in Order, Conflict and Community in Classical Athens*, 105-24, Cambridge.
Goldhill, S.D. (2011), *Classical Antiquity and Victorian Culture: Art, Opera, Fiction, and the Proclamation of Modernity*, Princeton.
Goldhill, S.D. (2022), *What Is a Jewish Classicist? Essays on the Personal Voice and Disciplinary Politics*, London.
Gombrich, E.H. (1960), *Art and Illusion*, London.
Gomme, A.W., A. Andrewes, and K.J. Dover (1945-81), *A Historical Commentary on Thucydides*, 5 vols, Oxford.
Gordon, M.C. (1945), *The Life of George S. Gordon 1881-1942*, London.
Gould, J. (1958-9), 'Languages and literature', *Oxford Magazine* 77: 382-6.
Gould, J. (1978), 'Greek popular morality', review of Dover (1974), *Classical Review* 28: 285-7.
Gow, A.S.F. (1952), *Theocritus: Edited with a Translation and Commentary*, 2nd edn, 2 vols, Cambridge.
Grafton, A.T. (1992), 'Germany and the West 1830-1900', in Dover, ed. (1992), 224-45.
Graham, A.J. (1992), 'Thucydides 7.13.2 and the crews of Athenian triremes', *Transactions of the American Philological Association* 122: 257-70.
Graham, A.J. (1998), 'Thucydides 7.13.2 and the crews of Athenian triremes: an addendum', *Transactions of the American Philological Association* 128: 89-114.
Greenberg, D.F. (1988), *The Construction of Homosexuality*, Chicago.
Greer, G. (1970), *The Female Eunuch*, London.
Grethlein, J. (2008), 'Eine herodoteische Deutung der sizilischen Expedition (Thuc. 7.87.5f)?', *Hermes* 136: 129-42.
Griffin, J. (1986), 'Words and speakers in Homer', *Journal of Hellenic Studies* 106: 36-57.
Griffith, M. (2007), 'Gilbert Murray on Greek literature: the Great/Greek man's burden', in Stray, ed. (2007b), 51-80.
Groot, A.W. de (1921), *Der antike Prosarhythmus. I*, Groningen.
Grundy, G.B. (1945), *Fifty-five Years at Oxford: An Unconventional Autobiography*, London.
Guarducci, M. (1961), 'Epigraphical appendix', in G.M.A. Richter, *The Archaic Gravestones of Attica*, 153-72, London.
Gutzwiller, K.J. (1996), 'The evidence for Theocritean poetry books', in A. Harder, R. Regtuit, G. Wakker, eds, *Theocritus*, 119-48, Groningen.
Hackforth, R. (1952), *Plato's Phaedrus*, Cambridge.
Halliwell, S. (2011), 'Kenneth Dover and the Greeks', Hellenic Society memorial lecture: https://risweb.st-andrews.ac.uk/portal/en/activities/kenneth-dover-and-the-greeks(0b21e2cb-d9d1-4740-9424-7d451f686d8d).html
Halliwell, S. (2016a), '*Eros* and life values in Plato's *Symposium*', in M. Tulli and M. Erler, eds, *Plato in Symposium: Selected Papers from the 10th Symposium Platonicum*, 3-13, Sankt Augustin.

Bibliography

Halliwell, S. (2016b), 'Foreword: the book and its author', in Dover (2016), vii–xiv.
Halperin, D.M. (1990), *One Hundred Years of Homosexuality*, London.
Halperin, D.M. (2002), *How to Do the History of Homosexuality*, Chicago.
Halperin, D.M. (2015), 'Epilogue: not fade away', in Blondell and Ormand, eds, 308–28.
Halperin, D.M., J.J. Winkler, and F.I. Zeitlin, eds (1990), *Before Sexuality: The Construction of Erotic Experience in the Ancient Greek World*, Princeton.
Hammond, N.G.L. (1966), review of Dover (1965b), *Journal of Hellenic Studies* 86: 186–7.
Handley, E.W. (1976), 'Ρυθμέω', *Bulletin of the Institute of Classical Studies* 23: 58.
Hare, R.M. (1952), *The Language of Morals*, Oxford.
Harris, E.M. (2014), 'Nicias' illegal proposal in the debate about the Sicilian expedition (Thuc. 6.14)', *Classical Philology* 109: 66–72.
Harris, J. (1994), 'The arts and social sciences, 1939–1970', in Harrison, ed. (1994b), 217–49.
Harrison, B. (1994a), 'The Kenneth Dover I knew', *Times Higher Education Supplement*, 23 December: 16–17.
Harrison, B., ed. (1994b), *The History of the University of Oxford*, vol. 8: *The Twentieth Century*, Oxford.
Harrison, S.J. (1994), 'Robert George Murdoch Nisbet', *Biographical Memoirs of Fellows of the British Academy* 13: 365–82.
Harrison, S.J. and C. Pelling, eds (2021), *Classical Scholarship and its History: Essays in Honour of Christopher Stray*, Berlin.
Hartsock, N. (1983), 'The feminist standpoint: developing the ground for a specifically feminist historical materialism', in S. Harding and M.B. Hintikka, eds, *Discovering Reality. Feminist Perspectives on Epistemology, Metaphysics, Methodology, and Philosophy of Science*, 283–310, New York.
Healey, D. (1989), *The Time of My Life*, London.
Hedreen, G. (2016), *The Image of the Artist in Archaic and Classical Greece*, Cambridge.
Heinemann, A, (2016), *Der Gott des Gelages: Dionysos, Satyrn und Mänaden auf attischem Trinkgeschirr des 5. Jahrhunderts v. Chr.*, Berlin.
Heitland, W.E. (1926), *After Many Years: A Tale of Experiences and Impressions Gathered in the Course of an Obscure Life*, Cambridge.
Henderson, I. (1960), 'The teacher of Greek', in Smith and Toynbee, eds, 125–48.
Henderson, J. (2006), *'Oxford Reds': Classic Commentaries on Latin Classics*, London.
Henderson, J. (2007), 'The "Euripides reds" series: Best-laid plans at OUP', in C.A. Stray, ed., *Classical Books: Scholarship and Publishing in Britain since 1800*, 143–75.
Henry, M.M. (1995), *Prisoner of History: Aspasia of Miletus and Her Biographical Tradition*, Oxford.
Herter, H. (1968), *Thukydides* (Wege der Forschung), Darmstadt.
Hickson, A. (1995), *The Poisoned Bowl: Sex, Repression and the Public School*, London.
Higham, T. (1949), 'Introduction', in J.G. Barrington-Ward et al., eds, *Some Oxford Compositions*, Oxford.
Highet, G. (1976), *The Immortal Profession: The Joys of Teaching and Learning*, New York.
Hilliard, C. (2021), *A Matter of Obscenity: The Politics of Censorship in Modern England*, Princeton.
Hirst, F.W. (1947), *In the Golden Days*, London.
Hobden, F. (2013), *The Symposion in Ancient Greek Thought and Society*, Cambridge.
Hornblower, S. (2004), *Thucydides and Pindar*, Oxford.
Hornblower, S. (2008), *A Commentary on Thucydides*, vol. iii, Oxford.
Howard-Johnston, J.D., 'A Chronicle of Corpus Christi College, Oxford. 1971–2009', (unpublished manuscript).
Hudson-Williams, H.Ll. (1962), 'Greek style', *Classical Review* 12: 238–9.
Humbert, J. (1960), *Syntaxe grecque*, 2nd edn, Paris.

Hunter, R. (1996), *Theocritus and the Archaeology of Greek Poetry*, Cambridge.
Hunter, R. (1999), *Theocritus. A Selection*, Cambridge.
Hunter, R. (2004), *Plato's Symposium*, Oxford.
Hunter, R. (2008), *On Coming After. Studies in Post-Classical Greek Literature and its Reception*, Berlin.
Hunter, R. (2015), 'Sweet Stesichorus: Theocritus 18 and the *Helen* revisited', in P.J. Finglass and A. Kelly, eds, *Stesichorus in Context*, 145–63, Cambridge.
Hunter, R. (2021), 'Theocritus and the bucolic Homer', in P. Kyriakou, E. Sistakou and A. Rengakos, eds, *Brill's Companion to Theocritus*, 223–41, Leiden.
Hunter, V.J. (1973), *Thucydides: The Artful Reporter*, Toronto.
Hutchinson, G.O. (2018), *Plutarch's Rhythmic Prose*, Oxford.
Ingleheart, J. (2015), 'Introduction. Romosexuality: Rome, homosexuality and reception', in J. Ingleheart, ed., *Ancient Rome and the Construction of Modern Homosexual Identities*, 1–35, Oxford.
Ingleheart, J. (2018), *Masculine Plural: Queer Classics, Sex and Education*, Oxford.
Jakobson, R. (1966–90), *Selected Writings*, 8 vols, The Hague/Berlin.
Janko, R. (2012), 'πρῶτόν τε καὶ ὕστατον αἰὲν ἀείδειν. Relative chronology and the literary history of the early Greek epos', in Ø. Andersen and D.T.T. Haug, eds, *Relative Chronology in Early Greek Poetry*, 20–43, Oxford.
Jarratt, S.C. (2014), 'Untimely historiography? Foucault's "Greco-Latin trip"', *Rhetoric Society Quarterly* 44: 220–33.
Jebb, C. (1907), *The Life and Letters of Sir Richard Claverhouse Jebb*, Cambridge.
Jeffries, L. (2019), 'Literary variation', in B. Aarts, J. Bowie and G. Popova, eds, *The Oxford Handbook of English Grammar*, 673–91, Oxford.
Jeffries, L. and D. MacIntyre (2010), *Stylistics*. Cambridge.
Jenkyns, R.J.A. (1997), 'The beginnings of Greats, 1800–1872: I Classical studies', in Brock and Curthoys, eds (1997), 513–20.
Jenkyns, R.J.A. (2000), 'Classical studies, 1872–1914', in Brock and Curthoys, eds (2000), 327–31.
Jew, D., R. Osborne and M. Scott, eds (2016), *M.I. Finley: An Ancient Historian and his Impact*, Cambridge.
Jones, J. (1962), *On Aristotle and Greek Tragedy*, London.
Jones, P.V. (2007), *Reading Greek*, 2nd edn, Cambridge.
Jowett, B. (1848), *Suggestions for an Improvement of the Examination Statute*, Oxford.
Kallet, L. (2001), *Money and the Corrosion of Power in Thucydides: The Sicilian Expedition and its Aftermath*, Berkeley.
Kallet, L. (2006), 'Thucydides' workshop of history and utility outside the text', in A. Rengakos and A. Tsakmakis, eds, *Brill's Companion to Thucydides*, 335–68, Leiden.
Kapparis, A. (2022), 'Dover's "pseudo-sexuality" and the Athenian laws on male prostitutes in politics', in A. Serafim, G. Katzanzidis, and K. Demetriou, eds, *Sex in the Ancient City*, 21–42, Berlin.
Karlen, A. (1971), *Sexuality and Homosexuality*, London.
Kaster, R.A. (1988), *Guardians of Language: The Grammarian and Society in Late Antiquity*, Berkeley.
Kennedy, R.F. (2014), *Immigrant Women in Athens: Gender, Ethnicity, and Citizenship in the Classical City*, New York.
Keuls, E. (1985), *The Reign of the Phallus*, New York.
Kilmer, M. (1993), *Greek Erotica on Attic Red-Figure Vases*, London.
Kinsey, A.C., W.B. Pomeroy, and C.E. Martin (1948), *Sexual Behavior in the Human Male*, London.
Kitson, M. and J. Shearman (1967), *Studies in Renaissance and Baroque Art Presented to Anthony Blunt on his 60th Birthday*, London.

Knight, W.F.J. (1938), review of Denniston (1934), *American Journal of Philology* 59: 490–4.
Koerner R. (1995), *Inschriftliche Gesetzestexte der frühen griechischen Polis*, ed. K. Hallof, Berlin.
Kölligan, D. (2007), *Suppletion und Defektivität im griechischen Verbum*, Bremen.
Konstan, D. (1997), *Friendship in the Classical World*, Cambridge.
Kytzler, B., K. Rudolph and R. Rüpke, eds (1994), *Eduard Norden (1868-1941). Ein deutscher Gelehrter jüdischer Herkunft*, Stuttgart.
Labov, W. (1972), *Sociolinguistic Patterns*, Oxford.
Lampe, G.W.H. (1971), *A Patristic Greek Lexicon*, Oxford.
Lape, S. (2006), 'The psychology of prostitution in Aeschines' speech against Timarchus', in C.A. Faraone and L. McClure, eds, *Prostitutes and Courtesans in the Ancient World*, Madison WI, 139–60.
Lape, S. (2010), *Race and Citizen Identity in the Classical Athenian Democracy*, Cambridge.
Larmour, D.H.J., P.A. Miller, and C. Platter, eds (1998), *Rethinking Sexuality: Foucault and Classical Antiquity*, Princeton.
Lear. A. (2014), 'Ancient pederasty', in T. Hubbard, ed., *A Companion to Greek and Roman Sexualities*, 102–27, Chichester.
Lear, A. (2015), 'Was pederasty problematized?', in Masterson, Rabinowitz and Robson, eds (2015), 115–36.
Lear, A. and E. Cantarella (2008), *Images of Ancient Greek Pederasty: Boys Were Their Gods*, London.
Lebeck, A. (1971), *The Oresteia: A Study in Language and Structure*, Washington DC.
Lebrecht Schmidt, P. (1995), 'Zwischen Anpassungsdruck und Autonomiestreben: die deutsche Latinistik vom Beginn bis in die 20er Jahre des 20. Jahrhunderts', in H. Flashar and S. Vogt, eds, *Altertumswissenschaft in den 20er Jahren: Neue Fragen und Impulse*, 115–82, Stuttgart.
Ledger, G.R. (1989), *Recounting Plato. A Computer Analysis of Plato's Style*, Oxford.
Leckie, P.R. (1989), *Bluff Your Way in the Classics*, Horsham.
Lesky, A. (1966), 'Decision and responsibility in the tragedy of Aeschylus', *Journal of Hellenic Studies* 86: 78–85.
Levene, D.S. (2010), *Livy on the Hannibalic War*, Oxford.
Levinson, J. (2005), 'Erotic art and pornographic pictures', *Philosophy and Literature* 29: 228–40.
Lewis, B. (2016), *Wolfenden's Witnesses: Homosexuality in Postwar Britain*, New York.
Lewis, C.S. (1955), *Surprised by Joy*, London.
Lewis, D.M. (1977), review of O. Aurenche, *Les Groupes d'Alcibiade, de Léogoras et de Teucros: remarques sur la vie politique athénienne en 415 av. J. C.* (Paris, 1974), *Classical Review* 27: 74–5.
Lewis, S. (1997), 'Shifting images: Athenian women in Etruria', in T. Cornell and K. Lomas, eds, *Gender and Ethnicity in Ancient Italy*, 141–54, London.
Lewis, S. (1998/9), 'Slaves as viewers and users of Athenian pottery', *Hephaistos* 16/17: 71–90.
Lewis, S. (2002), *The Athenian Woman*, London.
Lhôte, E. (2006), *Les lamelles oraculaires de Dodone*, Geneva.
Licht, H. (1925-8), *Sittengeschichte Griechenlands*, 3 vols, Dresden.
Lightfoot, J.L. (2019), 'Martin Litchfield West', *ODNB*.
Lilja, S. (1968), *On the Style of the Earliest Greek Prose*, Helsinki.
Lipscomb, B. (2021), *The Women Are Up to Something: How Elizabeth Anscombe, Philippa Foot, Mary Midgley, and Iris Murdoch Revolutionized Ethics*, New York.
Lissarrague, F. (1990), *The Aesthetics of the Greek Banquet*, Princeton.
Lissarrague, F. (2013), *La cité des satyrs*, Paris.
Livingstone, R.W. (1912), *The Greek Genius and its Meaning to Us*, Oxford.
Lloyd-Jones, H. (1956), 'Literae Humaniores in Oxford', *Cambridge Review* 77: 611–13.
Lloyd-Jones, H. (1971), *The Justice of Zeus*, Berkeley.
Lloyd-Jones, H. (1982), *Blood for the Ghosts: Classical Influences in the Nineteenth and Twentieth Centuries*, London.

Lloyd-Jones, H. (1989), review of Dover (1988a), *Classical Review* 39: 370–2.
Loepfe, A. (1940), *Die Wortstellung im griechischen Sprechsatz erklärt an Stücken aus Platon und Menander*, Freiburg.
López Eire, A. (1991), *Ático, koiné y áticismo: Estudios sobre Aristófanes y Libanio*, Murcia.
López Eire, A. (1993), 'De l'attique à la koiné', in C. Brixhe, ed., *La Koiné grecque antique, vol. i: Une langue introuvable?* (Études anciennes, 10), 41–57, Nancy.
López Eire, A. (1994), 'Historia del Ático a través de sus inscripciones, I', *Zephyrus* 47: 157–88.
López Eire, A. (1996), *La lengua coloquial de la comedia aristofanica*, Murcia.
López Eire, A. (1998), 'Historia del Ático a través de sus inscripciones, II', *Zephyrus* 51: 175–94.
López Eire, A. (1999a), 'Nouvelles données à propos de l'histoire de l'attique', in Cassio, ed. (1999), 73–107.
López Eire, A. (1999b), 'Historia del Ático a través de sus inscripciones, III', *Zephyrus* 52: 221–38.
López Eire, A. (2004), 'Registros lingüísticos en la comedia aristofánica', in A. López Eire and A. Ramos Guerreira, eds, *Registros lingüísticos en las lenguas clásicas*, Classica Salmanticensia III, 103–47, Salamanca.
Loraux, N. (1993), 'Éloge d'anachronisme en histoire', *Le genre humain* 27: 23–39.
Love, H. (2007), *Feeling Backward: Loss and the Politics of Queer History*, Cambridge Mass.
Luraghi, N. (2010), 'The local scripts from nature to culture', *Classical Antiquity* 29: 68–91.
Luraghi, N. (2021), 'Sounds, signs, and boundaries. Perspectives on early Greek alphabetic writing', in R. Parker and P.M. Steele, eds, *The Early Greek Alphabets: Origin, Diffusion, Uses*, 32–57, Oxford.
Luraghi, S. (2010), 'The rise (and possible downfall) of configurationality', in S. Luraghi and V. Bubeník, eds, *The Continuum Companion to Historical Linguistics*, 212–29, London.
Lynch, K. (2009), 'Erotic images on Attic vases: markets and meanings', in J. Oakley and O. Palagia, eds, *Athenian Potters and Painters* II, 159–65, Oxford.
Lynch, K. (2011), *The Symposium Context: Pottery from a Late Archaic House near the Athenian Agora*, Hesperia supplement 46, Athens.
Lynch, K. (2017), 'Reception, intention and Attic vases', in L. Nevett, ed., *Theoretical Approaches to the Archaeology of Ancient Greece*, 124–42, Ann Arbor.
Mac Cumhaill, C. and R. Wiseman (2022), *Metaphysical Animals: How Four Women Brought Philosophy Back to Life*, London.
McDonald, P. (1991), *Louis MacNeice: The Poet in his Contexts*, Oxford.
McDonald, P. (2019), 'The deaths of tragedy: The *Agamemnon* of MacNeice, Dodds, and Yeats', in Stray, Pelling and Harrison, eds, 228–43.
MacDowell, D.M. (1971), *Aristophanes Wasps*, Oxford.
MacDowell, D.M. (1976), '"Hybris" in Athens', *Greece and Rome* 23, 14–31.
MacDowell, D.M. (1978), *The Law in Classical Athens*, London.
[Mackail, J.W.] (1912), 'The Greek genius', review of Livingstone (1912), *Times Literary Supplement* 545: 249–50.
Macleod, C.W. (1983), *Collected Essays*, Oxford.
MacNeice, L. (1965), *The Strings are False: An Unfinished Autobiography*. London.
MacNeice, L. (1966), *Collected Poems*, ed. E.R. Dodds, London.
Maes, H. and J. Levinson, eds (2012), *Art and Pornography: Philosophical Essays*, Oxford.
Mag Uidhuir, C. and J. Pratt (2012), 'Pornography at the edge: depiction, fiction and sexual predilection', in Maes and Levinson, eds (2012), 137–60.
Marconi, C., ed. (2004a), *Greek Vases: Images, Contexts and Controversies*, Leiden.
Marconi, C. (2004b), 'Images of a warrior on a group of Athenian vases and their public', in Marconi ed. (2004a), 27–40.
Marcus, S. (1966), *The Other Victorians*, London.
Marett, R.R. (1941), *A Jerseyman at Oxford*, London.

Bibliography

Martin, S., ed. (1995), *Colin Haycraft 1929-1994: Maverick Publisher*, London.
Maslow, A.H. (1937), 'Dominance-feeling, behavior, and status', *Psychological Review* 44: 404-29.
Masters, W. and V. Johnson (1966), *Human Sexual Response*, Boston.
Masters, W. and V. Johnson (1970), *Human Sexual Inadequacy*, Boston.
Masters, W. and V. Johnson (1974), *The Pleasure Bond*, Boston.
Masters, W. and V. Johnson (1979), *Homosexuality in Perspective*, Boston.
Masterson, M. (2014), *Man to Man: Desire, Homosociality and Authority in Late-Roman Manhood*, Columbus Ohio.
Masterson, M., N.S. Rabinowitz, and J. Robson, eds (2015), *Sex in Antiquity: Exploring Gender and Sexuality in the Ancient World*, New York.
Masterson, M. and J. Robson (2016), 'Foreword: the book and its influence', in Dover (2016), xv-xxiv.
Matić, D. (2003), 'Topic, focus and discourse structure: ancient Greek word order', *Studies in Language* 27: 573-633.
Matzner, S. (2010), 'From uranians to homosexuals: philhellenism, Greek homoeroticism and gay emancipation in Germany 1835-1915', *Classical Receptions Journal* 2: 60-91.
Matzner, S. (2015), 'Of that I know many examples... On the relationship of Greek theory and Roman practices in Karl Heinrich Ulrichs's writings on the third sex', in J. Ingleheart, ed., *Ancient Rome and the Construction of Modern Homosexual Identities*, 93-108, Oxford.
Matzner, S. (2016), 'Queer unhistoricism: scholars, metalepsis and interventions of the unruly past', in S. Butler, ed., *Deep Classics: Rethinking Classical Reception*, 179-202, London.
Mayr-Harting, H. (2012), 'Henry Chadwick', *ODNB*.
Meiggs, R. (1982), 'Robert Maxwell Ogilvie', *Proceedings of the British Academy* 68: 627-36.
Meritt, B.D., H.T. Wade-Gery, and M.F. McGregor (1939-53), *The Athenian Tribute Lists*, 4 vols, Princeton.
Meyer, C. (2018), 'Foucault's clay feet: ancient Greek vases in modern theories of sex', *History Workshop Journal* 85: 143-68.
Meyer, C. and A. Petsalis-Diomidis, eds (forthcoming), *Drawing the Greek Vase: Classical Reception Between Art and Archaeology*, Oxford.
Midgley, M. (2005), *The Owl of Minerva: A Memoir*, London.
Mill, J.S. (1965), *Collected Works*, vol. iii, ed. J.M. Robson, Toronto.
Miller, P.N., ed. (2007), *Momigliano and Antiquarianism: Foundations of the Modern Cultural Sciences*, Toronto.
Minon, S. (2009), 'La stèle diglosse de Sigée en Troade (*IG* I^3 1508, ca. 550 a.C.)', in B. Bortulussi, M. Keller, S. Minon, L. Sznajder, eds, *Traduire, transposer, transmettre dans l'antiquité gréco-romaine*, 1-14, Paris.
Mitchell, B. (2009), *Looking Back: On Faith, Philosophy and Friends in Oxford*, Ongar.
Morgan, T. (2007), *Popular Morality in the Early Roman Empire*, Cambridge.
Morpurgo Davies, A. (1999), 'Contatti interdialettali: il formulario epigrafico', in Cassio, ed. (1999), 7-33.
Murray, G. (1897), *A History of Ancient Greek Literature*, London.
Murray, G. (1907), *The Rise of the Greek Epic*, Oxford.
Murray, G. (1908), 'The early Greek epic', in R.R. Marett, ed., *Anthropology and the Classics*, 66-92, Oxford.
Murray, G. (1909), *The Interpretation of Ancient Greek Literature*, Oxford.
Murray, G. (1913) *Euripides and his Age*, London.
Murray, G. (1946), *Greek Studies*, Oxford.
Murray, O. (1997), 'The beginnings of Greats, 1800-1872: II Ancient History', in Brock and Curthoys, eds (1997), 520-42.
Murray, O. (2000), 'Ancient History, 1872-1914', in Brock and Curthoys, eds (2000), 333-60.
Murray, O. (2008), review of Miller (2007), *The English Historical Review* 123: 414-16.
Murray, O. (2011), 'Ancient history in the eighteenth century', in A. Lianeri, ed., *The Western Time*

of Ancient History: Historiographical Encounters with the Greek and Roman Pasts, 301–6, Cambridge.
Neer, R. (2002), *Style and Politics in Athenian Vase-Painting*, Cambridge.
Neer, R. (2012), *Art and Archaeology of the Greek World*, London.
Norden, E. (1958), *Die antike Kunstprosa*, 2 vols, Stuttgart.
Nussbaum, M.C. (1997), 'A stoic's confessions', *Arion* 4: 149–60.
Nussbaum, M.C. (2010), 'Foreword' in Williams (2010), ix–xiv.
Oakley, J.H. (2020), *A Guide to Scenes of Daily Life on Athenian Vases*, Madison WI.
Oborne, P. (2021), *The Assault on Truth*, London.
Ogilvie, R.M. (1965), *A Commentary on Livy Books 1–5*, Oxford.
Olin, M. (1992), *Forms of Representation in Alois Riegl's Theory of Art*, University Park PA.
Olson, S.D. (2002), *Aristophanes Acharnians*, Oxford.
Oman, C.W.C. (1941), *Memories of Victorian Oxford and of Some Early Years*, London.
Ormand, K. (2018), *Controlling Desires: Sexuality in Ancient Greece and Rome*, Austin TX.
Ormand, K. and R. Blondell (2015), 'One hundred and twenty-five years of homosexuality', in Blondell and Ormand, eds, 1–22.
Orrells, D. (2011), *Classical Culture and Modern Masculinity*, Oxford.
Orrells, D. (2012), 'Greek love, orientalism and race: intersections in classical reception', *The Cambridge Classical Journal* 58: 194–230.
Orrells, D. (2015), *Sex: Antiquity and Its Legacy*, London.
Osborne, R. (1996), 'Pots, trade and the archaic Greek economy', *Antiquity* 70: 31–44.
Osborne, R. (1998), *Archaic and Classical Greek Art*, Oxford.
Osborne, R. (2001), 'Why did Athenian pots appeal to the Etruscans?', *World Archaeology* 33: 277–95.
Osborne, R. (2004), 'Images of a warrior on a group of Athenian vases and their public', in Marconi ed. (2004a), 41–54.
Osborne, R (2007), 'What travelled with Greek pottery?', *Mediterranean Historical Review* 22: 85–95.
Osborne, R. (2017), 'Classical presentism', *Past & Present* 234: 217–26.
Osborne, R. (2018a), 'Imaginary intercourse: an illustrated history of Greek pederasty', in P. Christesen, D.S. Allen, and P. Millett, eds, *How To Do Things With History*, 313–38, Oxford.
Osborne, R. (2018b), *The Transformation of Athens: Painted Pottery and the Creation of Greece*, Princeton.
Osborne, R. and P.J. Rhodes (2017), *Greek Historical Inscriptions 478–404 BC*, Oxford.
Owen, A.S. (1919–20), 'Classical Moderations and Literae Humaniores', *Oxford Magazine* 38: 198.
Padel, R. (1992), *In and Out of the Mind: Greek Images of the Tragic Self*, Princeton.
Panofsky, E. (1939), *Studies in Iconology*, Oxford.
Panofsky E. (1955), *Meaning in the Visual Arts*, Chicago.
Papillon, T.L. (1880), *Oxford Scholarship and Honour Moderations*, Oxford.
Parker, H. (2011), 'Sex, popular beliefs and culture', in M. Golden and P. Toohey, eds, *A Cultural History of Sexuality in the Classical World*, 125–44, Oxford.
Parker, H. (2015), 'Vaseworld: depiction and description of sex at Athens', in Blondell and Ormand, eds, 23–142.
Pater, W. (1877), *Studies in the Renaissance*, London.
Patrick, H. (2019), 'A brief history of women's arrival at Corpus', *The Pelican Record* 55: 19–24.
Patzer, H. (1982), *Die griechische Knabenliebe*, Wiesbaden.
Pelling, C. (2000), *Literary Texts and the Greek Historian*, London.
Pelling, C. (2013), 'Intertextuality, plausibility, and interpretation', *Histos* 7: 1–20 = https://research.ncl.ac.uk/histos/Histos_7_2013.html.
Pelling, C. (2021), 'Gomme's *Thucydides* and the idea of the historical commentary', in Harrison and Pelling, eds, 219–47.

Bibliography

Pelling, C. (2022a), *Thucydides: The Peloponnesian War Book VI*, Cambridge.
Pelling, C. (2022b), *Thucydides: The Peloponnesian War Book VII*, Cambridge.
Peradotto, J. and J.P. Sullivan, eds (1984), *Women in the Ancient World: The Arethusa Papers*, Albany.
Perry, B.E. (1964), *Secundus, the Silent Philosopher: The Greek Life of Secundus*, Ithaca NY.
Pickering, P.E. (2000), 'Verbal repetition in *Prometheus* and Greek tragedy generally', *Bulletin of the Institute of Classical Studies* 44: 81–101.
Plass, P. (1978), 'Plato's pregnant lover', *Symbolae Osloenses* 53: 47–55.
Pomeroy, S.B. (1975), *Goddesses, Whores, Wives and Slaves*, New York.
Popper, K. (1945), *The Open Society and Its Enemies: Volume 1, The Spell of Plato*, London.
Porter, K. and J. Weeks (1991), *Between the Acts: Lives of Homosexual Men 1885–1967*, London.
Poster, M. (1986), 'Foucault and the tyranny of Greece', in D.C. Hoy, ed., *Foucault: A Critical Reader*, 205–20, Oxford.
Postgate, R. (1958), 'Portrait of a classical scholar', *The Listener* 60 (11 Sept.): 378–9.
Pothou, V. (2009), *La place et le rôle de la digression dans l'œuvre de Thucydide* (Historia Einzelschr. 203), Stuttgart.
Poultney, J.W. (1962), review of Dover (1960), *American Journal of Philology* 83: 324–6.
Pritchett, W.K. (1993), *The Liar School of Herodotus*, Amsterdam.
Probert, P. (2010), review of Baechle (2007) and Dik (2007), *Mnemosyne* 63: 304–14.
Raile, A.L. (penname of E.P. Warren) (1928–30), *A Defence of Uranian Love*, 3 vols, London [privately printed].
Raynaud, S. (1990), *Il circolo linguistico di Praga (1926–1939). Radici storiche e apporti teorici*, Milan.
Reiter, H.A. (1991), *Athen und die Poleis des Delisch-Attischen Seebundes*, Regensburg.
Reitter, P. and C. Wellmon, eds (2021), *Permanent Crisis: the Humanities in a Disenchanted Age*, Chicago.
Reusser, C. (2002), *Vasen für Etrurien. Verbreitung und Funktionen attischer Keramik im Etrurien des 6. und 5. Jahrhunderts vor Christus*, 2 vols, Zurich.
Rhodes, P.J. (1984), review of Gomme, Andrewes, Dover (1945–81) vol. v, *Journal of Hellenic Studies* 104: 204–5.
Richlin, A. (1991), 'Zeus and Metis: Foucault, feminism, classics', *Helios* 18: 160–80.
Richlin, A., ed. (1992), *Pornography and Representation in Greece and Rome*, Oxford.
Riegl, A. (1901), *Spätrömische Kunstindustrie*, Vienna.
Rijksbaron, A. (1997), *New Approaches to Greek Particles*, Amsterdam.
Ringe, D. and J.F. Eska (2013), *Historical Linguistics. Toward a Twenty-First Century Reintegration*, Cambridge.
Rocke, M. (1996), *Forbidden Friendships: Homosexuality and Male Culture in Renaissance Florence*, New York.
Rohy, V. (2009), *Anachronism and its Others: Sexuality, Race, Temporality*, Albany NY.
Rood, T. (1998), *Thucydides: Narrative and Interpretation*, Oxford.
Rood, T. (2022), 'A.E. Zimmern, Thucydides, and the emergence of modern disciplines', in I. Matijašić and L. Iori, eds, *Thucydides in the Age of Extremes*, History of Classical Scholarship Supplement, at https://www.hcsjournal.org/ojs/index.php/hcs/issue/view/Supplements.
Rood, T., C. Atack, and T. Phillips (2020), *Anachronism and Antiquity*, London.
Rosenkranz, B. (1930), 'Der lokale Grundton and die persönliche Eigenart in der Sprache des Thukydides und der älteren attischen Redner', *Indogermanische Forschungen*: 127–78.
Rosenmeyer, T. (1969), *The Green Cabinet: Theocritus and the European Pastoral Lyric*, Berkeley.
Ross, I. (2013), *Oscar Wilde and Ancient Greece*, Cambridge.
Rowe, C.J. (1998), *Plato Symposium*, Warminster.
Rowe, C.J. (2007), *Plato and the Art of Philosophical Writing*, Cambridge.
Rudd, N. (1972), 'Introduction', in N. Rudd, ed., *Essays on Classical Literature*, Cambridge, vii–xvii.

Bibliography

Rüegg, W., ed. (2003), *Meeting the Challenges of the Future: A Discussion Between 'The Two Cultures'*, Florence.
Russell, D.A. (1989), 'Light from Attic skies', review of Dover (1987) and (1988a), *Oxford Magazine*, 2nd week Trinity Term, 14–15.
Russell, D.A. (1991), *An Anthology of Greek Prose*, Oxford.
Russell, D.A. (1992), *Dio Chrysostom. Orations VII, XII, XXXVI*, Cambridge.
Russell, D.A. (2007), 'The study of classical literature at Oxford, 1936–1988: II. Times change', in Stray, ed. (2007a), 225–38.
Russell, D.A. (2010), 'Sir Kenneth Dover' [obituary], *The Times*, 9 March 2010, 59–60.
Russell, D.A. and F.S. Halliwell (2012), 'Kenneth James Dover 1920–2010', *Biographical Memoirs of Fellows of the British Academy* 11: 153–75 [available online at https://www.thebritishacademy.ac.uk/publishing/memoirs/11/dover-kenneth-james-1920-2010/].
Rusten, J.S., ed. (2009), *Oxford Readings in Thucydides*, Oxford.
Rutherford, E. (2020), 'The Politics and Culture of Gender in British Universities, 1860–1935', PhD thesis, Columbia University.
Rutherford, R.B. (2012), *Greek Tragic Style*, Oxford.
Ryle, G. (1949), *The Concept of Mind*, London.
Salter, G. (2019), *Art and Masculinity in Post-War Britain: Reconstructing Home*, London.
Salter, G. (2022), 'Looking queerly at postwar masculinity', in J. Alison, H. Floe, and C. Flint, eds, *Postwar Modern: New Art in Britain*, London, 49–53.
Sandbach, F.H. (1981), review of Dover (1980), *Classical Review* 31: 126–7.
Sanders, E. (2014), *Envy and Jealousy in Classical Athens*, Oxford.
Sansone, D. (1998), review of Dover (1997a), *Bryn Mawr Classical Review* 98.6.24.
Sapsford, T. (2015), 'The wages of effeminacy? Kinaidoi in Greek documents from Egypt', *Eugesta* 5: 103–23.
Sapsford, T. (2022), *Performing the Kinaidos: Unmanly Men in Ancient Mediterranean Cultures*, Oxford.
Sargent, J.Y. and T.F. Dallin (1900), *Materials and Models for Greek Prose Composition*, London.
Saunders, T.J. (1991), *Plato's Penal Code. Tradition, Controversy, and Reform in Greek Penology*, Oxford.
Scheppers, F. (2011), *The Colon Hypothesis. Word Order, Discourse Segmentation and Discourse Coherence in Ancient Greek*, Brussels.
Schnapp, A. (1980), review of Dover (1978), *Annales* 5: 934–6.
Schofield, Malcolm (2003), 'The presidential addresses', in Stray, ed. (2003), 193–208.
Schofield, Michael (1960), *A Minority: A Report on the Life of the Male Homosexual in Great Britain*, London. (published under the name 'Gordon Westwood')
Schröder, W.A. (1999), *Der Altertumswissenschaftler Eduard Norden*, Hildesheim, Zürich and New York.
Schwyzer, E. and A. Debrunner (1950), *Griechische Grammatik. Syntax und syntaktische Stilistik*, Munich.
Scott, D. (1987), 'Platonic *anamnesis* revisited', *Classical Quarterly* 37: 346–66.
Screech, T. (2009), *Sex and the Floating World: Erotic Images in Japan 1700–1820*, London.
Sedgwick, E.K. (1985), *Between Men: English literature and male homosocial desire*, New York.
Sedgwick, E.K. (1990), *Epistemology of the Closet*, Berkeley CA.
Sedgwick, E.K. (2003), *Touching Feeling: Affect, Pedagogy, Performativity*, Durham NC.
Shapiro, H.A. (1992), 'Eros in love: pederasty and pornography in Greece', in Richlin ed., 53–72.
Shapiro, H.A. (2000), 'Leagros and Euphronios: painting pederasty in Athens', in T. Hubbard, ed., *Greek Love Reconsidered*, 12–32, New York.
Shapiro, J. (2015), 'Pederasty and the popular audience', in Blondell and Ormand, eds, 177–207.
Sheffield, F.C.C. (2001), 'Psychic pregnancy and Platonic epistemology', *Oxford Studies in Ancient Philosophy* 20: 1–33.

Bibliography

Sheffield, F.C.C. (2006), 'The role of the earlier speeches in the *Symposium*: Plato's endoxic method?', in J.H. Lesher, D. Nails, and F.C.C. Sheffield, eds, *Plato's Symposium: Issues in Interpretation and Reception*, 23–46, Cambridge Mass.
Shuter, W. (2003), 'Pater, Wilde, Douglas and the impact of "Greats"', *English Literature in Transition, 1880–1920* 46: 250–78.
Slater, W.J. (1986), *Aristophanis Byzantii Fragmenta*, Berlin.
Small, H. (2013), *The Value of the Humanities*, Oxford.
Smith, J. and A. Toynbee, eds (1960), *Gilbert Murray: An Unfinished Autobiography. With Contributions by His Friends*, London.
Snow, C.P. (1964), *The Two Cultures*, 2nd edn, with Introduction by S. Collini, Cambridge.
Sotirova, V., ed. (2016), *Bloomsbury Companion to Stylistics*, London.
Sourvinou-Inwood, C. (1991), *'Reading' Greek Culture: Texts and Images, Rituals and Myths*, Oxford.
Spatharas, D. (2006), 'Persuasive ΓΕΛΩΣ: public speaking and the use of laughter', *Mnemosyne* 59: 374–87.
Spivey, N. (1991), 'Greek vases in Etruria', in N. Spivey and T. Rasmussen, eds, *Looking at Greek Vases*, 131–50, Cambridge.
Stahl, H.-P. (1966), *Thukydides: die Stellung des Menschen im geschichtlichen Prozeß*, Munich; Engl. trans. with new final chapter, *Thucydides: Man's Place in History* (Swansea, 2003).
Stahl, H.-P. (2003), see Stahl (1966).
Stansbury-O'Donnell, M. (2006), *Vase-Painting, Gender and Social Identity in Archaic Athens*, Cambridge.
Stehle, E. (1997), *Performance and Gender in Ancient Greece*, Princeton.
Steiner, A. (2007), *Reading Greek Vases*, Cambridge.
Stewart, A. (1997), *Art, Desire and the Body in Ancient Greece*, Cambridge.
Strasburger, H. (1958), 'Thukydides und die politische Selbstdarstellung der Athener', *Hermes* 88: 17–40 [reprinted in Herter (1968) 498–530 and trans. in Rusten (2009), 191–209].
Stray, C.A. (1996), review of Dover (1994), *Classical Review* 46: 195–6.
Stray, C.A. (1998), *Classics Transformed: Schools, Universities, and Society in England, 1830–1960*, Oxford.
Stray, C.A., ed. (2003), *The Classical Association: The First Century 1903–2003*, Oxford.
Stray, C.A., ed. (2007a), *Oxford Classics: Teaching and Learning 1800–2000*, London.
Stray, C.A., ed. (2007b), *Gilbert Murray Reassessed: Hellenism, Theatre, and International Politics*, Oxford.
Stray, C.A. (2012), 'The Oxford Latin Dictionary: a historical introduction', in P.G.W. Glare, ed., *The Oxford Latin Dictionary*, 2nd edn, x–xvii, Oxford.
Stray, C.A. (2016), 'A teutonic monster in Oxford: the making of Fraenkel's *Agamemnon*', in C.S. Kraus and C.A. Stray, eds, *Classical Commentaries: Explorations in a Scholarly Genre*, 39–57, Oxford.
Stray, C.A. (2018), *Classics in Britain: Scholarship, Education, and Publishing 1800–2000*, Oxford.
Stray, C.A. (2019), 'An Irishman abroad', in Stray, Pelling and Harrison, eds, 10–35.
Stray, C.A. (2023), 'The making of William Whewell', in L.M. Verburgt, ed., *William Whewell: Victorian Polymath*, Pittsburgh.
Stray, C.A. and C.B.R. Pelling (2019), 'Introduction: a missing person?', in Stray, Pelling and Harrison, eds, 1–9.
Stray, C.A., C.B.R. Pelling and S.J. Harrison, eds (2019), *Rediscovering E. R. Dodds*, Oxford.
Sullivan, J.P. (1964), 'The Classics in England', review of R.M. Ogilvie, *Latin and Greek*, *Arion* 3: 127–36.
Sutcliffe, P. (1978), *The Oxford University Press: an Informal History*, Oxford.
Sutton, R. (1992), 'Pornography and persuasion on Attic Pottery', in Richlin ed., 3–35.

Sutton, R. (2014), 'A type γ courting scene for Alan: the Spitzer Amphora at Bryn Mawr College', in A. Avramidou and D. Demetrious, eds, *Approaching the Ancient Artifact: Representation, Narrative, and Function. A Festschrift in Honor of H. Alan Shapiro*, 319–33, Berlin.
Svensson, C. (1986), *Karaktertegning og sætningsstruktur hos Menander*, Copenhagen.
Świeczkowski, W. (1962), *Word Order Patterning in Middle English*, The Hague.
Symonds, J.A. (1908), *A Problem in Greek Ethics: Being an Inquiry into the Phenomenon of Sexual Inversion, Addressed Especially to Medical Psychologists and Jurists*, London.
Thomas, O.R.H. (2020), *The Homeric Hymn to Hermes*, Cambridge.
Thorp, J. (1992), 'The social construction of homosexuality', *Phoenix* 46: 54–61.
Threatte, L. (1980), *The Grammar of Attic Inscriptions*, i: *Phonology*, Berlin.
Threatte, L. (1996) *The Grammar of Attic Inscriptions*, ii: *Morphology*, Berlin.
Threatte, L. (2015), 'The Phanodikos inscription from Sigeum', in A.P. Matthaiou and N. Papazarkadas, eds, *Ἄξων: Studies in Honor of Ronald S. Stroud*, 105–23, Athens.
Thumb, A. (1909), *Handbuch der griechischen Dialekte*, Heidelberg.
Todd, C. (2012), 'Imagination, fantasy and sexual desire', in Maes and Levinson, eds, 95–115.
Todhunter, I. (1876), *William Whewell, DD, Master of Trinity College, Cambridge*, London.
Tompkins, D.P. (1972), 'Stylistic characterization in Thucydides: Nicias and Alcibiades', *Yale Classical Studies* 22: 181–214.
Tompkins, D.P. (2013), 'The language of Pericles', in A. Tsakmakis and M. Tamiolaki, eds, *Thucydides between History and Literature* (Trends in Classics suppl. 17), 447–64, Berlin.
Tompkins, D.P. (2015), 'Gorgias in the real world: Hermocrates on interstate stasis and the defense of Sicily', in C.A. Clark, E. Foster, and J.P. Hallett, eds, *Kinesis: the Ancient Depiction of Gesture, Motion, and Emotion*, 116–27, Ann Arbor.
Topper, K. (2012), *The Imagery of the Athenian Symposium*, Cambridge.
Trenkner, S. (1958), *The Greek Novella in the Classical Period*, Cambridge.
Trenkner, S. (1960), *Le style KAI dans le récit attique oral*, Assen.
Tribe, K. (2022), *Constructing Economic Science: The Invention of a Discipline 1850–1950*, Oxford.
Tsakmakis, A. (1995), *Thukydides über die Vergangenheit*, Tübingen.
Tsakmakis, A. (1996), 'Thukydides VI.54.1 und Herodot', *Philologus* 140: 201–13.
Tsingarida, A. and D. Viviers, eds (2013), *Pottery Markets in the Ancient Greek World (8th-1st Centuries AD)*, Brussels.
Turner, F.M. (1981), *The Greek Heritage in Victorian Britain*, New Haven.
Tyrrall, S., ed. (2021), *Compositions in Honour of Anthony Bowen*, Cambridge.
[University of Oxford] (1872), *The New Examination Statutes together with the Decrees of Convocation and Regulations of the Boards of Studies at present in force relating thereto*, Oxford.
[University of Oxford] (1888), *The Student's Handbook to the University and Colleges of Oxford*, 9th edn, Oxford.
[University of Oxford] (1906), *The Student's Handbook to the University and Colleges of Oxford*, 17th edn, Oxford.
[University of Oxford] (1939), *Handbook to the University of Oxford*, Oxford.
Usher, S., and D. Najok (1982), 'A statistical study of authorship in the Corpus Lysiacum', *Computers and the Humanities* 16: 85–105.
Vanderpool, E. (1942), 'An archaic inscribed stele from Marathon', *Hesperia* 11: 329–37.
Vanderpool, E. (1984), 'Regulations for the Herakleian games at Marathon', in A.L. Boegehold, ed., *Studies Presented to Sterling Dow on His Eightieth Birthday*, 295–6, Durham NC.
Van Effenterre, H. and F. Ruzé (1994), *Nomima: recueil d'inscriptions politiques et juridiques de l'archaïsme grec*, Rome.
Vanggaard, T. (1972), *Phallós: A Symbol and its History in the Male World*, London.
Vatri, A. (2017), *Orality and Performance in Classical Attic Prose: A Linguistic Approach*, Oxford.
Verity, A., trans. (2002), *Theocritus Idylls*, with an Introduction and Explanatory Notes by R. Hunter, Oxford.

Bibliography

Vernant, J.-P. (1996), *Mythe et pensée chez les grecs*, new edn, Paris.
Vernant, J.-P. (2006), *Myth and Thought Among the Greeks*, trans. J. Lloyd, New York.
Vickers, M. and D.N. Briggs (2007), 'Aggression and abuse in fifth-century Athens: a case study', in G. Rousseau, ed., *Children and Sexuality: From the Greeks to the Great War*, 41–69, Basingstoke.
Vickers, M. and D. Gill (1994), *Artful Crafts: Ancient Silverware and Pottery*, Oxford.
Vincent, E. (2018), *A.E. Housman: Hero of the Hidden Life*, Woodbridge.
Vorberg, G. (1926), *Ars erotica veterum: ein Beitrag zum Geschlechsleben des Altertums*, Stuttgart.
Vorberg, G. (1928), *Glossarium Eroticum*, Stuttgart.
Wackernagel, J. (1913), 'Lateinisch-Griechisches', *Indogermanische Forschungen* 31: 251–71.
Wackernagel, J. (1916), *Sprachliche Untersuchungen zu Homer*, Göttingen.
Wackernagel, J. (1953–79), *Kleine Schriften*, 3 vols, Göttingen.
Wackernagel, J. (2009), *Lectures on Syntax, with Special Reference to Greek, Latin, and Germanic*, ed. D. Langslow, Oxford.
Walbank, M.B. (1970), *Athenian Proxenies of the Fifth Century B.C.* Doctoral thesis at the University of British Columbia.
Walbank, M.B. (1978), *Athenian Proxenies of the Fifth Century B.C.*, Toronto.
Walker, T. (2019), '"The lonely flight of mind": W.B. Yeats, Louis MacNeice, and the metaphysical poetry of Dodds's scholarship', in Stray, Pelling and Harrison, eds, 210–27.
Walsh, J. (2009), 'A study in reception: the British debates over Aristophanes' politics and influence', *Classical Receptions Journal* 1.1: 55–72.
Walsh, W.H. (2000), 'The zenith of Greats', in Brock and Curthoys, eds (2000), 311–26.
'Walter' (1972), *My Secret Life*, ed. G. Grimley, London. (First published c.1888–95.)
Ward, J. (2022), *Postwar Modern: New Art in Britain, 1945–1965*, London.
Warnock, M. (2000), *A Memoir: People and Places*, London.
Waters, C. (2012), 'The homosexual as a social being in Britain, 1945–1968', *Journal of British Studies* 51: 685–710.
Weber, M. (1921), *Wirtschaft und Gesellschaft: Grundriss der verstehenden Soziologie*, Tübingen.
Webster, T.B.L. (1972), *Potter and Patron in Classical Athens*, London.
Weeks, J. (1990), *Coming Out: Homosexual Politics in Britain from the Nineteenth Century to the Present*, revised edn, London.
Weeks, J. (2007), *The World We Have Won: The Remaking of Erotic and Intimate life*, London.
Weeks, J. (2012), *Sex, Politics and Society: The Regulation of Sexuality Since 1800*, 3rd edn, Harlow.
Wender, D. (1973), 'Plato: misogynist, paedophile, feminist', *Arethusa* 6: 75–90.
West, D.J. (1960), *Homosexuality*, revised edn, Harmondsworth.
West, D.J. (1977), *Homosexuality Re-examined*, 4th edn, London.
West, F. (1984), *Gilbert Murray: A Life*, London.
West, M.L. (1966), *Hesiod, Theogony*, Oxford.
West, M.L. (1997), *The East Face of Helicon: West Asiatic Elements in Greek Poetry and Myth*, Oxford.
Westlake, H. D. (1966), review of Dover (1965a and b), *Classical Review* 16: 26–8.
Westlake, H. D. (1972), review of Gomme, Andrewes, Dover (1945–81) vol. iv, *Classical Review* 22: 188–91.
Westwood, G. (2020), *The Rhetoric of the Past in Demosthenes and Aeschines: Oratory, History, and Politics in Classical Athens*, Oxford.
Whitmarsh, T. (2016), 'Textual orientation: how a work of old-school philology inspired the gay rights movement', review of Dover (2016), *Times Literary Supplement* 5913 (29 July), 14–15.
Willett, G. (2019), 'Homosexual politics in the British world: toward a transnational understanding', in G. Brady and M. Seymour, eds, *From Sodomy Laws to Same-Sex Marriage: International Perspectives Since 1789*, 141–55, London.
Willi, A. ed. (2002), *The Language of Greek Comedy*, Oxford.

Bibliography

Willi, A. (2003), *The Languages of Aristophanes*, Oxford.
Willi, A. (2010), 'Attic as the language of the Classics', in C.C. Caragounis, ed., *Greek: A Language in Evolution*, 101–18, Hildesheim.
Williams, B., ed. (1979), *Report of the Committee on Obscenity and Film Censorship*, London.
Williams, B. (1993), *Shame and Necessity*, Berkeley.
Williams, B. (2006), *Philosophy as a Humanistic Discipline*, ed. A.W. Moore, Princeton.
Williams, C.A. (2010), *Roman Homosexuality*, 2nd edn, Oxford.
Wilson, D. (1987), *Gilbert Murray OM 1866–1957*, Oxford.
Wimsatt, W.K. Jr and M.C. Beardsley (1946), 'The intentional fallacy', *Sewanee Review* 54.3: 468–88.
Windelband, W. (1980), 'Rectorial address, Strasbourg, 1894', trans. G. Oakes, *History and Theory* 19: 169–85.
Winkler, J.J. (1990), *The Constraints of Desire: The Anthropology of Sex and Gender in Ancient Greece*, New York.
Wohl, V. (2002), *Love Among the Ruins: The Erotics of Democracy in Classical Athens*, Princeton.
Wolfenden, J. (1957), *Report of the Committee on Homosexual Offences and Prostitution*, London.
Wood, C. (2000), *The Vienna School Reader*, New York.
Woodman, A.J. (1988), *Rhetoric in Classical Historiography*, London.
Worman, N. (2008), *Abusive Mouths in Classical Athens*, Cambridge.
Wright, P. with P. Greengrass (1987), *Spycatcher: The Candid Autobiography of a Senior Intelligence Officer*, New York.
Wrigley, A. (2011), *Performing Greek Drama in Oxford and on Tour with the Balliol Players*, Exeter.
Wyatt, F. and H.L. Teubner (1944), 'German psychology under the Nazis 1933–1940', *Psychological Review* 51: 229–47.
Yates, V.L. (2005), '"Anterastai": competition in eros and politics in classical Athens', *Arethusa* 38: 33–47.
Young, D. (1969), *St Andrews: Town and Gown, Royal and Ancient*, London.
Zanker, A.T. (2014), 'Decline and *Kunstprosa*: Velleius Paterculus and Eduard Norden', in M. Formisano and T. Fuhrer, eds, *Décadence: 'decline and fall' or 'other antiquity'?*, 299–324, Heidelberg.
Zieliński, T. (1904), *Das Clauselgesetz in Ciceros Reden*, Leipzig.

INDEX

Ackermann, Rudolph (prints of Oxford) 74
'Actors of Dionysus' 329–30
Adkins, Arthur 135, 149, 151, 153, 154, 157, 163, 184, 292, 301
Aeschines, *Against Timarchus* 183, 186, 187, 190, 194, 204
Aeschylus 15, 43, 54, 170, 241, 271
    Agamemnon 168–9; *see also* Fraenkel, *Agamemnon* seminar
    Eumenides 39, 170
Alexander's successors 17
Allen, W. Sidney 90, 92
All Souls College, Oxford 84, 176, 184
Anaxagoras 257
Andrewes, Antony 21, 91, 113, 115–17
Antiphon 20, 114, 255, 269, 278
Apollonius Rhodius 49, 237, 246
Archilochus 266
Arethusa (journal) 183
Aristophanes 21, 25, 38, 43, 68, 69, 115, 173–5, 177, 217
    Birds 37, 53, 199
    Clouds 54, 183, 217
    Frogs 4, 53, 54
    Knights 188
    Lysistrata 244
    Thesmophoriazusae 257–8
    Wasps 255–6
Aristotle 135, 152–3, 277
    Poetics 34, 35, 54
Arnold-Baker, James 103
Aston, Judith 72, 74, 76
Aston, Trevor 62, 63, 67, 70–8, 101, 104–6, 320, 321–2, 324
    battels, unpaid 73
    circumstances of suicide 74–6, 77–8
    divorce 75
    excessive library expenditure 72, 73–4, 77
    house in Spain 74
    spells in Warneford Hospital 62, 74, 75
Attic and Ionic dialects 251, 254–5, 258–63
Ayer, A.J. 47, 142, 143

Bailey, Cyril 15, 28
Balliol College, Oxford 51, 57, 61, 81, 239, 318, 319, 323
    Dover as Fellow 20–1, 40, 42, 181, 237, 293, 298
    Dover as Senior Tutor 2, 21
    Dover as undergraduate 15–19, 35–7, 40, 106, 172
Balliol Players 37
Barrett, W. Spencer 23, 24, 30, 114, 173
Barrington-Ward, John (J.G.) 17
Barron, John 58
Bawden, Charles 92
Bean, George 5, 14, 15
Beard, Geoffrey 72
Beard, Mary 7, 171, 176
Beattie, Arthur 54
Beazley, Sir John 198, 205–18, 225, 226
Beck, Maximilian 2, 16, 28
Beckwith, John 86
Benson, Arthur 99
Berlin, Isaiah 45, 48, 82, 88
Bethe, Erich 191
Blake, Deborah 104, 108, 231
Blake, Lord (Robert) 90, 92, 108
Blundell, Mary Whitlock 161
Blunden, Edmund 37–8
Blunt, Anthony 81–98, 320, 326
    Dover's acquaintance with 84
    friend of Louis MacNeice 82
Blunt, Rev. Stanley 82
Blunt, Wilfred Scawen 83
Bond, Godfrey 63
Bourdieu, Pierre 224–5
Bowie, Ewen 323
    on a double entendre in Aristophanes 69–70
Bowra, Maurice 21, 30, 41, 48, 271
Boyle, Andrew, *Climate of Treason* 84
Bremmer, Jan 194–5
Briand, Aristide 38
Bridges, Margaret 79
British Academy 81–98, 293
Brooke, Henry 84
Brown, Catherine (née Dover) 27, 58
Browning, Robert 21, 29
Bullock, Alan (Lord) 78
Burckhardt, Jacob 187
Burgess, Guy 83, 84, 85
Burkert, Walter 297, 311
Burn, Andrew 14
Burnet, John 53
Burstall, Christopher 308

Index

Bush, Geoffrey 37
Butler, Samuel 99
Byron, Lord 167
Bywater, Ingram 7

Cairncross, John 83
Cairns, Douglas 161
Cairns, Francis 238
Cairo City, SS 14
Callimachus 237, 246
Cambridge Apostles 83
Cambridge University
    Dover's visits to 21, 249
    Regius chair of Greek 6, 7, 25
Campbell, Brian 75
Campbell, Lewis 53
Campbell, Malcolm 55, 249
Cannadine, David 95
Carey, Chris 70
Carnes, Jeffrey 188
Carter, Christopher 55
Cartledge, Paul 104, 194–5
Cartledge, Ben, on school classical reading 271
Case, Thomas 33
Casson, Stanley 14
Catullus 17, 39
Cavander, Kenneth 20
centenaries 1
Chadwick, Henry 101
    footnote dedicated to his memory 107
Chadwick, Owen 87
Charles-Edwards, Thomas 72, 73, 75, 77–8
Christie, Ian 89, 90, 92
Cicero 32, 33, 38, 277, 282
Clare, Anthony 322
Clark, Sir Kenneth 83
Classical Association 42, 291, 293, 295–7, 299, 308
    Classical Journals Board 82
composition, prose/verse 5, 7, 15, 20, 33, 38, 53, 246, 271–2, 276, 281–2, 298, 311
Connor, W.R. 116
Cooper, David 74, 77
Corpus Christi College, Cambridge 318
Corpus Christi College, Oxford 4, 61–80, 293
    Assistant Librarian 74, 76–7
    and Barclays Bank 319, 321
    'Chronicle' of, *see* Howard-Johnston, James
    College Office 72
    condom dispenser, JCR request for 64
    Corpus chair of Latin 4, 21, 61, 62, 172
    Dean 72
    Domestic Bursar 73, 317
    Fellows' Building 72, 73, 75
    food, improved during Keith Thomas's presidency 67
    golfers, admission of 65
    Governing Body 64, 74–5, 316, 317–18, 320
    History (Charles-Edwards and Reid) 77–8
    Joint (staff-student) committee 82, 317–18
    Junior Common Room 64, 65, 68, 105, 319
    library 72, 74, 77
    Middle Common Room 63–4
    Netherhale mansion 71
    No. 3 Merton Street 72–3
    President's study 72
    Senior Common Room 63, 71, 72, 73
    Senior Tutor 61, 70, 77, 318
    Tutor for Admissions 65
    Visitations 74, 320
    Warren praelectorship 22, 61
    women, admission of 62, 64–5, 69, 316
Courtauld Institute 83, 84, 88
Cox, James 321
Craik, Elizabeth 51
Crook, John 89, 97
Crossman, Richard 142
Cunningham, Valentine 68, 76

Davidson, James 183, 186, 188, 189, 192, 193, 195
Davidson, May 62
Davies, Anna Morpurgo 107, 322
Davies, John (J.K.) 116
Demosthenes (Athenian general) 119, 128, 130
Demosthenes (orator) 32, 33, 118, 121, 153, 162, 190, 261
Denniston, J.D. 33, 41, 271, 274
    Greek Particles 7, 20, 115, 275–6, 277–8
    Greek typewriter 20
Denniston, Mary 274
Denyer, Nicholas 66
De Romilly, Jacqueline 127, 164
Devereux, George 176, 184
Dik, Helma 274
Dodds, E.R. 5, 6, 15, 23–4, 37, 41, 46–7, 62, 172–3, 176, 177, 292, 293, 308–9, 327
    The Greeks and the Irrational 149, 150, 157, 327
    Missing Persons 2, 16, 99–100
Donaldson, James 53
Dorian origin of pederasty 183, 191, 195
Douglas-Home, Alec 84
Dover, Alan 66
Dover, Audrey (née Latimer) 20, 58, 63, 143, 315–16, 322, 323, 325, 329–30
    on the price of carrots 67
Dover, Dorothy ('Dully') 13, 81
Dover, Kenneth
    anthropological interests 18, 42, 151, 169, 176, 195, 218, 250–1, 292, 294, 301, 304, 306–7, 312, 313
    as art historian 205
    Bowra lecture (1977) 7

Index

British Academy memoir of 2, 95, 106, 181, 188
British Academy, presidency of 81–98
canonical model of the classical rejected 240, 299, 306
chairmanship of committees 43, 57, 49, 81–2, 85, 87, 93–5
Chancellor, University of St Andrews 2, 57, 327, 328
childhood fantasies 5, 13–15
Classics, justifications of 291–313
Corpus Christi College, Oxford, presidency of 61–80, 316–23
Cromer prize 18
empiricism 4, 95, 131, 132, 142, 155, 186, 252, 292
family 3, 315–16; *see also* parents, relationship with
feed-pipe model of history 294–5, 300
FIEC lecture (1979) 291, 295–6
Gaisford prize 3, 15–16, 36
gardening 67, 58, 315–16, 323–4, 330
Hertford prize 4, 16
historian of Greek language 251–70
humanities, conception of 126, 292, 295, 297–305
inscriptions, study of 19, 21–3, 24, 113–14, 120, 121, 154, 246, 251–70
language, views on nature of 251–4, 295, 303, 304–5, 321–2, 325
liberalism 316–20
lifestyle 59, 315–16
masturbation 100, 102, 106, 107, 142, 197, 324, 330
Mediterranean landscapes, response to 70, 79, 100, 141–2, 330
military service 4, 6, 18, 25, 36, 40, 120, 164, 188
monkeys, fascination with 15, 189, 196; *see also* Wimpee
moral experience, personal 151, 292
musical interests 5, 13, 17, 28, 146, 327
nickname, 'Ben' (Ben Dover) 67
old age, feelings about 323
parents, relationship with 2–4, 13, 16–17, 115; *see also* Dover, Dorothy *and* Dover, Percy
philosophy, antipathy to 16, 19, 78, 95, 131–47, 149, 152, 153, 155, 159, 168–9, 171–2, 175, 184, 185–6, 241, 300, 312
poems, his own 18, 25–7
'poetical humbug', lack of 167
pragmatist in linguistics 154, 251
psychoanalysis, views of 176, 292, 309; *see also* Freud, Sigmund
rationalism 113, 175, 190, 281–2, 320–1, 325, 327, 331
realism 37, 81, 120, 168, 173, 175, 204–5, 209–12, 215, 217, 219–22, 246–7
religion, attitudes to 57, 93, 101, 161, 327

remoteness 70
'Retrospect' (account of Blunt affair) 86, 88, 91–4, 95
Sather lectures, Berkeley 9, 58, 293; *see also* Lysias
scarlet fever 13
schooling 5, 13, 36, 172, 237, 239, 271, 302–3; *see also* St Paul's School
'stemmatic' diagram of interests 2, 196, 272–3, 283, 313
style, his own 7–8, 328
teaching methods 54, 55–6, 66, 68, 272–3, 276–7, 301, 325
theorizing, resistance to 4, 154, 162–3, 252, 292, 300, 301, 308–9
typewriter, attachment to 58
undergraduate career 15–19, 31–50
unfinished novel (*Paul's Rock*) 18
US visits (Berkeley, Cornell, Harvard, Stanford) 41, 58, 115, 179, 200, 275, 284, 293
WORKS (selected):
Ancient Greek Literature (ed.) 69, 113
Aristophanes Clouds 54, 67, 69, 115, 173–4, 217
Aristophanes Frogs 4, 58, 66, 173, 284
Aristophanic Comedy 67, 69, 174
The Evolution of Greek Prose Style 8, 113, 117, 125, 127, 251–70, 271–87
Greek Homosexuality 2, 65, 67, 95, 136, 157, 162, 181–201, 203–35, 310, 317, 328
Greek Popular Morality 69, 98, 127, 135, 149–65, 170–1, 184, 186, 292, 301
Greek Word Order 54, 113, 115, 251, 253, 273, 275, 278, 279, 284
The Greeks (book and TV series) 56–7, 120, 291, 305, 308
The Greeks and their Legacy 113, 177, 240, 291
Historical Commentary on Thucydides 113–30
Marginal Comment xii, 2, 7, 25, 36–40, 75, 85–8, 91–3, 99–109, 118, 120, 150, 171, 192, 291, 322, 323, 324–5, 326, and *passim*
Perceptions of the Ancient Greeks (ed.) 31, 313
Plato Symposium, see s.v. Plato
Theocritus: Select Poems 69, 237–50, 263
Dover, Percy 2, 58, 81, 325
Dover, Wendy 66, 315–16
Dover Committee (on Oxford admissions system) 80, 320
Dover-Foucault paradigm, *see* Foucault, Michel
Duckworth (publishers) 99, 103–4, 108, 231
Dummett, Michael 94, 104
Dunbar, Nan 52, 55
Dundee, University College (later Queen's College) 52–3
Dylan, Bob 327

Easterling, Patricia 70
Eden, Anthony 62

Index

Ehrenberg, Victor 175
Ehrman, John 90
Eliot, T.S. 37
Enkvist, Nils Erik 278
Ephesus 71
Ephorus 191
Epicharmos/-us 263–4
Esperanto 18
Euripides 41, 42, 43, 54, 56, 137, 178, 241
    Bacchae 24, 245
    Hecuba/Hekabe 271, 329
    Hippolytus/-os 114, 137, 329–30
Evening Standard 102–3

Farnell, L.R. 33
Feldman, Hilary, *see* O'Shea, Hilary
Festschrifts 84, 170
    Dover's (*Owls to Athens*) 51, 57–8, 328
Finley, Moses 5, 152, 160, 298, 300, 311
Fisher, Nick (N.R.E.) 161
Fleck, Rosemary 71
Florence, Renaissance 186
Forster, E.M. 85
Fortune, Reo 18
Foucault, Michel 95, 185, 189–90, 192–3, 195–6, 203, 217
Fox, Matthew 194
Foxhall, Lin 193
Fraenkel, Eduard 4, 5, 15–16, 19, 21, 23, 42, 105, 172–4, 240, 279, 292, 326
    Agamemnon seminar 16, 37, 81, 105, 172, 326
Fraser, Peter 239
Frazer, Sir James 7
Freud, Sigmund 176, 184, 301; *see also* Dover, Kenneth, psychoanalysis

Gardner, Dame Helen 88–9
Gash, Norman 90, 92
George, Peter 55
German scholarship 15, 19, 31, 40, 326; *see also* Fraenkel, Eduard
Gifford, Douglas 326
Gilgamesh 296
Glenmorangie 73
Goldhill, Simon 4
Gomme, A.W. 113–15, 116, 121
Gould, John (J.P.A.) 34, 161, 312
Gow, A.S.F. 107, 241, 243–5, 246–7, 249
Gower, L.C.B. (Jim) 89, 91
Grafton, Anthony 31
grammarians, good 294
Gratwick, Adrian 55
Gray, Dorothea 114
Greats (Literae Humaniores) 5, 16–17, 18–19, 20, 21, 32–5, 37, 40, 43, 44, 172, 184; *see also* Mods

Greek culture *vis-à-vis* Near East 296–7
Greek drama 167–79; *see also* Aeschylus, Aristophanes, Epicharmus, Euripides, Menander, Sophocles
Greek homosexuality, *see* Dover, Kenneth, *Greek Homosexuality*
Greek language 251–70, 271–87
Greek *vs* Latin 14, 239–40
Greek miracle, the; *see* Devereux, George
Greer, Germaine 203
Griffin, Jasper 17–18, 57, 69, 101–2, 108, 249
Grundy, George 99
Gurney, Oliver 92

Haldane, J.B.S. 15
Haldane, J.S. 15
Hall, Derek 61, 317
Hall, Ursula 55
Halliwell, Stephen 8, 57, 151, 184, 205, 232, 273
    British Academy memoir of Dover 2, 95, 106, 181, 188
Halperin, David 181, 193–4
Hammond, N.G.L. 122
Hardie, Frank 65, 72
Hardy, Thomas 37
Hare, Richard M. 29, 61, 75
Harris, Roy 104
Harrison, Sir Brian 68–9, 75, 77, 106
Harrison, Jane 310
Haycraft, Colin 103–4, 108, 231
Healey, Ana(stasia) 58, 106
Healey, Denis 37
Hegel, G.W.F. 16
Heinemann (publishers) 103
Heitland, William 99
Hellenic and Roman Societies, Joint Library of 105
Hellenic Studies, Society for the Promotion of 59, 66, 82, 293
Hellenistic poetry 237–50; *see also* Callimachus and Theocritus
Henderson's bookshop, St Andrews 53
Henry, Alan 55
Herodotus 54, 125, 126, 169, 253, 259, 261, 279, 280
Hesiod 19, 20, 297
Heymans, Gerard 2
Hill, Ron 77, 321
Hobsbawm, Eric 87
Hollis, Sir Roger 83–4
Homer 32, 33, 43, 54, 140, 142, 245, 259, 262–3, 271, 297, 301
Honour Moderations, *see* Mods
Horace 34, 327
Housman, A.E. 7
Howard, Lady Mary 100
Howard, Michael 87
Howard, Philip 309, 322

Index

Howard-Johnston, James 70, 71, 73, 74
Hubbard, Margaret 238
humanism 195, 292, 308
Humphries, Mark 105
Hunter, Virginia 115–16
Huxley, George 89

Institute of Classical Studies, London 58, 105
intentional fallacy, the 167
intercrural sex 189, 212, 213, 215, 217, 232–3
Ion of Chios 259
Istanbul 14, 71
ithyphallicism, variable display of in vase paintings 207, 212, 214–15, 231

Jackson, Henry 7
Jakobson, Roman 278
James, Alan 237
James, Clive 308
James, Robert 5
Jebb, Caroline 99
Jebb, Richard 6, 7
Jenkyns, Richard 18
Jessiman, Tom 53
Jocelyn, Harry 5
Joint Association of Classical Teachers (JACT) 27, 293
    Reading Greek 66, 272, 277, 293
Joll, James 91
Journal of Hellenic Studies 70, 79
Jowett, Benjamin 7, 33, 99, 142

Kant, Immanuel 151, 163, 302
Karlen, Arlo 183, 189
Kaster, Robert 30
Keir, David 81
Kennedy, Benjamin Hall 99
Kenney, Ted 248
Kidd, Ian 52, 55, 276
Kinsey Reports 182
Kitto, H.D.F. 45
Knight, W.F. Jackson 21
Knox, Sir Malcolm 53, 81
Konstan, David 161
Kray, Reginald 105
Kyoto University, Japan 51

Lasko, Peter 88, 95
Latimer, Audrey, *see* Dover, Audrey
Lattimore, Richmond 157
Leake, David 324
Lear, Andrew 186
Leavis, F.R. 37
Lebeck, Anne 170
Leckie, Ross 66, 105–6
lending libraries 23

Lepper, Frank 61–2
Lesky, Albin 168–9
Leverhulme Research Awards Committee 84
Lindsay, A.D. 20, 40, 81, 318
Linear B 54
Literae Humaniores, *see* Greats
literary criticism 238
    Dover's attitude to 31, 114, 115–16, 122, 167, 176, 253
    in Mods 32, 34, 40, 44
Livas family 14
Liverpool (Leeds) Latin Seminars, *see* Cairns, Francis
Livingstone, R.W. 41, 42
Lloyd-Jones, Sir Hugh 5, 18, 21–2, 23–4, 25, 34, 41, 104, 239
    The Justice of Zeus 149, 157
Locke, John 132, 135
Lodge, David 284
Loggan, *Oxonia Illustrata* 74
Long, Leo 83
'Longinus', *On the Sublime* 121
Loraux, Nicole 187
Lorimer, W.L. 52–3
Lowell, Robert 170
Lucian 68, 71
Lysias 21, 56, 101, 162, 186, 257, 282, 326

MacDowell, Douglas 149, 162, 164
Mackie, John 91
Maclean, Donald 84, 85
Macmillan, Harold 23, 62–3
MacNeice, Louis 47, 82
    Autumn Journal 176–7, 312
    The Strings are False 99
Mann, F.A. 86
Mao Tse-Tung 143
Marshall, Morrison 55
Martin, Arthur 83
Marx, Karl 18, 292, 298, 301
Maslow, Ivan 189
Masters and Johnson 203, 230
Masterson, Mark 194
Meiggs, Russell 5, 19, 21, 23, 29, 40, 81, 113–14, 120, 210, 253
Melanesian/Oceanic languages 7, 13, 18, 23, 101, 307
Melluish, T.W. 14
Menander 114, 240, 273, 284, 286
Meritt, Benjamin 19
MI5 83–4
Miliband, David 318, 319
Mill, John Stuart 316
Millar, Sir Fergus 102–3
Mitchison, Naomi 15
Mitford, Terence 52, 326

359

Index

Mods (Honour Moderations) 5, 15–19, 20–1, 31–49, 54, 114, 172, 237, 246
    cross-temporal perspectives in 35
    General Paper(s) 32, 34, 38
    vis-à-vis Greats 16, 19, 20
    Special Subjects 32–6
    wartime version 18, 37
    see also literary criticism, in Mods
Momigliano, Arnaldo 1, 19, 20, 24–5
Moncur, David 67–8
Mosley, Oswald 83
Mossman, Judith 66–7
Murdoch, Iris 29, 46, 326
Murray, Gilbert 6, 7, 8, 23, 31, 37, 99, 173
    Dover's relationship to 40–4
Murray, Oswyn 1, 6, 8
Myres, John 14

Napoleon 38
Nemrut Dağı 71
New Criticism 167
Newman, Cardinal 302
Nisbet, Robin 20, 46, 61, 62, 63, 73, 77
    Nisbet and Hubbard on Horace, *Odes I* 238
Norden, Eduard, *Die antike Kunstprosa* 276, 277
Nussbaum, Martha 106, 145, 192

Ogilvie, Robert 55, 101, 103, 104, 328
Osborne, Robin 189
O'Shea, Hilary 57, 101, 102
Otis, Brooks 170
Owen, Sir Geoffrey 29
Owen, Gwil (G.E.L.) 172
Oxford Book of Greek Verse 42
Oxford Latin Dictionary 22, 29, 274
Oxford Magazine 33
Oxford, University of
    admission of women to men's colleges 64–5, 316
    Bodleian Library 23
    Classics degree 6, 16, 20–1, 24, 43–4, 63; see also Mods *and* Greats
    History of the University of Oxford 71
    Oxford University Press 99, 100, 101–3, 104, 106, 125
    PPE (Politics, Philosophy, and Economics) 32, 40
    Regius chair of Greek 4–6, 22–4, 31, 43, 62, 172, 181, 285, 293
    student Classical Society 18
    Student Handbook 33, 34, 36

Padel, Ruth 72, 312
paedophilia 218
Page, Thomas Ethelbert 38, 99
Pamuk, Orhan 281

Panofsky, Erwin 224
Past and Present (journal) 62, 71
Pater, Walter 218
Patzer, Harold 195
Pausanias (Spartan regent) 169–70
penetration and Greek homosexuality 188–90, 217–18
Petropoulos, John 70
Pfeiffer, Rudolf 237, 238
Philby, Kim 84
photography and vase painting 205–6, 208, 219–23
Pindar 54, 239, 241, 256, 271
Pitt, William, the Younger 38
Platnauer, Maurice 248, 271
Plato 54, 103, 152–3, 156, 157, 186, 189, 256, 258, 271, 301, 305
    Charmides 191
    Phaedo 133–4, 136
    Phaedrus 100, 102, 131, 135–6, 142, 186, 187
    Symposium 4, 100, 125, 131–47, 173, 175, 183, 186, 190, 191, 272
Plumb, J.H. (Jack) 82, 85, 90, 92–4
Plutarch 285
Pomeroy, Sarah 149
Pool, Phoebe 84
Popper, Karl 142
pornography 189, 208, 219–20, 222, 224
Postgate, John Percival 25
Poussin 84
presentism 185, 187, 190, 294, 302
Presocratic philosophy 152, 241
Propertius 39

Queen Elizabeth II, coronation of 21
Queen Elizabeth the Queen Mother 83
Queen's Gallery, Buckingham Palace 83
Quine, Willard Van Orman 66

Rathbone, Christopher 325, 326
Rawson, Elizabeth 75
Reckford, Kenneth 4
Rees, Goronwy 84, 85
Reid, Robert 55
Riegl, Alois 224–5
Rijksbaron, A. 275
Robbins, Lionel (Lord) 88–9, 90, 91, 94
Roberts, Colin 89
Robinson, Richard 327
Rohy, Valerie 187
Romans, Epistle to the 22
Rose, H.J. 52, 53
Rosenmeyer, Thomas 239
Rudd, Niall 44
Russell, Donald 5, 16, 18, 19, 21, 25, 58, 63, 114, 188, 293
    British Academy memoir of Dover 2, 95, 106, 181

reactions to *Marginal Comment* 67, 102, 106, 321
work on Greek prose 275–7, 282

St Andrews, University of 5, 24, 25, 51–9, 63, 293
    Classics degree 52, 54, 55, 56
    Dover as Dean of Arts 2, 23, 57, 82, 318
    Greek department 52, 55
    Humanity (Latin) department 51, 52
    residences 81
    staff-student council 56
    student Classical Society 24
    student counselling 56
    summer school in Classics 56
    university library 23
St Leonards School (St Andrews) 328, 329, 330
St Paul's School, London 5, 14, 292, 298, 325
    Classical syllabus at 237, 239, 271
    paedophilia at 218
Samosata, *see* Lucian
Sandbach, F.H. 114
Sappho 167, 244
Schama, Simon 118
Schnapp, Alain 190
Schofield, Michael 183, 187
Scotland, Classics in 6, 25, 51–60, 63, 293
Sedgwick, Eve Kosofsky 194, 196
Sexual Offences Act 1967 182
Shakespeare, William 35, 167–8
Shefton, Brian 21
Shunga (Japanese erotic prints) 220
Skeat, Theodore 89
Smith, T.B. 89
Snow, C.P. 292, 297–8, 299, 305
Socrates 15, 301
    in Plato 131–48, 153, 187, 188, 191, 194
Some Oxford Compositions 271
Sophocles 54, 119, 271
    Ajax 302
    Antigone 303
    Philoctetes 304, 307
    Trachiniae 170
Southern, Richard 94
Sparta, homosexuality at 15, 191, 195–6
Stahl, Hans-Peter 116
statistical analysis of Greek 113, 117, 273–8, 281
Ste. Croix, Geoffrey de 92
Stephens, Sir David 23
Stesichorus 244–5
Straight, Michael 83
Stratheden hospital, St Andrews 55
Stuttard, David 8
style, Greek 271–87
Suez campaign 62
Sullivan, J.P. 49
Symonds, John Addington 218

Taylor, Alan (A.J.P.) 87, 91, 94
Taylor, Christopher (C.C.W.) 61, 77
Tennyson, *The Lady of Shalott* 65
Teubner (publishers) 20
textual criticism 32–4, 36, 39, 114, 125, 257
Thatcher, Margaret 84, 101, 188, 317, 319
Theocritus 43, 49, 69, 237–50, 263
Theognis 183
Thomas, Sir Keith 4, 64, 67, 103, 317, 318, 322–3
Thompson, D'Arcy Wentworth 52
Thomson, George 18
Thucydides 40, 113–30, 154–5, 169, 176, 253, 255, 271–3, 281
    and Dover's conception of history 295–6, 300, 312
    Dover's affinity with 113, 121
    Dover's teaching of 54, 114
    Thukydidesfrage 117
Times Literary Supplement 41, 43, 84, 284
Tompkins, Dan 119
Toynbee, Arnold 41
Trenkner, Sophie (Zofia) 274–5, 279
Trinity College, Cambridge 7, 83, 85, 249
Trubetzkoy, Nicolai 278
Two Cultures debate, *see* Snow, C.P.

Urmson, O. (Jim) 61

Vanderpool, Eugene 263
vase painting and Greek homosexuality 203–35
Vergil/Virgil 6, 17, 18, 38, 237–8, 271, 307
Vernant, Jean-Pierre 301
Verrall, A.W. 99
Vian, Francis 238
Virgil, *see* Vergil
Vlastos, Gregory 172

Wade-Gery, Theodore 4, 15, 19, 21
'Walter' 118
Warren, Edward Perry 218
Watson, William 85
Watt, Bill (W.S.) 173
Webster, Charles 74, 76
Webster, T.B.L. (Tom) 23
Weeks, Jeffrey 182–3, 185
Weiskittel, Ford 64
Wells, Frederick 173
West, Donald 182, 183, 187
West, Martin L. 20, 58, 69, 297
Westlake, H.D. 122
Whewell, William 99
Whitman, Walt 35
Whitmarsh, Tim 168
Whitting, Philip 5, 14
Wilamowitz-Moellendorff, Ulrich von 173, 249
Wild, Don 73

Index

Wilde, Oscar 35, 142, 218
Willi, Andreas 267, 279
Williams, Bernard 171–2, 184, 203
    Williams Committee on obscenity 203, 219
Williams, Craig 194
Williams, Gordon 21, 51, 55
Wimpee 5, 13–14; *see also* monkeys
Winchester College 22
Winkler, John J. 193–4
Wolfenden Report 182–3, 230
Wollheim, Richard 87
women philosophers in Oxford 19
Women's Studies 183, 193

Woodman, Tony (A.J.) 116
Woodward, Peter 55
Wordsworth, William 35
Wright, Peter 83
    Spycatcher 84
Wright, T. Erskine 52

Xenophon 117, 154, 188, 189, 195, 253, 263, 282

Yates, Velvet 194
Young, Douglas 52, 53, 54, 301

zero-sum competition 187, 190, 193–4

www.ingramcontent.com/pod-product-compliance
Lightning Source LLC
Chambersburg PA
CBHW071757300426
44116CB00009B/1112